THE ESSENTIAL SCOTS DICTIONARY

Scots-English English-Scots

Edited by
Iseabail Macleod
and
Pauline Cairns

Edinburgh University Press

© The Scottish National Dictionary Association Ltd 1996

Edinburgh University Press Ltd
22 George Square, Edinburgh

First published under the title *Scots School Dictionary*
1996 by Chambers, 1999 by Polygon at Edinburgh
This edition published 2004 by Edinburgh University Press

Reprinted 2006, 2009

Printed and bound in Great Britain by CPI Antony Rowe

A CIP Record for this book is
available from the British Library

ISBN 978 0 7486 2201 6 (paperback)

Other SLD publications:
  The Scottish National Dictionary 1931–76
  The Dictionary of the Older Scottish Tongue 1931–2002
    These are combined as *The Dictionary of the Scots Language*
    (www.dsl.ac.uk) 2004
  The Concise Scots Dictionary 1986
  The Pocket Scots Dictionary 1988
  The Scots Thesaurus 1990
  The Concise English-Scots Dictionary 1993
  The Grammar Broonie 2000

Contents

Introduction

The main aim of this dictionary is to provide a convenient, easy-to-use Scots-English/English-Scots dictionary to encourage native Scots speakers, Scots learners, and particulary younger Scots to use the Scots language, whether in reading, writing or simply talking to their friends. This dictionary is suitable for use in schools with upper primary and lower secondary pupils. We have tried to cover basic vocabulary, giving emphasis to words which pupils are likely to meet in a modern, largely urban environment, without totally neglecting rural vocabulary which has tended to dominate earlier dictionaries.

Efforts have been made to ensure a high coordination between the Scots-English and the English-Scots sides of the Dictionary, but a one-to-one correspondence was not considered necessary. There are many words included only in the Scots-English side because readers are likely to meet them in stories and poems, but omitted from the English-Scots side as they are unlikely to use them themselves. There are also words such as 'abeelitie' which are easy enough to understand but readers may need help if they want to use them; these are included in the English-Scots side only.

How to use the dictionary

How are the entries organized?
Longer entries may be divided into parts of speech (noun, verb etc) and/or meanings (introduced by numbers in bold type), *eg*

> **blatter** *v* **1** talk a lot, noisily and fast. **2** (*of rain, hail etc*) rattle, beat with violence.
>
> *n* **1** a loud rattling or rustling sound. **2** a storm of rain, hail etc.

In a few very long entries more space is given to these sections; see, for example, **kittle** in the Scots-English section.
The main part of the entry is sometimes followed by:

> (1) derivatives of the headword, *eg* **darger** under **darg**
>
> (2) compounds, *eg* **kailyaird** under **kail**
>
> (3) phrases, *eg* **gie's yer crack** under **crack**.

Examples are sometimes added to make the definitions clearer, *eg 'Dinna fash yersel'* under **fash**. In some entries, words are added, in italics and sometimes in brackets, to help you to understand the meaning or to find out which Scots word to use, *eg*

> **wheel** *n* (*in machinery*) whurl; (*on wheelbarrow*) trinnle.

Grammar

Main headwords are given a part-of-speech label; here is a list of them:

n (noun)	*adj* (adjective)
v (verb)	*adv* (adverb)
past tense	*preposition*
past participle	*conjunction*
present participle	*interjection*

When there is a distinctively Scots form of a verb it is given as follows:

ding *v*, *past tense* **dang, dung** ...

gae, go *v*, *past tense* **gaed, geed** SHETLAND, ORKNEY, N, **gied**; *past participle* **gane, geen** SHETLAND, ORKNEY, N ...

Distinctively Scots plural forms are also given:

ee, eye *n*, *pl also* **een**

Spelling

Scots has a very wide variety of different spellings, as you will see if you look at the *Concise Scots Dictionary* or, even more so, the ten-volume *Scottish National Dictionary*. In this little dictionary there has of course been no space for more than a very few different spellings. You will usually find only the commonest Scots spelling, one or two variants, sometimes from different regions, and the English spelling if it is often found with a Scots meaning, *eg* **cairrie, carry**.

If you can't find the word you want under a particular spelling, try skimming the same page and those next to it for a slightly different spelling under which it may be entered. The following suggestions will give an idea of many of the commoner ways in which the spellings may vary and which are worth trying if you do not find the word at once:

Omit a final -e	For lik see **like**
Try single instead of double consonants	For tittlin see **titlin**
or double instead of single consonant	For smedum see **smeddum**
Try double instead of single vowel	For beke see **beek**

Sometimes different spelling possibilities are shown by using brackets. For example **tra(u)chle** means that some people use **trauchle** and others use **trachle**.

Cross-references

We have noted that some words are given in more than one spelling. So that you can find all of these, cross-references are given for the second, third etc. For example: **ca, caw, call** *v* **1** call. ... Later you will find: **call** *see* **ca**. and further on still **caw** *see* **ca**.

Thus if you want to know what **caw** means, you look at the entry for **ca**. When a word is printed in bold type in the middle of a definition, that usually means that you will find an entry for it in this dictionary, *eg*

bannock ... a round flat cake, ... baked on a **girdle**.

Time and place

Most of the words you will find in this dictionary are still widely used throughout Scotland, but there are a very few which have been put in because you might come across them in stories about the past; they have been clearly labelled, *eg*

claymore *n* (*in past times*) a large Highland sword.

Some words, spellings or meanings are used only or mainly in one part of Scotland and these have been given a regional label, for example SHETLAND, ABERDEEN or NE for North-East. The maps on pp. x and xi will show you what areas these labels cover. Most of them are on Map 1, which shows the main dialect areas; a few are on Map 2, giving the old counties of Scotland, which stopped being our local-government units in 1975. EDINBURGH, GLASGOW, ABERDEEN and DUNDEE are used occasionally for words which belong to these cities. Here is a list of the areas mentioned in the Dictionary. (It runs roughly north to south on the map of Scotland.) You can see where most of these areas are on Maps 1 and 2 on pages x and xi, and one or two are given further explanations below:

SHETLAND
ORKNEY
CAITHNESS
ROSS
N
NE
ABERDEEN usually refers to the old county of Aberdeenshire, but occasionally means the town.
ANGUS
DUNDEE
CENTRAL
E CENTRAL
FIFE
EDINBURGH
SE refers to words which are used both in the part of the E CENTRAL area which lies south of the Forth and also in SOUTH.
WEST
ARGYLL
GLASGOW
AYRSHIRE
SW
SOUTH
ULSTER Many Lowland Scots moved to Ulster in the 17th century, taking their Scots language with them, and the dialects there still have strong Scots features.
HIGHLAND, HEBRIDES Scots is spoken much less in the Highlands and in the Western Isles (the area with no shading on Map 1), but there are a few words from these areas in the Dictionary, marked as above.

If you would like to know more about where words are used, you can look in the bigger dictionaries, the *Concise Scots Dictionary* and the ten-volume *Scottish National Dictionary*.

Which words to use

As well as telling you when and where words are used, the dictionary sometimes gives you an idea of what kind of word to use. For example a SLANG word is one you would usually use only when talking to friends. You would not use it in a school essay (though it might come into the dialogue of a story or play you were writing), *eg*

cludgie *n* (*slang*) a lavatory.

There is also RHYMING SLANG in Scots, used as above. For example **corn beef** meaning **deef**, as in 'Are you corn beef? Can ye no hear me?'

HUMOROUS means that the word is usually only used jokingly, *eg*

squeak *n* (*humorous*) a local newspaper.

GIPSY/ORIGINALLY GYPSY means that the word came from the language of the gipsies or other travelling people, but many of these have become more widely used, especially in South-East Scotland. For example **gadgie** means 'man' in gipsy language, but if you live in Edinburgh you are very likely to have heard it used by other people.

LITERARY - Some words are used mainly in poetry or in other literary words, *eg*

aiblins *n* (*literary*) perhaps.

How to pronounce Scots words

The spellings in the Dictionary will give you a good idea of modern Scots pronunciation, but where they might not make it clear, further notes are given to help you, *eg* **ay, aye** [rhymes with 'eye'], **rowan** [-ow- as in 'cow']. The stressed syllable is shown with bold type *eg* **jalouse** [ja**looze**]. The following notes may help you to pronounce the words in the Dictionary:

(1) **ng** in Scots, *eg* in **ingle**, **ingan**, **hunger**, is pronounced as in English 'sing', not as in English 'single'.

(2) In Scots, **ch** in the middle or at the end of a word is most often sounded as in **loch** or **dreich** or in the place-names **Buchan** or **Brechin**.

(3) At the beginning of a word, **ch** has its usual English sound as in 'cheese'. Where this pronunciation occurs later in a word, it is usually spelt -tch- in this Dictionary, eg *fleetch*.

(4) **gh**, which is normally found only in the middle or at the end of a word, has the same sound as **ch** in (2) above.

(5) **th** in Scots has the same two pronunciations as in English, one as in 'the, that, breathe', the other as in 'thank, thin, three, teeth'.

(6) **wh** is pronounced *hw-*, not *w-* as in southern English, eg *wheen* [pronounced hween].

(7) In some dialects north of the Tay, the k in initial **kn-** in *eg* **knife** is or was pronounced either as *k-* or, near the Tay, as *t-*, so that *knife* in these dialects is pronounced either k(e)nife or t(e)nife; similarly with the **g** in **gn-** as in *gnash* in some of the same dialects; elsewhere **kn-** and **gn-** are pronounced simply as n- as in English.

(8) **ui** varies with the dialect: in some dialects (*eg* Shetland, Orkney, Angus, South Scots), the pronunciation is similar to the vowel of French 'peu' or German 'schön'

in East Fife and neighbouring dialects, the pronunciation is like *a* in Scottish Standard English 'late' or 'blade' or *ai* in 'pair' or *ay* in 'day'

in many other dialects, the pronunciation in some words is like *ai*, so that **puir** is pronounced like **pair**, but in other words like *i* in English 'bit', so that *buit* is pronounced like 'bit'

in the Northern mainland dialects this sound does not occur; -**ee**- is used instead, as in **beet** for 'boot'.

(9) **oo** as in Scottish Standard English 'groove' or 'moon'.

(10) **ey** as in *gey* (very) is the same as the vowel in the Scots (and Scottish Standard English) pronunciation of 'mine' or 'tile'.

(11) *Stress*. In Scots, in words of more than one syllable, stress is usually on the same syllable as it would be in English, *eg* words such as *hoolet* have stress on the first syllable, but prefixes such as *dis-* in *disjaskit* or *un-* in *unbraw* are usually unstressed.

Further information on Scots pronunciation can be found in the other dictionaries (listed on p xii).

The Scots language

Scots is a very old language with an interesting history, closely linked with its neighbour English. They are both descended from Old English, but Scots comes from a northern form of it which reached the south-east of what is now Scotland some time in the seventh century. By this time too the Scots had come from Ireland with their Gaelic language, and they gradually began to extend their power till by the eleventh century the King of Scots ruled over most of what is now mainland Scotland, with Gaelic as the leading language. However from the eleventh century, strong influences came from England. Many Anglo-Norman noble families and monasteries moved up from north-east England. Although their own language was Norman-French, that of their servants and followers was a form of northern English with strong Scandinavian influence (still noticeable in modern Scots in words such as *graith*, *lowp* and *nieve*). This developing language, then known as *Inglis*, spread very rapidly, especially through trade in the newly-founded burghs, soon reaching most of the east and south-west of the country.

There were many influences from other European languages. Norse, that is Scandinavian, words have been noted already. Norse had an even greater influence in Shetland, Orkney and part of Caithness, where a Norse language, known as Norn, was spoken up to the 17th century, and this is obvious in their modern dialects.

In the Middle Ages Scotland traded a great deal with the Low Countries (now the Netherlands and Belgium) and their language gave us words like *loon*, *pinkie*, *golf* and *scone*. French influence was very strong, especially at the time of what became known as the Auld Alliance (between 1295 and 1560) when Scotland and France were allies. Examples of French words in Scots are *fash*, *ashet*, *leal* and *aumrie*. Many Latin words were used, especially legal ones, and indeed some still are, such as *homologate* (ratify), *sederunt*. It is often said that there are not many words of Gaelic origin in Scots, considering the two languages have lived for so long in one country, but you will find quite a few, especially words to do with landscape, such as *ben*, *glen* and *strath*.

In the early days most writing was in Latin, but there are written records in Scots from the late fourteenth century onwards; one of the earliest literary works was Barbour's *Brus*, a narrative poem on King Robert the Bruce and his exploits in the wars against English invasions at the beginning of that century.

By the early sixteenth century, Scots, as it was now called, was well on the way to becoming an all-purpose national language for Scotland, just as modern English was developing in England. (Gaelic was by now confined to western and northern areas and to the Western Isles.) Scots reached a fine literary flowering in the poetry of Robert Henryson, William Dunbar and Gavin Douglas, whose works were well-known in Europe. But after the Scottish Reformation in 1560, Scotland began to look to Protestant England rather than to Catholic France. In the absence of a Scots translation of the Bible, an English one was used in churches, creating a severe obstacle to the written use of Scots in many important areas of society.

With the Union of the Crowns of Scotland and England in 1603 the court of James VI moved to London, and with it went many of the writers, thus removing much of the focus of literary life. After the Union of the Parliaments in 1707, English became the language of government and of polite society though the vast majority of people continued to speak Scots. Many however tried to make their speech more English and took lessons from English people. Others made up lists of words to avoid in order to sound English.

In schools, efforts were made for a very long time to stop children using their own Scots language and to make them speak only English. This was because their parents and teachers thought speaking English was necessary if they were to communicate in a wider world. Nowadays however we know that people can learn English, which is an international language, for this purpose and keep their Scots as well. So why is it important to preserve the Scots language? As we have seen, Scots has a long and fascinating history and has produced marvellous literary works from early times right down to the present day. Also there are many things which you can say in Scots which are much more difficult to express in English. Just try to find one English word for *swither*, *dreich*, *fushionless* or *dwam* and you will see how hard it is. Lots of books, games and charts have been produced lately to help in the teaching of Scots in schools and we hope that this dictionary will add to these.

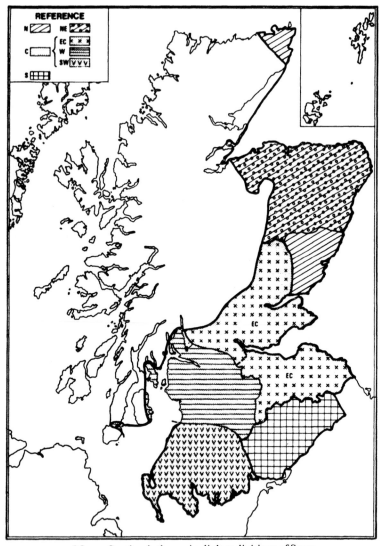

Map 1 Scotland: the main dialect divisions of Scots

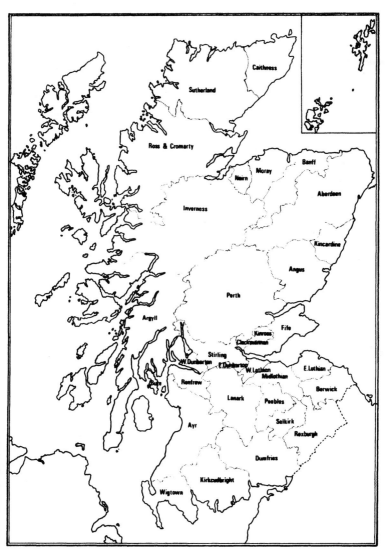

Map 2 Scotland: pre-1975 counties

Acknowledgements

We would like to thank all those who have given advice on the educational aptness of this piece of lexicography, in particular Ronald Renton and the Schools Committee of the Association for Scottish Literary Studies, Jim McGonigal, Claire Milne, Andrew Purves, Lesley Rowson and Leslie Wheeler. We are deeply grateful to the following for suggestions from different dialect areas: Mary Robertson (Shetland); Margaret Flaws (Orkney); Gordon Booth (North-East), Kate Armstrong (Angus); John Hodgart (Ayrshire); Liz Niven, Charlotte Bennie (South-West); Jan Deans (South). Last but not least we would like to thank Timothy Cairns for useful comments from the point of view of a school pupil.

The quality of the dictionary has been much enhanced by careful checking and keying by Majella Hackett, checking by Ivor Normand and Susan Rennie, and keying by Bettina Isensee and Joanne Highet. Thanks are also due to the staff of Larousse plc, in particular to Catherine Schwarz for helpful comments.

The editors are as ever grateful to all their predecessors, especially to David Murison whose work underlies the dictionaries from the former SNDA.

Funding of dictionaries is an ever-present problem and we are very grateful to all who contributed to this dictionary. It was made possible by generous grants from the Scottish Office, the European Commission, many local authorities (in particular Grampian Region), the Halley Stewart Trust and the James Wood Trust.

We acknowledge with thanks the generous voluntary help that SNDA received, in particular from SNDA's Secretary and Treasurer, Henry Pirie, and its Executive Council under the Chairmanship of Sir Kenneth Alexander; our sincere thanks are due to the fund-raising committee: Sheila Davies, Betty Philip, Jessie Purves and the late Ann Aikman Smith.

Scottish Language Dictionaries Ltd

Scottish Language Dictionaries Limited is a charitable limited company, formed in 2002 from a union between the Scottish National Dictionary Association Ltd, the lexicographers of Scots from about 1700 onwards, and the Dictionary of the Older Scottish Tongue (DOST) which was concerned with Scots from its earliest beginnings up to about 1700.

The ten volumes of the Scottish National Dictionary and twelve volumes of DOST are now available online at www.dsl.ac.uk.

SLD is constantly monitoring the language and recording language change. If you would like to help, or would like more information, please see our main website at www.sldl.org.uk and our schools website at www.scuilwab.org.uk or write to:

Scottish Language Dictionaries Ltd
27 George Square
Edinburgh
EH8 9LD
Scotland

Abbreviations

adj	adjective	etc	et cetera	E	East	S	South
adv	adverb	n	noun	N	North	SE	South-East
eg	for example	pl	plural	NE	North-East	SW	South-West
ie	that is	v	verb				

A

A *see* **Ah.**

a', all, aw, aa, aal *adj* **1** all. **2** every.

  a'bodie everybody.

  a'bodie's bodle a general favourite.

  a(w)kin kind every kind (of).

  a'ways, a'weys in all directions.

aafu *see* **awfu.**

aal *see* **a', auld.**

aback *adv* **1** back; away, off. **2** behind.

abeen *see* **abuin.**

abeese *see* **abuise.**

able, yibble SOUTH, **yable** SOUTH *adj* **1** able. **2** physically fit, strong. **3** having an appetite (for).

ablow *preposition, adv* under, below.

a'bodie *see* **a'.**

aboon *see* **abuin.**

aboot *adv, preposition* **1** about. **2** on the move, going about (especially after an illness).

  aboot it about the same.

abreist *adv* abreast.

abstrack *v* abstract.

abuin, aboon, abeen N *adv, preposition* **1** above. **2** in good spirits, in or into better condition.

abuise, abeese N *v* abuse.

academy *n* (*now mainly in names*) a secondary school: '*Largs Academy*'.

accep *v* accept.

ach!, auch! *interjection* exclamation of impatience, disappointment, contempt etc.

ack *v, n* act.

ackwart *adj* awkward.

acquant, acquent *adj* acquaint(ed).

adae, adee N, **ado** *v* **1 whit's adae?, fat's adee?** N what's going on? **2 whit's adae wi ye?** N, **fat's adee wi ye?** N what's the matter with you?

advocate *n* (*law*) **1** a professional pleader in a court of justice, a barrister. **2** a solicitor ABERDEEN.

ae, yae WEST, SOUTH *adj* **1** (*numeral*) one. **2** the same: '*aw ae kind*'. **3** only: '*oor ae wean*'. **4 the ae** the very . . . : '*the ae warst wumman*'. **5** a certain: '*ae day*'. Compare **ane**[1].

aefauld *adj* **1** single. **2** simple, sincere; honest, faithful; single-minded.

  Aefauldlie (*letters*) Yours sincerely.

aesins *see* **easins.**

aet *see* **eat.**

ae wey *see* **wey**[1].

aff, off *adv* off.

  preposition **1** off. **2** away (from a place).

affcome the way something turns out, result; escape.

affgo start, outset.

aff-loof offhand.

affpit 1 excuse, reason for delay. **2** a delay. **3** a person who or thing which delays.

affset 1 an ornament. **2** an outset, a start.

afftak 1 a mocking remark. **2** a person who ridicules others, a mimic.

aff an on 1 undecided, changeable, unsettled. **2** (*of health*) sometimes better, sometimes worse.

aff o(f) off, from, away from: '*He fell aff o the wa*'.

affeck *v* affect.

affuird *v* afford.

afore *adv* **1** (*of time*) before, previously. **2** (*of place*) before, in front; in advance. **3** (*of a clock*) fast.

  preposition **1** (*of time*) before, earlier than. **2** (*of place*) before, in front of; in advance of; into the presence of.

  conjunction **1** (*of time*) before. **2** rather than.

aft *see* **aften.**

aften, aft *literary in poetry, adv* often.

after *see* **efter.**

agaln, agane [rhymes with 'lane'] *adv* **1** again. **2** back: '*I cam aw the wey again*'. **3** later: '*I'll get it again*'.
preposition **1** against. **2** in preparation for (a particular time etc). **3** (*of time*) towards, by.
conjunction in preparation for a particular time etc when; until.

age *n*: **be ages wi** be the same age as.

agin *preposition* against.

aglee *see* **agley.**

agley, aglee [rhymes with 'gey' or 'me'] *adv* off the straight, wrong.

Ah, A *pronoun* I.

aheld *adv* ahead.

ahent *see* **ahin.**

ahin, ahint, ahent *adv* **1** behind, remaining, at the back, following. **2** in your past life, in time past. **3** at a later time, late, too late. **4** (*of a clock*) slow.
preposition behind; later than, after; too late for; in view of.

aiblins *adv* (*literary*) perhaps.

aicht *see* **aucht**[1], **aucht**[2].

aifter *see* **efter.**

aik *n* an oak.

ail *v*: **whit ails ye (at)? 1** what objection have you (to)?: '*What ails ye at ma Da?*'. **2** what's the matter with you?

ain *adj* (your) own.
  my *etc* **ainsel** myself etc.

aince, yince, wance *adv* once.

aipple, epple *n* an apple.

airch *n* an arch.

airgument *see* **argie.**

airieplane *n* an aeroplane.

airm, erm *n* an arm.
  mak a lang airm *see* **lang.**

airmie *n* army.

airn *n*, *v* iron.

airra *see* **arrae.**

airt[1] *n* art, skill.

airt[2] *n* **1** a point of the compass: '*frae aw the airts*'. **2** a direction, way, manner.

v **1** direct, guide to a place; set facing or moving in a certain direction; urge forward. **2** make (for), take the road (for).

airticle *n* an article.

ais *see* **ass.**

ait, yit E CENTRAL, SOUTH *n* oat.

aither, ether, edder SHETLAND, N
pronoun either.

aither *see* **ither.**

aix *n* an ax.

aizle *n* an ember; a spark.

ajee *adv* **1** to one side, aside, off the straight. **2** (*of a door etc*) ajar, partly open. **3** off the straight; in a disturbed state.

akin kind *see* **a'.**

Alan *n* an Arctic skua SHETLAND, ORKNEY.

Alan-hawk, scootie-allan names given to several sea birds, *eg* an Arctic skua.

alane, aleen SHETLAND, ORKNEY, NE
adj alone.

alang *adv* along.

ald *see* **auld.**

ale, yill, eel SHETLAND, ORKNEY, Ile N
n **1** ale. **2** lemonade, fizzy water NE.

aleen *see* **alane.**

aleeven, aleevent *see* **eleeven.**

all *see* **a'.**

Allan-hawk *see* **Alan.**

aller, arn *n* alder.

alloo *v* allow.

amaist *adv* almost.

amang, among, amo *preposition* **1** among. **2** in(to) the midst of, amid.

ambeetious *adj* ambitious.

amissin *adj* missing.

amna, amnae *see* **be.**

amo, among *see* **amang.**

an *see* **and, than.**

an a, an aw *see* **and.**

and, an *conjunction* and.
  an aw, an a 1 and everything or everyone else. **2** besides, as well: '*I want a piece an aw*'. **3** '*strong an a as she is*': although she is so strong.

ane[1], **yin**, **een** SHETLAND, ORKNEY, N *numeral* one. *Compare* **ae.**

ane[2] *indefinite article* (*in past times*) a, an.

aneath *preposition* under, below, beneath.

anent *preposition* concerning, about.

anidder *see* **anither.**

anither, **anidder** SHETLAND, NE *adj, pronoun* another.

Annicker's midden *n* a shambles, a mess.

annoonce *v* announce.

antrin *adj* occasional; odd, peculiar, strange.

anxeeitie *n* anxiety.

apen *see* **open.**

appeteet *n* appetite.

Aprile *see* **Averil.**

aquavitae [akwaveetay] *n* spirits, whisky.

Arbroath smokie *see* **smokie.**

a'ready, **areddies** *adv* already.

argie [g- as in 'get'] *v* argue, especially aggressively.

argie-bargie *n* a quarrel, haggling. *v* dispute, haggle.

airgument an argument NE.

ark *n* a chest, especially a large one for storing grain etc.

arn *see* **aller.**

arna, **arnae** *see* **be.**

aroon, **aroond** *adv* around.

arra *see* **arrae.**

arrae, **arra** WEST, **airra** NE *n, v* arrow.

artifeecial *adj* artificial.

asheer *see* **asseer.**

ashet *n* 1 an oval serving plate, especially for a joint. 2 a pie-dish WEST.

aside *adv* close by.
preposition beside; close to, in comparison with.

ask[1], **ax** *v* ask.

ask for ask after.

ask[2], **esk** *n* a newt.

asklent *adv* aslant, astray.

ass, **ais**, **ess** *n* ash, ashes.

asseer, **asheer** *v* assure NE.

astragal *n* a glazing bar in a window.

at[1], **it** *preposition*: **be at someone** bother or hurt someone.

be at someone about something talk to a person about a thing; keep finding fault with, tease someone.

whit are ye at? what do you mean?

at[2], **it** NE *relative pronoun, conjunction* that.

at *see* **that.**

aten *see* **eat.**

athegither *see* **awthegither.**

athoot *preposition, also* **ithoot** without.
adv outside.
conjunction unless.

athort *preposition, adv* 1 across; from one side of (a place or thing) to the other. 2 across in various directions; all over.

attercap *see* **ettercap.**

atterie *adj* 1 infected, festering. 2 grim, angry, forbidding; stormy.

atweel *adv* certainly, indeed.

atween *preposition* between.

(a)tween han(d)s, at intervals; in the meantime: '*Ah'll get a cup o tea atween hands*'.

atweesh *preposition* between.

auch *see* **ach.**

aucht[1], **aicht**, **echt**, **eight** *numeral* 1 eight. 2 eighth.

eightsome a group of eight people or things, often of a dance, especially a reel; the reel itself: **eightsome reel.**

aucht[2], **aicht** ORKNEY, NE *v* 1 owe, be owing. 2 own, possess.

aul *see* **auld.**

auld, **aul**, **ald**, **aal** N, **owl(d)** SHETLAND, ORKNEY, CAITHNESS, ROSS, ARGYLL, ULSTER, **old** *adj* 1 old.

2 the same, usual: '*Pate will still be the auld man*'.

3 (*indicating family relationships*) great-: '*auld uncle*'; grand-: '*auld mither*'; oldest: '*auld brither*'.

4 (*of bread*) stale.

5 referring to the devil: '*Auld Nick*'; '*the Auld Man*'.

the auld enemy the English.

auld-farran(t) **1** old-fashioned, quaint. **2** (*of children*) having the ways of older people; precocious.

auld-fashioned 1 old-fashioned. **2** (*of children or young people*) = **auld-farrant** 2.

the Old Firm Rangers and Celtic football teams considered together.

auld lang syne *see* **lang.**

auld maid's bairn (*proverb*) an improbably well-behaved child which a spinster has in mind when criticizing the children of others.

Auld Reekie nickname for Edinburgh.

auld-warl(d) *adj* antique.

auld wife, auld yin (*contemptuous*) your mother; your wife.

Auld Year the previous year; the year that is about to end; the last few days of the year.

aumrle *n* a cupboard, pantry, usually a separate piece of furniture.

auntie *n* an aunt.

Auntie Beenie a rather old-fashioned-looking woman or her clothes: '*She wears Auntie Beenie claes*'.

ava *adv* at all.

Averil, Aprile *n* April.

aw! *interjection* oh!

aw *see* **a'.**

awa, away *adv* **1** away. **2** on, along: '*Come awa to yer bed*'. **3** dead; wasted, made very thin: '*He's awa tae skin and bone*'. **4** asleep.

interjection exclamation expressing surprise, disbelief etc: '*awa wi ye!*'.

awa fae past, unable to: '*He wis awa fae speakin*'.

awa wi't done for; out of your senses; lost; dead.

awa wi ye! go away!

awaird *n*, *v* award.

awaur *adj* aware.

a'ways *see* **a'.**

awe, owe, yaw NE *v* **1** owe. **2** own, possess.

wha is aucht . . . ? who owns . . . ?

aweel *adv* (*used to introduce a remark*) well: '*Aweel, Jamie, what think ye?*'.

a'wey *see* **wey**[1].

a weys, a'weys *see* **a'.**

awfie *see* **awfu.**

awfu, awfie, aafu NE *adj* **1** awful. **2** shocking; ugly; remarkable; difficult; very great.

adv very, extremely; very much.

an awfu . . . a great many . . .

awkin kind *see* **a'.**

awn, own *v* **1** own. **2** recognize as a relation or friend; have to do with; attend to; come into contact with.

awthegither, athegither *adv* altogether.

aw wey, aw weys *see* **wey**[1].

ay, aye [rhymes with 'eye'] *interjection* **1** yes. **2** (*as a greeting, sometimes sarcastic*) hello, well there you are: '*Ay ay Souter!*'. **3 ay ay** just so, that's it.

ay *see* **aye.**

aye, ay [rhymes with 'gey'] *adv* **1** always, continually; at all times. **2** still; all the same.

Yours aye (*in letters*) Yours sincerely.

aye *see* **ay.**

ayeweys *adv* always.

ayont *see* **beyont.**

ax *see* **ask**[1].

B

ba[1], **baa, baw, ball** *n* **1** a ball. **2** football; **the Ba** the annual game of football formerly played in some areas on Shrove Tuesday. **3 the Ba** a game of handball played on certain annual holidays in the Borders and Orkney.
baw-faced round-faced; stupid.
bawheid a fool, an idiot.
the ba's up on the slates there's trouble now, the fat's in the fire.
ba[2], **baa, baw** *v* hush (a child) to sleep.
baw baw(s), beddie baw(s) child's word for bed or going to sleep.
baa *see* **ba**[1], **ba**[2].
bab at the bowster, babbitie bowster *n* a children's game differing according to district.
bachle *see* **bauchle.**
back *v* address (a letter).
backart(s) backwards.
backie 1 a carry on the back; a piggyback. **2** a backyard.
backin an address (on a letter).
backlins backwards.
back coort a backyard.
backdoor trot diarrhoea.
back end the end of harvest, late autumn.
back-ganglin a relapse.
backland the back of a piece of ground; the building on it; a house behind another.
backset something which keeps you back, slows down progress, causes a relapse in an illness.
backsey name for various parts of a loin of beef etc.
backside 1 the back part of a building; the outside space next to it. **2 backsides** the parts of a town off the main streets.
backside foremaist *see* **foremaist.**

at the back o not long after: '*at the back o six*'.
back an fore backwards and forwards.
come up yer back come into your mind, fit in with what you intend to do.
backet *n* a box for fuel, ashes etc; a dustbin.
backie, bawkie *n* a bat (the animal).
bad, baud *adj* **1** bad. **2** unwell, in pain, physically ill.
badly ill, not very well.
the bad man *see* **man.**
the bad place hell.
no bad pretty well; pretty good: '*She's no bad at the cookin*'; attractive.
bad *see* **bide.**
badder *see* **bather.**
badderlocks *npl* a kind of edible seaweed.
baff[1] *n* a blow (with something soft).
baff[2], **baffle** *n* a slipper.
baggie[1] *n* a swede.
baggie[2], **baggie mennen** *n* a kind of large minnow.
bahookie *see* **behoochie.**
baikie[1] *n* a square container for ashes, coal, rubbish etc.
baikie[2] *n* a peg to which a tether is fastened NE.
baille, bylie *n* **1** a town magistrate next in rank to the **provost. 2** the person in charge of the cows on a farm.
baird, beard *n* a beard.
bairdie 1 *also* **chinnie bairdie** the rubbing of a man's rough chin against a child or woman's chin or cheek. **2** a kind of stickleback. **3** *also* **bairdie lotchie** a loach.
bairge[1] *v* speak loudly and angrily.

bairge[2] *v* move clumsily, violently and noisily.

bairn *n* **1** *also* **bairnie** a child; a baby; someone's child. **2 the Bairns** nickname for Falkirk football team.

v make pregnant.

bairnlie, bairnlik(e) childlike; childish.

baist, beast *n, also* **beastie,** *pl also* **beas, bease 1** a beast. **2** a cow, bull, calf, ox. **3** a creature of any sort, a bird, fish, insect etc, (body- and head-)louse etc.

v beat, get the better of, do better than.

beastie held a person with head lice.

bait *n* a boat N.

baith, both *adj, pronoun* both.

baith the twa (o them) both (of them).

bake, byaak NE *v, past tense* **beuk** NE; *past participle* **baken** bake.

n a thick or soft biscuit.

bake-board a baking board.

balderrie [ba**l**derrie] *n* any of several types of wild orchid.

ball *see* **ba**[1].

ballant *n* a ballad.

ballop *n* the opening in the front of men's trousers.

Balmoral *n* a kind of bonnet with a **toorie** on the crown and a band, worn to one side.

baloo [ba**loo**] *n* word used to hush a child to sleep; a lullaby.

bambor *numeral* (*children's rhymes*) five.

bammer *see* **bampot.**

bampot, bammer *n* a fool, a stupid or crazy person.

ban *see* **band**[1], **band**[2].

banannie *n* a banana.

band[1]**, ban, baun(d)** *n* **1** a band, something which binds. **2 bands** the two short white linen strips hanging from a minister's collar.

band[2]**, ban, baun(d)** *n* a band, a company, group.

band *see* **bind.**

bane, been N *n* a bone.

bang *v* be better than, beat, thrash.

bank, baunk *n* a bank.

Bankies *npl*: **the Bankies** nickname for Clydebank football team.

bannet *see* **bonnet.**

bannie, banno *see* **bannock.**

bannock, bannie, banno ORKNEY *n* a round flat cake, often of oat-, barley- or pease-meal, baked on a **girdle.**

banshee *n* a female spirit, often connected with a family, whose wail was thought to forecast death or disaster.

banstickle *n* a stickleback.

bap *n* a bread roll, varying locally in shape, size and texture.

v walk in a plodding, flat-footed way.

bar[1]**, baur** *n, v* bar.

bar-the-door *n* the game of **leave-o.**

bar[2]**, baur** *n* a joke, humorous situation, practical joke.

bard *n* a poet; a strolling singer or player.

barefit, berfit, barfit N *adj* barefoot(ed).

barles (in your) bare feet.

barken *v* clot, harden or plaster over, blacken.

barley, baurlie *n* (*mainly in children's games*) a truce, pause.

barley play a cry for truce in games.

cry (a) barley call for a truce.

barley-bree *n* malt liquor, whisky.

barra, barrae, borra *n* **1** a (hand-)barrow. **2** a supermarket trolley.

barrie *adj* fine, excellent, very good; big; smart in appearance: '*That wis a barrie picture last night*'; '*He looked barrie in his new suit*'.

bash *v* beat, smash.

n a heavy blow (which will smash something).

on the bash out on a spree, having a drinking bout.

bass *n* a mat of coarse straw etc, especially a doormat.

bastart *n* a bastard.

adj, also **bastardin** devilish.

6

bate *v, past tense, past participle* **bate**
beat.

n something which is much better
than something else.

bather, budder SHETLAND, N, **badder**
SHETLAND, N *v, n* bother.

batter *v* paste (to a wall, together),
stiffen as with paste.

n **1** a paste or glue. **2 batters** the
covers of a book.

bauch [-ch as in 'loch'] *adj* **1** poor,
weak, not very good. **2** (*of a knife
etc*) blunt. **3** (*of ice*) thawed, not
slippery.

bauchle, bachle *v* walk clumsily,
wear (shoes) out of shape.

n **1** an old shoe, especially one worn
down at the heel. **2** an old, useless,
worn-out person or thing. **3** an untidy
or clumsy person.

baud *see* **bad.**

baudrons *n* **1** affectionate name for a
cat. **2** a hare.

bauk *n* **1** a balk, an unploughed ridge;
a wooden beam. **2** a crossbeam, rafter. **3** the beam of a pair of scales.

baul *see* **bauld.**

bauld, baul *adj* bald: '*bauldie-heidit*'.

baun, baund *see* **band**[1], **band**[2].

baunk *see* **bank.**

baur *see* **bar**[1], **bar**[2].

baurber *n* a barber.

baurlie *see* **barley.**

baw *see* **ba**[1], **ba**[2].

baw baw, baw baws *see* **ba**[2].

bawbee *n* **1** a coin, originally valued at
six pennies in old Scots money,
equivalent to a halfpenny sterling. **2**
a halfpenny. **3 bawbees** money.

bawd *n* a hare.

bawkie *see* **backie.**

bawsant *adj* (*of an animal*) having a
white mark or streak on the face.

bawtie *n* a hare, a rabbit SOUTH.

be, bey SOUTH [rhymes with 'gey'] *v,
past tense also* (**I, he, she, it**) **wes, wis,
wus, wur;** (**we, you, they**) **wur, war.**
ur (*emphatic*) are, am: '*Ah'm ur*' WEST.

amnae, amna am not.

isnae, isna is not.

arnae, arna, urnae are not.

wasnae, wasna, wisnae, wisna was
not.

wernae, werna, wurnae were not.

be *see* **by.**

bead *n* a glass or quantity of spirits:
'*He had a good bead in him yesterday*'.

beadle *n* a church officer.

beal, beel *v* **1** fester. **2** (be) fill(ed) with
pain, rage etc.

bealin *n* a festering sore, boil, pimple
etc.

adj **1** festering. **2** furiously angry.

bealach [*Gaelic* beealach] *n* (*especially
mountaineering*) a narrow mountain
pass.

beamer *n* a blushing face: '*get a beamer*'.

bear *see* **bere.**

beard *see* **baird.**

beas, bease, beast *see* **baist.**

beck *n, v* bow, curtsy.

bed *n* **beds** the spaces chalked on the
ground for playing **peever**[1]; the game
itself.

beddie baw, beddie baws *see* **ba**[2].

bedfast bedridden.

bee-baw-babbetie *n* a (kissing) game
or dance.

beef *n* any butcher's meat.

beek *v* **1** warm (yourself). **2** (*of the sun*)
shine brightly.

beel *see* **beal.**

been *see* **bane.**

beerial *n* burial NE.

beerie *v* bury.

beest *n* the first milk of a cow after
calving.

beet *v* supply something missing to
(something), *eg* replace hooks on (a
fishing line).

beet *see* **buit**[1], **buit**[2].

beetle *see* **bittle.**

beezer *n* (*informally*) a thing or person bigger or better than usual.

begeck *v* deceive, disappoint.

begowk *v* outwit.

behaud *v* behold.

behoochie, bahookie *n* (*often to children*) the behind, backside, bottom.

beis *see* **by.**

belang *v* **1** belong. **2** own, possess. **3** belong to (a place) be a native of: '*He belangs Glesca*'.

beld *adj* bald.

bell *n* a bubble.

bell heather *see* **heather.**

bellies *n, also as double pl* **bellises** bellows.

belloch *v* bellow, roar.

belly *n*: **belly-blind** blind man's buff; the blindfolded person in it.

belly-flaucht flat on your face or stomach; headlong.

belt *n* **1 the belt** = **the tawse. 2** a blow, a hit.

belted *see* **Galloway.**

ben[1] *adv* in or towards the inner part of a house etc; in or to the best room or another room; inside.
preposition through (a house) towards the inner part; in or to the best room or another room: '*ben the hoose*'.
n the inner room, the best room.

ben[2] *n* a mountain, hill, one of the higher Scottish mountains.

bennel *n* any long reedy grass.

bent *n* **1** bent, a kind of coarse grass. **2 bents** sandy hillocks covered with bent.

bere, bear *n* a hardier and coarser kind of barley.

berfit *see* **barefit.**

berries *npl*: **the berries** berry-picking.

besom, bizzom *n* **1** any broom; a besom. **2** a term of contempt for a person, especially a woman: '*ye wee besom ye*'.

bessie *n* a bad-mannered, bad-tempered woman or girl NE.

best maid *n* a bridesmaid.

bethankit *n* grace after a meal.

better *adj* completely recovered from an illness.

betterness improvement in health.

beuk *see* **bake, buik.**

bew *see* **blue.**

bewaur *v* beware.

bey *see* **be.**

beyond *see* **beyont.**

beyont, ayont, beyond *preposition, adv* **1** beyond. **2** (*of time, number, degree*) above, more than etc.

Bhoys *see* **boy.**

bibble *see* **bubble.**

bick *n* a female dog.

bicker[1] *v* move quickly and noisily.
n a (street- or school-)fight; a quarrel.

bicker[2] *n* a beaker, a (wooden) drinking cup; a (porridge) bowl.

bid *v* invite (to a wedding etc).

biddin 1 a command. **2** an invitation.

bide *v, past tense* **bidit, bad;** *past participle* **bidit, bidden 1** remain, stay (especially temporarily), dwell, reside. **2** await, stay for. **3** put up with, stand. *n* pain NE.

bidie-in a person who lives with another of the opposite sex without marriage NE.

bield *n, v* shelter.

bien [been] *adj* **1** in good condition. **2** comfortable(-looking), pleasant, cosy. **3** well-to-do, well-off. **4** (*of a house etc*) well-stocked.

big[1] *adj* conceited, swollen-headed.

big hoose the main house of the **laird** on an estate.

big miss a great loss by death, or by the departure of a friend.

big sma faimilie a large family of young children.

big[2] *v, past tense* **biggit, bug;** *past participle* **biggit** build, construct.

biggin 1 (the act of) building. **2** a building; (*in place names*): '*Newbiggin*'.

bile[1] *v, n* boil.

bilin, boilin a boiled sweet.

bile[2] *n* a boil, an infected swelling.

bilf *n* a sturdy young man NE.

bill *see* **bul.**

billet *n* a bullet.

billie *n* **1** a fellow, lad. **2** a lover. **3** a close friend; **grand billies** on very friendly terms.

Billy *n* (*contemptuous*) a Protestant, Orangeman GLASGOW.

bin *see* **bind.**

bind, bin [rhymes with 'tin(ned)'] *v*, *past tense also* **band;** *past participle also* **bun(d) 1** bind. **2** tether.
n **bin** humour, mood NE.

neither tae haud nor bind beyond control.

bine *see* **boyne.**

bing *n* **1** a heap or pile. **2** a slag-heap.

binger a horse or dog that loses a race.

bink *n* **1** a bench. **2** a wall rack or shelf for dishes etc; a kitchen dresser.

bird, burd *n* **1** a bird. **2** a lady, woman; a girl. **3** term of endearment, especially to a child.

burd-alane quite alone.

birk *n* **1** a birch tree. **2 birks** a small wood consisting mainly of birches.

birkie *n* a smart (usually young) fellow.
adj lively, spirited.

birl *v* revolve quickly, whirl round, dance; make a rattling or whirring sound.
n **1** a turn, twist, revolving movement. **2** a whistle; the sound made by a whistle.

birr[1] *n* **1** force, energy, bustling activity. **2** enthusiasm. **3** a whirring sound.

birr[2] *n*: **in a birr** (*of hair etc*) standing up on end.

birse *n* **1** bristles, (a) bristle. **2** anger, temper: '*His birse is up*'.

birsie 1 bristly; hairy. **2** hot-tempered, passionate.

birsle *v* **1** scorch. **2** toast; warm thoroughly.

(weel-)birselt well-cooked, fried until crisp.

birst, burst, brust *v, past tense also* **burstit;** *past participle also* **burstit, burs(t)en** burst.

n **1** a burst. **2** an injury caused by over-exertion. **3** a bout of drunkenness. **4** a big feed, *often* **a hunger or a burst** scarcity or plenty.

bit *n* your job.

bittie, bittock a small piece; a short distance or time.

a bittie somewhat, rather: '*She's a bittie slow*'.

I cannae get oot o the bit I can't make any progress, I'm stuck.

come to the bit come to the point of decision.

bit *see* **buit**[1], **but.**

bittle, beetle *n* **1** a beetle, a mallet. **2** a kitchen utensil for mashing potatoes etc.

bizz *v* **1** buzz. **2** (*of liquids*) hiss, fizz.
n a state of commotion, bustle.

bizzom *see* **besom.**

bla *see* **blaw**[1].

black *n* **blacks** mourning clothes.
adv **1** completely, utterly. **2** intensely, extremely: '*black affrontit*'.

blackie a blackbird.

blackberry the blackcurrant.

black bun a very rich spiced fruit cake, baked in a pastry crust and eaten at **Hogmanay.**

black cock a male black grouse.

black man 1 (*in threats made to children*) the bogeyman, the Devil.
2 a kind of toffee or other dark-coloured sweet.
3 an ice-cream with a plain wafer on one side and a marshmallow-filled wafer with chocolate edges on the other.
4 a piece of black matter in the nose.

black-strippit ba a striped boiled sweet, a bull's eye.

black sugar liquorice (juice).

black thief *see* **thief.**

blade *n* a leaf of cabbage, turnip, tobacco etc; a tea-leaf.

blae *adj* **1** blue; bluish; dark bluish grey. **2** bluish from cold, bloodlessness etc.

blaes a bluish-grey hardened clay, soft slate or shale.

blaeberry a bilberry.

blaln *n* a scar from a sore or wound; a weal.

blame *n* fault: '*It's no ma blame*'.

blash *n* **1** a splash of liquid etc. **2** a heavy shower of rain etc. **3** a weak mixture of drink, soup etc.

blashle 1 rainy, wet, gusty. **2** (*of food or drink*) weak.

blast *n* **1** a smoke, a puff of a pipe. **2** a stroke, a sudden attack of illness.

blate *adj* **1** timid, modest, shy: '*Ye needna be sae blate*'. **2** dull, stupid, easily deceived. **3** (*of crops*) backward in growth.

blatter *v* **1** talk a lot, noisily and fast. **2** (*of rain, hail etc*) rattle, beat with violence.

n **1** a loud rattling or rustling noise. **2** a storm of rain, hail etc.

blaud *v* damage, by harsh or careless treatment, injure.

blaw[1]**, bla, blow, byauve** [beeauve] NE *v* **1** blow. **2** boast; exaggerate. **3** (*draughts*) take a piece from (your opponent).

n **1** a blowing (of a horn etc). **2** a puff (of a pipe). **3** boasting, a boast; a boaster.

blawdoon a backdraught in a chimney or fireplace.

blaw[2] *n* a blow, a stroke.

blaw[3] *n* blossom.

blear *v*: **blear someone's ee** deceive someone.

blearle *adj* watery-eyed.

n liquid food, gruel.

bleck *n* **1** blacking (for leather). **2** (a small piece of) soot or smut. **3** a black person. **4** scoundrel, rascal.

v make black, blacken, dirty.

bleed *see* **bluld.**

bleem *see* **blulm.**

bleeter *see* **blooter.**

bleeze *n, v* blaze.

bleezln (fou) very drunk.

blenk *see* **blink.**

blether[1] *v* talk foolishly or too much (about nothing or about something untrue).

n **1 blethers** foolish talk, nonsense; long-winded (boasting) talk. **2 blethers!** nonsense!, rubbish! **3** a talk, a chat. **4** a person who talks foolishly or too much.

bletheratlon, bletherle foolish talk.

blether(an)skate a silly, foolish person (who talks too much).

blether[2] *n* a bladder.

bllb *n* a weak watery helping of tea, soup etc NE.

blld *see* **bluld.**

blide *see* **blithe.**

bliffert *see* **bluffert.**

blln, blind *adj* **1** blind. **2** (*of mist etc*) dense NE. **3** (*especially of a cow's teat*) having no opening.

v **1** blind. **2** close (the eyes) as in sleep NE.

blln drift drifting snow.

blln(d) falr (*often of albinos*) extremely fair.

blln(d) Harrle blindman's buff.

blln lump a boil which does not come to a head.

blink, blenk *v* make eyes at (someone), stare at.

n **1** a (pleasant) glance, brief look. **2** a short time, moment. **3** a wink of sleep.

blinker 1 the eye. **2 blinkers** eyelashes.

blinkle a (pocket) torch.

blirt *v* cry, weep, burst into tears.

bliss *v* bless.

blithe, blide SHETLAND, ORKNEY *adj* **1** blithe. **2** cheerful, glad, in good spirits.

blob *n* a drop of moisture, a bubble.

block, hammer and nail *n* a children's game.

blood *see* **bluld.**

bloom *see* **blulm.**

blooter, blulter, bleeter NE *n* a big,

clumsy, useless person; a foolish talker.

v **1** talk foolishly; blurt out. **2** bungle, make a mess of.

blootert very tired; drunk.

ɔlow *see* **blaw**[1].

ɔlowst [rhymes with 'oust'] *v, n* brag, boast.

ɔlue, bew, blyew [bleeoo] *adj, n* blue.

bluebell 1 a harebell. **2** an English bluebell.

blue keeker *see* **keek**.

ɔluffert, bliffert *n* **1** a squall (of wind and rain). **2** a blow, slap NE.

ɔluid, blid, bleed N, **blood** *n* blood.

v (cause to) bleed.

bluidshed bloodshot.

ɔluim, bleem N, **bloom** *n* **1** bloom. **2** a potato top.

ɔluiter *see* **blooter**.

ɔlybe NE *n* a large quantity of liquid, especially of spirits.

v drink heavily.

ɔlyew *see* **blue**.

ɔoadle *see* **bodle**.

ɔoak, boke, byock NE, **bock** *v* vomit, retch, belch.

n **1** a retch, a belch. **2** a feeling of sickness or disgust.

gie (someone) the (dry) boak cause to feel sick, retch or vomit; disgust.

ɔoakle *n* a piece of hard matter in the nose.

ɔoax *see* **box**.

ɔoay *see* **boy**.

ɔob *n* a dance.

ɔocht *v, past tense, past participle* bought.

ɔock *see* **boak**.

ɔockle SHETLAND, ORKNEY, N *n* a hobgoblin; a scarecrow.

ɔodach [boddach] *n* an old man.

ɔoddom *n, v* bottom SHETLAND, ORKNEY, NE.

ɔode *n* **1** an offer, a bid (especially at an auction). **2** the price asked by a seller; the offer of goods at a certain rate.

ɔodie, boadie, buddie *n* a person, a human being: (*referring to someone else or yourself*): 'Could ye no leave a bodie in peace?'.

bodle *n* **1** (*in past times*) a small copper coin. **2 no worth a bodle** not worth anything.

bog *v*: **bog-bleater** a bittern.

bog-cotton cotton-grass.

bogie *n*: **the game's a bogie** a call to cancel a game and start again when there has been a fault.

bogle *n* **1** an ugly or terrifying ghost; a cause of annoyance. **2** a scarecrow.

boillin *see* **bile**[1].

boke *see* **boak**.

bole *n* **1** a recess in a wall, later one used as a cupboard; a small opening in a wall. **2** a pay-desk window.

bo-man *n* a bogyman.

bonnet, bannet, bunnet *n* a soft flat brimless cap worn by men and boys, often one with a peak.

bonnetie a boys' game played with bonnets.

bonnie *adj* **1** beautiful, pretty. **2** (*of boys or men*) handsome, attractive. **3** good, excellent, fine. **4** great, considerable.

bonnie penny a high price.

a bonnie wheen *see* **wheen**.

bonspiel *n* a match or contest, now a curling match.

bonxie *n* a great skua SHETLAND, ORKNEY.

boo, bow *v* **1** bow (as a sign of respect etc). **2** bend, curve; become bent or crooked. **3** cause to bend.

boo-backit hump-backed.

boodle *n* a ghost, hobgoblin; a scarecrow NE.

boof *see* **buff**[1].

book *see* **bulk**.

bool[1] [-oo-] *n* **1** a bowl, the ball used in bowls; **bools** the game itself. **2** a ball or rounded object, *eg* a round stone, a round sweet. **3** a marble.

hae a bool in yer mou speak in an affected way.

bool^2 *n* a curved band, forming the handle of a pot, bucket etc.

boolie, bowlie [-ow- as in 'cow'] *adj* crooked, bent.

n a bowlegged person.

bowlie-backit hump-backed; round-shouldered.

bowlie-leggit bow-legged.

boon *n* a bound, boundary, limit.

boorach *n* **1** a heap; a crowd, group, swarm. **2** *also* **boorachie** a muddle, mess N, HIGHLAND.

boord *see* **buird**.

boordly, boorly *see* **buirdly**.

boortree *n* an elder tree.

bootch *n*, *v* botch, bungle, muddle.

border *n*: **the Borders** the area lying between the Scottish-English border and Lothian.

bore *n* a hole, *eg* a shelter or hiding-place; an opening.

v press (against etc).

borestone, borestane 1 a stone bored to hold a flagstaff. **2** a boundary stone.

borra *see* **barra**.

bosie *n* **1** a hug, cuddle. **2** a bosom.

boss *adj* **1** hollow; empty. **2** without money or brains.

both *see* **baith**.

bothy *n* **1** a rough hut used as temporary accommodation *eg* by shepherds, salmon-fishers, mountaineers. **2** permanent living quarters for workmen, especially a separate building on a farm to house unmarried male farmworkers.

v live in a **bothy**.

boucht^1, **bucht** *n* a sheepfold.

boucht^2 *v*, *past tense, past participle* bought.

bouet *n* a (hand) lantern.

bouff, bowf *n* a contemptuous term for a big person NE.

bouk^1 [-oo-] *n* **1** the carcass of a slaughtered animal. **2** the body of a person (living or dead).

bouk^2 [-oo-] *n* size, quantity.

boukit 1 -sized, in size: '*little-boukit, muckle-boukit*'. **2** bulky.

bow^1 [rhymes with 'cow'] *n* **1** a bow (the weapon). **2** an arch, especially of a bridge, an arched gateway *in place-names, eg* **Netherbow**.

bowdie(-leggit) bandy-legged.

bow-backit hump-backed.

bowbrig an arched bridge.

no bow an ee not close your eyes, not sleep.

bow^2 [rhymes with 'cow'] *n* a buoy.

bow *see* **boo**.

bowdie, bowdie-leggit *see* **bow**^{1}.

bowf *v* **1** (*especially of a large dog*) bark; make a loud dull sound. **2** cough loudly.

bowf *see* **bouff**.

bowfin *adj* smelly.

bowie [-ow- as in 'cow'] *n* **1** a broad, shallow dish, bowl or small tub. **2** a barrel for water or ale.

bow-kail [-ow- as in 'cow'] *n* cabbage.

bowl [-ow- as in 'cow'] *n, in Scots used also where English prefers* basin: '*puddin bowl*'.

bowlie a small bowl.

bowlie *see* **bool**^{2}.

bowsie *adj* big, fat, puffed up.

bowster *n* a bolster.

bowsterous [-ow-] *adj* boisterous, fierce; rowdy.

bowstock *n* a cabbage with a properly-developed heart NE.

bowt *n, v* bolt.

box, boax *n* (*informal*) an accordion or melodeon.

box-bed a bed enclosed in wooden panelling, the front having either sliding panels, hinged doors, or curtains.

on the box receiving weekly assistance from a poor fund, more recently from social services.

boy, boay *n* **1** a man of any age; a bachelor of any age still living with his parents. **2** an apprentice. **3** **the Bhoys** nickname for Celtic football team.

boyne, bine *n* a shallow tub; a wash-tub.

bra *see* **braw.**

brace *n* a fireplace; a mantelpiece.

brae *n* **1** the (steep or sloping) bank of a river or lake or shore of the sea. **2** a bank or stretch of ground rising fairly steeply; a hillside; a road with a steep gradient. **3** the brow of a hill. **4** an upland, mountainous district: **the Braes o Balquhidder.**

gae doon the brae go to ruin; (*of an old person*) become physically weaker.

braid, broad *adj* broad.

braid oot unrestrainedly, without hiding anything.

braid Scots the Scots language (*see* **Scots**).

braid Scotland in the whole (breadth) of Scotland.

brain *v* hurt, especially by a blow to the head, wound, beat severely.

braird *see* **breird.**

braith *n* breath.

brak, brek *n* ,*v*, *past tense also* **brak;** *past participle* **brukken** break.

broken 1 ruined, bankrupt. **2** (*of milk*) curdled.

brakefast, brakfast *n* breakfast.

bramble, brammle *n* a blackberry; its bush.

brammed-up *adj* dressed-up.

brammer *n* an attractive woman.

brammle *see* **bramble.**

brander *n* **1** a gridiron. **2** a framework used in construction work; a trestle. **3** the iron grating over an entrance to a drain etc.

brang *see* **brocht.**

branks *n* **1** a kind of bridle or halter, originally with wooden side-pieces. **2** (*in past times*) an instrument of public punishment, an iron bridle and gag. **3** mumps.

pit the branks on restrain, cut (someone) down to size.

brash *n* **1** a short bout of illness. **2** a sudden gust of wind or burst of rain.

brat *n* **1** a (poor or ragged) garment. **2** a bib, pinafore; a (worker's) coarse apron.

brattle *n* **1** a loud clatter, a rattle, *eg* of horses' hooves. **2** a peal of thunder. **3** a short rush.

v clatter, clash, rattle.

braw, bra *adj* **1** fine, handsome, good-looking; well-dressed. **2** very good, excellent, fine. **3** (*of sums of money etc*) considerable: '*It cost a braw penny*'.

adv **1** well, finely. **2** very.

brawlie 1 very well, excellently. **2** well, in good health.

braws 1 good clothes, your best clothes. **2** beautiful or good things.

Braw Lad, Braw Lass the young man and girl chosen annually by the people of Galashiels to represent the burgh at the **Braw Lads' Gathering** on 29 June.

braxy *n* a usually fatal intestinal disease of sheep.

bread *see* **breid.**

brecham *n* a horse-collar.

bree *n* **1** a liquid in which something has been steeped or boiled, stock; soup, gravy. **2** whisky. **3** liquid or moisture of any kind.

breed *n* breadth.

breed *see* **brod**[3].

breek *n, pl* **breeks 1** trousers; underpants, knickers. **2** a forked stick such as is used for a catapult.

v tuck up (a dress etc) especially for rough work.

breekums 1 (very) short trousers; knee-breeches. **2** affectionate term for a little boy.

pull up yer breeks pull up your socks.

breem *n* broom (the plant) NE.

breenge *v* rush forward recklessly or carelessly; plunge; make a violent effort.

n a violent or clumsy rush, a dash, a plunge.

breengin pushing, sharp-tongued; bustling.

breer *n* brier.

breet NE *n* **1** a brute. **2** a (poor etc) fellow, creature.

breether *see* **brither**.

breid, bread *n* **1** bread. **2** an oatcake N.

breird, braird *n* the first shoots of grain etc.

v germinate, sprout.

breist *n* a breast.

v spring up or forward; climb.

in a breist abreast.

brek *see* **brak**.

brent *adj* (*of the brow*) smooth, unwrinkled.

bress *n* brass.

brewster *n* a brewer.

bricht *adj* bright.

bridder *see* **brither**.

bridle *n*: **Forfar bridle** a kind of pie made of a circle of pastry folded over, with a filling of meat, onions etc.

brief *n* (*law*) an official document; a summons; a legal writ.

brig *n* a bridge.

brinkie-broo *n* (*used to children*) the forehead NE.

brither, breether NE, **bridder** SHETLAND *n* a brother.

brither-dochter a niece on your brother's side.

brither-son a nephew on your brother's side.

brittle *adj* difficult.

brizz *v*, *n* bruise.

broad *see* **braid**.

broch [-ch as in 'loch'] *n* **1** a **burgh; the Broch** used as a proper name for the nearest town, *now only Fraserburgh, Aberdeenshire or Burghhead, Banffshire*. **2** a late prehistoric structure, consisting of a large round tower with hollow stone-built walls; (not, as once supposed, built by the **Picts**). **3** a halo round the sun or the moon, the latter indicating bad weather. **4** (*curling*) a circle round the tee NE.

brocht *past tense, also* **brung, brang** brought.

past participle, also **brung** brought.

brock[1] *n* **1** a badger. **2** contemptuous term for a person.

brock[2], **bruck** SHETLAND, ORKNEY *n* broken or small pieces; rubbish; leftovers.

brockit *adj* **1** having black and white stripes or spots. **2** streaked with dirt; filthy.

brod[1] *n* **1** something with a point, a goad, a spur. **2** a prod or prick with a sharp instrument etc.

brod[2] *n* **1** a board. **2** a table spread for a meal. **3** a games board, now especially a draughtboard. **4** a committee etc. **5** a (church) collection plate.

brod[3], **breed** NE *n* a brood.

brog *n* a tool for boring.

brogue *n* a heavy shoe, especially one decorated with a distinctive pierced pattern along the seams.

broken *see* **brak**.

broo[1] *n* **1** a liquid, especially that in which something has been boiled. **2** liquid or moisture of any kind.

broo[2] *n* a brow.

broo *see* **buroo**.

brook *v* make black or dirty.

n soot on pots, kettle etc.

broon *adj*, *n* brown.

broonie, brownie a good fairy, supposed to carry out household tasks in the night; a goblin.

brose *n* **1** a dish of oat- or pease-meal mixed with boiling water or milk, with salt and butter etc added. **2** a meal of which **brose** was the chief ingredient; your living, livelihood.

brosie 1 covered or fed with **brose**. **2** stout (with too much food or drink).

brosie-heidit fat and inactive NE.

broth *n* a thick soup made from mutton, barley and vegetables, Scotch broth.

browden adj: **browden on** extremely fond of.

v **browden (on)** be fond (of), be intent (on).

brownie see **broon.**

bruck see **brock**[2].

bruckle adj easily broken, brittle; crumbling.

brukken see **brak.**

brung see **brocht.**

brunt see **burn**[2].

brust see **birst.**

bubble, bibble n **1** a bubble. **2** mucus from the nose.

v **1** bubble. **2** weep in a loud snivelling way.

bubblie adj **1** snotty, dirty with nasal mucus. **2** tearful, snivelling.

n a tearful person.

bubbly jock a turkey cock.

sair hauden doon by the bubbly jock overwhelmed with too much to do.

bucht see **boucht**[1].

bucket n **1** a quantity of drink: '*He taks a guid bucket*'. **2** a dustbin; a wastepaper basket.

bucket-scranner a scrounger in dustbins.

buckie[1] n **1** an edible shellfish, usually a whelk; its shell. **2** a snail-shell. **3** something of little value: '*It's no worth a buckie*'.

buckie[2] n a hip, the fruit of the wild rose.

Buckie n: **gae tae Buckie (an bottle skate)!** go to hell!, get lost! NE.

budder see **bather.**

buddle see **bodle.**

buff[1], **boof** n a blow (making a dull sound).

v strike, beat.

buff[2] n silly talk.

buffets npl mumps.

bug see **big**[2].

buik, book, beuk, byeuk [beeook] n **1** a book. **2** a record book or register. **3** the Bible; the reading of the Bible, family worship.

v book.

buik-lair learning, education.

buird, boord, byoord [beeoord] NE n **1** a board. **2** a table, often one spread for a meal.

buirdly, boor(d)ly adj **1** burly. **2** rough NE.

buit[1], **bit, beet** N n a boot.

buit[2], **beet** N n: **tae the buit** in addition, into the bargain, to boot.

bul [rhymes with 'Mull'], **bill** n a bull.

bullie a bullfinch.

bullax n an axe, hatchet N.

buller n **1** a bubble; a whirlpool; a bubbling or boiling up of water: **the Bullers of Buchan.** **2** a roar, bellow.

bullox v spoil, make a mess of.

n a mess.

bum v **1** make a humming or buzzing noise.

2 make a droning sound.

3 brag, boast.

4 go on vigorously NE.

n **1** a humming or droning sound.

2 a person who reads, sings or plays badly.

3 a musical note NE.

4 a boastful person.

bummer 1 an insect that makes a humming noise, especially a bumblebee or bluebottle.

2 a humming top.

3 a factory siren.

4 a thing or person (or animal) which is very large or wonderful of its kind.

bummin very good, worth boasting about NE.

bumbee a bumblebee.

bum-clock a humming beetle.

bumbaze v perplex, confuse, bamboozle.

bumfle adj (*of a person*) lumpy in shape.

bumfle v **1** puff out, bulge. **2** roll up untidily; rumple up: '*aw bumfelt up*'.

n an untidy bundle; a pucker, untidy fold, especially in cloth.

bumflie, bumfelt bundled up,

rumpled; untidily put on: '*Yer under-skirt's aw bumflie*'.

bummle *v* **1** (*of a bee*) hum. **2** read, play or sing badly; stutter, stammer; speak carelessly.

n **1** a wild bee. **2** a bungle, a mess.

bumps *npl* **1** *usually* **gie someone his or her bumps** mark a child's birthday by thumping him or her on the back, a thump for every year of age. **2** very fast turns of a skipping rope.

bun[1] *n* **1** a bun; in Scotland now usually less sweet than in England. **2** = **black bun** (*see* **black**).

bun[2] *n* the tail of a hare or rabbit.

bun, bund *see* **bind**.

bung *v* throw violently, hurl.

n the act of throwing forcibly.

in a bung in a temper, in the sulks NE.

bung-fu *adj* **1** completely full. **2** very drunk.

bunker *n* **1** a chest or box, often one used also as a seat. **2** a small sandpit, now especially on a golf-course. **3** a storage receptacle for household coal.

bunnet *see* **bonnet**.

bur *n* the tongue or top edge of the upper of a shoe SHETLAND, N.

burd *see* **bird**.

burgh *n* (*until 1975*) a borough, a town with special privileges conferred by charter and having a corporation.

burn[1] *n* a stream, brook.

burn[2] *v, past tense, past participle* **brunt** burn.

burnie (*child's word*) hot.

Burns: **Burns Night** 25 January, the anniversary of the birth of the poet Robert Burns.

Burns Supper a celebration meal, held annually to commemorate the birth of Robert Burns.

buroo, broo *n* the Unemployment Benefit Office; unemployment benefit received from it; a job centre.

on the broo on the dole.

bursen, burst, bursten, burstit *see* **birst**.

buss *n* **1** a bush. **2** a clump of some low-growing plant, *eg* heather, rushes. **3** a mass of seaweed on sunken rocks.

but *preposition* **1** *also* **bit**. **2** out or away from the speaker or spectator; over; across, through (a house etc).

adv **1** in or towards the outer part of a house etc; into the kitchen or outer room; out. **2** though: '*It wisnae me but*'.

conjunction, also **bit** but.

adj **1** outer, outside; of the **but**. **2** of the parlour or best room NE.

n the kitchen or outer room, especially of a **but and ben**.

but and ben *adv* **1** in (or to) both the outer and inner parts, backwards and forwards, to and fro; everywhere. **2** at opposite ends (of the same house, passage or landing).

n a two-roomed cottage.

but the hoose **1** the kitchen or outer end of a **but and ben** N. **2** the best room NE.

butch [rhymes with 'hutch'] *v* butcher, slaughter (an animal) for meat.

butchermeat *n* butcher's meat.

butt[1] *n* a ridge or strip of ploughed land.

butt[2] *n* **1** ground for archery practice. **2** (*grouse-shooting*) a wall or bank of earth erected to hide the guns.

butter *n, v*: **buttered** made with butter as an ingredient: '*buttered bannocks*'.

butterie a butter biscuit; a bread roll made of a high-fat, croissant-like dough.

buttons *npl,* **buttony** *n* a boys' game rather like marbles, but played with buttons with different names and values.

by, be *preposition* **1** by. **2** in comparison with, as distinct from: '*Archie was auld by me*'. **3** except, besides: '*There's monie folk by him*'. **4** (*of age, quality etc*) past: '*by their best*'. **5** concerning, about: '*I ken nothing worse by him*'.

adv **1** by. **2** nearby; present: '*wi a'bodie by*'.

conjunction **1** by the time that, as soon as: '*I was drookit by I made the scuil*'. **2** compared with (what); than: '*He's caulder by he was*'.

by's, bels *preposition* **1** except; instead of. **2** compared with.

by-common out of the ordinary, unusual.

bygane 1 (*of* (*a period of*) *time*) past; ago: '*these seven year bygane*'. **2** (*of actions, things*) belonging to past time; done etc in the past.

byganes things of the past or done in the past, especially past offences or injuries.

bygaun passing by.

in the bygaun in the passing, incidentally.

by my certle *see* **certle.**

by-ordlnar *adj* extraordinary, unusual.

adv extraordinarily, unusually.

by yersel out of your mind, beside yourself.

by wl over and done with, finished.

byaak *see* **bake.**

byauve *see* **blaw**[1].

byeuk *see* **bulk.**

byke *n* **1** a bees', wasps' or ants' nest; a beehive. **2** a swarm, especially of people.

v (*of bees*) swarm NE.

bylle *see* **ballle.**

byock *see* **boak.**

byoord *see* **bulrd.**

byre *n* a cowshed.

C

ca[1], **caa, caw, call** *v* **1** call. **2** order (a drink). **3** call (a person) names. **4** urge on (by calling), drive (animals). **5** drive (a vehicle etc). **6** bring home (turnips etc) from the fields. **7 ca awa** be driven; drive, proceed; keep going, plod on. **8** hammer in or on. **9** knock, push. **10** set or keep in motion (*eg* a skipping rope). **11** turn (a handle). **12** ransack, search NE.
n **1** a call. **2** a hurry. **3** a knock, blow. **4** a search. **5** the motion of waves. **6** a turn, *eg* of a skipping rope.
ca cannie *see* **cannie.**
caw the feet fae knock (a person) over; astonish.
ca for someone call on, visit.
ca someone for name after: '*He's cawed for his grandpa*'.
ca someone for everything heap insults on someone.
ca oot dislocate.
ca throu *v* **1** work vigorously. **2** pull through (an illness).
ca-throu *n* **1** drive, energy. **2** a disturbance. **3** (*of clothes*) a slight or preliminary wash. **4** a search.
ca[2] *n* a calf.
caa *see* **ca**[1].
caal *see* **cauld.**
cabal *n* NE **1** a group who meet for a gossip or a drink. **2** a violent dispute.
cabbie-labbie *n* a quarrel, uproar.
cabbitch *n* a cabbage.
caber *n* a heavy pole, a long slender tree-trunk.
toss the caber throw the heavy pole, as in **Highland Games.**
cack, cackie, kach *n* human excrement.
caddie[1] *n* a bottle-fed lamb SHETLAND, ORKNEY.

caddie[2] *n* **1** (*golf*) an attendant who carries a player's clubs. **2** a trolley for a golf-bag.
v act as a **caddie** *n* 1.
cadge *v* **1** peddle wares. **2** carry loads, parcels etc.
cadger *n* **1** a travelling dealer, especially in fish; a carrier, a carter. **2** a bad-tempered person NE.
cadger's news stale news.
cadie *n* a man's cap.
caff, cauf *n* chaff, often used for stuffing mattresses etc.
caffle *see* **cauf**[1].
cahootchie *n* rubber.
caibin *n* a cabin.
cailleach [kallyach, kailyach] *n* **1** an old woman. **2** the last sheaf of corn cut at harvest. **3** the harvest festival.
caip *see* **kep**[1].
cair *v* **1** stir N. **2** scrape or rake up N.
caird[1], **cyaard** NE *n* **1** a tinker; a tramp; a rough person: '*Stoap chummin aboot wi thae cairds.*' **2** a person who scolds N.
caird[2], **card** *n* **1** a card. **2** *also* **cairt** a playing card. **3** a chart, map. **4** a photograph.
cairn *n* **1** a pyramid of loose stones, as a boundary-marker or other landmark, often now on the tops of mountains or as a memorial; a heap of stones in general. **2 Cairn (terrier)** a type of small West Highland terrier, now a separate breed.
cairngorm *n* a yellowish semi-precious stone.
cairpet *n* a carpet.
cairriage *n* a carriage.
cairrie, carry *v* carry.
n **1** a (heavy) weight, burden. **2** a lift in a vehicle: '*Gie's a cairrie doon the*

road. **3** the motion of the clouds; the clouds in motion.

cairried **1** carried away, elated. **2** conceited. **3** delirious.

cairrie-oot (a portion of) food or drink bought in a restaurant or pub to be eaten or drunk elsewhere.

cairt *n* cart.

cairter a carter.

cairtie a child's home-made cart.

cairt *see* **caird**².

cake, kyaak NE [keeak] *n* **1** a cake, often an oatcake. **2** cake, fruit loaf etc given to children or visitors at New Year.

cald *see* **cauld**.

call *see* **ca**¹.

callan *see* **callant**.

callant, callan *n* **1** a youth, fellow. **2** an affectionate or familiar term for an older man NE.

caller *adj* **1** (*of fish, vegetables etc*) fresh, just caught or gathered: '*caller herrin*'. **2** (*of air, water etc*) cool, fresh, refreshing. **3** healthy, vigorous.

caller oo *see* **oo**².

cam, came *see* **come**.

caman *n* the club or stick used in the game of **shinty**.

camceil, camsile *n* a sloping ceiling or roof WEST.

cammock *n* a crooked staff or stick NE.

camshachle *see* **camshauchle**.

camshauchle, camshachle *adj* distorted, bent, twisted, disordered.

camsile *see* **camceil**.

camstairie *adj* perverse, unruly, quarrelsome.

can *v:* **cannae, canna** cannot.

n skill, knowledge, ability N.

cud *v, past tense* could.

cudnae, cudna could not.

canaul *n* a canal WEST.

candibrod *n* sugar-candy.

canker *n* a bad temper.

v fret; become bad-tempered NE.

canker(i)t **1** cross, ill-natured. **2** (*of weather*) threatening, stormy NE.

canna, cannae *see* **can**.

cannas *n* canvas NE.

cannie *adj* **1** cautious, careful, prudent.

2 skilful.

3 favourable, lucky.

4 frugal, sparing.

5 gentle, quiet, steady.

6 pleasant; good, kind.

7 comfortable, easy.

ca cannie go warily, act with care.

no cannie unnatural, supernatural.

cannie, caunie WEST *n* a candle.

cantie *adj* **1** lively, cheerful, pleasant. **2** small and neat. **3** comfortable.

cantle¹ *n* NE **1** a corner, projection, ledge. **2** (the crown of) the head.

cantle² *v:* **cantle up** **1** brighten. **2** recover your health or spirits. **3** bristle with anger.

cantrip *n* **1** a spell, charm; magic, *mainly* **cast cantrips**. **2** a trick, antic, piece of mischief.

cap, caup *n* a (wooden) cup or bowl.

capercailzie [capperkaylie] *n* a woodgrouse, a kind of large game bird.

capernoitie *adj* capricious, crazy; drunk, giddy; irritable.

car, caur *adj* left (hand or side), left-handed.

car *see* **caur**¹.

carb *n, v* wrangle, quarrel.

card *see* **caird**.

carefae *see* **carefu**.

carefu, carefae *adj* careful.

carfuffle, curfuffle *v* put into confusion or disorder.

n **1** a disorder, mess. **2** a disagreement, quarrel. **3** a fuss.

car-handit *see* **corrie-fistit**.

cark *n* care, anxiety NE.

carl-doddie *see* **curl-doddie**.

carle *n* a man, fellow, a chap; a man of the common people, a peasant or labourer.

   the auld carle the Devil.

carline *n* **1** a (usually old) woman; a

witch. **2** last sheaf of corn on a harvest field.

carnaptious *adj* irritable, quarrelsome.

carrant *n* **1** an expedition, a sudden journey. **2** a social gathering, wild party; an uproar.

carrie-handit *see* **corrie-fistit**.

carry *see* **cairrie**.

carsackie *n* an overall.

carse *n* land along the banks of a river.

casket *n* an apple-core: '*Gie's a bite o yer casket*'.

cassie *see* **causey**.

cassin *see* **cast**.

cast, kest, kiest NE *v, past tense also* **kiest** NE, **cuist;** *past participle also* **casten, cassin, cuisten 1** cast.

2 dig, cut (peats etc); dig, clear out (a ditch etc).

3 (*of animals*) give birth to.

4 (*of bees*) swarm.

5 (*of a horse*) throw (its rider).

6 toss (the head).

7 throw (off) clothes etc.

8 sow (seed).

n **1** a cast.

2 a turn or twist.

3 your fortune, fate.

4 an opportunity, chance NE.

5 a friendly turn; help.

6 appearance, a look.

casten (*of colours*) faded.

cast aboot manage, arrange, look after NE.

cast cantrips *see* **cantrip**.

cast something at someone reproach someone with something.

cast oot disagree, quarrel.

cast something up to someone reproach someone with something: '*She's always castin it up that Ah lied tae her*'.

castock *n* a stalk of **kail** or cabbage.

cat *n*: **cattle 1** the game of tip-cat. **2** a catapult.

cat's een the germander speedwell.

cat's face a round of six scones etc.

cat's lick a hasty superficial wash.

cat-wittit 1 hare-brained, unbalanced. **2** spiteful; short-tempered.

cat and bat, cat and dog the game of tip-cat.

catch *v, past tense also* **catchit, caucht, cotch** catch.

n **1** a hold, grasp. **2** a sharp pain, a stitch.

catchers a game played with a ball, or a bat and ball.

catchie clappie a kind of ball game.

catterbatter *n* a quarrel, disagreement FIFE, SOUTH.

cattle *see* **cat**.

cattle *n* **1** lice, fleas etc. **2** birds and beasts in general NE. **3** a term of contempt for people.

cattle beas(ts) livestock.

caucht *see* **catch**.

cauf[1], **caffie** NE *n* a calf.

cauf grund, cauf kintra the place of your birth and early life.

cauf [2] *n* the calf (of the leg).

cauf *see* **caff**.

cauk, kalk NE, PERTH *n* chalk, lime.

caul *see* **cauld**.

cauld, caul, cald, caal N, **cowl(d)** SHETLAND, ORKNEY, CAITHNESS, ROSS, ARGYLL, ULSTER, **cold** *adj, n* cold.

cauldit suffering from a cold.

cauldrif(e) 1 cold, likely to feel cold. **2** cold in manner; indifferent.

caul(d) kail het again 1 re-heated **broth** or other food. **2** a stale story etc.

caunie *see* **cannie**.

caup *see* **cap**.

caur[1], **car** *n* a car; a tramcar.

caur[2] *npl* calves NE.

caur *see* **car**.

cause, kis *conjunction* because.

causey, cassie *n* **1** a paved area, a roadway, street, pavement, mainly cobblestones. **2** the paved area around a farmhouse.

v pave.

croon o the causey the middle of the road; a conspicuous, respectable or leading position.

caution [rhymes with 'nation'] *n* (*law*) bail.

cavie *n* a children's game, prisoners' base NE.

caw *see* **ca**[1].

ceilidh *n* [**kaily**] **1** originally an informal social gathering among neighbours, with or without singing, playing instruments, storytelling etc; a visit, chat, gossip HIGHLAND. **2** an organized evening entertainment (in a hall, hotel etc) of Scottish music etc. *v* visit, chat.

certie, (by) my certie *adv, interjection* to be sure.

chaave *see* **tyauve**.

chack[1], **check** *n* **1** a check. **2** a groove or notch. **3 check** a door-key.
v **1** check. **2** make a **chack 2** on (a board etc). **3 check** scold, reprove: '*Check thae bairns fur drawin on the wa*'.

chack[2] *v* **1** snap shut; bite. **2** make a clicking noise; (*of the teeth*) chatter NE. **3** *also* **check** catch (*eg* fingers in a door), hack, chop.
n **1** *also* **check** a cut or hack; a bruise, nip. **2** a snack.

chack[3] *n* check, checked fabric.

chacks *see* **chuck**.

chaff *v* chafe, rub, wear.

chaffie *n* a chaffinch.

chaft *n* **chafts 1** jaws. **2** cheeks.
chaft blade 1 the jaw-bone. **2** the cheek-bone.

chairge *n* **1** a charge. **2** an expense, a cost.

champ *v* trample; crush, pound, mash.
champit tatties mashed potatoes.

chance *n* **chances** tips, perks.
no chancie 1 unfortunate, unlucky. **2** not to be relied on, dangerous: '*It's no chancie gaun hame late*'.

change *see* **chynge**.

channel *n* **1** a gutter. **2** *also* **channer** shingle, gravel.

chanter *n* the melody pipe of the bagpipes; a separate pipe for practising on.

chantie *n* a chamber-pot; a W.C. pedestal.

chap, shap SHETLAND, N *n* **1** a knock, blow. **2** a stroke of a clock or bell.
v **1** knock, strike.
2 (*dominoes or card games*) tap on the table as a sign that you cannot play at your turn.
3 tap at a door or a window.
4 mash (vegetables).
5 chop.
6 choose; pick sides.
7 strike a bargain with; agree to (a bargain).

chapper 1 a door knocker. **2** a tool for pounding NE.

chappit tatties mashed potatoes.

chap han(d)s shake hands.

chape *adj* cheap.

chaps, chips NE *v* **1** pick out, choose. **2** choose (sides for a game).
chaps me I claim, I prefer: '*Chaps me this een*'.

chark *see* **chirk**.

chase *v* hurry: '*Chasin aw ower the toon*'.

chasie 1 a game of tig. **2** a kind of marbles game.

chat[1] *n* impudence, impertinent talk.

chat[2] *n* a snack; a morsel.

chate *see* **cheat**.

chatter *v* shatter.

chattert *adj* nibbled; frayed, tattered.

chattit *adj* chafed, frayed NE.

chaumer *n* **1** a chamber. **2** a private room, originally a bedroom, latterly also the parlour. **3** a sleeping place for farmworkers.

chaw[1] *v* **1** *also* **chow** chew. **2** provoke, vex; make jealous.
n **1** *also* **chow** chew. **2** a disappointment, snub; a cutting reply.

chaw[2] *n* a jaw, a talk, gossip, lecture N.

chaw see **haw**[1].

cheat, chate NE v **1** cheat. **2** I'm
cheated, it cheats me I'm very much
mistaken: '*He's a hamely chiel yon, or
I'm cheated*'.

cheatrie cheating, deceit, fraud.

check see **chack**[1], **chack**[2].

cheek n the side of something, *eg* of a
door, fireplace.

cheen, chine NE n a chain.

cheenge see **chynge**.

cheenie n china.

cheep v **1** whisper; make a pitiful
sound. **2** squeak, creak.
n **1 no a cheep** not a whisper, hint,
word. **2** *also* **cheeper** a light kiss:
'*Gie's a wee cheeper*'.

cheer, chyre n a chair.

cheese n: **no say cheese** not mention,
keep quiet about something.

cheese see **chuse**.

cheet, cheetie(-pussy) n a cat; a call
to a cat.

cheuch see **teuch**.

chib n a knife (as a weapon).
v injure with a knife.

chice see **chuse**.

chief n the head of a **clan** or feudal
community.
adj friendly, on close terms.

chiel see **chield**.

chield, chiel n **1** a lad, (young) man,
fellow. **2** a young woman FIFE.

child, chile n, pl **childer** a child.
children's hearing a system set up in
Scotland in 1971 to deal with children
in difficulties, for example because of
lack of parental care, truancy, criminal
behaviour. A hearing takes place before a panel of three specially-trained
volunteers, drawn from the children's
panel for the area. At the hearing the
panel members discuss with the child
and his/her parents what the difficulties are in order to make the best
decisions about the child's future.

chimbley, chimley n **1** a chimney. **2** a
grate, hearth, fireplace NE.

chimbley-heid a mantelpiece.

chincough [rhymes with 'loch']
whooping cough.

chine see **cheen**.

chingle, jingle n shingle.

chinnie bairdie see **bairdie**.

chippit *adj* (*of fruit etc*) damaged.

chips see **chaps**.

chirk, chark v make a harsh, unpleasant noise.

chirl, churl v, n chirp, warble, murmur.

chirm n a bird's call, chirp.
v **1** warble, murmur. **2** fret, complain.

chirple v twitter N.

chirt v squeeze, press, squirt.

chist n chest.

chitter v **1** chatter, shiver (with cold
etc). **2** (*of birds*) twitter.
chitterin bit, chitterie bite a snack
eaten after swimming.

chock v choke.

choice see **chuse**.

chollers npl **1** the jowls, a double chin.
2 the gills of a fish. **3** the wattles of a
cock SW, SOUTH.

chookie CENTRAL, **chuckie** NE,
COAST n **1** a chicken, a bird. **2** a
fool. **3** term of endearment, especially to a child.

chore [choray, chore] v steal E CEN-
TRAL, SOUTH.

chow see **chaw**[1].

chowk [-ow- as in 'cow'] v choke SW,
SOUTH.

chowks npl the cheeks, jaws.

chowl [-ow- as in 'cow'] n jowl.

chowp n: **nae a chowp** not a single
word NE.

christen see **kirsten**.

Christmas n a Christmas present,
Christmas box: '*There yer Christmas*'.

chuck, juck n **1** a pebble (or occasionally a marble). **2 chucks** *also* **chacks** a
game involving throwing and catch-
ing pebbles.
chuckie (stane) a small stone, a pebble.

chucken *n* a chicken.

chuckie *see* **chookie.**

chuddle *n* chewing gum NE.

chug, teug *v, n* tug.

chum *v* accompany as a friend: '*Ah'll chum ye tae the shops*'; associate (with).

churl *see* **chirl.**

chuse, choice *v, also* **cheese, chyse** NE, E CENTRAL choose. *n, also* **chice** a choice.

chynge, cheenge, change *n* **1** a change. **2** exchange, trade; custom, business NE. *v* **1** change. **2** exchange. **3** (*of food*) go bad, deteriorate N.

 chynge yer feet put on dry shoes and socks or stockings.

 chynge yersel change your clothes.

chyre *see* **cheer.**

chyse *see* **chuse.**

cinner, shinner *n* a cinder.

claa *see* **clowe**[2].

clabber, glabber *n* mud, clay.

clabbydhu *n* a (large) mussel WEST.

clachan *n* a (small) villlage.

clacht *see* **claught.**

clack *n* **1** a sharp sound. **2** *also* **cleck** gossip, chatter, insolence.

claddin *n* cladding boarding; lining with such.

claes, clathes *npl* clothes.

 claes pole 1 a clothes-prop. **2** a fixed pole to which the clothes-line is attached.

 claes raip a clothes-line.

clag, cleg *v* **1** smear (with mud, clay etc). **2** clog, block up. *n* **1** a lump or mass of clay, mud, snow etc. **2** a quantity of any kind of soft (sticky) food.

 claggle sticky; (*of weather*) producing heavy, sticky soil.

 claggum treacle toffee.

claik[1] *n* **1** a shrill, raucous bird-cry. **2** (a) gossip. *v* **1** (*of birds*) cry. **2** (*of children*) cry continuously and impatiently. **3** gossip, chatter.

claik[2] *v* smear, dirty (with something sticky) NE.

claik[3] *n* barnacle.

clairt *see* **clart.**

claith *n* **1** cloth. **2** clothing.

clam[1], **clam shell** *n* a scallop (shell).

clam[2] *adj* sticky, damp, clammy.

clam, clamb *see* **clim.**

clamihewit *n* **1** a blow, a thrashing. **2** an uproar, a hubbub.

clamjamfrie, clanjamfrie *n* **1** a crowd of people; rabble, riff-raff. **2** rubbish, junk.

clamp[1] *n, v* patch.

clamp[2], **clamper** *v* walk noisily or heavily, clump.

clan *n* a local or family group, especially in the Highlands or Borders.

clang *see* **cling.**

clanjamfrie *see* **clamjamfrie.**

clap *n* **1** a heavy blow. **2** an affectionate pat. *v* **1** pat affectionately. **2** press down, flatten. **3 clap doon** flop, crouch (down).

 clappit-in (*of the face*) sunken through illness etc.

clapshot *n* potatoes and turnip mashed together *originally* ORKNEY.

clarsach *n* a wire-strung Highland or Irish harp.

clart, clairt, clert *n* **1** mud. **2** a lump of something unpleasant. **3** a big, dirty, untidy person. *v* **1** smear, dirty: '*clartit wi dubs*'. **2** act in a slovenly, dirty way; work with dirty or sticky substances.

 clartie, clairtie, clertie dirty, muddy; sticky.

clash *n* **1** a blow, collision. **2** a mass of something soft or moist; a downpour. **3** chatter, talk, gossip. **4** a tale, story. *v* **1** strike, slap. **2** slam (a door). **3** throw forcefully or noisily (especially anything wet or liquid).

4 (*often of rain*) fall with a crash or splash.

5 tell tales, gossip, chatter.

adv with a crash, bump.

clashmaclavers *npl* gossip, idle tales.

clash-pyot a tell-tale.

clat *n* a lump, clot, especially of something soft.

clatch *n* **1** a splashing sound. **2** a wet mass, clot. **3** a dirty, untidy person, a slut; a fat clumsy woman.

v move with a splashing or squelching sound.

clathes *see* **claes.**

clatter *n, often* **clatters** gossip, scandal; rumours.

v **1** gossip, talk scandal. **2** (*of birds*) chatter, call.

claucht *see* **claught, cleek.**

claught, cla(u)cht *n, v* clutch, grasp, grab.

claut *n* **1** a claw. **2** a clutch, hold. **3** a hoe; an implement for scraping dung, dirt etc. **4** a handful; a lump.

v scrape; clean by scraping, rake.

claver[1] *v, n* gossip.

claver[2], **clivver** *n* clover.

claw *see* **clowe**[2].

claymore *n* (*in past times*) a large Highland sword.

clean *adj* pure, absolute, complete.

cleck *v* **1** hatch. **2** give birth to. **3** invent; conceive.

cleckin 1 the act of hatching or giving birth. **2** a brood, litter: of animals; (*contemptuously*) of human beings.

cleck *see* **clack.**

cled *see* **cleed.**

cleed, clethe *v, past tense, past participle* **cled, cleed 1** clothe. **2** cover thickly; fill.

cleek, click *n* **1** a hook.

2 a salmon gaff.

3 a latch, a catch.

4 the hooked piece of iron used by children for guiding a **gird**[1].

5 a boyfriend or girlfriend.

v, past tense, past participle **cleekit,**

claucht 1 seize, snatch, take for yourself.

2 lay hold of, clutch.

3 hook, catch or fasten with a hook.

4 link arms, walk arm in arm with.

5 (*dancing*) link arms and whirl around.

6 get off with (a person of the opposite sex).

cleekit crocheted.

cleek in wi associate, be intimate with.

cleesh *v, n* whip SOUTH.

cleg, gled SOUTH *n* a gadfly, horsefly.

cleg *see* **clag.**

clep, clip *n* **1** a clip. **2** (*fishing*) a gaff. **3** an adjustable iron handle for suspending a pot over the fire.

clert *see* **clart.**

clethe *see* **cleed.**

cleuch *n* **1** a gorge, ravine. **2** a cliff, crag.

cleuk, clook [kleeook] *n* **1** a claw. **2** a hand. **3** *mainly* **cleuks** clutches.

clever, clivver, cluvver *adj* **1** clever. **2** swift, quick. **3** handsome, well-made. **4** (*of people or things*) good, nice.

click *see* **cleek.**

clift[1] *n* a cliff.

clift[2] *n* **1** a plank, board. **2** a cleft; a cave.

clim *v, past tense* **clam, clamb, climmed** climb.

clinch *v, n* limp.

cling *v, past tense* **clang;** *past participle* **clung** shrink, contract; shrivel.

clink[1] *n* **1** money, cash. **2** a blow.

v **1** strike, slap, beat. **2** move quickly, hurry.

clink doon 1 flop, sit or fall suddenly. **2** dump, deposit.

in a clink in a flash.

clink[2] *v* clench, rivet.

clint *n* a cliff, crag, precipice.

clip *n* **1** a colt. **2** a cheeky or mischievous child, usually a girl.

clip *see* **clep.**

clippin *n* the shearing of sheep.

clipshear *n* an earwig.

clish *v* repeat gossip.

clish-clash idle talk, gossip.

clishmaclaver(s) idle talk, gossip; endless talk.

clitter-clatter *n* **1** a rattling, clattering noise, a continuous crackle. **2** noisy, lively talk, senseless chatter.

clivver *see* **claver**², **clever.**

cloak *n* a clock.

cloak *see* **clock**¹.

clocher [-ch as in 'loch'] *n* **1** bronchial mucus. **2** a rough or wheezing cough. *v* cough, clear the throat.

clock¹, **cloak** *n* the clucking sound made by a broody hen. *v* **1** brood, sit on, hatch (eggs). **2** sit idly for a long time.

clocker a broody hen.

clockin the desire to brood; the desire to marry.

clockin hen 1 a broody hen. **2** a woman past the age of childbearing. **3** a woman during the time of having and rearing a family.

clock², **cloke** *n* a beetle, especially a large one.

clo(c)ker a (large) beetle, a cockroach.

clock³ *n, v* cloak.

clod *n* **1** a sod. **2** a peat. **3** a (usually wheaten) loaf. *v* **1** pelt with missiles. **2** throw.

clog *n* a log or block of wood.

cloit, clyte *n* a sudden heavy fall. *v* fall heavily or suddenly.

cloiter *v* **1** do dirty, wet work. **2** work in a dirty, disgusting way, especially in liquids.

cloke *see* **clock**².

clomph, clumph *v* walk heavily.

clood *see* **clud.**

cloof *see* **cluif.**

clook *see* **cleuk.**

cloor *n* **1** a blow. **2** a lump, swelling caused by a blow. **3** a hollow, dent, especially in metal. *v* **1** batter, thump; damage, disfigure. **2** dent. **3** dress or chisel (stone).

cloot¹ *n* **1** a piece of cloth, a rag, often a dishcloth; a bandage. **2** (*mainly* **cloots**, *often contemptuous*) clothes. **3** a baby's nappy. **4** a patch. *v* patch, mend (clothes); repair (pans, footwear etc) with a metal plate.

clootie made of cloths or rags: '*clootie rug*'.

clootie dumpling a **dumpling** wrapped in a cloth and boiled.

clootie rug floor rug made of rags.

a tongue that wad clip cloots a sharp tongue.

cloot² *n* a blow. *v* strike, slap.

cloot³ *n* **1** one of the divisions in the hoof of cloven-footed animals; the whole hoof. **2** **auld Cloot(s), (auld) Clootie** the Devil.

clorach NE *v* **1** work in a slovenly way. **2** clear the throat noisily. **3** sit lazily by the fire as if ill.

close¹ *adj* (*of work etc*) constant, relentless. *v* be stuffed up, have difficulty breathing because of asthma, bronchitis etc.

close² *n* **1** an enclosure, courtyard. **2** a farmyard. **3** an **entry,** passageway, alley. **4** the **entry** to a **tenement,** the passageway giving access to the **common stair.**

close mou the entrance to a **close.**

it's a(w) up a closie (wi) it is a hopeless position, it is a poor outlook (for).

in the wrang close in a really tight spot, badly mistaken.

closhach NE *n* **1** the carcass of a fowl. **2** a mass of something, especially semi-liquid. **3** a hoard of money.

clowe¹ [rhymes with 'cow'] *n* a clove, the spice.

clowe², **claa** SHETLAND, ORKNEY, N, **claw** *n* **1** a claw. **2** a scratching, (often of the head as a sign of mild astonishment). *v* **1** claw. **2** scratch gently; scratch (the head) as a sign of astonishment etc. **3**

scrape; clean out, empty. **4** beat, strike.

claw aff do (something speedily or eagerly).

claw someone's back flatter someone, get into someone's good books.

claw someone's hide punish, beat.

gar (someone) claw whaur it's no yeukie give (someone) a thrashing.

no claw an auld man's held not live into old age.

clud, clood *n* a cloud.

cludgie *n* (*slang*) a lavatory.

clulf, cloof *n* a hoof, originally cloven.

clumph *see* **clomph**.

clung *see* **cling**.

clunk *n* **1** a hollow, gurgling sound made by liquid in motion. **2** a plopping or popping sound.

cluvver *see* **clever**.

clyack *n* **1** the last sheaf of corn at the harvest. **2** the harvest-home (festival).

Clyde *n*: **Ah didna come up the Clyde on a banana boat** I'm no fool.

clype[1] *v* **1** *also* **clype on** tell tales, inform against someone. **2** report, tell. **3** be talkative, gossip.

n **1** a tell-tale. **2** (a piece of) gossip, a lie.

clype[2] NE *n* **1** a large, messy mass. **2** a big, awkward or ugly person.

clype[3] *n* a heavy, noisy fall; a blow NE.

clyte *v* strike, rap (your knuckles) against a hard object.

clyte *see* **cloit**.

coachbell, scodgebell, switchbell *n* an earwig.

coag *see* **cog**[1].

coal, coil *n* coal.

coalie-back, coilie buckle a piggyback ride.

coarn *see* **corn**.

coarum *see* **quorum**.

coat, cot, cwite NE *n* **1** a coat. **2** *mainly* **coats, cwites** NE a petticoat; a skirt.

cob *v* beat, strike.

coble[1], **cowble** *v* rock.

coble[2] *n* a short, flat-bottomed rowing boat, used especially in salmon-fishing.

cock *n*: **cockle leekie, cock-a-leekie** chicken and leek soup.

cocks and hens name for the buds, stems or seeds of various plants, and of games played with them.

cocker *v* rock, totter, walk unsteadily.

cockleleerie *n* **1** the crowing of a cock. **2** the cock itself.

cockle *v* totter, be unsteady.

cod[1] *n* a cushion, pillow.

cod[2] *n* a pod or husk (of peas, beans).

coff *v, past tense, past participle* **coft** buy.

cog[1], **coag** *n* a (wooden) container, a tub, pail or bowl.

cog[2] *n* a wedge or support.

coggle *v* rock, totter, shake.

coggle unsteady, easily overturned.

coil *see* **cwile**.

cold *see* **cauld**.

cole *n* a haystack.

coif *v* fill in, stop up.

coil *see* **coal**.

colleague [colleague] *v* associate, be friendly with (for purposes of crime or mischief), plot.

college *n*: **the college** (a) university: *'She's at the college now'*.

collie *n* a sheepdog, usually black (and white).

collieshangie *n* **1** a noisy quarrel, uproar. **2** a dog-fight.

collogue [collogue] *n* **1** a whispered conversation, private interview. **2** a discussion; a conference.

v **1** talk together, chat. **2** be in league, have an understanding with, scheme.

collop *n* a (thin) slice of meat.

comatee *n* a committee.

come *v, past tense, past participle* **cam, came, come** come.

come awa(y) 1 *also* **c'wa** NE (*usually in commands*) come along. **2** (*of seeds, plants*) germinate, grow rapidly.

come back on a person (*of food*)

repeat: '*Liver an ingans aye comes back on me*'.

come hame be born NE.

come in collapse.

come in by come in, draw near: '*Come in by, beside the fire*'.

come o become of (someone), happen to: '*Whit come o that boyfriend o yours?*'.

come on (*usually command*) come along.

come ower 1 (*usually of misfortune*) happen to (a person). **2** repeat, make mention of.

come tae 1 calm down. **2** become reconciled; comply. **3** come near NE.

come the time *eg* **five years come the time** five years old on your next birthday; five years on the anniversary (of an event).

come through recover from an illness.

a week *etc* **come Monday** a week etc on Monday.

commands, commans *npl* the Ten Commandments.

common *adj*: **Common Riding** the **Riding of the Marches** (see **ride**) in certain towns, *eg* Selkirk, Hawick.

common stair *n* the communal staircase into a block of flats etc.

compear *v* appear before a court or other authority.

complain *see* **compleen**.

compleen, complain *v* **1** complain. **2** be ailing, unwell.

complouter *v* **1** agree, fit in (with). **2** mix with.

conceit, consait *n* **1** conceit. **2** an idea, opinion, notion. **3** a good opinion (of yourself etc): '*hae a guid conceit o yersel*'. **4** a fancy article, a quaint or dainty thing or person.

conceitie 1 conceited, vain. **2** witty, apt. **3** neat, dainty.

conflummix *n* an unwelcome surprise.

connach *v* waste; spoil; consume.

consait *see* **conceit**.

conteen *v* contain.

conteena *v* continue.

conter *preposition* against.

adj opposite.

v oppose, contradict, thwart: '*Dinna ye conter yer ma!*'.

contermacious *adj* perverse, self-willed, obstinate: '*That's a contermacious wee bairn*'.

contrair *adj, adv, n* contrary.

v go contrary to, oppose, contradict.

convener *n* **1** a person who convenes a meeting. **2** the chairperson of a committee, *eg* a local council.

conversation (sweetie), conversation (lozenge) *n* a flat sweet of varying shape with a message on it.

convoy [convoy] *v* **1** escort, accompany, conduct. **2** carry, transport (goods etc). **3** convey.

n the escorting or accompanying of a person on his way; company: '*Gie's a convoy up the road*'.

coo *n* a cow; *pl* **kye, coos** cows.

cooard *n* a coward.

cooard(l)ie cowardly.

cooardie lick a blow given as a challenge to fight.

cood[1], **cweed** NE *n* cud.

cood[2], **cweed** NE *n* **1** a shallow tub, a wooden dish or basin, especially for milk. **2** a large tub for washing, storage, carrying.

coof *n* **1** a fool. **2** a useless person. **3** a lout. **4** a coward.

cook *v* disappear suddenly from view; dart in and out of sight.

cook *see* **culk**.

cookie *n* **1** a plain bun. **2** a prostitute.

coom[1] *n* soot; coal-dust, **dross**; peat-dust; fine turf mould.

v dirty, blacken, stain.

coom[2] *n* the sloping part of an attic ceiling.

coomed vaulted, arched; (*of a ceiling*) sloping.

coomcell *v* lath and plaster (a ceiling). *n* a sloping ceiling or roof.

coomcelled having a sloping ceiling.

coonger *v* **1** keep in order, scold. **2** overawe, threaten.

coont, count, cwint NE *v* **1** count. **2** do arithmetic. **3** settle accounts with.
n **1** a count. **2** **coonts** arithmetic, sums.

coont kin wi compare your pedigree with that of, claim relationship with.

coonter-lowper *n* a shop-assistant.

coop *n* a small heap.

coor *v* **1** cower. **2** bend, lower, fold.
coorie 1 stoop, bend, crouch down; cringe. **2 coorie in** snuggle, nestle.

coorgie *n* a blow or push given as a challenge to fight.

coorse[1] *adj* **1** coarse, rude, vulgar. **2** (*of weather*) foul, stormy. **3** (*of persons*) wicked, bad, naughty; rough, awkward. **4** hard, trying; disagreeable NE.

coorse[2] *n* a course.
in coorse 1 of course. **2** in due course.

coort *n* **1** a court. **2** a (covered) enclosure for cattle.
v go out with, court: '*He's coortin a braw lassie*'.

cooshie-doo *see* **cushat**.

coot, cweet *n* a guillemot NE.

cooter *n* **1** a coulter. **2** a nose.

cooter *see* **culter.**

cootie *n* (*of fowls*) having feathered legs.

copy *n* a copy-book, exercise book.

Corbett *n* a Scottish mountain of between 2500-3000 ft (762-914 metres approximately).

corbie *n* **1** a raven. **2** a rook. **3** a carrion crow; a hooded crow.
corbie messenger a slow or unfaithful messenger.
corbie stanes = **crawsteps.**
be a gone corbie be a goner, be done for.

cord *n* one of the ropes (held by close relatives and friends of the deceased) by which the coffin is lowered into the grave.

cordiner *n* a shoemaker.

core *n* **1** a team of **curlers. 2** a (convivial) party or company.

cork *n* an overseer, master, employer; a person in authority.

corkie *n* a feather-brained person.

corn, coarn *n* **1** oats. **2** a single grain.
v **1** feed (a horse or poultry) with oats or grain. **2** (*of people or poultry*) take food etc NE.
corn beef deaf *rhyming slang for* '*deef*'.
corn kist a storage-bin for corn.
corn kister a type of song sung at farmworkers' gatherings.
corn yaird a stackyard.

cornet *n* a standard-bearer in some **Riding of the Marches** ceremonies.

coronach *n* a funeral lament; a dirge.

corp *n* **1** a corpse. **2** the deceased.
corp candle a will-o'-the-wisp.

corrie *n* a hollow on the side of a mountain or between mountains.

corrie-fistit, carrie-handit, car-handit *adj* left-handed; awkward.

corrieneuchin [-ch- as in 'dreich'] *n* an intimate converation.

cors *see* **cross.**

cosh *adj* snug, comfortable; friendly, intimate.

cosy *adj* **1** (*of people*) warm and comfortable, well wrapped-up. **2** (*of places*) sheltered, providing comfort and protection.

cot *n*: **cottar** a tenant occupying a cottage with or without land attached to it; a married farmworker who has a cottage as part of his contract.
cot-folk those who live in farm cottages.
cot hoose a (farmworker's) cottage.

cot *see* **coat.**

cotch *see* **catch.**

cottar *see* **cot.**

count *see* **coont.**

countra, kintra, cwintry N *n* **1** country. **2** a district; its inhabitants; the territory of a **clan.**

countra clash the gossip of the district.

countra Jock a farmworker.

couple, kipple *n* **1** a couple. **2** a pair of rafters, forming a V-shaped roof support; one of these, a principal rafter.

couthie [coothie] *adj* **1** agreeable, sociable, friendly, sympathetic. **2** (*of places or things*) comfortable, snug, neat; agreeable.

cow *n* a hobgoblin; a frightening creature.

cowble *see* **coble**[1].

cowe[1] *n* **1** a twig or branch; a tufted stem of heather. **2** a broom, especially one used in curling.

cowe[2] *v* **1** poll, crop; cut (hair). **2** cut, cut short. **3** do better than, outdo. *n* a haircut.

cowe aw, cowe awthing be better than everything: '*That cowes aw*'.

cower *v* recover, get well from.

cowk *v* retch.

cowl, cowld *see* **cauld.**

cowp[1] *n* **1** an upset, overturning; a fall. **2** a rubbish tip. *v* **1** upset, overturn; ruin. **2** tilt up; empty by upturning. **3** swallow, drink (quickly). **4** overbalance, fall over, capsize; go bankrupt.

cowp the creels 1 turn a somersault, fall head over heels. **2** upset the plans or get the better (of) NE.

cowp the laidle play seesaw.

cowp[2] *v* buy, trade (goods, horses); barter, exchange.

cowper 1 a trader, dealer. **2** a horse-dealer.

cowp-cairt *n* **1** a closed cart. **2** a tipping cart.

cowshus *adj* cautious.

cowt *n* **1** a colt. **2** a rough, awkward person. **3** an adolescent.

cra *see* **craw**[1], **craw**[2].

crabbit *adj* in a bad temper, cross; bad-tempered.

crack *v* **1** boast, brag. **2** talk, gossip. **3** hit, strike: '*Ah'll crack yer jaw*'.

n **1** (*mainly*) **cracks** loud boasts or brags.

2 a talk, gossip, conversation; a story, tale.

3 an entertaining talker, a gossip.

4 a 'go', a **shot** in a game etc.

cracker 1 a boaster.

2 a talker, gossip.

3 crackers pieces of bone or wood used as castanets.

4 the lash of a whip.

crack like a (pen-)gun *etc* talk in a lively way, chatter loudly.

gie's yer crack(s) give me your news.

in a crack in a jiffy, immediately.

craft *see* **croft.**

crag *see* **craig**[1].

craig[1], **crag** *n* **1** a crag, rock; cliff. **2** a projecting spur of rock.

craig[2] *n* **1** the neck. **2** the throat, gullet. **craigit** -necked, *eg*: **(lang-)craigit heron** a heron NE.

craighle, crechle [-ch- , -gh- as -ch in 'dreich'] *v* cough drily or huskily; wheeze.

craik *v* **1** (*of birds*) utter a harsh cry, croak. **2** (*of things*) creak. **3** ask persistently, clamour. **4** grumble, complain. *n* **1** the harsh cry of a bird, especially a corncrake. **2** a corncrake.

craitur *n* **1** a creature. **2** whisky.

cran[1] *n* **1** a crane (the bird). **2** a heron. **3** a swift.

cran[2] *n* a crane (the machine).

cran[3] *n* (*until the 1970s: measure of fresh, uncleaned herrings*) one barrel, latterly fixed at 37.5 gallons (170.48 litres).

cran[4] *n* a tap.

cranachan *n* a dish made by mixing toasted oatmeal into whipped cream, sometimes adding fruit or other flavouring.

crane *n* a cranberry.

crank[1] *n* a harsh noise.

crank[2] *adj* difficult.

crankle unsteady, insecure, unreliable.

crannie *n* the little finger N.

crannog *n* an ancient lake dwelling.

cranreuch [**kran**rooch] *n* hoar-frost.

crap, crop *n* **1** a crop. **2** the top of a tree or plant. **3** the stomach.

crappit heids stuffed haddock's heads.

craw in someone's crap irritate, annoy; henpeck; give cause for regret.

crap *see* **creep.**

crappin *n* a dish of fish livers etc cooked in a fish head SHETLAND.

craw[1], **cra** *n* a crow, the bird; a rook.

crawsteps step-like projections up the sloping edge of a gable.

craw-taes 1 crow's feet, wrinkles at the corner of the eye. **2** creeping crowfoot; bird's foot trefoil; the English bluebell, wild hyacinth.

craw's waddin *etc* a large assembly of crows.

sit like craws in the mist sit in the dark.

craw[2], **cra** *n* a crow, a crowing of a cock.

craw in someone's crap *see* **crap.**

cray *see* **crue.**

crechle *see* **craighle.**

creek *n*: **creek o day** break of day, dawn NE.

creel *n* **1** a deep basket for carrying peats, fish etc. **2** a fish-trap, lobster-pot.

in a creel in confusion or perplexity; mad.

creen *see* **croon**[2].

creep *v, past tense* **creepit, crap;** *past participle* **creepit, cruppen** creep.

creeple *n* a low stool; a footstool.

cruppen doon shrunk or bent with age.

cattle creep a passage for animals under a railway or motorway.

cauld creep(s) gooseflesh, the creeps.

creep afore ye gang (*proverb*) walk before you run.

creep in 1 (*of daylight hours*) shorten. **2** grow smaller, shrink.

creep oot (*of hours of darkness*) lengthen.

creep ower swarm, be infested (with vermin).

creep thegither shrink, huddle up with cold or age.

creesh *n* fat, grease, tallow.

v **1** grease; oil; lubricate. **2** beat, thrash.

creeshie greasy; fat; dirty.

creesh someone's luif pay, tip, bribe someone.

crib[1] *n* a hen-coop.

crib[2] *n* a curb, kerb.

crimpet *n* a crumpet NE; NB in Scotland usually refers to a large, thin dropped scone.

crine *v* shrink, shrivel.

cripple *adj* lame.

v walk lamely, hobble.

crit *see* **croot.**

crivvens! *interjection* goodness!

crochle NE *v* limp.

crock[1] *n* an old ewe.

crock[2] *n* an earthenware container for foodstuffs, *eg* milk, salt, butter.

crockaneetion *adj* smithereens NE.

croft, craft NE *n* a croft; a smallholding.

crofter, crafter a person who occupies a smallholding.

croichle *n* a cough.

crood *see* **crud.**

croodle, crowdle FIFE *v* cower; nestle.

croodlin doo *n* **1** a wood-pigeon NE. **2** a term of endearment.

crook *see* **cruik.**

croon[1] *n* a crown.

croon[2], **creen** NE *v* **1** bellow, roar. **2** lament, mourn; wail. **3** sing in a low tone; mutter, hum.

n a wail, lament, mournful song.

croop, crowp *v* **1** (*of birds, especially crows*) croak, caw. **2** speak hoarsely. **3** grumble.

croose *adj* **1** bold, courageous, spirited. **2** confident, self-satisfied; cheerful. **3** conceited, arrogant, proud. **4** cosy, comfortable.

craw croose boast, talk loudly and confidently.

croot, crit *n* a small, puny child or young animal.

crop *see* **crap.**

cross, cors *n* 1 a cross. 2 a market cross; a market-place.

cross-fit a starfish.

crotal *see* **crottle.**

crottle, crotal *n* a dye-producing lichen.

crowdie[1] *n* oatmeal and water mixed and eaten raw.

cream crowdie = **cranachan.**

crowdie[2] *n* a kind of soft cheese.

crowdle *see* **croodle.**

crowl *v* crawl.

crowp *see* **croop.**

crub *v, n* curb.

crud, crood *n, mainly* **cruds** curds.

crudle curdle.

crue, cray *n* an animal pen or fold, *eg* a pigsty.

cruik, crook *n* 1 a crook. 2 a hook.

cruikit 1 crooked. 2 lame.

no cruik a finger not make the least effort.

cruisie *n* (*in past times*) an open, boat-shaped lamp with a rush wick; a candleholder.

cruive *n* 1 a fish-trap in a river or estuary. 2 a pen, fold, *eg* a pigsty, a hen-coop.

crulge *v* cower, crouch.

crummock *n* a stick with a crooked head, a shepherd's crook.

crump *v* 1 crunch, munch. 2 crackle. *adj, also* **crumple, crumshie** NE (*especially of ice*) crisp, brittle.

crunkle, grunkle NE *v* crinkle, wrinkle, crackle.

crunt *n* a heavy blow SW.

cruppen *see* **creep.**

cry *v* 1 call on (a person) for help etc. 2 summon. 3 call, give a name to. 4 **be cried** have your marriage banns proclaimed. 5 be in labour.

n 1 a call, summons: '*Just gie's a cry*

if ye want oniething'. 2 **cries** the proclamation of banns of marriage: '*Pit in the cries*'. 3 the distance a call can carry. 4 a short visit (in passing), *usually* **gie (someone) a cry (in).**

cry in (by) call in, visit: '*I'll cry in by yer hoose*'.

cry names call (someone) names.

cry on, cry up to call in on, visit.

cud *see* **can.**

cuddie[1] *n* 1 a donkey. 2 a horse. 3 a joiner's trestle. 4 a gymnasium horse.

cuddy-lowp(-the-dyke) the game of leapfrog.

cuddie[2] *n* a young coalfish.

cuddle *v* 1 squat, sit close. 2 **cuddle up tae** approach someone to coax or wheedle. 3 throw or place a marble close to the target.

cude *adj* hare-brained.

cudna, cudnae *see* **can.**

cuff[1] *n*: **cuff o the neck** the nape or scruff of the neck.

cuff[2] *v* 1 winnow for the first time. 2 remove a layer of soil with a rake from (a piece of ground) before sowing, replacing it afterwards.

culk, cook *v* 1 cook. 2 **cook** coax.

cull, cweel NE *adj, v* cool.

culst, culsten *see* **cast.**

cult, cweet NE *n* an ankle.

culter, cooter *v* 1 nurse, pamper, look after carefully. 2 coax, wheedle.

Cullen skink *n* a smoked-fish soup.

cullie *see* **culyie.**

culpable homicide *n* (*law*) manslaughter.

culyie, cullie *v* 1 fondle. 2 cherish. 3 coax, entice.

cummer, kimmer *n* 1 a godmother. 2 *also* **gimmer** a female friend; a gossip. 3 a midwife. 4 a girl, lass.

cundie *n* 1 a covered drain, the entrance to a drain. 2 a street-gutter. 3 a tunnel, passage.

cunning *n* a rabbit.

cunyie *n* a coin.

curcuddoch [curcuddoch] *adv* sitting close together or side by side.

curdoo *v* coo (as a pigeon); make love.

curfuffle *see* **carfuffle**.

curl *v* play at **curling**.

  curler a person who plays at **curling**.

  curling a game played by sliding heavy stones on ice.

  curling stone the smooth rounded stone, now usually of polished granite, used in **curling**.

  curl-doddie, carl-doddie *n* name for various plants with a rounded flowerhead, *eg* devilsbit scabious, ribwort plantain, clover.

  curly green(s), curly kail curly colewort.

curmur [kurmur] *v* make a low rumbling or murmuring sound; purr.

curn *n* a currant.

curpin *n* **1** a horse's crupper. **2** the behind or rump.

curran *n* a currant.

currie *n* a small stool.

currieboram *n* a confused, noisy or frightened crowd NE.

currie-wurrie *n* a violent dispute.

cushat, cooshie-doo *n* **1** a wood-pigeon. **2** a term of endearment.

cut *v, past tense, past participle also* **cuttit** cut.

  n **1** a measure of linen or woollen yarn. **2** temper, (bad) humour: '*He's in bad cut*'. **3** a group of sheep divided from the rest.

cuttin laif bread old enough to be easily cut.

cuttit 1 cut. **2** curt, abrupt.

cutchack *n* a small, blazing, coal or peat fire NE.

cuttance *n* **1** an account, description; news NE. **2 no cuttance** no encouragement.

  rin the cutter carry out liquor from a public house or brewery unobserved.

cutty *adj* short, stumpy.

  n **1** a short, dumpy girl. **2** affectionate name for a child. **3** a mischievous or disobedient girl. **4** contemptuous term for a woman. **5** = **cutty-pipe**. **6** a hare.

  cutty clay, cutty pipe a short, stumpy (clay) pipe.

  cutty quine contemptuous term for a woman NE.

  cutty sark in Burns' 'Tam o' Shanter', the name of a witch who wore a very short garment.

  cutty stool a low, usually three-legged, stool.

  cutty wran a wren.

c'wa *see* **come**.

cweed *see* **cood**[1], **cood**[2].

cweel *see* **cull**.

cweet *see* **coot, cult**.

cwile, kyle, coil *n* the small heap into which hay is gathered after being cut.

cwint *see* **coont**.

cwintry *see* **countra**.

cwite *see* **coat**.

cyaard *see* **caird**[1].

D

da *see* **the.**

dab *v* **1** peck. **2** pierce slightly, stab: '*Dab the lid wi a fork afore ye pit it in the microwave*'. **3** aim (a marble etc) at. **4** push, shove.

n **1** a blow, slap. **2** melted fat, gravy etc in which potatoes are dipped.

dabber a very large marble sw, SOUTH.

dabble a game played with marbles or tops.

dabbitie 1 a (small) ornament. **2** a game played with small cut-out pictures.

no lat dab not to give information (that . . .).

daberlacks *npl, mainly* NE **1** = **badderlocks** a kind of seaweed. **2** wet, dirty scraps of cloth etc. **3** hair in lank, tangled, separate locks. **4** a tall, unattractive person.

dacent *adj* decent.

dachle *see* **dackle.**

dacker¹, daiker *v* **1** bargain. **2** walk slowly, aimlessly or weakly. **3** be doing undemanding work. **4** dither.

dacker² *v* search (a house, person) for stolen goods etc (by official warrant) NE.

dackle, dachle NE *v* hesitate, dawdle, go slowly NE.

dad *see* **daud.**

dadderie *n* hard work, drudgery SHETLAND.

dae, do, dee *v, past tense* **done** *past participle* **duin, deen** NE, **don** SHETLAND do.

dis does.

disnae, disna does not.

dinnae, dinna, (*emphatic*) **divnae, divna** do not.

didnae, didna did not.

doer a person who acts for another; a **factor,** agent.

be daein 1 be content, satisfied. **2 I canna be daein wi it** I can't put up with it.

daff *v* act playfully or foolishly.

daffin, dafferie fun; foolish behaviour, teasing, 'chatting up'.

daft *adj* **1** foolish, stupid, lacking intelligence. **2** crazy, insane; lacking commonsense. **3** frivolous, thoughtless. **4 daft aboot** extremely fond of, crazy about: '*daft aboot cream cakes*'.

daftie 1 a mentally handicapped person. **2** a fool.

daft days 1 a time of merrymaking and fun; your youth. **2** the period of festivity at Christmas and New Year.

daft Erchie a gullible person; one easily tricked.

daft on 1 enthusiastic about: '*daft on cars*'. **2** in love with, crazy about (someone).

act the daft laddie *or* **lassie** pretend to be stupid, play the fool.

dag¹ *n, mainly* NE **1** thin, drizzling rain. **2** a heavy shower of rain.

dag!², dag on('t)!, dog on it! *interjection* damn it!

daich *see* **daigh.**

daidle¹, *also* **daidlie** *n* **1** a (child's) pinafore or bib. **2** an apron. **3** a table napkin WEST.

daidle² *v* **1** idle, waste time; potter about. **2** waddle; stagger.

daidle³ *v* dirty, wet (your clothes etc) NE.

daidle⁴ *v* dandle, fondle (a child).

daigh [-gh as -ch], **daich** *n* **1** dough. **2** a mixture of meal and hot water used as chicken food.

dalghie 1 doughy. **2** (*of people*) inactive, lacking in spirit.

dalgie *n* a kind of marbles game.

dalk *v, mainly* NE **1** deck, adorn. **2** smooth down (the hair etc).

dalker *see* **dacker**[1].

dalmen *adj* rare, occasional.

dalnner *see* **denner**.

dainty *adj* **1** pleasant, agreeable. **2** large, fair-sized; (*of time*) considerable.

dalth *n* death: '*Sure as daith*'.

dale[1] *n* **1** a deal. **2** a part, portion, share.

dale[2] *n* **1** a deal, plank. **2** a shelf. **3** a (high) diving-board at a swimming pool CENTRAL.

dale[3] *n* a goal, stopping place or base in a game.

dall, dallie *n* a doll.

dam *n*: **the dambrod, the dams** the game of draughts NE.

dame *n* **1** a (farmer's) wife, housewife. **2** a young (unmarried) woman NE.

Dan, Dannie boy *n* (*contemptuous*) nickname for a Roman Catholic CENTRAL.

dance *v*: **the (Merry) Dancers** the Northern Lights, Aurora Borealis.

dander, daun(d)er *v* stroll, saunter.

dang *v, interjection* damn.

dang *see* **ding**.

Dannie boy *see* **Dan**.

darg *n* **1** a day's work. **2** work: '*the day's darg*'. **3** the product of a day's work.
v work, toil.
darger a casual unskilled labourer.

dark, dawrk WEST, **derk** *adj, n* dark.

Dark Blues *npl* nickname for Dundee football team.

darn *see* **dern**.

dask, desk *n* a pew.

dass, dess *n* **1** a ledge on a hillside. **2** a layer in a pile of hay etc.

dat *see* **that**.

daud, dad, dod *v* **1** strike heavily, beat; jolt: '*Daud the washin machine*

tae start it'. **2** dash, bump about, thud. **3** pelt; bespatter. **4** (*of wind, rain etc*) blow in gusts, drive. **5** bang, slam (a door).
n **1** a heavy blow, thud. **2** a large piece, lump, quantity (knocked off): '*a daud o cheese*'.

daunder, dauner *see* **dander**.

daunton *v* subdue, suppress, overcome; challenge, defy.

daur *n, v* dare.

daut *v* pet, fondle, make much of.
dautie a pet, darling.

dave *see* **deave**.

daver *v* **1** wander aimlessly or dazedly. **2** stun, stupefy; chill.

daw[1] *n, v* dawn.

daw[2] *n* a lazy person; a slut.

dawkie *adj* drizzly.

dawrk *see* **dark**.

de *see* **the, there**.

dead *see* **deid**.

deaf *see* **deef**.

deas *n* **1** a dais. **2** a desk or pew in a church. **3** a seat also used as a table or bed.

deasil *n* the custom of walking following the sun (*ie* clockwise) round a person or thing to bring good luck.

deave, dave *v* **1** deafen: '*Ye'll deave me wi yon loud music!*'. **2** annoy (with noise or talk); bore: '*deaved wi the minister's sermon*'.

dee *v* die.

dee *see* **dae, thou, thy**.

Dee *n*: **the Dees** nickname for Dundee football team.

deedle *see* **diddle**[2].

deef, deaf *adj* **1** deaf. **2** (*of soil etc*) poor, unproductive.

deefenin sound-proofing (of a building) by pugging.

deefie *n* a deaf person.
adj (*of sound*) dull; (*of a ball etc*) without bounce.
v ignore (a person): '*Dinnae deefie me when I'm talkin tae ye*'.

deef nit a nut without a kernel; an

unimportant person or thing: '*He's nae deef nit*'.

deek *v* catch sight of, see.
n a glimpse, a look: '*Tak a deek at that*'.

deem *n* NE **1** a dame. **2** an elderly woman. **3** a young woman; an unmarried woman. **4** a kitchenmaid on a farm.

deen *see* **dae.**

deep plate *n* a soup plate or similarly-shaped smaller dish.

deevil *see* **deil.**

defait, defeat *adj* **1** defeated. **2** exhausted, worn out NE.

defamation *n* Scots law term covering both libel and slander in English law.

defeat *see* **defait.**

defender *n* (*law*) a defendant, latterly only in a civil case.

deg *v* strike (a sharp-pointed object) quickly into something NE.

deid, dead *adj* dead.
n death; the cause of (someone's) death.

deid-ill a fatal illness.

deid-kist a coffin.

deid man's bells the foxglove.

deid thraw death throe.

i the deid thraw NE **1** between hot and cold. **2** between one state and another; undecided.

deil, deevil, divil *n* a devil.

deil's bird a magpie.

deil's buckle an awkward, obstinate person.

deevilock a little devil, imp NE.

deil's dizzen thirteen.

deil a . . . not a . . . , never a . . .

deil ane not one; no one at all.

deil kens goodness knows: '*Deil kens whaur it's gane*'.

deil (may) care no matter; for all that.

delf[1] *n* a place dug out; a hole or pit.

delf[2] *n* everyday china.

dell *v* delve, dig SHETLAND, ORKNEY, N.

delt *v* pet, spoil NE.

dem *v* dam NE.

dem *see* **them.**

demain, demean *v* treat badly, injure NE.

den[1] *n* a narrow valley, especially one with trees.

den[2] *n* **1** (*games*) a base, place of safety. **2** the forecastle of a herring boat.

denner, dainner NE, **dinner** *n* dinner.
v dine, have dinner; give dinner to.

dinner scull *n* a school lunch hall.

dentylion *n* a dandelion.

deochandorus [d(ee)ochandorus] *n* a drink taken before leaving.

depooperit *adj* poor, without money SHETLAND.

depute [depute] *adj, following the noun* appointed or acting as a deputy: '*advocate depute*'.
n a deputy.

der *see* **their, there.**

dere *see* **there.**

derf *adj* **1** bold, daring, hardy. **2** (*of things*) hard, rough, violent.

derk *see* **dark.**

dern, darn *adj* **1** secret, hidden. **2** (*in past times*) dark, dreary.
v hide; go into hiding.

dert *n, v* dart.

desk *see* **dask.**

dess *see* **dass.**

destrick *n* a district.

District Court the lowest criminal court in Scotland.

deuk, jeuk *n* a duck.

deval [deval] *v* stop, leave off; relax.

dewgs, juggins *npl* small pieces, shreds: '*We used tae call toy money juggins*'.

dey [rhymes with 'gay' or (NE) with 'gey'], **tae** *n* **1** child's word for father. **2** a grandfather.

dey *see* **there.**

deyd [-ey- as in 'gey'] *n* a grandfather; a grandmother NE.

dib *see* **dub.**

diced *adj* having a chequered pattern: '*Polismen wear diced hats*'.

diced up trim and neat.

dicht, dight [rhymes with 'fricht' or (especially Orkney) with 'light'] *v* **1** wipe or rub clean and dry (quickly). **2** clean (up) (quickly) by sweeping, removing dust etc, make tidy. **3** sift or winnow. **4** scold, thrash.

n **1** a wipe, a quick wash; a rub: '*Gie yer face a dicht*'. **2** a blow, smack; a heavy defeat.

dichtin a beating, *eg* in a game.

diddle[1] *v* **1** dance with a jigging movement. **2** move (the elbow) to and fro in fiddling; fiddle. **3** dandle (a child).

diddle[2], **deedle** *v* sing without words.

diddle[3] *v* busy yourself without getting much done.

didna, didnae *see* **dae**.

diet[1] *n* **1** a church service: '*diet o worship*'. **2** a day or date fixed for a meeting (*eg* of a court), or for a market.

diet[2] *n* a meal.

differ *v* quarrel, dispute.

n **1** a difference of opinion; a disagreement. **2** a difference.

dight *see* **dicht**.

dilgit, dulget *n* a lump; an untidy heap or bundle NE.

dill *v* soothe, quieten down, die away.

dilse *n* dulse, a kind of edible seaweed.

din[1] *n* **1** loud talk or discussion; a fuss, disturbance. **2** a report, rumour; a scandal.

din[2] *adj* **1** mousy(-coloured). **2** dark-complexioned, sallow.

dine *n* dinner; dinnertime.

ding *v*, *past tense* **dang, dung;** *past participle* **dung 1** knock, beat or strike (with heavy blows); defeat, overcome (with blows); beat, get the better of.

2 (*of rain, wind etc*) beat or fall heavily and violently.

3 drive (with violence).

4 strike, force, drive from.

n a knock or blow, a smart push.

gae yer dinger go at something very vigorously or boisterously.

dinge *v* dent, bruise.

dingle *v* tingle.

dingle-doosie *n* a lighted stick etc waved rapidly by a child to make patterns of light.

dink *adj* **1** *also* **dinkie** neat, trim, finely dressed, dainty. **2** prim, precise; haughty.

dinna, dinnae *see* **dae**.

dinner *see* **denner**.

dinnle *v* **1** shake, vibrate. **2** (*of bells, thunder etc*) peal, roll, drone. **3** tingle with cold or pain; twinge.

dint *n* affection, liking.

dip[1] *n* melted fat in which potatoes are dipped.

dip[2] *v* sit down SHETLAND.

dir *see* **there**.

dird *n* a hard blow, knock; a sharp or stunning fall, a bump; a bounce, romp NE.

v push violently, bump; bounce, jolt NE.

dirdum *n* **1** a loud noise, quarrelling, uproar. **2** a quandary, problem. **3** blame; punishment, a scolding.

dirk, durk *n* **1** a short dagger worn in the belt by Highlanders, now as part of the Highland dress. **2** a stab, prod SHETLAND.

v stab with a **dirk**.

dirl *v* **1** vibrate, rattle; ring when struck; whirl. **2** pierce or (cause to) tingle with emotion or pain.

n **1** a knock causing such; a shock, clatter.

2 the pain caused by such a blow; a tingling sensation.

3 a vibrating motion or noise, a clatter or rattle.

4 a gust (of wind) SHETLAND, N.

5 a hurry, bustle SHETLAND, N.

dirlie-bane funny bone.

dirl aff recite, sing, play continuously.

dirl up strike up (a song, tune), play vigorously.

dirt *v* defecate on: '*He's dirtit hissel*'.
n nonsense SHETLAND.

dirten NE **1** dirtied, filthy, soiled with excrement. **2** mean, contemptible; conceited.

dis *see* **dae, this.**

discreet *adj* polite, well-behaved.

disjaskit *adj* **1** dejected, downcast, depressed. **2** exhausted, worn out; weary-looking. **3** dilapidated, neglected, untidy.

disna, disnae *see* **dae.**

dist *see* **dust.**

district *see* **destrick.**

dit *v* shut, close; obstruct, block.

divil *see* **deil.**

divna, divnae *see* **dae.**

divot [divvot] *n* **1** a turf, sod, peat. **2** a thick clumsy piece of bread etc. **3** a stupid person.

dixie *n* a sharp scolding ORKNEY, NE.

dizzen *n* a dozen.

dizzie *n*: **gie someone a dizzie** stand someone up.

do *see* **dae.**

doaken *see* **docken.**

dob *v, n* prick.

dobbie, dooble *n* a dull, stupid, clumsy person.

dochter, dother *n* a daughter.

dock *n* **1** the buttocks. **2** the rear or butt-end of something. **3** a haircut.
v dock, shorten (clothes).

dockit (*of speech or temper*) clipped, short.

docken, doaken *n* **1** a dock plant. **2** something of no value or significance: '*no worth a docken*'.

doctor *n* a kind of minnow.

dod! *mild exclamation* God!

dod *see* **daud.**

doddie *n* a hornless bull, cow or sheep.

dods *npl* a fit of the sulks.

  tak the dods sulk.

doer *see* **dae.**

dog *see* **dug.**

doilt *adj* **1** dazed, confused, stupid. **2** wearied, grief-stricken.

doist, dyst *n* a heavy blow; a thud, bump, crash.
v fall, sit or throw (down) with a thud, bump.

doit[1] *n* **1** (*in past times*) a small copper coin. **2** something of little value: '*no worth a doit*'.

doit[2], **dyte** *v* **1** act foolishly, be crazed or confused in mind. **2** walk with a stumbling or short step NE.
n a stupid person, a fool.

doitert witless, especially in old age.

doitit not in sound mind, foolish, silly, senile.

doll *n* a portion, large piece, especially of dung.

dominie *n* a schoolmaster.

don, done *see* **dae.**

donnert *adj* dull, stupid, witless, especially in old age.

donsie *adj* unfortunate, luckless.

doo *n* **1** a dove, pigeon. **2** term of endearment: '*ma wee doo*'.

doocot a dovecote.

dooble *see* **dobbie.**

dooble *adj, adv, n* double.

doodle[1] *v* dandle, lull (a child).

doodle[2] *n* a musical instrument made from a reed SOUTH.
v play (a wind instrument, especially a **doodle** or the bagpipes).

dook[1] *v* **1** duck. **2** bathe. **3** baptize as a Baptist.
n **1** a duck (into water). **2** a bathe. **3** a drenching, soaking. **4** liquid into which something is dipped: '*breid an dook*'.

dookie up hoist up.

dook for aipples (*Halloween game*) try to get hold of apples floating in a tub etc with your teeth, by dipping your head in the water and without using your hands.

dook[2] *n* **1** a wooden peg etc driven into a wall to hold a nail. **2** a plug, a bung of a cask, boat etc.
v insert such wooden pegs etc in (a wall).

dool[1], **dule** *n* grief, distress.

dool[2], **dult** *n* (*games*) the goal or place of safety WEST.

doolie *n* **1** a hobgoblin, ghost. **2** a stupid, dithering, nervous person.

doon[1] *adv* **1** down. **2** **doon o** below. **3** (*of a river*) in flood.

doonie a member of the **hand-ball** (*see* **hand**) team playing towards the downward goal, the **doonies** usually coming from the lower part of the town ORKNEY, SOUTH; *see also* **uppie.**

doon-by down there, in the neighbourhood.

doon-haud a handicap, something that prevents you rising in the world.

Doonhamers nickname for the inhabitants of Dumfries, and for Queen of South football team.

doon leukin sullen.

doon mooth a sad expression; *see also* **mooth.**

doon-set(tin) **1** a (good etc) settlement, *eg* on marriage. **2** (*of food etc*) a (grand etc) spread.

doon-sit(tin) the action of settling in a place NE.

doon the watter down the river (of pleasure trips or resorts on the Clyde).

gae doon the brae go downhill in health, fortune etc.

doon[2] *n* down, soft feathers.

doop *v* stoop, bend, duck.

doop o day the close of day.

door *n*: **door-cheek** a door-post; a door, doorway.

door-stane a flagstone in front of the door; the threshold.

he hisnae been ower the door he hasn't been outside or out of the house.

tak the door wi ye go out and shut the door as you go.

doose *v* strike, knock, thrash.

doosht *n* a dull, heavy blow, a push; a thud.

doot, doubt *v* **1** doubt. **2** fear, be afraid, suspect: '*Ah doot he'll no be back*'. **3** expect, rather think.

Ah hae ma doots I am doubtful.

dooth *see* **douth.**

dorb *n* a peck; a prod NE.

Doric *n, adj* (of, in) the Scots language, now usually referring to North-East Scots.

dorro *n* (*fishing*) a kind of handline SHETLAND.

dort *n*: **tak the dorts** sulk, go into a huff.

dortie **1** bad-tempered, sulky; cheeky; haughty. **2** difficult to please. **3** feeble, delicate, sickly.

dose *n* a large quantity or number.

a dose o the caul(d) a cold.

doss[1] *adj* spruce, neat, tidy.

doss[2] *n* a knot or bow (of ribbon etc) N.

doss[3] *v* toss or pay down (money) NE.

dot *n* a small person, especially a child. *v* walk with short, quick steps; wander without plan.

dother *see* **dochter.**

dotter *v* walk unsteadily, stagger.

dotterel *n* an idiot.

dottert *adj* stupid, feeble-minded (from old age).

dottle[1] *n* **1** a very small thing or person. **2** the plug of tobacco in a pipe after smoking. **3** a cigarette end. **4** the core of a boil etc.

dottle[2] *v* be in or fall into a state of dotage, become or make crazy.

dottelt senile.

doubt *see* **doot.**

douce [rhymes with 'goose'] *adj* **1** sweet, pleasant, lovable. **2** sedate, sober, respectable. **3** neat, tidy, comfortable.

dour [rhymes with 'moor'] *adj* **1** dull, humourless, sullen. **2** hard, stern, severe, determined. **3** slow, sluggish, reluctant. **4** (*of weather*) bleak, gloomy. **5** (*of land*) hard, barren.

douth, dooth, dowth SOUTH *adj* **1** depressed. **2** gloomy, dreary, dark.

dove [rhymes with 'cove'] v become drowsy, doze.

dover[1] v 1 doze off, snooze. 2 wander hesitatingly, walk unsteadily.

dover[2] numeral (children's rhymes) nine.

dowe[1] v be able or willing, have the strength or ability (to do something).

doweless feeble, lacking in strength or energy.

dowe[2] v fade away, wither.

dowf, duff adj 1 dull, spiritless; stupid; weary. 2 sad, melancholy. 3 (of a sound) dull, hollow. 4 (of a part of the body) numb, insensitive SHETLAND.

n 1 a stupid or gloomy person. 2 a dull blow with something soft.

dowg see **dug**.

dowle adj 1 sad, dismal; dull. 2 weak, delicate, ailing.

dowp n 1 the buttocks. 2 the seat of a pair of trousers. 3 the bottom or end of something, eg an eggshell.

dowt n a cigarette-end.

dowth see **douth**.

doze v 1 stupefy, stun. 2 spin (a top) so fast that it appears not to move: 'Doze yer peerie'.

dozent adj (in past times) stupefied, dazed, physically weakened (through age, drink etc).

draa see **draw**.

drabble, draible v 1 dirty (your clothes, boots etc). 2 spill. 3 (of rain) drizzle NE.

n 1 a spot of dirt. 2 a small quantity of liquid food. 3 rubbish, especially something too small for use.

drackle see **draik**.

draft see **draucht**.

drag n 1 a large heavy harrow. 2 also **draig** the motion of the tide.

draggle see **draigle**.

draible see **drabble**.

draig see **drag**.

draigle, draggle v 1 bedraggle, dirty,

muddy. 2 mix (flour, meal etc) with water NE. 3 move slowly or wearily.

n a dirty, untidy person.

draigelt soaked through, drenched.

draigon n 1 a dragon. 2 a paper kite.

draik v drench, soak.

drackle damp, wet, misty.

dram n a drink of spirits; in Scotland, a drink of any size, usually whisky.

drammock n a mixture of raw oatmeal and cold water.

drap, drop n 1 a drop. 2 a very small quantity. 3 the dripping of water or the line down which it drops from the eaves of a house. 4 **draps** small shot, pellets.

v 1 drop. 2 stop (work); stop (raining). 3 rain slightly, drizzle.

drop(ped) scone a Scottish **pancake**.

a drapple a drink.

no a drap's bluid not a blood relation.

draucht, draft n 1 a draught. 2 a load. 3 the guts of an animal. 4 a sheep etc taken out of the flock.

v 1 break in, harness (a horse) NE. 2 line off (land) with the plough by straight furrows.

drave[1] n 1 a drove. 2 the annual herring fishing. 3 a shoal of fish; a catch.

drave[2], **dreeve** NE past tense, past participle drove.

draw, draa SHETLAND, ORKNEY, N v 1 aim (a blow); raise (your hand, foot etc) in attack. 2 **draw tae, draw till** head for; come to like (someone). 3 (of tea) infuse, become infused.

n a puff at a pipe, a smoke.

draw straes cast lots.

dree v endure, suffer (pain, misfortune): 'dree yer weird' suffer your fate.

dreel n, v drill, furrow.

dreep v 1 drip. 2 drain, strain (eg potatoes after boiling). 3 come off (a wall etc) by letting yourself down to the full stretch of the arms and dropping.

dreepin roast, dripping roast a constant source of income.

Sammy dreep a 'drip', a spiritless, ineffective person.

dreeve *see* **drave**[2].

dreg[1] *v* dredge (shellfish etc).

dreg[2] *v* drag.

dreich *adj* **1** dreary, dull, bleak: '*The weather's gey dreich the day*'; long, boring, uninteresting. **2** slow; backward; slow to pay debts. **3** depressed.

dreid *v* **1** dread. **2** suspect, fear.

dress *v* **1** iron (cloth). **2** neuter (a cat).

drib[1] *n* **1** a drop, a small quantity of liquid. **2 dribs** dregs.
v extract the last drops of milk from (a cow).

drib[2] *v* beat, thrash; scold NE.

dribble *v* **1** tipple, drink. **2** drizzle.

driddle *v* **1** walk slowly or uncertainly; dawdle, saunter. **2** potter, idle, waste time. **3** spill, dribble. **4** play the fiddle, strum.

drite *v* defecate.
n dirt, excrement.

drochle *see* **droich**.

drog *n* a drug.

droich [-ch as in 'dreich'] *n* a dwarf, a stunted person.

drochle a small (dumpy) person or animal.

drone *n* the bass pipe of the bagpipes.

drook *n*: **drookin** a drenching, soaking.
adj dripping with moisture.

drookit, drookelt drenched, soaked; steeped.

drookit stour mud.

droon *v* drown.

drooth *see* **drouth**.

drop *see* **drap**.

dross *n* coal-dust, small coal.

droucht [-oo-] *n* drought; drying breezy weather.

drouchtit parched.

drouchtie dry NE.

drouth, drooth *n* **1** drought; drying breezy weather. **2** thirst. **3** a drunk, a habitual drinker.

droothie 1 (*of the weather*) dry. **2** thirsty, addicted to drinking.

drove road *n* a road or track used for driving cattle or sheep to markets.

drowe[1] [rhymes with 'cow'] *n* a cold, wet mist, a drizzle.

drowe[2] [rhymes with 'cow'] *n* an attack of illness, a fainting fit; a spasm of anxiety.

drucken *adj* drunken.

drug *v* pull forcibly, drag.

drum *adj* sad, dejected, sulky.

drumlie *adj* **1** (*of streams or water*) troubled, clouded, muddy; (*of alcohol*) full of sediment. **2** (*of the weather*) cloudy, gloomy. **3** troubled, muddled, confused.

drumlin *n* a long mound of glacial deposit, higher at one end.

drunk *past tense* drank.

drunts *npl* the sulks, a fit of ill-humour.

drush *n* powdery waste, *eg* of peat NE.

dry *adj*: **dry dyke** = **dry-stane dyke**.

dry shave the rubbing of another's cheek with an unshaven chin or with the fingers.

dry-stane dyke a stone wall built without mortar.

dry-stane dyker a person who builds such walls

du *see* **thou**.

dub, dib *n* **1** a pool, especially of muddy or stagnant water; a pond. **2** a small pool, especially of rain water, a puddle. **3** (*humorous*) the ocean. **4** a sea pool. **5 dubs** mud.

dubble muddy.

dud *n* **1 duds** ragged clothes, rags, tatters. **2** a coarse cloth for domestic purposes, *eg* a dish-cloth.

duddie ragged, tattered.

duff *see* **dowf**.

duffie *n* a lavatory SOUTH.

dug, dog, dowg *n* a dog.

dog('s) flourish one of the various umbelliferous plants.

dog('s) hip the fruit of the dog-rose, the rosehip.

duin *see* **dae.**

dule *see* **dool**[1].

dulget *see* **dilget.**

dult *n* **1** a dolt. **2** the pupil at the bottom of the class.

dult *see* **dool**[2].

dumfooner *v* amaze.

dump *v* **1** beat, thump, kick. **2** walk with short, heavy steps, stump about. *n* **1** a blow, a thump, a thud. **2** *usually* **gie someone his or her dumps** mark a child's birthday by thumping him or her on the back, a thump for every year of age.

dumplin *n* **1** a kind of rich, boiled or steamed fruit püdding. **2** a small, plump child.

dunch *v* **1** punch, thump, bump. **2** (*of animals*) butt. *n* **1** a blow, a bump, a nudge. **2** a butt from an animal.

dunder *see* **dunner.**

dung *see* **ding.**

dunk *adj* dank, damp, moist.

dunner, dunder *v* **1** make a noise like thunder, rumble, bang. **2** move quickly and noisily.

dunnie *n* an underground cellar or passage in an old **tenement** building; a basement WEST.

dunt *n* **1** a heavy, dull-sounding blow or stroke, a knock.

2 the wound caused by such.

3 a dent.

4 a heavy fall, thud, bump; the sound of such.

5 a throb or quickened beat of the heart.

6 a blow, a shock, disappointment.

7 an insult.

8 a chance, opportunity, occasion SHETLAND.

9 a lump, a large piece.

v **1** beat, stamp, thump, bump, knock (with a dull sound).

2 (*of the heart*) throb, beat rapidly or violently; (*of a sore*) throb.

3 stamp down (herrings) in a barrel.

4 shake together the contents of (*eg* a sack) by knocking on the ground.

5 crush or dent by striking.

gie the heavy dunt tae get rid of (a person).

dunter *n* **1** a porpoise; a dolphin. **2** an eider duck SHETLAND, ORKNEY.

durk *n* a large clumsy thing or person.

durk *see* **dirk.**

dush *v* push or strike with force, butt.

dust, dist ORKNEY, NE *n* **1** dust. **2** particles of meal and husk.

dux *n* the best pupil in a school, class or subject.

dwabble *see* **dwaible.**

dwaible, dwabble, dweeble *adj* **1** flexible, flabby, soft. **2** weak, feeble, shaky.

dwaiblie shaky, wobbly, weak.

dwall *v* dwell.

dwam *n* **1** a daze; a daydream. **2** a swoon, a fainting fit; a sudden attack of illness.

dwam ower fall asleep.

dwamie sickly, faint; dreamy.

dwang *n* **1** a wooden strut or bar; an iron lever. **2** toil.

v **1** worry, harass, subject to pressure. **2** toil, work hard.

dweeble *see* **dwaible.**

dwine *v* pine, waste away, fail in health; fade, wither.

dy *see* **thy.**

dyke *n* **1** a wall of stones, turf etc. **2** a hedge SW.

v surround with a dyke.

dyker a builder of **dykes.**

dyst *see* **doist.**

dyte *see* **dolt**[2].

E

e *see* **he, the.**

ear *n* a year.

earwig *n* an earwig.
v eavesdrop.

Earl o Hell *n* the Devil: '*It's as black as the Earl o Hell's waistcoat*'.

earn, yirn *n* an eagle; a sea-eagle SHETLAND, ORKNEY.

earn *see* **yirn.**

easement *n* personal comfort; relief from physical discomfort.

easins, aesins *npl* the eaves of a building (or of a haystack).

east *adv, adj* 1 east. 2 in one of two possible directions: '*Move that ashet a bittie east*'.
preposition in an easterly direction along: '*east the road*'.

easter 1 eastern, lying towards the east, the more easterly of two places. 2 the east wind.

eastlins eastward NE.

easy-osie *adj* (*of people*) easy-going, inclined to be lazy; (*of things*) involving the minimum of effort.

eat, ett, aet *v, past tense* **ett;** *past participle also* **ett, etten, aten** SW eat.

ebb *n* the foreshore.
adj shallow, lacking in depth, scant.

echt *see* **aucht**[1].

edder, ether *n* a straw-rope used in thatching a haystack NE.

edder *see* **aither, ether**[1], **ether**[2].

Edinburrae *n* Edinburgh.

Edinburgh rock a stick-shaped sweet made of sugar, cream of tartar, water and various flavourings, originally made in Edinburgh.

ee, eye *n, pl also* **een** 1 an eye. 2 an opening, *eg* an opening through which water passes, the hole in the centre of a millstone. 3 regard, liking, craving.

een peeper (*child's word*) eye.

eehole an eyesocket.

pit oot a person's ee get an advantage over.

ee *see* **the.**

eechie [-ch- as in 'dreich'] **(n)or ochie** [-ch- as in 'loch']: **neither eechie nor ochie** neither one thing nor another; absolutely nothing.

eejit, eediot *n* an idiot.

eeksie-peeksie, icksy-picksy NE *adj* much alike, six and half-a-dozen.

eel *see* **ale.**

Eel *see* **Yule.**

eelie *see* **ely, ile.**

eemage *n* 1 an image. 2 a ghost of your former self, a pitiful figure.

eemir *see* **humour.**

eemock, emot *n* an ant.

een *see* **ane**[1], **ee, even**[1].

e'en *see* **even**[2].

eence *adv* once SHETLAND, ORKNEY, NE.

eendle, eentie *numeral* (*words used in children's rhymes*) one.

eenin *see* **eening.**

eening, eenin *n* evening.

eenoo, ivnoo NE, **evenoo** *adv* 1 just now, at the present time, a moment ago. 2 in a short time, soon, at once.

eentie *see* **eendle.**

eer *see* **yer.**

eeran *see* **eerant.**

eerant, eeran, errand *n* 1 an errand. 2 **errands** purchases, parcels, shopping.

eerie *adj* afraid, especially affected by fear of the supernatural.

eese, eeseless *see* **use.**

eeswal *see* **usual.**

eetle ottle *n* words used in counting-out rhymes: '*eetle ottle black bottle, eetle ottle oot*'.

eft *adv* **1** aft. **2** towards the rear of something.

efter, alfter, after *preposition* **1** after. **2** (*in telling time*) past: '*hauf an oor efter ten*'.

efterhin after(wards).

efterins 1 the last drops of milk taken while milking. **2** final results, consequences; remainder.

efternuin, efterneen N **1** afternoon. **2** a meal taken during the afternoon.

egg *n*: **aff (o) yer eggs 1** mistaken. **2** nervous.

eight *see* **aucht**[1].

eik[1] *n* **1** the natural grease in sheep's wool SOUTH. **2** human perspiration SOUTH.

eik[2] *n* an addition, extension, increase; an additional part or piece.
   v increase, add (to), supplement.

eild *n* **1** old age. **2** antiquity, long ago.
   within eild under age.

eild *see* **yeld**.

eibuck *n* an elbow.

eider *n* (*in the Presbyterian Churches*) a person appointed to take part in church management.

eidritch *adj* **1** of or like elves etc. **2** weird, ghostly, strange, unearthly.

eleeven, aleeven *numeral* eleven.

eleevent, aleevent eleventh.

Elfin *n* **1** fairyland, the land of the elves. **2** Hell.

else *adv* **1** otherwise. **2** already, previously.

ely, eelie *v* disappear, vanish gradually.

Embro *n* Edinburgh.

emdy *see* **onie**.

emerteen *n* an ant NE.

emot *see* **eemock**.

en, end, eyn NE *n* **1** an end. **2** a room; one room of a two-roomed cottage.
   v **1** end. **2** stand on end. **3** kill; die.

endless obstinately long-winded.

en(d)rig the land at the end of the furrow on which the plough is turned.

endweys forward, straight ahead; successfully.

endlang, enlang *adv* **1** right along, straight on. **2** lengthwise, at full length.

eneuch *adj, adv, n* enough.

Englified *adj* anglicized (in speech or manner).

English and Scots *n* a children's game imitating the old Border Raids.

enlang *see* **endlang**.

entry *n* **1** an alley or covered passage, usually in or between houses. **2** the front doorway of a house; an entrance-lobby or porch, especially in a block of flats. **3** the entrance to an avenue leading to a house; the avenue itself.

epple *see* **aipple**.

equal-aqual *adj* equally balanced, alike, similar, quits.

erd *n* earth; *see also* **yird**.

ere *adv* early, soon.
   conjunction before, until SHETLAND, NE.

erethestreen the night before last.

erle *see* **herle**.

erm *see* **airm**.

err *see* **there**.

errand *see* **eerant**.

erse *n* **1** the arse. **2** the hinterland, the interior.

esh *n* ash(-tree or -wood).

esk *see* **ask**[2], **yesk**.

esp *n* an aspen tree.

ess *see* **ass**.

estreen *see* **yestreen**.

ether[1], **edder** *n* an adder.

ether[2], **edder** NE *n* an udder.

ether *see* **aither, edder**.

ett *see* **eat**.

etter *n* pus; venom, poison.
   v fester.

ettercap, attercap *n* **1** a spider. **2** a spiteful or nasty person.

ettle *v* **1** plan or intend to do; aim; try to reach; attempt, try.

2 try to express, get at: '*Whit are ye ettlin at?*'.

3 desire very much, be eager for: '*The*

bairns are aye ettlin fur mair pocket money'.
4 ettle tae dae be about to.
n **1** your aim, object. **2** an effort, attempt.
even[1], **een** *n* evening.
at een in the evening.
even[2], **e'en** *adj, adv* **1** even. **2** just, simply.
v **1** even. **2** estimate, compare with, liken to.
evenly smooth, even, level.
evendoon 1 (*of rain*) straight, perpendicular. **2** sheer, absolute, downright. **3** honest, frank, sincere.
even on continuously, without stopping, straight on.
evenoo *see* **eenoo.**
ever, ivver *adv* ever.

everly constantly, perpetually.
ewe gowan *see* **gowan.**
excaise, exkeese NE *n, v* excuse.
exerceese *n* an exercise.
exkeese *see* **excaise.**
expensive *adj* extravagant: '*Whit an expensive pairtie Ah went tae yesterday!'*.
export *n* a better-quality, stronger beer, slightly darker in colour than **heavy.**
explore *n* an exploration.
eydent *adj* **1** diligent, busy. **2** conscientious, careful, attentive. **3** (*of rain*) continuous, persistent.
eye *see* **ee.**
eyn *see* **en.**
eyntment *n* ointment.
eywiz *adv* always.

F

fa, faa, faw, fall *v, n* fall.
  fa awa 1 waste away, go down in health. **2** faint SHETLAND, NE.
  fa by take ill.
  fa ower fall asleep: '*When ye're auld it's hard tae fa ower*'.
  fa-tae a lean-to building.
  fa wi bairn become pregnant.
fa *see* **wha.**
faa *see* **fa.**
faal *see* **whaal.**
faap *see* **whaup**[1].
face *n*: **facie** bold; impudent, cheeky.
  face caird a court card.
  the face o clay any person alive.
  put a face in put in an appearance.
  torn face *see* **teir.**
facile *adj* (*law*) easily influenced by others; weak-minded.
fack *n* a fact.
factor *n* a person appointed to manage property for its owner.
faddom *n, v* fathom.
fader *see* **faither.**
fadge *n* **1** a kind of round thick loaf or bun. **2** a kind of potato scone ULSTER.
fae[1] *n* a foe.
fae[2]**, frae, thrae** SE, **fra** SOUTH *preposition* from.
  conjunction from the time that, as soon as.
faem *n, v* foam.
faggot *n* term of abuse for a messy, clumsy or irritating woman or child.
falk *n* **1** a fold of a garment NE. **2** a plaid, wrap, shawl. **3** a strand of rope N.
  v **1** fold, tuck (cloth or garment) around. **2** coil (a rope or line).
fail *n* turf as a material for building or roofing; a piece of turf, a sod.
faimilie, faimlie *n* a family.

fain *adj* **1** loving, affectionate, amorous. **2** **fain o** fond of.
fair[1] *adj* complete, absolute, utter: '*Ye're a fair disgrace*'.
  adv completely, simply; directly.
  v (*of weather*) clear (up): '*Ah hope it fairs up fur the gairden pairtie*'.
  the Fair City Perth.
  fair hornie *see* **horn.**
  fair-spoken frank, friendly.
fair[2] *n*: **the Fair** the annual summer holiday, especially **the Glasgow Fair.**
fairin(g) a present, often food from a fair or at a festive season.
  gie someone his or her fairins punish someone.
fairm *see* **ferm.**
fairnytickle *see* **ferntickle.**
faisible, feasible *adj* **1** (*of things*) neat, tidily made; satisfactory. **2** (*of people*) neat, tidy; respectable, decent.
faither, fader SHETLAND, NE *n* a father.
  v **1** father. **2** show who your father is by resemblance etc.
faize[1] *v* unravel, fray.
faize[2] *v* **1** annoy, ruffle NE. **2** make an impression on.
fall *see* **fa, faw.**
false *see* **fause.**
fan *see* **whan.**
fang *see* **whang.**
fank[1] *n* a coil of rope, noose, tangle.
  v tangle, twist.
fank[2] *n* a sheepfold.
fankle *v* tangle, mix up: '*It's aw fankelt*'.
  n a tangle, muddle.
fantoosh *adj* flashy, ultra-fashionable.
far, fer SOUTH, **faur** *adj* far.
  far ben 1 friendly, intimate, in great favour. **2** (*of the eyes*) dreamy, far

away. **3** having deep or specialized knowledge.

far oot 1 on bad terms, not friendly. **2** distant in relationship.

far ower too much.

far seen far-sighted; deeply-skilled.

far throu 1 (*of clothes etc*) finished, worn out. **2** very ill, at death's door.

far *see* **whar.**

farce *n* a funny story, a joke.

fardel *n* **1** a three-cornered cake, especially an oatcake. **2** a large slice or piece of food NE.

farin *n* food, fare.

farl *n* a three-cornered piece of oatcake, scone etc.

fash *v* trouble, annoy, anger, inconvenience: '*Dinna fash yersel*'.

n trouble, pains, annoyance, bother.

no fash yer thoum *see* **thoum.**

fashious *adj* **1** troublesome, annoying. **2** fractious, bad-tempered: '*a fashious auld man*'.

fastern's een *n* Shrove Tuesday.

fat[1] *n* a vat.

fat[2]**, fattle, fatum** *adj* (*marbles*) applied to marbles in a ring game which are disqualified if they come to rest inside the ring.

fat *see* **what**[1].

fatna *see* **whitna.**

fatterals *npl* ribbon ends; anything loose and trailing.

fattie, fatum *see* **fat**[2].

fauch *n* a fallow field.

fauchie *n, adj* **1** pale (brown). **2** pasty-faced, sickly looking.

faul *see* **fauld**[1]**, fauld**[2].

fauld[1]**, faul** *n* **1** a fold (of cloth etc). **2** a strand (of rope).

v **1** fold. **2** shut, close. **3** (*of the legs etc*) double up, bend under you.

fauld[2]**, faul** *n* a fold, a pen (for animals).

fault *see* **faut.**

faur *see* **far.**

fause, false *adj* false.

false face a face-shaped mask.

faut, fault *n* **1** a fault. **2** a want, lack. **3** harm, injury SHETLAND, NE.

v find fault with, blame.

favour *n*: **for onie favour** for goodness' sake.

faw, fall *n* a falling mouse- or rat-trap.

faw *see* **fa.**

fear *n* a fright, a scare.

v frighten, scare.

feart, feared frightened.

feardie, feartie a coward: '*That big feardie will no go tae the dentist*'.

feasible *see* **faisible.**

feat *adj* neat, trim.

Februar *n* February.

fecht *v, past tense* **focht**, *past participle* **focht, fochten 1** fight. **2** wrestle, kick or fling the limbs about.

n a fight.

fechter a fighter.

a bonnie fechter a good or fearless fighter, especially for a good cause.

feck *n* **1** the majority. **2** a (great etc) quantity, number, amount: '*That's a feck a messages*'.

feckfu effective, capable, efficient.

fedder *n* a feather SHETLAND, ORKNEY.

fee *n* an engagement as a servant.

feein market one where the farmers engaged servants.

feech! [-ch as in 'dreich'] *interjection* expression of disgust, pain or impatience.

feechie foul, dirty, disgusting.

feel[1] *v* sense by smell or taste.

feel[2] *adj* cosy, neat; comfortable; soft, smooth to the touch.

feel *see* **fuil.**

feem NE *n* **1** fume. **2** a state of sudden heat, a sweat. **3** a state of agitation or rage.

feenish *v, n* finish.

feerich [-ch as in 'dreich'] NE *n* **1** ability, activity. **2** a state of agitation, excitement, rage or panic.

Feersday *see* **Fuirsday.**

feesant *n* a pheasant.

feeze *v* **1** twist, screw, cause to revolve. **2** wriggle (the body), wag (the tail). **3** work hard. **4** get yourself into another's favour.

fegs!, *also* **by (my) fegs!, guid fegs!** *interjection* indeed!, goodness!

feifteen *numeral* fifteen.

feifteent fifteenth.

fell[1] *n* a (steep, rocky) hill; a stretch of hill-moor.

fell[2] *v* **1** slaughter, kill. **2** injure, thrash.

fell[3] *adj* **1** fierce, cruel, ruthless. **2** severe, acute. **3** extremely strong, big, loud etc. **4** energetic and capable, sturdy. **5** clever, shrewd.
adv **1** extremely, greatly, very. **2** vigorously, energetically; sternly.

fella, fellae SE *n* a fellow.

feltie, feltiefiler [feltie-fleeer] *n* a field-fare.

fend *v* **1** defend, protect, shelter. **2** provide with food, sustenance. **3** support yourself.
n **1** a defence, resistance. **2** an effort, attempt: '*We'll hae tae mak a fend*'.

fent[1] *n* a slit or opening in a garment.

fent[2] *v, n* faint.

fer *see* **far**.

fere[1] *adj* healthy, sturdy; sound.

fere[2] *n* a companion, comrade.

ferile *n* **1** a strange sight, a marvel, a curiosity, wonder. **2** a piece of (surprising) news; an object of gossip.
v wonder, marvel, be surprised (at).

ferm, fairm *n, v* farm.

ferm toon a farm and the buildings round about.

fern *n* bracken.

ferntickle, fairnytickle *n* a freckle.

fernyear *n* last year; the preceding year.

ferrier *n* **1** a farrier. **2** a veterinary surgeon.

ferry *v* farrow, produce young.

ferry-lowper *n* an incomer to Orkney.

fesh, fess *v* **1** fetch. **2 fesh up** bring up, rear NE. **3 fesh on** bring forward, advance NE.

fest *adj* **1** fast. **2** busy, occupied NE.

fettle *adj* suitable.

feugle *see* **fuggle**.

fey[1] [rhymes with 'gey'] *adj* **1** (*of people*) fated to die, doomed, especially as forecast by peculiar, usually excited behaviour; (*more vaguely*) otherworldly. **2** behaving in an excited or irresponsible way: '*She's been richt fey since her bairn wis born*'.

fey[2] N, **fy** NE [rhymes with 'gey' or 'my'] *n* whey.

fey[3] *n* a field SW.

ficher [-ch- as in 'dreich'] *v* fumble, fiddle nervously with the fingers: '*Stoap ficherin wi that an help me!*'.

fickle *adj* difficult, tricky.
v puzzle, perplex.

fiddler's biddin *n* a last minute invitation.

fidge *v* fidget; move restlessly from excitement; twitch, itch.

fient *n* a fiend.

fient (a) . . . , the fient (a) . . . devil a . . . , never a . . . : '*fient a bit*'.

fift *numeral* fifth.

figmaleerie *see* **whigmaleerie**.

file *see* **while**.

files *see* **whiles**.

filk *see* **whilk**.

fill *v* pour out.

filler a funnel for pouring liquids through.

fin *see* **find**.

find, fin *v, past tense, past participle* **fun(d)** **1** feel, be conscious of. **2** feel with the fingers, grope. **3** be aware of (a smell or taste).

fine *adj* **1** comfortable, contented; in good health. **2** pleasant-mannered, likeable.
adv very well, very much: '*I like it fine*'.
finean(d). . . very, properly, really. . . : '*fine an tight*'.

finick *n* a fussy person.

Finnan, Finnan haddie *n* a haddock cured with the smoke of green wood, peat or turf.

fir tap, fir yowe *n* a fir-cone.

fire *n* **1** fuel. **2** a foreign body in the eye. *v* **1** bake (oatcakes, scones, etc) by browning in an oven or over a flame: '*weel fired rolls*'. **2** inflame (a part of the body) by chafing. **3** heat (a house): '*Keep the house fired*'.

firies very fast turns of a skipping rope ANGUS.

fire-flaucht (flashes of) lightning.

fire-raising (*law*) arson.

fireside tartan *see* **tartan**.

gae on fire catch fire.

firm *see* **furm**.

first *adj*: **first fit** *n* the first person to enter a house on New Year's morning, considered to bring good (or bad) luck for the year.
v be the first to visit (a person) in the New Year; go on a round of such visits.

first floor the ground floor of a building; ground-floor flat: '*I need a first floor fur ma wheelchair*'.

Monday *etc* **first** next Monday etc, Monday immediately following.

firth *n* a wide inlet of the sea; an estuary: '*Firth of Forth*'.

fir yowe *see* **fir tap**.

fiscal *n* = **procurator fiscal**.

fish, fush *n* **1** fish. **2** a salmon. **3** white fish, as opposed to herring.

fit, foot *n* **1** a foot. **2** a foothold, step: '*lose yer fit*'.

fitter patter, move restlessly.

fit fowk pedestrians, especially those going to church, market etc on foot.

fit-road a footpath.

chynge yer feet change your footwear.

mak yer feet yer freends leave quickly.

fit *see* **what**[1].

fite *see* **white**[1], **white**[2].

fither *see* **whither**.

fitin *n* a whiting NE.

five-stanes *npl* the game of **chucks** played with five stones or pebbles.

fivver *n* fever, often scarlet fever.

fizz *v* make a fuss, bustle; be in a towering rage.

flacht *see* **flaucht**.

flae *n* **1** a fly. **2** a flea.

flaff *v* **1** flap, flutter. **2** (*of the wind*) blow in gusts.

flair *see* **fluir**.

flam *see* **flan**.

flan, flam *n* **1** a gust of wind (blowing smoke down a chimney). **2** a sudden squall of wind.

flannen *n* flannel.

flap *v* fall down flat suddenly.

flash *n* a tab of cloth on the garter of a kilt stocking.

flat, flet *adj* flat.
n **1** a flat. **2** a storey (of a house). **3** a saucer.

flaucht, flacht *n* a burst of flame, a flash of lightning; a snowflake.

flauchter peel turf from the ground.

flauntie *adj* capricious, flighty: '*a flauntie wee lassie*'.

flech [-ch as in 'dreich'] *n* **1** a flea. **2** a restless, active person.
v rid of fleas.

flee[1] *v* fly.

fleein very drunk.

flee[2] *n* a fly, an insect.

let that flee stick tae the wa drop a particular (embarrassing) subject.

fleem *n* phlegm.

fleer *see* **fluir**.

fleet *v* float SHETLAND.
n a set of nets or lines carried by a single boat.

fleetch *v* coax, flatter, beg.

fleg *v* **1** frighten, scare. **2** drive away. **3** take fright, be scared: '*I wis real fleggit*'.
n a fright, a scare.

flesh *n* butcher's meat.

flesher a butcher.

flet *see* **flat**.

fleuk, fluke *n* a flounder, flat fish.

fley [rhymes with 'gey'] *v* frighten, scare; drive off by frightening.

flichan *n* a snowflake.

flicht[1] *n* flight, the act of flying.

flicht[2] *n* flight, the act of fleeing.

flicht[3] *n* a flake, a small speck of soot, dust, snow etc.

flichter *v* 1 (*of birds*) flutter, fly awkwardly; (*of people*) rush about excitedly. 2 (*of the heart*) flutter, quiver, palpitate: '*That speeder fair made ma hert flichter*'. 3 (*of light*) flicker.

fling *v* 1 kick. 2 dance, especially a Scottish dance. 3 jerk sideways as a sign that you are not pleased. 4 jilt: '*He flung her last week*'.

n 1 a kick. 2 being jilted: '*get the fling*'.

flisk *v* 1 dart from place to place, caper, frisk. 2 whisk.

fliskie *adj* 1 restless, flighty, skittish. 2 (*of a horse*) apt to kick.

flist *v* 1 whizz; explode with a sharp hiss or puff. 2 fly into a rage NE. 3 boast, brag; exaggerate N.

flit *v* remove, transport from one place to another, *eg* to another house; move (tethered animals) to fresh grazing.

flittin 1 the act of moving from one house to another. 2 goods, especially household goods, when being moved.

floan NE *v* 1 show affection, especially sloppily. 2 lounge, loaf.

flocht *n* a flutter, a state of excitement; a bustle, a flurry, a great hurry.

flochter *v* 1 flutter, flap; spread open, sprawl. 2 fluster.

flooer, flower, flour *n* 1 a flower. 2 a bunch of flowers, a bouquet: '*Get a flooer fur Mother's Day*'. 3 flour.

flourish *n, v* blossom.

flow *n* very wet boggy ground.

flower *see* **flooer**.

fluff *v* puff, blow.

fluffer *v* flutter, flap: '*Ah hate when moths fluffer*'.

fluir, flair, fleer NE *n* floor.

fluke *see* **fleuk**.

fluther *v, n* flutter.

flype[1] *v* 1 fold back; turn (socks etc) wholly or partially inside out. 2 tear off (the skin) in strips, peel. 3 (*of the tongue, lip etc*) curl.

flype[2] *v* fall heavily.

flyte *v* scold, rail at; quarrel violently. *n* a scolding (match).

flyting 1 scolding, quarrelling using abusive language. 2 (*in past times*) a contest between poets in mutual abuse.

fob *v* pant with heat or exertion NE.

focht, fochten *see* **fecht**.

fodge *n* a fat, clumsy person SE.

fog *n* moss, lichen.

v 1 gather moss NE. 2 save money.

foggie bee a kind of wild bee.

folk *see* **fowk**.

folla, follae *v* follow.

follower *n* the young of an animal, especially one still dependent on its mother.

folp *see* **whalp**.

fond *adj* 1 foolishly keen, infatuated; easily tricked, 2 eager, glad (to do etc).

foo SHETLAND, NE *adv* 1 how. 2 why, for what reason: '*Foo are ye deein at?*'.

foo *see* **hoo**[1].

fool[1] *n* a fowl, bird.

fool[2] *adj* 1 foul. 2 dirty; unwashed.

foon *see* **foond**.

foond, foon *v* 1 found. 2 base your opinion or conduct on. 3 be based or established on.

n 1 *usually in pl* **foon(d)s** a foundation, base. 2 a fund of money NE.

foon(d)er *v* 1 founder. 2 collapse, break down because of drink, exhaustion, illness etc. 3 strike down (a person, animal etc).

n 1 a collapse, breakdown in health. 2 a severe chill.

foord *see* **fuird**.

foosht *see* **foost**.

foosome *adj* 1 filthy, nasty, horrible NE. 2 (*of food*) filling, over-rich SHETLAND, NE.

foost, foosht NE *v* become or smell mouldy.

n a mouldy condition or smell.

foostle, fooshtle NE *adj* mouldy.

foostle *n* a kind of large thick bread roll.

foot *see* **fit.**

footer *n* **1** a slacker, a muddling, aimless person. **2** a troublesome, fiddling job. **3** an annoying person N.

v **1** potter, trifle, work in a fiddling, unskilled way. **2** thwart, inconvenience.

footerie (*of a person*) fussy, inept; (*of a task*) trivial; fiddling, time-wasting.

footh *n* plenty, abundance, an ample supply.

footie *adj* **1** mean, despicable, underhand. **2** obscene, indecent.

for, fur *preposition* **1** for. **2** because of, as a result of, through. **3** *with* **to** *expressing purpose*: '*She went out for to buy some*'. **4 be for** want (to have): '*Are ye fur puddin?*'. **5** for fear of, to prevent: '*He winna wait for missin the bus*'.

foraneen *see* **forenuin.**

forby *adv* **1** besides, in addition, as well. **2** extraordinarily.

preposition **1** in addition to. **2** except. **3** compared with, relative to. **4** beside, beyond.

forder *v* **1** further. **2** make progress, succeed.

adj further.

fore *n*: **tae the fore 1** on hand, in reserve. **2** alive, still in existence: '*Is he still tae the fore?*'. **3** in advance, ahead.

fore-end *n* the first or front part or portion (of something); the beginning or earlier part (of a period of time).

forefolk *npl* ancestors, forefathers.

forehaimmer *n* a sledge-hammer.

forehand *adj* **1** (*of payments, now only of rents*) made in advance. **2** first, foremost, leading.

foreheld *n* a forehead.

foremaist *adj, adv* foremost.

backside foremaist back to front; inside out.

forenent *preposition* opposite to, in front of.

forenicht *n* the evening; (*latterly especially*) the winter evening as a time for entertainment.

forenuin, foraneen NE *n* forenoon, morning.

foreside *n* the front or front part of something.

forestair *n* an outside staircase.

Forfar bridle *see* **bridle.**

forfauchelt *adj* worn out, exhausted.

forfeuchin *see* **forfochen.**

forfochen, forfochten, forfeuchin SE *adj* exhausted: '*sair forfochen*'.

forgaither *v* **1** assemble, gather together, congregate. **2** meet, fall in with, often by chance.

forget *n* (an instance of) forgetfulness, absent-mindedness.

forgettle forgetful.

forgie *v* forgive.

forhoo *v* (*mainly of a bird*) leave, abandon (a nest).

forjeskit *adj* exhausted, worn out.

fork *n* **1** a forkful. **2** a thorough search.

v **1** *mainly* **fork for** search, hunt for (money, work etc). **2** fend for yourself.

forker, forkie, forkietail an earwig.

forkie golach *see* **golach.**

forlaithie *n* a surfeit, an excess (of something); a feeling of revulsion NE.

forleet *v* neglect, leave behind, abandon.

forrit *adv* **1** forward. **2** available for sale, on the market.

adj **1** forward. **2** (*of a clock etc*) fast. **3** present, at hand.

forritsome forward, impudent, bold.

fotch *v* shift, turn, change the position of.

fother *n, v* fodder.

fou, ful, full *adj* **1** full. **2** full of food, well-fed. **3 fou** drunk: '*fou as a puggie*'; '*roarin fou*'. **4 fou** comfortably well-off, well-provided for. **5** proud, pompous, conceited.

adv fully, very, exceedingly.

n a fill, your fill, a full load.

foumart, thoumart *n* **1** a polecat; a ferret; a weasel. **2** term of abuse NE.

four, fourt *see* **fower.**

fowe *n* a pitchfork.

v **1** lift or toss straw, hay etc with a fork. **2** kick about restlessly, especially in bed NE.

fower, four *numeral* four.

fowersie a game in which a set or group of four stones etc have to be picked up while another is thrown up in the air.

fowersome 1 a group of four persons or things. **2** *also* **foursome reel** a reel danced by four people.

fowert, fourt *adj* fourth.

fowk, folk *n* **1** folk. **2** people, persons, mankind. **3** the inhabitants of a place. **4** the members of your family, community etc. **5** individual persons: '*Here's twae folks fae Glasgow*'.

foze *see* **wheeze.**

fozie *adj* **1** (*often of overgrown or rotten vegetables*) soft, spongy. **2** (*of rope etc*) ragged, frayed NE. **3** fat, flabby, out of condition. **4** unintelligent, dull, stupid.

fra, frae *see* **fae**².

fraik *n* **1** flattery; affectionate fussing. **2** a flatterer, a wheedler. **3** a slight illness about which too much fuss is made.

v **1** flatter, make a fuss of, pamper. **2** pretend to be ill, make a fuss about a minor illness.

fraise *see* **phrase.**

frame *n* **1** a square or hoop of wood hung from the shoulders on which to carry pails. **2** a painfully thin person or animal.

frase *see* **phrase.**

fraucht *n* a load, a burden; as much as can be carried or transported at one time by one person.

frawart *adj* contrary, perverse; adverse, unfavourable.

free, frei SOUTH *adj* **1** free. **2** single, unmarried. **3** ready, willing. **4** (*of pastry etc*) brittle, crumbly.

v **1** free. **2** clear (someone of a suspicion etc). **3** (*games, mainly hide-and-seek etc*) put (someone) out of the game by reaching 'home' first.

freen *see* **freend.**

freend, freen *n* **1** a friend. **2** a relative. **be freends tae** be related to NE.

freenge *n* fringe.

freest *n* frost NE.

freet¹ *v* rub, chafe, injure.

freet² *n* **1** fruit CAITHNESS, NE. **2** milk produce CAITHNESS.

frei *see* **free.**

freit *n* **1** **freits** superstitious beliefs, observances or acts. **2** a superstitious saying.

freith *n* **1** froth, foam, lather. **2** a hasty wash given to clothes.

fremd, fremmit *adj* **1** strange, unfamiliar, foreign; unrelated. **2** strange, unusual, uncommon. **3** strange in manner, distant, aloof.

the fremd strangers, the world at large.

French *adj*: **French cake** a kind of small sponge cake, iced and decorated. **French loaf** a kind of sweetened loaf giving a heart-shaped slice.

frequent [frequent] *v* associate, keep company (with).

fresh *adj* **1** (*mainly of a heavy drinker*) sober. **2** (*of weather*) not frosty, thawing. **3** (*of animals*) thriving, fattening. *n* (the setting in of) a thaw, a period of frost-free weather.

v **1** thaw NE. **2** pack (herring) in ice ungutted, to be eaten fresh.

freuch *adj* dry and brittle, liable to break NE.

Freuchie *n*: **gae tae Freuchie (an fry mice)!** get lost!

fricht *n* fright.

v *also* **frichten** frighten, terrify: '*Ye frichtit me!*'.

frizz *v* (*of cloth etc*) fray, wear out.

fro *n* froth, foam.

front *n* the front garden.

in front of (*of time*) before; prior to.

froon *v, n* frown.

frost *n* ice: '*He slippit on the frost*'.

v protect (a horse) from slipping on ice by spiking its shoes.

frothie *see* **furth.**

frowe [rhymes with 'cow'] *n* a big buxom woman NE.

frugal *adj* frank, kindly, hospitable SHETLAND, CAITHNESS, NE.

frull *n, v* frill.

frush *adj* **1** crumbly. **2** (*of wood, cloth etc*) brittle, decayed, rotten. **3** frank, bold, rash. **4** tender, easily hurt or destroyed, frail.

fry *n* **1** a small number of fish for frying especially when presented as a gift: '*Here a fry o haddies tae ye*'. **2** a state of worry or distraction, a disturbance.

fud *n* **1** the buttocks. **2** the tail of an animal: '*a mappie's fud*'. **3** the female genitals.

v frisk about; walk briskly or with a short, quick step.

fudder *see* **whidder.**

fuff *v* **1** puff (smoke or vapour), hiss. **2** go off in a huff or rage.

interjection exclamation indicating an explosive noise, or expressing contempt, fsst!, bah!

fuffle impatient.

fuffle *v* ruffle, disarrange (clothes etc). *n* fuss, violent exertion.

fuftie *numeral* fifty.

fuggle, feugle NE *n* **1** a small bundle of hay, rags etc, especially one used to stop up a hole. **2** an unburnt plug of tobacco in a pipe.

fugie [f(ee)oojie] *n* **1** a runaway, a fugitive; a coward. **2** a challenge to fight given by one schoolboy to another. **3** a truant from school.

v, mainly **fugie the scull** play truant NE.

fuld *n* food.

full, feel N *n* a fool. *adj* foolish, silly.

fuird, f(y)oord N *n, v* ford.

Fuirsday, Feersday NE *n* Thursday.

ful, full *see* **fou.**

fummle *v, n* fumble.

fummle *see* **whummle.**

fun *see* **find, whin**[1]**, whin**[2]**.**

funcle *adj* fancy NE.

funcle pieces cakes NE.

fund *see* **find.**

fung, funk *v* **1** (*especially of a restive horse*) kick. **2** throw violently and abruptly, toss, fling. **3** strike with the hands or feet NE. **4** fly up or along at high speed and with a buzzing noise, whizz. **5** fly into a temper or rage, sulk NE.

funny *n* a game, usually of marbles, played for fun, where no score is kept and all winnings are restored to the loser.

fup *see* **whip.**

fuppertie jig *n* a trick, dodge NE.

fur coat an nae knickers *adj* above yourself, snobbish.

fur *see* **for, furr.**

furl *see* **whirl.**

furm, firm *v, n* form.

furr, fur *n* **1** a furrow made by the plough; the strip of earth turned over in the process. **2** a deep furrow etc cut by the plough to act as a drain. **3** the act of furrowing, a ploughing.

v **1** plough, make furrows in. **2** make drills in or for, draw soil around (plants), earth up.

furth *adv* **1** forth. **2** outside, out of doors, in(to) the open air SHETLAND, NE.

preposition out of, from, outside.

n the open air NE.

furthie, frothie NE **1** forward, bold; go-ahead, energetic; impulsive NE. **2** generous, hospitable.

furth the gait candid(ly), honest(ly), straightforward(ly) NE.

furth o out of, outside, away from, beyond the confines or limits of: '*furth o Scotland*'.

the furth out of doors, in the open, away from home NE.

fush *see* **fish.**

fushion *n* **1** the nourishing or sustaining element in food or drink.
2 physical strength, energy; bodily sensation, power of feeling NE.
3 mental or spiritual force or energy; strength of character, power NE.

fushionless 1 spiritless, faint-hearted, lacking vigour or ability.
2 (*of people*) physically weak, without energy; numb, without feeling.
3 (*of things*) without strength or durability; weak from decay.
4 (*of actions, speech etc*) dull, uninspired.
5 (*of food*) lacking in nourishment, tasteless, insipid.
6 (*of plants*) without sap or pith, dried, withered.

fushnach *see* **fussoch.**

fusker *n* a whisker, moustache NE.

fuskie *see* **whisky.**

fusper *v, n* whisper NE.

fussle *see* **whistle.**

fussoch, fushnach sw *n* **1** waste straw, grass etc sw. **2** a loose bundle of something NE.

fussy *adj* affected in dress or manner, dressy.

futher *see* **whidder.**

futley *see* **whittle**[2].

futrat *see* **whitrat.**

futtle *see* **whittle**[1].

fuzzle *adj* effervescent, hissing, fizzing NE.

fy *see* **fey**[2].

fyke *v* **1** move about restlessly, fidget.
2 fret, be anxious or troubled.
3 exert yourself, take trouble or pains (with).
4 bustle about, fiddle, make a fuss about nothing.
n **1** a restless movement, a twitch; **fykes** the itch, the fidgets, (a fit of) restlessness.
2 a fuss, bustle, excitement.
3 trouble, bother, worry; **fykes** small worries.
4 an intricate and usually trivial piece of work.
5 a whim, a fussy fad.
6 a fussy, fastidious person.

fykie 1 (*of people*) restless, fidgety, finicky. **2** (*of a task etc*) tricky, troublesome, intricate and difficult to manage.

mak a fyke make a fuss (about).

fyle *v* **1** make dirty, soil. **2** soil with excrement. **3** defecate.

fyle yer finger wi have to do with, meddle with (something).

fyle the stamack upset the stomach, make you sick.

fylies *see* **whiles.**

fyoord *see* **fuird.**

fyow *adj* few N.

G

gaan *see* **gae.**

gab[1] *n* **1** speech, conversation, way of speaking. **2** entertaining talk, chat, cheek. **3** a chatterbox, gossip.

v talk, chatter.

gabble chatty; fluent.

gab[2] *n* a mouth, beak.

steek yer gab! hold your tongue!, shut up!

gaberlunyie *n* (*in past times*) a beggar, a tramp.

gadder *see* **galther.**

gadgie *n* a man, fellow SE.

gae, go; *see also* **gang** *v, past tense* **gaed, geed** SHETLAND, ORKNEY, N, **gled;** *past participle* **gane, geen** SHETLAND, ORKNEY, N; *present participle* **gaun, gaein, gaan** N, **gyaun** SHETLAND, NE, **gyan** SHETLAND, NE **1** go. **2** cover on foot, walk. **3** (*of animals*) graze NE.

n **go** a fuss, bother; a state: '*in a go*'.

gane 1 past, ago: '*Sunday gane a week*'. **2 nae farrer gane (than)** as recently (as): '*Nae farrer gane than yesterday she telt me . . .*'. **3** over, more than (a certain age): '*He's eighteen gane*'; '*She's gane forty-twa*'. **4** mad, crazy.

gaun (*of a child*) at the walking stage.

gaun(-aboot) bodie a tramp.

gaunae going to.

gaun yersel! (*to encourage someone*) come on!

gae awa 1 die. **2** faint. **3** expressing impatience, disbelief etc: '*Gae awa wi ye*'.

gae back get worse, run down, fall off: '*Grannie's gane back since granda died*'.

gae by someone's door pass someone's house without calling in, shun.

gae done be used up or worn out, come to an end.

gae giey *see* **giey.**

gae in shrink.

gae in twa break in two, snap NE.

gae in wi agree with: '*She aye gaes in wi the boss*'.

gae intae open and search (a bag etc).

gae ower be beyond a person's power or control; get the better of (someone).

gae tae shut, close.

gae thegither 1 come together, close. **2** (*of lovers*) court.

gae throu 1 waste, *especially* **gae throu't** become bankrupt, penniless. **2** bungle, muddle (speech) *mainly* N.

gae throu the fluir be overcome with shame, embarrassment, astonishment.

gae wi 1 keep company with, court (a lover). **2** go pleasantly or smoothly for.

Gael *n* a Highlander, a Gaelic-speaker.

Gaelic [**ga**lick, **gay**lick] the Celtic language of the Highlands and Islands.

gaff *n* a guffaw, a hearty laugh.

v **1** guffaw, laugh heartily. **2** babble, chatter.

gaffaw *n* a guffaw, a hearty laugh.

v laugh loudly and heartily or coarsely, guffaw.

gaig *n* **1** a crack, chink. **2** a chap in the hand.

gaillie, gellie *n* **1** a galley, a kind of ship. **2** a garret, especially in a **bothy;** a **bothy** NE.

gaily *see* **gey.**

gainer *see* **ganner.**

gair *n* a gore, a triangular piece of cloth or opening in a garment.

gairie bee the black and yellow striped wild bee SOUTH.

gaird *n, v* guard.

gairden *n* a garden.

gairdener a gardener.

gairdener's ga(i)rtens ribbon-grass.

gairten *see* **garten.**

gaishon *n* a thin, starved-looking person, a 'skeleton' SW, SOUTH.

gaislin *n* a gosling.

gait *n* a goat.

gait *see* **furth.**

gaither, gedder NE, **gadder** SHETLAND, **gather** *v* 1 gather. 2 save. 3 make a collection (of money contributions). 4 collect your wits, pull yourself together, get better, improve in health.

gaithert, weel-gaithert rich, well-to-do.

gaitherin *n* gathering.

Highland Gathering = Highland Games (*see* **game** 2).

gaivel *see* **gavel.**

Galatian, Galoshan *n* 1 (*in past times*) a play performed by boy **guisers** at **Hogmanay** or at **Halloween.** 2 the name of the hero in such a play. 3 an actor in such a play.

gale *see* **gavel, gell².**

gallant [galant] *v* gad about, gallivant; flirt.

Gallovidian *adj* of Galloway. *n* a native of Galloway.

Galloway *n* 1 a small sturdy type of horse. 2 a breed of hornless cattle.

belted Galloway a breed of **Galloway** cattle with a broad white band round a black body.

gallus, gallows *n* gallows. *adj* 1 wicked *mainly* WEST. 2 **gallus** wild, unmanageable, bold; mischievous, cheeky. 3 very good, excellent WEST.

galluses trouser braces.

Galoshan *see* **Galatian.**

galshach *n, mainly* **galshachs** NE 1 sweets, titbits. 2 trashy (especially sweet) food. 3 luxuries, treats.

galt *see* **gaut.**

game, gemm *n* 1 a game. 2 **games** *often* **Highland Games** a meeting consisting of athletics, piping and dancing, held originally in the Highland area.

gamie, gemmie a gamekeeper.

game watcher a gamekeeper NE.

gams *npl* 1 (large) teeth NE. 2 the jaws.

gan *v* go.

gan on aboot make a fuss about.

gane *see* **gae.**

gang, ging NE, **gyang** [geeang] NE, **geeng** SHETLAND; *see also* **gae** *v* go. *n* 1 a journey, trip (especially when carrying goods). 2 a load, the quantity that can be carried at one time, especially of water. 3 way of walking. 4 a row in knitting, plaiting or weaving SHETLAND, ORKNEY, CAITHNESS.

gangrel(l) 1 a tramp: '*a gangrel bodie*'. 2 a toddler N.

gang awa faint.

gang doon the hill grow old.

gang done be used up or worn out, come to an end NE.

gang oot amang fowk work as a charwoman, washerwoman etc in private houses.

gang ower overcome.

gang throu waste.

gang thegither (*of lovers*) court.

ganner, gainer *n* a gander. *v* wander about aimlessly or foolishly.

gansey, genzie *n* a guernsey, a jersey, especially one worn by fishermen.

gansh *v* 1 (*of a dog*) snatch (at), snap, snarl. 2 stammer.

gant *v, n* yawn.

gantry *n* a bottle stand in a bar.

gapus *see* **gaup.**

gar¹ *n* filth.

gar² *v* 1 make (a person or thing do something): '*Gar him come*'. 2 give instructions, take steps (to do or make something).

gardy *n* 1 the arm NE. 2 **gardies** hands or fists (raised to fight).

gardyloo *interjection* (*in past times*) a warning call that waste, dirty water etc was about to be poured into the street from an upper storey EDINBURGH.

garron *n* **1** a small sturdy type of horse, used especially for rough hill work. **2** an old, worn-out horse **3** a strong, thickset man or sturdy boy NE.

garten, gairten *n* a garter.

get the green garten said about an older sister or brother when a younger one marries first.

gash[1] *n* chat, talk, impudent language. *adj* talkative.

gash[2] *adj* **1** shrewd, wise. **2** well or neatly dressed, respectable.

gate *n* **1** a way, road, path.

2 a street (*now mainly in street names*). **3** way, direction.

4 -where, *eg* **nae gate** nowhere, **somegate** somewhere.

5 length of a way, distance.

6 -how, rate, *eg* **(at) onie gate** at any rate, **nae gate** in no way.

7 a way of behaving, manner NE.

gate en(d) a neighbourhood.

gang yer gate go on your way.

gang yer ain gate follow your own opinions.

in the gate on the way, along the road NE.

oot o the gate out of the way.

oot the gate on your way, along the road, up the road.

tak the gate set off.

gate-slap *n* an opening, gateway.

gather *see* **galther.**

gauger *n* an exciseman.

gaun, gaunae *see* **gae.**

gaup, gowp *v* **1** gawp, stare openmouthed, gape. **2** eat greedily, devour.

n **1 gaup, gauple** a fool, a person who gapes. **2 gowp** a stare NE.

gauplt, gowplt stupid, silly.

gawpus, gapus a fool, a clumsy stupid lout.

gaut SHETLAND, ORKNEY, N, **galt** *n* a pig, usually a boar or hog.

gavel, galvel, gale NE *n* a gable.

gavelock, gellock SW *n* **1** a crowbar, lever. **2** an earwig or other similar insect.

gaw *n* **1** a gall, a sore etc. **2** a defect, mark *eg* a gap in woven cloth.

gawk *n, also* **gawkie** an awkward, clumsy person, a fool.

v **1** *also* **gawkie** play the fool, flirt. **2** wander aimlessly, idle. **3** stare idly or vacantly.

gawkit stupid, clumsy.

gawpus *see* **gaup.**

gawsie *adj* **1** (*of people*) plump, fresh-complexioned, cheery, handsome. **2** (*of animals*) handsome, in good condition. **3** (*of things*) large; handsome, showy.

gean *n* a wild cherry.

gear *n* **1** possessions, goods, money, *often* **goods an(d) gear. 2** livestock, cattle. **3** stuff, material. **4** worthless things, rubbish N.

guid gear gangs in sma bulk applied to a small but capable person, or to something small but valuable.

gebble *n* **1** the crop of a bird E CENTRAL. **2** a person's stomach. **3** a person's mouth, a bird's beak.

geck *v* **1 geck at** mock at, scoff at. **2** toss the head scornfully, raise the head proudly. **3** stare rudely. **4** turn the head in a flirty or foolish way NE.

gedder *see* **galther.**

gee [g- as in 'get'] *n* a fit of temper, a mood, fancy.

tak the gee take offence, sulk.

gee *see* **jee.**

geed *see* **gae.**

geem [g- as in 'get'] *n* the gum (in the mouth) NE.

geen *see* **gae.**

geeng *see* **gang.**

geese *see* **guse, gussie.**

geesie *see* **gussie.**

geet *see* **get.**

geg[1] [g- as in 'get'] *n* a gag, trick.

geg[2] [g- as in 'get'] *n* the thing (*eg a penknife, a piece of wood*) used in the game of **smuggle the geg** a children's game, the aim of the two teams respectively being to protect or capture the **geg**.

geggie[1] [g- as in 'get'] *n* a travelling theatre show.

geggie[2] *n* the mouth.

geing, ging [g- as in 'get'] *n* human excrement; filth.

gell[1] [g- as in 'get'] *n* a crack (in wood). **gelled** (*of unseasoned wood*) split or cracked in drying.

gell[2], **gale** *n* **1** a gale. **2 in a gale** in a state of excitement from anger, joy etc. **3** *mainly* **gell** a brawl, row, squabble.

gellie *see* **gaillie**.

gellock *see* **gavelock**.

gemm, gemmie *see* **game**.

General Assembly *n* (*Presbyterian Churches*) the highest church court.

gentie [jentie] FIFE, NE *adj* **1** neat, dainty, graceful. **2** genteel; courteous, well-bred.

genzie *see* **gansey**.

geo, gyo *n* an inlet of the sea with steep sides SHETLAND, ORKNEY, CAITHNESS.

'Gers *npl* nickname for Rangers football team.

get, git *v, past tense* **got, goat;** *past participle* **got, goat, gotten 1** get. **2** find, get by looking: '*Ye'll get it in ma pooch*'. **3** marry: '*Who did Tibbie get?*'. **4** be called, be addressed as: '*Mackenzie's ma name but I aye get Jock fae her*'. **5** be able, be allowed, manage (to do something): '*I couldna get sleepin*'; '*Can I get downstairs?*'. **6** be struck, get a hit NE: '*I got i the lug wi a steen*'. **7** become: '*He's gey auld gettin*'.
n, also **gyte, geet** NE **1** a child, young of animals etc. **2** a brat; a bastard.

get by 1 avoid, do without SHETLAND, NE. **2** get past.

get on to be, get on for get a job as, be promoted to.

get on tae scold, nag.

get oot wi let out (a roar).

get ower 1 last out NE. **2** get the upper hand of.

get (it) ower the fingers be told off.

get roon master, get the hang of, manage to do.

get throu escape, recover from.

get up in years grow old.

get well up rise in position, succeed.

gey [g- as in 'get'] *adv* considerably, very; rather, fairly: '*gey far*'.
adj **1** excellent, splendid. **2** wild, wicked. **3** (*of quantity or amount*) fairly large, considerable, good (-sized), great: '*a gey few*'.

gaily, geylies 1 pretty, rather; very. **2** fairly well, pretty well, pretty nearly. **3** (*of health*) well enough, fairly well.

gey an(d) rather, very: '*gey an handy*'.

a gey wheen *see* **wheen**.

ghaist, ghaistie NE *n* **1** a ghost. **2** contemptuous term for a nasty (looking) person or for a sickly or undersized person.

ghillie *see* **gillie**.

gib, gibble *n* a cat; a tom-cat, especially a neutered male.

gibberie[1] *n* gingerbread N.

gibberie[2] *n* a kind of marbles game N.

gibble *see* **gib**.

gibble-gabble [g- as in 'get'] *n* chatter.

gibbles [g- as in 'get'] *npl* tools, things. **gibblet** [g- as in 'get'] a tool, utensil.

gie [g- as in 'get'], **give** *v* **1** give. **2** strike.

gied, gien *past tense* gave; *past participle* given.

gie's give us, give me: '*Gie's a len o yer bike*'.

gimme give me.

given 1 (*usually implying exasperation*) 'blasted': '*I had tae sit twa given hours*'. **2 given name** first name, Christian name.

gie ower give up, abandon SHETLAND, NE.

gled *see* **gae, gle.**

glen *see* **gle.**

glf [g- as in 'get'] *conjunction* if *literary.*

glff-gaff [g- as in 'get'] *n* **1** helping each other, give and take, fair exchange. **2** exchange of talk.

v exchange (especially words).

glg *see* **jeeg.**

glgot [jiggot] *n* a leg (of lamb, pork etc).

glll [g- as in 'get'] *n* a ravine, gully.

glllle, ghlllle [g- as in 'get'] *n* a sportsman's attendant, usually in deerstalking or angling in the Highlands.

v act as a sportsman's attendant.

gllly-gawpus [g- as in 'get'] *n* a stupid person, a fool NE.

gllple [g- as in 'get'] *n* a lively young girl, a tomboy.

gllravage [g- as in 'get'] *v* **1** eat and drink greedily. **2** enjoy yourself noisily, create a disturbance. **3** rove about, especially to plunder.

n **1** merry-making, horseplay, commotion. **2** a state of confusion, a disturbance.

glm [jim] *adj* neat, spruce NE.

glmmer [g- as in 'get'] *n* a year-old ewe.

glmmer *see* **cummer.**

gln[1] [g- as in 'get'] *conjunction* **1** if, whether: '*gin you please sir*'. **2** oh that, if only: '*Oh gin they were awa!*'.

gln[2] *preposition* **1** by, before: '*gin ten o'clock*'. **2** in readiness NE: '*gin Yeel*'. **3** than NE.

conjunction by the time that, when, before, until: '*Gin we get there, it'll be dark*'.

glng *see* **gang, gelng.**

glnge *n* ginger.

glngebreld *n* gingerbread.

glnger *n* lemonade, fizzy water of any flavour WEST.

glnk [g- as in 'get'] *n* **1** a trick, notion NE. **2** a habit.

glrd[1] [g- as in 'get'] *n* **1** a band or hoop for a barrel. **2** a child's hoop.

glrd[2] [g- as in 'get'] *n* a knock, blow.

v **1** rush (at), do vigorously. **2** push, force.

glrdle [g- as in 'get'] *n* an iron plate used for baking, traditionally circular with a hooped handle for hanging over a fire.

glrdle scone a scone baked on a **glrdle**, frying pan or hotplate.

llke a hon on a het glrdle restless(ly), anxious(ly), impatient(ly).

glrn[1] [g- as in 'get'] *v* **1** complain, whine, grumble.

2 screw up (the face) or gnash (the teeth) in rage or disapproval.

3 snarl, grimace.

4 grin, sneer.

5 (*of clothes*) gape.

6 (*of soil*) crack.

n **1** a whine, whimper; whining; grumbling.

2 a snarl.

3 a bad-tempered person.

glrnle *adj* bad-tempered: '*The bairn's girnie because she's teethin*'.

n a bad-tempered person.

glrn[2] [g- as in 'get'] *n, v* snare.

glrnel *n* a storage chest for meal.

glrse, gress *n* **1** grass. **2 glrse** a stalk or blade of grass NE.

v **1** pasture (animals). **2** grass.

glrsle grassy.

glrsle *n* **1** gristle. **2** a small piece of crisp or caked porridge etc.

glrth *n* a hoop.

gurthle very fat; heavy.

glt *see* **get.**

glltter *see* **gutter.**

glve *see* **gle.**

glzlntles *npl* division sums.

glzzen [g- as in 'get'] *adj* **1** (*of wooden containers*) cracked, leaky. **2** dry, patched, shrivelled. /

glzzent [g- as in 'get'] *adj* (over)full; soaked NE.

glabber *see* **clabber.**

glack *n* **1** a hollow between hills, a ravine. **2** an angle or fork, *eg* the fork of a tree NE.

glaff *see* **gliff.**

glag *n* a gurgling or choking noise. *v* make such a noise.

glaid *see* **glid.**

glaik *n* a silly, thoughtless person.

glaikie thoughtless, foolish N.

glaikit 1 foolish, stupid; thoughtless. **2** (*especially of a child*) too fond, clinging.

glaim *n* **1** gleam. **2** a flame.

glaister *n* a thin covering of snow or ice.

glaizie *adj* **1** glittering, shiny. **2** (*of sunshine*) bright but watery, indicating more rain.

glamour *n* magic, enchantment, witchcraft.

v **1** bewitch; dazzle. **2** deceive.

glamp *n*, *v* snatch.

glance on *v* occur to: '*It glanced on me aw at yince*'.

Glasgow *see* **Glesca.**

glass *see* **gless.**

Glaswegian *n, adj* (of) a native or inhabitant of Glasgow.

glaum *v* **1** snatch, grab (at). **2** seize or snatch at with the jaws. **3** grope. *n* a clutch or grab, usually unsuccessful.

glaur *n* **1** soft, sticky mud; ooze, slime. **2** contemptuous term for a person or thing.

v make muddy, dirty; make slimy or slippery.

glaurie muddy, dirty.

glaursel completely covered with mud SOUTH.

glebe *n* a piece of land given to a parish minister for his use, in addition to his **stipend.**

gled *n* **1** a kite, the bird. **2** applied to other birds of prey, mainly the buzzard. **3** a greedy person.

gled *see* **cleg.**

gledge *v* squint, look sidelong. *n* **1** a squint, a sidelong look. **2** a glimpse.

gleed *n* **1** a live coal or peat, an ember.

2 a spark, glimmer of fire or light. **3** a glowing fire.

gleem-glam *see* **glim-glam.**

gleet *v, n* (*mainly in poetry*) glitter, shine.

gleg *adj* **1** quick, sharp, keen: '*gleg o ee; gleg i the hearin*'. **2** quick of movement; nimble. **3** keen, smart, alert, quick-witted: '*gleg in the uptak*'. **4** lively; merry. **5** (*of cutting implements*) sharp-pointed, keen-edged. **6** (*of mechanisms*) smooth-working, quick-acting.

adv keenly, sharply.

glegness sharpness, keenness, cleverness.

gleg-eared with ears cocked.

gleg-eed sharp-eyed.

gleg-gabbit smooth-tongued, talkative, glib.

as gleg as a gled as keen or eager as a hawk; very hungry.

glen *n* a (narrow) valley, usually a river valley.

glent, glint *v* **1** gleam, glint, shine, sparkle. **2** glance, peep.

n **1** a gleam, glint, flash of light, a faint glitter. **2** a look, glance. **3** a glimpse. **4** a slight suspicion, a flash of intuition.

glintin dawn, daybreak.

Glesca, Glasgow *n* Glasgow.

Glesca keelie contemptuous term for a (rough and tough) Glaswegian.

Glesca kiss a headbutt (to the face).

Glesca screwdriver a hammer.

gless, glass *n* glass.

glessack a small glass marble CAITHNESS.

glessie 1 a home-made sweet, a kind of toffee. **2** *also* **glesser** a glass marble.

talk gless haunles speak (over-)politely with an affected accent.

gley [rhymes with 'gey'] *v* **1** squint, cast a sideways glance. **2** look with one eye, take aim NE.

n **1** a squint, a sideways or sly look, a glance; a squint in the eye. **2** being off the straight, irregularity; error NE. **3** aim, the act of aiming NE.

adj squint-eyed.

adv off the straight, *often* **gae gley.**

gley(e)d 1 squint-eyed, having a squint. **2** off the straight, slanting, crooked.

gleytness 1 having a squint, being squint-eyed. **2** being off the straight.

be aff the gley be wide of the mark, be wrong.

glib *adj* **1** smooth, slippery. **2** smart, cunning. **3** talkative, fluent (without being insincere).

adv smoothly, easily, readily.

glib-gabbit, glib-moued talkative, fluent; gossipy; smooth-tongued.

glid, glaid *adj* moving smoothly; slippery.

gliff, glaff *v* **1** frighten, startle. **2 gliff** glance (at), look at hurriedly.

n **1** a hurried or startled glance; a glimpse.

2 a moment, a short while.

3 a very slight resemblance.

4 a flash, glint.

5 a slight attack, touch (of an illness): '*a gliff o the cauld*'.

6 a whiff, puff, breath of air; a gust, blast of hot or cold air.

7 a sudden fright, a scare, a shock.

glim-glam, gleem-glam *n* the game of blind-man's buff NE.

glimmer *v* (*of the eyes*) be dazzled; blink, wink, look unsteadily.

glint *see* **glent.**

glisk *v* **1** glance (at). **2** gleam, glimmer SHETLAND.

n **1** a glance, peep, glimpse. **2** a gleam, sparkle, flash. **3** a moment, twinkling. **4** a momentary sensation or reaction; a short spell; a whiff, trace. **5** a resemblance, a slight similarity.

a glisk o cauld a slight cold.

glit, glut *n* **1** filth; slimy, greasy or sticky material. **2** mucus, discharge from a wound etc. **3** slimy vegetation

found in ponds etc. **4** slime on fish or decomposing meat.

glittie 1 slimy, greasy, oily. **2** smooth, slippery SW, SOUTH.

gloam *v* become dusk, darken.

n twilight, a faint light.

gloamin *n* dusk.

glob *n* a blob.

glock *v* (*of liquids*) gurgle.

glog *v* **1** swallow, gulp down. **2** gurgle.

n **1** a gulp NE. **2** a gurgling noise.

gloss *n* **1** (*of a fire*) a bright glow. **2** a doze.

v doze.

glossy (*of a fire*) glowing clear.

glowe *n, v* glow.

glower *v* **1** stare, gaze intently. **2** be drunk to the point of being glassy-eyed. **3** scowl.

n **1** a wide-eyed stare, an intent look. **2** a scowl, a fierce look.

glugger *v* gurgle N.

gluive *n* a glove.

glumph *v* be glum, sulk, look gloomy.

n a sulky or gloomy person.

glumsh *v* be or look sulky or gloomy, grumble, whine.

n a sulky, sullen, bad-tempered mood, look or reaction.

adj **1** sulky, cross-looking NE. **2** sad.

glunsh[1] *v* look cross, scowl; grumble, snap at.

n a cross look, scowl.

adj sulky, cross, bad-tempered.

glunsh[2] *v* gobble, gulp food.

glut *n, v* gulp.

glut *see* **glit.**

gnap *v* **1** bite, gnaw NE. **2** speak affectedly.

n a bite of food NE.

gnap(-at)-the-win thin oatcakes, light bread or other light food NE.

gneck *n* a notch NE.

gnib *adj* quick in action or speed.

gnipper and gnapper *adv* bit by bit, every bit NE.

gnyauve [(g)neeawve] *v* gnaw N.

go *see* **gae.**

goam *v* pay attention to, notice; recognize, greet.

goamless stupid.

goat *see* **get.**

gob[1], **gub** *n* the mouth; a bird's beak.

gobstopper a large, round, hard sweet.

gob[2] *n* a mass or lump, usually of something soft.

v spit.

gog *n* (*games*) the tee or mark in curling, marbles etc.

goggle *n* (*child's word*) **1** an egg. **2** a baby bird.

goggles *npl* blinkers for horses NE.

golach *n* **1** an insect *eg* an earwig, a kind of beetle. **2** contemptuous term for a person N.

forkie golach NE, **hornie golach, horned golach** an earwig.

goldie *see* **gowd.**

golf *see* **gowf**[1]**.**

goller *v* **1** roar, shout, bawl. **2** gurgle. *n* **1** a shout, roar. **2** an outburst (of oaths). **3** a loud laugh. **4** a gurgle.

gollie *v* **1** roar, shout, bawl. **2** scold. **3** weep noisily.

n a shout, roar.

gollop *v, n* gulp.

gomerel *n* a fool, stupid person.

goo[1] *n* **1** a strong, lasting, often nasty taste. **2** a nasty smell. **3** a liking, taste for.

gooie tasty, having a distinctive flavour.

goo[2] *n* a gull N.

goo[3] *v* (*of a baby*) coo.

good *see* **guid.**

goods an(d) gear *see* **gear.**

goold *see* **gowd.**

goolie *see* **goo**[1]**.**

goon *n* **1** a gown. **2** *usually* **goonie** a night-gown, nightshirt, especially a child's one.

goor, gurr SHETLAND, ORKNEY, CAITHNESS *n* **1** mucus, waxy matter, especially in the eye. **2** mud, dirt; muddy, stagnant water. **3** slush in running water SHETLAND, NE.

v (*of streams in thaw*) become choked with snow and ice NE.

goose *see* **guse.**

gooster *see* **gowster.**

gorb *n* **1** *also* **gorbie, gorblin** NE a baby bird. **2** *also* **gorbie** an infant. **3** a greedy person.

v eat greedily SW, ULSTER.

gorbie *v* gobble up, eat ravenously.

gorblin *see* **gorb.**

gorge *v* choke up (a channel) with mud, snow etc.

gorlin *n* **1** a baby bird. **2** a very young person, especially a boy SW.

gorroch *v* **1** mix, stir, (something soft and messy) SW. **2** make a mess of, spoil SW.

n a trampled muddy spot.

got *see* **get.**

gote, gwite NE *n* **1** a ditch, drain etc. **2** a narrow rocky inlet of the sea, a channel.

gotten *see* **get.**

goudle, gowdie *n* Gouda (cheese).

gove *v* **1** stare, gaze; stare stupidly. **2** wander aimlessly about. **3** (*of animals*) start (with fright), toss the head.

govie an awkward or silly person.

govie!, govie dick!, govie ding! *interjection* exclamation of surprise.

gowan [-ow- as in 'cow'] *n* **1** *also* **ewe gowan, May gowan** a daisy. **2** *also* **(large) white gowan** an ox-eye daisy or marguerite.

horse gowan name for various wild flowers, *eg* a daisy, a dandelion.

yella gowan name for various yellow wild flowers, *eg* a buttercup, marigold.

gowd [-ow- as in 'cow'], **goold** *n* gold.

gowden golden.

gowdie 1 *also* **goldie** a goldfinch. **2** one of various fishes, *eg* a gurnard. **3**

gowdie (duck) a golden-eyed duck SHETLAND.

gowdspink a goldfinch.

gowdie *see* **goudle.**

gowf[1] [-ow- as in 'cow'], **golf** *n* golf.

gowf links a golf course by the sea-shore.

gowf stick a golf club.

gowf[2] *v* hit, strike, slap.

gowk [-ow- as in 'cow'] *n* **1** *also* **gowk-oo** the cuckoo. **2** a fool. **3** a joke, trick, especially an April Fool's Day joke.

v **1** fool, deceive, often in connection with April fooling. **2** wander about aimlessly.

gowkie stupid.

gowkit foolish.

April Gowk an April fool.

gowk('s) day April Fools' Day.

gowk('s) errand a fool's errand.

gowk's meat wood sorrel.

gowk('s)-spit(tle(s)) cuckoo spit.

gowk('s) storm a brief storm; a spring storm coinciding with the arrival of the cuckoo.

gowk's thimmles a harebell, a bluebell.

(the) gowk and (the) titlin two unlikely companions, *eg* a tall and a short person seen together.

gowl [-ow- as in 'cow'] *v* **1** howl, yell, roar, weep noisily. **2** scold angrily. **3** scowl.

n a yell, howl, bellow, growl.

gowp[1] [-ow- as in 'cow'] *v* **1** (*of the heart or pulse*) beat strongly or wildly. **2** (*of sores or pains*) throb, ache violently.

n a throb of pain.

gowp[2] [-ow- as in 'cow'] *v, n* gulp.

gowp[3] [-ow- as in 'cow'] *v* scoop up (*eg* water), wash with the hands, hollow out.

gowp *see* **gaup.**

gowpen [-ow- as in 'cow'] *n, also* **gowpenfu 1** as much as can be held in the two hands held together. **2** cupped hands.

gowd in gowpens untold wealth, lots of money.

gowst *v* boast.

n a gust.

gowster [-ow- as in 'cow'], **gooster** ORKNEY *v* boast.

n **1** a wild, violent, boasting or swaggering person. **2** a violent outburst.

gowst(e)rous 1 hearty, vigorous. **2** (*of weather*) dark and stormy.

gowsterie wet and windy.

gowstie [-ow- as in 'cow'] *adj* **1** (*of places, buildings*) vast, dreary, cheerless. **2** (*of people*) unhealthy(-looking).

grab *n* **1** a thing grabbed, plunder. **2** a good bargain, an advantage, often one got dishonestly. **3** a mean or greedy person.

grabble greedy.

grabble *n, v* grab, grope.

gracie *adj* religious, virtuous, well-behaved.

grain[1] *n* **1** a branch, offshoot *eg* of a tree; of a stream, river; of a valley. **2** a prong (of a fork, salmon spear etc).

grain[2] *v* **1** groan. **2** complain, grumble; be unwell.

graip[1] *n* a large fork used in farming and gardening.

v fork up.

graip[2] *v* grope.

graith *v* prepare, make ready (*eg* a horse for riding or work).

n **1** materials or equipment; tools, machinery; equipment belonging to a mechanism, *eg* a mill, plough, loom. **2** the rigging or tackle of a ship. **3** furnishings, belongings. **4** the trappings, harness etc for a horse. **5** possessions, wealth, money. **6** (*fishing*) the attachment by which the hook is hung from the line NE. **7** a soapy lather; dirty, used soapsuds.

gralloch *n* **1** a deer's guts. **2** the removal of the guts from a deer.

v remove the guts from a deer.

grand billies *see* **billie.**

granich [-ch as in 'dreich'] *v* sicken, disgust NE.

grannie *n* **1** a chimney-cowl. **2** the last sheaf cut at harvest-time ULSTER. **3** a hairy caterpillar, the larva of the tiger moth sw. **4** used in contemptuous exclamations: '*We could've improvised a sledge.*' '*Improvised yer grannie!*'.

v (*in a game*) defeat heavily, often without the loser scoring.

grannie('s) bairn a grandchild, especially one brought up by its grandmother and spoilt.

grannie('s) mutch(es) 1 columbine. **2** snapdragon.

grannie mutch(ie) nickname for an old woman or for an old-fashioned little girl.

grannie's sooker a peppermint sweet, a **pan drop.**

grannie's tartan *see* **tartan.**

grannie at address as 'granny': '*Dinna you grannie at me!*'.

grapple *v* **1** drag (water) for a corpse. **2** grope.

grappling a method of catching salmon by means of a special arrangement of hooks.

grapus *n* the Devil, a hobgoblin NE.

grat *see* **greet.**

gravat [gra*vat*, grau*vat*] *n* a (woollen) scarf.

graveyaird *n*: **graveyaird deserter** a sickly-looking person NE.

graveyaird hoast a very bad cough, a churchyard cough.

gray *adj* grey.

v **1** dawn SHETLAND, ORKNEY, NE. **2** cover with a thin sprinkling of snow sw.

grayback 1 a hooded crow. **2** a flounder NE, FIFE. **3** a salmon or salmon trout in the autumn run sw, SOUTH. **4** an immature herring gull or lesser black-backed gull.

gray face a cross-bred sheep, black-faced crossed with Leicester.

gray hen a female black grouse.

gray paper brown paper SHETLAND.

great, gryte NE *adj* **1** great. **2** big, stout SHETLAND, NE. **3** (*of a river*) in flood,

high. **4** friendly, close: '*He's great wi the new boss*'.

great-hertit filled with emotion, ready to cry, sorrowful.

gree[1] *v* **1** make peace between (people); settle (something). **2** come to terms, make an agreement. **3** be or live in harmony, be friends; be of one mind. **4** correspond, fit.

greeable peaceable, kindly, agreeable.

greement agreement, harmony.

gree[2] *n* first place, victory; the prize, *often* **bear the gree** win the prize *now literary.*

green[1] *adj* **1** covered with grass, grassy. **2** young, youthful, full of life. **3** (*of milk*) new, fresh, especially milk from a newly calved cow. **4** (*of a cow*) recently calved. **5** (*of manure*) fresh, unrotted.

n **1** grassy ground; the grassy ground forming part of the grounds of a building *eg* **kirk green, back green, drying green. 2 greens** green vegetables, especially **kail.**

greenich(t)ie greenish.

greenie pole a clothes-prop.

green grape (*contemptuous*) a Catholic *rhyming slang* (*for '*pape*'*).

green lady 1 a ghost (believed to be a sign of death). **2** a Health Visitor (in certain towns).

green lintie, greenie the greenfinch.

green[2] *v* **1** long (for). **2** (*of a pregnant woman*) have a craving (for particular foods): '*When she wis expectin she wis aye greenin fur ice-cream*'.

greep *see* **grulp.**

greeshach *adj* shivery; chilly N.

greeshoch *n* a glowing fire of red-hot embers, the embers themselves, especially of a peat fire.

greet *v, past tense* **grat, gret;** *past participle* **grat, gret, grutten** weep, cry; complain; grumble.

n a sob; a fit of weeping.

greetie *adj* **1** weepy. **2** inclined to rain, showery.

n a child's whimper.

greetin ee a watering eye.

greetin face a person who usually looks miserable or tearful.

greetin fou at the tearful stage of drunkenness.

greetin meetin a farewell meeting, especially the last meeting of a council before an election.

greetin Teenie a cry-baby; a person who is always complaining.

get yer greet oot relieve your feelings by weeping.

gress *see* **girse**.

gret *see* **greet**.

grew *n* **1** *also* **grew hound** a greyhound. **2 the grews** greyhound racing.

grice *n* a pig, especially a young pig.

grieve *n* the overseer or head-workman on a farm; a farm-bailiff.

grilse *n* a young salmon on its first return to fresh water.

grime, grim *v* sprinkle, fleck, cover thinly especially with snow SW, SOUTH.

adj, only **grim** grey, roan, mottled black and white; grimy.

grip, grup *v, past tense* **gruppit**; *past participle* **gruppen, gruppit 1** grip. **2** catch, seize. **3** get the better of, outsmart NE.

n **1** grip. **2** a handclasp; sometimes one used between members of a secret society, *eg* the Freemasons. **3 grips** someone's embrace or clutches. **4** *usually* **grips** sharp pains, especially colic, gripes. **5 the grip** (*building industry*) a system of sub-contracting work to casual labour, the 'lump'.

gripple mean, miserly, greedy; likely to cheat.

grip in pinch, make narrow or tighter SHETLAND, NE.

grip tae, grip till grab, hold on to; stick close to SHETLAND, NE.

hae a guid grip o (the) gear 1 be well off. **2** be mean.

hae a guid grip o Scotland have large (flat) feet.

haud the grip keep a firm hold; hold to your faith or purpose; last.

slip the grip die NE.

grip *see* **gruip**.

groatie, groatie-buckle *n* a kind of cowrie shell SHETLAND, NE.

groff *adj* coarse SHETLAND, N.

groosie *see* **gruse**.

groozle *v* breathe heavily, grunt.

groser, groset, gros(s)art *n* a gooseberry.

ground *see* **grund**.

grounge *see* **grunch**.

growe [rhymes with 'cow'] *v* grow.

growthe weeds, overgrown plants.

growthie 1 (*of weather*) warm and moist, encouraging growth. **2** (*of plants*) growing fast and thick; weedy. **3** (*of persons or animals*) well-grown, thriving.

grown-up overgrown, choked with weeds etc.

growze *see* **gruse**.

grub *v* grasp at (money).

grubber a large heavy hammer.

grudge *v* complain, be unhappy, discontented or unwilling.

grue[1] *v* **1** feel horror or terror, shudder, shrink in horror or fear. **2** (*of the flesh, heart, blood etc*) creep, quake, run cold with horror or fear. **3** shiver from cold. **4** make a face.

n a shudder, shiver, feeling of horror or disgust.

it gars me grue it makes my blood run cold.

tak the grue (at) become disgusted or fed up (with).

grue[2] *n* melting snow and ice found on rivers in early spring.

gruel *n* **1** porridge, especially thin porridge SHETLAND, ORKNEY. **2** food made of oatmeal; any food.

gruggle *v, n* rumple, crease NE.

gruip, grip, greep *n* **1** the gutter in a **byre. 2** a field drainage ditch ORKNEY, NE.

v (*carpentry*) cut a groove in (a board) for fitting into a corresponding 'tongue'.

grummel, gummie *n* rubbish, rubble; mud, sediment.

v make muddy.

grumlie, gumlie muddy, full of dregs or gravel; confused, gloomy.

grummie *v* grumble.

n **1** grumble. **2** a grudge, complaint, quarrel.

grummlie 1 bad-tempered, grumbling. **2** (*of weather*) unsettled, blustery NE.

grumph *n* **1** a grunt. **2** name for a pig. **3** a grumbler, complainer.

v grunt; grumble.

grumphie *n* (name for) a pig.

v grunt like a pig.

adj grumpy, bad-tempered.

grun *see* **grund.**

grunch, grounge SOUTH *v* **1** grumble; object, refuse SOUTH. **2** growl, grunt ORKNEY.

n a grumble, grunt, growl SOUTH.

grund, grun, ground *n* **1** ground.

2 the bottom or lowest part of anything.

3 the bottom of the sea.

4 the bottom, root (of a matter), text (of a sermon).

5 the pit of the stomach.

6 farm-land, a farm, an estate.

7 ground reserved for the burial of a person or family.

8 (*piping*) the main theme in **pibroch.**

grund ebb 1 the ebb-tide at its lowest, low water SHETLAND, NE. **2** the lowest part of the foreshore CAITHNESS, NE.

grunkle *see* **crunkle.**

gruntie *n* (*humorous*) a pig.

gruntle *n* **1** the snout, usually of a pig. **2** (*contemptuous, of a person*) the nose and mouth, the face or head. **3** a grunt.

v grunt, groan.

grunyie *n* the snout of an animal or (*contemptuous*) of a person.

grup, gruppen *see* **grip.**

gruse, growze *v, n* shiver, shudder.

groosie shivery.

grush *n* grit, fine gravel.

grushie *adj* **1** (*of a child*) thriving. **2** (*of plants*) thick, abundant.

grutten *see* **greet.**

gry *n* (*gypsy*) a horse.

gryte *see* **great.**

gub *see* **gob.**

guddle *v* **1** catch (fish) with the hands by groping under the stones or banks of a stream. **2** do dirty, messy work. **3** do things in a careless, messy way, mess about, make a mess.

n **1** a mess, muddle, confusion. **2** a person who does things in a messy way. **3** hard, dirty or messy work. **4** a crowbar. **5** a pointed iron bar for making holes for fenceposts.

gudge *n* **1** a gouge. **2** anything short and thick, especially a short, strong, thickset person NE.

v **1** gouge. **2** raise or separate by driving in wedges NE.

gudgle short and thickset, squat.

guess *n* a riddle, puzzle.

guest *n* an object thought to foretell the arrival of a stranger SHETLAND, ORKNEY.

guff[1] *n* a fool.

guffie stupid.

guff[2] *n* **1** a (usually unpleasant) smell or whiff. **2** a taste, after-taste. **3** a puff, whiff, current of air etc.

v give off a smell, steam, smoke etc.

guffie fat, flabby or chubby about the cheeks.

guff[3] *n* **1** a grunting, snuffling sound (of a pig); a low bark SHETLAND. **2** a suppressed laugh, a snort CAITHNESS.

v **1** snort, snuffle SHETLAND, ORKNEY. **2** cackle with laughter; babble, talk foolishly. **3** belch.

guffie name for a pig.

guga [googa] *n* a young gannet HEBRIDES.

guld, gweed NE, **good** *adj* **1** good. **2**

(*of people*) respectable, of high social standing. **3** (*of clothes*) best; (*of rooms*) the best, used on formal occasions. **4** -in-law, *eg* **guid brither** brother-in-law.

n **1** good. **2** God: '*He feared the Guid*'.

guidlie 1 goodly. **2** godly, pious NE.

a guid bit a long time.

(the) Guid Book the Bible.

guideen (*greeting*) good evening.

the guid fowk(s) the fairies, brownies etc.

guid gaun going well, active, flourishing.

a guid (fyow) mair a good many more NE.

guid man 1 the guid man (*mainly child's word*) God. **2** term of address used between equals who do not know each other well. **3** the head of the household. **4** a husband. **5** the Devil.

the guid place Heaven.

guidsire, gutcher a grandfather.

guid wife 1 (*as a polite term of address*) the mistress of a house, a wife. **2** the mistress (of a particular place, especially a farm). **3** the landlady of an inn. **4** a wife.

guidwillie willing, ready; generous, hearty.

guid words children's prayers etc.

as guid (as) (*of price, value, measure*) as much (as), practically: '*as guid as five*'.

(be)come guid for guarantee.

dae guid get good results, thrive, prosper.

get the guid o get what advantage or benefit is to be had from (a thing): '*Ye'll get the guid o that soup if ye eat it hot*'.

guid an weel well and good, so be it.

ken the guid o realize or enjoy the benefits of.

guide *v* **1** run (an organization etc); direct, manage, control (something). **2** manage, use (money etc, well, sparingly etc). **3** treat, use, handle, care for (people (especially children) or animals). **4** behave (yourself): '*Young fowk winna guide theirsels*'.

n a manager, controller, usually of money or property SHETLAND, NE.

guider 1 a manager, administrator. **2** a home-made children's cart steered by a rope E CENTRAL.

gull, guid *n* a corn marigold.

guilt *n*: **tak guilt tae yersel** feel or show guilt, be conscience-stricken.

guise, gy ORKNEY *n* a masquerade; a piece of fun.

v **1** disguise. **2** **guisin** going about as a **guiser**.

guiser *n* **1** masquerader, now especially one of a party of children who go in disguise from door to door offering entertainment in return for gifts or money, especially at **Halloween.** **2** an odd-looking person NE.

v go about as a **guiser.**

hae a guise (wi) have (a bit of) fun (with) SHETLAND, NE.

Guiser Jarl the chief **guiser** at **Up-Helly-Aa** SHETLAND.

guiss *v* guess.

guld *see* **gull.**

gull *n* a thin cold mist and a chilly breeze NE.

gullet *n* **1** a narrow, deep channel or rocky inlet. **2** a gully, ravine.

gullie *n, also* **gullie knife** a large knife. **gulliegaw** wound, cut, gash N.

gulsa, gulshichs *see* **gulsoch.**

gulsoch, gulsa SHETLAND *n* **1** jaundice. **2** over-eating; feeling of sickness caused by this NE. **3** **gulshichs** sweet cakes, sweets NE.

gum¹ *n* **1** mist, haze, condensation on glass N. **2** *also* **yella gum** jaundice, especially in the newborn. **3** a disagreement, ill-will.

v become misted over NE.

gum² *n* coal dust CENTRAL.

gumlie, gummie *see* **grummel.**

gump, gumph *v* search, grope for; especially **guddle** (fish).

gumph, gump *n* **1** *also* **gumphie** a fool. **2 gumphs** the sulks, *often* **tak the gumphs.**

gumph *see* **gump.**

gumsh *v* munch NE.

gun *n* a tobacco pipe.

be great guns (wi) be close friends.

gunch [gunsh] *n* a thick piece, a hunk.

gundie[1], **gunnle** *n* a father-lasher NE.

gundie[2] *n* toffee.

gunk *n* a bitter disappointment, *often* **do a gunk (on someone), gie (someone) the gunk** cause (someone) pain, unhappiness, disappoint; jilt.

gunnie *see* **gundie**[1].

gurl *v* **1** (*of the wind*) roar, howl. **2** growl. **3** (*of water*) gurgle.

adj **1** (*of weather, wind etc*) cold, stormy, wild. **2** (*of people*) bad-tempered, surly.

n **1** a gale, squall. **2** a growl, a snarl. **3** a gurgle.

gurlie 1 (*of weather etc*) stormy, threatening, bitter. **2** (*of people*) bad-tempered, surly. **3** (*of dogs*) growling, snarling NE. **4** gurgling.

gurr *v* growl, snarl.

gurrie 1 a dogfight, brawl. **2** a hurry, a bustle, a state of confusion.

gurr *see* **goor.**

gurthie *see* **girth.**

guse, geese, goose *n* **1** a goose. **2 goose** (*piping*) a bagpipe with a **chanter** but no drones.

guse-grass 1 goose-grass, cleavers. **2** brome grass.

gus-gus *see* **gussie.**

gushet *n* **1** a gusset. **2** a breast-pocket of a jacket or coat. **3** *also* **gushet-neuk** a triangular piece of land, especially between neighbouring properties; an odd corner of land; a nook. **4** the corner of a building, a corner in a building.

gussie, gees(i)e *n* **1** a pig, especially a young pig or sow. **2** *also* **gus-gus** a call to pigs. **3** a fat person. **4** a segment of an orange ANGUS.

gust *n* taste.

v **1** taste (food, drink etc). **2** *often* **gust the gab** whet the appetite, fill the mouth with tasty food or drink. **3** smell (strongly, bad).

gustie tasty, savoury.

gut *n*: **guts** *v* eat greedily or gluttonously.

gutser 1 a very greedy person NE. **2** a belly-flop.

gutsie greedy.

gutsin overeating.

gutter a woman employed in gutting fish.

guttle *adj* **1** thick; very fat; pot-bellied. **2** fond of good eating, greedy.

n **1** a pot-bellied person SW, SOUTH. **2** a minnow.

gutcher *see* **guidsire** (*under* **guid**).

gutter, gitter *n* **1 gutters, gitters** mud, muddy puddles. **2** the doing of something in an unskilful or dirty way. **3** a muddle, mess. **4** a stupid, awkward or messy worker.

v **1** do something in a dirty, messy or unskilful way. **2** potter about, waste time. **3** talk nonsense, gabble.

gutterie, gitterie muddy, messy.

guttie *n* anything made of rubber: **1** *also* **guttie ba** a golfball; **2 guttie** a catapult; **3 gutties** gymshoes, plimsolls.

guttie-perkie rubber.

guy *v* guide, steer NE.

n **guys** the handlebars of a bicycle.

guzzle *n* a bout of excessive eating and drinking.

v take by the throat, throttle.

gweed *see* **guid.**

gwite *see* **gote.**

gy *see* **guise.**

gyan *see* **gae.**

gyang *see* **gang.**

gyaun *see* **gae.**

gyo *see* **geo.**

gype [g- as in 'get'] *v* **1** stare foolishly or open-mouthed. **2** play the fool; make a fool of.
n a foolish, awkward person, a silly person.

gyper NE *v* talk nonsense.
n nonsense; fun.

gypit silly, foolish.

gyte [g- as in 'get'] *adj* **1** mad, insane; mad with rage, pain etc: '*gang gyte*'. **2** mad with longing, love-sick. **3** (*of things*) nonsensical, crazy; **gang gyte** go to pot, go awry.

gyter NE *n* **1** nonsense, foolish talk. **2** a stupid, talkative person.
v talk a great deal in a silly way.

gyte *see* **get.**

H

ha *n* **1** a hall. **2** *also* **ha hoose** a farmhouse as opposed to the farm cottages; a mansion-house.

ha *see* **hae.**

haaf *n* deep sea (fishing) SHETLAND.

haar *n* **1** a cold mist or fog, especially an east-coast sea fog. **2** a cold easterly wind.

haarie 1 misty, foggy. **2** (*of wind*) cold, piercing.

haar-frost *n* hoar-frost.

habber *v* **1** stammer, stutter SHETLAND, N. **2** snarl; make a gobbling noise N.

habble *v* **1** hobble. **2** confuse. **3** tangle (thread etc).
n **1** a difficulty, problem. **2** a scuffle, fight.

habit and repute *adj* (*mainly law*) held to be or regarded as (married to etc): '*She's his wife by habit and repute*'.

hack, hawk *n* **1** a crack or chap in the skin. **2** a joiner's adze; a miner's pick-ended hammer. **3** a pronged tool for breaking up or raking the soil etc. **4** (*curling*) a metal footplate to steady the player's foot. **5** a notch on a graded scale; a certain amount (of time, distance) NE: '*Wullie's late! Aye, he's aye a hack ahint!*'.
v **1** chop up (meat, firewood etc). **2** (*of the skin*) crack, chap, roughen.

hackin stock a chopping block.

hackit ugly, unattractive.

tak doon a hack take (someone) down a peg.

hackle *see* **heckle.**

hacky duck, hucky-duck *n* a children's game in which two teams take it in turn to leap on the lined-up backs of their opponents E CENTRAL.

had *see* **haud.**

haddie, haddo, hoddock NE *n* a haddock.

hae, have, ha, hiv *v, past tense* **hid, haid;** *past participle* **hid, haid, haen 1** have. **2** put, bring, take, send: '*Mrs B has her compliments to you*'.

his, hes has.

hisnae, hisna, hasnae, hasna has not.

hinnae, hinna, hivnae, hivna have not: '*Ye hinna goat a clue!*'.

be well had be well off.

haet: deil a haet, (the) flent a haet devil a bit!, not a bit!

no a haet not the smallest amount.

haiveless 1 shiftless, incapable, careless, extravagant N. **2** senseless, meaningless.

haffet *n* **1** the cheek, the temple. **2** a side-lock of hair. **3** the wooden side of a **box-bed,** chair etc.

hag *v* hack, cut, chop wood.
n **1** a notch, hack. **2** brushwood; felled wood used for fuel. **3** a hollow of marshy ground, *eg* where channels have been made or peats cut. **4** a hillock of firmer ground in a bog. **5** a ledge of turf overhanging a stream SW, SOUTH.

hagger *v* cut clumsily, hack NE.
n a deeply jagged cut NE.

haggis *n* a traditional Scottish dish of sheep's guts, oatmeal etc.

haggle, haigle SOUTH *v* **1** cut unevenly, hack. **2** stumble forward, struggle on SOUTH. **3** carry (something heavy) with difficulty SOUTH.

haid *see* **hae.**

haigle *see* **haggle.**

halk *v* **1** trudge; wander aimlessly. **2** carry or drag with difficulty. **3** treat roughly, drive hard.

n a person or animal given to roaming about, usually on the scrounge.

be on the halk for be on the lookout for.

halk *see* **heck.**

hail[1]**, whole** *adj* **1** sound, in a healthy state; wholesome; robust, vigorous. **2** uninjured, undamaged in body or mind. **3** (*of things*) whole, complete, undamaged.

adv wholly, completely, fully.

n the whole, the full number or amount.

haillie wholly, completely.

hail-heartit undaunted, stalwart.

hail-heidit unhurt; (*of things*) complete, entire N.

gang hail-heidit for give your entire energy to.

hailscart unscathed, scotfree.

hail-skinnt having an undamaged skin.

hail-tear at full speed.

hail watter a downpour.

get hail o recover from.

hail at the hert in good spirits.

hail[2] *n* **1** the winning of a goal; a goal. **2** the shout when a goal is scored. **3** the goal area.

hail the dool(s) score a goal; be the winner; celebrate.

hail[3] *v* **1** haul, drag, pull (up) SHET-LAND, NE. **2** flow, run down, pour.

haillie *see* **hail**[1].

haimmer *n* a hammer.

haims, hems *npl* part of the collar of a draught horse.

pit the haims on curb, keep in order: '*Pit the haims on thae bairns!*'.

hain *v* **1** *also* **hain in** save (up), be thrifty, hoard. **2** keep from harm, protect. **3** enclose by a hedge or fence; keep unused.

hainin an enclosed piece of ground.

hainch *n* **1** a haunch. **2** an underhand throw. **3** a halt or limp. **4** a 'leg-up'; a help up with a heavy object.

v **1** throw a stone etc by jerking the

arm against the thigh. **2** walk jerkily or with a limp.

haingle *v* move about feebly; loiter, hang about.

adj slovenly, careless; lazy, not inclined to work.

haip *see* **heap.**

hair[1] *n*: **hairy** *adj* (*especially of work*) untidy, slovenly.

n a woman slum-dweller; a woman of loose morals, a prostitute; (*contemptuous*) a young woman: '*a wee hairy*'.

hairy grannie a large hairy caterpillar.

hairy-mooldit covered with mould, mouldy.

hairy oobit *see* **oobit.**

hairy tatties a dish made of mashed potatoes and flaked dried fish NE.

hair[2] *n* hoar.

hair moul(d) the mould on cheese, bread, jam etc exposed to damp.

hairstane a large, grey, moss-covered stone, especially one conspicuously fixed as a boundary mark NE.

hairbour *see* **herbour.**

hairm, herm *v*, *n* harm.

hairp, herp, harp *n* **1** a harp. **2** a sieve, riddle. **3** a shovel with spars used *eg* for digging up potatoes etc.

hairst, hervest *n* **1** harvest. **2** a harvest job. **3** the autumn.

hae a day in hairst wi someone have a score to settle with someone; owe someone a favour.

hairt *see* **hert.**

haister *v* **1** cook too hastily, scorch. **2** annoy, pester SW.

hait, het, heat *v*, *n* heat.

get a heat make (yourself) warm.

heat the hoose hold a housewarming.

halt *see* **het**[1].

halthen *adj* heathen.

n **1** a heathen. **2** an awkward person or thing.

halveless *see* **hae.**

halver *v* **1** talk in a foolish or silly way,

speak nonsense. **2** make a fuss about nothing, pretend to be busy. **3** dawdle, potter about; lounge.

n **1** **halvers** nonsense, gossip, chatter. **2** a piece of nonsense, a foolish notion. **3** a gossip, a chat. **4** a person who talks nonsense. **5** a state of fussy indecision; a person in this state, an idler.

haiverel *n* **1** a foolishly chattering person, a fool. **2** a lazy person.

adj **1** too talkative, speaking foolishly. **2** foolish, stupid.

haiverin *adj* nonsensical, gossiping, babbling.

n a chatter, gossip, nonsense: '*Stop yer haiverin*'.

halzer *v* dry (partially), air in the open, bleach (newly-washed clothes etc).

half, hauf *n* **1** a half. **2** a part; one of two unequal parts; one of three or more divisions or portions. **3** a half measure of a specified amount, especially of whisky˙ = a half-gill; **a wee hauf** a quarter gill, a small whisky. **4** (*of time: with the preceding hour*), *eg* **half-five** = half past five; (*now rarely with the following hour*), *eg* **half five** = half past four.

adj, adv half.

v **1** divide into two equal parts, halve; go halves with. **2** divide into more than two equal shares.

halver, haufer *n, usually* **halvers 1** a half-portion, a share. **2** *also* **halfies** exclamation used especially by children when claiming a half share in a find.

v halve, divide equally.

gae halvers share equally.

halfie a half-holiday (from school).

halfies *see* **halver** 2 above.

halflin 1 a half-grown boy, especially a farmworker. **2** a half-mature herring.

halflins 1 half, partly, almost. **2** halfway, mid-way.

half-chackit half-witted.

half-cousin the child of your parent's cousin, a second cousin.

half gaits halfway.

half gone about the middle period of pregnancy.

half-hoose a semi-detached house NE.

half-loaf a loaf of bread (of the standard modern size).

half-road(s) halfway.

halfways halfway; partly.

a . . . and a half something which is large or extraordinary of its kind: '*a letter and a half*'.

a hauf and a hauf a small whisky with a half pint of beer as a chaser.

half an atween neither one nor the other, not quite.

halie *adj* holy.

hallaby [hallabie] *n* nonsense word, used only in a children's counting rhyme.

hallan *n* **1** (*in past times*) an inner wall, partition, or door-screen between the door and the fireplace. **2** a similar partition in a **byre** or stable, or between the living-room and the **byre.**

hallanshaker a beggar, a vagabond, tramp.

hallion *n* a slovenly-looking or clumsy person, a rascal, a clown.

hallirackit *see* **hallock.**

hallock *n* a thoughtless giddy young woman or girl or occasionally young man.

adj crazy, hare-brained; uncouth, noisy NE.

v behave in a crazy, wild or irresponsible way.

hallockit, hallirackit (*especially of a girl or young woman*) crazy, hare-brained, uncouth, noisy.

hallow[1] *adj, n, v* hollow.

hallow[2] *adj* All Saints.

Hallowday All Saints' Day.

Halloween 31 October, the eve of All Saints' Day, the last day of the year in the old Celtic calendar, associated with witches and the powers of darkness, and celebrated with bonfires, telling the future etc; now a children's festival when they go around as **guisers** often with turnip lanterns; *see also* **dook for aipples** (*under* **dook**[1]).

halver *see* **half.**

ham *n* bacon.

ham-a-haddie *n* **1** a confused or unlikely story or situation. **2** a mix-up, a fuss.

hame *n* home.

adv **1** home. **2** at home. **3 bring hame** bring into the world; give birth to; **come hame** come into the world, be born.

hamelie 1 homely. **2** friendly, kind, courteous.

hameward, hameart belonging to or made at home, homely.

hamewith homewards.

hamecomin 1 a coming or return home. **2** the festivities that take place on the arrival of a bride at her new home. **3** a birth.

hame-drauchit NE **1** selfish, keen to help yourself or your home. **2** homesick: fond of, or drawn to home.

hamefare the journey of the bride to her new home; the festivities on that occasion.

hame-gaun 1 a return (journey), the act of going home. **2** death; burial.

hame-made *n* a home-made article. *adj* homely, countrified, unrefined.

hameower *adv* homewards.

adj **1** (*of speech*) homely, simple, in Scots. **2** plain, simple.

hamlt *adj* **1** home-produced, homegrown. **2** home-loving, homely, familiar, rough-and-ready, untidy.

Hampden (roar) *n* the score (in a game) *rhyming slang*.

han *see* **hand.**

hanch *v* **1** snap (at), show the teeth, snatch. **2** eat greedily and noisily, munch.

hand, han, haun(d) *n* **1** a hand. **2**

direction, neighbourhood: '*near han*'. **3** a handle.

handle 1 (*child's word*) a hand. **2** a small wooden tub, especially a milk-pail.

han(d)less awkward, clumsy, incompetent, slow.

handy 1 ready with the hands. **2** (*of an animal*) quiet to handle. **3 nae handy** not easy to do or put up with; awful(ly), excessive(ly): '*at a rate nae handy*'.

han(d)ba 1 hand-ball. **2** a team game played in the Borders.

han(d)ban(d) the wristband or cuff of a shirt.

hand-breed a hand's breadth.

hand-cloot a towel.

handlawhile a short space of time.

handlin a handline.

hand-waled handpicked, carefully selected, choice.

handwrite handwriting, penmanship.

aboot hand(s) at hand, near.

aff someone's han on someone's authority, on someone's initiative.

amang yer hands 1 at spare moments, at intervals. **2** in your possession.

(a)tween hands in the interval.

behind the hand after the event.

for yer ain hands for your own part, for your own interest.

hae through hand(s) deal with, discuss or investigate thoroughly; crossexamine.

hand for nieve hand in hand, side by side; hand in glove.

hand(s) ower heids indiscriminately.

hand-roon-tea a tea at which people are served individually and not seated at a table.

in hand (*of a sum of money*) in cash.

in hands wi occupied with, busy with.

keep in hand keep in suspense; delay.

pit hand tae yersel commit suicide.

pit oot yer hand help yourself at table.

plt tae yer hand lend a hand, buckle to.

there's my hand I assure you.

handle *see* **hannle.**

handsel, hansel *n* **1** a gift intended to bring good luck to something new or a new beginning, *eg* the New Year, a new house, a new baby. **2** the money received by a trader for his first sale, thought to bring good luck.

v **1** to give or offer a **handsel** at the beginning of a year or day, or to mark some special occasion. **2** start (something) off with some ceremony or gift to bring luck. **3** celebrate the first use of (something) with a **handsel**; use for the first time; be the first to try, test or taste (something).

Handsel Monday the first Monday of the New Year, formerly a holiday.

hang *see* **hing.**

hangrell *n* a stick, arm etc on which something is hung, *eg* the gallows, a tree branch for holding bridles etc in a stable.

hanker *v* hang about expectantly; hesitate.

hannle, haunle, handle *n* a handle.

handlin 1 a piece of business. **2** a (difficult) task. **3** a share in some affair, a hand in something. **4** a rounding up and penning of sheep for dipping, shearing etc. **5** an entertainment, meeting, party, social gathering.

hansel *see* **handsel.**

hantle *adj* convenient, handy.

hantle *n* a considerable quantity (of things), a large number (of people), a great deal.

hap[1] *v* **1** cover, surround, so as to shelter or to hide.

2 cover over *eg* with earth, straw etc as a protection against cold or wet; pile (earth) on; thatch; bury.

3 wrap a garment round (a person), wrap (a person) up in clothes: '*weel happit*'; tuck up (in bed).

4 clothe, dress.

5 make up a (fire) so as to keep it burning for a considerable time.

n **1** a covering, especially a protection against the weather. **2** a wrap, shawl, or **plaid**; a warm outer garment; a bed-quilt or blanket.

hapwarm a warm wrap or thick outer garment.

hap[2], **hop** *v* **1** hop, jump. **2** walk with a limp.

hoppin beds, hap-the-beds hopscotch.

hap, step and lowp hop, step and jump.

happen *v* happen to.

happenin casual, occasional, chance.

happer *n* **1** a hopper (in a mill). **2** a basket or container, especially one for seed.

happy *adj* lucky, fortunate.

hapshackle *v* hobble (a horse etc), tie up (an animal) to prevent it from straying.

n a hobble for tethering a horse etc, a fetter, shackle.

hard, herd *adj* **1** hard. **2** (*of alcoholic drink*) strong, undiluted, raw. **3** close-fisted, stingy.

n **1** difficulty, hardship; **if hard comes tae hard** if the worst comes to the worst. **2** **gae throu the hard** experience hardship or misfortune. **3** spirits, especially whisky.

adv **1** hard. **2** tightly, firmly, securely.

harden (up) (*of the weather*) clear up, become settled after rain.

hardie 1 a kind of white bread roll with a hard surface ANGUS. **2** a hard sort of butter biscuit NE; a variety made in Cupar and popular as ship's biscuits FIFE.

hardlies, hardlins hardly, scarcely.

hard breid 1 a kind of thin oatcake. **2** stale bread, especially for making into breadcrumbs.

hard fish dried or salt fish.

hard neck brass neck.

hard-set wilful, obstinate.

the hard stuff whisky.

hard up 1 (*of people*) in poor health, unwell. **2** (*of things*) in bad condition, in a bad state of repair.

hard *see* **hear.**

hardy *adj* **1** bold. **2** in good health. **3** frosty.

hare *n*: **harebell** a single-bell-shaped blue flower, the bluebell of Scotland.

hare('s) lug a kind of angling fly.

harlgals *npl* the guts, especially of an animal or fowl.

hark *v* **1** listen (to), hearken: '*Hark till him!*'. **2** whisper, mutter SHETLAND, ORKNEY, N.

n a whisper.

harl[1] *v* **1** drag (violently or roughly), pull, haul.

2 drag yourself, trail; move slowly, with dragging feet.

3 troll for fish with a fly or minnow for bait.

4 gather by trailing or dragging, scrape (together).

n **1** what has been gathered as by dragging or scraping; an amount of something, large or small.

2 a rake or scraper used *eg* for scraping up soft mud etc.

3 the act of dragging, a tug.

4 a dirty, untidy or coarse person.

harl[2] *v* roughcast with lime and small stones.

n a mixture of sand and lime used for roughcasting.

harn[1] *n* **harns** brains, the brain, intelligence.

harn[2] *v* roast on embers, toast, make crisp, bake.

harnish, herness *n* **1** harness. **2** (*weaving*) the mounting of a loom.

harp *see* **hairp.**

harra, harrow *n* a harrow.

dee i(n) the harrows die in harness, die while still working.

harry *see* **herrie.**

hash *v* **1** slash, hack, mangle.

2 slice, cut up, chop; munch, chew.

3 spoil, destroy.

4 overwork, harass.

5 be hashed be pressed, be harassed.

6 talk too much, talk nonsense.

7 move or work in a muddling, rushing way.

n **1** contemptuous term for a person.

2 a heap, a large quantity; a crowd.

3 a row, uproar, brawl.

4 nonsense.

5 a rush or excessive pressure of work; work done hastily, carelessly.

6 a strong wind, especially along with rain.

hasher 1 an implement used to slice up turnips for fodder. **2** a careless, hustling person.

hashie 1 (*of people*) slapdash, careless or slovenly in dress, work or habits: '*hashie wi shoes*'. **2** (*of weather*) wet, wet and windy, stormy.

hashie-bashie a marbles game in which smaller marbles are knocked out of holes by striking them with a larger one.

hashter work done in a slovenly way, or badly arranged.

hask *v* give a short dry cough.

hasna, hasnae *see* **hae.**

hass *see* **hause.**

hassock *n* **1** a large round tuft of peat used as a seat. **2** a shock of bushy hair.

haste *see* **heest.**

hat *n* a layer of froth etc forming on the surface of a liquid.

like a hatter with maximum energy, like mad.

hattie name of various games involving a hat or cap.

hat *see* **hit**[1].

hatter *v* **1** batter, bruise; treat roughly. **2** harass, vex, overtire. **3** collect in crowds, swarm. **4** move confusedly or laboriously; work in a careless way.

n **1** a mixed collection, a confused heap; a state of disorder. **2** a difficulty; a struggle, a fluster SOUTH. **3** a skin rash.

hattle *see* **hat.**

hauch *v* cough, especially in order to clear the throat.

n **1** a gasp, a forcible breath, especially on a surface before polishing NE. **2** a soft loose cough; a clearing of the throat.

haud, had, hold, howl(d) SHETLAND, ORKNEY, CAITHNESS, ROSS, ARGYLL, ULSTER *v* NB *This verb is often used where English has* keep: **1** hold.

2 keep, go on: '*We'll haud content*'.

3 continue, keep (in health): '*Hoo are ye haudin yersel?*'.

4 keep, cause to continue to be or do something.

5 go on your way, go in a certain direction; continue on or along (your way etc).

6 wager, bet.

7 hauds ye I accept your wager NE.

8 stop; restrain yourself: '*Haud you there!*'.

9 restrain, keep back: '*Wha could haud their temper?*'.

10 burden, afflict, *often* **hauden doon**: '*a young woman sair hauden doon wi a sma faimilie*'.

11 keep, maintain (people or animals); keep (provisions etc) in store. *n* **1** a hold.

2 property: **house and haud** house and home.

3 a support, prop.

4 a den of an animal, *eg* a rabbit-hole.

haudin 1 a holding; a small farm or house held on lease. **2** possession, means of support. **3** furniture, equipment; the stock of a farm SOUTH.

haud aff (o) yersel look after yourself, defend yourself or your own interests NE.

haud again hold back; resist.

haud at 1 keep at (something). **2** nag.

haud awa 1 keep away, keep out or off. **2** continue on your way, go away.

haud by 1 pass by, keep away from. **2** have (little etc) respect for.

haud-doon a handicap, burden.

haud yer feet keep (on) your feet.

haud for aim at, make for.

haud forrit continue to improve (in health).

haud in *n* a stinting, a lack.

v **1** hold in. **2** (*of a container*) hold the contents, not leak or spill. **3** *also* **haud in aboot** bring or come closer; save, economize, be miserly.

haud in aboot keep in order, keep a check on.

haud in wi keep in with.

haud yer mooth! be silent!, keep quiet!

haud on 1 carry on, keep up. **2** supply, keep adding or putting on: '*Haud the peats on the fire*'.

haud oot 1 keep out. **2** keep up. **3** live (in a place).

haud tae 1 (*especially of a door*) (keep) shut. **2** keep hard at work.

haud till keep saying.

haud up hold up.

haud up wi keep pace with; keep in touch with.

haud a wee wait a little, stop for a moment.

haud wi own up to.

in a haud in difficulties, in trouble.

on haud on fire: '*Yer lum's on haud*'.

see's a haud o give, hand over, catch hold of.

neither tae haud nor tae bind beyond control.

hauf *see* **half.**

haugh [-gh as -ch in 'loch'] *n* a piece of level ground on the banks of a river, river-meadow land.

haul *n* a very large quantity.

haun, haund *see* **hand.**

haunie *see* **hannie.**

haunt *n* a custom, habit, practice.

haurd *see* **hear.**

hause, hass *n* **1** the neck. **2** the throat, gullet. **3** a narrow place: a neck of land; a narrow stretch of water. **4** a narrow neck-like part, *eg* of an axle.

hausebane the collarbone.

hausepipe the throat, windpipe.

gae doon (intae) the wrong hause (*of food etc*) go down the wrong way.

have *see* **hae, heave.**

haver *n* oats, the oat.

haw[1], **chaw** *n* a haw, hawthorn(-berry).

haw-splitter a peashooter sw.

haw[2], **hyaave** [heeaave] NE *adj* of a pale, wan colouring, tinged with blue or green NE.

Hawick ba *n* **1** (*in past times*) a game played at Shrovetide in the River Teviot. **2** a round, brown, mint-flavoured boiled sweet made in Hawick.

hawk *see* **hack.**

hawkie *n* a cow with a white face; any cow; pet name for a favourite cow.

hawkit *adj* **1** (*of animals*) spotted or streaked with white; white-faced NE. **2** (*of people*) foolish, stupid, harum-scarum.

hay *see* **hey**[1].

hazel *v* beat or thrash, as with a hazel stick.

hazel oil a caning, a sound beating (with a hazel stick).

hazy *adj* weak in the mind, mentally unbalanced.

he, e, hei SOUTH *personal pronoun* **1** he, it. **2** used by a wife of her husband or a servant of his or her master.
n a man, a male person NE.

head, headicks and pinticks *see* **heid.**

heal[1] *n* health, physical well-being.

heal[2] *v* hide, conceal; keep secret.

heap, halp *n* **1** a heap. **2** a great deal, a lot: '*a heap better*'. **3** a slovenly woman; a coarse rough person.

be heid o the heap be in the forefront, take first place.

hear *v*, *past tense, past participle* **hard, haurd** hear.

hearer a person who listens to the preaching of a certain **minister**, a churchgoer.

hearin(g) 1 a scolding. **2** *see* **children's hearing** (*under* **child**).

hear yer ears hear yourself speak.

hear till him *etc!* just listen to him etc!

hearken *v* **1** *also* **hearken tae** eavesdrop, play the eavesdropper. **2** listen to, hear with attention. **3** **hearken someone his lessons** *etc* hear someone repeat lessons etc. **4** whisper (something). **5** (*of the wind*) blow gently.

heart *see* **hert.**

heat *see* **hait.**

heather, hedder SHETLAND, ORKNEY, NE *n* heather.

heathery 1 heather-covered; of or like heather. **2** rough, shaggy, untidy.

heathery heid (a person with) a tousled or shaggy head of hair.

heather bell the flower of the heather.

heather-bleater a snipe.

bell heather a kind of heath with bell-shaped flowerlets; *loosely, also* cross-leaved heath.

set the heather on fire cause a great fuss or sensation.

heave, have [rhymes with 'shave'] ORKNEY, NE *v* **1** heave. **2** throw, pitch, toss (without implying effort or strain as in English). **3** rise up above the surface, come into view.
n **the heave** the sack (from a job).

gie someone the heave 1 push, shove. **2** sack or dismiss from a job. **3** give up a sweetheart.

heavy *adj* **1** *also* **heavy-footed** pregnant. **2** (*of a river*) swollen. **3** (*of a drink, mainly of spirits*) large.
n a kind of beer corresponding to English bitter.

be heavy on, be a heavy neibour on be hard on (clothes), consume a great deal of (food, drink).

hech! [-ch as in 'dreich'] *interjection* exclamation of sorrow, fatigue, pain, surprise or contempt: '*hech me!*'; '*hech sirs!*'.

v pant, breathe hard or uneasily SOUTH.

hech how! exclamation of weariness or regret.

(the) auld hech how the old routine.

hechle [-ch- as in dreich] *v* **1** pant, breathe quickly. **2** walk or move with difficulty.

heck, haik *n* a rack, a slatted wooden or iron framework, *eg* for fodder in a stable etc, or placed in or across a stream.

v eat greedily E CENTRAL, SOUTH.

hecker a glutton, a hearty eater E CENTRAL, SOUTH.

live at heck and manger live extravagantly, be in clover.

heckle *n* **1** *also* **hackle** a hackle, heckle, flax-comb; the long neck-feathers of a cock etc. **2** a severe beating, sharp criticism; a person who gives this. **3** *also* **hackle** a cockade of hackle-feathers dyed in various colours and worn in the bonnets of certain Scottish regiments.

v **1** dress (flax etc) with a **heckle. 2** speak sharply (to), scold severely.

heckle(d) biscuit a type of hard biscuit made in Angus with a pinhole surface.

be (kept) on heckle-pins be (kept) in suspense or on tenterhooks.

heckum-peckum *n* a type of artificial fly used for trout-fishing.

hedder *see* **heather.**

heed *v*: **never heed** never mind, don't bother.

heed *see* **huld.**

heedrum hodrum *n* Gaelic music *contemptuous.*

heefer *adj* **1** a young cow, the precise meaning varying considerably as to whether or not the animal has calved, or how often she has calved. **2** a large clumsy person, usually a woman: '*Ye big heefer!*'.

heel *n* the rind or last portion of a cheese; each end of a loaf of bread, especially when cut off the loaf.

cowp by the heels lay low.

gie heels tae cause to hurry; (*curling*) make the progress of (a stone) more rapid by sweeping the ice in front of it.

heels ower gowdie, heelster gowdie, heelster heid(s) head-over-heels, topsy-turvy, upside-down.

take yer heels take to your heels, run away.

heelie *see* **huilie.**

heeliegoleerie *adv* topsy-turvy, in a state of confusion.

heelster gowdie, heelster heid(s) *see* **heel.**

heerin *see* **herrin.**

heest, hist, haste *v, n* haste.

hasty brose a kind of quickly-made **brose** NE.

haste ye back! 'come back again soon!', an invitation to visit again.

heeturi (*children's rhymes*) *numeral* six.

heeze, hize NE, **heyze** *v* **1** hoist, lift, raise (up).

2 raise, lift up (someone's spirits etc).

3 carry (a person) to a place; hurry (a person) off.

4 hurry.

5 dance in a lively way; make merry NE.

6 swarm with.

n **1** a heave, a hitch up.

2 an aid, encouragement, a helping hand.

3 a romp; a practical joke, a teasing NE.

heezle, hizle NE a heave, a hitch-up.

heezle-hozle a game in which two players stand back, interlink arms, and, stooping alternately, raise each other from the ground SOUTH.

heyzer [rhymes with 'miser'] a clothes-prop NE.

heezel *see* **hissel.**

heffer *v* laugh heartily, guffaw E CEN-
TRAL.

heft[1] *n* a haft.

   hae heft an blade in yer hand have
complete control, have the whip hand
NE.

heft[2] *v* **1** accustom (sheep or cattle) to a
new pasture. **2** (*of animals*) become
accustomed to a new pasture; (*of
people*) become settled (in a place,
occupation etc).

n **1** a pasture which animals have
become familiar with; attachment to
a particular pasture. **2** the number of
sheep that graze on such a pasture.

hei *see* **he.**

heich, high *adj* **1** high.

2 tall.

3 occupying the higher situation, situated above another of its kind; situated in the upper part or on the upper
floor of a building.

4 arrogant, proud, snobbish.

5 in high spirits, lively, excitable.

6 out of your mind, raving in delirium
NE.

7 north SW.

adv **1** high. **2** loudly, in a loud voice. **3**
proudly, haughtily, disdainfully.

n a hill, height, an eminence, upland.

Higher (*secondary education*) at a
more advanced level, of both a State
examination and the certificate
awarded to the successful candidates: '*Higher English*'; one of these
examinations or certificates: '*I got two
Highers*'.

**High Court = High Court of Justi-
ciary** (*see* **justiciary**); NB in England,
High Court refers to the supreme civil
court.

high English the awkward, affected
form of English used by Scots trying
to imitate 'correct' English.

heich-heidit arrogant, proud, snobbish.

high kirk the principal church in a town
or region, *eg* St Giles in Edinburgh.

High School name for the principal
secondary school in many Scottish
towns.

high shooder a piggyback on the
shoulders.

high tea *see* **tea.**

high tig *see* **tig.**

up tae high doh in a state of extremely agitated excitement.

heichen, hichten *v* heighten.

heicht, hicht *n* **1** height. **2** a high place,
a hilltop. **3** (*of behaviour, emotion etc*)
a high pitch.

v raise higher, heighten.

heid, head *n* **1** the head. **2** (*bowls and
curling*) that part of the game in which
all the stones or bowls on both sides
are played to one end of the rink. **3**
the highest point of a street etc: '*heid o
the Walk*'.

v head, lead, top.

headicks and pinticks a game played
with pins.

heidie *adj* **1** headstrong, passionate,
impetuous, violent; proud, haughty. **2**
clever. **3** apt to make you giddy or
dizzy.

n **1** a headmaster. **2** (*in ball games*) a
header.

heidmaist topmost, highest up.

heid-banger an idiot, a very stupid
person.

heid bummer (*often sarcastic*) a manager, a prominent or important person.

heid-heich with the head high,
proudly, confidently, with dignity.

heid rig(g) the ridge of land at the end
of a field on which a horse and plough
etc are turned.

heid room (*power*) authority.

heidsheaf 1 the last sheaf of grain
placed on top of a **stook** or rick. **2** the
finishing touch; the last straw NE.

heid yin, high heid yin a leader, a
person in authority.

aff at the heid, awa in the heid off
your head.

be at heid an aix wi be involved with NE.

get yer heid in yer hands (*usually in threats*) get a severe scolding or punishment.

heids an heels completely, wholly.

heids an thraws (*of things arranged in a row*) with alternating head and feet or top and bottom; in disorder or confusion, higgledy-piggledy.

in the heid o busied or occupied with, deeply involved in.

on the heid o 1 immediately after, on top of SHETLAND, NE. **2** = **in the heid o.**

on the heids o in confirmation of; on the strength of; over, concerning.

ower the heid(s) o because of, on account of, concerning.

pit *or* **stick the heid on** head-butt.

tak yer heid *see* **tak.**

wi yer heid under yer oxter looking downcast, sorry for yourself.

heidie craw *see* **huid.**

heidiepeer *adj* of equal height or age.

heist *see* **hyste.**

helm *n* **1** a helmet. **2** a crowd, noisy gathering NE.

help *v, n*: **helper, helpender** NE **1** a helper. **2** a **minister's** or teacher's assistant.

helplie helpful; willing to help.

help ma bob! exclamation of astonishment or exasperation CENTRAL.

hempie *n* **1** a rogue, a person deserving to be hanged. **2** a mischievous or unruly person, now especially a girl. *adj* wild, roguish.

hems *see* **haims.**

hen *n* **1** a hen, *often used where English uses* chicken: '*hen broth*'. **2** term of address for a girl or woman. **3** a dare, a challenge.

v **1** chicken out. **2** challenge, dare.

henner LOTHIAN **1** an acrobatic or gymnastic feat. **2** a dare, a challenge.

hennie timid, cowardly.

hen-cavie, hen-crae a hencoop.

hen's eeran a fool's errand.

hen('s) flesh goose-flesh.

hen-hertit chicken-hearted.

hen-laft a hen roost; the roof-joists of a house and the space above them.

hen-picks NE, **hen plooks** SOUTH = **hen's flesh.**

hen-taed, hen-toed pigeon-toed.

hen's taes (*of bad handwriting*) scrawls.

hen-wife 1 a woman who has charge of or deals in poultry. **2** a man who concerns himself about matters usually left to women.

hae a memory like a hen have a bad memory.

like a hen on a het girdle impatient.

see (somebody) by the hens' dish see (somebody) part of the way home.

hender *see* **hinder**[2].

hennie *see* **hen.**

hent *see* **hint**[1].

her *see* **hir.**

herbour, hairbour *n* harbour.

herd, hird *n* a person who tends or watches over sheep or cattle, a shepherd.

v **1** watch over (sheep or cattle). **2** watch over, attend to. **3** keep (someone) away from. **4** keep (land) clear of animals.

herd *see* **hard.**

here! *interjection* exclamation expressing surprise.

hereanent (*now mainly law*) concerning this matter; in regard to what has just been said.

herle, erle *n* a heron E CENTRAL.

herm *see* **hairm.**

hern, huron *n* a heron SOUTH.

herness *see* **harnish.**

heronshew *n* a heron.

herp *see* **hairp.**

herrie, harry *v* **1** harry, rob, plunder. **2** rob (a nest) of eggs or young, or (a beehive) of its honey. **3** make poor.

herrin, heerin NE *n* a herring.

hersel, herself *pronoun* **1** herself. **2**

name for the female head of any institution, *eg* the mistress of the house, a female boss.

hert, hairt, heart *n* **1** the heart. **2** the stomach SHETLAND, ORKNEY, NE. **3 (the) Hearts = Heart of Midlothian.**

hert(e)nin encouragement; strengthening.

hertie 1 hearty, cordial.

2 drunk, tipsy.

3 fond of fun and good company, cheerful.

4 generous *often sarcastic*: '*My, but ye're hertie*' (of someone giving a small amount).

5 having a good appetite.

6 suffering from a weak heart.

hertalane lonely.

hertless 1 disheartened, dejected. **2** cheerless, dismal, discouraging.

hert-dry thoroughly dry NE.

hert-glad very glad, delighted.

hert-hale (*of the body*) sound, healthy.

hert-hunger 1 a ravenous desire for food NE. **2** a longing for affection SHETLAND, NE.

hert-lazy exceptionally lazy.

hert-likin affection, love SHETLAND, NE.

hert-sair *n* pain or grief of heart; a great annoyance, constant grief. *adj* heartsore.

hert-scaud 1 heartburn. **2** a feeling of disgust. **3** a source of bitter grief, trouble, disappointment NE.

hertsome 1 encouraging, animating; cheering, attractive, pleasant. **2** (*of a meal*) substantial, hearty. **3** merry, lively.

hert-sorry deeply grieved.

hert-stoun(d) a pain at the heart.

gar someone's hert rise make someone sick.

hae yer hert an yer ee in be extremely interested in, be eager to possess.

the hert o corn one of the best, a good fellow.

Heart of Midlothian 1 name for the old **Tolbooth** of Edinburgh (demolished 1817), now the site of this marked by a heart-shaped arrangement of cobbles in the roadway. **2** name of one of the Edinburgh football teams.

hervest *see* **hairst.**

hesp[1] *n* a hasp, clasp.

v fasten with a hasp, fix.

buckled wi ae hasp tarred with the same brush, birds of a feather.

hesp[2] *n* a length of yarn, a skein of wool etc.

a raivelt hesp a confused state of affairs, a difficult situation.

het[1]**, hot, hait** *adj* **1** hot. **2** warm, comfortable.

het hert a heart suffering from bitter disappointment; the disappointment itself.

het-skinned bad-tempered, fiery.

gie (someone) a het skin give (someone) a sound thrashing.

gie (someone) it het (an reekin) scold or beat (someone) severely.

het[2] *pronoun* it, the person who chases etc in children's games.

het *see* **hait, hit**[1].

heuch [heeooch, heeuch] *n* **1** a precipice, cliff, a steep bank. **2** a **glen** or ravine with steep, overhanging sides. **3** a pit, mineshaft, quarry(-face).

heuk [heeook, heeuk] *n* a hook.

heukbane [heeook-] *n* the hipbone; a cut of beef from that part of the animal (corresponding to English rump steak).

hey[1] [rhymes with 'gey'], **hay** *n* **1** hay. **2** the hay harvest.

hey-fowk haymakers.

hey![2] [rhymes with 'gey'] *interjection* hey!

v exclaim **hey**; call with a shout.

gie hey-ma-nannie scold or punish vigorously.

heyze *see* **heeze.**

Hi-bees *see* **Hibs.**

Hibs, Hi-bees *npl* nicknames for the Edinburgh football team Hibernian.

hicht *see* **heicht.**

hichten *see* **heichen.**

hick[1] *n* a hiccup, hiccuping NE.
v **1** hiccup. **2** catch the breath before bursting into tears; sob noisily SOUTH.

hick[2] *v* **1** delay, hestitate; waver, haggle in bargaining SW, SOUTH. **2** hesitate in speaking NE.

hickertie-pickertie *adv* higgledy-piggledy.

hid *see* **hae.**

hidder *see* **hither.**

hiddle *v* **1** hide, conceal. **2** nestle closely, take shelter NE.
hiddlie hidden, sheltered, remote.
hidlin hidden, secret; secretive.

hidle *adj* carefully hidden; very suitable for hiding anything or anyone in. *n, also* **hidle-go** the game of hide-and-seek; the call given by a player to indicate that he or she is ready to be looked for.
hidle-hole a hiding place.

hidlin *see* **hiddle.**

hidlins *adv* secretly, stealthily.
npl hiding places, refuge.

hidmist *see* **hindmaist.**

hielan *see* **hieland.**

hieland, hielan, highland *n*: **the Hielan(d)s, Highlands** the mountainous district of Scotland lying north and west of the **Highland line.**
adj of or like the Highlands or Highlanders *eg* **1** (*of sports, dancing etc*) originally from the **Highlands. 2** (*of the language of the Highlands*) **Gaelic,** in **Gaelic, Gaelic**-speaking. **3** of the character (supposed to be) typical of Highlanders; (1) warmly hospitable; (2) having an exaggerated sense of birth and descent; (3) uncouth, unskilled, inelegant, *often* **no sae hieland** not too bad(ly); (4) naive, impractical, 'green', *often* **no sae hieland. 4** of breeds of animals from the Highlands.

Hielander, Highlander 1 a native or inhabitant of the Highlands. **2** a soldier in one of the **Highland regiments. 3** one of the Highland breeds of cattle.

Highland dance a dance, based on traditional figures, performed as a spectacle, usually solo.

Hielan Donald nickname for a Highlander.

Highland fling a solo **Highland dance.**

Highland Games, Highland Gathering *see* **game** *n* 2.

Highland line name for the imaginary boundary between the **Highlands** and **Lowlands** (*see* **lawland**) of Scotland.

Highland pony one of a breed of ponies originating in the Highlands.

high *see* **heich.**

highland *see* **hielan.**

Hi Hi *n* nickname for Third Lanark football team.

hilch *v* **1** limp, hobble, lurch. **2 hilch up** move with a jerk; hitch up (a load on your back).
n a limp; an uneven way of walking.

hill, hull *n* **1** a hill. **2** an (artificial) mound. **3** a moor where rough grazing rights are shared by the community. **4** any piece of rough grazing on a farm.
hillock, hullock 1 a fat, sluggish person. **2** a large quantity NE.
hill-run 1 (*especially of wild moorland*) hilly, upland. **2** (*of people*) uncultured, rough.

hilt *n*: **(neither) hilt (n)or hair** nothing at all, not a trace.

himsel, himself, hissel *pronoun* **1** himself. **2** name for the head or chief male person in any body or institution, a male boss.

hin *see* **hint**[1].

hind, hyne *n* **1** a farm-servant, a ploughman. **2** a married skilled farm-worker who occupies a farm-cottage.

hind *see* **hint**[1], **hyne**.

hinder[1], **hinner** *adj* **1** (*of time*) last, (recently) past sw. **2** (*of place*) coming from or situated behind, in the rear etc.

hinderend, hinneren 1 the later or final part, the back portion of anything. **2** the end, (*especially of life or time*) the concluding part. **3** (*of people*) the behind, the backside. **4** the remains of something, refuse, the worst of something.

the hinderend o aa the last straw NE.

at the hinderend in the long run, finally; on the Day of Judgment.

lauch yer hinderend die laughing NE.

hinder[2], **hinner, hender** *v* **1** hinder, detain, prevent, delay. **2** linger, dawdle SHETLAND, NE. **3** waste (time) SHETLAND, NE.

n a hindrance, obstruction.

hindersome obstructive, troublesome.

you'll no hinder me tae dae ... nothing could (have) prevent(ed) me from doing . . .

hindmaist, hinmaist, hindmost, hidmist SHETLAND *adj* **1** last, furthest behind, in the rear. **2** last, final.

n the last, the farthest back; (of time) the close, the end.

hin-en *see* **hint**[1].

hing, hang *v* **1** hang. **2** lean (out of a window) in order to watch events in the street. **3** be in a poor state of health.

n **1** hang. **2** the act of leaning out of a window as in *v* 2.

hinger 1 a device by which something is hung. **2 hingers** hanging drapery, curtains, a tapestry.

hinger-in a person who perseveres, a conscientious, hard-working person.

hangie the hangman.

hingin-like, hingie ill-looking.

hingin-luggit dejected, depressed, ashamed.

hingin mince 1 sausages *humorous*. **2** a

non-existent thing, an absurdity.

hingin-mou'd dejected, sulky NE.

hangit hanged (by a court of law).

hing by yer ain held be self-reliant.

hing in carry out a task with energy, persevere; hurry.

hing yer lugs look dejected or ashamed.

hing on 1 linger expectantly, wait. **2** delay or hinder (someone) in doing something, keep (someone) waiting NE.

hing-on (a source or period of) delay, boredom or weariness; a hindrance.

hing tae join in, attach yourself (to someone or something).

hing-tee a mistress, girlfriend N.

hing-thegither cliquey.

ill-hung-thegither clumsily built; dressed without care or taste.

hing up (*of weather*) keep dry.

on the hing in the balance.

hingmy *see* **thing**.

hinkum sneevie *see* **hinkum sneevlie**.

hinkum sneevlie, hinkum sneevie *n* a silly stupid person; an underhand person, a tell-tale NE.

hinmaist *see* **hindmaist**.

hinna, hinnae *see* **hae**.

hinner *see* **hinder**[1], **hinder**[2].

hinneren *see* **hinder**[1].

hinnie, honey *n* **1** honey. **2** a term of endearment.

adj sweet as honey.

hinnie-pear a sweet pear.

aw hinnie an jo(e) all smiles, extremely pleasant: '*He wis aw hinnie an jo when Ah saw him yesterday*'.

hint[1], **hind, hin, hent** *adj* belonging to or at the back, rear.

n the back, rear; (*of time*) the end; the period immediately following.

adv, preposition behind.

hint-en(d), hin-en the back part, the last part of; the hindquarters.

hint-han(d) slow, careless, late.

hint-side the rear.

hint-side foremaist back to front, backwards.

hint the han stored for future use.

hint² *n*: **neither hint nor hair** nothing at all NE.

hip¹ *n* a projecting piece of land.

hippin a baby's nappy.

hippit 1 hipped. **2** *also* **hip-grippit** having a feeling of stiffness or overstrain in the lower back, hips or thighs.

hip² *v* **1** miss, skip, pass over, not take into account. **2** hop, skip SOUTH.

n the act of hopping, a hop SOUTH.

hippertie-skippertie light, frivolous NE.

hippitie with a limp, lamely; lame, crippled.

hippans *npl* hips, the fruit of the wild rose NE.

hir, her, hur *pronoun* her; *see also* **she.**

hird *see* **herd.**

hiring fair, hiring market *n* a fair or market held for the purpose of engaging farmworkers.

hirple *v* limp, hobble.

hirsel¹ *n* **1** a herd or flock, now only a flock of sheep. **2** an area of land to be grazed by a flock of sheep under the care of one shepherd.

hirsel² *v* **1** move with a rustling or grating noise NE.

2 move along awkwardly or without getting up, slither, cause to slide along or down; shuffle.

3 hurry, bustle.

4 wheeze, breathe noisily.

n **1** the act of moving the body sideways in a sitting position, a slithering, hitching motion. **2** the sliding motion of something slipping or being shifted with difficulty. **3** a wheeze.

hirsel yont move further up or along to make room for others, move over or away.

hirst *n* **1** a barren piece of ground. **2** *also* **hist** a great number (of people), a great quantity (of things), a heap (of objects) NE.

hirstle, histle (*of soil*) dry and stony, barren.

hirtch NE *v* **1** move jerkily, edge forward. **2** sidle.

n a slight sideways push or jerky motion, a hitch; a shrug of the shoulders.

hish¹, hiss *v* **1** make a hissing sound in order to drive (an animal) away etc. **2** make (*eg* a dog) attack.

hish² *interjection* **1** be quiet! **2** a soothing sound, especially for rocking a child to sleep.

hish-hash *n* a muddle, confusion.

hishie, hushie *n* a very quiet sound, a whisper.

v lull to sleep, sing a lullaby.

neither hishie (n)or w(h)ishie not the slightest sound.

hisna, hisnae *see* **hae.**

Hi-Spy *n* (the call used in) the game of hide-and-seek.

hiss *see* **hish¹.**

hissel, hizzle NE, **heezel** SOUTH *n* hazel.

hissel *see* **himsel.**

hist *see* **heest, hirst.**

hit¹ *v, past tense also* **hut, het, hat;** *past participle also* **hutten, hitten, hut** hit.

hit² *n* 'it' in children's games.

hit *see* **it.**

hitch *v* hobble, limp.

n the little hop made in playing hopscotch.

hitchie-koo *n* a ball game NE.

hither, hidder SHETLAND *adv* hither.

hither an yon(t) *adv* this way and that. *adj* untidy; careless; muddled, separated.

hiv *see* **hae.**

hives *npl* **1** a skin rash; any childish illness without distinctive symptoms. **2** inflammation of the bowels in children.

hivna, hivnae *see* **hae.**

hiz *see* **us.**

hize *see* **heeze.**

hizzle, hussie *n* **1** a housewife. **2** a

woman, especially a frivolous woman; a servant girl. **3** a woman of bad character. **4 hussle** a pocket-case for needles, thread etc.

hizzle *see* **hissel.**

ho *n*: **nae (ither) ho but** no (other) choice, no hope but NE.

hoaliday *n* a holiday.

hoast, host *n* **1** a cough. **2** something of little value or which causes no difficulty.

v **1** cough. **2 hoast up** get something off your chest.

hoatch *see* **hotch.**

hobble *v* **1** rock, bob up and down. **2** *also* **hubble** shake with laughter NE. **3** swarm with living creatures.

n **1** a shaking. **2** a difficulty, predicament. **3** *also* **hubble** a scuffle.

hobble bog a quagmire NE.

hoch[1] [rhymes with 'loch'] *n* **1** the hough, hock, the hind-leg of an animal. **2** *now usually* **hough** a hind-leg joint of meat, the shin. **3** (*usually of people*) the hollow behind the knee-joint, the (back of the) thigh.

v hamstring; put a stop to; overthrow, defeat.

hoch band a hobble, a strap tied to an animal's leg to restrict its movement.

hoch![2] [rhymes with 'loch'] *interjection* exclamation expressing weariness, regret or disapproval.

hoch aye expression of agreement (especially when you don't really want to say yes).

hochie *v* walk slowly, awkwardly, hobble, totter.

n **1** an awkward shifting of position. **2** a clumsy, awkward, messy person.

hochmagandle *n* sex(ual intercourse).

hodden *n* **1** a type of coarse, undyed, greyish woollen cloth. **2** rustic, homely.

hodden gray 1 wool or woollen cloth of the natural undyed colour. **2** a person dressed in a simple rustic fashion; a homely, unaffected person.

hoddle *v* waddle, hobble; walk quickly.

hoddock *see* **haddle.**

hodge *v* **1** move awkwardly, hobble along SHETLAND, ORKNEY, NE. **2** fidget NE. **3** shake, especially with laughing NE. **4** hitch up, tug, heave SHETLAND, NE.

n a shove, push SHETLAND, NE.

hog *see* **hogg.**

hogg, hog 1 *also* **hogget** a young sheep. **2** (*curling*) a stone which does not pass over the **hogg-score.**

hogg-score (*curling*) either of the two distance lines drawn across the rink over which every scoring shot must pass.

hogger, hugger *n* **1** a coarse stocking without a foot, worn as a gaiter. **2** an old stocking-leg used to keep money in; a hoard.

hogget *see* **hogg.**

Hogmanay *n* **1** 31 December, New Year's Eve. **2** a New Year's gift; any form of hospitality, especially a drink given to celebrate the New Year, or money given to tradesmen and employees on that day: '*Gie them their Hogmanay*'.

hoise *v* raise, heave up.

hold *see* **haud.**

hole *n* **1 holes, holie** a kind of marbles game. **2** a small bay. **3** a shallow pool, a puddle.

v **1** dig (up), loosen (*eg* potatoes) from the ground. **2** *often* **hole on, hole about** linger, linger too long in one place or at one task. **3** wear into holes.

holiepied full of holes especially of open-work embroidery NE.

hole i(n) the wa 1 a small house etc often between two larger buildings. **2** a **box-bed,** a bed in a recess.

hollin *n* holly, a holly-tree NE.

holm *n* a small island SHETLAND, ORKNEY.

honest *adj* of good character and standing, worthy.

honesty decency, a mark of respectability; (*of clothes etc*) best.

the Honest Lad, the Honest Lass the leading participants in the annual festival in Musselburgh.

the Honest Men nickname for Ayr United football team.

honey *see* **hinnie.**

hoo[1], **how, foo** NE *adj* **1** how. **2** why.
hoo an aw be however, nevertheless.
hoo's aw wi ye? how are you?
hoo that? in what way, how?

hoo[2] *v* **1** scare (birds or straying animals) away from growing crops; scare (people etc) away NE. **2** shout to attract attention. **3** (*of an owl*) hoot; hoot like an owl.

hoo[3], **how** *n* a cap.

hooch! [-ch as in 'dreich'] *interjection* exclamation expressing excitement shouted by dancers during a **reel.**
v **1** cry **hooch,** shout. **2** shout with laughter. **3** breathe hard on an object before polishing it NE.

hood *see* **huid.**

hoole *v* exchange, barter.

hooker-doon *n* a cloth cap with a peak.

hookie *n*: **by the hookie** a mild oath.

hool *see* **hull.**

hoolet *n* **1** an owl. **2** (*insulting*) a person showing real or imagined characteristics of an owl (*eg* stupidity).
v **1** henpeck. **2** go about with a miserable expression; be solitary.

hoolie *see* **hullie.**

hoon, hoond *see* **hound.**

hoop *see* **howp.**

hoops! *interjection* exclamation encouraging someone to rise or to lift something heavy.

hoor *see* **hure.**

hoose, house *n* **1** a house. **2** a flat. **3** (*curling and carpet-bowls*) the circle round the **tee** within which the stones etc must lie to be counted in the score.

v **1** house. **2** take, put, or drive (mainly animals) into a house; shelter. **3** store (goods) etc NE.

housing scheme *see* **scheme.**

hoose ba the game of rounders.

hoose devil a person who behaves badly at home.

hoose-en(d) 1 the end or gable of a house. **2** a stout or heavily-built person.

hoose-fast housebound.

hoose-gear household furnishings or equipment.

hoose-heatin a house-warming.

hoose-heid the roof of a house.

hoose-side a big clumsy person.

hoose-tied = **hoose-fast.**

yer hoose at hame your home.

hoot!, hoots! *interjection* exclamation expressing disagreement, impatience etc.

hoozle *see* **hose**[1].

hop *see* **hap**[2].

hope[1] *n, mainly* SOUTH **1** a small valley or hollow in the hills. **2** a hill.

hope[2], **howp** *n* a small bay or haven *now in place-names.*

hope *see* **howp.**

horl *n* **1** a whorl, a small wheel. **2** the metal tag or point of a bootlace.

horn *n* a horn or something resembling a horn, *eg* a handle; a spout.

horned golach an earwig.

horner an earwig NE.

hornie 1 *mainly* **Auld Hornie** nickname for the Devil. **2** a policeman. **3** a cow (of a horned breed). **4** a form of the game of tig. **5 fair hornie** fair play.

hornie golach an earwig.

horn daft quite mad.

horn-dry (*of clothes*) thoroughly dry.

horn-idle having nothing to do, completely unemployed.

auld i the horn getting on in years and experience, wise, shrewd.

get oot yer horns begin to behave more freely or boldly.

hae yer horn in someone's hip criticize severely, oppose.

lang i the horn = **auld i the horn.**

horoyally *n* a **ceilidh,** a singsong, an uproarious party HIGHLAND.

horse *n* a trestle, a support, as used by masons to support scaffolding.

be sic mannie, sic horsie be all of one kind, be birds of a feather.

horse-buckie a large whelk.

horse gowan *see* **gowan.**

horse-mussel a (large freshwater) mussel SHETLAND, N.

hose[1] *n* **1** the socket for the handle on any metal implement, *eg* a rake. **2** the sheath enclosing an ear of corn.

hozle, hoozle the socket into which the handle of a hammer, fork, golf club etc is fitted.

hose-fish a cuttlefish.

hose[2] *v* swallow greedily NE.

hoshen, hushion *n* a footless stocking used to cover legs or arms in cold weather.

host *see* **hoast.**

hot, hut *n* **1** a small heap. **2** a small stack of corn etc to protect the crop temporarily from the weather before it is removed to the stackyard.

v **1** heap up, heap together. **2** put up (sheaves) in small stacks as a protective measure against weather etc.

hot *see* **het**[1].

hotch, hoatch *v* **1** jerk up and down, bob. **2** fidget, hitch about with impatience or discomfort. **3** heave with laughter. **4** cause to move jerkily, shrug, hitch up; shift along in a sitting position to make room for others.

n **1** a jerk, jolt, bounce, hitch, shrug; a twitch. **2** a big, fat, clumsy woman; a slut.

hotchin, hoatchin 1 seething, overrun (with), infested. **2** restless with impatience, extremely eager.

hotter *v* **1** jerk, jolt about. **2** walk unsteadily, totter. **3** bubble, boil

steadily. **4** shudder, shiver with cold or fear, shake with laughter or excitement. **5** crowd together, swarm.

n **1** a shaking or jolting, a rattling sound. **2** the bubbling made by boiling liquid. **3** a shiver; a start; a quiver(ing) NE. **4** a confused heap.

hotterel a mass of festering sores NE.

hottle *n* a hotel.

hough *see* **hoch**[1].

houn *see* **hound.**

hound, houn, hoon(d) *n* a dog; a hunting dog.

v **1** hound. **2** (*of a male dog*) run about from place to place after females.

house *see* **hoose.**

house an haud *see* **haud.**

hove *v* **1** raise. **2** throw, fling. **3** rise. **4** swell; expand.

hovie (*of bread etc*) well-risen.

hover *v* pause, wait a little.

hover a blink wait a little.

how *see* **hoo**[1], **hoo**[3].

howd NE *v* **1** sway, rock, bump up and down. **2** (*of a boat or ship*) pitch, bob up and down.

n a lurching, rocking movement from side to side.

howder, howther *v* rock, jolt, bump NE.

n **1** (*of a boat*) a rocking, jolting, sideways motion NE. **2** a blast of wind, a blustering wind NE.

howdle move with a rocking or bumping motion, limp.

howdie, howdie wife *n* a midwife; formerly an untrained sick-nurse; a woman who laid out the dead.

howdiein 1 a birth. **2** midwifery.

howe[1] *n* **1** a hollow, depression, a low-lying piece of ground. **2** a hollow, a hollow space, a cavity.

adj **1** hollow, lying in a hollow, deep-set, sunken. **2** hungry, famished.

howe backit round-shouldered; hollow-backed.

be in the howes be depressed.

howe o (the) winter midwinter.

howe², **hyowe** [heeow] N *n*, *v* hoe.

howf *n* **1** a favourite haunt, a meeting place, often a public house, sometimes a rough one. **2** a rough shelter or refuge; a natural or improvised shelter used by mountaineers. **3** a burial ground, often a private one.
v **1** live, dwell; go to or visit often. **2** take shelter or refuge.

howk *v* **1** dig (ground), dig (a trench etc), uproot. **2** investigate. **3** unearth, extricate. **4** hollow out, scrape or scoop out the inside of (something). **5** mine (coal), quarry (stone).

howl, howld *see* **haud.**

howp, hoop SHETLAND, ORKNEY, **hope** *n*, *v* hope.
I hope! would you believe it! '*I hope he'd forgotten the key!*'.
na howp bit no alternative but.

howp *see* **hope².**

howther *see* **howd.**

hozle *see* **hose¹.**

hubble *see* **hobble.**

hucky-duck *see* **hacky duck.**

hudder, huther *v* heap together in disorder; throw on (clothes) hastily or untidily.
n **1** an untidy worker or person. **2** a confused crowd or heap.

hudderie, hutherie 1 *also* **hudderie-dudderie** dirty or untidy in appearance or habits. **2** (*mainly of hair*) untidy.

hudge *n* a large quantity, a vast amount (of money etc).
v mass, heap up NE.

hudge-mudge secrecy; furtive whispering (especially behind someone's back) NE.

hugger NE *v* **1** shudder, shiver, hug yourself (to keep warm). **2** crowd or huddle together as a protection against cold. **3** (*of clothes*) slip down or hang untidily.

huggert, huggerin 1 round-shouldered. **2** huddled up or shrunk with cold, pinched-looking.

hugger *see* **hogger.**

huggerie-muggerie *adj* furtive; disorderly, untidy.

hugmahush *n* a slovenly person; a lout NE.

huld, heed NE, **hood** *n*, *v* hood.

huidie, hoodie craw, heidie craw SHETLAND, N **1** a hooded crow. **2** a carrion crow.

hull, hool, hull *n* **1** a hull, pod, shell etc. **2** the skin of a person or animal.
v shell (peas etc), husk.

hullie, hoolie, heelie NE *adj* moderate, slow, cautious, careful.
adv moderately, slowly, gently.
interjection be careful!, go slow!, have patience!
v pause, halt, hesitate.

hull *see* **hill, hull.**

hulster *v* **1** hoist a load onto your back; struggle along under a heavy burden. **2** walk heavily as if laden NE. **3** have on too many clothes.

hum¹ *v* **1** *also* **hummie** chew partially. **2** eat greedily, crunch NE.

hum² *v*: **hum an hae, humph an hae** hesitate.

humbug *n* a nuisance NE.

hum-drum *adj* in low spirits; sullen.

humf *see* **humph¹, humph².**

humlock *n* **1** common hemlock or other umbelliferous plants such as cow parsnip. **2** a dried hemlock stalk used as a peashooter.

hummel *adj* (*of cattle*) having no horns.

hum(m)el doddie NE *adj* hornless.
n a woollen mitten.

hummle *see* **hum¹.**

humour, eemir NE *n* **1** humour. **2** matter or pus from a wound or sore. **3** a skin eruption.

hump *see* **humph¹.**

humph¹, humf, hump *n* **1** a hump, a curvature of the spine, a hump-back. **2** the act of carrying a heavy load.
v **1** carry about (a heavy burden), lift up (something heavy). **2** move around

with difficulty under the weight of a heavy load.

humphed hunched.

humphie *adj, also* **humphie-backit** having a hump, hunchbacked.

n, also **humphie-back** a hunchbacked person.

come up yer humph come into your head, occur to you to do something.

humph², **humf** *n* **1** a bad smell of something going bad. **2** a high flavour, a taste of foodstuff going bad.

humphie having a bad smell or a high taste.

humph an hae *see* **hum²**.

humple¹, **humplock** WEST *n* a small heap or mound, a hillock.

humple² *v* walk unevenly or haltingly; hobble.

humplock *see* **humple¹**.

hunch *v* heave or shove with the shoulder.

hunchie a hunchback.

hunch-cuddy-hunch a boys' team game.

hund *n* a dog.

hunder, hunner *n* a hundred.

hunger *v* starve.

hungert starved(-looking).

hungry mean, miserly; greedy.

a hunger or burst scarcity or plenty.

hunker *v*: **hunker doon 1** squat; crouch. **2** huddle, sit or settle yourself in a crouching or cramped position.

n **on yer hunkers 1** in(to) a squatting position. **2** in a quandary; on your last legs.

hunker-bane the thigh bone.

hunker-slide 1 slide on ice in a crouched position. **2** get out of a duty or a promise.

hunner *see* **hunder**.

Huns *npl* insulting nickname for Rangers football team, especially by Celtic fans.

hunt *v*: **hunt (th)e gowk** go on a fool's errand, be made a fool of, especially an April fool.

huntiegowk 1 the game of April fool, a fool's errand especially on April Fool's Day. **2** April Fool's Day. **3** an April fool, a person sent on a fool's errand.

hunt the staigie a children's game in which one player has to catch the others NE.

hur *see* **hir, she**.

hurcheon *n* **1** a hedgehog. **2** a rough, untidy person.

hurdies *npl* the buttocks, hips, haunches of human beings or animals.

ower the hurdies in difficulties, deep (in debt).

hure, hoor *n* a whore, prostitute.

hurkle *v* **1** crouch. **2** walk with the body in a crouching position; stumble along, stagger NE. **3** yield, give in NE.

hurkle-backit hunchbacked, misshapen.

hurkle-bane the hip-bone.

hurl¹ *v* **1** dash, hurtle, fall from a height. **2** convey in a wheeled vehicle, drive, push or pull along on wheels. **3** move on wheels, trundle along, ride in a wheeled vehicle.

n **1** a ride or drive in a wheeled vehicle, a lift along the road. **2** a violent rush forwards or downwards, *eg* of falling stones or wind.

hurlie 1 *also* **hurl-barra** a wheel-barrow; a handcart. **2** *also* **hurlie bed** a bed on wheels. **3** *also* **hurlie-cairt** a child's homemade cart.

hurl² *v* **1** make a deep rumbling hollow sound, as of rushing water. **2** wheeze SHETLAND, ORKNEY, NE.

n a rumbling or grating noise; thunder.

huron *see* **hern**.

hurroo *n* an excited, high-spirited, disorderly gathering, an uproar.

hurry *n* **1** a disturbance, riot, quarrel. **2** a scolding. **3** a rush of work, an exceptionally busy time.

hurried harassed, hard pressed.

hurry-burry a tumult, confusion.

In a couple of hurries without delay.

In a hurry suddenly, unexpectedly.

tak yer hurry (In yer han) take your time.

hush *n* **1** a rushing, gushing sound SHETLAND, ORKNEY. **2** a whisper, a slight sound; a rumour NE. **3** a large quantity.

hushie *see* **hishie**.

hushie-ba *interjection, n* an expression for lulling a child to sleep.

hushion *see* **hoshen**.

hushle[1] *v* fidget or move about awkwardly or restlessly NE.

n **1** a heap, an untidy bunch or mass. **2** an untidy, carelessly-dressed person. **3** a rustling sound NE.

hushle[2] *n* a strong, drying, gusty wind.

hushloch *see* **hushoch**.

hushoch, hushloch *n* a confused heap, a tangled mass, a loose quantity of something.

husk *v* cough violently.

hussie *see* **hizzie**.

hut *see* **hit**[1], **hot**, **It**.

hutch *n* (*mining*) the box-like container in which coal is carried from the coal face.

huther *see* **hudder**.

hutten *see* **hit**[1].

hyaave *see* **haw**[2].

hyke *v* **1** move with a jerk. **2** sway, rock, swing.

hyne, hind *adv* **1** (*of place*) *also* **hyndie(s)** (*mainly child's word*) NE, hence, away, far (off), at a distance. **2** far on, late NE.

hyne *see* **hind**.

hyowe *see* **howe**[2].

hypal *n* a broken-down or worthless, rough person or animal.

hype *n* a big unattractive person N.

hyste, heist [rhymes with 'diced'] *v* hoist.

hyte *adj* **1** mad, excited, enraged. **2** excessively or madly keen.

gae hyte go mad with rage or passion, fly into a hysterical state.

hyter NE *v* walk unsteadily, lurch; stumble, trip.

n **1** a lurch, a stumble NE. **2** a stupid person.

adv with weak or uncertain stumbling step; in a state of ruin.

hythe *n* a harbour, a landing place, an inlet among the rocks NE.

I

I *see* **In.**

ice shoggle *n* an icicle.

icksy-picksy *see* **eeksie-peeksie.**

idder *see* **ither.**

idderwise *see* **itherwise.**

idleset *n* **1** idleness, laziness. **2** lack of work, unemployment.

ignorant *adj* bad-mannered, rude, presumptuous.

ile, uille, eelie NE *n, v* oil.

eelie dolly an oil lamp NE.

uillie pig an oil barrrel etc.

awa for ile ruined, done for.

ile *see* **ale.**

ilk[1] *adj* the same thing or person, the same place, estate or name, especially in names of landowners: '*Grant of that ilk*' (= Grant of Grant).

ilk[2] *adj* each, every (of two or more). *pronoun* each one, every one.

ilk ane each one of two or more, everybody, all and sundry.

ilka, likie N *pronoun* each, every (of two or more).

ilka ane each one, everyone.

ilkaday *adj* ordinary, everyday as opposed to Sunday or festive: '*ilkaday claes*'.

n a weekday NE.

ill, uill *adj, adv* **1** (*of people*) evil, wicked, bad. **2** (*of behaviour, language*) bad, hostile. **3** unwholesome, harmful. **4** harsh, severe, cruel. **5** difficult, troublesome. **6** awkward, inexpert, having difficulty (in). **7** (*often in curses*) unlucky; unfriendly, hostile. **8** poor in quality, scanty. **9** (*of weather*) stormy. *n* **1** harm, injury, mischief from natural or supernatural causes. **2** illness, disease. **3** badness, malice.

ill-aff 1 badly off, poor. **2** miserable, badly-treated. **3** (*confused*) at a loss.

ill-contrivit mischievous, badly behaved.

ill-daer 1 an evildoer, a wicked person. **2** a sickly animal.

ill-deedie mischievous, wicked.

ill-ee 1 the evil eye. **2** a longing, yearning NE.

ill-faured 1 ugly, not good-looking, unbecoming. **2** bad-mannered, bad-tempered, coarse. **3** hateful, obnoxious, unpleasant. **4** poor in quality, unattractive, scruffy SHETLAND, ORKNEY, NE.

ill-hertit malevolent, greedy, mean.

ill-less harmless, innocent.

ill-mou'd insolent, impudent.

ill-set nasty, bad-tempered, cruel.

ill-thochtit *see* **thocht.**

ill-tongue a malevolent or abusive tongue; bad language, slander.

ill-trickit apt to play tricks, mischievous NE: '*He's an ill-trickit loon*'.

ill-will *n, v* hate.

ill-willie bad-tempered, unfriendly, mean.

ill aboot keen on, fond of.

ill for inclined to (some bad habit etc).

ill tae dae wi difficult to please or humour.

imsh *see* **nimsh.**

in, I *preposition* **1** in.

2 into.

3 on, upon, along.

4 with: '*provided in a living*'.

5 as: '*in a gift*'.

adv **1** (*leaving out certain verbs*): '*The dog wants in*'.

2 (*of a gathering, meeting etc*) assembled, in session: '*The scuil's in*'.

3 under your breath, in a whisper: '*said in tae hersel*'.

4 alert, attentive.

n (*children's games*) (one of) the side which is in possession of the goal or home, or whose turn it is to play.

in o in, into, inside.

inbring *v* import to a place.

inby, in by *adv* **1** from outside to inside, further in. **2** inside, in the inner part (of a house etc), at someone's house. **3** in the farmland nearest the farm-building.

Inch *n* (*mainly in place-names*) **1** a small island. **2** a piece of rising ground in the middle of a plain. **3** a stretch of low-lying land near a river or other water, sometimes cut off at high tide.

income *n* **1** an entrance, arrival. **2** an illness etc with no obvious cause; a swelling, abscess, festering sore; a sharp attack of pain: '*Oh whit an income in ma back!*'.

India Pale Ale *see* **pale ale.**

induct *v* (*Presbyterian churches*) install (an ordained **minister**) in a charge.

indwaller *n* a resident, inhabitant.

ingaither *v* **1** collect (money, dues etc). **2** gather in, harvest (crops).

ingan [ing- as in 'sing'] *n* an onion.

ingang [**in**gang] *n* **1** a lack, shortage. **2** an entrance, entry.

ingaun *n* **1** an entrance, way in. **2** the assembling in a building, especially for a church service. **3** entry to a new tenancy: '*We goat an ingaun tae wir new hoose*'.

ingine [in**gine**] *n* **1** an engine. **2** natural cleverness, wit, genius, ingenuity.

ingle *n* a fire on a hearth; an open hearth, the fireside, a chimney corner.

ingle-neuk the fireside, chimney corner.

ink-fish *n* a squid.

inklin *n* **1** a small amount. **2** an inclination, a slight desire SHETLAND, ORKNEY, N.

in-kneed *adj* knock-kneed.

inlaik *n* a lack, shortage, reduction.

inlat, inlet *n* **1** an inlet. **2** an entrance,

avenue. **3** an encouragement, opportunity, welcome.

inower [-ow-] *preposition* **1** in, inside, within. **2** over (a fence or boundary) into the inside area.

inpit, input *v* put in.

n a share, contribution.

inquire *v* **1** **inquire at** inquire of, ask for information from. **2** **inquire for** ask about the health of (a person).

insteid *adv* instead.

intae, intil *preposition* **1** into. **2** in, within.

be intae 1 find fault with, scold. **2** hook (a fish).

speak intae yersel speak under your breath.

intaed, intoed *adj* with turned-in toes, pigeon-toed.

intak, intake *v* take in.

n **1** a narrowing, *eg* the number of stitches decreased in knitting. **2** the act of taking in, *eg* food, harvest. **3** a fraud, deception.

interdict *n* (*law*) a court order prohibiting some action complained of as illegal or wrongful, until the question of right is tried in the proper court.

v prohibit or restrain from an action by an **interdict.**

interim interdict a provisional **interdict** (which can be granted without the participation of the **defender**).

intil *preposition* **1** into. **2** in, inside, forming a part or ingredient of.

intimation *n* (*from the pulpit*) an announcement.

intimmers *npl* **1** the mechanism, the works. **2** (*humorous*) the stomach, bowels etc.

into *see* **intae.**

intoed *see* **intaed.**

is *adv* as.

is *see* **this.**

isna, isnae *see* **be.**

iss *see* **this.**

it, hit, hut *pronoun* it.

awa wi't, by wi't ruined in health or fortune; mad, insane.

It *see* **at**^{1}, **at**^{2}.

itchy-coo *n* anything causing a tickling, *eg* the prickly seeds of the dogrose put by children down each other's backs.

ither, other, aither, idder SHETLAND, NE *adj, pronoun* **1** other. **2** further, additional, more: '*ither twa*'.

ithergates, ither-roads *see* **itherwise.**

itherwise, ithergates, ither-roads, idderwise SHETLAND, NE *adv* otherwise.

ithoot *see* **athoot.**

ivery *adj* every.

ivnoo *see* **eenoo.**

ivver *see* **ever.**

iz *see* **us.**

J

ja *see* **jaw.**

jabb *v* weary NE.

jabble *v* **1** splash. **2** (*of the sea*) become choppy.
n **1** a liquid and sediment stirred up together, especially a weak mixture, *eg* of tea or soup. **2** a choppy area of water.

jack, jeck, jaik *n* **1** = **Jock** *n* 1 NE. **2** a jack. **3 jacks** small stones, bones or metal objects used in the game of **chucks** or knuckle-bones; the game itself. **4** *also* **jackie** a jackdaw.

jack easy indifferent; easy-going, offhand.

jad *see* **jaud.**

jag *v* **1** *also* **jog** prick, pierce. **2** inject.
n **1** *also* **jog** a prick; a sharp blow, prod; an injection, inoculation. **2** a prickle, a thorn; something causing a sting, *eg* on a nettle.

jaggle prickly, piercing; (*of nettles*) stinging.

the Jags nickname for a football team with *thistle* in its name, *mainly* Partick Thistle.

jaicket *n* a jacket.

jaik *see* **jack.**

jail *see* **jile.**

jalouse [jalooze] *v* suspect, be suspicious.

jam *v* **1** mend, patch SHETLAND, ORKNEY. **2** put in a quandary, cause to be at a loss. **3** inconvenience.

jandies *n* jaundice.

Janet Jo *n* children's singing game.

janitor *n*, *also informal* **jannie** *n* a caretaker of a public building, especially a school.

Januar *n* January.

jap *see* **jaup.**

jarg *see* **jirg**².

jaud, jad *n* term of abuse for a horse or other animal; a woman; an old or useless article.

jaup, jap *v* **1** (*of water etc*) dash, splash, spill. **2** splash, spatter with water, mud etc.
n **1** the splashing of the sea, a breaker, a choppy sea. **2** a splash (of water, mud etc). **3** contemptuous term for a small quantity, a drop (of drink, alcohol) NE.

jaupit exhausted, wearied.

jaur *n* a jar WEST.

jaurie *n* an earthenware marble.

jaw, ja *v* pour, splash; (*of liquid*) dash, splash.
n **1** a wave, breaker NE. **2** a rush, outpouring, splash; liquid splashed or thrown. **3** a drink.

jaw-box a sink; a drain.

jaw-hole a sewer.

jaw-lock *n* lockjaw.

jeck¹ *v*, *mainly* **jeck up** give up, throw away.

jeck² *v* move smoothly; fit in (with).

jeck *see* **jack.**

Jeddart *see* **Jethart.**

jee, gee *v* move, budge; move to one side or another, swerve; raise.
n a move, a sideways turn.

jeed off the straight.

(no) jee yer ginger (not) bother your head.

jeedge NE *n* a judge.
v **1** judge. **2** swear, curse.

jeeg, jig *n* **1** a jig. **2 jeegs** carryings-on, capers NE.
v **1** jig. **2** creak, make a creaking noise. **3** *also* **gig** move briskly.

jeeger an odd or eccentric person.

the jiggin dancing, a dance.

jeegle jiggle.

jeeglie unsteady, shaky.

jeel *n* **1** jelly. **2** extreme coldness. **3** a
chill.

v freeze, congeal; (*of jelly etc*) set.

jeelie, jelly *n* **1** jelly. **2** jam.

jeelie-heidit stupid.

jeelie-jaur, jeelie-can, jeelie-mug
NE a jam-pot.

jeelie neb, jeelie nose a bloody nose.

jeelie pan a very large pan for making jam or jelly.

**jeelie piece, piece an jeelie, piece
on jeelie** bread and jam.

jeest *see* **juist.**

jeet *see* **jute.**

jelly *see* **jeelie.**

Jennie *see* **Jenny.**

Jenny, Jinny, Jennie *n* **1** a woman,
especially a country girl. **2** a man who
occupies himself with what are regarded as female concerns; an effeminate man. **3 jennies** callipers.

Jennie a'thing(s) a female owner of a
small general store; her shop.

Jennie's blue een speedwell.

Jennie-hun(d)er-feet a centipede.

Jennie-lang-legs a cranefly, daddy-
long-legs.

Jennie-monie-feet = **Jennie-hun-
der-feet.**

Jennie muck a working woman; a
female farmworker NE.

Jennie-nettle(s) 1 = **Jennie-lang-
legs. 2** a stinging nettle.

Jennie spinner = **Jennie-lang-legs.**

jerk *see* **jirg**[1].

Jerusalem traveller *n* a louse.

Jessie *n* contemptuous term for an
effeminate man or boy: '*a big Jessie*'.

Jethart, Jeddart *n* Jedburgh.

Jethart snails a kind of mint-flavoured boiled sweet from Jedburgh.

jeuk *see* **deuk.**

jibber *n* silly talk, idle chatter.

jibble *v* spill (a liquid) by shaking its
container.

n **1** a splash, the splashing or lapping
of liquid. **2** a small quantity of a liquid
etc.

jig *see* **jeeg.**

jile, jail *n* jail.

get the jile be sent to prison.

jillet *n* a flighty girl, a flirt.

jilp, jilt *v* splash, spill.

n **1** a small quantity of liquid splashed
or spilt. **2** a small quantity of liquid,
especially a thin or insipid drink NE.

jilt *n* contemptuous term for a girl or
young woman.

jilt *see* **jilp.**

Jimmie *n* **1** very familiar form of
address to a man, usually a stranger. **2 jimmie,** *often* **mealie Jimmie**
an oatmeal **pudding.**

jimp *adj* **1** slender, small, neat, dainty.
2 (*of clothes*) close-fitting, too small. **3**
scanty, barely adequate, sparing.

adv scarcely, barely.

v give short or scant measure.

jimpit 1 on the short side. **2** scanty.

jine, join *v* **1** join. **2** become a com-
municant of (a particular religious
denomination): '*joined member*'. **3**
begin (work).

n the clubbing together of several
people to buy drink; a social gathering or outing.

jiner, joiner a woodworker, carpenter.

jing-bang *n* a considerable number,
usually **the haill jing-bang** the whole
lot.

jingle *see* **chingle.**

jingo-ring *n* a children's singing game.

jings *npl*: **(by) jings!** *interjection* a mild
exclamation.

jink[1] *v* **1** turn quickly, move or dodge
nimbly.

2 move along in quick, sudden or
jerky movements, dart, zigzag.

3 dodge; cheat, trick.

4 dodge (school etc), play truant.

n **1** a quick or sudden twisting movement, a jerk.

2 a coil, twist, kink.

3 the act of dodging someone; a
dodge, trick.

4 *mainly* **jinks** playful tricks or frolics.
5 jinks *or* **jinkie** a chasing game.

jink² *n* a chink, a crack.

jinkie *see* **jink¹**.

Jinny *see* **Jenny**.

jint [rhymes with 'pint'] *n, v* joint: '*a big jint o lamb*'.

jirble *v* **1** splash. **2** pour out unsteadily in small quantities.

jirg¹, jerk NE *v* make a squelching or splashing sound, gurgle.

jirg², jarg *v* **1** creak, grate, jar. **2** grate, grind (the teeth).

jist *see* **juist**.

jo, joe *n* **1** (*term of endearment*) sweetheart, dear, darling: '*ma jo*'. **2** a sweetheart, lover, usually male.

joab *see* **job¹**.

joater *see* **jotter**.

job¹, joab *n* a job.

jobbie, joabie (*child's word*) faeces.

job² *v* pierce, prick.
n a prick; a prickle.

jobbie prickly; (*of nettles*) stinging.

Jock *n* **1** a man, a fellow, especially a countryman, a farmworker. **2** (nickname for) a soldier in one of the Scottish regiments.

Jockie 1 = **Jock**. **2** a tramp.

Jockie blindie, Jockie blind-man blindman's buff.

Jock Tamson's bairns the human race, common humanity; a group of people united by a common interest: '*We're aw Jock Tamson's bairns*'.

jockteleg *n* a penknife.

joco [joco] *adj* cheerful, merry, pleased with yourself.

joe *see* **jo**.

jog *see* **jag**.

John *n*: **Johnnie a'thing(s)** an owner of a small general store; his shop.

John Barleycorn personification of barley as the grain from which malt liquor is made; whisky or ale.

John o Gro(a)t's buckie the cowrie shell.

joice *n* juice.

join *see* **jine**.

joke *v* make a joke against, tease.
jokie jocular, fond of a joke.

jonick *adj* genuine, honest, fair, just.

joogle¹ *v* joggle, shake, wrestle.
n a joggle, a shaking.

joogle² *v* juggle.

jooter *v* saunter, totter.

joskin *n* a country bumpkin, farmworker.

jossle *v* shake, totter.

jot *n* **jots** small pieces of work, odd jobs NE.
v do light work, potter (about) NE.

jotter, joater *n* **1** a rough notebook, now especially a school exercise book. **2** an odd-job-man; a dawdler.
v do odd jobs or light work; work in a dawdling way.
get yer jotters be sacked, get the sack.

joug [-oo-] *n* **1** a jug. **2** a mug or drinking vessel.

jougs *npl* (*in past times*) an iron collar for punishment.

jouk [rhymes with 'hook'] *v* **1** duck, dodge a blow etc.
2 duck out of sight, hide.
3 bow; behave (too) humbly.
4 cower, crouch.
5 avoid (someone or something).
6 play truant.
7 appear and disappear quickly, dodge in and out, dart, flicker.
8 dodge by trickery, cheat, deceive.
n **1** a quick, ducking or dodging movement. **2** a bow etc. **3** a trick.
joukerie-pawk(e)rie trickery, deceit, roguery.

jowe [rhymes with 'cow'] *n* **1** a single peal or stroke of a bell; the ringing of a bell. **2** the swell of water or waves. **3** a swing, swinging.
v **1** ring. **2** rock, swing. **3** spill (a liquid) from a container.

jowel *n* a jewel NE.

juck *see* **chuck**.

judgement *n* reason, sense, wits, sanity: '*oot o his judgement*'.

juggins *see* **dewgs.**

juist, just, jist, jeest NE *adv, adj* **1** just. **2** really, simply, no less than; truly: '*Ye didna go!*' '*I did just.*'

jummle *v* **1** jumble, mix up, get mixed up with, confuse. **2** agitate, shake, churn. **3** make a churning or confused noise.

jummlie turbid, muddy.

jumpin-rope *n* a skipping rope.

jundie *n* a steady pace.

junt *n* **1** a large lump of something NE. **2** a squat, clumsy person NE.

just *see* **juist.**

justiciary *n*: **High Court of Justiciary,** *often* **High Court** the highest criminal court in Scotland.

jute, jeet NE *n* **1** weak or sour ale; bad whisky. **2** any insipid drink, dregs, weak tea etc.

K

kach *see* **cack.**

kae, kyaw [keeaw] NE, SW *n* **1** a jack-daw. **2** its call.

kail, kale *n* **1** a green vegetable, a kind of cabbage, especially the curly variety (often served boiled and mashed); cabbage.
2 soup made with this vegetable as a main ingredient; soup made of other ingredients, with the name of the main ingredient added, *eg* **pea kail, salmon kail.**
3 a main meal, dinner: '*Come an get yer kail!*'.

kail time dinner-time.

kailworm a caterpillar.

kailyaird 1 a cabbage garden, a kitchen garden. **2** a type of sentimental Scottish fiction popular in the late 19th and early 20th centuries.

earn saut tae yer kail make a (good) living.

kalk *see* **cauk.**

kame *n* **1** a comb. **2** a combing. **3** a narrow ridge.
v comb.

Katie bairdie *n* **1** a loach. **2** a woman with a beard or moustache.

keb *see* **ked.**

kebbuck *n* a cheese, a whole cheese, especially home-made.

keck *n* the sharp cackling sound made by a bird.

keckle *v* **1** (*of hens etc*) cackle. **2** laugh noisily; giggle. **3** laugh with joy or excitement SHETLAND, NE.

ked, keb *n* a sheep-tick.

keech, kich [-ch as in 'dreich'] *n* **1** excrement, filth or dirt of any kind. **2** exclamation of disgust, a warning, often to a child, not to touch something dirty.

v defecate.

keechie filthy, dirty, nasty.

keechie [-ch- as in 'dreich'] *v* giggle, titter.

keeger *v* mix up messily, mess about; work in a slovenly or ineffective way NE.

kéehoy [keehoy], **keehow** [keehow] NE *n* the call in the game of hide-and-seek; the game itself.

keek *v, n* peep, glance: '*He keekit in the door*'.

keeker 1 an eye. **2** *also* **blue keeker** a black eye. **3** a peeping Tom.

keekin glass a mirror.

keek-bo *n* the game of peep-bo.
exclamation, also **keekie-bo 1** used in the game when the player in hiding has been seen. **2** used in similar play with a young child.

keek hole a chink or peep-hole.

keek o day sunrise, peep of day.

keek an hide = **keek-bo.**

keek *see* **kick.**

keelick, keelup *n* a blow, stroke, a thud.

keelie *n* a rough male city-dweller, a tough, especially from the Glasgow area.

keelin *n* a cod.

keelivine *n* a (lead) pencil.

keelup *see* **keelick.**

keen *adj* **1** lively, brisk; eager. **2** (*curling, of ice*) crisp, smooth. **3** greedy, miserly. **4** (*of prices*) highly competitive.

be keen o be eager for, be fond of.

keeng *n* a king.

keep *v* **1** tend, take care of. **2** fare (as regards health): '*Hoo are ye keepin?*'. **3** keep going (talk, noise etc) NE.
n **keeps** a game of marbles in which the winnings are kept SW.

keppit, keepit *past tense, past participle* kept.

keepie-in a pupil kept in after school as a punishment.

keepie-up a game of keeping a ball in the air by means of the feet, knees or head.

keep-up upkeep.

keep a calm souch *see* **souch**.

keep aff o yersel stand up for yourself.

keep in aboot restrain, keep in order.

keep in yer hand 1 restrain yourself, stop yourself striking. **2** be stingy.

keep someone's pootch provide someone with pocket money.

keep up 1 stay awake. **2** (*of weather*) stay fine.

keer *n, v* cure NE.

keetchin *see* **kitchen**.

keethin *see* **kythe**.

keevee *v*: **on the keevee** on the alert; in high spirits; worked up.

kelp *n* **1** a mischievous young person SOUTH. **2** a big raw-boned youth NE.

kelpie *n* a (horse-shaped) water demon, found in rivers and fords.

Kelso Laddie *n* the leading male participant in the Kelso **Riding of the Marches**.

kelt *n* a salmon or sea-trout on its way back to the sea after spawning.

kelter *v* wriggle, struggle.

Kelvinside (accent) *n* a very affected, over-refined pronunciation of Scottish English GLASGOW.

kemp, kyemp SHETLAND *v* struggle, strive; compete.

kemple a bold or pugnacious person; a lively child.

ken *v, past tense, past participle* **kent** know.

n knowledge, acquaintance, comprehension, insight.

kennin 1 recognition, acquaintance; teaching, understanding. **2** a very small amount.

kenmark a distinguishing mark, a mark of ownership on an animal.

(guid) kens whit *etc* goodness knows what etc.

lat ken announce.

kennle, kinnle *v* kindle.

kennlin, kinnlin, kinnlers NE kindling.

kenspeckle *adj* easily recognizable, conspicuous, familiar.

kep[1], **caip** *n* a cap.

kep[2] *v* **1** catch (a falling object or liquid).

2 stop, head off; ward off (a blow).

3 meet; (*of a train, bus etc*) connect with (another).

4 keep, contain, guard.

5 hold (the hair) up with a band, comb etc.

n **1** a catch, especially with the hands. **2** the heading off of animals.

kepper 1 a person who is good at catching. **2** a thing which is easy to catch. **3 keppers, kepples = catchers**.

kep again check, turn back.

keriositie, kerious *see* **kwerious**.

kest *see* **cast**.

kettle *n* **1** a large cooking pot. **2** *also* **kettlie** the game of hopscotch.

key *n* **1** mood, humour. **2 keys** (*in children's games*) a state of or call for truce.

kich *see* **keech**.

kicher[1] [-ch- as in 'dreich'] *v* have a short, persistent, tickling cough.

kicher[2] [-ch- as in 'dreich'] *v, n* titter.

kick, keek SHETLAND, ORKNEY *v* **1** kick. **2** show off, walk haughtily NE.

n **1** a kick. **2** something newfangled. **3** a trick, caper. **4** a habit, whim NE. **5 kicks** airs, manners NE.

kick-ba football.

kick the can(nie) *etc* a game in which a player hunts for others while preventing any of them creeping out to kick a can etc.

kick bonnetie (kick) a game played by

kicking a cap or bonnet until the owner can substitute another which is in turn kicked.

kiest *see* **cast.**

kill[1] *n* a kiln.

kill[2] *v* **1** thrash, beat; hurt badly. **2** overcome from weariness.

Killie *n* nickname for Kilmarnock football team.

kilt[1] *v* **1** tuck (up) (your clothes). **2** lift (up), suspend (a thing); hang (a person).

n a part of modern male Highland dress, a kind of skirt, usually of tartan cloth, reaching to the knee and thickly pleated at the back.

kilted dressed in a kilt.

high-kiltit having your skirts well tucked up; immodest, indecent.

kiltie, kiltie cauld bum *or* **dowp** a wearer of the **kilt**; a soldier in a Highland regiment.

kilt[2] *v* overturn, upset.

kilter *n* good spirits.

kim *adj* spirited, lively NE.

kimmer *see* **cummer.**

kin *n* a kinsman, relation.

adj related, akin.

kin *see* **kind.**

kinch *n* **1** a twist or doubling in a rope, a kink; a loop, noose, running knot. **2** a tight corner, a difficult problem.

v **1** twist a loop in (a rope) with a stick to tighten it. **2** tie up.

kind, kin *v* **1** **kind tae** be like, resemble, take after SOUTH. **2** sort, arrange according to kind.

adv somewhat, rather: '*an odd kind chiel*'.

(a) kind o, kin o, kinna somewhat, rather.

yon kind not quite normal or proper; not worth much; in indifferent health.

kink *v* gasp or choke convulsively; suffer an attack of coughing, especially whooping-cough; choke with laughter.

n a catching of the breath as in whooping-cough; a fit of coughing; a violent and irrepressible fit of laughter.

kink cough, kink hoast whooping-cough.

kin-kind *n* kind, sort, description NE.

kinnie *see* **kennie.**

kintra *see* **countra.**

kip[1] *n* a jutting or projecting point on a hill; a peak *mainly* SOUTH.

kippit (*of a nose, or a cow's horn*) turned or tilted up.

kip[2] *v* play truant from school.

kip the scull (a) truant.

kipple *see* **couple.**

kirk *n* church, now as **the Kirk** often used to refer to the Church of Scotland.

v: **be kirked** go to or be received in church, especially for the first time after a wedding, birth, family funeral, or (*of a council*) after election.

kirkie enthusiastically devoted to church affairs.

kirk claes Sunday clothes.

kirk session (*Presbyterian Churches*) the lowest court, consisting of the **minister** and the **elders** of a congregation.

kirkyaird hoast a very bad cough, a churchyard cough.

come into the body of the kirk (*of a person sitting etc apart*) come forward and join the main company.

kirn[1] *n* **1** a churn. **2** a natural feature resembling a churn in noise, motion or shape. **3** a churning motion, a confused stirring. **4** a sloppy or muddy mess; a muddle.

v **1** churn. **2** stir, mix up with a churning motion. **3** cause to turn or rotate; bore with a drill or circular chisel. **4** search, hunt or poke about; work with your hands in a sloppy, purposeless or disgusting way. **5** (*of a crowd*) swarm, mill about.

kirn[2] *n* **1** a celebration marking the end of the harvest, a harvest-home. **2** the last sheaf or handful of corn of the harvest.

kirn baby, kirn doilie the decorated female effigy made from the last sheaf or handful of corn to be cut, a corndolly.

kirn supper the celebration held when the corn is cut.

kirnel *n* **1** a kernel. **2** a lump under the skin; a swollen gland.

kirr *adj* cheerful; self-satisfied sw.

kirsen *see* **kirsten.**

kirsten, kirsen, christen *v* christen.

kirstenin piece, christening bit, christening piece a slice of cake, cheese and a coin offered to the first person to see a baby after its christening.

kis *see* **cause.**

kist *n* **1** a chest, a large box. **2** the chest, the part of the body. **3** a coffin.

v **1** put in a coffin. **2** place in a box or chest, store.

kist o whustles 1 a church organ. **2** a wheezy chest.

kit *n* **1** a small tub. **2** a fair amount SOUTH.

kitchen, keetchin *n, also* **kitchie 1** a kitchen. **2** anything served in addition to a plain food such as bread or potatoes.

v **1** add flavour to, season. **2** make (something) go far, use sparingly.

kitchie deem a kitchen maid NE.

kith *n* a person's acquaintances, neighbours and relations.

kithin *see* **kythe.**

kittie *n* **1** familiar or contemptuous term for a woman or girl. **2** the jack in the game of bowls. **3** a kittiwake.

kittie cat the piece of wood etc hit by the sticks in **shinty** SOUTH.

kittie[1] *v* **1** tickle.

2 please; make excited; arouse sexually.

3 poke, stir (a fire).

4 annoy, tease.

5 scold.

6 (*of the wind*) freshen, blow more strongly and gustily NE.

7 (*of people*) become angry, moved or annoyed.

8 (*of a horse*) become restless.

9 (*of circumstances, health etc*) improve NE.

10 set (the strings of a musical instrument) in motion, tune (up), strike up (a tune).

11 puzzle.

n **1** a tickle.

2 an irritation (of the throat).

3 a pleasurable excitement.

4 a stir, a poke (of a fire).

5 a difficult feat.

6 a polish, shine NE.

adj **1** ticklish, tickly. **2** touchy, easily upset or offended, difficult to deal with. **3** hard to deal with, tricky, puzzling, difficult.

kittlie 1 tickly, causing a tickling sensation; itchy, ticklish. **2** troublesome, difficult, ticklish; puzzling.

kittle cattle people (or animals) who are unmanageable, capricious, difficult.

kittle[2] *v* (*of cats*) kitten; (*of small animals*) produce young.

kittlin *n* a kitten.

kivver *v, n* cover.

kizzen *n* a cousin.

knab, nabb *n* a person of importance or prestige, a snob.

knab *see* **knap**[2], **nabb.**

knack, nack *v* **1** make a sharp crackling noise; snap (the fingers); break or snap with a sharp sound. **2** strike or slash sharply. **3** chatter (away).

n a sharp noise; a sharp blow, a crack ORKNEY, NE.

knackle, nackle *adj* **1** nimble, smart; trim, neatly-built, spruce. **2** deft, ingenious, skilful. **3** witty, pleasant, funny.

knag, nag *n* **1** a knot or spur sticking out from a tree. **2** a peg etc for hanging things on.

knap[1], **nap** *n* **1** a rounded knob, a lump or bump. **2** a tassel, *eg* on a hat. **3** the point of the elbow; the kneecap. **4** a shin of beef. **5** a hillock, knoll.

knapple lumpy, bumpy NE.

knap[2], **knab** *v* **1** knock, strike sharply, rap. **2** break sharply, snag. **3** break or snap with the teeth, munch, eat greedily.

n **1** a sharp knock or blow. **2** a snap, bite.

knapper 1 a stone-breaker. **2** a small hammer used by stone breakers.

knap[3] *n* a sturdy lad; a chap NE.

kned *v* knead.

knee *v* bend so as to form a knee-shaped angle.

kneef *mainly* N *adj* **1** mentally or physically alert, agile. **2** fit, in sound health and spirits.

kneep *n* a lump NE.

kneevle *n* a bit, lump.

kneggum *n* strong, disagreeable taste or flavour.

knell *n* an echoing sound, as of gunshot NE.

knick, nick *v* **1** make a cracking, clicking or ticking sound. **2** break, snap. **3** (*marbles*) propel smartly with thumb and forefinger.

knidge *v* rub, squeeze, press, especially with the knee SHETLAND, N.

kniffe *n* a children's game in which each player tries to stick an open knife into the ground by sliding or tossing it from different parts of the body.

knip[1] *n* a little, mischievous boy or girl N.

knip[2] *v* pull to pieces, break off, snap.

knock[1], **nock** *n* a clock.

knock[2] *n* a hillock.

knolt[1], **knyte** NE *n* **1** a large piece, a lump NE. **2** a knob, a bump; a bunion.

knolt[2], **nolt** *n* a sharp blow, a knock. *v* **1** knock, beat. **2** hobble, walk stiffly and jerkily.

knoose *see* **knuse**.

knot *n* **1** a lump, a broken-off chunk; a lump in porridge. **2** a sturdy, thickset person or animal. **3** a joint in the stem of a plant.

v form or grow into lumps.

knotless futile, aimless, ineffective.

a knotless threid 1 a thread that has no knot and tends to slip. **2** an aimless, useless, futile person or thing: '*He wis staunin there lik a knotless threid*'.

knowe [rhymes with 'cow'] *n* a little hill, a knoll.

knuckle, nickle *n* **1** a knuckle. **2** (*measure*) the length of the second finger from tip to knuckle. **3** (*marbles*) the flick given to the striking marble; the marble so played NE.

knurl *n* a bump.

knuse, knoose, noose, noozle *v* squeeze, press down, bruise; cuddle; pummel, drub, hit hard.

knyte *see* **knolt**[1].

kwerious, kerious *adj* curious NE.

keriositie *n* curiosity NE.

kyaak *see* **cake**.

kyauve [keeauve] SHETLAND, N *v* **1** toil, wrestle laboriously, struggle with. **2** move or toss restlessly, tumble about, wrestle in fun SHETLAND, NE. **3** knead NE.

n a struggle, exertion, a turmoil.

kyaw *see* **kae**.

kye *see* **coo**.

kyemp *see* **kemp**.

kyle[1] *n* a narrow strait or arm of the sea.

kyle[2] *n* **1** a ninepin or skittle; **(the) kyles** ninepins, skittles. **2** a chance, opportunity.

kyle *see* **cwile**.

kype *n* **1** a small scooped-out hollow in the ground, used in the game of marbles. **2** a game played with marbles aimed at a hole in the ground.

kyte NE *n* the stomach, belly.

kytie fat, pot-bellied.

up the kyte pregnant.

kythe *v* show, display; appear.

kithin, keethin NE appearance.

kythe to, kythe wi take after; be attracted to.

L

lab *n* **1** a lump; a bit; a shred. **2** a blow, stroke. **3** a kind of marbles game.
v **1** beat, strike. **2** throw.
lab *see* **laib.**
labour, lawbour *n* **1** labour. **2** farm work, tilling the ground.
v **1** labour. **2** cultivate, till.
lab-sided *adj* lop-sided.
labster *see* **lapster.**
lace, liss SHETLAND *n* (a) lace.
lacer *n* a lace, especially a boot-lace.
lach *see* **lauch.**
lachter, lauchter *n* **1** the eggs laid by a fowl. **2** a hatch or brood of chickens.
lad, lawd *n* **1** a lad. **2** a youth. **3** a male child, a son. **4** a boyfriend. **5** the young bachelor chosen as the leading male participant in some annual local festivals.
lad bairn a son.
lad o pairts a promising boy, a talented youth.
lade, lead *n* a channel bringing water to a mill; a mill-race.
lady, leddy *n* **1** a lady. **2** estate title given to a female landowner or wife of a landowner: '*Lady Leithhall*'.
ladyhen a lark SHETLAND.
leddy launners a ladybird.
lady's thummles a foxglove.
laen *see* **len.**
laft, loft *n* **1** a loft. **2** the upper storey of a two-storey building. **3** a gallery in a church.
v **1** provide (a building) with a loft by flooring joists. **2** (cause to) rise off the ground.
lag *adj* lingering, slow.
lagammachie *see* **lamgammachie.**
lagger *v* **1** make wet or muddy. **2** sink in soft ground.
n mud.

laggin, leggin *n* the edge or bottom of something, *eg* the staves beyond the bottom of a barrel.
laib, lab N *v* lick up, lap, gobble.
n **1** a mouthful, especially of liquid. **2** an untidy piece of clothing NE. **3** a rigmarole NE.
laibach *v, n* babble, chatter NE.
laich [-ch in 'dreich'], **law, low** *adj* **1** low. **2** in the lower part of a building.
n **1** a stretch of low-lying ground *often in place-names*. **2** the low side or lowest part of something.
laid, load *n* **1** a load. **2** a measure of quantity varying according to district and to what is measured. **3** a heavy attack (of cold).
laidron *n* a rascal, a lazy, untidy person.
laif, loaf *n* **1** a loaf. **2** bread, especially wheat-flour bread.
laif breid wheat-flour bread (as opposed to oatcakes).
laif *see* **leaf.**
laig, lyaag [leeagg] *v, n* chatter, gossip NE.
laik[1] *n* a small marble used as a stake in a game NE.
laik[2] *v* leak.
laip, lep SHETLAND, ORKNEY *v* lap.
n **1** the act of lapping. **2** a mouthful or small amount (of liquid). **3** a quick wash, a swill.
lair[1] *n* **1** a person's bed. **2** a place where animals lie down, a fold. **3** a burial place or grave; a burial space reserved by a person or family in a graveyard or church.
lair[2] *n* **1** mud. **2** a muddy, wet place NE.
v (cause to) sink in mud etc.
lair[3], **lear** *n* learning, knowledge, education.

102

laird *n* **1** the landlord of landed property or an estate. **2** an owner of property, especially a house-owner.

auld laird the present laird, where there is a male heir.

young laird the male heir of a **laird**.

lairge, large *adj* **1** large. **2** generous NE.

laith *adj* unwilling, reluctant, loath.
n ill-will, loathing, scorn ORKNEY.
v loathe.

lake *see* **leck.**

laidie *n*: **gie someone laidie** give someone a thrashing or a scolding.
gie it laidie do something vigorously or enthusiastically: '*Gie it laidie on the piano*'.

lallan, lalland *n* **1** Lallans the Scots language; *now* a literary variety used by writers.
adj **1** Lowland. **2** Scots in speech (as opposed to Gaelic- or English-speaking).

lamb *n* **1** a lamb. **2** *often* **lambie, lammie, my wee lamb** affectionate term of address, especially to a child.

lamb's lugs the name of several plants, *eg* the hoary plantain.

lammie-meh pet name for a lamb.

lame, leem SHETLAND, ORKNEY *n* **1** earthenware, china. **2** a piece of broken crockery, especially one used as a toy.

lament *n* a song about the death of someone; a tune for such a song, especially one played on the bagpipes.

lamgammachie, lagammachie *n* a long rigmarole NE.

Lammas *n* 1 Aug, a Scottish quarter day.

lammie *see* **lamb.**

lamp *v* **1** stride along, take long springing steps. **2** limp, hobble.

lan *see* **land.**

lance *n* a surgeon's lancet, a scalpel.

land, lan, laun(d) *n* **1** land. **2** the fields as opposed to the buildings of a farm. **3** a holding of land, a building site; a

building on this, a **tenement.**

lander a tumble, fall on the ground.

landlord the head of the family where you are a guest, your host.

land moose a field vole.

land o the leal *see* **leal.**

landart *see* **landward.**

landward, landart *adj* **1** in, toward or in the direction of the country as opposed to the town. **2** in or of the country as opposed to (a particular) town. **3** awkward, uncouth, countrified.

lane[1] *n* a marshy meadow; a slow-moving, winding stream SW.

lane[2]**, leen** NE, **lone** *adj* **1** lone. **2** on your own, alone: '*He went his lane*'.

lanelie, lanerlie lonely.

lang, long *adj* **1** long. **2** tall. **3** (*of prices*) high NE.

lang ale a soft drink NE.

lang back long ago.

lang-heid shrewdness; a shrewd or wise person.

lang kent familiar.

lang leeks a variety of the game of leap-frog.

long lie a lie-in.

lang lugs 1 a person with long ears. **2** a donkey. **3** a hare.

lang-luggit 1 long-eared. **2** shrewd.

lang-nebbit 1 having a long **neb,** snout etc. **2** (*of things*) long, tapering, pointed. **3** sharp, having an eye to your own advantage. **4** inquisitive, critical. **5** (*of words*) long, over-learned.

langsome 1 lengthy, boringly long. **2** (*of people*) slow, taking a long time. **3** lonely, bored.

lang syne *adv* long ago, long since.
n old times, memories of the past, old friendship.

auld lang syne 1 = **lang syne. 2** the song or tune of this name, now especially Burns' song and its tune, played and sung at the close of social gatherings and at midnight on **Hogmanay.**

lang drink (o watter) a tall lanky, often useless person.

lang may yer lum reek said to wish someone luck and prosperity.

mak a lang airm stretch out and help yourself: '*Dinnae mak sic a lang airm when we've goat veesitors*'.

langer *see* **langour**.

langle *n* a hobble, tether for an animal.

v **1** hobble (an animal). **2** hinder, frustrate.

langour, langer [rhymes with 'hanger'] *n* boredom, low spirits.

had oot o langer entertain, be company for SHETLAND, ORKNEY, NE.

langsome *see* **lang**.

lanimer [lannimer] *n* a boundary, especially of **burgh** lands.

Lanimer Day the day etc of celebrations accompanying the annual **Riding of the Marches** in Lanark.

lap, lape *see* **leap**.

lapper[1] *v* **1** clot, curdle: '*lappert*'. **2** (*of water*) freeze. **3** cover with or become covered with blood etc.

n **1** a clot or clots, especially of milk or blood. **2** melting, slushy snow sw, SOUTH.

lapper[2] *v, n* lap, ripple.

lapster, labster *n* a lobster.

lapster creel a lobster trap.

large *see* **lairge**.

larick *n* a larch tree.

larick *see* **laverock**.

larkie *n* the game of hide-and-seek.

larrie *n* a lorry.

laskit *n* elastic.

lass, lassie *n* **1** *also* **lassock, lassock-ie** a girl. **2** (*familiar*) a woman. **3** an unmarried woman. **4** a daughter. **5** a female servant. **6** girlfriend. **7** **lass** the leading female participant in various local festivals.

lass(ie) bairn, lass wean a daughter.

lass(ie) boy an effeminate boy.

lass o pairts a promising, talented girl.

lat, let *v, past tense* **lat, loot, leet** NE; *past participle* **lat, latten, letten** let.

lat aff break wind.

lat at hit out at.

lat bat = **lat on**.

lat be leave alone.

lat doon 1 lower the price of. **2** (*of a cow*) give (milk). **3** swallow. **4** (*knitting*) drop (a stitch).

lat on 1 no lat on not show that you know (about something). **2** pretend.

lat ower swallow.

lat see 1 let see, show. **2** pass, hand over.

latch[1] *n* a wet muddy place, patch of bog.

latch[2] *v* delay; lag.

latchet *n* a small loop of string, thread, wire etc.

lauch, lach *v, past tense* **leuch, laucht**; *past participle* **lauchen** NE, **laucht** laugh.

lauchter *see* **lachter**.

laun, laund *see* **land**.

lave[1] *n* the rest, the remainder.

lave[2] *v* bale, remove (water) with a bucket.

lave *see* **lea**.

laverock, larick [laivrock, lairick] *n* a skylark.

law[1] *n*: **lawer, lawvyer** a lawyer.

law-agent a solicitor.

law lord one of the judges of the **Court of Session**.

law[2] *n* a rounded hill, often in an isolated position.

law *see* **laich**.

lawbour *see* **labour**.

lawd *see* **lad**.

lawin *n* a bill in a public house; a person's share of this.

lawland, lowland *n*: **the Lowlands** any part or all of Scotland east and south of the **Highland Line**.

adj belonging to the **Lowlands** of Scotland. *See also* **lallan**.

Lawlander a person from the **Lowlands**.

lawvyer *see* **law**[1].

lay *v* **1** *used where English has* put, place, set etc. **2** flatten (crops) by wind or rain. **3** re-steel (a tool etc). **4 lay up** start knitting (something) SHETLAND, ORKNEY.

n a mood SHETLAND.

be laid aside be out of action because of illness.

lay aff talk at length and confidently (about).

lay at strike at, beat.

lay by 1 lay aside, discard. **2** set aside, reserve. **3** (cause to) stop or rest. **4 be laid by** be out of action through illness.

lay in 1 set to work energetically. **2** fold (something) down or over on itself; turn up (a hem).

lay intae eat greedily.

lay on 1 (*of rain or snow*) fall heavily. **2** eat heartily.

lay till, lay tae 1 start to eat. **2** beat. **3** set to, work vigorously. **4** close (a door) SHETLAND, ORKNEY, NE.

laylock *n* lilac.

lea, lave *v* leave.

lead *see* **lade**.

leaf, laif *n* **1** a leaf. **2** one of the segments of an orange.

leal *adj* **1** loyal, faithful; constant. **2** honest, law-abiding.

land o the leal land of the faithful, Heaven.

leam *n* (a gleam of) light.

v shine, glitter, flash.

lean *v* lie down, take a seat.

leap *v, past tense* **lap, lape, leaplt;** *past participle* **luppen, leaplt 1** leap. **2** split, burst open, especially of potatoes being boiled in their skins.

lear *v* learn.

lear *see* **lair**[3].

lea rig *n* (*now only in poetry*) a strip of grass left untilled in a ploughed field.

learn *v* teach.

leash *n* **1** a long piece of string, thread etc. **2** a stroke of a lash.

v **1** lash, flog SHETLAND. **2** move or work quickly or energetically SHETLAND, N.

leather, ledder SHETLAND, ORKNEY, NE *n* **1** leather. **2** the skin, hide. **3** a heavy blow.

v **1** beat, thrash. **2** do something fast and energetically.

leave *v* permit, allow.

n **1** permission to a pupil to leave the classroom during a school lesson; the playtime interval in school. **2** dismissal.

leave piece a snack eaten during a school break.

leave-o, leavie-o NE *n* a children's game in which one side hunts out and captures the members of the other.

leck, lake *v* **1** leak. **2** (*of rainfall*) fall in showers.

ledder *n* a ladder.

ledder *see* **leather**.

leddy *see* **lady**.

lee, lie *v* **1** lie, tell lies. **2** say something wrong without meaning to.

leesome incredible, shocking SW, SOUTH.

lee on tell a lie about, slander.

leem *see* **lame, lulm**.

leemlt *n, v* limit.

leen *see* **lane**[2].

leep *v* **1** heat or cook partially. **2** sit lazily by a fire.

leeplt 1 warmed up; scalded. **2** fond of warmth and comfort, soft, not hardy.

leerle *n* (*in past times*) **1** a lamplighter. **2** a lamp.

leerle *see* **lyre**.

leerle-la *n* the call of the cock; a cock.

v crow, cry like a cock.

leero *see* **lyre**.

leerup *n* a sharp blow or smack, a lash.

leesome[1] *adj* **1** pleasant, lovable. **2** (*of weather*) fine, mild and bright.

leesome[2] *adj* morally or legally permissable; right, just.

leesome *see* **lee.**

leet[1] *n* a list of selected candidates for a post.

long leet a first list of selected candidates to be further selected into a **short leet,** the final list for a post.

leet[2] *v* **1** give a sign that you know or are taking notice; pay attention. **2** make mention, pass on information.

leet *see* **lat.**

leetanie *n* a long rigmarole SHETLAND, NE.

leetera *numeral* (*in children's games*) six.

leeterarie *adj* literary.

leeve, live *v* live.

leevin 1 a person, anyone. **2** food.

livin-like lively, in good health.

leeve aff live on.

left-fitter *n* (*contemptuous*) a Roman Catholic.

leg, leig NE *n* a leg.

v walk at a quick pace, run.

leg aff set off, leave.

leg on walk or work energetically or quickly.

on the leg on the move.

pit legs an airms tae add to (a story).

tak leg(s) run off, clear out.

tak leg bail run away.

leggin *see* **laggin.**

leid[1] *n* **1** lead, the metal. **2** one of the lead-weights of a pendulum-clock.

leidie a handmade lead marble or counter for the game of **buttons.**

leid[2] *n* **1** a language. **2** a long rambling story; something told over and over again.

leig *see* **leg.**

leister [**leester**] *n* a pronged spear used (now illegally) for salmon fishing.

lek *see* **like**[1].

lempit *n* a limpet.

len, lend, laen SHETLAND, ORKNEY *v* **1** lend. **2** give (a blow).

n a loan: '*Gie's a len o yer bike*'.

lench *v* launch.

lend *see* **len.**

length *see* **lenth.**

lenth, length *n* **1** distance; amount: '*this lenth*' as far as this. **2** a person's height.

at lang lenth, at lenth an lang at last, in the end.

fa breadth an lenth fall your full length.

gae yer lenth let yourself go, follow your feelings as far as you can or dare.

see (someone) the lenth o accompany (someone) part of the way home.

lep *see* **laip.**

lerb *n* a lick, a mouthful of liquid NE.

less!, less a less! *interjection* alas! SHETLAND.

lest[1] *adj* last, final.

lest[2] *v* last.

n ability to last.

lestie lasting.

let *see* **lat.**

leuch *see* **lauch.**

leuk, luck, look *v* **1** look. **2** look at, examine.

n **1** a look. **2** a look or visit to see or examine something, *often* **a leuk o** *or* **a leuk to.**

leuk efter take notice of NE.

leuk the gate o take an interest in; visit.

leuk ower 1 look after, take care of. **2** pass over, forgive.

leuk ower the door go outside, especially after an illness.

leuk ower the windae lean out of the window and look out.

no look the road someone is on take no interest in, ignore.

leuk see! look here!

leuk till, leuk to look at.

lew, loo *adj* lukewarm.

n a warmth, especially inside a (corn or hay) stack.

lewder, louder [**loo**der] *n* a wooden lever, a crowbar.

licht[1], **light** *adj* **1** light. **2** *also* **lichtie** the will-o'-the-wisp (regarded as an omen of death) NE.

licht[2], **light** *adj* **1** light, not heavy. **2** dizzy, light-headed. **3 licht on** not taking too much of.

n a kind of alcoholic beer.

v **1** light, lighten. **2** make light, lighten, ease. **3 licht on, light till** set upon, attack; scold.

lichtlie *adv* lightly.

v, also **lichtlifie** make light of, insult.

lichtfit, licht-set light-footed, nimble.

lichtsome 1 carefree, cheerful. **2** cheering, pleasant. **3** light on your feet.

lat licht admit; make known.

lick *n* **1** a very small amount. **2** a hard blow; **licks** a thrashing. **3** a smart pace, a burst of speed.

adv with a heavy thud.

gie something big licks do something vigorously.

lickerie, liquorie *n* liquorice.

lickerie stick liquorice root chewed by children as a **sweetie** WEST.

lie *v, past participle* **lien** [lïyen] NE **1** be ill in bed. **2** (*of the tongue or speech*) be still, silent.

n **1** the act of lying, especially in bed. **2** the place where you lie.

lyin money ready cash.

lyin time a period of time worked by an employee at the beginning of a new job for which he or she is not immediately paid, wages being kept until the person leaves the job.

lie doon go to bed because you are ill.

lie *see* **iee.**

life *n*: **lifie** full of life, lively.

livin an lifelike hale and hearty.

lift[1] *n* the sky, the heavens.

lift[2] *v* **1** (*knitting*) pick up (stitches). **2** (*of the police*) arrest, take into custody. **3** take up out of the ground (*eg* a crop of corn, potatoes). **4** mention (especially a person's name).

5 take (a lady) up to dance; be the first couple on the dance floor. **6** raise (the spirits). **7** get up, stand up and move off NE. **8** collect and carry away (goods or people). **9** collect (money, rents etc). **10** collect or gather. **11** take up or cash (money etc), withdraw (money from a bank). **12** serve (a dish at table).

n **1** the act of lifting. **2** help, encouragement. **3** a rising swell in the sea. **4** a load, burden; a large amount. **5** a theft; what is stolen.

gie a lift tae, lend a lift tae give a helping hand to, encourage.

lift an lay pick things up and lay them down again.

lift yer hand (tae) hit, strike.

lift yer lines (*in the Presbyterian churches*) leave a certain congregation.

lig *v* lie, rest *literary*.

liggat *n* a self-closing (farm) gate SW.

light *see* **licht**[1], **licht**[2].

lik *see* **like**[1], **like**[2].

like[1], **lik, lek** SHETLAND, CAITHNESS *adj, comparative* **liker, mair liker 1** like. **2 liker** more apt, more appropriate: '*Mair liker it tae wear a dress insteid o trousers*'. **3** likely, probable: '*It's like Ah'll go tae Spain for ma hoalidays*'. **4** likely to, apparently on the point of: '*They're like to quarrel*'.

adv **1** like. **2** so to speak, as it were: '*jist for the day like*'. **3** likely, probably: '*We'll ken very like in the course of a week*'. **4** as if about (to do something): '*greetin like tae brak her hert*'.

n **1** like. **2 the like** that very thing, indeed; **no the like** nothing of the sort, not at all: '*Ye're sleepin — I'm no the like*'.

v **1** love (a person of the opposite sex).
2 be llken tae be likely or about to,
look like doing or being: '*Ah'm liken
tae cook dinner the nicht*'.

llkely, llkly NE *adj* **1** likely. **2** good-
looking, handsome. **3** capable or
competent in manner; suitable.
adv probably.
n likelihood, probability, chance.

llken tae, llken wl associate (a person) with (another person or thing),
think of in connection with: '*Ah liken
pancakes tae ma mither*'.

**no tae leave a body ln the llkeness o
a dog** call someone everything that is
bad.

be llke yer meat look well-fed.

be llke yersel 1 be unchanged in
appearance. **2** act up to your reputation.

llke², **llk** *v* love, have a strong affection
for (especially a person of the oppo-
site sex).

llkely, llkly *see* **llke**¹.

lllt *v* **1** sing in a low clear voice, sweetly,
cheerfully; sing a tune without the
words. **2** move in a lively way, skip,
dance.
n **1** a lively, sweet or rhythmical song;
the tune for this. **2** a rhythm (in music
or speech).

llly *n* a narcissus, especially the common daffodil or the pheasant's eye
varieties, often **white llly, yella llly.**

llmb *n*: **llmb o the dell** an imp, a rascal.

llme *n* mortar, cement: **stone and llme**
masonry, buidings.

llmmer *n* **1** general term of contempt
for a woman, a female animal or a
thing. **2** a loose woman; a man's
mistress; a whore. **3** (*of a mischievous
child*) a rascal. **4** a rascal, scoundrel.

lln *v* stop, pause SHETLAND.

llne¹ *n* **1** (*marbles*) a straight line
scored on the ground.

2 a line of written authorization: **a
doctor's llne** one stating that you are
unfit for work.

3 an account with a shop; a bill: '*Pit it
on the line*'.
4 a prescription.
5 a note requesting or explaining a
child's absence from school etc.
6 a shopping list.
7 a betting slip.
8 llnes a certificate of church membership.

llner a line-fishing boat.

llney (*marbles*) a game played with a
llne.

llne² *v*: **llne someone's lulf** grease
someone's palm, bribe someone.

llney *see* **llne**¹.

llngel¹ *n* the waxed thread used by
shoemakers.

llngel-backlt having a long, weak,
limp back.

llngel² *n* **1** a length of rope or cord *eg*
for hobbling an animal. **2** any long,
thin thing or person.

llnk¹ *n* **1** a link in the chain from which
the pot-hook hung in the fireplace. **2** a
joint of the body, especially in the
backbone. **3 llnks** a string of sausages
or black puddings. **4 llnks** loops of a
winding stream or river, the land enclosed by such: '*Links of Forth*'.
v **1** go arm in arm; give your arm to. **2**
place (a pot) on or take (it) off the
pot-hook on the **llnks.**

llnk² *v* **1** move fast or easily, trip along.
2 skip, dance NE. **3** work vigorously.

llnkle a deceitful person; a rogue.

llnks *npl* **1** a stretch of open rolling
ground covered with grass or gorse,
usually near the seashore. **2** a golf-
course (originally on seaside **llnks**) as
at St Andrews.

llnn¹ *n* **1** a waterfall. **2** a deep and
narrow gorge SW, SOUTH.

llnn² *n* the pool below a waterfall.

llnt *n* **1** a flax plant. **2** linen thread.
llnt-white (*of hair*) very fair, flaxen-
blond.

llntel *n* **1** a mantelpiece. **2** the threshold
of a door.

lintie *n* **1** a linnet: '*singin like a lintie*'. **2** a lively merry girl.

lip *n* the edge of a stream, pool etc.
v **1** touch with the lips, taste. **2** break, notch or chip (a blade).
lippin-fou, lip-fou full to the brim, overflowing.

lippen *v* **1** trust, depend on. **2** expect confidently, count on.

lipper *v* **1** (*of water*) ripple, be ruffled. **2** be full almost to overflowing.

lipple *n* an old Scots measure of dry capacity.

lippen-fou *see* **lip**.

liquorie *see* **lickerie**.

lirk[1] *n* **1** a crease, rumple or fold; wrinkle. **2** a fold of the body, a joint. **3** a fold or hollow in a hill, a ravine. **4** an unusual trait of character NE.

lirk[2] *v* lurk NE.

lisk *n* the groin.

liss *see* **lace**.

lith *n* **1** a joint in a finger or toe, a small part of the body. **2** one of the divisions of an orange, onion etc, a joint, slice.

lithe *adj* **1** (*of a place etc*) calm, sheltered, snug. **2** (*of people etc*) gentle, kindly NE.
n shelter, protection from the weather; a sheltered spot.
v **1** shelter from the weather NE. **2** thicken (soup, porridge etc) with oatmeal etc NE.

lithocks a kind of gruel made from fine oatmeal and buttermilk.

little *adj*: **littlin, little ane** a child.
little-boukit 1 small in body or bulk, shrunken. **2** of little importance, insignificant NE.
little fowk(s) the fairies.
little wee *see* **wee**.
little worth (*of a person*) worthless, feeble.

live *see* **leeve**.

livin an lifelike *see* **life**.

load *see* **laid**.

loaf *see* **laif**.

loan, loanin *n* a grassy (cattle-)track through fields.

loass *see* **loss**.

loch *n* **1** a lake, pond (applied to all natural lakes in Scotland, except the Lake of Menteith, Perthshire); a **sea-loch**. **2** a small pool or puddle.
lochan a little **loch**.

Lochgelly *n* a leather strap formerly used for punishing children, manufactured in Lochgelly, Fife.

lockfast *adj* shut and locked, under lock and key.

loft *see* **laft**.

logan *n* a collection *eg* of coins, marbles (scattered for children to scramble for) NE.

londies *see* **Londoners**.

Londoners, Lononers, londies *npl* a skipping game with two ropes SHETLAND, NE.

lone *see* **lane**[2].

long *see* **lang**.

longie *n* a guillemot SHETLAND.

Lononers *see* **Londoners**.

loo *see* **lew, luve**.

lood, loud *adj* loud.
lood oot out loud, in a loud voice.
lood-spoken loud-voiced.

looder *see* **lowder**.

loof *see* **luif**.

look *see* **leuk**.

loom *n* **1** *also* **loomie** a red-throated diver ORKNEY. **2** a guillemot SHETLAND.

loon *n* **1** a boy, youth, a fellow, chap, lad.
2 a male child, a son, a baby boy.
3 a young farmworker; (*among workmen*) a boy who does the odd jobs.
4 a rogue, rascal.
5 nickname for a native of Forfar N.
6 the Loons nickname for Forfar Athletic football team.

loonder, lunner *v* **1** hit with heavy blows. **2** work with energy and speed (at).

loop *n* **1** (*knitting*) a stitch. **2** any natural bend etc, *eg* the winding of a river.

loople deceitful, crafty.

loop *see* **lowp**.

loorach *n* **1** something tattered or trailing. **2** an untidy person.

loorie *adj* (*of the sky*) dull, overcast, threatening rain.

loose *n* a louse.

loose *see* **lowse**.

loosome *see* **luve**.

loot *v* bend the body, stoop, duck; bow.

loot-shoothered round-shouldered.

loot *see* **lat**.

lootch *v, n* stoop, slouch.

Lord Lyon, Lord Lyon King of Arms *n* the chief officer of arms of Scotland and head of the **Lyon Court**.

lorie! *interjection* lord! SHETLAND, OR- KNEY, N.

lorin, lorin scarf *n* a cormorant.

Lorne sausage *n* a sliced sausage.

losh! *exclamation* Lord!

loss, loass *v* lose.

loss the held fly into a temper.

loud *see* **lood**.

louder *see* **lewder**.

lovanentie! *interjection* dear me!, good gracious!

lovie *see* **luve**.

low *see* **laich**.

lowden [-ow- as in 'cow'] *v* (*of sound, the wind etc*) lessen, quieten, die down.

lowder, lyowder [l(ee)owder], **looder** *v* **1** loiter, idle. **2** walk heavily as if weary, plod; move clumsily or lazily.

lowe [rhymes with 'cow'] *n* **1** a flame. **2** fire; a fire indoors or out, a blaze. **3** a glow, as of fire etc or of feeling.

v **1** burn with a bright light, blaze. **2** gleam, glow, flare. **3** be blazing with love, excitement etc.

lowland *see* **lawland**.

lown [rhymes with 'down'] *adj* **1** (*of the wind*) calm; (*of weather*) calm, still; (*of a place*) sheltered, snug. **2** (*of places etc*) peaceful, undisturbed. **3** (*of people*) subdued, restrained; (*of sounds*) quiet, hushed.

n **1** a peaceful sheltered spot. **2** calm, unclouded weather. **3** peace, quietness.

v shelter (from the wind).

lowp, lup SHETLAND, ORKNEY, **loop** SHETLAND, ORKNEY *v* **1** leap, jump, spring.

2 spring to your feet, spring to atten- tion.

3 start or jump with pain, surprise, shock.

4 dance, hop about.

5 walk with a long springing step, bound.

6 (*of the heart, blood etc*) throb, race.

7 (*of things*) spring or fly (in some direction); pop out of.

8 (*of frost*) thaw, break N.

n **1** a leap, jump, spring. **2** a throb, start. **3** a place where a river is crossed; a shelf in a river-bed over which fish may leap up-river.

lowpen *past participle* leapt.

lowpin infested.

lowp the cuddle leapfrog.

lowse [-ow- as in 'cow'], **loose** *adj* **1** loose. **2** immoral; dishonest, lawless. **3** not tied or fastened together. **4** (*of clothes*) unfastened, loose-fitting.

adv loose.

v **1** loose. **2** unbind (an animal). **3** stop work or other activity. **4** become loose or free, become unfastened. **5** let yourself go, explode (in anger at someone).

lowsed 1 freed, *eg* from the day's work. **2** tired, weary.

lowsen loosen.

lowsin time time to stop work, the end of the working day.

lubbard *n* a lout SW, SOUTH.

luck[1] *n* a piece of luck or good fortune.

v have good fortune; succeed.

luckie *adj* full, more than the stan- dard amount.

n 1 (*familiar, of an elderly woman*) old Mrs . . . : '*Luckie Broon*'. 2 a midwife. 3 a landlady, hostess of a tavern. 4 a grandmother NE.

lucky box a child's savings-bank.

lucky dad(d)ie a grandfather NE.

lucky minnie a grandmother.

lucky minnie's oo cotton grass SHETLAND, ORKNEY.

lucky poke a lucky bag, lucky dip.

lucky pot a lottery.

luck('s) penny a sum of money given for luck.

luck² *v* entice SHETLAND.

luck *see* **leuk.**

lucken *adj* 1 (*of the hand or foot*) closed tight, clenched. 2 (*of cabbages etc*) having a firm heart. 3 (*of fish*) gutted, but not split right down to the tail.

luckenbooth a booth or covered stall which could be locked up, common in medieval Scottish towns.

luckenbooth brooch a heart-shaped, silver brooch originally used as a love token.

lug *n* 1 an ear. 2 a part of something which sticks out, *eg* a flap of a cap; a handle of a cup etc; a flap of a shoe; spike etc on a tool. 3 a chimney corner.

luggie a container with one or two handles, *eg* a wooden porridge bowl.

lug-chair a wing chair.

at yer lug at your side, close by.

hae the wrang soo by the lug have hit on the wrong person or thing; have the wrong end of the stick.

lay yer lug bet (that . . .).

(oot) ower the lugs over head and ears, completely absorbed: '*oot ower the lugs wi that book*'.

lulf, loof *n* 1 in the palm of the hand. 2 the paw, foot or hoof of an animal SW.

lulffie a punishment stroke on the hand.

aff lulf offhand.

crack lulfs shake hands in friendship.

lulm, leem N *n* 1 an instrument or tool of any kind. 2 an open container, a tub, bowl. 3 a loom, a weaving loom.

lum *n* 1 a chimney. 2 the whole chimney and fireplace, chimney corner and surroundings. 3 the funnel of a steamship or locomotive. 4 a long passage through a cliff; a rock chimney. 5 *also* **lum hat** a top hat, a tall silk hat.

lumber *v* get off with (a person of the opposite sex).

n a person of the opposite sex, a boyfriend or girlfriend.

lump *n* a lot, a large amount: '*He got a lump o money fur that wee job*'.

lunkie-hole *n* a hole in a wall to let sheep pass through.

lunner *see* **loonder.**

lunt¹ *n* 1 a match, a light. 2 a column of fire and smoke, a puff of smoke or steam etc.

v catch fire, burn, blaze; smoke, give out puffs of smoke, smoke (a pipe).

lunt² *v* walk with a springy step, walk briskly.

lup *see* **lowp.**

luppen *see* **leap.**

luve, loo *v, n* love.

lovie a sweetheart, lover; (*child's word*) a hug.

loosome loveable, beautiful.

lyaag *see* **laig.**

lyart [liyart] *adj* 1 (*of the hair*) streaked with white, silver. 2 multi-coloured.

lyke SHETLAND, N *n* 1 a corpse, an unburied body. 2 a watch kept over a corpse until burial, a wake.

Lyon *n* informal name for the **Lord Lyon (King of Arms)**, the chief officer of arms of Scotland, head of the **Lyon Court.**

Lyon Court the College of Arms in Scotland.

lyowder *see* **lowder.**

lyre ORKNEY, **lyrie** SHETLAND, **leerie** SHETLAND, **leero** ORKNEY *n* a Manx shearwater.

lythe *n* a pollack.

M

ma, mi, my *possessive adj* my; used with certain nouns where English omits: '*Ah'm gaun tae ma bed*'.

maa *see* **maw**[1], **maw**[2].

Mac *n* form of address to a man, usually a stranger (not necessarily a Scotsman).

machair [-ch- as in 'loch'] *n* **1** a stretch of low-lying land next to the sands at the seashore HEBRIDES. **2 the Machairs** the land bordering the Solway Firth or Luce Bay.

macht *see* **maucht.**

Mackay *n*: **the real Mackay** the genuine article, the true original.

mad *adj* annoyed, angry.

made *see* **mak.**

mae[1] [may] *adj, adv* more.

mae[2], **meh** *v, n* baa, bleat.

magerfu, magerful *see* **maugre.**

maggie *n* a magpie.

Maggie *see* **Meg.**

maggot *n* a whim, fancy, bee in your bonnet.

maggotie, maggotive NE perverse, changeable.

magink [-g- as in 'get'] *n* a queer-looking object or creature.

magowk *v* make an April fool of.

magowk's day April Fool's Day WEST, SW.

maid *see* **maithe.**

maiden *n* (*in past times*) a guillotine.

maik[1] *n* a halfpenny.

as daft as a maik watch completely silly.

maik[2] *n* the equal of a person or thing.

main *adj*: **main door** a door giving access only to a private house, as opposed to a common entrance to a block of flats.

main door flat, main door (house) a ground-floor flat of a block of flats, which has a door to itself direct from the street.

mainner *n* manner.

mains *n* **1** the home farm of an estate. **2** as part of a farm name: '*the Mains of Shaws*'; '*Morton Mains*'. **3** name for the farmer of a **mains** NE. **4** the outbuildings of a farm.

mair, more *adj* **1** more. **2** larger in physical size. **3** *with a comparative*: '*mair aulder*'; '*mair nearer*'.

mair nor more than.

maister an mair, mistress an mair a domineering master or mistress, one with the whip hand.

mair *see* **muir.**

mairch, merch *v, n* (*walk*) march.

mairch *see* **march.**

Mairch, Merch *n* (the month of) March.

mairriage, merr(i)age, marriage *n* **1** marriage. **2** a large gathering of birds, especially rooks. **3 mairriage braws** wedding clothes.

mairry, merry *v* marry.

marriet on, merrit on married to.

mairt *see* **mart**[2].

mairtin *n* a (house)martin.

mairtyr *n* **1** a martyr. **2** a disgusting mess, a dirty confusion N.

v **1** martyr. **2** hurt or wound severely. **3** cover with dirt.

maisies, mizzles NE, E CENTRAL *n* measles.

maist *adj* **1** most. **2** (*of people*) chief, most powerful, greatest. **3** (*of things*) chief, principal.

adv **1** most. **2** for the most part, mostly. **3** almost.

maist han(d) almost entirely SHETLAND, NE.

maistlie 1 most of all, especially. **2** almost, nearly.

maistlins almost, nearly.

maister, master *n* **1** a master. **2** the landlord of a tenant. **3** a schoolmaster; **the maister** the only or principal teacher in a small rural community. **4 Master** title for the male heir of some Scottish noble or landed families.

maisterfu(l) powerful, big, strong.

malt *see* **meat.**

maithe, maid *n* a maggot; an egg or grub of a bluebottle.

maitter *n, v* matter.

mak (a) maitter make a fuss.

there is no (muckle) maitter it doesn't (much) matter.

major-mindit *adj* haughty, proud, high-minded.

mak, make *v, past tense, past participle* **made, mak(k)it 1** make. **2** matter, be important N: '*It disna mak a fig*'. **3** prepare (ground) for sowing. **4** (*of food or drink in the process of cooking*) thicken, set, infuse. **5** (*of dung*) mature. **6** (*of the weather*) produce or threaten: '*It maks rain*'.
n make, form, shape.

made distressed, upset *eg* because of overwork or worry NE.

made diet a cooked meal SHETLAND, NE.

made lee a deliberate lie.

made tie a man's bow-tie sold with the bow ready tied.

sair made hard to put to it, sorely harassed.

makar a poet, often referring to one of the 15th and early 16th century Scots poets.

mak a better o improve upon, do better: '*We canna mak a better o't, I suppose*'.

mak by make money or gain advantage by, profit ORKNEY, NE.

mak doon 1 dilute the strength of (spirits). **2** prepare (a bed) by turning down the bedclothes. **3** grind, reduce into smaller fragments.

makdoon a garment altered to suit a smaller wearer.

mak for 1 prepare for, be on the point of. **2** (*of weather*) show signs of, 'look like': '*It's makkin for snaw*'.

mak intae make or force your way into.

mak or meddle, mak or mell interfere, meddle.

mak naethin o it (*of an ill person*) fail to show signs of improvement.

mak o fuss over, make much of.

mak on pretend.

mak-on a pretence, humbug; an impostor SHETLAND, NE.

mak oot 1 achieve successfully, manage: '*It's terrible steep tae climb but we made it oot*'. **2** make a living, keep going, succeed. **3** make up (weight).

mak siccar *see* **sicker.**

mak tae, mak till go towards.

mak up 1 make rich, establish successfully in life. **2** make (a bed). **3 mak it up** plan, contrive, arrange: '*We made it up to meet him*'; plan to get married: '*That couple — I doot they're makkin it up*'.

mak up on overtake, catch up with.

malafooster [malafooster] *v* destroy.

malagrooze [malagrooze] *v* spoil, injure, hurt NE.

male *n* a meal.

male *see* **meal.**

malky *n* a razor (as a weapon).
v slash with a razor *rhyming slang* (*for* '*Malcolm Fraser*').

mallimoke *n* a fulmar SHETLAND, OR-KNEY, CAITHNESS.

malt *see* **maut.**

mam *n* child's word for mother.

mammie mother.

mammie-keekie a spoilt child SW, SOUTH.

mament *n* a moment.

mammie *see* **mam.**

man, maun *n* **1** a man. **2** a husband.

3 used to show surprise, displeasure or irony: '*Maun, Will, I'm dumfoonert*'.

4 mjn, mon as an exclamation: '*C'mon min!*'.

mannie 1 a little man.

2 affectionate term for a small boy.

3 contemptuous term for an adult.

4 any man in charge; a skipper NE.

5 one who is 'it' in a game NE.

man-big, man-grown adult, grown to manhood.

man bodie an adult man, a man as opposed to a woman.

man-keeper 1 a newt or water-lizard SW, ULSTER. **2** a common lizard SW, SOUTH, ULSTER.

men-folk men; the men of a particular family or the male workers on a farm.

the Auld Man, the bad man, the black man the Devil.

man o business a lawyer.

be man o yer malt have a healthy appetite and digestion.

man *see* **maun**[2].

manage *see* **manish**.

mane *n* **1** a moan. **2** a complaint, grouse.

v **1** mourn, lament. **2** indicate pain or injury by flinching, or by ostentatiously nursing (the affected part). **3** pity or show sympathy towards (a person or his misfortune). **4** moan, utter a mournful sound E CENTRAL.

mak (a) mane 1 lament, mourn. **2** complain, grumble.

mang, myang *v* be extremely eager or anxious, long (for) NE.

manish, manage *v* **1** manage. **2** succeed in reaching: '*Did ye manage Glesca despite the snaw?*'.

mankit *adj* mutilated, damaged.

manse *n* the house provided for the parish **minister.**

a son or daughter of the manse a son or daughter of a Presbyterian minister.

mant *v, n* (have) a speech impediment, stammer, stutter.

many *see* **monie.**

map *v* nibble with twitching lips, as a rabbit does.

mapple, map-map pet name for a rabbit.

mapple('s)-mou(s) name for various plants especially of the figwort family, which have blossoms in the shape of a rabbit's mouth.

mappit *adj* stupid, thick-headed; exhausted, worn out NE, E CENTRAL.

mar *n* an obstruction, hindrance.

v obstruct.

march, merch, mairch *n* **1** marches, a boundary or frontier. **2** the Anglo-Scottish Border. **3** a boundary(-line): '*march dyke*'; '*march stane*'.

v **1** have a common boundary (with). **2** border, form the boundary of: '*The same hedge marched the twa estates*'.

Riding of the Marches *see* **ride.**

mardle *n* a large number, a crowd NE.

mark, merk *n* a mark.

v **1** mark. **2** note down. **3** take aim.

markit notable, distinguished.

marl *n* **1** a mottle, a mottled or veined pattern. **2** **mirls** measles NE.

marlie, mirlie mottled or variegated in pattern.

maroonjous [maroonjes] *adj* wild, obstinate NE.

Maroons *npl* nickname for **Heart of Midlothian** (*see* **hert**) football team.

marriage *see* **mairriage.**

marrot *n* a guillemot; a razorbill.

marrow, morrow *n* **1** a comrade, companion. **2** a marriage partner. **3** another of the same kind, *eg* one of a pair: '*a pair o buits that wisnae marrows*'. **4** a match, equal: '*I've nivver seen his marrow*'.

v **1** enter into partnership, combine. **2** **marrow wi** marry. **3** match, equal.

marrowless 1 matchless, unequalled. **2** (*of gloves etc*) odd, not matching.

mart[1] *n* **1** a market. **2** a building used for agricultural auctions; the periodical sales themselves.

mart[2], **mairt, mert** *n* **1** an ox or cow fattened for slaughter. **2** any other animal or bird to be salted or dried for winter meat. **3** a clumsy, inactive person NE.

masel, masell, mysel *pronoun* myself.

mash[1] *n* a heavy two-faced hammer.

mash[2] *n* mesh (of a net).

mashlum *n* mixed grains (and pulses) grown and ground together.

mask[1] *v* **1** mash (malt); brew (ale etc). **2** make or infuse (tea). **3** (*of tea*) brew.
  maskin pot a teapot.

mask[2] *n* mesh (of a net) SHETLAND, N.

massacker [ma**sacker**] *n* **1** massacre. **2** severe injury; destruction.
  v **1** massacre. **2** maul, bruise, beat (a person). **3** spoil (something) by rough treatment.

massie *adj* bumptious, proud.

master *see* **maister.**

mat *n* a thick bedcover.

match *n* a bout or fit of . . . : '*a greetin match*'.

mattrass [matras] *n* a mattress.

mauchless *see* **maucht.**

maucht, macht [-ch- as in 'loch'] *n* **1** ability, power, capacity. **2** physical strength.
  mauchtless,   mauchless   feeble, powerless.

maugre *v* act in despite of; master, spite NE.

magerfu(l) domineering, wilful NE.

mauk *n* a maggot.
  maukie maggoty; filthy.
  maukit 1 (*especially of sheep*) maggoty. **2** filthy. **3** exhausted SOUTH.
  mauk flee a bluebottle.

maukin *n* **1** a hare. **2** an awkward, half-grown girl; a young servant.

maukit *see* **mauk.**

maumie *adj* **1** (*of fruit etc*) ripe, mellow. **2** (*of a liquid*) thick and smooth. **3** (*of weather*) soft, mild. **4** mellow, pleasant.

maun[1] *v* **1** must. **2** (*missing out* 'go' *etc*): '*I maun awa in*'.

mauna must not.

maun-be an unavoidable necessity.

maun[2], **man** *v* manage, succeed; control.

maun *see* **man.**

maut, malt *n* **1** malt. **2** malt whisky.
  malt whisky whisky distilled from malted barley in a pot-still, as opposed to a blended whisky (made mainly from grain).

mavie *see* **mavis.**

mavis, mavie *n* a song-thrush.

maw[1], **maa** SHETLAND, SOUTH *v, past tense* **mawit, meuw** SW, SOUTH; *past participle* **mawn** mow, cut (hay etc) with a scythe.

maw[2], **maa** SHETLAND, ORKNEY *n* a seagull, *eg* the common gull, herring gull.

maw[3] *n* informal name for a mother.

mawn *see* **maw**[1].

mawsie *adj* warm, thick, comfortable. *n* a warm woollen jersey etc.

May gowan *see* **gowan.**

maybe, mebbe, mibbie *adv* **1** perhaps, possibly. **2** (*of quantity or measurement*) approximately: '*maybe half a mile*'.
  n a possibility: '*A maybe is no aye a honey bee*'.
  maybe aye and maybe hooch aye perhaps it was or perhaps it wasn't, perhaps yes, perhaps no.

meal, male *n* meal, especially oatmeal as distinct from other kinds, *eg* **barley-meal, pease-meal.**
  mealie dumplin a round **pudding** of oatmeal and fat with seasoning, boiled or steamed.
  mealie Jimmie *see* **Jimmie.**
  mealie pudding a sausage-shaped
  mealie dumplin, a **white pudding.**

mean *adj* possessed jointly or in common, joint-.

meantime *adv* **1** meanwhile. **2** for the time being, at present.

mear *n* **1** a mare, a female horse. **2** a wooden frame used as a trestle to support scaffolding.

Tamson's mear shanks's pony, on foot.

meat, malt n **1** meat. **2** food in general, for people or animals.
v **1** provide food for, feed. **2** eat a meal, get your meals.

meat-hail having a healthy appetite.

meat tea high tea.

llk(e) yer malt looking well fed.

mebbe see **maybe**.

meddle see **middle**.

meechle [-ch- as in 'dreich'] adj mean, stingy.

meed see **muld**.

meedow, meeddle mainly E CENTRAL n **1** (a) meadow. **2** marshy grassland where the natural coarse grasses are often cut for hay.

meefle see **multh**.

meel, meelack, meelackle, meeld see **muld**.

meen see **muln**.

meenister see **minister**.

meenit, minute, minent n **1** a minute. **2** an interval or recreation time; a teabreak NE.

meer see **mulr**.

meeserable, miserable adj **1** miserable. **2** mean, stingy, miserly.

meesick n music NE.

meet v: **meet in wi** meet (with), encounter.

meeve see **mulve**.

Meg, Maggle, Meggle n a rather unsophisticated girl, a rough country girl.

Meggle(-lickle)-spinnie a spider N.

Meg(gie) wi the monie feet a centipede.

megrim n a crazy idea, a whim.

megstie mel, mextlel interjection exclamation of surprise, distress or disapproval.

meh see **mae**[2].

melchie see **multh**.

melkle see **muckle**.

melth n **1** a boundary (marker). **2** a landmark used by sailors to steer by.

mell[1] v **1** mix, mingle, blend. **2** meddle, interfere (in something, with a person).

mell[2] n **1** a heavy hammer, a maul. **2** a heavy blow. **3** **mell wl** have sexual intercourse with.
v strike (as) with a heavy hammer.

melt n **1** (of an animal) the spleen. **2** the milt of a male fish.
v thrash.

menadge, menodge [menadge, menodge] n a kind of savings club to which each member contributes a fixed sum weekly for a stated period.

he couldnae run a menodge he is so inefficient that he couldn't organize anything.

mend v **1** reform, improve. **2** restore to health, heal. **3** **mend o** recover from (an illness). **4** (of a wound, disease etc) get better. **5** fatten.

past mendin beyond repair.

mends n, also **a mends** compensation.

mennen, mennent see **minnon**.

menodge see **menadge**.

mense n **1** honour, credit. **2** dignity; moderation; courtesy, hospitality. **3** something which brings you credit or honour. **4** common sense, intelligence.

mensefu polite, sensible; respectable.

menseless 1 unmannerly. **2** greedy, grasping. **3** stupid, foolish. **4** (of prices etc) unreasonably high.

menyie n **1** a group of followers; a body of troops. **2** a crowd, a rabble. **3** a large or mixed collection of things N.

mercat n a market.

merch see **malrch, march**.

Merch see **Malrch**.

merchant n **1** also **general merchant** a retail shopkeeper, especially of a grocery and general store. **2** a customer, buyer NE.

mergh [-gh as -ch in 'loch'], **mergie** SHETLAND, ORKNEY n marrow.

merk see **mark**.

merl *see* **merle.**

merle, merl *n* a blackbird.

merrage, merriage *see* **mairriage.**

merry *adj*: **merry dancers** the northern lights, aurora borealis SHETLAND, ORKNEY, N.

merry-ma-tanzie phrase found in the chorus of a children's ring game etc.

merry *see* **mairry.**

merse *n* **1 the Merse** the district of Berwickshire lying between the Lammermuirs and the Tweed; *also* the whole of the county of Berwickshire. **2** flat land by a river, especially on the Solway SW.

mert *see* **mart**[2].

mesmerise *v* surprise, astonish.

message *n* an errand: '*gae a message*'. **messages** purchases, your shopping. **message boy** an errand-boy.

go the messages do the shopping.

messan *n* **1** a dog, mongrel. **2** contemptuous term for a person.

methery *numeral* (*in children's rhymes*) four.

mettle *adj* spirited, lively.

meuw *see* **maw**[1].

mextie *see* **megstie.**

Mey [rhymes with 'gey'] *n* May, the month.

mey-flooer the primrose SHETLAND, ORKNEY, ULSTER.

as mim as a Mey puddock very prim and proper.

mi *see* **ma.**

miauve *v, n* miaow NE.

mibbie *see* **maybe.**

mich *see* **much.**

Michael, mickey *n* a chamber-pot.

micht *v* might.

michtie *adj* **1** mighty. **2** disgraceful, scandalous NE.

michtie (me)! exclamation of surprise or impatience.

mickey *see* **Michael.**

mickle *see* **muckle.**

midden *n* **1** a dunghill, compost heap, refuse heap. **2** a domestic ashpit. **3** a

dustbin. **4** a muddle, mess. **5** a dirty, slovenly person. **6** a gluttonous person or animal NE.

like straw hingin fae a midden (*of* hair) very untidy.

midder *see* **mither.**

middle, meddle *v* **1** meddle. **2** interfere with, bother, harm. **3** have to do with.

middlin *adj* **1** of medium size or quality. **2** fair, tolerable.

midge, mudge HIGHLAND *n* **1** a midge. **2** a small unimportant person or animal.

midge *see* **mudge.**

midgie *n* (domestic) rubbish: '*midgie men*'.

midgie-motor refuse-collector's lorry.

midgie-raker a scrounger in dustbins.

mids *n* the middle, centre, midst.

mill, mull, miln *n* **1** a mill. **2** a snuffbox. **3** *also* **mullie** a tin box with a lid NE.

millart, mullert NE a miller NE.

mill-lade a channel bringing water to a mill.

mim *adj* prim and proper, affected.

mim-mou'd very prim in eating or speaking.

as mim as a Mey puddock *see* **Mey.**

mimp *v* **1** to speak or act affectedly. **2** eat with the mouth nearly closed.

min *see* **man, muin.**

minch, mince *v, n* **1** mince. **2** nonsense: '*That's jist mince*'.

minshie a crumb, morsel NE.

thick as mince very stupid.

yer heid's fou o mince you're stupid.

mind, mine *n* **1** mind. **2** a memory, recollection N.

v **1** remember, recollect.

2 remember (a person) in a will, give (someone) a small gift.

3 remind (a person) (of).

4 pass on one person's greetings to another: '*Mind me tae yer mither*'.

5 mind yersell careful!, watch out!

mindin 1 a small gift (made by way of remembrance). **2** a memory, recollection.

hae mind (o) remember, have recollection (of).

keep mind (o) bear in mind, take heed (of).

mineer [mineer] *n* an uproar, a noisy gathering, a fuss NE.

minent *see* **meenit**.

mines *pronoun* mine, my one(s).

ming *n* a smell.

mingin 1 *also* **mingle** smelly, stinking. **2** very drunk.

minister, meenister *n* a clergyman, especially of the Church of Scotland.

mink, munk *n* **1** a noose, loop. **2** a cow's tether; a horse's halter.

minker a ragamuffin, vagrant.

minnie *n* a mother *affectionate name*.

minnon, mennen(t) SOUTH *n* a minnow; any small freshwater fish.

minshie *see* **mince**.

mint *v* **1** intend, attempt (to do), aim at, to etc. **2** plan, attempt (something). **3** brandish (a weapon), aim (a blow), threaten (a person). **4** suggest, hint (at). **5** mention, speak of.
n **1** an attempt, effort, intention. **2** a pretended blow.

minute *see* **meenit**.

miraculous *adj* **1** very drunk. **2** clumsy, loutish N.

mird *v*: **mird wi** meddle with, have dealings with; sport with.

mire-duck *n* a wild duck, a mallard.

mirk *adj* dark, black, gloomy.
n darkness, night, twilight.
v darken.

mirkness darkness.

mirkle dark, dirty.

mirkie *adj* merry, mischievous.

mirl *see* **murl**.

mirlie *see* **marl**.

mirligoes *npl* vertigo, dizziness.

mirls *see* **marl**.

misbehadden *adj* out-of-place, impolite SHETLAND, NE.

misbelieve *v* disbelieve, doubt.

misca, miscaw, miscall *v* **1** call (a person) bad names, abuse verbally, denounce. **2** slander. **3** mispronounce.

miscairrie *v* miscarry.

miscall, miscaw *see* **misca**.

mischancie *adj* unlucky, ill-fated, risky, dangerous.

mischief *n* **1** misfortune, trouble. **2** a physical injury.

mischieve *v* injure, beat (a person), treat cruelly SHETLAND, NE.

misdoot *v* **1** distrust, doubt. **2** suspect, be afraid (that).
n a doubt, suspicion, fear.

miserable *see* **meeserable**.

misert *n* a miser.
adj mean, miserly.

misert pig a child's (earthenware) moneybox SHETLAND.

misfit *v* offend NE.

misfortune *n* illicit sex; an illegitimate child.

misfortunat unfortunate, unlucky.

misgae *v* go wrong, fail NE.

misguide *v* **1** treat badly, neglect; bring up badly or cruelly. **2** waste, mismanage.

mishanter [mishanter] *n* **1** disaster; misfortune. **2** a physical injury.

misken *v* **1** fail to recognize or identify SHETLAND, NE. **2** have mistaken ideas of your own importance.

mislearit *adj* **1** misinformed, mistaken. **2** ill-bred, rude, selfish, greedy.

mislippen *v* **1** distrust, doubt, suspect. **2** neglect, overlook. **3** deceive, lead astray.

misluck *n* bad luck, misfortune.

misluckit dogged with bad luck, unfortunate NE.

mismak *v* **1** prepare or cook (food) badly. **2 mismak yersel** disturb yourself, trouble yourself.

misrestit *adj* suffering from loss of sleep.

miss *v* **1** fail; fail to happen. **2** avoid, escape. **3** escape the notice of. **4** pass over, skip, *eg* in reading. **5** miss something good by not being there: '*Ye really missed yersel at the pairtie last nicht*'.

n a loss, want: '*She'll be a big miss when she leaves this job*'.

misslie [**miss**lie] *adj* alone, lonely because of the absence of a usual companion.

mistak, mistake *v* **1** mistake. **2** do wrong. **3** make a mistake, go wrong.

n **1** a mistake. **2** illicit sex.

mistaen *adj* misunderstood.

in a mistak *adj* mistaken.

adv by mistake.

mistime *v* keep irregular hours, depart from routine NE.

mistress *n* **1** before the name of a married woman, = Mrs. **2** your own or another person's wife. **3** term of address to an older woman, implying respect.

mite *n* **1** a small clay marble. **2** the smaller size of button used in the game of **buttons; mites** the game itself.

mith *v* might NE.

mither, midder SHETLAND, NE *n* mother.

mither's bairn a spoilt child.

mither's pet the youngest child; a spoilt child.

mitten *n* **1** any kind of glove. **2** a small squat person NE.

v grab hold of, seize SHETLAND, NE.

mittle *n* injure, physically harm.

mixter-maxter, mixtie-maxtie *n* a jumble of objects, a mixture, confusion.

adj mixed; jumbled; in a state of confusion.

mizzer *v, n* measure SHETLAND, NE.

mizzles *see* **maisles.**

moch[1] *n* a moth.

v be infested with moths NE.

moch-etten moth-eaten; infested with woodworm.

moch[2] *n* a warm moist atmosphere, close misty weather.

adj = **mochie** 1.

v (*of corn, meat, etc*) become fusty or rotten NE.

mochie 1 (*of weather*) humid; misty and oppressive. **2** (*of stored articles*) spoiled by damp, mouldy NE.

moger, mooger *v* work in a slovenly or messy way.

moggan *n* a coarse, footless stocking; a stocking foot worn as a slipper ORKNEY, N.

moldert *adj* confused, dazed, especially as a result of blows, drink, mental strain etc.

mole *v, also* **mollach** loiter, wander idly NE.

molie a mole-catcher.

molligrant *n* a complaint; *often* **molligrants** a fit of sulks, a state of dissatisfaction.

v complain, grumble.

mon *preposition* among NE.

mon *see* **man.**

Monanday *n* Monday.

monie, many *adj* **1** many. **2** big, great, considerable: '*many company*'.

monie's the . . . many a . . .

moniment *n* **1** a monument. **2** a rascal; a silly person.

monkey *n* a tool with a ratchet for tensing fencing wire.

monkey-chip a kind of marbles game.

month, mounth, mount *n* **1** *usually* **the Mounth** name for the mountains at the eastern end of the Grampians. **2** a stretch of hilly or high ground; a mountain, hill, moor.

moo *see* **mou.**

moog *see* **mug**[1].

mooger *see* **moger.**

mool *see* **moul**[2], **mulid.**

moold, mooler *see* **mulid.**

moolie *see* **moul**[1].

moolin *see* **mulid.**

moon *see* **muin.**

moop *see* **moup.**

moor *see* **muir.**

moose, mouse *n* **1** a mouse. **2** a small

lead weight tied to a cord, used by joiners to guide cords into a sash window and by electricians to drop wires.

mouser a moustache.

mouse moulding a narrow moulding filling the angle between floor and skirting board or wall.

moose web, moose wab a spider's web, cobweb.

moot *v* hint SHETLAND, NE.
n a whisper, hint SHETLAND, NE.

moot *see* **mout**.

mooth, mou, mouth *n* **1** a mouth. **2** an entrance to an enclosed place or stretch of country. **3** the beginning (of a season, event etc). **4** a talkative boastful person.
v tell, utter, mention.

moothie a mouth-organ.

moothfae, moufae a mouthful.

ask if someone has a mooth invite someone to eat or drink.

doon o mooth in low spirits.

fin yer mou put food in your mouth.

mopple *see* **moup**.

more *see* **mair**.

morn *n* **1 the morn** tomorrow, (on) the following morning or day. **2 the morn's morn** tomorrow morning; **the morn's nicht** tomorrow night.

the morn-come-never the end of time.

mornin *n* morning.

morning roll a soft bread roll.

Morningside (accent) *n* a very affected, over-refined pronunciation of Scottish English EDINBURGH.

morra *n*: **the morra** tomorrow.

the morra's morn tomorrow morning.

morrow *see* **marrow**.

mortal *adj* extremely drunk.
adv very, *especially* **mortal drunk**.

mosh *n* (*marbles*) a hollow scooped in the ground in which the target marble is placed.

moss *n* **1** boggy ground, moorland. **2** a peat bog. **3** peat.

mossy boggy, peaty.

moss bluiter a snipe.

moss cheeper a meadow pipit.

mosscrop cotton grass.

most *n* a mast NE.

mote *n* a mound or hillock.

mottle *adj* smutty SHETLAND, NE.

mou, moo *n* a large heap of grain, hay etc.

mou *see* **mooth**.

moul[1]**, mould, moulit** [-oo-] *adj* mouldy.

moulie, moolie *adj* **1** mouldy; little used. **2** mean, stingy.

moul[2]**, mool** [rhymes with 'pool'] *n* a chilblain, especially a broken one on the heel.

mould *see* **moul**[1]**, mulld**.

mount *see* **month, munt**[1]**, munt**[2].

mounth *see* **month**.

moup, mowp, moop *v* **1** twitch the lips; nibble (at); munch (at); mumble. **2** live with sw.
n, also **mopple, mup-mup** familiar or child's word for a rabbit.

mouse *see* **moose**.

mout, moot [rhymes with 'soot'] *v* **1** moult. **2** fritter away, use up bit by bit. **3** crumble away, decay slowly.

mouth *see* **mooth**.

mowd *n* a clothes-moth.

mowdie, mowdiewarp *see* **mowdiewort**.

mowdiewort, mowdie, mowdiewarp *n* **1** a mole. **2** a sneaking, underhand person. **3** a slow-witted or slovenly person. **4** a mole on the skin, a wart.
v **mowdie** loiter or prowl about sw.

mowdieman a mole-catcher.

mowp *see* **moup**.

mows [rhymes with 'cows'] NE *npl* a joke, a laughing matter.
adj safe, harmless.

nae mows no laughing matter; serious, dangerous, uncanny.

moyen *n* **1** power to influence, steps taken NE. **2** a forewarning, news in advance, *usually* **get (a) moyen(s) o** NE.

v **1** direct, guide (something); persuade (someone) NE. **2** recommend, back (a person) NE.

mak moyen(s) take steps (towards something), use influence NE.

moze *v* decay, become musty or mouldy SHETLAND, ORKNEY, CAITHNESS.

mozie decayed, fusty, mouldy.

much, mich HIGHLAND *adj, n, adv* much.

much aboot it much the same.

no mak much o it show little improvement in an illness, job etc.

muck *n* **1** dung, farmyard manure. **2** dirt, filth; refuse, rubbish.

v **1** clear of dirt, clean out; clean dung out of (a **byre** etc). **2** spread with dung, fertilize. **3** clutter up, spoil the appearance of SHETLAND, NE.

muck flee a bluebottle; dung-fly.

muck midden a dunghill.

as drunk as muck very drunk.

muckle, meikle, mickle *adj* **1** large, great. **2** much, a great deal of. **3** full-grown, adult. **4** of high rank or social standing; self-important. **5** (*of letters of the alphabet*) capital SHETLAND, NE.

adv much, greatly, very.

n a large quantity, a great deal.

muckle-boukit 1 physically big and broad, burly. **2** pregnant.

muckle furth the open air, the outdoors NE.

muckle pot the largest cooking pot, a cauldron.

I've seen as muckle as . . . I would not be surprised if . . .

man-muckle,   wumman-muckle grown-up.

monie a mickle maks a muckle every little helps.

muckle aboot it much the same, without change.

no mak muckle o't show little improvement in an illness, job etc.

mudge, midge *v* (cause to) move, shift.

n **1** a movement. **2** a sound, a whisper; a rumour.

mudgins movements, especially of the features, grimaces.

mudge *see* **midge.**

mug¹**, moog** N *n* a mug.

mugger a tinker.

mug² *n* (*marbles*) **1** a hole in the ground used as a target. **2** *usually* **muggie** a game played using such a target.

mug³ *n* drizzling rain, often with mist or fog NE.

v, also **muggie** drizzle NE.

muggy drizzling, wet and misty NE.

muld, meed NE *n* a mood.

mulf *see* **multh.**

mulid, meel(d) NE, **mool(d), mould** *n* **1** mould, earth etc. **2** soil, lumps of earth. **3** *usually* **mools** the grave.

v **mool, meel** NE **1** crumble (one substance with another). **2** crumble down, reduce to small pieces.

moolie a marble of burnt clay.

adj liable to crumble, crumbling.

moolin NE, **meelack(ie), mullin** a crumb, a small fragment.

mulider, mooler moulder.

muildie, moolie earthy, deep in the soil.

muin, meen NE, **min, moon** *n* **1** a moon. **2** a (lunar) month SOUTH. **3** a very long period of time. **4** a goldcrest SOUTH.

muinlicht flittin a secret removal during the night.

muir, meer NE, **mair, moor** *n* **1** a moor. **2** rough, uncultivated heathery land considered as part of an estate. **3** open ground held (usually) by a community, the common.

muirburn the controlled burning of moorland to clear the way for new growth.

muircheeper a meadow pipit.

muircock a male red grouse.

muir duck a wild duck, a mallard.
muir fowl a red grouse.
muirhen a female red grouse.
throu the muir a severe scolding.
muith, muif SHETLAND, ORKNEY, SOUTH *n* a warm moist atmosphere, oppressive humid weather, oppressive heat SHETLAND, ORKNEY.
adj, also **muithie, meefie, meichie** [-ch- as in 'dreich'] (*of the atmosphere*) oppressively close and humid.
muive, meeve NE *v, n* move.
mulberry *n* whitebeam.
mull[1] *n* (*in place-names*) a headland, promontory.
mull[2] *n* the mouth or muzzle of an animal or a person SHETLAND, ORKNEY, FIFE.
mull, mullert, mullie *see* **mill.**
mullin *see* **mulid.**
multi *n* a high-rise flat.
mummie *v* mumble.
mump *v* **1** nibble like a rabbit. **2** mumble, mutter. **3** grumble, complain. **4** sulk, mope around; loaf around.
n a word, a whisper, the merest suggestion NE.
adj depressed, sullen.
munk *see* **mink.**
munsie NE *n* **1** an odd-looking or ridiculously-dressed person. **2** the jack or knave in a set of playing cards.
mak a munsie o reduce to a ridiculous or sorry state, spoil.
munt[1]**, mount** *v* **1** mount. **2** prepare to set off; depart.

muntin(g) equipment, dress, especially a bride's trousseau.
munt[2]**, mount** *n* **1** a mount, a hill. **2** a low tree-covered hill.
mup-mup *see* **moup.**
murder *see* **murther.**
murl, mirl *v, often* **murl doon 1** crumble, ruin. **2** crumble away, moulder.
n, also **murlack** a crumb, fragment.
murlie crumbly, friable.
murlin *n* a crumb, fragment.
adj crumbling, mouldering.
murn *v* **1** mourn. **2** complain, show resentment, grumble.
murnin mourning.
mak (a) murn for lament, bewail NE.
murr *v* make a continuous murmuring sound; (*of a cat*) purr; growl NE.
murther, murder *n* murder.
v **1** murder. **2** harass, torment, distress.
murtherer murderer.
mutch *n* **1** a kind of hood usually of linen etc, worn *eg* by women by night or day, especially a close-fitting cap worn by married women. **2** an old woman.
grannie('s) mutches, grannie mutchie *see* **grannie.**
my *see* **ma.**
myang *see* **mang.**
myowt [meeowt] *n* a sound, a whisper, especially of complaint or protest NE: '*nae a myowt oot o the bairns*'.
mysel *see* **masel.**

N

na[1], **naw** *adv* no.

na[2], **nae** *adv, mainly used with verbs* not, *eg* **canna, dinnae.**

na[3], **nae, no** NE *adv* now, then: '*Let me see nae*'.

naar *see* **nar.**

nab *n* a peg or nail on which to hang things.

nabal *n* a miser.
adj grasping, mean NE.

nabb, knab *n* a hillock, summit.

nabb *see* **knab.**

nack *see* **knack.**

nacket[1] *n* a small, neat person.

nacket[2] *n* a packed lunch.

nackle *see* **knackle.**

nae[1] *adv* no, not any.
   nae gate *see* **gate.**
   nae neen not any NE.
   naethin(g) nothing.

nae[2] NE *adv* not: '*He's nae here*'.
   nae bit no more than, just.

nae[3] *adv* nay, no.

nae *see* **na**[2], **na**[3].

naesay *see* **na-say.**

naethin, naething *see* **nae**[1].

naewey *see* **wey**[1].

nag *see* **knag.**

naidder *see* **naither.**

naig *n* a horse.

nail *v* 1 clinch (an argument or bargain). 2 hit, kill.
   aff at the nail off your head, deranged.

nain *adj* (your) own.
   ma *etc* **nainsell** myself etc: '*aw by ma nainsell*'.

naipkin, neepyin *n* 1 a napkin. 2 a handkerchief; a neckerchief.

nairra, nairrae *adj* narrow.
   nairra-begaun miserly.
   nairra-boukit thin, lean.

naistie *see* **nestie.**

naither, naidder SHETLAND, N *adv, conjunction* neither.

naitherins *with another negative* either NE: '*Ah dinna like naitherins o them*'.

naitur *n* nature.

naked *see* **nakit.**

nakit, nyakit NE [neeakkit], **naked** *adj* 1 naked. 2 thin, lean. 3 (*of alcoholic drink*) neat.

name, nem, neem SHETLAND, CAITHNESS *n* a name.

namelie noted, famed.

namer, namie one of the two chief players in a children's guessing game.

name dochter, name son a girl or boy who has been called after someone.

name faither, name mither the man or woman after whom someone is named.

caw (someone) oot o his *or* **her name** call (someone) names.

in the name (o a(w))!, in the name o the wee man! exclamation of impatience.

nane, neen SHETLAND, N, **none** *pronoun* 1 none. 2 neither (of two).
adj none.
adv not at all: '*He can draw nane*'.

nap *n*: **tak the nap aff** make fun of, mock.

nap *see* **knap**[1].

naperie *n* table linen.

napple *adj* (*of ale etc*) foaming, strong.

nar, naar SHETLAND, NE *adj* 1 near or left-hand (side). 2 nearer, closer to the speaker.
adv 1 nearer, closer. 2 near, close by NE. 3 nearly, almost.
preposition close to, beside.

narrer nearer.

narrest nearest.

nar *see* **nor**[1].

narr, nyarr [neearr] NE *v* **1** (*of a dog*) snarl. **2** (*of people*) be discontented or complaining.

na-say, naesay *n* a refusal, denial.

v refuse, deny.

nash *v* hurry.

nash-gab *n* too much cheeky talk SOUTH.

natch *n* a notch.

nate *see* **neat**.

natter, nyatter NE *v* chatter, nag, grouse.

n **1** grousing, nagging talk; aimless chatter. **2** a bad-tempered, nagging person; a chatterer.

naw *see* **na**[1].

near *adv* nearly, almost: '*Ah near died laughin*'; only just.

adj closely related by blood or family ties.

v draw near (to), approach.

nearlins almost SHETLAND, NE.

near aboot(s) 1 close by. **2** almost, by and large.

near-begaun miserly.

nearby *adv* **1** close at hand. **2** nearly.

preposition near, beside.

near cut a short cut.

near hand *adv* **1** near at hand, close by. **2** almost, all but.

adj close, near, neighbouring.

preposition near, close.

near-hand cut a short cut.

as near nearly (as good), near enough.

near the bane miserly.

near the bit 1 miserly. **2** pretty well correct.

neat, nate *adj* **1** neat. **2** (*of people*) trim, smart. **3** exact, precise.

neb *n* **1** the beak of a bird. **2** a person's nose; the whole face. **3** any projecting tip or point, *eg* of a finger or toe, the tongue, a piece of land, the point of a pencil.

v **1** (*of birds*) tap with the beak. **2** put a point on (a pencil etc).

nebbie 1 biting, sharp; smart. **2** brusque, sharp in manner. **3** cheeky. **4** inquisitive.

nebfu a beakful; a small quantity, a drop.

necessar *adj* necessary.

neck *n* **1** the collar of a coat or shirt. **2** the throat, gullet.

(in) spite o yer neck in defiance of your efforts, wishes etc.

nedder *see* **nether**.

need *v, n*: **hae mair need to do** ought rather to do, would be better to.

no oot o (the) need o still in need of.

he will need to he had better.

needcessitie *n* necessity, need.

needle *v* move like a needle rapidly through, or in and out.

neem *see* **name**.

neen *see* **nane, nuin**.

neep *n* **1** a turnip; *in Scotland,* usually a swede. **2** a head. **3** a turnip watch.

v **1** feed (cattle) with turnips. **2** sow (land) with turnips.

neep-heid a stupid person.

neep lantern a turnip-lantern.

neepyin *see* **naipkin**.

Neer, Ne'erday *see* **New-year**.

neese *see* **niz**.

neet *n* a nit, the egg of a louse, now mainly a head louse.

neetie *n* a mean or disobliging person.

adj stingy.

neeze *v, n* sneeze.

neffie *see* **nevoy**.

negleck *v, n* neglect.

neibour, neiper NE, **neighbour** *n* **1** a neighbour. **2** a husband or wife, a bedfellow, partner. **3** (*of people or things*) a match, one of a set or pair.

v **neibour wi** be near; cooperate with; associate with; match, form a set with.

neibourheid 1 friendly relations between neighbours. **2** neighbourly relations within a community. **3** a neighbourhood.

neibourless (*of one of a pair*) lacking the other: '*a neibourless glove*'.

neir *n* a kidney.

neist *adj, adv, preposition* next, nearest.

nem *see* **name**.

nervish *adj* nervous, easily agitated.

nesh *adj* soft, fragile, sensitive.

ness *n* a headland.

nestle, naistle *adj* nasty.

nether, nedder SHETLAND, ORKNEY *adj* under, lower, *eg* of the lower of two farms of the same name.

nettercap, netterie *n* a spider.

nettle *n*: **on nettles** on tenterhooks, impatient, bad-tempered.

neuk *n* **1** a nook. **2** a projecting point of land, especially into the sea. **3** an angle of a building; the corner of a street. **4** an outlying or remote place.

neukit 1 having corners; crooked. **2** cantankerous NE.

the East Neuk the eastern corner of Fife.

nevel *n* a sharp blow with the fist, a punch.

v **1** punch, pummel, batter. **2** squeeze, pinch SHETLAND.

never, nivver *adv* never.

nivver a not a single.

nevoy, neffie *n* **1** a nephew. **2** a grandson, a great-grandson.

new *adv* newly, recently, just.

newlins newly, recently.

newfangle a novelty, something new.

new-farrant novel, new-fangled NE.

news *n, v* talk, conversation; gossip.

newsie gossipy, talkative.

New-year, Neer *n* **1** the New Year. **2** a gift, or a drink or food given in hospitality at the New Year.

New-year('s) day, Ne'erday [neerday], **Noor's Day 1** New Year's Day. **2** = **New-year**: '*Gie them their Ne'erday*'.

next, nixt *adj* **1** next. **2** (*with names of days or months*) the next but one: '*Friday first . . . Friday next*'.

nib *n* **1** = **neb**. **2** a nip, a prod.

nibbie a walking stick with a hooked handle SW, SOUTH.

nibble *v* fiddle with.

nicher [-ch- as in 'dreich'], **nicker** *v, n* **1** (*of horse*) snicker, neigh. **2** snigger.

nicht, night *n* night.

v **1** **be nichtit** be overtaken by night NE. **2** pass the night.

the nicht afore the morn the eve of an important occasion, *eg* one of the **Common Ridings**.

nick *n* **1** one of the notches or growth-rings on an animal's horns. **2** a narrow gap in a range of hills. **3** a broken-off piece, a scrap.

v **1** cut off; cut short. **2** catch, seize. **3** imprison. **4** cheat, trick.

nickie an oatcake or bun with an indented edge.

nick *see* **knick**.

nicker *see* **nicher**.

nickie-tams *npl* a pair of straps or pieces of string, used by farmworkers to tie their trousers below the knees, to keep the legs above their knees clean.

nickle *see* **knuckle**.

nickle naething *n* nothing, originally as used in games.

nickum *n* a scamp, a rogue, a mischievous boy.

nid nid noddin, nid noddin *present participle* nodding repeatedly, as when dozing.

nidder *see* **nither**.

nieve *n* **1** a fist. **2** **nieves** fisticuffs.

nievie-nievie-nicknack first line of a rhyme in a children's guessing game.

niggar *n* a miser.

night *see* **nicht**.

nimm *interjection* (*exclamation by or to a child*) yum-yum.

nimmie *adj* nimble.

nimp, nyim [neelmm] *n* a small bit, a little: '*jist a nimp*'.

nimsh, imsh *n* a tiny piece.

nine *numeral*: **ninesie** the ninth movement in a game of **chuckles.**

nint ninth.

ninesome a group of nine.

nineteen(t) *adj* nineteenth.

(up) to the nine(s) to perfection: '*That steak's done up to the nines*'.

nip *n* **1** sharpness of taste. **2** a fragment, a small piece, a pinch.

v **1** (*baking*) pinch dough at its edges. **2** (*especially of animals*) nibble; graze. **3** (*cause to*) tingle or smart. **4** get the better of (in bargaining), cheat sw. **5** seize, catch; snatch.

nippit 1 bad-tempered. **2** (*of clothes*) tight-fitting. **3** mean. **4** narrow-minded. **5** pinched with hunger.

nippitie quick and jerky.

nippy 1 (*of taste*) sharp: '*nippy sweetie*'; hot, spicy: '*nippy curry*'. **2** short-tempered, abrupt. **3** forward, cheeky, cunning: '*That wee lassie's right nippy*'.

nippy-sweetie *n* a sharp-tongued, bad-tempered person.

adj primly disapproving: '*She gied him a nippy-sweetie look*'.

nip-lug backbiting, squabbling.

nip-nebs Jack Frost.

nipscart a mean, stingy person.

nirlie *adj* **1** dwarfish, stunted SHETLAND, ORKNEY. **2** (*of cold*) pinching, nipping.

nit *n* a nut.

nitch *n* a notch, small cut.

nither, nidder *v* **1** pinch with cold or hunger SOUTH. **2** shrink or huddle as with cold, shiver.

nivver *see* **never.**

nixt *see* **next.**

niz NE, **neese** (*now humorous*) *n* the nose.

nizwise far-seeing, perceptive NE.

njirr *see* **nurr.**

no *adv* not.

no bad pretty good.

no cannie risky, unlucky.

no weel, nae weel ill.

no *see* **na**³.

nocht *n* nought, nothing.

adv not.

nochtie 1 (*of people*) good for nothing, insignificant. **2** (*of things*) small, worthless, unfit.

nock *see* **knock**¹.

noit *see* **knoit**².

noille *n* a canal WEST.

none *see* **nane.**

noo *adv* now.

noo(s) an than(s), noo an aan NE now and then, from time to time NE.

noonal well then!, now then!, really!

the noo just now; just a moment ago; in a moment, soon.

noop *n* a cloudberry N, SOUTH.

Noor's Day *see* **New-year.**

noose, noozle *see* **knuse.**

nor¹, **nar** NE, SOUTH *conjunction* **1** nor. **2** than: '*better nor that*'. **3** that . . . not, (but) that NE: '*Nae wonder nor you're thin*'.

nor² *conjunction* **1** used to emphasize negative answers: '*Is it sore?*' '*No, nor sore*'. **2** followed by another negative: '*Ye nor me havena been there*'.

nor- *see* **north.**

norie *n* a puffin SHETLAND.

norlan, norland *see* **north.**

Norn *n, adj* (of) the Norse language formerly spoken in Shetland and Orkney, now surviving only in their dialect.

Norroway *n* Norway SHETLAND, ORKNEY, NE.

norter *n* **1** nurture. **2** rigorous discipline, rough treatment NE.

v **1** nurture. **2** discipline, punish NE.

north, nor- *n* **1** the north. **2** the north and north-east of Scotland.

northart northward, to the north SHETLAND, ORKNEY, NE.

northlins towards the north, in a northerly direction.

norlan(d) (*a person from*) the north or north-east of Scotland.

note *n* a one-pound banknote.

notice *v* heed, watch; tend, see to SHETLAND, ORKNEY, NE.
n care, attentive help SHETLAND, NE.

notion *n*: **a notion o** a liking or affection for (a person).

novelle [novel] *n* a novel.

nowt[1] *n* **1** cattle. **2** an ox NE. **3** a big, clumsy person, a blockhead.
nowt beast a cow, bull, calf, ox NE.

nowt[2] *n* **1** nought, nothing SOUTH. **2** **nowts** (*marbles*) a shout by an opponent preventing the player from firing from any spot he or she chooses SW, SOUTH.

nowther *adj, pronoun* neither.
nowther nor neither.

nozzle *see* **knuse.**

nuin, neen N *n* noon.

nummer *n, v* number.

numptie *n* an idiot, stupid person.

nurr, njirr [neeirr] SHETLAND, ORKNEY, CAITHNESS *v* **1** growl like an angry dog, snarl like a cat. **2** (*of a cat*) purr.
n the growl of an angry dog.

nurrin growling, snarling; fault-finding.

nyaff [neeaff] *v* **1** (*of a small dog*) yelp, yap. **2** talk senselessly or irritatingly.
n **1** a small, puny, unimportant person; a small, conceited, impudent person. **2** a worthless person: '*She's gaun oot wi a wee nyaff*'.

nyakit *see* **nakit.**

nyarb [neearb] *v* be discontented or complaining NE.

nyarr *see* **narr.**

nyatter *see* **natter.**

nyim *see* **nimp.**

O

o *preposition* of; about.

O *see* **ordinar.**

oam, yoam *n* **1** steam. **2** a warm smell, *eg* from cooking. **3** a warm stuffy atmosphere.

oan *see* **on.**

oar *v* row (a boat).

oarie boat a rowing boat.

obleege *v* oblige.

obleegement, obligement an act of kindness, a favour.

observe *n* an observation; a remark, comment.

och! *interjection* expression of sorrow, pain, regret, or of annoyance, weariness etc.

och aye yes indeed.

ocht[1], **owt** *n* aught, anything; nothing: '*It cost ocht*'.

ocht[2] *v* ought.

o'er *see* **ower.**

o'ercome *see* **owercome.**

off *see* **aff.**

offer *v* threaten; make as if (to . . .); try: '*If he offers tae fight — hit him!*'.

old *see* **auld.**

on, oan *preposition* **1** about, concerning: '*Dae ye mind on that man?*'. **2** supported by, with: '*gae on a stick*'. **3** to: **cry** *etc* **on** attract the attention of (someone) by calling out: '*That's yer mither shoutin on ye*'. **4** for: '*Wait on me!*'.

on aboot talking about, harping on: '*Whit's she on aboot?*'.

on for, on wi eager for.

on *see* **yon.**

oncairrie *n* a fuss, carry-on.

oncome *n* **1** the beginning of something; progress in something. **2** a heavy fall of rain or snow. **3** a sharp attack of illness SOUTH.

onding *n* **1** a heavy continuous fall of rain or snow. **2** an attack, outburst.

onfa *see* **onfaw.**

onfaw, onfa *n* **1** a heavy fall of rain or snow. **2** an attack of a disease. **3** a beginning.

ongaeins, ongauns *npl* goings-on, (wild or rowdy) behaviour: '*Whit an ongauns in the close last night!*'.

ongang *n* **1** the setting in motion of machinery, especially a mill NE. **2** rowdy behaviour NE.

ongauns *see* **ongaeins.**

onie *adj, adv* **1** any. **2** in any way, at all: '*Can ye fish onie?*'.

oniebodie, emdy anybody.

oniewey(s), onie road anyway; anywhere.

onless *see* **unless.**

oo[1], **ool, woo** *n* **1** wool. **2** oos, oose, ooze woollen fluff, dust; fluff from cotton etc.

oosie, oossie, oozie fluffy, dusty; furry; having a good nap or pile.

oother, ooder fluff from wool, cotton etc when it begins to fray.

a(w) ae oo all one wool; all the same; equal.

oo[2] *n*: **caller oo** (*in street cries*) fresh oysters.

oo *see* **us.**

oobit *n*: **hairy oobit** a hairy caterpillar.

ooder *see* **oo**[1].

oof[1] *n* a wolf.

oof[2] *n* a small unimportant creature; a stupid fool, idiot.

oogile *see* **ugly.**

ook SHETLAND, NE, **wick** NE *n* a week.

ool *n* an owl.

v **1** treat harshly, bully; wreck the health of. **2** feel low or depressed.

ool *see* **oo**[1].

oolet n an owl.

oople stiffle, oopsie doople see **up**.

oor[1] n an hour.

oor[2]**, wir, wur, weer** NE adj our.

oor ane, oor yin my wife; my husband.

oorich, oorichie see **oorie**.

oorie, oorich(ie) adj **1** dismal, gloomy, miserable-looking from cold, illness etc; (of weather) dull and chilly, raw. **2** uncanny, strange: 'It's oorie in a graveyaird at nicht'.

oorlich miserable-looking from cold, hunger or illness; damp, raw, bleak; (of things) sad and depressing, eerie.

oorit adj cold, shivery; tired or ill-looking.

oorlich see **oorie**.

oos, oose, oossie see **oo**[1].

oot, out adv **1** out.

2 (of a cup etc) emptied: 'Is yer cup oot?'.

3 (of a gathering of people etc) away and out of the building; (of the meeting itself) over, finished: 'The scuil was oot'.

4 (especially of your age) fully, quite NE: 'I'm fifty oot'.

preposition **1** out of, from.

2 along, up (a road) in an outward direction away from the speaker: 'oot the wey homeward'.

adj **1** out, outlying etc: 'the oot glens'. **2** (working) out of doors or in the fields, eg **ootwork(er), oot-girl**.

oot aboot out of doors, out in the garden or fields, quite far from your home.

oot at out of, from (a door, window etc).

oot on, ooten out of, outside.

oot o out of, from out of, beyond.

oot ower preposition **1** (of motion) outwards and over; over the top of; over to the other side of; across; out of.

2 (of position) above, over, on top of; bent over (a drink, task etc); on the other side of, on either side of.

adv **1** at a distance; aside; apart. **2** out of bed, up.

oot ower the door out of doors.

oots an ins ins and outs, details (of something).

ootby adv **1** outwards; out and a little way off; away from the shore, out at sea. **2** out of doors, outside, out in the fields. **3** away from home, not near. **4** in the outer part of a room, away from the fire.

adj outlying, out of the way, distant, away from the main or central part, eg from a farm's main buildings.

ootcast n a quarrel.

ootcome n **1** the result, effect. **2** produce, product; profit.

ootgan see **ootgane**.

ootgane adj (of a time or age) past, fully: 'a laddie, no twenty-twae ootgane'.

ootga(u)n, outgoing adj **1** (of a tenant) outgoing, removing, leaving. **2** (of the tide) ebbing.

ootgang n **1** an outgoing, departure. **2** expense, outlay.

ootgate n a way out.

ootgaun see **ootgane**.

oother see **oo**[1].

ootland, ootlin n an outsider, stranger, outcast.

ootlay v (of a hen) lay away from the regular nest.

ootlin see **ootland**.

ootmaist adj furthest away.

ootrel, outeral n a person from a different place or family; a stranger, incomer.

ootset n an ornament.

oot-stair n an outside stair on a house up to an upper flat.

ootwith see **outwith**.

ooze, oozie see **oo**[1].

open, apen adj **1** open. **2** free (to do . . .).

n an opening, gap, space.

or preposition **1** before. **2** until.

conjunction **1** before; until. **2** sooner than, rather than.

oranger *n* an orange.

ordain *see* **ordeen.**

ordeen, ordain *v* **1** ordain. **2 ordain** (*Presbyterian churches*) admit (an **elder** or deacon) to office.

orders *npl* your gear, all that you need for some purpose: '*aw yer orders*'.

ordinar, ordnar, ordinary *adj* **1** ordinary.

2 ordinary (*Scottish universities*) in the Faculties of Arts and Science, of the general courses in any particular subject, passes in a certain number of which lead either to an **Ordinary Degree** or to the higher classes of an Honours course; *also* **Ordinary Degree** an academic degree gained by a number of passes in **ordinary** courses.

3 (*up until the late 1980s*) **Ordinary, O** (*secondary education*) at a less advanced level, of a state examination, the course leading to it or the certificate awarded to successful candidates; **O (Grade)** one of these examinations, courses or certificates.

n **1** ordinary.

2 the usual state of things; what is normal or usual to a person etc: '*He's in his ordinar*'.

for ordinar usually, as a rule.

nae ordinar unusual(ly), extraordinar(il)y: '*There was a fuss nae ordinar*'.

orp *v* grumble, complain.

orra *adj* **1** spare, unemployed; (*of one of a pair*) without a partner; unmatched, odd; extra. **2** occasional, appearing here and there; (*of a job*) casual, unskilled; (*of a person or animal*) doing casual or unskilled work: '*orra baist*'. **3** miscellaneous, odd. **4** strange, uncommon. **5** worthless, shabby, disreputable.

n what is left over; an article not in use; **orras** odds and ends.

orral a scrap, fragment; **orrals** bits and pieces, odds and ends; leftovers.

orraman, orra loon NE a person who does odd jobs, especially on a farm.

ort *n, usually* **orts** what is useless and has been thrown away; leavings, leftovers.

v throw away; refuse; use wastefully.

other *see* **ither.**

out *see* **oot.**

outeral *see* **ootrel.**

outgoing *see* **ootgane.**

outwith, ootwith *preposition* outside, out of, beyond; out of the control of; away from: '*outwith the city boundary*'.

adv outside, out of doors, outwards.

ovven *see* **une.**

over[1] *numeral* (*children's rhymes*) a numeral, *probably* eight.

over[2] *adj* upper, higher, especially in place-names, *eg* the upper or higher of two farms of the same name.

over *see* **ower.**

overhead *see* **owerheid.**

owdience *n* an audience SHETLAND, NE.

owe *see* **awe.**

ower, o'er, over *preposition* **1** over. **2** (down) from, out of, out at (a door, window etc). **3** showing position or direction, *eg* **ower abuin** over there above. **4** (*of time*) well on, late. **5** off to sleep.

owerance control.

owerlie, overly *adv* **1** carelessly, in a casual way, by chance. **2** too (much). *adj* **1** superficial, casual, careless. **2** excessive, exaggerated; unusual.

ower a(w) **1** all over, everywhere. **2** above all else, most of all.

ower the heid o in spite of, without the permission of.

owerby *adv* over, across at or to a place (at a distance from the speaker), over there.

owercome, o'ercome *n* **1** a sudden

attack of illness. **2** a refrain (of a song), a chorus; a phrase or a saying which is often repeated.

owerend *v* turn up, set on end, tip up; turn topsy-turvy.

owergae *v* **1** overflow, cover over (with weeds, dirt etc). **2** overpower, get the better of. **3** (*of time*) pass.

owerheld, overhead *adv* **1** at an average rate per item; overall. **2** in confusion; untidily SHETLAND, NE.

owerset *v* translate.

owertaen *adj* made helpless, overcome, stupefied, especially by drink.

owerturn *n* **1** a chorus of a song; a repetition of a story. **2** (*in a business*) turnover.

owerword *n* a chorus of a poem or song; a repeated saying.

owl, owld *see* **auld.**

own *see* **awn.**

owsen *npl* oxen NE.

owt *see* **ocht**[1].

owthor *n* an author.

oxter *n* **1** the armpit; the under part of the (upper) arm. **2** the corresponding part of an animal, the underside of its shoulder. **3** the corresponding part of a garment; the armhole.

v **1** take, lead, support by the arm. **2** hold, carry under the arm. **3** cuddle, embrace. **4** elbow, shove, jostle.

under yer oxter under your arm, in your armpit.

P

Pace *n* Easter.
  Pace Egg Day Easter Monday.
  Pace Day Easter Sunday SHETLAND, ORKNEY, NE.
pack *adj* on close and friendly terms WEST, SOUTH, ULSTER.
packman *n* a travelling merchant, a pedlar.
pad *n* **1** a footpath, a narrow, unsurfaced track or way. **2** a pass through hills etc.
  v travel on foot, trot along steadily.
paddle, paddock *see* **puddock**.
Paddy *n*: **Paddy's Market 1** a street market in Glasgow (originally much used by the Irish). **2** any confused scene, an untidy room etc.
  Paddy's Milestone name for Ailsa Craig, a rocky island in the Firth of Clyde.
paewae *adj* pale, sickly, drooping.
paice *see* **peace**.
paidle[1] *v* **1** paddle. **2** move with short quick steps, toddle. **3** press or beat with the feet, trample.
paidle[2] *n* a long-handled tool for weeding, scraping earth etc; a hoe.
  v scrape (floors etc) clean; use a hoe.
paidle[3] *n* a lumpfish.
paik *v* **1** beat, thrash, punish. **2** trudge, tramp along.
  n **1** a blow, stroke, thump. **2 get yer paiks** get the punishment you deserve.
painch *n* **1** a paunch. **2 painches** the bowels or guts of a person or animal.
paint *see* **pent**.
paip *n* **1** the stone or kernel of a fruit; a dried cherrystone used as a counter in children's games. **2 the paips** a game played with cherrystones as counters and stakes.

pair, perr *n* **1** a pair. **2** a set, not limited to two, of related objects, *eg* **pair o bagpipes, pair o beads, pair o cairds**. **3** a single object viewed as a collection *eg* **pair of blankets** one large blanket used folded in two.
paircel, parcel *n* **1** a parcel. **2** a small company; a group, herd, flock.
pairish *n* a parish.
pairk *see* **park**.
pairt, part *n* **1** a part. **2** a place, neighbourhood SHETLAND, ORKNEY, NE.
  v **1** part. **2** divide into parts, share.
  pairt wi bairn give birth to a premature or stillborn baby; suffer a miscarriage.
pairtie, pertie *n* a party.
pairtner, pertner *n* a partner.
pairtrick *see* **paitrick**.
Paisley *n* with reference to the thread and textile industries of Paisley, the town near Glasgow, or shawls of the **Paisley pattern**; the pattern itself or any fabric bearing it.
  Paisley buddie a native of Paisley.
  Paisley pattern a colourful pattern based on Hindu and Arabic designs, originally used in the **Paisley shawl**.
  Paisley screwdriver (*humorous*) a hammer WEST.
  Paisley shawl a shawl of the **Paisley pattern** made of cashmere and wool or silk, or cotton and wool, very popular in the 19th century.
paitrick, pairtrick *n* a partridge.
paittern, pattren *n* a pattern.
palaiver *see* **palaver**.
palaver, palaiver *n* **1** a palaver. **2** a fuss. **3** a fussy person.
  v behave in a silly way, fiddle about; waste time.

pale *n* a small shovel or scoop for taking samples of food, especially cheese.

pale ale, India Pale Ale *n* a kind of beer less strong than **heavy**.

palie *adj* **1** thin, pale and sickly-looking, listless. **2** stunted, underdeveloped, delicate. **3** deformed, lame; paralysed.

pall *n* a pole, a strong post, especially a mooring post.

v **1** puzzle; surprise; frustrate SHETLAND, ORKNEY, NE. **2** go beyond, beat SHETLAND, NE: '*That palls aa*'.

pallall, pallie *n* **1** *also* **pallalls** the game of hopscotch. **2** the counter with which it is played.

pallo *see* **pellock**.

palmie, pawmie *n* a hit with a **tawse** or cane on the palm of the hand.

pan *n* the skull, the cranium.

v (*of soil*) become solid so that rain does not flow through.

pan breid bread baked in a pan or tin.

pancake a small, round, flat cake, made by dropping thick batter onto a **girdle**, frying pan etc, smaller and thicker than an English pancake, usually eaten cold with butter, jam etc.

pan drop a round peppermint **sweetie**, a mint imperial.

pan-jotral(s) (a dish made from) odds and ends of food.

pan loaf 1 a loaf with a smooth crust, baked in a pan or tin. **2** an affected way of speaking to impress others.

knock yer pan in work very hard, exert yourself to the point of exhaustion.

pandle *n* a hit with a cane or **tawse** on the palm of the hand.

panel *n* (*law*) a prisoner at the bar, the accused.

pang *v* **1** pack tight, cram full. **2** cram (the stomach) with food.

pani *n* water; rain *gipsy* SOUTH.

panshit *n* a state of excitement, panic, muddle NE.

pant *n* a piece of fun, a prank.

pap[1] *n* **1** the uvula: '*pap o the hause*'. **2** a conical hill. **3** one of the segments of an orange. **4** a sea anemone.

pap[2]**, pop** *v* **1** pop. **2** touch or strike lightly and smartly. **3** beat, thrash. **4** aim, throw, shoot; strike with a missile.

pape *n* **1** the pope. **2** contemptuous term for a Roman Catholic CENTRAL, ULSTER.

papple, popple *v* **1** flow, bubble up. **2** (*of fat*) sizzle, sputter.

parade *see* **parawd**.

parawd, parade *n* **1** a parade. **2** a procession, march.

parcel *see* **paircel**.

Paris bun *n* a sweet, sugar-topped, sponge-like bun.

park, perk, pairk *n* **1** a park. **2** an area of enclosed farmground, a field.

parkie child's word for a park-keeper or attendant.

parkin, perkin *n* a hard, round, spiced biscuit.

parlie *n* (*games*) a truce, a respite.

parr *n* a young salmon with dark stripes on its side before the **smolt** stage.

parrafin *n* an outfit, get-up.

parritch *n* porridge.

as plain as parritch as clear as crystal.

auld claes an parritch your usual daily routine, the daily grind: '*It's back tae auld claes an parritch the morn*'.

save yer breath tae cool yer parritch save your breath; hold your tongue.

parry *v* **1** waste time, dawdle or delay in order to avoid action. **2 parry wi** meddle with, have dealings with.

part *see* **pairt**.

partan *n* **1** the common edible crab. **2** an ugly, bad-tempered or stupid person.

parteecular, parteeclar, particular

adj **1** private, confidential. **2** clean, hygienic, especially in cooking.
adv particularly.

pass *n* **1** a pace, a step. **2** a lane between factory machines or between pews in a church.

past *adv* on one side, out of the way; over, done with.
adj **1** (*after a date etc*) last: '*I hivna seen him this year past*'. **2** having reached a specified age on your last birthday: '*Wee Bob's nine past*'.

lay past, pit past, set past put away, set aside for later use.

no (be able to) see past someone be obsessed with someone's virtues or merits: '*She cannae see past her boss*'.

past aw unspeakable, beyond belief, into!erable.

pat, pot *n* **1** a pot. **2** hopscotch NE. **3** *also* **pottle** a clay or earthenware marble NE.

pottit heid, pottit hoch a dish made of meat from the head or shin of a cow or pig, boiled, shredded and served cold in a jelly made from the stock.

pat *see* **pit**.

path *see* **peth**.

pattren *see* **paittern**.

pauchle, pochle *n* **1** a bundle, a small load. **2** something taken by an employee from his or her employer without permission. **3** a swindle, a piece of trickery, a fiddle.
v **1** be guilty of a minor dishonesty, cheat. **2** steal. **3** shuffle (playing cards).

pavey-waveys *n* a girls' skipping game in which the rope is made to wave.

paw *n* pa, dad.

pawkie[1] *adj* **1** having a matter-of-fact, humorously critical outlook on life, with a sly, quiet wit. **2** roguish; lively, merry. **3** cunning and stubborn; astute.

pawkie[2] *n* a mitten.

pawmie *see* **palmie**.

pawnd *n* **1** a pawn, a pledge. **2** a pawnshop: '*Tak it tae the pawnd*'.

pawpie *n* child's word for grandfather.

pawt *v* strike the ground with the foot, stamp in rage; (*of a horse etc*) paw (the ground).

pay *see* **pey**.

peace, paice *n* **1** peace. **2** *in phrases eg* **I wish tae peace** I wish to God; **surely tae peace** surely to God.

bide at peace! (*to a child*) sit still!, don't fidget!

gie me peace! leave me alone!, don't disturb me!

pearl *n* purl, a stitch in knitting.

pease, piz(z) *n* peas: '*pease brose*'.

pizzer a pea NE.

peasie a small marble.

peat *n* **1** peat; a piece of this dried for fuel. **2 the peats** the work of digging and preparing peat for fuel.

peat hag a hole or pit left in an old peat-working.

pech *v* **1** puff, pant, gasp for breath. **2** move or work so as to pant or gasp with the effort.
3 breathe slowly, sigh, groan.
n **1** a pant, gasp; your breath.
2 an asthmatic wheeze, a breathless cough.
3 a sigh of weariness, relief, satisfaction etc.

pechie short-winded, asthmatic, wheezy.

pecht out of breath.

a sair pech a weary effort, an exhausting struggle.

pecht *see* **pict**.

pee-the-bed *n* a dandelion.

peedie *see* **peerie**.

peek[1] *n* the cry of a small animal or bird, a piping noise, a cheep.
v **1** cheep, chirp, cry feebly. **2** complain, whimper NE.

peek[2] *n* a tiny point of light, a little tongue of flame.

peel[1] *v* skin (your leg, arm etc), usually by accident.

peeler a small crab at shell-casting time.

peel[2] *v* equal, match; (*in curling, bowls etc*) tie, have equal scores.

stan(d) peels have equal scores.

peel[3] *n* (*in past times*) a stockade; the ground enclosed by it; fortified house or small defensive tower.

peel[4] *n* a pill, a tablet.

peel *see* **pull**.

peelie *adj*: **peelie-wallie** sickly, feeble, thin and ill-looking.

poelie-wersh sickly, delicate; insipid SOUTH.

peen[1], **pin** *n* **1** a pin. See also **praen**. **2** (*in past times*) a kind of door-knocker consisting of a ring rattled up and down a serrated rod. **3** a small, neat person or animal. **4** a mood, frame of mind: '*in an angry pin*'.

v **1** pin. **2** strike with a small missile; pelt. **3** move quickly ORKNEY, N.

peen-held 1 the young fry of the minnow or stickleback. **2** a stupid person.

pinheld (oat)meal coarsely ground oatmeal.

pin-leg a wooden leg.

full pin at full speed.

peen[2] *n* a pane, a sheet of glass NE.

peen[3] *n* a sloping point at the end of a roof.

peenge *v* **1** whine, complain, whimper. **2** droop, mope, look cold and miserable.

n a feeble, sickly-looking person; a fretful child.

peengie, peeng(e)in 1 bad-tempered, moaning. **2** sickly-looking, puny.

peenie *n* **1** a pinafore, especially one worn by children; an apron. **2** (*child's word*) the tummy.

peeoy *n* a schoolchild's home-made firework.

peep *n* a small flame from a gas-cooker jet.

pit someone's gas at a peep put someone in his or her place.

peer, perr WEST *n* a pear.

peerie 1 a child's spinning top. **2** a fir cone. **3** a small stone marble NE.

peerie-heel a high, sharply-pointed heel of a shoe, a stiletto heel.

peerie-heidit in a state of mental confusion.

peer *see* **pulr**.

peerie SHETLAND, **peedie** ORKNEY, CAITHNESS, FIFE *adj* small, little, tiny.

peerie-weerie *adj* = **peerie**.

n a tiny creature.

peerie-winkie (*in nursery rhymes*) the little finger or toe.

peerle *see* **peer**.

peesie *adj* (*slang and child's word*) excellent.

peesie *see* **peesweep**.

peesweep, peewee, peeweet, peesie *n* a lapwing.

peesie-weesie sharp-featured; shrill-voiced, complaining.

peety, pity *n, v* pity.

it's a peety o 1 it's a pity about. **2** it's a bad lookout for (you); it serves (you) right.

peety me! exclamation of surprise, disgust etc.

peever[1] *n* **1** the flat stone used in the game of hopscotch. **2** **peever(s)** the game itself.

peever(ie) beds the chalked square on which the game is played.

peever[2] *n* a very small marble.

peewee, peeweet *see* **peesweep**.

pellock, pallo ORKNEY *n* **1** a porpoise. **2** something bulky and clumsy; a short fat person.

pen *n* a pointed conical hill SOUTH: '*Ettrick Pen*'.

pen *see* **pend**.

pend, pen(n) *n* **1** an arch (of a bridge, gateway etc). **2** an arched passageway or **entry,** especially one leading into the back-court of a block of houses. **3** a covered drain or sewer; the grating over it.

penny *n* money: '*a bonnie penny*'.

penny-book(ie), penny-buff a child's first school book; *hence* the first class in a school.

penny wedding (*in past times*) a wedding at which guests contributed a small sum of money (for food and drink) towards the cost, the surplus being given to the couple as a gift.

a bonnie penny a considerable sum of money.

pent, paint *v* paint.

n **1** paint. **2** the painted woodwork of a room or building, the paintwork.

penurious, perneurious NE *adj* **1** bad-tempered, whining NE. **2** attentive to detail NE.

perfit *adj* perfect.

perish *v* squander (money), wreck (a ship etc); finish (food or drink).

perisht (wi cauld) feeling very cold.

perjink *adj* **1** trim, neat, smart in appearance. **2** prim, strait-laced. **3** exact, precise, fussy.

perk *n* a pole, or rod, especially one projecting from a wall or window on which clothes were hung to dry; latterly, an indoor drying rail or rope.

perk *see* **park.**

perkin *see* **parkin.**

perlaig *n* trash, rubbish, rubbishy food NE.

perlicket *n* a trace, scrap NE.

perneurious *see* **penurious.**

pernicketie *adj* **1** very precise, obsessed by detail, fussy. **2** cantankerous, touchy, bad-tempered. **3** (*of things*) requiring close attention or great care, fiddling, troublesome.

perr *see* **pair, peer.**

pertle *see* **pairtle.**

pertner *see* **pairtner.**

pest *v* pester.

pet, pet day *n* a day of sunshine in a spell of bad weather.

pet *see* **pit.**

peter *n*: **come the peter ower** act in a domineering way over, dictate to.

pit the peter on put a firm and sudden stop to.

Peter *n*: **peter(ie)-dick, peter(-a)-dick** a rhythmic pattern of two or three short beats followed by one long, *eg* in a dance step.

Peter's thoom, Peter's mark one of the black marks behind the gills of a haddock.

peth, path *n* **1** a cleft on a steep hill; a steep track into a ravine and up the other side. **2** a path.

petticoat tails *npl* triangular shortbread biscuits.

pettit lip *n* a sulky expression: '*hing the pettit lip*'.

pettle *v* pet, pamper, stroke SOUTH.

peuch, pyoch [peeoch, peeoach] *interjection, n* **1** (*imitating the sound of the wind etc*) puff! **2** (*expressing impatience, disgust, disbelief etc*) pooh! **3** a light blast of air, a puff of wind or breath.

peuchle, pyocher **1** fuss about or work ineffectually. **2** cough in a choking, asthmatic way.

peuther *v* fuss about doing nothing.

pewl *v* **1** whine, complain, pule. **2** (*of animals*) be in a weak state; (*of people*) be half-alive, scrape a bare living.

n **1** a wailing cry; a moan. **2** a seagull.

pey [rhymes with 'gey'], **pay** *v* **1** pay. **2** beat, punish: '*Ah'll pey ye*'. **3** pay for: '*It'll help tae pey the coal*'.

n **1** pay. **2** a blow, punishment.

pey aff pay for others' drink etc.

pey someone's dock spank, smack.

photie *n* a photograph.

phrase, fra(i)se *n* **1** an elaborate, flowery speech, flattery. **2** something false and misleading.

v **1** phrase. **2** flatter, praise, often insincerely NE.

phrasie, fraisie **1** gushing. **2** too fussy.

pibroch [peebroch] *n* the music of the Scottish bagpipes, now limited to traditional marches, salutes, laments etc; a piece of this, consisting of a theme and a series of variations.

piccatarrie *see* **pictarnie.**

picher [-ch- as in 'dreich'] *n* **1** a state of confusion or muddle. **2** a useless person, a person who is usually in a flap.

v work in a disorganized way, muddle along.

pick[1] *v* **1** be a petty thief, pilfer. **2** question (someone), pick someone's brains.

n **1** a pecking; (a quantity of) food. **2** a small quantity.

pick-thank *n* a person who seeks favour, a sneak.

adj ungrateful, unappreciative.

pick someone up get someone's meaning.

pick[2] *v* **1** throw, hurl, drive. **2** **pick on** pitch on, choose.

n a marble, thrown instead of being rolled NE.

pick[3] *n*: **hae a pick at** have a dislike for, bear (someone) a grudge.

pick[4] *n* a spade in playing cards NE.

pickie *n* a children's chasing game: '*high pickie*'; '*green pickie*' SHET- LAND, ORKNEY.

pickit *adj* roughened, pitted, uneven.

pickle, puckle *n* **1** a small amount, a little, a few. **2** a grain of oats, barley or wheat. **3** a small particle or grain; a speck.

pickman *n* a miner.

pickmaw *n* a black-headed gull.

pict, pecht *n* **1** **Pict** one of an ancient people who inhabited parts of Scot- land. **2** contemptuous term for a small undersized person.

pictarnie, piccatarrie *n* **1** a common or arctic tern. **2** a black-headed gull. **3** a thin wretched-looking person; a bad-tempered person.

picter *n* a picture.

pie *v* peer closely, squint.

pie-eyed cross-eyed, drunk.

piece *n* **1** a piece of food, a snack, now usually a piece of bread, scone etc with butter, jam etc. **2** **the piece** each: '*20p the piece*'. **3** **a piece** a little, rather. **4** a short distance.

piece box a box for a (lunchtime) snack.

piece denner a lunchtime snack of sandwiches etc.

piece poke the bag in which a snack is carried.

piece-time, piecie-time NE a break for a meal or snack.

pig *n* **1** a(n earthenware) container, a pot, jar. **2** an earthenware moneybox, now sometimes shaped like the ani- mal. **3** an earthenware hot-water bot- tle. **4** earthenware as a material; a piece of this.

tae pigs an whustles to pieces, to ruin.

pike *n* **1** a pointed tip or end; a spike. **2** a thorn or prickle on a plant; a spine or quill of an animal.

v **1** steal, pilfer. **2** make thin, reduce to skin and bone. **3** nibble, pick (at food). **4** provide with a pointed end.

pikie spiked, jagged, barbed.

pikit weer barbed wire NE.

pile[1] *n* a snowflake.

pile[2] *v* increase the speed of a swing, scooter etc by moving the body or feet.

piler a child's home-made cart moved this way.

pilk *v* **1** pick out, shell, peel. **2** pilfer, steal.

pillan *see* **piller.**

piller, pillan *n* a small crab at the shell-casting stage, useful for bait.

pin *see* **peen**[1].

pinch *v* **1** spend or give meanly, stint. **2** move (a heavy object) by levering.

n a crowbar.

pincher 1 pinchers tweezers, pliers etc. **2** a crowbar.

pine *n* suffering, distress, pain SHET- LAND, NE.

v waste away from disease.

pingle *v* **1** struggle, exert yourself, work hard. **2** dabble or meddle (with), work in a lazy way.
n **1** a contest, disagreement. **2** an effort, struggle.

pink[1], **pinkie** *n* a primrose.

pink[2] *v* **1** drip (with a sharp, tinkling sound). **2** strike making a tiny sharp sound, a ping.

pinkie *n* **1** the little finger. **2** something very small.

pinkie *see* **pink**[1].

pint, point *n* **1** a point. **2** a tagged length of cord etc, *eg* a shoe- or bootlace.
v point.

pintit, pointit precise, (over-)attentive to detail, exact.

pintle *n* the penis.

pipe *n* **1** *also* **the pipes** the Scottish bagpipe(s). **2** a large ripe acorn with its stalk SE.
v pipe; play (a tune) on the bagpipes.

piper 1 a piper, especially one who plays the bagpipes. **2** an unsplit, half-dried haddock NE.

piper's biddin a last-minute invitation.

piper's news out-of-date news.

pipe band a band made up of **pipers** and drummers with a drum-major.

pipe major, pipie (*informal*) the leader of a **pipe band**; as a military title, the equivalent of the regimental bandmaster in an English regiment.

pirl, purl *v* **1** twist, twirl, coil, curl; roll, whirl.
2 (*in football etc*) drive (the ball) with quick light strokes or kicks NE.
3 spin, whirl round, swirl.
4 fumble.
5 move or work idly or half-heartedly.
n **1** a curl, twist, coil. **2** a knot of hair, a bun. **3** a swirl, a ripple, gentle breeze.

pirlie *adj* curly, curled, twisted SOUTH.
n something very small.

pirlie pig a circular, earthenware moneybox.

pirn *n* **1** a small spool, a reel of or for thread. **2** (*weaving*) a spool for holding the weft yarn in the shuttle, a bobbin. **3** the reel of a fishing rod.

pirr[1] *n* a tern.

pirr-maw a black-headed gull.

pirr[2] *n* **1** a sudden sharp breeze; a gentle breath of wind SHETLAND, NE. **2** a sudden burst of activity; a panic, rage.
v **1** (*of liquid*) ripple; flow, stream. **2** tremble with anger, fizz with rage.

pirrie unpredictable, unreliable; quick-tempered.

pirr-maw *see* **pirr**[1].

pish *v* **1** piss. **2** gush, rush, splash.

pish-minnie SW, SOUTH, **pismire** an ant.

pish-the-bed a dandelion.

Piskie *n* informal name for a member of the Scottish Episcopal Church.

pismire *see* **pish**.

piss *n* a call to a cat or kitten.

pit, put, pet *v, past tense also* **pit, pat;** *past participle also* **pit, pitten, putten 1** put. **2** *used where English has* send, make, take etc: '*Ah wis juist pittin aff ma claes*'.

pit aff waste time.

pit awa 1 dismiss, sack. **2** bury. **3 pit yersel awa** commit suicide.

pit by 1 put by, set aside. **2** complete; spend time, stay. **3** make do with, tide (yourself) over with.

pit on impress, impose on, fool.

pit-on insincerity, pretence.

pitten-on affected, conceited, insincere.

weel pit(ten)-on finely dressed.

pit-past a hasty meal, a quick meal.

pit tae close (a door) (without locking).

pitawtie, potato *n* a potato.

pitawtie bogle a scarecrow.

potato scone = tattie scone.

pitcher *n* **1** the flat stone etc used in the

game of hopscotch; the game itself. **2** a marble which is thrown rather than rolled NE.

pitten *see* **pit.**

pity *see* **peety.**

piz *see* **pease.**

pizen *see* **pooshion.**

pizz *see* **pease.**

plack *n* **1** money, cash; your worldly wealth. **2** (*in past times*) a small coin.

plackless hard-up.

no worth a plack worth nothing.

plaid *n* a length of (tartan) woollen cloth, formerly worn as an outer garment, now part of the ceremonial dress of members of **pipe bands.**

plain *adj* (*of ground*) without hills, water etc; open; (*of any surface*) flat, level.

plainie (*games*) a movement in its simplest form, before variations etc are introduced.

plain breid bread baked as a **plain loaf.**

plain loaf a flat-sided white loaf with a hard black crust on top and a brown crust at the bottom, a batch loaf.

plainstanes a pavement; a paved area surrounding a town's market or **toon hoose.**

plaister, plaster *n* **1** plaster. **2** a person who thrusts himself on the attention or company of others, a flatterer. **3** a mess, a shambles.

v make a mess, work unsystematically.

plait *see* **plet.**

plane *n* a sycamore.

plank *v* **1** set down, place (decisively, with a thump). **2** put in a secret place, hide for later use.

n a hoard (for later use).

plapper NE *v* **1** (*of a liquid*) bubble and plop when boiling. **2** splash about in water.

plash *n* **1** a splash. **2** a sudden sharp downpour of rain; a heavy shower. **3** a weak tasteless liquid or drink; a large quantity of a liquid.

v **1** splash, squelch; (*of rain etc*) fall in torrents, lash. **2** splash with liquid, wet, drench. **3** walk on waterlogged ground, squelch along.

plashie 1 causing splashes; waterlogged, soaking wet. **2** rainy, showery.

plaster *see* **plaister.**

plat, plet *adj* **1** flat, level, even. **2** direct, clear, downright.

adv **1** flat; flat on the ground. **2** straight; directly.

n, also **plettie** DUNDEE a landing (on a stair).

platch[1] *n* **1** a splashing, stamping in water or mud; a splash of mud etc. **2** a large spot, a patch.

v **1** splash, cover with mud. **2** go about or work in a sloppy way, potter.

platchie wet, muddy.

platchin soaking SOUTH.

platch[2] *v* walk in an awkward flat-footed or heavy clumsy way.

play *v* **1** **play yersel** amuse yourself; waste time. **2** (*of a liquid or its container*) boil. **3** *where English uses* 'go': '*The door played clink*'.

n **1** a game, sport, pastime. **2** **the play** time off school or work.

playock a toy.

play piece a mid-morning snack at school.

plead *v, past tense, past participle also* **pled 1** plead. **2** argue, debate in a court of law.

pleasant *see* **pleesant.**

pleasure *see* **pleesure.**

pleat *n* a pigtail, plait.

pled *see* **plead.**

pleep *n* a sea-bird with a thin, high-pitched cry, *eg* an oyster-catcher, a redshank.

pleesant, pleasant *adj* **1** pleasant. **2** humorous, witty, merry.

pleesure, pleasure *n* pleasure.

v please, give pleasure to, satisfy.

plenish *v* furnish (a house).

plenishin furniture, household equipment.

plenty *n* a great number (of): '*Plenty o them play fitba*'.

plet, plait *v* **1** plait. **2** cross or fold (your legs or arms). **3** fold. **4** twist.
n a pleat in a garment, a fold, crease.

plet *see* **plat.**

pleuch [pleeooch], **plew, ploo** *n*, *v* plough.

pleuchie a ploughman.

plink *n* a short sharp sound like that made by a taut string.

pliskie *n* **1** a practical joke, a trick. **2** a plight, predicament. **3** a wild idea, a bee in your bonnet.

plivver *n* a plover.

ploo *see* **pleuch.**

plook *n* **1** a pimple; a boil. **2** a growth, a swelling. **3** a knob.

plookie, plookit pimply.

ploom *n* **1** a plum. **2** the fruit of the potato-plant (growing above the ground).

ploot *see* **plowt.**

plot, plowt *v* **1** scald something with boiling water to clean it; bathe (a sore) in very hot water; overheat, burn. **2** become very hot.
n **1** a scalding, putting into boiling water. **2** an overheated state, a sweat, swelter.

plowd *v* **1** *also* **plowder** walk in a heavy-footed way, plod along. **2** work on for a long time, plod NE.

plowp *n*, *v* plop.

plowster *v* work messily in mud etc, flounder about SOUTH.

plowt, ploot *v* **1** plunge into (a liquid). **2** set down suddenly and heavily. **3** fall heavily. **4** squelch along. **5** (*of a liquid*) fall with a splash; (*of rain*) pelt down.
n **1** a noisy fall or plunge; a splash, plop. **2** a heavy shower, a downpour of rain.

plowt *see* **plot.**

plowter, plyter NE *v* **1** dabble with hands or feet in a liquid, splash aimlessly in mud or water. **2** work or act idly or aimlessly, potter or fiddle about.
n **1** the act of working or walking in wetness or mud; a messy task; a botched job.
2 a splash, dashing of liquid.
3 a wet, muddy place.
4 a sloppy or sticky mess of food etc.
5 a messy, inefficient worker.

ploy *n* **1** an undertaking; a piece of business, a scheme. **2** a light-hearted plan for your own amusement, a piece of fun, a trick.

pluff, pyuff NE [peeuff] *adv* with a puff, whoof!
n **1** a mild explosion, a whiff or puff of air, smoke. **2** a tube used as a pea-shooter or as a simple form of bellows.
v **1** blow out by puffing air. **2** swell up, puff out.

pluffer a pea-shooter.

pluffie *adj* plump, puffy, fleshy.
n a kind of toffee made fluffy and brittle by the addition of bicarbonate of soda, puff candy.

plug *v* dodge (school), play truant.

plump *v* **1** (*of rain*) fall heavily, pour. **2** (*of a (semi-)liquid*) make a loud bubbling noise.
n a heavy downpour of rain, often following thunder.

plunk[1] *adv* with a dull, heavy sound, plump; in a sudden way, quickly.
n **1** a heavy fall, plump or plunge; the sound of this.
2 a popping sound, *eg* of a cork being drawn from a bottle.
3 a sharp forward jerk or thrust, a flick, *eg* with the forefinger and thumb on a marble.
v **1** fall with a dull heavy sound, usually into water etc, plop.
2 make a plopping or gurgling noise.
3 drop into water, plop, put down with a thump.

4 propel (a marble) with a thrust or jerk.

5 strike with a dull thud, thump.

6 pluck (the strings of a musical instrument) to make a popping or twanging noise.

plunker a heavy clay, glass or metal marble.

plunkie 1 a game of marbles played as in **plunk**[1] *n* **3**. **2** a kind of **sweetie** made of treacle or syrup and flour NE.

plunk[2] *v* dodge (school), play truant.

plype *n* (the noise of) a sudden dash of water; a sudden heavy shower of rain NE.

v **1** drop suddenly into a liquid, plunge or splash in mud or water NE. **2** dabble ‧ or work messily and carelessly NE. **3** walk on wet or muddy ground NE.

plyter *see* **plowter**.

poatch *v* **1** stir, poke, push, prod. **2** reduce to mush by messing about with NE: *'The baby's poatchin his porridge'*. **3** mess about SOUTH.

pochle *see* **pauchle**.

pock *see* **poke**.

podlie *n* **1** the young of the coalfish; a pollack, a **lythe**. **2** a tadpole. **3** a red-breasted minnow.

point *see* **pint**.

poke, pock, pyock NE [peeock] *n* **1** a bag, a small sack; a shopkeeper's paper bag. **2** a kind of fishing net.

be on yer ain pock neuk be relying on your own resources.

poke puddin 1 a **dumpling** or steamed pudding cooked in a bag. **2** a nickname for an Englishman.

poke shakkins 1 the last child of a large family. **2** the smallest pig in a litter.

pokey-hat *n* an ice-cream cone.

policies *npl* the enclosed grounds of a large house, the park of an estate.

polis *n* **1** the police. **2** a policeman: *'There a polis comin'*.

poll *see* **powe**[1].

pollywag *n* a tadpole.

poochie *adj* proud, self-assured, cocky NE.

pooder *see* **poother**.

pook *v* **1** pluck, twitch, tug. **2** remove the feathers from, pluck (a fowl).

n **1** a plucking motion, a twitch, tug. **2** what is to be plucked (off), *eg* wool from a sheep, fluff; a mouthful, bite; a small quantity, a little. **3** a moulting condition in birds.

pookie dejected-looking, thin and unhealthy-looking.

pookit plucked; having a miserable appearance, thin-looking; shabby.

in the pook 1 (*of birds*) moulting. **2** not very well, below par.

pook *see* **powk**.

poolie *n* a louse.

pooplt *n* a pulpit.

poor, pour *v* **1** pour. **2** empty (a container) by pouring out its contents; pour the liquid from (boiled food, especially potatoes): *'Poor the tatties noo'*.

n a heavy shower of rain.

poorie 1 a jug, especially a cream jug. **2** a small oilcan with a spout.

poor ooti the shout by children at a wedding for coins to be scattered in the street.

poor-oot such a scattering of coins.

poor (the) tea pour out tea.

pooshion, pushion, pizen *n* **1** poison. **2** a nasty person or thing.

adj unpleasant, detestable.

v **1** poison. **2** make unpleasant, spoil; make (food) uneatable.

pooss *see* **push**.

poost, powst *n* strength, power, force SOUTH.

poot, powt *n* **1** a poult, a young (game-) bird. **2** *also* **pootie** a small haddock.

pootch *n* **1** a pouch. **2** a pocket in a garment. **3** the pocket as containing your money, your purse or finances.

v **1** put into your pocket; steal, pocket. **2** eat greedily, gulp down NE.

poother, pooder, powder *n* powder.
v **1** powder. **2** sprinkle (food) with salt
or spices to preserve it.

pootherie, pooderie powdery.

pop *see* **pap²**.

popple *see* **papple**.

porr *v* prod, poke, thrust at sw.

port *n* a gateway, entrance, especially
of a walled town or a castle *now only
in place-names*.

porter biscuit *n* a large round flattish
bun.

pose *v* place (an object) in a particular
position, *eg* with the aim of hiding it,
save up: '*Pose the bairns' Christmas
praisents*'.
n, also **posie** a quantity, pile, hoard,
collection of money or valuables.

posh, poshie *n* child's word for porridge.

posie *see* **pose**.

positive *adj* determined, obstinate.

post, postie *n* a postman.

pot *see* **pat**.

potato *see* **pitawtie**.

pottage, pottitch *n* porridge; your
breakfast, food in general NE.

potterlowe *n* a broken or ruined condition, smithereens, pulp NE: '*gane tae
potterlowe*'.

pottie *see* **pat**.

pottitch *see* **pottage**.

pou, pul, pull *v* **1** pull. **2** pluck (fruit,
flowers etc). **3** strip (a bird) of feathers, pluck (a fowl). **4** extract (a tooth).
5 (*of a chimney etc*) have a strong
draught, draw.
like pullin teeth extremely difficult
(to get a response etc).

pour *see* **poor**.

povereese *v* reduce to poverty, exhaust (land etc) by overworking.

powder *see* **poother**.

powe¹ [rhymes with 'cow'], **poll** *n* the
head.

powe² [rhymes with 'cow'] *n* **1** a slow-
moving stream flowing through flat
land. **2** a pool of water; a puddle.

poweheld [-ow- as in 'cow'] *n* a tadpole.

powk [-ow- as in 'cow'], **pook** *v* **1** poke.
2 dig in a careless, clumsy way NE.

powl [-ow- as in 'cow'] *n* a pole.

pownie [-ow- as in 'cow'] *n* **1** a pony. **2**
a carpenter's trestle.

powst *see* **poost**.

powt [-ow- as in 'cow'] *v* **1** poke, prod.
2 walk heavily, plod NE.

powt *see* **poot**.

powter [-ow- as in 'cow'] *v* **1** poke or
prod repeatedly. **2** potter. **3** paddle or
poke about in a liquid.

praisent *see* **present**.

pran NE *v* **1** crush, squeeze, pulp,
pound. **2** bruise, beat, punish.

prap, prop *n* **1** a prop. **2** something set
up as a marker, *eg* as a boundary-
mark, a memorial, a target for shooting at, a guide in ploughing.
v **1** prop. **2** mark (a boundary etc) by
means of **praps**.

prattick, prottick *n* **1** a piece of mischief, trick NE. **2** an undertaking;
scheme, trick, dodge NE.

preceese *adj* precise.
adv exactly, precisely.

pree *v* **1** to try out, sample. **2** try by
tasting.
pree (someone's) mou *or* **lips** kiss.

preen, prin *n* a metal pin; something
of very little value. *See also* **peen**¹.
v fasten with a pin, pin.

preen-cod a pin-cushion.

preen-held 1 a pin-head; something
of very little value or importance. **2**
the young of the minnow.

preen-heidit stupid, of low intelligence.

preen-tae 1 a person or thing attached to another. **2** an unlawful
sexual partner.
be sittin on preens be very nervous,
be on tenterhooks.

prent *n* **1** print. **2** a pat of butter.
v print.
speak lik a prent buik speak with an

air of knowledge; speak in an affected way.

preparatory service *n* a church service held before communion.

presbytery *n* a church court above the **kirk session** (*see* **kirk**); the area represented by such.

present *n, also* **praisent** a present. *v* (*Presbyterian Churches*) offer (a child) for baptism.

give in a present give as a present, make a present of.

presently *adv* now, at this moment, at present.

preses [preesiz] *n* the person who presides at a meeting etc, the chairperson, president; the leader.

press *n* a large (wall-)cupboard.

pretty, protty NE *adj* **1** pretty. **2** (*of people*) fine, good-looking, dignified; (*of men*) courageous, manly; (*of women*) well-built; (*of animals*) sturdy, in good condition; (*of things*) well-made, attractive.

price *n*: **be the price o someone** serve someone right.

prickle *n* a prickling or stinging sensation.

pridefu *adj* snobbish.

prief *see* **pruif**.

prieve *see* **pruive**.

prig *v* **1** haggle over a price; drive a hard bargain; beat down a price. **2** plead with (someone) for (something).

prime *v* fill, stuff, load.

primp *v* **1** make prim and over-neat. **2** behave or talk affectedly. *adj* prim, conceited.

primsie *adj* self-consciously correct, strait-laced, old-maidish.

prin *see* **preen**.

prink *v* **1** make smart or pretty. **2** strut, move with a swagger.

prinkie fussy, ostentatious, conceited.

prinkle *v* **1** have pins and needles, tingle, thrill. **2** twinkle, glitter, sparkle; (*of a boiling pot*) bubble, simmer.

privy hedge *n* a privet hedge.

procurator fiscal *n* the public prosecutor in a **Sheriff Court** (*see* **sheriff**), who also carries out some of the duties of an English coroner.

Prod, Proddie *n* contemptuous term for a Protestant.

prog *n* **1** a piercing weapon or instrument. **2** a thorn, spine, prickle. **3** a stab, thrust, poke etc. *v* stab, pierce, prick; poke, prod, jab.

prood, proud *adj* **1** proud. **2** pleased, glad. **3** (*of an object or surface*) set higher than its immediate surroundings: '*a proud roof*'.

proof *see* **pruif**.

prop *see* **prap**.

prottick *see* **prattick**.

protty *see* **pretty**.

proud *see* **prood**.

prove, proven *see* **pruive**.

providin, providing *n* (*in past times*) the household articles laid aside by a young woman before her weddding.

provost *n* **1** the head of a Scottish **burgh**.

pruif, proof, prief *n* proof.

pruive, prove, prieve *v, past tense* **pruivit**; *past participle* **proven** **1** prove. **2** try out, put to the test, sample; try by tasting.

public room *n* a room in a house which visitors are received and entertained, *eg* a sitting room, dining room.

puckle *see* **pickle**.

pud *n* **1** a small, neat, often plump person or animal. **2** name for a pig.

puddin [rhymes with 'sudden'] *n* **1** a pudding. **2** a kind of sausage made from the stomach or guts of a sheep, pig etc, oatmeal; onions, seasoning etc: '*white puddin*'. **3** **puddins** guts (of people or animals). **4** a stupid or clumsy person.

keep the puddin het keep the pot boiling, keep going.

puddock, paddock, paddie *n* **1** a frog,

a toad. **2** a spiteful arrogant person; a clumsy, ungainly or ugly person. **3** a flat, wooden platform for transporting heavy loads of hay etc.

puddock('s) crud(d)les frogspawn.

puddock stuil, puddock steel NE a mushroom; a toadstool.

be in the puddock hair be very young.

puff *v* boast, brag.

puffer (*until the 1960s or 70s*) a small steamboat which carried cargo around the west coast of Scotland.

puggelt, puggled *adj* exhausted, done for, at the end of your resources.

puggie[1] *n* **1** a monkey. **2** contemptuous term for a person.

as fou as a puggie extremely drunk.

loss yer puggie lose your temper.

puggie[2] *n* **1** (*marbles*) a hole into which the marbles are rolled.
2 the bank, jackpot or pool in a game of cards etc WEST.
3 a fruit-machine: '*We're gaunnae play on the puggies*'.
4 a cash dispenser at a bank.

puggled *see* **puggelt**.

puil, peel NE *n* a pool.

puir, peer NE *adj* poor.

mak a puir mou(th) plead poverty as an excuse for meanness, claim to be poor when in fact you are quite well-off.

puirtith *n* (*literary*) poverty.

pul, pull *see* **pou**.

pump *n* breaking of wind.
v break wind.

pumphal NE *n* **1** an enclosure for animals. **2** a kind of square church pew.

pun *see* **pund**[1].

punce *n* **1** a pounce. **2** a light blow, a nudge, poke.
v **1** pounce. **2** poke, jog.

pund[1], **pun** *n* (*in money or weight*) a pound.

pund[2] *n* a pound, an enclosure for animals.

punt-up *n* a hoist up WEST.

pupple *n* a poppy.

pupple show *n* a puppet show, a Punch-and-Judy show.

mak a pupple-show o yersel make a fool of yourself.

purfelt *adj* fat and asthmatic, plump and wheezing.

purl *n* a pearl.

purl *see* **pirl**.

purls *npl* small balls of sheep or rabbit dung.

purple *adj, n* purple.

purpose *adj* well-ordered, tidy, methodical; tidy-looking.

pursurer *n* (*law*) the active party in a civil action, the prosecutor.

push [rhymes with 'mush'], **pooss** *v* **1** push. **2** urge, egg on.

pushion *see* **pooshion**.

puss, pussie *n* a hare.

put *see* **pit**.

putt, put *v* **1** push, shove; nudge gently, prod; butt. **2** (*athletics*) hurl (a stone or heavy metal ball). **3** (*golf*) strike (the ball) as in **putt** *n* 2.
n **1** a gentle touch or push. **2** (*golf*) the gentle tapping stroke used to move the ball across the **green**[1] and into the hole. **3** (*athletics*) the movement by which a weight is propelled.

putten *see* **pit**.

pyoch, pyocher *see* **peuch**.

pyock *see* **poke**.

pyot *n* **1** a magpie. **2** a chattering, irresponsible person.
adj **1** like a magpie in colouring, multi-coloured. **2** (*of speech*) loud, empty.

pyuff *see* **pluff**.

Q

qua *see* **quaw.**

qualch *n* a shallow two-handled cup, originally made of wood, sometimes decorated with or made entirely of silver, now mainly ornamental and used for trophies etc.

qualk *v* quack NE.

qualstion *see* **question.**

quak *v* quake.

quakin-bog a quagmire.

qualifying examination, *informally* **the quallie** *n* (*until the 1960s*) an examination at the end of primary education which decided which type of secondary education pupils should have.

quarrel[1] [-a- as in 'cat'] *n* **1** a stone-quarry. **2** stone etc taken from a quarry.

quarrel[2] *v* find fault with, criticize.

quarter *n* a quarter-pound.

quat [-a- as in 'cat'] *v* **1** leave, abandon; give up. **2** stop.

quat *see* **quit.**

quate, quiet *adj* **1** quiet. **2** secret, private. **3** (*of weather*) still, calm.

quate wi ye! be quiet!

quate *see* **quit.**

quaw, qua *n* a bog, quagmire, marsh.

queek *v* squeak, cheep.

queen *n*: **make a queen's chair** carry someone seated on the crossed and joined arms of two other people.

Queen Mary a children's ring dance accompanied by a song beginning with these words.

queen o (the) meadow meadow-sweet.

Queen of the South 1 nickname for the town of Dumfries. **2** official name for the Dumfries football team. **3** the Dumfries schoolgirl chosen as the festival queen at the annual local **Riding of the Marches.**

queer *adj* considerable, very great: '*a queer lot o money*'.

queerie *adj* rather strange NE.

n an oddity, a queer thing or person: '*Her boyfriend's a richt queerie*'.

queerlositie *n* a curiosity, something strange.

queern *see* **quern**[1].

queesitive *adj* inquisitive.

quern[1], **queern** *n* **1** a hand-milling stone, a quern. **2** the stomach of a fowl, the gizzard.

quern[2] NE *n* a small seed, granule.

querny (*of honey, sugar etc*) coarse NE, grainy.

question, qualstion, queystion 1 a question. **2** (*expresssing doubt or wonder*) I wonder, goodness knows: '*Quaistion if he can find the road*'.

quey, queyock *n* a heifer.

queystion *see* **question.**

quick *adj* swarming, infested: '*This hoose is quick wi mice*'.

quick water the current (of a river), running water SW, SOUTH.

quicken *see* **quickens.**

quickens, quicken *npl* couch grass.

quiet *see* **quate.**

quine, quinie *n*, *now* NE **1** a young (unmarried) woman, a girl; a female child; a daughter. **2** a female servant. **3** a female sweetheart. **4** a bold, impudent woman, a slut.

quink goose *n* a brent goose; a greylag goose ORKNEY.

quinkins *npl* **1** dregs or leavings, scum of a liquid, charred traces of food stuck to the pan. **2** a worthless trifle.

quirk *n* a riddle, catch question, an arithmetical problem.

v trick, get the better of, cheat.

quirky 1 intricate, twisted, complicated. **2** cunning, resourceful, tricky.

quit *v, past tense* **quat, quate;** *past participle* **quat 1** give up, stop. **2** free, aquit.

adj, also **quat** quit, free.

quoit *v* play at the game of curling, play a curling stone.

quorum, coarum NE *n* **1** a quorum. **2** a gathering, especially of friends for social purposes, a company NE.

R

ra *see* **raw**[1], **raw**[2].

Rab *see* **Rob**.

rabbit's sugar *n* child's word for the seeds of the common sorrel NE.

rabble *see* **raible**.

race[1] *n* a run, a hurried journey; a flying visit; a short run before jumping.

race[2] *n* a set (of articles used together) NE.

rack *v* **1** stretch, pull, increase in length. **2** twist, wrench, dislocate.
n **1** a sprain, wrench, dislocation. **2** a stretch of a river; a ford in a river. **3** a path, track.

rackle *n* **1** a chain. **2** the rattling, jingling noise made by a chain NE.

rackless *adj* reckless.

rackon *v* reckon.

rade *see* **ride**.

radge *adj* **1** *also* **radgie** mad, violently excited, furious. **2** *also* **radgie** sexually excited. **3** silly, weak-minded.

tak a radge have a fit of rage.

radical *n* a wild person, a rogue, rascal.

rael, real *adj* **1** real. **2** (*of character*) honest, genuine.
adv very, extremely.

raep *v* reap.

raff *n* plenty, a large number.

raffle NE **1** abundant, generous. **2** thriving, flourishing.

raft *n* a rafter.

rag[1] *n* **1** a rough projection on a surface, *eg* after sawing. **2** a lean, scraggy animal or fish.

ragger a rag-collector N.

raggie *adj*, *also* **raggetie** ragged.

raggit ragged.

raggle make an uneven cut in, cut jaggedly.

ragglish erratic; uncertain; wild, unreliable NE.

ragnail a loose piece of skin or broken nail at the side of a fingernail, a hangnail.

ragweed ragwort.

loss the rag lose your temper.

rag[2] *v* scold severely.

hae a rag oot o enjoy a joke at the expense of, get a laugh out of.

tak the rag (oot) o make fun of, make a fool of.

rag[3] *n* a wet mist, drizzle SHETLAND, ORKNEY, NE.

raggetie, raggle *see* **rag**[1].

raggle[1] *v* cut a groove in stone (or wood) to receive another stone etc, *eg* in stairs.

raggle[2] *v* wrangle, dispute NE.

raggle, ragglish *see* **rag**[1].

raible, rabble *n* **1** a disorganized rigmarole; nonsensical talk. **2** a carelessly-built or ruinous building etc.
v utter (a torrent of words), speak or read hastily and indistinctly.

raik *v* **1** move, go forward, especially with speed. **2** journey, go; walk, stroll. **3** range over, wander through. **4** work energetically and speedily NE.
n **1** the act of going; a journey; a long or tiring walk; a stroll. **2** a journey; a trip, run. **3** as much as can be carried in one load. **4** (*of food*) a spoonful; a helping. **5** speed.

ralp[1], **rope** *n* **1** rope. **2** a straw or hay rope. **3** a clothes-line.

ralp[2] *v, n* rip NE.

rair, roar *v* **1** roar.
2 (*of animals or birds not thought of as roaring*) call loudly.
3 call, summon with a loud shout; pay a flying visit: '*roar in tae ma mother's*'.

4 (*of a curling stone*) make a roaring noise as it moves on the ice.

5 weep, cry, usually, but not necessarily, loudly, *often* **roar and greet**.

n **1** roar. **2** a call, as to a neighbour in passing, a short visit: '*Gie's a roar in when yer passin'*.

roarie 1 loud, noisy, roaring. **2** drunk. **3** (*of colours*) bright, showy; glaring, garish, loud: '*Ye cannae wear that roarie dress tae a funeral*'.

roarin game the game of curling.

raise *v* **1** arouse, rouse from sleep. **2** infuriate, drive into a frenzy.

n a state of extreme bad temper, a frenzy.

raised infuriated, wild, over-excited.

raison *see* **rizzon**.

raither, redder SHETLAND, NE *adv* rather.

raivel, rile sw *v* **1** get into a tangle or confusion; muddle, disorder. **2** ramble, be delirious. **3** confuse, perplex. **4** bamboozle, outwit SHETLAND, NE.

n **1** a muddle, tangle, confusion. **2** a broken or frayed thread, a loose end.

raivelt tangled, confused, in difficulties; rambling, delirious.

raivelt hesp a knotty problem, a state of confusion.

rake *v* **1** rake, especially stalks of corn left on a harvested field. **2** search (a person): '*Ye'll get raked at the polis office*'.

n **1** a hoard, what has been gathered together. **2** a grasping, hoarding person. **3** a very thin person.

ramble *see* **rammle**.

rame *v* **1** repeat, recite something; drone on monotonously; harp on. **2** talk nonsense, rave.

ramfeezle, ramfoozle *v* muddle, confuse; exhaust.

rammle *n* a free-for-all, violent disturbance, scuffle: '*a stairheid rammie*'.

rammish, ramse ORKNEY *adj* mad, crazy, uncontrolled.

rammle, ramble *v* **1** ramble. **2** wander

about aimlessly, especially under the influence of drink.

ramp *v* **1** (*of plants*) climb, ramble. **2** romp boisterously. **3** stamp, beat the floor with the feet.

rampage *n* an outburst of rage.

ramscooter *v* beat, drive off in terror.

ramse *see* **rammish**.

ramsh *adj* **1** (*of food*) unpleasant, coarse. **2** (*of people*) brusque, badtempered NE. **3** (*of yarn*) rough and coarse-textured.

ramstam *adj* headstrong, rash, heedless.

n a headstrong, impetuous person or action.

adv recklessly, headlong.

ramstougar [ram-**stooger**] *adj* rough in manner, boisterous, disorderly.

rance *n* **1** a prop, wooden post or bar used *eg* across the legs of a chair. **2** a bar used for securing a door or as a crossbar of a fence.

v **1** prop up (a building etc). **2** close up, fasten firmly to prevent movement.

rander, render *v* **1** render. **2** talk idly or nonsensically, ramble.

n **1** a great talker. **2** senseless talk. **3** order, restraint. **4** dripping (from meat).

randle *adj* **1** rough, aggressive. **2** (*of a woman*) loud-voiced, coarse and aggressive. **3** boisterous, wild. **4** (*of language*) coarse, uncouth; obscene.

n **1** a (rude) beggar, a ruffian. **2** a beggar-woman; any foul-mouthed, brawling, bad-tempered woman; an immoral woman. **3** a boisterous, mischievous person. **4** a romp, frolic.

range *see* **reenge, rinse**.

rank *v* get ready, prepare, dress before going out NE.

rannoch *n* fern; bracken.

ranshackle *v* search minutely, ransack.

ransom *n* a very high price or rent.

rant *v* **1** romp, make merry. **2** play or

sing a lively tune, especially for a dance. **3** make a great fuss, complain at length.

n **1** a romp, boisterous or riotous merry-making NE. **2** a festive gathering with music and dancing. **3** a lively tune or song, especially one for an energetic dance.

rantin merry, uproarious.

rantinlie merrily, uproariously.

ranter *v* sew together, darn, mend (hastily or roughly).

rap *v* **1** dash, thump, knock, strike or fall with a sharp thud. **2** fall rapidly in a shower or in drops SHETLAND. **3** make a rapping or banging noise SHETLAND, NE.

in a rap in an instant, in a moment.

raploch *n, also* **raploch grey** coarse, undyed, woollen cloth; a garment made of this.

adj ordinary; home-made; rough-and-ready.

rapture *n* a fit, especially of rage.

rash¹, **thrash, thresh** *n* a rush, the plant.

rashie *n* = **rash.**

adj made of rushes; overgrown with rushes.

Rashiecoat name of the heroine of a Scottish version of *Cinderella*, who wore a coat of rushes.

rash² *adj* active, agile, vigorous.

rasp *n* a raspberry.

rat *n* a rut, a groove, deep scratch SOUTH.

ratch¹ *v* range about ravenously; prowl SOUTH.

ratch² *v* damage by rough usage, tear, scratch.

rat's tail, rat tail *n* greater plantain; its seedhead.

rattle *v* **1** strike or beat repeatedly: '*Ah'll rattle yer jaw*'. **2** do with great haste and without care.

rattlestane (*in children's rhymes*) a hailstone.

ratton, rottan *n* **1** a rat. **2** term of

contempt or endearment for a person.

rauchle *n* a loose, untidy heap; something ramshackle.

rauchle *see* **raucle.**

raucht *see* **reak.**

raucle, rauchle *adj* **1** bold, rash. **2** strong, sturdy, hard, stern, grim. **3** rough, crude, tough.

rave *n* a person who talks too much and nonsensically, a windbag.

rave *see* **rive.**

raverie *n* NE **1** raving, nonsense, foolish talk. **2** a rumour, a piece of gossip.

raw¹, **ra, row** *n* **1** a row, a line. **2** a row of houses, especially of miners' or farmworkers' cottages; a street of such houses: '*miners' raw*'.

v set up in a row, arrange in a line.

raw², **ra** *adj, n* raw.

rax *v* **1** stretch yourself after sleep etc; stretch (a cramped limb etc).

2 put (yourself) to great effort, overexert, strain; sprain (a limb).

3 stretch in order to lengthen etc, pull out.

4 raise (the head or eyes) in order to look or listen; reach out (the hand or arm); stretch out, crane (the neck).

5 reach, stretch out to take or grasp (something); help yourself to (food).

6 hand (a person an object): '*Rax me ower the breid*'; deal (a person a blow).

7 stretch, expand; (*of the day, time*) stretch out.

rax *see* **rex.**

reach *v* retch, try to vomit.

read *v* interpret (a dream, riddle etc), foretell the future.

n a loan (of a book etc) for the purpose of reading it: '*Can Ah get a read o yer buik?*'.

readin sweetie = **conversation lozenge.**

ready *adj* apt, liable, likely to: '*ready makin mistakes*'.

v **1** make ready, prepare. **2** cook (food), prepare (a meal).

readily probably; likely; naturally.

reak, reck SHETLAND *v, past participle also* **raucht 1** reach. **2** reach for. **3** deliver (a blow).

real *see* **rael.**

ream *n* **1** cream. **2** the froth on top of ale NE.

v **1** (*of milk*) form cream. **2** skim the cream off (milk). **3** form a froth or foam. **4** be full of a frothy liquid; bubble over.

   reamie 1 creamy; made of or with cream. **2** frothing.

reboon *see* **reboond.**

reboond, reboon *n* **1** rebound. **2** a loud explosive noise, *eg* a gunshot. **3** a scolding.

receipt *n* **1** a (medical) prescription or preparation. **2** a recipe.

reck *see* **reak.**

rector *n* **1** a high-ranking university official; now a public figure elected by the students. **2** a headteacher of a secondary school. **3** a clergyman in charge of a full congregation of the Scottish Episcopal Church.

red *see* **redd¹, reid.**

redd¹ *v, past tense, past participle* **red(d) 1** free, rid, relieve.

2 clear (a space, the way), make room; clear out (a ditch, channel etc); clear (the throat, nose, stomach etc); clear (a fireplace, tobacco pipe) of ashes, poke up or out.

3 clear away, remove (from).

4 disentangle, unravel, sort out.

5 *also* **redd up** arrange; settle (affairs etc); clear up, sort out (problems, difficulties etc).

6 put an end to (fighting).

7 *also* **redd up** put in order, tidy up.

n **1** the act of cleaning away or tidying up; a putting in order; a cleaning, tidying. **2** rubbish etc which has been or is to be cleared away. **3** a combing and arranging of the hair.

   reddin up 1 a tidying. **2** a scolding.

redd² *n* **1** fish- or frog-spawn. **2** the rut

in a riverbed made by salmon for spawning in.

redder *see* **raither.**

ree¹, reeve, reed *n* **1** a yard for storing coal. **2** an enclosure or pen for animals.

ree² *adj* **1** tipsy. **2** over-excited, delirious, crazy.

ree³ *n* a medium-sized sieve or riddle for cleaning grain, peas, etc.

reed *see* **ree¹.**

reef *see* **ruif.**

reek, rick NE *n* **1** smoke. **2** mist, especially a morning mist rising from the ground. **3** the act of smoking a pipe etc, a smoke, a whiff, puff.

v **1** (*of a house etc*) have smoke coming out of the chimney. **2** (*of a chimney*) give out smoke; fail to give out smoke properly, sending it back into the room. **3** (*of hot liquid, damp hay etc*) give off vapour or steam. **4** show anger, fume.

   reekie, rickie 1 smoky, smoke-filled; blackened by smoke. **2** of or like smoke; misty, damp.

   reekie-mire a hollowed cabbage-stalk packed with oily waste, used to blow smoke into a house as a prank NE.

   reekit 1 blackened with smoke or soot. **2** (*of food*) smoke-cured; smoke tainted.

reel *n* **1** a lively dance for two, three or four couples; the music to which it is danced. **2** a noise, crash, peal.

v **1** wind (yarn etc) on a reel; fill (a spool) with thread. **2** (*of the eyes*) roll with excitement, greed etc. **3** (*of the head*) be in a whirl, become confused. **4** dance to a **reel**; do a figure-of-eight travelling movement.

   reel-rall a state of confusion.

reemage *see* **reemish.**

reemis, reemish *n* NE **1** a resounding crash or rumble. **2** a scuffle, din, clatter. **3** a heavy blow or beating.

reemish, reemage *v* search noisily, poke around NE.

reemish *see* **reemis.**

reen *see* **rind**[1].

reenge *v* **1** wander over, travel through. **2** *also* **range** search (a place) widely and thoroughly. **3** poke ashes from (a fire). **4** bustle about noisily.

n **1** range, distance. **2** a thorough search.

reenge *see* **rinse.**

reerle *n* a row, uproar NE.

reese *see* **roose**[3].

reeshle *see* **reesle.**

reeshtle *see* **roost.**

reesle, reeshle *v* **1** rustle. **2** (*of wind etc*) whistle. **3** (*of doors, crockery etc*) clatter, rattle. **4** rap at (a door). **5** move about noisily or with a clatter, crash about. **6** go through with a scuffling noise, rummage through. **7** move or shake (an object) so as to make it rustle or rattle. **8** beat, thrash. **9** shake, stir.

reest[1] *v* cure (fish, ham etc) by drying or smoking.

n a framework on which fish, meat etc is smoked.

reest[2] *v* **1** arrest, seize (goods), especially for debt. **2** bring to a halt. **3** cover or damp down (a fire) for the night. **4** stop and refuse to move.

reest[3] *n* the mould-board of a plough.

reet *see* **rult**[1].

reeve *v, past tense, past participle* **reft** tear, grab, snatch forcibly (at).

reeve *see* **ree**[1].

reevin *adj* blaze NE.

reezle *adj* light-headed, especially from drink, tipsy.

refeese *see* **refuise.**

reft *see* **reeve, reive.**

refuise, refeese NE *v* refuse.

n a refusal.

regaird *v, n* regard.

regairdless 1 heedless, uncaring. **2** regardless.

regibus [rejibus] *n* a children's game, involving one side trying to catch the other side's caps NE.

reid, rid, red *adj* red.

ridder, riddle = red face.

reidle a red clay marble WEST.

red-arsle a bee with red markings behind.

red biddy (*slang*) a mixture of cheap red wine and methylated spirit or other alcohol; any cheap red wine.

red brae the gullet.

red face a blushing face, as a sign of embarrassment or shame.

red fish 1 a male salmon at spawning time when it turns reddish. **2** (*used where the name 'salmon' is taboo*) salmon in general.

reid mad furiously angry.

reid nakit stark naked.

reid road the gullet.

red wuld stark staring mad, beside yourself with rage.

reird *n* a noisy breaking of wind NE.

reive *v, past tense, past participle also* **reft 1** rob, plunder. **2** take away; steal.

reiver 1 (*in past times*) a plunderer, robber, especially one riding on a raid. **2 Reiver** the chief male participant in the annual festival at Duns, Berwickshire.

Reiver's Lass the female partner of the **Reiver** (as in 2).

release *n* a variety of the game of tig in which players who have been touched by the catcher may be released by the touch of an uncaught player.

remainder *n* a remnant of cloth at the end of a bale.

remeeve *see* **remuve.**

remeld *n* remedy, redress.

remember *v* **1 remember o, remember on** have memory of, recollect. **2** remind (a person) of or about. **3 remember something to someone** remember to repay someone for something.

remorse *v* express regret or remorse (about) NE.

remove *see* **remuve.**

remuve [-u- as -ui- in 'guid'], **remeeve** NE, **remove** *v* **1** remove. **2** (*of a landlord*) force (a tenant) to quit his holding. **3** (*of a tenant*) quit a property.

renaig *v* refuse to do work; shirk, shy away from a responsibility, engagement or challenge.

render *see* **rander.**

repeat *v* refund, repay.

replenish *v* repair, renovate.

reset *v* **1** receive, give shelter or protection to (especially a criminal, enemy, fugitive etc). **2** receive (stolen goods), usually with the intention of reselling.

n (*law*) the receiving of stolen goods, often **reset of theft.**

resetter a person who **resets,** a fence.

residenter *n* a resident, inhabitant, especially one of long standing.

respeck, respect *n* **1** respect. **2** affectionate esteem; **show respect** attend someone's funeral.

v **1** respect. **2** regard affectionately, esteem.

restrick *v* restrict.

retiral *n* retirement from office etc.

rex, rax *n* a children's chasing game.

rheumatise [**room**ateez] *n* rheumatism.

rheums [rooms] *npl* rheumatic pains.

rhyme *v* repeat, drone on monotonously; talk nonsense.

rhymeless without good reason, meaningless; (*of people*) irresponsible, reckless, ineffective.

rib *n* **1** a horizontal roof-timber joining rafters. **2 ribs** the bars of a grate.

ribble-rabble *adv* in a state of great confusion.

n a rabble.

richt, right *adj* **1** right. **2 no richt** not in your right mind; simple-minded; abnormal. **3** sober, living in a well-behaved way.

adv **1** right. **2** very, exceedingly. **3** thoroughly, very much, very well NE. **4** adequately, properly, satisfactorily.

ken the richt side o a bawbee *etc* be knowing with money, be good at getting the best value for money.

richt an very, completely.

richt eneuch comfortably off, well provided for.

richt noo immediately.

richt oot outright: '*He telt me richt oot*'.

the richt way o't the true account or story, the genuine version.

rick *see* **reek.**

ricket *n* a noisy disturbance, racket, row.

ricketie 1 a kind of wooden rattle, now used by children and football supporters. **2** a ratchet brace or drill.

rickle[1], **ruckle** *n* **1** a heap, pile, collection especially an untidy one.

2 an old or miserable building: '*rickle o stanes*'; a ramshackle or broken-down object; a very thin, miserable-looking person or animal, *often* a **rickle o banes.**

3 an untidy collection or building.

4 a dry-stone wall.

5 a small temporary stack of grain or hay.

6 a small heap of peats or turfs, stacked loosely for drying.

v **1** pile together loosely; build loosely or insecurely. **2** build (grain) into small temporary ricks. **3** stack (peats) loosely for drying.

ricklie badly-built, rickety.

rickle[2] *v, n* rattle, clattering.

rickmatick *n*: **the hale rickmatick** the whole lot.

rid *see* **reid.**

ride *v, past tense also* **rade 1** ride out on a foray, especially in the Borders. **2** fix (the boundaries of land etc) by riding round them.

Riding of the Marches the traditional

ceremony of riding round the boundaries of common land to inspect landmarks, boundary stones etc, latterly the focus of an annual local festival in certain, especially Border towns.

ride-out one of a series of rehearsal rides of a section of the boundaries in the weeks before the **Riding of the Marches.**

rife *adj* **1** plentiful, abundant. **2 rife wi** having plenty of, well supplied with, rich in.

adv plentifully, abundantly.

-rif(e) having plenty of, notable for, liable to, *eg* **cauldrife** cold, likely to get cold; **waukrife** not sleeping.

rift[1] *v* **1** belch. **2** exaggerate, brag.

n **1** a belch. **2** an exaggerated account; a boast.

riftin fou full to bursting point of food.

rift[2] *n* a cleft, split in a rock etc.

rig[1] *n* **1** the back or backbone of a person or animal. **2** a (white) strip running along the back of an animal. **3** a ridge of high ground, a long, narrow hill.

riggin *n* **1** = **rig** 1. **2** the ridge of a roof; the roof; the materials of which it is made. **3** the top, the highest part of a wall, a cornstack. **4** the top of a stretch of high ground; a high ridge of land.

rig-bane the backbone, spine.

rig[2] *n*: **on the rig** out for fun or mischief.

rig[3] *n* the smallest animal or weakling of a litter.

right *see* **richt.**

riglin *n* an undersized or weak animal or person; the smallest animal in a litter.

rile *see* **raivel.**

rime *n* **1** hoar-frost. **2** a frosty haze or mist.

rimple *n, v* wrinkle; ripple.

rim-ram *adj* confused, higgledy-piggledy, disordered NE.

rimwale *n* a board round the gunwale of a boat.

rin, run *v, past tense, past participle* **run 1** run. **2** (*of a dog*) move sheep at a brisk pace SW, SOUTH. **2** be covered with water, mud etc, be awash; leak. **3** (*of milk*) curdle. **4** hold (the hands etc) under running water, swill. **5** (*bowls*) drive (another bowl or the jack) away with a strong shot.

n **1** a flow of water. **2** the course of a river or stream, a river valley. **3** a run.

rinner a runner.

run-knot a slip-knot which has been pulled tight.

rinaboot *adj* runabout, roving.

n a tramp, rover; a restless person, a gadabout.

rin ahin 1 run close behind or at the heels of. **2** be in arrears, fall into debt.

rin the cutter bring home alcoholic drink secretly.

rin eerants go on errands.

rin the hills roam about in a wild, unrestrained way, rush or gad about.

rin in by, run in to pay a short visit to (a person).

rin-a-mile (*game*) a variation on hide-and-seek.

rin oot (*of a container*) leak.

rin-there-oot a tramp, roving person NE.

rinagate *n* a fugitive, rascal.

rind[1] *n* **1** *also* **reen** N a strip or slat of wood, a piece of beading. **2** the edge, *eg* of a strip of land.

rind[2] *v* melt down, render (fat, tallow), clarify (butter etc).

rind[3] *n* hoar-frost.

rind *see* **ruind.**

ring[1] *n* (*marbles*) **the ring, ringie** a circle on the ground used as a target; a game using such a target.

v put a metal tyre round the rim of (a wheel).

ring[2] *v* **1** give a resounding blow to. **2** (*of ice etc*) make a ringing sound.

n **1** the striking of a clock, the stroke.

2 a resounding blow.

ringle a ringing, jingling sound.

ring³ *v* reign.

ringin *adj* **1** domineering. **2** out-and-out, downright.

adv forcefully, with ease NE.

rink *n* **1** (*curling, quoits*) the marked-out area of play.

2 a stretch of ice etc for skating.

3 the team forming a side in a game.

4 (*curling*) a game, one of a series of games making up a match.

5 a restless, especially noisy, prowling or hunting NE.

6 a rattling noise NE.

v **1** range or prowl about restlessly and especially noisily NE. **2** search thoroughly, rummage (in) NE. **3** climb, clamber NE.

rinse, reenge, range *v* **1** rinse. **2** clean (a pan etc) by scraping or scrubbing, scour. **3** *only* **rinse** wash down (a meal) with liquor NE.

n **1** a rinse. **2** a scourer made of heather twigs.

rin-there-oot *see* **rin.**

rip *n* a handful of unthreshed grain or hay.

ripe *v* **1** search thoroughly (especially for stolen property); hunt through. **2** rummage through, turn out the contents of (a pocket, etc); pick a pocket. **3** rifle, plunder. **4** clear (the bars of a fireplace etc) of ash; clear a pipe of ash. **5** strip (*eg* berries from a bush).

n a poke, stir to clear an obstruction.

rippet *n* **1** a noisy disturbance, uproar; the sound of boisterous merrymaking. **2** a row, noisy quarrel.

v create a row or disturbance, quarrel loudly.

ripture *n* a rupture.

rise *v* **1** get out of bed in the morning. **2** cause to rise up, lift up; bring about, produce.

n the act of getting out of bed.

risp *v* **1** file, smooth off with a file; cut or saw roughly. **2** grind together,

grind (the teeth) NE. **3** make a harsh grating sound.

n **1** a coarse file or rasp. **2** a harsh grating sound. **3** a knock (at a door).

rissom *n* **1** a single head or ear of oats. **2 no a rissom** not the smallest amount.

rit, rut *v* scratch, score, groove; make a cut in.

n **1** a scratch, score, groove. **2** a sheepmark in the form of a slit in the ear etc.

rither *n* a rudder.

rive *v, past tense also* **rave** **1** tear, rip. **2** burst, crack, split.

3 wrench, pull apart, break up (into pieces).

4 wrench or force out, dig up.

5 pull or tug roughly or vigorously.

6 tear (the hair), especially in grief or anguish.

7 tear at or maul an opponent in a fight.

8 (*of wind*) blow violently SHETLAND, N.

9 work with a tugging or tearing motion or very hard.

10 rive at tear into (food).

11 force your way forward.

n **1** a tear, rip, scratch. **2** an uprooting, break; breaking off. **3** a pull, jerk, wrench, grab; a hug. **4** a bite, a large mouthful; a good feed. **5** a large quantity or company NE.

rizzar *n* a redcurrant.

rizzert *adj* **1** (*of haddock*) sun-dried. **2** (*of clothes*) sun-dried, thoroughly aired.

rizzon NE, **raison** *n, v* reason.

oot o (aa) rizzon unreasonable.

oot o yer reason out of your mind.

rizzon or nane with or without reason on your side; obstinately NE.

road *n* **1** *often* **roadie** an unsurfaced road. **2** a direction, route. **3** a way, method, manner. **4** a condition, state NE.

v **1** travel on a road, set out on a

journey NE. **2** send (a person) off (on an errand or in a particular direction) NE.

roadit on the road, off on a journey; (*of a child*) able to walk NE.

road-en(d) the junction where a side road meets a main road.

a(w) roads everywhere.

aw the road all the way: '*Ah'll tak this court case aw the road*.

get the road be dismissed.

hae yer ain road go your own way.

in the road in your way, causing inconvenience.

nae road by no means, in no possible way.

on the road (*of a woman*) pregnant.

onie road anyway, anyhow.

oot o yer road out of your way.

oot o the road o unaccustomed to.

tae the road recovered after an illness, able to be about again NE.

tak in the road travel along the road, cover the distance, especially at speed NE.

tak the road set off (on a journey).

roar *see* **rair**.

roast, rost *v, past participle also* **roast-in** roast.

roastit 1 uncomfortably hot. **2** (*of cheese*) toasted.

Rob, Rab *n* **1** familiar form of Robert. **2 the Rabs** nickname for Kirkintilloch Rob Roy football team.

Robbie-rin-the-hedge goose-grass.

Rob Roy (tartan) a red-and-black checked pattern in cloth.

robbie *see* **robin**.

robin, robbie *n* **1** child's word for the penis. **2** a wren SHETLAND.

robin-rin-the-hedge, robin-roon-the-hedge goose-grass SW, SOUTH.

roch *see* **ruch**.

rochian [-ch- as in 'loch'] *n* a ruffian.

rock¹, roke *n* **1** a rock. **2** a curling-stone. **3** *also* **rock partan** the common edible crab.

rockie pebbly.

rock bool a round, hard, candied-sugar sweet.

rock cod (fish) a cod which lives amongst rocks.

rock-halibut a coal-fish NE.

rock turbot the flesh of the catfish or wolf-fish.

rock² *v* stagger or reel in walking.

rockie row, rocketie-row with a rocking or rolling motion.

rodden *n* the berry of the **rowan** N.

as soor as roddens very sour or bitter.

roddie *n* familiar name for a rhododendron.

roit *see* **royet**.

roke *see* **rock¹**.

roll *see* **rowe¹**.

rone *n* the horizontal gutter for rainwater, running along the eaves of a roof; a **rone pipe**.

rone pipe the vertical pipe for draining water from the **rone**; a **rone**.

roof *see* **ruif**.

rook *n* **1** a rook, but in Scotland more usually called a **craw¹**. **2** (*especially marbles*) a complete loss.

v **1** plunder, clean out; steal. **2** rob (a bird's nest) of eggs. **3** (*marbles*) win (all the opponent's marbles).

rookie (*marbles*) a game in which the winner takes all.

rook *see* **rouk**.

rookettie *interjection, also* **rookettie-coo** the call of a pigeon.

rookettie doo a tame pigeon.

room *n* **1** an estate; land rented from a landowner, a farm. **2** (*originally*) the apartment of a **but and ben** not used as the kitchen; *hence* a sitting-room, best room.

room-end the end of a **but and ben** away from the kitchen.

room an kitchen a dwelling, usually a flat, consisting of a kitchen/living-room and another room.

roon *see* **roond**.

roond, roon, roun(d) *adj, adv, v* round.

n **1** a round. **2** a round turret. **3** a circular sheepfold. **4 the roond** the surrounding country, neighbourhood. **5 the round o the clock** twelve hours. **6** *also* **roundsteak** a cut of meat, especially beef, taken from the hindquarter.

roop *see* **roup²**, **roup³**.

roose¹, **rouse** [rhymes with 'choose'] *v* **1** rouse. **2** move with violence or speed, rush SHETLAND, NE. **3** become agitated, excited or enraged.

roose², **rouse** [rhymes with 'choose'] *v* **1** sprinkle (fish) with salt to cure them. **2** sprinkle with water; water with a watering-can NE.

rooser a watering-can.

roose³, **ruise**, **reese** NE *v* praise, flatter.

n praise, flattery; boasting; a boast.

roost *n* **1** rust. **2 no a roost** not a brass farthing.

roostie, **reeshtie** NE **1** rusty. **2** (*of the throat or voice*) rough, dry; hoarse.

root *see* **rowt**.

rope *see* **raip¹**.

roset *n* resin, rosin.
v rub with resin; rub (a fiddle-bow) with rosin.

rosidandrum *n* rhododendron.

rosie *n* reddish marble.

rost *see* **roast**.

rottan *see* **rattan**.

rough *see* **ruch**.

rouk, rowk, rook *n* mist, fog.
roukie misty and muggy.

roun, round *see* **roond**.

roup¹ [-ou- as -ow- in 'cow'] *v* **1** sell or let by public auction. **2** sell up, especially turn out (a bankrupt) and sell his or her effects.

n a sale or let by public auction.

roup², **roop** [-oo-] *v* shout, roar; croak.
n hoarseness, huskiness, any inflamed condition of the throat.

roupie, roupit hoarse, rough.

roup³, **roop** [-oo-] *v* **1** plunder, rob, deprive of everything. **2** prune very severely. **3** take (the marbles of a defeated opponent) in a game of **roopie**, in which the winner claims all the loser's marbles.

roupie, roupit *see* **roup²**.

rouse *see* **roose¹**, **roose²**.

rout [-oo-] *v* (*of the sea, winds, thunder etc*) roar, rumble.

rove¹ *v* wander in thought or speech, be delirious, rave.

rove² *v* (*of a fire*) burn well, blaze NE.

row *see* **raw¹**.

rowan [-ow- as in 'cow'] *n* **1** *also* **rowan tree** the mountain ash. **2** *also* **rowan berry** the fruit of the mountain ash.

rowe¹, **roll** [-ow- as in 'cow'] *v* **1** roll. **2** wheel, convey in a wheeled vehicle. **3** trundle (*eg* a **girl¹**) forward. **4** play (a bowl or curling-stone); (*of bowls*) roll towards the jack. **5** wind, twist, twine. **6** wrap up or in; wrap around. **7** wind up (a clock etc). **8 be rowed intae** be involved in. **9** move about with a rolling or staggering gait, stumble along. **10** move about, fidget, toss and turn restlessly. **11** (*of sheep*) roll over on the back.
n a roll.

rower a rolling pin, often a ribbed or grooved one.

rowie a flaky bread roll made with a lot of butter NE.

rollie-pin (*games*) a rolling action of the hands between the bouncing and catching of a ball.

rowe-chow *v* (*especially of children at play*) roll, tumble.
adj rolling, revolving; mixed up, tangled.

rowe-chow tobacco a game in which a chain of children coil round a large child and all sway to and fro shouting the name of the game until they fall in a noisy heap.

rowe² [-ow- as in 'cow'] *v* (*of a boat*) move along in the water easily or smoothly.

rowk *see* **rouk.**

rowst[1] [-ow- as in 'cow'] *v, n* shout, roar, bellow.

rowst[2] [-ow- as in 'cow'] *v* arouse, stir to action.

rowt, root *v* **1** (*of cattle*) bellow, roar. **2** (*of other animals*) roar, cry. **3** shout, make a great noise. **4** play on (a horn); toot. **5** break wind.

rowth *n* plenty, abundance, profusion. *adj, also* **rowthie** plentiful, abundant, profuse.

royet, roit NE *adj* **1** (*especially of children*) wild, mischievous. **2** (*of weather*) wild, stormy, variable NE. *n* an unruly, troublesome person or animal.

rub *v* (*bowls, curling*) move (a stone or bowl) aside by knocking gently against it with another.

rubbage *n* rubbish.

ruch, roch, rough *adj* **1** rough. **2** (*of sheep*) unshorn, unclipped. **3** (*of grass or crops*) strong, luxuriant. **4** abundant; plentifully supplied, especially with good plain food. **5** foulmouthed, indecent, dirty. *n* **1** rough. **2** rough ground. **3** the major part of something.

ruck *n* a (small, temporary) hay- or cornstack.

ruckle *n* a stone; a marble SOUTH.

ruckle[1] *v* make a rattling, gurgling or roaring sound, especially of the breathing of a dying person.

ruckle[2] *v* wrinkle, crease, work into folds.

ruckle *see* **rickle**[1].

rudas [rhymes with 'Judas'] *n*: **auld rudas** a coarse or masculine-looking woman; a bad-tempered hag NE. *adj* **1** (*of a woman*) ugly, cantankerous, witch-like. **2** wild, undisciplined, irresponsible NE.

rue *v* **1 rue on** have pity on, feel compassion for. **2** regret a promise, bargain etc, withdraw from a bargain or contract.

rug *v* **1** pull vigorously or forcibly, tug, drag, draw. **2** (*of pain, hunger etc*) ache, nag NE. *n* **1** a pull, a rough, hasty tug. **2** a tug on a fishing line, a bite. **3** a strong undercurrent in the sea, a strong tide. **4** a twinge of nerves or emotions. **5** a knot or tangle of hair. **6** a bargain, especially one which takes unfair advantage of the seller.

rug an rive 1 pull or tug vigorously; struggle, tussle. **2** rob, plunder.

rulf, reef NE, **roof** *n* **1** a roof. **2** the ceiling of a room.

rulf-tree 1 the main beam or ridge of a roof. **2** a house, home.

ruind, rind *n* the border or selvage of a web of cloth; a strip of cloth.

rulse *see* **roose**[3].

rult[1], **reet** N *n* **1** a root. **2** a dried tree root used as firewood, especially one dug up from a bog.

rult[2] *v* **1** root, dig up with the snout. **2** rummage, search.

rumble *see* **rummle.**

rumgumption, rummle-gumption *n* common sense, understanding, shrewdness.

rummle, rumble *v* **1** rumble. **2** knock violently or throw stones (at a door) as a prank. **3** strike or beat severely; jolt, handle roughly. **4** toss about restlessly in bed. **5** stir or shake vigorously; mash (potatoes); scramble (eggs). **6** search through (carelessly). *n* **1** a rumble. **2** a movement causing a rumbling sound; a vigorous stir; a rough jolting; a resounding blow or whack. **3** a rough knocking or beating. **4** a ruin SHETLAND, NE.

rummlie 1 (*of soil*) rough and stony; loose and crumbly. **2** (*of the mind*) disordered.

rummle(de)thump 1 mashed potatoes with cabbage (or turnip). **2** mashed potatoes with milk, butter and seasoning sw. **3** = **skirlie** (*under* **skirl**).

rummle-gumption *see* **rumgumption.**

rump *n* in Scotland, a cut of beef corresponding to English topside and silverside, now usually called **round-steak.**

v **1** cut, clip or crop very short. **2** eat down to the roots. **3** plunder; steal; (*marbles*) win (all your opponent's marbles).

rump and stump completely.

run *see* **rin.**

runch *see* **wranch.**

rung *n* **1** a strong stick. **2** a blow with a stick; a thump. **3** contemptuous term for a bad-tempered person; a large, ugly person or animal; a thin, scraggy animal.

v **1** make or fit with spans or rungs. **2** beat with a stick, cudgel.

runkle *v* **1** wrinkle. **2** crease, rumple, crush. **3** twist, curl.

n a wrinkle; a crease.

runkelt, runkle creased, crumpled.

runt *n* **1** an old or decayed tree-stump. **2** the hardened, withered stem of a cabbage or **kail** plant. **3** an apple core. **4** a short, thickset person; an under-sized person or animal.

runtit 1 stunted in growth. **2** completely deprived of your possessions, made bankrupt; (*marbles*) having lost all your marbles to your opponent NE.

rut *see* **rit.**

S

s *see* **us**.

saat *see* **saut**.

Sabbath, Sawbath *n* (*especially among older speakers*) Sunday as a day of the week without reference to its religious significance.

sacrament *n*: **the Sacraments** the period Thursday to the following Monday including the Communion and other services HEBRIDES, HIGHLAND.

sad, sod N *adj* **1** sad. **2** (*of bread or pastry*) not risen, heavy.
v (*of a haystack, soil etc*) sink or settle down, shrink, become solid.

sae, so *adv* **1** so. **2 so it is** *etc* indeed it is etc: '*You're a wee dodger, so you are!*'.

sae bein('s) provided that, since.

saft, soft *adj* **1** soft. **2** (*of weather*) mild, not frosty; thawing. **3** wet, rainy, damp.
n a thaw; rain, moisture.

saftie 1 a softie, a weak, stupid person. **2** *also* **saft biscuit** a kind of plain floury bun or roll with a dent in the middle. **3** *also* **saftick** an edible crab which has lost its shell, often used for bait NE. **4** a soft slipper.

up someone's saft side into someone's favour.

hae a saft side tae have a special liking for.

saicant *adj, n* second.

saidle, seddle *n, v* saddle.

saikless *adj* harmless, silly.

sail *n* a ride in a cart or other vehicle or on horseback.
v **1** be covered with liquid: '*The kitchen's sailin*'. **2** ride or drive in a vehicle.

sain *v* protect from harm by a sign, especially the sign of the cross, bless.

saint, saunt *n* **1** a saint. **2 the Saints** nickname for **St Johnstone** and **St Mirren** football teams.

St Johnstone official name for the Perth football team.

St Mirren official name for the Paisley football team.

saip *n* soap.

saip(ie) graith, saipie sapples soapy lather.

sair, sore *adj* **1** sore.

2 causing pain, distress or strain: '*It's sair on the back*'; '*a sair sicht*'; '*a sair disaster*'.

3 (*of a battle, struggle etc*) hard, severe, fierce, now often of life in general: **it's a sair fecht.**

4 (*of the weather*) severe, stormy.

5 (*of something unpleasant etc*) serious, considerable, sorry: '*a sair come-doon*'.

6 (*of the head*) aching, painful, throbbing.

7 (*of the heart*) aching, sorrowful.

8 (*of people*) harsh.

9 sair on destructive, harmful, giving hard wear or usage to: '*She's sair on her claes*'.

adv **1** sorely, severely, so as to cause pain or suffering.

2 in a distressed way: '*greetin sair*'.

3 hard, with great effort: '*sair won*'.

4 with all your strength or feeling.

5 very much, greatly, extremely: '*sair forfochen*'.

sair aff badly off, very hard up.

sair duin (*of meat*) well-done, overcooked.

sair hand 1 a mess, a piece of badly-done work. **2** a large thick slice of bread with butter or jam.

sair held 1 a headache. **2** *also* **sair**

heidle a small plain cake with a paper band round it.

sair hert a sad state of mind; a great disappointment.

sair teeth toothache.

sair wame stomach-ache.

sair awa wi't worn out by illness, hard usage etc.

sair *see* **serve.**

sairgint *n* a sergeant.

sairie *adj* sorry.

sairious *adj* serious.

saison, sizzon NE *n* a season.

saithe *n* a full-grown coalfish in its third or fourth year.

saitin *n* satin.

saitisfee *v* satisfy.

sake *n*: **for onie sake** for Heaven's sake.

sald *see* **sell.**

sall *v* shall.

past tense **sud** SHETLAND, **sid** NE, **shid** NE should.

sudna SHETLAND, **sidna** NE, **shidna** NE, **shouldnae, shouldna** should not.

shanna shall not.

salt *see* **saut.**

same *n* fat, especially of pigs, grease, lard.

Sammy dreep *see* **dreep.**

san, sanal *see* **sand.**

sand, san, saun(d) *n*: **san(d)al, san(d)le** a sand-eel.

sannie = **sandshoe.**

sandy laverock a ringed plover.

sand lowper a sand flea.

sandshoe a plimsoll, gym shoe.

Sandle, Sawnie *n* **1** shortened forms of Alexander. **2** a young man, especially a countryman. **3** *often* **auld Sandle** the Devil.

sandle *see* **sand.**

sang, song *n* **1** a song. **2** the noise of the sea breaking on the shore. **3** a fuss, outcry: '*mak a sang aboot*'.

the end o an auld sang the last of an old custom, institution etc, the end of an era.

sanie *see* **sand.**

sanshach *adj* **1** wily, shrewd. **2** disdainful, surly NE. **3** irritable. **4** (*of people*) pleasant NE.

sap[1] *n* (an amount of) something to drink, to be taken with food SHETLAND, ORKNEY, N.

sap[2] *n* **1** a sop. **2 saps** pieces of bread etc soaked or boiled in milk etc.

sapsie *adj* like **saps**, soft, sloppy; effeminate.

n a soft, weak-willed person.

sapple *adj* **1** (*of meat*) juicy. **2** (*of people*) plump, fleshy. **3** wet, soggy, sodden. **4** (*of food*) soft, soggy, like **saps** (*see* **sap**[2]). **5** (*of a kiss*) soft, long-drawn out.

sapple *v* soak with water, rain etc; steep (clothes) in soapy water.

n, also **sapples** soapy lather.

sapsie *see* **sap**[2].

serk, serk *n* **1** a man's shirt. **2** (*in past times*) a woman's long, loose vest.

a sarkfu o sair banes a person stiff or sore from hard work or from a beating.

sarkin roof boarding.

Sassenach *adj* English(-speaking); formerly also used by Highlanders of Lowlanders.

n an English person.

sassenger *n* a sausage.

sate *n* a seat.

sattle *v, n* settle.

sauch [-ch as in 'loch'] *n* a willow, willow wood.

saucy *adj* **1** vain, conceited. **2** fussy about food or dress.

sauf *adj* safe.

v save.

saul, sowl *n* **1** a soul. **2** spirit, courage.

the (wee) sowl term of pity used *eg* to a hurt child, sometimes used sarcastically.

saumon *n* a salmon.

saumon lowp 1 a salmon leap. **2** a kind of leapfrog.

saun, saund *see* **sand.**

saunt *see* **saint.**

saur *v* have a certain taste or smell.

n **1** taste. **2** a slight wind, gentle breeze.

saurless 1 tasteless. **2** lacking in wit, spirit, energy NE.

saut, saat, salt *n* salt.

adj **1** salt. **2** (*of experience etc*) painful, severe, bitter. **3** (*of prices etc*) dear, stinging. **4** (*of speech, manner*) harsh, unkind sw.

v **1** salt. **2** punish, treat severely; overcharge, sting.

saw, shaw NE, **shaave** NE *v* SOW.

Sawbath *see* **Sabbath.**

Sawnie *see* **Sandie.**

sax, six *numeral* six.

sixsie a move in à game of **chuckies.**

sixsome a group of six (people), *eg* in a dance.

saxt, sixt sixth.

saxteen sixteen.

saxteen(t) sixteenth.

saxtie sixty.

six(es) and sax(es) very much alike, six and half a dozen.

say *v* say.

n **1** what is said; a remark, piece of gossip. **2** a saying, proverb SHETLAND, ORKNEY, N.

say ae wey (wi) agree (with).

say awa(y) *v* **1** say on, speak your mind. **2** say grace before a meal.

n a long rigmarole.

say wi agree with.

scab *n*: **scabble-heid** a person with head lice.

scabbit 1 scabbed. **2** (*of land*) bare, infertile. **3** (*of a person*) mean, worthless.

scad *see* **scaud.**

scaff[1] *n* a light boat, skiff.

scaff[2] *v* **1** scrounge, go about looking for (food) to pick up. **2** wander about.

n a low-class person, low-class people: '*Stay awa fae that scaff*'.

scaffie *n* a street-sweeper, refuse-collector.

scaffie cairt a refuse-collector's cart or lorry.

scailie, scallie, skylie *n* **1** a slate. **2** (*in past times*) a slate pencil.

scal, scald *see* **scauld.**

scald *see* **scaud.**

scallie *see* **scailie.**

scallion *n* a spring onion.

scam *v* burn slightly, scorch, singe.

n **1** a burn, singe. **2** a spot, crack, injury.

scance *v* scan, analyse, look carefully.

n **1** a quick look. **2** a gleam, a brief appearance.

scant *n* lack, scarcity.

scantlins scarcely, hardly.

scar *adj, also* **skair** timid, shy, wild, apt to run away.

n a fright, scare.

v **1** scare, frighten. **2** take fright, run away in fear.

scarf *see* **scart**[3].

scart[1] *v* **1** scratch, scrape. **2** strike (a match). **3** mark (a paper) with a pen, scribble (a note etc). **4** make a scraping, grating noise.

n **1** a scratch. **2** a mark or scrape of a pen, a scribble. **3** a furrow or mark on the ground. **4** a grain, very small quantity.

scart[2] *n* a thin, shrunken person.

scart[3], **scarf, scrath** NE *n* a cormorant; a shag.

scash NE *v* **1** quarrel, squabble. **2** twist, turn to one side; shuffle along with the toes turned out.

scatter *v, n* (*at a wedding*) scatter(ing) coins in the street for children to scramble for.

scaud, scald, scad *v* **1** scald. **2** make (tea) sw, SOUTH. **3** *mainly* **scad** (*of cloth*) (cause to) become faded or shabby.

n **1** a scald. **2** a sore caused by rubbing of the skin. **3** tea. **4** a hurt to the feelings.

scalder a kind of jellyfish.

scaul *see* **scauld.**

scauld, scaul, scal(d) *n* **1** a scold, a scolding woman. **2** scolding, abuse. *v* scold.

scaup *n* **1** the scalp. **2** thin shallow soil; a piece of (bare) stony ground. **3** a bank for shellfish in the sea.

scaur[1], **sker** SOUTH *n* a steep rock, precipice.

scaur[2] *n*, *v* scar.

scaw *n* **1** a scaly skin disease. **2** a mass of barnacles.

scawt 1 having a skin disease; scabby, scruffy. **2** shabby, faded.

scent, sint *n* **1** scent. **2** a small quantity, drop, pinch.

scheme *n*, *also* **housing scheme 1** a local-authority housing estate. **2** a low-class person.

schemie *adj* shabby.

n a low-class person.

scholar *n* a school pupil.

scissor *n* a pair of scissors.

sclaff *v* **1** strike with the open hand or with something flat, slap. **2** walk in a flat-footed or shuffling way.

n **1** a blow from something flat, a falling flat, a thud. **2** (*golf*) a muffed shot when the club grazes the ground before hitting the ball. **3** a light loose-fitting shoe or slipper; an old worn-down shoe. **4** a thin flat piece of something.

sclaffer a big, clumsy, flat-footed person; a flat foot.

sclaffert 1 a blow from something flat N. **2** a clumsy flat-footed person NE.

sclammer[1] *v* clamber.

sclammer[2] *v*, *n* clamour NE.

sclatch *v* **1** smear or cover over with something wet or messy. **2** do something messily, clumsily or carelessly.

n **1** a large smudge, smear. **2** a mess. **3** a heavy fall (into water or mud), a slap, smack.

sclate, slate *n*, *v* slate.

slater a woodlouse.

want a slate be mentally defective.

sclender, sclinner NE *adj* slender.

sclice *n*, *v* slice.

sclidder *see* **slidder.**

sclim *v* climb.

sclinner *see* **sclender.**

sclutter *see* **slutter.**

scly *v* slide, skate (as) on ice.

sclype *see* **slype**[1].

scob *n* a twig, rod or slat of wood.

scodge, scodgie *n* **1** a servant who does light, rough or dirty work. **2** *also* **scodgie brat** a rough apron for dirty work.

v do rough work.

scodgebell *see* **coachbell.**

scomfish [**skum**fish] *v* **1** suffocate, choke, overpower with heat etc. **2** disgust, sicken.

scone *n* **1** a usually semi-sweet cake baked on a **girdle** etc or in an oven. **2** an oatcake SHETLAND. **3** a slap (with the flat of the hand), smack.

v **1** strike the surface of (something) with a flat object. **2** slap with the open hand, smack (especially a child's bottom): '*Shut up or Ah'll scone ye*'.

scondies a child's word for smacks, a spanking.

Wha stole yer scone? Why are you so glum?

scoo *see* **scull.**

scoor[1] *n* a shower of rain, especially with gusts of wind.

scoorie blustery with rain, wet and squally.

scoor[2] *n* **1** a run, rush, quick pace. **2** a blow, stroke, box (on the ear).

scoor[3] *v* **1** scour, cleanse. **2** clear out (the bowels, stomach). **3** scold severely.

scoor-oot (*at a wedding*) the scattering of coins in the street for children to scramble for.

scoorie *adj* **1** (*of people*) scruffy, disreputable-looking. **2** (*of clothes*) shabby, worn.

scoot[1] *v* **1** make (water etc) spout or spurt out, squirt. **2** (*of liquid*) spurt or squirt out.

n **1** a sudden gush or flow of water from a spout etc; the pipe from which it comes.
2 *also* **scooter** a squirt, syringe, especially one used as a water gun.
3 *also* **scooter** a peashooter, especially one made from a plant stem.
4 diarrhoea, especially of birds or animals.
5 contemptuous term for a person.
scootie worthless, scruffy; small, insignificant: '*That restaurant gies scootie wee portions*'.
scoot[2] *n* one of various seabirds, *eg* a razorbill, a guillemot.
scootie allan *see* **Alan**.
score[1] *n* **1** a stroke, scratch. **2** (*games*) a mark or line on the ground, *eg* the starting line. **3** a line, wrinkle on the skin; a scar left by a wound. **4** a parting in the hair.
score[2] *n* a crevice, cleft, gully in a cliff face.
gae ower the score go beyond what is reasonable.
scorie *n* a young gull SHETLAND, ORKNEY, CAITHNESS.
Scotch *see* **Scots**.
Scots, Scottish, Scotch *adj* **1** of or belonging to Scotland or the Scots.
2 used in Shetland and Orkney to refer to the mainland of Scotland.
3 *mainly* **Scots** of the Scottish legal system: '*Scots law*'.
4 speaking or expressed in **Scots**.
n the Scots language, the speech of Lowland Scotland; that treated in this dictionary.
Scotch convoy the accompanying of a guest a part or all of the way back to his or her home (sometimes with company back again).
Scotch horses a formation of children running etc with arms linked behind their backs.
scowder, scowther *v* **1** burn, scorch, singe; over-toast (bread etc). **2** (*of frost or rain*) wither (leaves etc). **3**

become scorched, burn. **4** rain or snow slightly.
n **1** a scorch, singe, burn. **2** a jellyfish (because of its burning sting). **3** a slight shower (of rain).
scowe *n* a flat-bottomed boat, *eg* a barge.
scowes [rhymes with 'cows'] *npl* **1** barrel staves. **2** splinters, shattered pieces.
scowf *see* **scowthe**.
scowthe, scowf *n* freedom, scope.
scowther *see* **scowder**.
scrachle *see* **scrauchle**.
scrae *n* a stunted, shrivelled, underdeveloped person or animal.
scramble *n* (*at a wedding*) the scattering of coins in the street for children to scramble for WEST, SW.
scran *n* **1** food. **2** scraps or leavings of food or other rubbish often got by begging or scrounging.
v scrounge about for (food etc); scrape together.
scrape *n*: **a scrape o the pen** a mark made by a pen; a hasty scribble or letter.
scrat *v* scratch, claw; make a scratching noise.
n a scratch, slight wound; the noise made by scratching.
scratcher *n* (*slang*) a bed: '*Get oot yer scratcher*'.
scrath *see* **scart**[3].
scrauchle, scrachle *v* scramble with hands and feet, climb hastily and clumsily.
scree[1] *n* a mass of loose stones on a steep hillside.
scree[2] *n* a riddle or sieve for grain, sand, coal etc.
screed *n* **1** a long narrow strip: (1) of cloth, paper etc; a torn piece; (2) of land. **2** (*often contemptuous*) a long speech or piece of writing. **3** a tear, slash; a scratch. **4** the sound of tearing etc; a grating, scraping noise.
v **1** tear, rip. **2** tear, come apart. **3**

make a shrill screeching noise. **4** *often* **screed aff** read, recite fluently, reel off.

sreef *see* **scrulf.**

screenge *v* **1** rub or scrub energetically. **2** whip, flog. **3** wander about aimlessly NE.

screeve *v* **1** graze (the skin), peel or tear off (a surface etc), scratch, scrape. **2** make a scraping or grating motion or sound.

scrieve[1] *v* **1** move along quickly and smoothly. **2** talk fluently for a long time.

scrieve[2] *v* **1** write, especially fluently and easily. **2** scratch a mark on (wood), *eg* to show the shape in which something is to be made.
n a piece of writing, a letter or its contents.

scrimp *adj* **1** in short supply. **2** (*of clothes*) short, tight. **3** (*of people*) having too little (of something). **4** mean, sparing.
v **1** stint, not give enough to. **2** cut down in amount; use (up) carefully or meanly. **3** be over-careful, mean.

scrimple scanty, inadequate.

scrimpit under-sized; mean; scanty.

scrog *n* a stunted or crooked bush or tree; a stump of such.

scroggie full of **scrogs,** covered with undergrowth.

scroll *n* a rough draft or copy; a writing-pad etc for rough drafts or notes.

scronach NE *n* a shrill cry, outcry, loud lamentation.
v shriek, yell, cry out.

scroo *n* a stack of corn, hay etc, or of corn sheaves SHETLAND, ORKNEY, N.

scrulf, screef NE *n* **1** scruff, scurf. **2** a hardened scab of skin, hair, dirt. **3** a thin surface layer, crust etc.

scrunt[1] *n* **1** something shrunken or worn down by use, age etc. **2** a thin, scraggy person; a poorly-developed plant. **3** a mean miserly person.

scruntie 1 *also* **scruntit** stunted, shrivelled, stumpy. **2** mean, miserly.

scrunt[2] *v* **1** scrape, scrub, scratch, grind. **2** plane (wood) roughly.

scud *v* **1** throw (a flat stone) so as to make it skip over the water, play ducks and drakes. **2** beat with the open hand or a strap, smack.
n a blow, smack, a stroke with the **tawse.**

scudder a driving shower of rain or snow NE.

scuddle a game like **shinty** or hockey; the club or the ball used in it N.

scuddle *adj* **1** naked, without clothes, or with one piece of clothing only. **2** miserable, scruffy, shabby-looking. **3** stingy, insufficient, too small NE.
n, also **scud 1** the bare skin, a state of nakedness: '*in his bare scuddie*'; '*in the scud*'. **2** a nestling, a young unfledged bird.

scuddle *v* **1** work messily. **2** dirty (your clothes), make shabby or shapeless NE.

scuddlin claes your second-best or working clothes.

scuff *v* **1** touch lightly in passing, draw your hand etc quickly over; brush off or away.
2 hit with a glancing blow.
3 shuffle, scuffle.
4 wear away (clothes), make worn and shabby.
n **1** a glancing or brushing stroke of the hand, a slight touch in passing, a hasty wipe. **2** a slight passing shower of rain. **3** riff-raff.

scuffin (*of clothes*) second-best.

scuffle 1 shabby, worn, mean-looking. **2** mean, miserly NE.

scug *v* **1** hide, screen. **2** shelter, protect. **3** take shelter (from). **4** hide, skulk.
n **1** shade, shelter, protection (of a rock etc). **2** a pretence, excuse.

scull [-ui- as in 'guid'], **skweel** NE, **skeel** N *n* a school.

learn the scull be a pupil at school.

sculp, sklp, skeep NE *n* **1** a scoop. **2** *mainly* **skip** the front brim of a hat, the peak of a cap.

skipplt bonnet a cloth cap with a peak.

sculdudderle *n* **1** sex. **2** obscenity, indecency, especially in language.

scull, scoo *n* a shallow, scoop-shaped basket.

scult *v* strike with the palm of the hand, slap, smack.

scum *n* a worthless, disreputable person.

v skim, remove scum (from).

scunge, squeenge NE *v* prowl or slink about (in search of something), scrounge.

scunner *v* **1** get a feeling of disgust or loathing, feel sick, have had more than enough. **2** feel disgust at, be sickened by, be bored by. **3** cause such feelings in (a person).

n **1** a feeling of disgust, sickness, dislike, loss of interest: '*tak a scunner at something*'. **2** something which or someone who causes loathing or disgust, a nuisance: '*She's jist a scunner*'.

scunneration something which causes dislike or disgust.

scunnert, scunnered disgusted, bored, fed up.

scunnersome sickening, disgusting, horrible.

scur, scurl *n* a scab on a sore or wound NE.

scurr *v* slither, slide, skate, skid NE.

scurrlevalg *n* a tramp, vagabond; an idle person, a slut; a lout.

v roam about aimlessly.

scurry, squeerle *v* roam about, prowl about like a dog on the hunt NE.

scush NE *v* shuffle.

n a shuffling, scuffing with the feet; the noise of this.

scutch *v* **1** graze the surface of one object with another, flick. **2** walk quickly with a light scuffling step.

scutter *v* **1** do something messily or carelessly; spill or splash about. **2** do troublesome, time-wasting, pointless work, fiddle about. **3** keep (someone) back with something unimportant or annoying.

n **1** the doing of work awkwardly or dirtily; a footling, time-consuming and annoying occupation. **2** a person who works in a muddled or dirty way.

scutterle troublesome; time-wasting, footling NE.

sea, sey MORAY COAST, SOUTH *n*: **sea loch** an arm of the sea, especially fiord-shaped.

sea maw a seagull.

sea pyot an oyster-catcher.

sea tangle *see* **tang**[1].

sea toon a seaport town or village.

seam *n* **1** a row of natural or artificial teeth: '*a seam o teeth*'. **2** the parting of the hair. **3** a piece of sewing or needlework. **4** any task, piece of work.

search *n* a sieve, strainer.

v put through a sieve, sift, strain.

seater *numeral* (*in children's rhymes*) seven.

secretar *n* a secretary.

seddle *see* **saidle**.

sederunt [sedayroont] *n* **1** a list of those present at a meeting. **2** an informal meeting or sitting.

see, sel SOUTH [rhymes with 'gey'] *v* **1** see.

2 look at.

3 take steps to: '*see tae get some mair*'.

4 hand, let (a person) have: '*see me the teapot*'.

5 introducing a person or thing about to be discussed: '*See him, he cannae drive*'.

seen, seed *past tense* saw.

seeln glass a mirror.

I've seen mysell (do(ing) something) I can remember . . . , I have often . . .

seestu you see, you understand.

see aboot look after, ask about (a person).

see after 1 look after (a person) **2** make enquiries for.

see someone far enough (*expression of annoyance*) wish that someone was out of the way, had not appeared: '*Ah could see him far enough*'.

see thegither see eye to eye, agree.

see till, see to look at.

seeck *adj* sick.

seed *n* **1** *also* **sid** particles of (oat-) bran, frequently used to make **sowans**. **2** a grain (of something).

seed *see* **see**.

seek¹, sik *v, past tense, past participle* **socht 1** seek.

2 search for, look for.

3 ask for, *eg* by begging or in order to buy or hire etc.

4 search (a place), look through.

5 invite (a person) (to come, to do etc).

6 to go, come etc to, in(to), away etc.

7 propose to (a woman).

8 wish, desire: '*I'm seekin tae gae*'.

9 bring, fetch SOUTH.

socht exhausted NE.

seek² *v* soak, ooze.

seemit *see* **semmit**.

seen *see* **see, suin, syne**.

seendil *adv* seldom.

seep *see* **sype**.

seerup *n* syrup.

seestu *see* **see**.

seet *see* **suit**.

seeven, siven N *numeral* seven.

seevent seventh.

seeventeen(t) seventeenth.

seeventie seventy.

seevensome a group of seven.

seg¹ *n* **1** sedge. **2** a yellow flag-iris.

seggan a wild iris.

seg² *v* sag.

seg³ *v* (*of sour fruit etc*) set (the teeth) on edge.

sel *see* **see**.

sell [-ee-] *n* happiness, good fortune.

sellie blessed, lucky, happy.

sel, self *pronoun, adj* self.

self-contained (*of houses or flats*) having their accommodation and entrance restricted to the use of one household.

selch *see* **silkie**.

self *see* **sel**.

selkie *see* **silkie**.

Selkirk bannock *n* a kind of rich fruit loaf, originally made as a speciality by Selkirk bakers.

sell *v, past tense, past participle* **selt, sald** SHETLAND sell.

semmit, simmit, seemit NE *n* a man's vest or undershirt.

semple *adj* simple.

ser *see* **serve**.

serk *see* **sark**.

serve, ser, sair *v* **1** serve. **2** (*of clothes*) fit, suit. **3** satisfy or content, especially with food or drink; satiate, give much to.

n **ser** your fill, enough.

saired satisfied, full up.

ill-saired not having enough food.

weel-saired well satisfied with food or drink.

sairin 1 your fill (especially of food). **2** enough of something unpleasant; a thorough beating.

servit *n* a table-napkin, serviette.

session *n* **1** = **kirk session** (*see* **kirk**). **2** (*schools and Scottish universities*) the part of the year during which teaching is carried on.

session clerk the clerk or secretary of a **kirk session**.

session house the room in or attached to a church, in which the **kirk session** meets.

Court of Session the highest civil court in Scotland.

set *v, past participle also* **setten** NE **1** set.

2 make to sit, seat, place on a seat.

3 sit, be seated.

4 (*of plants and animals*) stop growing, have the growth checked.

5 disgust, sicken NE.

6 guide in a certain direction NE.

7 leave (milk) standing for the cream to rise.

8 be suitable for, suit: '*It sets me tae hae a long lie at the weekend*'.

9 (*of a person*) look well in: '*She sets it weel*'.

n **1** a set, a young plant etc used for planting.

2 a check; a setback, a disappointment.

3 a feeling of disgust NE.

4 a carry-on, fuss.

5 the way in which a thing is set or arranged; a condition, state (of affairs).

6 (*of a person*) build, physique, kind.

7 a person's attitude.

8 the setting of a piece of music.

9 *usually* **sett** a checked pattern in cloth, especially (the arrangement of) the squares and stripes in a tartan.

adj **1** inclined, determined, obstinate, *often* **weel-set, ill-set**. **2** pleased NE.

set awa *v* set off, start on a journey. *n* a fuss; a row, scolding; a sending-off.

set by lay aside, clear away, set aside for future use.

set tae set upon, attack.

set up 1 earth up (a plant). **2** set (a chimney) on fire. **3 set him** *etc* **up** what a cheek!

set-up conceited, stuck up.

set up yer gab make impudent remarks.

Seturday *n* Saturday.

Seturday's penny *etc* pocket money given to a child.

severals *npl* several persons or things.

sey *see* **sea.**

sgian dubh *see* **skean dhu.**

shaave *see* **saw.**

shachle *see* **shauchle.**

shae, shee NE *n, pl also* **shuin** [-ui- as in 'guid'], **shoon, sheen** a shoe.

v, see also **shod 1** shoe. **2** fit with metal rims, studs, tips etc.

shae *see* **she.**

shalf *n* a sheaf.

shair, shuir, sheer NE *adj* sure.

shairn, sharn *n* dung, excrement, especially of cattle.

shairp, sharp, sherp *adj* **1** sharp. **2** (*of soil*) gravelly, open and loose.

n **1** the act of sharpening (a tool etc). **2** a frost-nail on a horse's shoe.

v sharpen.

shak *v, past tense* **shakkit, shuck**; *past participle* **shakken, shooken, shucken, shook** shake.

n a shake.

the shakers a fit of shaking, a state of terror.

the shakkins o the poke the last remnants; the last-born of a family; the smallest pig in a litter.

shak a fit dance.

shalder *n* an oyster-catcher SHETLAND, ORKNEY.

shall *see* **shell.**

sham, shan *v* twist the face, make a face, grimace.

shammle NE *v* **1** shamble, walk awkwardly. **2** twist, strain; twist (the face).

shan *adj* **1** of poor quality, bad, shabby: '*That wis a shan trick tae play on the wee boy*'. **2** shy, timid, frightened.

shan *see* **sham.**

shangie[1] *n* **1 shangies** handcuffs. **2** a forked stick used to make a catapult.

shangie[2] *n* a row, disturbance, fight.

shank *n* **1** a leg of meat.

2 the leg of a stocking; a stocking, sock, or any piece of clothing in the process of being knitted.

3 the stem or shaft of a spoon, brush, glass etc.

4 the stem or stalk of a tree, plant or fruit.

5 the lower part or sides of a cornstack.

v **1** walk, go on foot, cover on foot. **2** send away on foot. **3** knit stockings etc. **4** fit (a tool etc) with a **shank** or handle.

shanks'(s) naig(ie) shanks' pony, on foot.

shankie, shunkie *n* a lavatory.

shanna *see* **sall.**

shap *see* **chap, shaup.**

shape *v* cut (cloth) in a certain pattern or shape.

n **1** a dressmaking pattern, a pattern piece. **2** an attitude; manner.

mak a shape make an effort.

share *see* **shear.**

sharg, shargar *n* a small, stunted, weakly person or animal.

sharn *see* **shairn.**

sharp *see* **shairp.**

shauchle, shachle *v* **1** walk without lifting the feet, shuffle. **2** wear (a garment, shoes etc) out of shape.

n **1** a shuffling, clumsy walk. **2** an old worn-out shoe, slipper. **3** a weakly, stunted or deformed person or animal.

shauchlin, shauchlie 1 unsteady or weak on your feet, shuffling; knock-kneed; wearing worn-out shoes. **2** (*of shoes*) out of shape, down at heel and worn, badly-fitting.

shaul *see* **shauld.**

shauld, shaul *adj* **1** shallow, not deep. **2** shallow in character, empty-headed. *n* a shallow part in the sea or a river, a shoal.

shaup, shap *n* **1** the seed husk of peas, beans etc; a pea-pod. **2** an empty-headed, useless person. **3** **shaups** bits, smithereens NE.

v shell (pea-pods), take (peas) from the husks.

shaw[1], **show** *v* **1** show. **2** cut off the **shaws** of (turnips).

n **1** a show. **2** **shaws** the stalks and leaves of potatoes, turnips etc. **3** **the shows** a fair with roundabouts, side-shows etc.

shaw[2] *n* (*literary*) a small natural wood.

shaw *see* **saw.**

shawlie *n* **1** a small shawl or scarf. **2** (*in past times*) an urban working woman or girl.

she, shae, sheu SHETLAND, ORKNEY *pronoun* she: **1** used by a husband of his wife or by a servant of his or her mistress. **2** referring to a thing, *eg* a mill, bell, church, clock.

hir, hur her.

shear, share *v* **1** shear. **2** reap (corn), cut (crops) with a sickle.

n **1** the act of cutting (especially corn). **2** a cut edge, especially of a sheaf of corn NE.

shear moose a shrew.

shears *npl* (a pair of) scissors; (sheep-) clippers.

sheave *n* a slice of bread etc.

shed, sheed SHETLAND, ORKNEY, NE *v* **1** shed. **2** part or comb (the hair, a sheep's fleece etc) to one side or the other. **3** separate (lambs from ewes). *n* **1** a parting of the hair on the head or the wool on a sheep's back. **2** the act of sorting out sheep, as a test in sheepdog trials. **3** a separate piece of ground.

shee *see* **shae.**

sheed *see* **shed.**

sheel, shill *v* **1** shell (peas, grain etc), take out of the husk or pod. **2** cut (a mussel) from its shell. **3** win money, marbles etc from, swindle (a person). **4** shell out (money). **5** throw out or scatter right and left NE.

sheelins the grain removed from the husk by milling.

sheel *see* **shull.**

sheen *v* shine, gleam, glisten.

sheen *see* **shae.**

sheep *n*: **sheeple meh 1** a sheep. **2** a flower of the wild white clover.

sheep fank, sheep stell a (dry-stone) enclosure where sheep are gathered for shelter, dipping, shearing etc.

sheer *see* **shair.**

sheet *see* **shuit.**

shell, shall SHETLAND, ORKNEY, N *n* **1**

a shell. **2** a small saucer-shaped dish; a saucer.

sheltie *n* **1** a Shetland pony, one of a breed of very small horses, originally native to Shetland; also applied to any pony. **2** a Shetlander SHETLAND, ORKNEY, N.

shenachie [shenachie] *n* a storyteller (of Celtic/Gaelic tales).

shepherd's check, shepherd's tartan *n* (a cloth of) black-and-white check.

sheriff, shirra *n* **1** the chief judge of a **sheriffdom**. **2** a legal officer who presides over a **Sheriff Court** and also has other legal and certain administrative duties.

sheriffdom the area under the jurisdiction of a **sheriff**.

sheriff clerk the clerk of the **Sheriff Court**.

Sheriff Court a locally-based court which deals with both criminal and civil cases.

sheriff officer an official or messenger who carries out the warrants of a **sheriff**, serves writs etc.

sherp *see* **shairp**.

sherrack, shirrak *n* a noisy quarrel, rumpus.

v raise a riot about (a person); give (a person) a public dressing-down.

sheu *see* **she**.

sheuch [shooch, shuch] *n* **1** a ditch, a trench in the ground, especially for drainage. **2** a furrow. **3** a street gutter. *v* **1** dig, make a ditch or furrow (in). **2** lay (a plant etc) in the ground, especially in a temporary trench.

In a sheuch in a state of misery, ruined.

up the sheuch mistaken, in error.

shevel, showl, shile sw *adj* (*of the mouth*) twisted.

v **1** twist out of shape; screw up (the face). **2** twist the mouth, make a face from annoyance, pain, a bitter taste etc.

shew [shoo] *v* sew.

n the act of sewing; a spell of needlework.

shid, shidna *see* **sall**.

shiel *n* a temporary or rough hut or shed, especially one used by (salmon) fishermen or shepherds (and their animals), a **shieling**.

shielin(g) a high or remote summer pasture, usually with a shepherd's hut or huts; one of those huts.

shiffle *see* **shull**.

shift *v* **1** change places with NE. **2** change (your clothes, shoes etc); change the clothes of (another person), provide (someone) with (fresh clothes). **3** make a move in the game of draughts.

n **1** a change of situation, home or job. **2** each successive crop in a system of crop-rotation; the land or field on which this is grown. **3** a change of clothing. **4** a move in the game of draughts.

shift yer feet change your shoes and socks or stockings.

shilagie [shilaggie] *n* coltsfoot, especially its leaves used by juvenile smokers as a substitute for tobacco.

shile *see* **shevel**.

shilfa, shillie *n* a chaffinch.

shill *see* **sheel**.

shillie *see* **shilfa**.

shilpie *adj* thin, puny, pinched-looking.

shilpit *adj* **1** thin, puny, starved- or pinched-looking. **2** (*of drink*) insipid, thin SHETLAND. **3** sour, bitter; no longer fresh SHETLAND, ORKNEY, CAITHNESS.

shin *n* a ridge or steep hillface.

shine[1] *n* **1** a social gathering: '*tea shine*'; '*cookie shine*'. **2** a disturbance.

shine[2] *v* throw with force, fling SOUTH.

shinner *see* **cinner**.

shinty *n* **1** a game like hockey played towards **hails**[2], now mainly in the

Highlands. **2** the club or stick used in the game, a **caman**.

shirpit *adj* thin, shrunken, with sharp, drawn features.

shirra *see* **sheriff**.

shirrak *see* **sherrack**.

shite *n, v* shit.

shither *v, n* shiver, shudder SOUTH.

shive *n* a slice (of bread).

shivereens *npl* small bits.

shiverin bite, shivery bite *n* a small snack taken after swimming to stop shivering.

shoad *see* **shod**.

shock *n* a (paralytic) stroke.

shockle *n* an icicle.

shod, shoad *past tense, past participle of* **shae** shod.

v, past tense, past participle **shod(d)it** **1** put shoes on; shoe (a horse). **2** fit (a bootlace, spade etc) with a metal tip etc. **3** put iron toe- and heel-pieces on (a shoe), cover (shoe soles) with studs etc.

n **1** an iron tip etc on a (wooden) object to prevent wear. **2** a metal plate on the toe or heel of a shoe; a hobnail.

shog, shug, shoog *v* **1** shake, jog, cause to swing or rock. **2** *also* **shoggle** sway, swing, rock from side to side, wobble. **3** go at a leisurely but steady pace, jog along.

n **1** a jog, shake, nudge. **2** *also* **shoggle** a swinging or rocking; a swinging-rope; a child's swing.

shoggle shaky, unsteady, wobbly.

sho(g)gle boat a swingboat at a fair.

shoggle-shoo 1 a seesaw, the game of seesaw. **2** a swing.

shoogle, shoggle, shuggle *v* **1** wobble, move unsteadily, rock, sway. **2** shake, joggle, cause to totter or rock. **3** jog along, move unsteadily, shuffle. *n* **1** a shake, jog, jolt. **2** a swinging on a rope, tree branch etc.

shooglie shaky, unsteady, tottery.

shoo *see* **shue**.

shooder, shoother *n* a shoulder.

shooderie carrying a child on the shoulders: '*Gie me a shooderie*'.

shooer, shower *n* **1** a shower (of rain etc). **2** a pang of pain etc.

shoog, shoogle *see* **shog**.

shook, shooken *see* **shak**.

shoon *see* **shae**.

shoot, shuit, suit *v* **1** suit. **2** please, satisfy: '*He wisnae shootit*'. **3** look good (in a colour, piece of clothing): '*Ye suit blue*'; '*She suits that blouse*'.

n a suit.

shoot *see* **shuit**.

shoother *see* **shooder**.

shop, tchop NE *n* a shop.

shop door the front flap or fly of trousers.

shore[1] *n* a quay, landing place, harbour: '*the Perth shore*'.

shore[2] *n* a kind of marbles game.

shore[3] *v* **1** threaten. **2** scold SHETLAND.

short *adj, adv*: **shortlins, shortly 1** shortly. **2** recently.

shortcome a shortcoming; a shortage.

shortie shortbread.

short-set small and stockily-built.

shortsome lively and entertaining, cheerful, making time pass quickly.

short an lang in brief.

short (sin) syne a short time ago.

short in the trot, short in the pile in a bad temper, curt and rude.

shot, shottle NE *n* a brief loan; a turn: '*Gie's a shot o yer bike*'; '*shots each*'. *v* **1** shoot. **2** cast (lines or nets) NE. *interjection* a warning among children of the approach of a policeman, teacher etc.

shot *see* **shuit**.

shott *n* a young pig after weaning.

shotten *see* **shuit**.

shottle *see* **shot**.

shottle, shuttle *n* a small compartment at the top of a trunk, chest etc.

shouldna, shouldnae *see* **sall**.

show *see* **shaw**[1].

showd NE *v* swing to and fro, rock.
n a rocking, swaying motion; a swing.

shower *see* **shooer.**

showl *see* **shevel.**

shreed *n* a shred.

shrood *n* a shroud.

shrunkelt, shrunkled *adj* shrunken, shrivelled.

shuck, shucken *see* **shak.**

shue, shoo *v* **1** swing, rock or sway backwards and forwards. **2** back water SHETLAND, ORKNEY, CAITHNESS.

shuffle *see* **shull.**

shug *see* **shog.**

shuggar, succar, sugar *n* sugar.

sugaraille liquorice, especially when made up as a **sweetie;** a stick etc of liquorice.

sugaraille watter a children's drink made up by dissolving a piece of liquorice in water.

sugar bool, sugardoddle a round, striped, boiled **sweetie.**

sugar piece a slice of bread buttered and sprinkled with sugar.

shuggle *see* **shog.**

shull, sheel, shuffle, shiffle *n* a shovel.
v **1** shovel. **2** take away (someone's) store of something, clean (someone) out. **3** slide, shuffle (the feet).

shuln *see* **shae.**

shuir *see* **shair.**

shult, shoot, sheet N *v, past tense also* **sheetit** NE; *past participle also* **shotten, sheetit** NE **1** shoot. **2** position (a fishing-net) in water. **3** push, jerk forward.

shot *adj* **1** (*of plants*) run to seed. **2** *also* **shotten** (*of fish*) spawned. **3 shot o** rid of, free from.
n an inferior animal, especially a sheep, left over *eg* after a buyer's selection.

shot joint a joint deformed by rheumatism.

shult by manage somehow.

shult *see* **shoot.**

shunkle *see* **shankle.**

shut *v*: **shut tae** close (especially a door) properly.

shuttle *see* **shottle.**

sib *adj*: **sib tae 1** related by blood to, of the same family as. **2** of the same sort, connected (with). **3** bound by ties of affection, familiarity etc.

sic, sich *adj, pronoun* such.
adv so NE.

siccan 1 such, of such a kind, of a sort already mentioned. **2** what (a) . . . !, how . . . !: '*siccan a day!*'.

siclike *adj* **1** suchlike. **2** (*of health etc*) much about the same; so-so, indifferent.
adv similarly, in the same way.

sic-an-sae, sic-an-sic-like alike, similar, much of a muchness.

siccar *see* **sicker.**

sich *see* **sic.**

sicht, sight *n* **1** a sight. **2** a close look, examination. **3** the pupil (of the eye).
v **1** sight. **2** examine, inspect (*eg* a newborn animal for its sex).

a sicht for sair een a welcome or pleasing sight.

sicker *adj* **1** safe, free from danger etc. **2** firm, stable, fixed; held firm. **3** dependable, reliable. **4** careful, cautious, especially with money, wary. **5** (*of a blow*) hard, severe.

mak siccar make sure or certain.

siclike *see* **sic.**

sid *see* **sail, seed.**

side *n*: **sidelin(s), sidlings** *adv* **1** sideways, side on, to one side. **2** (*of speech or look*) indirectly.
adj **1** sidelong, moving or glancing sideways. **2** sloping, on a slope.
n a sloping piece of ground, a hillside.

sidleweys sideways.

sidna *see* **sail.**

siege *v* scold severely, storm at NE.

sight *see* **sicht.**

sik *see* **seek**[1].

sile[1] v pass (a liquid, especially milk) through a sieve, strain.

n a sieve, strainer, filter, especially for milk.

sile[2], **sill** n the newly-hatched young of fish, especially of herring.

silkie, selkie SHETLAND, ORKNEY, CAITHNESS, NE, **selch** [-ch as in 'dreich'] n a seal, the animal.

selkie folk, silkies seal people, imaginary seal-like sea creatures SHETLAND, ORKNEY.

sill see **sile**[2].

siller n 1 silver. 2 money.

sillered wealthy.

siller shakers quaking grass.

silly adj 1 helpless; weak, sickly, delicate; shaky. 2 mentally deficient.

silly cuddles the game of leapfrog.

simmen n a rope made of straw, heather, rushes etc, used with stone weights to hold down thatch on houses and stacks.

simmer, summer n summer.

simmer cowt a heat haze, the shimmering of the air on a hot day.

simmer's day a summer day.

simmer an winter go into (something) in great detail, be long-winded in telling a story.

simmit see **semmit**.

sin[1], **son** n a son.

Son of the Rock 1 a native of Dumbarton or Stirling. **2 the Sons (of the Rock)** nickname of Dumbarton football team.

sin[2] n pity, shame: 'It's a sin, so it is'.

sin yer soul become guilty of sin (especially by telling lies).

sin see **sun, syne**.

sinder, sinner v 1 part, separate, sunder. 2 single, hoe out (seedlings) NE.

sindrins a fork in the road.

sindrie, sinnerie 1 sundry. **2** separate, apart, distinct.

sing[1] n a whizzing blow, wallop.

sing dumb keep silent.

sing[2] v, past tense, past participle **singit, sung** singe.

singit stunted, shrivelled, puny.

single adj (in a fish-and-chip shop) not served with chips, by itself: 'single fish'; 'single puddin'.

v thin out (seedlings, especially turnips).

single en(d) a one-roomed flat or house.

sinner see **sinder**.

sinsyne see **syne**.

sint see **scent**.

sirple v sip continuously, go on drinking in small quantities, tipple SOUTH.

sister n: **sister bairn** the child of a parent's sister, a cousin CAITHNESS.

sister son a nephew, the son of your sister ORKNEY.

sit v, past tense also **sut**; past participle also **sitten, sutten 1** sit. **2** (of plants) stop growing, be stunted.

n a sinking or settling down of the surface of the ground or of something built on it.

sitten adj 1 (of tea) stewed, strong and bitter. 2 (of an egg) near to hatching.

sitten-doon (of a cold etc) persistent, chronic.

sit doon v settle yourself in a place or situation, make your home.

n 1 a chance or spell of being seated, a seat. 2 a home, settlement, a situation.

sit in draw your chair in (to a fire, a table).

sit-ooterie (humorous) a place where you can sit out, eg at a dance, outside at a restaurant, in a conservatory or in a patio.

sit see **suit**.

sitten see **sit**.

siven see **seeven**.

six, sixt see **sax**.

sizzon see **saison**.

skaich see **skech**.

skaik v smear, plaster with something soft and wet, streak, blotch NE.

skail v 1 (of a group, eg in a school,

church etc) break up, separate. **2** scatter (a group of people); chase; dismiss (a meeting, congregation). **3** pour out, spill (accidentally). **4** scatter, throw or spread about (a collection of things).

skair *n* a slanting cut or notch in a piece of wood by which it can be joined to another of similar shape.

skair *see* **scar**.

skaith *v, n* damage, hurt, harm.

skane *see* **skin**.

skean dhu, sgian dubh [**skee**an **doo**] *n* a small sheath-knife worn in the stocking as part of Highland dress.

skech, skaich *v* get (something) in an underhand way, scrounge.

n a scrounger, sponger.

on the skech on the prowl, scrounging.

skeeg *v* whip, strike, slap NE.

n a blow, smack, especially on the bottom NE.

skeel *n* **1** skill. **2** skill in healing (people or animals), especially by non-professionals.

v look carefully, especially for weather signs.

skeelie 1 skilled, experienced, practised. **2** having real or supposed skill in the art of healing.

skeelie wife a woman believed to have great or supernatural healing powers.

skeel *see* **scull**.

skeep *see* **sculp**.

skeer *v* scare.

adj, also **skeerie** nervous, fearful, agitated; flighty; mentally unstable.

skeet *see* **skite**[1].

skeetch *see* **sketch**.

skelch [-ch as in 'dreich'] *adj***1** (*of horses*) frisky, spirited, restless. **2** (*of people*) in high spirits, daft; shy, haughty.

skelchen 1 timid, easily scared, nervous NE. **2** fussy about food, easily upset NE.

skelb *n* **1** a thin flake, slice or splinter

of wood etc, especially in the skin. **2** any thin slice NE.

skelf[1] *n* a shelf SHETLAND, ORKNEY, N.

skelf[2] *n* **1** a thin slice, a flake; a splinter especially in the skin. **2** a small thin person.

skellie[1] *adj* **1** squinting, squint-eyed. **2** lop-sided.

n a squint in the eye; a sideways glance.

v **1** squint, be cross-eyed. **2** make a mistake, exaggerate.

skellie[2] *n* a ridge of rock running out to sea, usually covered at high tide.

skelloch[1] *n, v* shriek, scream, cry.

skelloch[2] *n* charlock or wild mustard.

skellum *n* a scamp, rogue, scoundrel.

skelp[1] *v* **1** strike, hit, especially with something flat, smack (someone's bottom); hit, drive with blows, kicks etc; beat, hammer. **2** work with great energy. **3** gallop, move quickly.

n **1** a blow, especially with a flat object, a smack. **2** a blast of wind, downpour of rain. **3** an attempt, try.

skelpin *adj* big of its kind: '*a skelpin ice-cream*'.

skelpit leatherin a thrashing, spanking.

skelp[2] *n* **1** a thin slice; a flake; a splinter, especially in the skin. **2** a large slice or chunk. **3** a long strip (of ground).

skelter *v* scurry, scamper, rush.

skemmels *npl* a slaughterhouse; a meat or fish market.

skemp *n* a scamp.

skep *n* **1** a basket, especially for grain, meal or potatoes. **2** a (straw) beehive.

v put (a swarm of bees) into a hive.

skepple, skep (bee) a hive- or honeybee.

sker *see* **scaur**[1].

skerrie *n* a rock in the sea, especially one covered at high tide.

sketch, skeetch, skytch [-y- as -ey in 'gey'] *n* **1** an ice-skate. **2** a turn or spell of skating.

v **1** skate. **2** (*of a stone*) skim along the surface of water; play at ducks and drakes.

skeetcher 1 the flat stone etc kicked in the game of **peever**[1]; the game itself. **2** a skimming stone. **3** *also* **skytcher** a skater; an ice-skate.

skeuch *see* **skew**.

skew, skyowe [skeeow] NE, **skeuch** [skeeooch] NE *v* **1** go off the straight, move sideways NE. **2** twist, turn sideways, screw round. **3** (*of the feet, legs*) splay, turn outwards NE. **4** (*of the eyes or glance*) squint naturally or on purpose. **5** fall out, disagree NE.
n **1** a twist, turn, sideways movement. **2** a squint, sidelong glance NE. **3** a quarrel, row NE.

skewl, skyowl [skeeool, skeeowl] *v* turn aside; twist.

skice *v* leave quickly and without being noticed NE.

skiddle[1], **skittle** *v* splash, squirt, spill.
n **1** a mess, muddle, especially with spilling of liquid. **2** a thin watery liquid, *eg* weak tea. **3** contemptuous term for a small thing, person, or animal.

skiddlie small, insignificant, unimportant.

skiddle[2] *v* move quickly and lightly.

skiff[1] *v* **1** move lightly, skim, glide, skip.
2 rain or snow very slightly.
3 do work carelessly.
4 touch lightly in passing, brush, graze.
5 throw along the surface; make (a flat stone) skip over water, or over the ground, play ducks and drakes.
n **1** a slight touch or graze in passing. **2** a slight gust of wind. **3** a slight touch (of an illness). **4** a slight shower of rain or snow.

skiffer, skiffle NE a flat stone used in playing ducks and drakes.

skiffin 1 a slight fall of snow. **2** a thin partition or screen.

skiffle *n* a slight shower of rain.
v (*eg of a stone on water*) skip or skim across.

skifflers the game of ducks and drakes.

skiff[2] *n* a type of small fishing boat with oars and a lugsail.

skiffle *see* **skiff**[1].

skift *v* **1** move lightly, skim, skip. **2** (*of rain or snow*) fall lightly.
n **1** a light shower of rain or snow. **2** a hurried dusting.

skifter 1 = **skift** *n* 1. **2** **skifters** the game of ducks and drakes.

skilt *v* move about quickly and lightly, dart, skip.

skime *n* **1** a glance, a quick or angry look. **2** a gleam of light, flash; a brief glimpse.

skimmer *v* **1** twinkle, gleam; be bright. **2** glide along easily and quickly.
n a light sprinkling, especially of snow or rain.

skin, skane SHETLAND *n* **1** skin. **2** (*slang*) a robbery; a swindle.

skinnin a small amount (taken or saved).

skin-the-cuddie a kind of leapfrog.

skink[1] *n* **1** a shin or knuckle of beef. **2** a soup, especially one made from this (*but see* **Cullen skink**).

skink[2] *v* pour.
n **1** drink, especially of a weak, wishy-washy kind. **2** a kind of thin, oatmeal-and-water gruel.

skinkin easily poured, thin, weak.

skinkle *v* glitter, gleam, sparkle.

skinny[1] *n* a bread roll.

skinny[2] *adj*: **skinnymalink(ie)** a thin, skinny person or animal.

skinny tattie a potato boiled in its skin.

skip[1] *v*: **skipple** *adj* (*of roads etc*) slippery, icy.
n a skipping game SW.

skip raip a skipping rope.

skip[2] *n* (*curling and bowls*) the captain of a rink or side.
v act as **skip** to a team.

skip *see* **sculp.**
skippack *see* **skipple.**
skipple, skippack *n* the game of tig N.
skire *adj* clear, bright.
v shine brightly, glitter; be gaudy, garish.
skirie bright, gaudy, garish (in colour) NE.
skirl *v* **1** scream, screech, shriek; cry or sing shrilly. **2** (*of bagpipes etc*) make a shrill sound. **3** crackle, sputter; (*especially in frying*) sizzle.
n **1** a scream or shriek. **2** the loud cry or whistle of a bird. **3** the shrill sound of bagpipes. **4** the sound of a strong wind. **5** a screeching, whirring or whistling noise.
skirlie, skirl-in-the-pan a dish of oatmeal and onions fried in a pan.
skirlie wheeter an oyster-catcher NE.
skirl nakit *adj* completely naked.
skirp NE *v* **1** sprinkle (water etc), splash in small drops. **2** (*of water, mud etc*) splash; rain slightly, spit.
n **1** a small drop, splash; a slight shower or spot of rain. **2** a small flying piece of metal, stone etc.
skirt *v* run away; elope; play truant from (school).
skirvin *n* a thin covering of soil, snow etc SOUTH.
skit *n* diarrhoea.
skite[1], **skeet** SHETLAND, ORKNEY *v* **1** slip or slide on a slippery surface; skate (on ice).
2 throw, send flying, make (something) shoot off at an angle; cause (a stone) to skip over the surface of water.
3 strike, hit.
4 dart through the air suddenly, forcibly and often at a slant.
adv with a sharp blow, with force or bounce.
adj off your head, daft NE.
n **1** a slip, skid.
2 a sudden sharp blow.
3 a spree, blow-out: '*on the skite*'.

4 shooting out or squirting liquid; a short sharp shower (of rain).
5 a yellowhammer NE.
6 a nasty person.
skiter a squirt, syringe; a pea- or water-shooter, especially one made from a plant stem.
skitle slippery.
skite[2] *v* have diarrhoea.
n, also **skiter** NE a nasty person.
skitter *n* **1** diarrhoea. **2** anything dirty or disgusting, a mess.
v **1** have diarrhoea. **2** waste time doing footling jobs, potter about aimlessly: '*skitterin aboot*'.
skitterie 1 trifling, small or inadequate. **2** (*of a task*) fiddly, time-consuming.
skitterie feltie a fieldfare.
in a skitter in a hurry, trying to do several things at once.
skittle *see* **skiddle**[1].
skive[1] *v* roam or prowl about (like a dog in search of food).
skive[2] *v* shave, pare, slice off a thin layer from.
skiver *n* a splinter of wood in the skin.
v pierce or stab as with a skewer.
skleff *adj* **1** shallow, flat; thin and flat. **2** equal, even (in a competition etc).
sklent *v* **1** *also* **slent** move at a slant, move sideways, zigzag. **2** slope, slant, lie to one side. **3** aim (something) sideways, send across. **4** look sideways, squint.
n **1** a slanting cut; a slope. **2** a sideways movement, change of direction. **3** a sidelong glance.
adj slanting, to one side.
skleush [skl(ee)**oosh**] *v* walk in a clumsy, shuffling or weary way N.
skliff *v* **1** walk with a heavy, shuffling step, scuffle. **2** strike with a glancing blow, rub against. **3** cut away the upper surface or covering of, pare, slice.
n **1** a shuffling, trailing way of walking. **2** a clumsy, worn-out shoe. **3** a blow with a flat surface, a swipe in

passing. **4** a segment, *eg* of the moon, of an orange.

skliffer a thin layer.

skllnter *v* splinter, break off in pieces or flakes.

sklone *n* a large amount of something soft.

sklyte *n* **1** a heavy fall, a thud NE. **2** a soft, wet, half-liquid mass NE. **3** a big, clumsy, slovenly person or animal NE. *v* **1** fall with a thud or thump; go with a clatter. **2** pour or throw liquid in a careless noisy way NE. **3** work messily or clumsily.

skook *v* **1** skulk. **2** avoid (in a skulking way). **3** scowl, look from under the eyebrows.
n a furtive look; a frown NE.

skool *v, n* scowl.

skoosh *v* gush in spurts or splashes, squirt; dart or move quickly with a swishing sound.
n **1** a splash, spurt, jet (of liquid). **2** lemonade etc.
adv with a splash or swish.

skoosher a device for sprinkling or spraying, a sprinkler.

skoosh car a tramcar WEST.

skoosh it do something easily.

skralch *v, n* screech, shriek, scream.

skrankle *adj* thin, scraggy, shrivelled.

skrauch *v* utter a shrill cry, scream, shout.

skreek, skrelch [-ch as in 'dreich'] *n*:
skreek o day first light, the crack of dawn.

skreek *see* **skrelch**.

skrelch, skreek *v, n* shriek, screech, scream.

skrelch *see* **skreek**.

skrink *v* shrink, shrivel up.

skrunklt *adj* shrunk(en), shrivelled.

skulk *v* play truant from (school) OR-KNEY, NE.

skweel *see* **scull**.

sky *n* daylight, sunlight, the sun, especially at dawn or sunset.
v NE **1** look towards the horizon,

shading your eyes with your hand. **2** shade (a patch of water) so as to see the bottom.

skybald NE *adj* **1** disreputable, worthless; ragged. **2** needy.

skylle *see* **scaille**.

skyowe *see* **skew**.

skyowl *see* **skewl**.

skytch *see* **sketch**.

slabber *v* **1** wet or stain with saliva or with food when eating.
2 wet with something messy and semi-liquid.
3 slaver, dribble; eat or drink noisily, sloppily.
4 make a snorting, bubbling sound.
5 work carelessly, messily or with something wet or messy.
6 talk drivel.
n **1** a greedy or noisy mouthful, a slobber. **2** something liquid or messy, especially food. **3** a messy person, a slobberer.

slack *n* **1** a hollow, especially between hills, a pass. **2** a low-lying, boggy, hollow area in the ground SOUTH.

slade *see* **slide**.

slae[1] *n* a sloe, blackthorn.

slae[2] *n* a slow- or blindworm.

slaiger *v* **1** smear with something soft and wet. **2** eat or drink messily. **3** walk messily in mud etc, plod wearily or carelessly.
n **1** a wet, soggy or slimy mess, a smear of sloppy food etc. **2** an act of daubing; careless, messy work.

slaigerin dirty, careless and messy.

slaik *v* **1** lick, slobber on. **2** (*especially of a pet animal*) lick (dishes) or eat (food) on the sly. **3** kiss, fondle over-sloppily. **4** smear, streak.
n **1** a lick with the tongue, a slobber-ing lick or kiss. **2** a careless wash, a hasty clean or wipe; a dirty, messy way of working.

slair *v* smear.

slairle *n* a smear, daub, a lick of paint.

adj messy in your eating habits.

slaister *v* **1** work messily or splash the hands about in a liquid; work awkwardly, clumsily.

2 eat or drink messily or greedily.

3 make messy, smear; smear (a substance) on a surface, spread or scatter messily.

n **1** a careless, dirty worker, a slut; a messy person, especially a messy eater.

2 a state of wetness and dirt, a splashy mess, dirty water, slops.

3 a disgusting mixture of foods etc.

4 a state of confusion.

slaisterin untidy, careless and messy.

slaisterie wet and dirty, muddy, slimy.

slaister kyte a messy eater, a greedy person.

siammachs *npl* spiders' webs NE.

slap[1], **slop** N *n* **1** a slap, a smack. **2** a large quantity.

v **1** slap, smack. **2** beat, go beyond.

full slap at full speed.

slap[2], **slop** *n* **1** a gap or opening in a wall, hedge etc. **2** a pass or shallow valley between hills. **3** a hole, missing part, a break in a pattern.

slaps *npl* slops, sloppy food etc.

slash *n* a splash, a violent dash, especially of something wet SHETLAND, NE.

v **1** throw (liquid) with a splash; hit with something wet. **2** rush violently, dash forward.

slate *see* **sclate**.

slaurie *v* spread or splash with mud etc.

slaver, slivver NE *v* **1** slaver. **2** talk nonsense, chatter in a silly way. **3** (*of lovers*) cuddle, pet.

n slaver, saliva.

slaw *adj* slow.

adv slowly.

sled *n* **1** a sledge. **2** a child's cart, usually made of short planks on the frame of an old pram.

sled *see* **slide**.

slee, sly *adj* **1** sly. **2** (*of people*) clever, skilled, expert; wise. **3** (*of things*) well-made.

sleek *adj* smooth and deceitful; cunning, self-seeking, sly.

v **1** smooth. **2** (*in measuring*) level off (especially grain or fruit) at the top of the container. **3** slink, sneak. **4** flatter, wheedle, curry favour with.

sleekit 1 smooth in manner; sly, cunning, not to be trusted. **2** smooth, having an even surface or glossy skin.

sleep *v* (*of a top*) spin so fast and so smoothly that it appears motionless.

sleepie men, sleepie things the little specks of matter which form in the eyes during sleep.

be sleepit oot have slept your fill.

sleep in oversleep.

sleesh *n* **1** a slice NE. **2** a swipe, cutting stroke.

sleetch, silke FIFE *n* mud or sludge left behind by the sea or a river.

slent *see* **sklent**.

slerp *v* **1** slobber, splutter messily, spit. **2** smear or daub with something wet or messy.

n **1** a slurp. **2** a slut, a slovenly woman.

slicht[1] *n* cunning, skill, sleight.

slicht[2] *adj* slight.

slid *adj* slippery, smooth.

slidden *see* **slide**.

slidder, sclidder *v* **1** slip, slide, slither. **2** move in a casual or lazy way.

n **1** a sliding, slithering movement, a skip, skid. **2** ice, an icy surface NE. **3** a narrow, stony, steep hollow or track down a hillside.

slidderie, sclidderie 1 slippery. **2** (*of food*) soft, sloppy. **3** insecure, unstable to stand on etc, shaky. **4** (*of people or actions*) sly, deceitful, unreliable.

slide *v, past tense also* **slade, sled;** *past participle also* **slidden 1** slide. **2** tell a mild lie, exaggerate NE.

slider an ice-cream wafer.

slidey, slidy slippery, very smooth.

slike *see* **sleetch.**

slim *adj* **1** (*of clothes, shoes etc*) flimsy, thin SHETLAND, NE. **2** sly, crafty, wily. *v, often* **slim ower** treat (work) carelessly, rush through (a job).

sling *v* walk with a long vigorous stride, swing along SOUTH.

slingers *npl* sausages.

slink *n* **1** contemptuous term for a person, a smooth crafty person. **2** a premature, stillborn or newly-born animal. *adj* thin, scraggy.

slunken weak- or starved-looking.

slip *v*: **slipper** a slippery state or condition; something which causes slipperiness, ice etc NE.

slippy slippery.

slip awa die quietly.

slip-by shoddy work.

slitter *v* **1** work or walk messily in water etc, splash about untidily; eat or drink messily. **2** smear with something wet or messy, make messy or stained. *n* **1** a sloppy mess, especially of food; a dirty untidy state. **2** an untidy or messy person.

slitterie wet and messy, sloppy.

slive *n* a thin slice, a sliver SE.

slivver *see* **slaver.**

sloch[1] *n* **1** an outer skin, slough. **2** the outer skin or husk of certain fruits or vegetables.

sloch[2] *v* swallow (food or drink) in a noisy slobbering way. *n* a noisy gulp of food or drink.

sloch *see* **slock**[2].

slock[1] *v* **1** quench (thirst etc), *often* **slock yer drouth. 2** satisfy the thirst of (a person or animal); satisfy the wishes or desires of. **3** slake (lime). **4** moisten, soak NE. **5** put out (a fire etc). *n* a drink.

slockin a drink, enough (drink) to quench your thirst.

slockit drunk NE.

slock[2], **sloch** *n* **1** a hollow between hills. **2** a long deep inlet of the sea.

slocken *v* **1** put out (fire, flame). **2** quench (thirst). **3** satisfy the thirst of (a person or animal). **4** celebrate with a drink. **5** moisten, soak. **6** slake (lime). **7** make a paste of (meal).

slockener a drink, a thirst-quencher.

slogger *n* a dirty or untidy person.

sloom *n* a dreamy or sleepy state, a daydream, a light or unsettled sleep NE.

sloonge, slunge *v* **1** idle or loaf about, walk in a slouching, lazy way. **2** hang about in the hope of getting food.

sloonge *see* **slunge.**

sloosh *n* **1** a sluice. **2** a dash of water, a splashing. *v* splash with water, flush.

slooster *v* work untidily or messily.

slootch *v* **1** slouch. **2** crouch, cower, skulk. *n* **1** a slouch. **2** an idle, work-shy person.

slop *see* **slap**[1], **slap**[2].

slorach *v* **1** eat or drink messily and noisily, slobber. **2** clear the throat loudly, breathe or speak through catarrh. *n* a wet disgusting mess (of something) NE.

slork *v* **1** make a slobbering noise, *eg* when eating; suck up (food or drink) noisily. **2** sniff, snort.

slorp *v* **1** eat or drink noisily and slobberingly. **2** (*of shoes, etc*) squelch.

slot *n* a bar or bolt for a door, window etc.

slubber *v* slobber, eat or drink in a noisy, gulping way. *n* a noisy, slobbering way of eating.

sluch *n* a slough, a wet, muddy place.

slug *n* a sleep, nap, rest.

slump[1] *v* treat (several things) as one, lump together. **at the slump, in a slump** taken as a whole, in total.

slump[2] *n* a marsh, boggy place.

slung *n* **1** a sling (for hurling stones). **2** a tall, lanky, stupid person; a rascal NE.

slunge, sloonge *v* **1** make a plunging movement or noise. **2** put into water, throw water over.
n a plunging movement, a splash made by a heavy object.

slunge *see* **sloonge**.

slunk *n* a wet and muddy hollow, a ditch.

slunken *see* **slink**.

slush *v* work in a messy or careless way SHETLAND, ORKNEY, CAITHNESS.

slutter, sclutter *v* **1** work in a messy, dirty way or in something messy. **2** slouch.
n **1** a mess, a mass of dirty (semi-) liquid. **2** a state of confusion, a muddle.

sly *see* **slee**.

slype[1], **sclype** *n* NE **1** a hard slap or smack. **2** contemptuous term for a man.

slype[2] *n* **1** a kind of wooden, wheelless platform for moving heavy loads. **2** a wooden runner by which barrels etc are unloaded from a lorry.

sma, small *adj* **1** small. **2** (*of people, animals*) slim, slender, slightly-built; (*of things*) narrow, thin. **3** fine, made up of small particles etc: '*sma rain*'. **4** (*of cloth, mesh*) fine in texture. **5** (*of the sea, a lake etc*) smooth, calm; (*of a river*) low, not in flood.
n **1** a small quantity or amount, a little, not much. **2 smas** small change NE.
adv quietly: '*Speak sma!*'.

smallie (*of people*) undersized, weakly; (*of things*) small, slight.

sma-boukit small, compact, shrunken.

sma faimllie a family of young children.

small fish fish such as haddock, herring etc, caught inshore.

sma oors, wee sma hours the very

early hours of the morning, just after midnight.

sma lines the lines used by inshore fishermen to catch **small fish**.

in smas in small amounts, piecemeal, little by little.

smacherie *n* **1** a large number of small objects or people NE. **2** a mixture of food, especially **sweeties** NE.

smack *v* kiss, especially in a loud hearty way.

smad *n* a small stain, smut, dirty mark; a very small quantity SHETLAND, NE.
v stain, soil SHETLAND, NE.

smalrg *v* smear with something oily or messy.

smairt, smart, smert *adj* smart.
smairter, smartle a lively and efficient person, one who is quick to understand and act.

small *see* **sma**.

smarrach *n* a confused crowd or collection, especially of children NE.

smart *see* **smairt**.

smash *n* a smashed or pulpy state.
smashle a kind of marbles game; a heavy marble used in this game.

smatchet *n* a small, worthless person (or animal), a cheeky or mischievous child SHETLAND, ORKNEY, N.

smatter *v* **1** smash, shatter. **2** work untidily, (appear to) be busy with trivial jobs.
n a small jumbled collection of people or things.

smeddum *n* **1** spirit, energy, drive, vigorous common sense and resourcefulness. **2** fine powder, *eg* a finely-ground meal, a medicinal powder.

smeek *n* **1** the fumes from something burning, smoke. **2** an unpleasant smell, a stuffy foul atmosphere. **3** a whiff, stifling puff of fumes; the act of smelling, a sniff.
v **1** affect or suffocate with smoke or soot, make smoky. **2** give off smoke or fumes.

smeek oot drive out (bees) with smoke fumes; smoke (out) people as a joke.

smeeker something for smoking out bees (or playing practical jokes).

smeerich [-ch as in 'dreich'] *n* a thin layer (of butter etc) N.

v make a mess of NE.

smeerless *see* **smerghless**.

smeeth *see* **smulth**.

smell *n* a small quantity, a taste (especially of drink).

smelt *n* a **smolt** (see **smowt**[1]), young salmon.

smerghless [smerchless], **smeerless** *adj* lacking in spirit or energy, feckless, stupid; (*of things*) uninteresting, insipid N.

smert *see* **smairt**.

smiddy *n* a smithy.

smirk[1] *v* smile in a pleasant friendly way, have a smiling expression; have a flirtatious smile.

n a pleasant smile, a friendly expression.

smirkle having a good-natured, friendly expression.

smirk[2] *n* a kiss NE.

smirr *n* a fine rain, drizzle, *often* **smirr o rain**.

v (*of rain or snow*) fall gently and softly in fine clouds, drizzle.

smirtle *v* smile in a knowing way, smirk; giggle, snigger.

smit *v* **1** affect (with (something bad)). **2** (*of an infectious disease or patient*) affect by contact, infect, taint.

n: **get the smit** be infected by a disease; fall in love.

smittin, smittle infectious.

smite *n* a small unimportant person, a weak creature NE.

smoch *n* thick choking smoke; thick fog.

smochie smoky; (*of the air*) close, sultry, stifling.

smokie, Arbroath smokie *n* an unsplit smoked haddock.

smolt *see* **smowt**[1].

smoochter *see* **smuchter**.

smooder *v* smoulder.

smook *v* slink or sneak (about (looking for something to steal)).

smook *see* **smulk**.

smool *v* **1** slink, sneak NE. **2** curry favour, suck up to, wheedle.

n (*often of a child*) a wheedler, a very small or unimportant person NE.

smoor *see* **smuir**.

smoorach *n* fine dust or powder, *eg* crumbled peat.

smoorach *see* **smoorich**.

smoorich, smoorach *v, n* kiss, hug, cuddle.

smore *v* **1** smother, suffocate (*eg* with smoke). **2** be smothered, choke. **3** block in or cover thickly with snow. **4** (*of snow, smoke etc*) fall or come out in a dense stifling cloud.

smorin (*of a head cold*) thick, choking, heavy.

be smorin wi the cauld have a very bad cold.

smowt[1], **smolt** *n* **1** a young salmon (or sea trout) between the **parr** and **grilse** stages. **2** a small child, animal or thing.

smowt[2] *n* a term used in games of marbles WEST, SW.

smuchter, smoochter *v* NE **1** smoulder, give off thick black smoke, burn slowly. **2** (*of rain, snow etc*) fall in a fine mist, drizzle.

n NE **1** thick smoke, *eg* from damp fuel; slight smoke from a fire not properly lit; a thick stuffy atmosphere. **2** a thin light mist or rain. **3** a thick choking cold, a heavy catarrh.

smudge *v* laugh quietly to yourself, smirk.

n a quiet laugh, a smirk.

smulk, smook *n* **1** smoke, fumes. **2** fine thick snow or rain ORKNEY, CAITHNESS, NE.

v **1** smoke, smoulder with thick smoke. **2** (expose to) smoke; cure (meat) by smoking; smoke out (bees).

smuir, smoor *v* **1** be choked, be suffocated, die, especially by being buried in a snowdrift. **2** suffocate, smother. **3** damp down (a fire) so that it smoulders quietly.

n a thick atmosphere, a dense cloud of smoke, snow, rain, mist.

smulth, smeeth NE *adj* smooth.

smush *v* break into very small pieces, crush, smash.

n a mass of tiny crushed pieces, something reduced to pulp or powder, *eg* over-boiled potatoes: '*The tatties are intae smush*'.

smyte, smytrie *n* contemptuous term for a collection of people (especially children) or small objects NE.

sna *see* **snaw.**

snab *n* a steep short slope, a rock that juts out.

snack[1] *n* a bite, snap, especially of a dog.

v snap with the teeth, bite.

snack[2] *adj* **1** (*of people*) nimble, active, quick, sharp. **2** clever, quick in mind.

snag *n* a titbit, especially a **sweetie** NE.

snagger *v* snore loudly.

snail *n* a slug.

snap *v* **1** snatch NE. **2** gobble (up), eat quickly or with pleasure.

n **1** a small piece, scrap, especially of food: '*Eat it up, every snap*'. **2** a sharp blow, a rap SHETLAND, N.

snapper *v* stumble, trip SHETLAND, NE.

snar *adj* severe, strict.

snash *n* cheek, abuse.

snashters *npl* contemptuous term for **sweeties,** cakes etc; junk food.

snaw, sna, snyauve [sneeawve] NE *n*, *v* snow.

snaw bree, snaw broo slush, often that carried down in rivers.

snaw flake a snow bunting.

snaw wreath a snowdrift.

like snaw aff a dyke (disappear) very quickly.

sneck[1]**, snick** *n* a latch, catch of a door etc.

v **1** latch, fasten (up) with a latch etc; make (a catch) fast. **2** shut (your mouth), shut up. **3** lock up or in, catch (something) in (a door), jam or squeeze between two objects. **4** switch or turn off (an electrical appliance).

sneck-draw(er) a crafty, deceitful person.

aff the sneck (*of a door etc*) unlatched, with the catch left off.

on the sneck latched but not locked, closed but not locked.

sneck[2] *n* **1** a notch, a slight cut; a mark in an animal's horn as a sign of age. **2** a dip in the ground, a saddle between hills.

v **1** cut sharply, cut into or off, prune, notch. **2** beat, be better than NE.

sneck[3]**, snick** *v* snatch, seize, steal.

n a greedy grasping person.

sned[1] *n* the shaft of a scythe, to which the blade is attached.

sned[2] *v* **1** chop, lop off (a branch); prune (a tree). **2** cut off the tops (and roots) of (turnips, thistles etc). **3** cut off, trim.

n a cut, cutting; a slash, slight wound; a lopping or pruning.

sneed *see* **snuid.**

sneel *see* **snuil.**

sneesh *n* (a pinch of) snuff.

v **1** take snuff. **2** sneeze.

sneeshin *n* snuff, a pinch of snuff; something of little value.

sneet *see* **snite**[1]**, snite**[3]**.**

sneeter *v* **1** giggle, snigger. **2** weep, blubber.

sneevil *v* **1** snivel. **2** speak through the nose, whine. **3** cringe, act insincerely.

n **1 the sneevils** a severe cold in the nose. **2** a nasal twang: a snuffle in your speech.

sneist *v* behave in a contemptuous way, be scornful.

n a taunt, look of contempt, cheek.

sneistie cheeky, sneering, sharp.

snell *adj* **1** (*of weather*) bitter, severe. **2** (*of a blow, fortune etc*) hard, severe. **3** severe in manner or speech. **4** sharp to the taste or smell, strong.

adv **1** (*of winds*) keenly, piercingly, with a nip. **2** harshly, unfeelingly, vigorously. **3** quickly, eagerly.

snib *v* **1** fasten (a door etc) with a catch. **2** cut (short or off), slice, cut into.

n **1** a catch, small bolt for a door etc. **2** a check, scolding; a calamity, setback.

snicher *v, n* snigger, titter.

snick *see* **sneck**[1], **sneck**[3].

snifter *v* **1** sniff; snivel, snuffle (*eg* with a cold); snort, snore. **2** (*of wind*) blow in strong gusts.

n **1** a (noisy) sniff from a cold, grief etc, a snivel, whimper, snigger. **2 the snifters** a (severe) head cold, catarrh, stuffed nose. **3** a strong blast, gust, flurry (of wind, sleet etc).

snigger *v* catch (salmon) illegally by dragging a cluster of weighted hooks along the river bed; fish (a pool) by this method.

snipe[1] *n* contemptuous term for a person.

sniple a kind of marbles game.

snipe[2] *n* a setback, a let-down, fraud NE.

v cheat, bring loss on NE.

snippit *adj* **1** quick in speech, sharp. **2** mean, giving short measure.

snirk *v* snort, wrinkle the nose, snigger.

n a snort, snigger.

snirlie *n* a gusty biting wind.

snirt *v* **1** snigger, make a noise through the nose when trying to stifle laughter; sneer. **2** snort.

n **1** a snigger, suppressed laugh. **2** a snort.

snitchers *npl* handcuffs.

snite[1], **sneet** *v* **1** blow (your nose), especially with the finger and thumb, wipe the nose. **2** snuff (a

candle), strike off (the burnt tip) NE.

n **1** a blowing or wiping of the nose SHETLAND, NE. **2** a sharp blow, especially on the nose.

snite someone's niz tweak someone's nose; take someone down a peg.

snite[2] *n* (*insulting*) a worthless person or thing.

snite[3], **sneet** *v* move about or work in a lazy, careless or dazed way NE.

snitter *v* laugh into yourself, giggle, snigger.

snocher *v* snort, snuffle.

n **1** a snort, snore. **2 the snochers** a severe nose cold.

snochie *v, n* snuffle.

snochies *n pl* snot NE.

snochter *n* nasal mucus.

snochter-dichter a handkerchief.

snod *adj* **1** smooth, level, evenly cut. **2** neat, trim, tidy. **3** comfortable, snug, at ease.

v **1** make trim or neat, tidy. **2** prune, cut, smooth, make level.

snod-up, snoddle-up a tidying, smartening.

snoit *v* snore.

snoke, snook, snowk *v* **1** sniff, smell, scent out (as a dog), poke with the nose. **2** hunt, nose your way, prowl.

snood *see* **snuid.**

snook *see* **snoke.**

snoot *n* **1** a snout. **2** contemptuous term for the nose, face, head. **3** the peak (of a cap). **4** (*slang*) a detective, policeman.

snootit (*of a cap*) peaked.

snoozle *v* **1** snooze. **2** snuggle.

snore *v* **1** (*of animals*) snort. **2** (*especially of wind, fire etc*) make a rushing, whirring, droning sound. **3** move at speed with a rushing, roaring sound. *n* a snort, roar, loud roaring or droning noise.

snork *v* snort, snore, snuffle.

snorl *n* **1** a knot, tangle, kink or twist in a thread, rope etc, a mix-up. **2** a difficulty, confusion.

v ruffle, wrinkle, twist, tangle.

snot *n* **1** the burnt wick of a candle NE. **2** contemptuous term for a person.

v snub, tell off.

snotter *n* **1** *mainly* **snotters** nasal mucus, especially when hanging from the nose. **2** the red skinny flaps on a turkey-cock's beak. **3** a telling-off. **4** a snuffle.

v **1** snuffle, snort. **2** snivel, weep noisily. **3** snooze, doze. **4** snub.

snotter box the nose.

snotter-dichter a handkerchief.

snotterie 1 slimy, running at the nose. **2** tearful, miserable: '*a snotterie wee bairn*'.

snowk *see* **snoke**.

snuffle *adj* sulky, touchy.

snuld, snood, sneed NE *n* **1** (*fishing*) the part of a sea-line to which the hook is attached. **2** (*in past times*) a ribbon etc worn round the hair by young unmarried women.

snull, sneel NE *n* a weak or cowardly person; a lazy person.

v **1** give way, cringe, act meanly, deceitfully or weakly. **2** show lack of energy.

snuve *v* slink, sneak, laze about.

snyauve *see* **snaw**.

so *see* **sae**.

soad *see* **sod**.

sober *adj* **1** poor, miserable NE. **2** small, slightly-built NE. **3** in poor health, sickly, weak.

socht *see* **seek**[1].

sock *n* a ploughshare.

sod, soad *n* **1** a sod. **2** a piece of turf used as fuel.

sod *see* **sad**.

sodger *n* **1** a soldier. **2 sodgers** the stems and flowerheads of plantain, especially ribwort plantain; a game played with these. **3** name for various small reddish-coloured creatures *eg* a ladybird, a red-breasted minnow. **4 sodgers** small sparks, *eg* on the edge

of burning paper; smuts of burning soot. **5** a wounded or injured child or animal.

v **1** soldier. **2** march in a stolid, dogged way, trudge.

sodie *n* soda.

sodie-heid contemptuous term for a scatterbrained person.

sodie-heidit scatterbrained.

soft *see* **saft**.

sole *n* the lower part, bottom or base of something, *eg* of a golf club, a curling-stone; the lower crust of a loaf of bread; the bottom rope of a fishing net; *see also* **windae-sole**.

solvendie *adj* (*of things*) firm, safe, sure.

some *adv* a little; very, a great deal: '*some glad*'; '*I'm some to blame*'.

somebit somewhere.

somegate 1 somewhere. **2** somehow, in some way.

someplace somewhere.

something somewhat, a little: '*She's something lazy*'.

somewey 1 somehow. **2** somewhere.

and some and more so: '*She's as bonnie as you and some*'.

son *see* **sin**[1].

song *see* **sang**.

sonnet *n* **1** a song. **2** a tale, a (tall) story, nonsense NE.

sonse *n* abundance, plenty; prosperity, good fortune.

sonsie 1 (*especially of women*) attractive: '*a real sonsie quine*'; (*of the figure*) plump, buxom; (*of young children*) chubby, sturdy.

2 fine, handsome, impressive, pleasant, cheery.

3 friendly, hearty, jolly; good, honest.

4 bringing good fortune; lucky.

5 big.

soo[1] *n* **1** a sow. **2** a pig. **3** *also* **soo stack** a ridge-shape *eg* a large oblong stack of hay.

soo's back a ridge (of land).

soo('s) cruive a pigsty.

soo[2] *v* ache.

sooder *see* **sowther.**

sook *v* 1 suck. 2 flow in a certain direction, as if drawn by suction. 3 suckle (a baby animal), breastfeed (a baby).

n 1 a person seeking favour, a toady. 2 a cheat, deception, swindle NE. 3 a stupid person.

auld wifie's sookers mint imperials, **pan drops.**

sookie *n* 1 a suckling. 2 (*contemptuous*) a petted or spoilt child. 3 clover; sometimes common red clover.

sookie soo the flower of the clover.

sookie soorocks wood sorrel.

sookin teuchit NE, **sookin turkey** *etc* a feeble or foolish person.

sook in flatter, try to get into someone's good books.

sook-the-papple (*contemptuous*) a fairly old but babyish child, a big baby; an effeminate person.

soom, sweem *v* swim.

n 1 a swim. 2 an extremely wet state, a flood.

soon *see* **soond**[1], **soond**[2], **soond**[3].

soond[1], **soon** *n* 1 a sound. 2 a rumour, report; gossip.

soond[2], **soon** *adj* 1 sound, in good condition. 2 smooth, even, level.

soond[3], **soon** *v* faint (away).

n a faint; faintness, *often* **in a soond** SHETLAND.

soop[1] *n* a small amount of liquid, a sip.

soop[2], **swype** NE, **sweep** *v* 1 sweep. 2 **soop** (*curling*) sweep (the ice) in the path of a curling-stone.

sweep-the-flair a move in the game of **chucks.**

soople *adj* 1 supple. 2 ingenious, cunning, crafty. 3 limp, helpless with laughter etc.

adv agilely.

soor, sour *adj* 1 sour. 2 (*of weather*) cold and wet, miserable.

soorock 1 name for various kinds of sorrel. 2 a sulky, bad-tempered person.

soor dook 1 buttermilk; yoghurt. 2 a bad-tempered, mean person.

soor face a gloomy, bad-tempered person.

soor ploom 1 a sharp-flavoured, round, green, boiled sweet. 2 a native of Galashiels.

soose *v* 1 strike, cuff, thump. 2 fall or sit (down) heavily.

n 1 a heavy blow, especially on the head, a thump. 2 (the sound of) a heavy fall.

soos(t)er something very large, a large amount: '*a big sooster*'.

sooth, south *n, adj, adv* south.

soothie left-handed.

Southron English.

sooth-moother an incomer to Shetland SHETLAND.

sooth awa, sooth by in the south.

sore *see* **sair.**

sorn *v, also* **sorn on** scrounge or sponge (on).

sorra, sorrow *n* 1 sorrow. 2 (the) Devil. 3 a rascal, a troublesome child, a pest of a person.

sorrafu 1 sorrowful. 2 troublesome.

sorra fa(w) ye *etc* used as a curse.

no hae yer sorra(s) tae seek have plenty of trouble on your hands.

sort *v* 1 put in order, arrange, tidy up; tidy (yourself).

2 repair, mend, fix up; heal.

3 neuter (an animal) SHETLAND, NE.

4 feed and litter (especially a horse).

5 attend to the wants of (a child or sick person).

6 deal with by punishment etc, put (a person) in his or her place, scold.

n a repair, a tidying-up.

sosh ANGUS, FIFE, **soshie** NE *n* a Co-operative Society shop.

soss[1] *n* 1 a mixture of food or drink, a wet, soggy mess of food. 2 a (very) wet state, a dirty wet mess; a muddle, confusion.

v 1 eat sloppy or messy food; eat in a messy way. 2 mix (especially liquids) in a messy way. **3** make wet and dirty; make a mess. **4** nurse over-tenderly, fuss over; pester.

soss[2] *n* a thud, a heavy awkward fall, a heavy blow.

sot, sut *adv* (*child's word after* 'not') so: '*It is not!*' '*It is sot!*'.

sotter *v* **1** boil, simmer, bubble or splutter in cooking. **2** sputter, crackle; come bubbling out. **3** work in a dirty unskilful way; handle in a disgusting way.

n **1** the noise made by something boiling, frying or bubbling up. **2** a state of wetness NE. **3** a mess, muddle.

souch [-oo-; -ch as in 'loch'] *n* **1** the sound of the wind, especially when long-drawn-out.

2 the rushing, roaring or murmuring of water.

3 a rustling or whizzing sound, as of an object moving rapidly through the air; a whizzing blow.

4 a deep sigh or gasp, heavy breathing, panting.

5 a song, tune.

6 the sound or pitch of a voice, an accent, way of speaking.

7 general feeling or opinion, attitude, style.

8 gossip, rumour, scandal.

9 an uproar, fuss.

v **1** (*of objects moving through the air*) whizz, buzz, drone, flap, whirr.

2 (*of leaves etc*) rustle, whisper; (*of water*) ripple, gurgle, make a slapping sound.

3 (*of wind*) make a rushing, moaning, murmuring sound.

4 breathe heavily, sigh, wheeze, splutter, gurgle.

5 souch awa die.

6 sing softly, hum, whistle.

keep a calm souch keep calm or still; keep quiet, hold your tongue.

sour *see* **soor.**

souter [-oo-] *n* **1** a shoemaker, cobbler.

2 a native of Selkirk or Forfar.

v cobble, make or mend shoes.

south *see* **sooth.**

sowans *npl* (*in past times*) a dish made from oat husks and fine meal steeped in water.

sowans nicht Christmas Eve NE.

sowder *see* **sowther.**

sowff *v* **1** sing, hum or whistle softly or under your breath NE. **2** (*of wind, water etc*) murmur; (*of a breeze or smoke*) puff gently.

sowl *see* **saul.**

sowp[1] *n* **1** a (small) amount of liquid, a sip, a large amount. **2** a drink; something to drink. **3** supper.

sowp[2] *v* soak, steep.

n **1** rain, wet weather. **2** wetness; a bog.

sowther, sowder, sooder *v* **1** solder. **2** unite in marriage; make (a marriage) NE. **3** settle, patch up (a quarrel etc).

spaad *n* a spade NE.

spad *v*: **spad on** walk energetically NE.

spae *v* **1** prophesy, predict, tell (fortunes). **2** read (someone's hand).

spaewife a female fortune-teller.

spag *n* a paw, hand, foot N.

spalk *n* **1** a spoke (of a wheel etc). **2** the perch of a bird's cage, a roosting bar. **3** one of the rungs of a ladder.

spall, spell *n* NE **1** a splinter, chip or sliver of wood; a wood-shaving; a thin strip of wood. **2** a splinter in the skin. **3** a wooden spill or taper used for lighting etc.

spairge *v* scatter, sprinkle, dash (water, mud etc) (about).

spalver *n* the opening in the front of trousers.

spak *see* **speak.**

spalebone *see* **spaul.**

spang[1] *n, v* span.

spangle a game played with marbles etc.

spang[2] *n* a pace, a long vigorous step or bound.

v stride out, walk with long steps, leap, bound.

spang-new, spankle-new *adj* brand-new.

spank *v* move quickly.

spanker a lively, fast-moving horse or person.

spankle lively, spirited.

spankle-new *see* **spang-new.**

spar *n* **1** a wooden bolt for securing a door. **2** a bar or rail of a wooden fence or gate NE. **3** a rung of a chair or ladder. **4** a perch in a birdcage.

sparred slatted.

spare *n* **1** the opening in the front of trousers. **2** the opening or slit in a skirt, petticoat etc.

spark, sperk SOUTH, **spirk** NE *n* **1** a spark. **2** a very small amount of (something liquid or semi-liquid), a drop, *eg* a raindrop, a spot of mud. *v* **1** spark. **2** light (a match etc). **3** splatter with liquid or mud. **4** throw out a fine spray. **5** rain slightly; spit with rain.

sparkle giving off sparks; bright, sharp, quick-witted; lively.

sparra, sparrie, sporrow SHETLAND, ORKNEY *n* a sparrow.

spat *n* a spot.

spate *n* **1** a heavy downpour (of rain). **2** a flood of tears. *v* rain heavily.

spaul, spauld *n* **1** the shoulder; the shoulder-bone. **2** a joint, a shoulder or leg (of mutton, beef etc); the wing or leg of a fowl.

spalebone a cut of beef from the shoulder.

spead *n* a spade NE.

speak, spike NE, **spick** NE *v, past tense* **spak 1** speak. **2** order (goods): '*I'll speak ma butcher meat fur the week*'. *n* **1** a speech, comment; a popular saying NE. **2** a story without much truth in it, nonsense SHETLAND, NE. **3** gossip. **4** a subject of conversation, the talk (of a place): '*She's been*

the speak o the toon since she wore that dress'.

speak back reply (in argument); talk back.

spean *v* **1** wean (an infant or suckling animal). **2** put (a person or animal) off food through disgust, fear etc. **3** draw (a person) away from (a habit, idea etc).

speariment *n* spearmint.

speckle *adj* wearing glasses.

speeder, spider *n* **1** a spider. **2 the Spiders** nickname for Queen's Park football team. **3** a trout-fly without wings.

speeder jenny SW, SOUTH, **speeder-legs** a daddy-long-legs.

speel[1] *n* **1** a spell (of time). **2** a time of rest or relaxation, a break in work. *v* take a turn at work for (someone).

speel[2] *v, n* climb.

speen *see* **spuin.**

speendrift *see* **spindrift.**

speerit *n* spirit.

speeshal *adj* special.

speet *n* a pointed stick on which fish are hung up to dry.

speir *v* **1** ask a question, inquire; ask too many questions.

2 speir for ask after (someone's health): '*Thanks fur speirin fur ma mither*'.

3 ask, put a question to (a person).

4 speir for make a proposal of marriage to.

5 invite.

6 speir oot search, track down, trace (by inquiry).

n **1** a question(ing), investigation. **2** a person who is continually asking questions.

speirin *adj* inquisitive, searching.

speirins *npl* **1** questioning, investigation, asking too many questions. **2** information, news.

spel *see* **speld.**

speld, spel *v* split, cut, slice open (especially of fish to dry).

spelder 1 spread or pull open or apart. **2** wrench or pull muscles by falling with the legs apart.

speldin SHETLAND, N, **speldrin** a split and dried (or smoked) fish, especially a haddock or whiting.

spelk *n* **1** a sharp splinter (of wood, glass etc); a small strip of wood. **2** a surgical splint.

v **1** splinter; fly about like splinters. **2** bind (*eg* a broken limb) with splints.

spell *n* spelling, a spelling lesson.

spell *see* **spail.**

spence *n* an inner room of a house, used as a sitting room, small bedroom etc, or for storage.

spent *adj* (*of a fish*) spawned, in poor condition after spawning.

spentacles *npl* spectacles.

sperk *see* **spark.**

speug, spug [sp(ee)ug] *n* **1** a sparrow. **2** a child, a small person etc.

spew *see* **spue.**

spice *n* pepper SHETLAND, ORKNEY, N.

spick *see* **speak.**

spicket, spigot *n* an outdoor tap.

spider *see* **speeder.**

spigot *see* **spicket.**

spike *see* **speak.**

spilk *v* shell (peas) NE.

spin *v* go well NE.

spinner 1 a daddy-long-legs. **2** a spider.

spinnin jenny 1 a daddy-long-legs. **2** a home-made spinning toy.

spin(nin) maggie a daddy-long-legs.

spin *see* **spuin.**

spindrift, speendrift NE *n* **1** spray whipped up by wind. **2** snow blown up from the ground NE.

spink[1] *n* name for various flowers, *eg* lady's smock, common primrose, maiden pink.

spink[2] *n* a chaffinch.

spirk *see* **spark.**

spirl *n* **1** a small slender shoot. **2** a tall, thin person.

spirlie *adj* slender, thin, spindly. *n* a slender person.

spit *v, past tense* **sput** spit.

spitten eemage exact image.

spitter *n* **1** a slight shower of rain or snow. **2** **spitters** small drops of wind-driven rain or snow.

splairge *v* **1** spatter, splash (a person etc). **2** sprinkle, splash (a liquid etc).

splashack *n* a plaice N.

splatch *n* a splodge, blot, a patch of colour, dirt etc.

splatter *v* **1** scatter, splash, spatter. **2** splash noisily, move with a clattering or rattling noise.

n a splashing (sound), a commotion.

spleet *v* split.

spleet new brand new SHETLAND, ORKNEY, N.

spleuchan *n* a (leather) pouch for tobacco or money.

spleuterie *adj* **1** weak and watery NE. **2** (*of weather*) wet, rainy.

spleyter [rhymes with 'tighter'] NE *n* **1** a splash of spilt liquid, a blot. **2** a wind-driven shower of rain, snow etc. *v* spill, spatter messily over an area.

splice *n* a sliver of wood, splinter.

split *v* part (the hair).

split new brand new.

splitter *n, v* splutter, splash.

splore *n* **1** a party. **2** a quarrel. **3** a prank, escapade. *v* **1** have a good time. **2** show off.

splurt *v* squirt.

spoatch SOUTH *v* **1** poach. **2** sponge, scrounge around for favours.

spoon *see* **spuin.**

spoot *n* **1** a spout, a pipe. **2** a natural spring of water streaming from the ground or from a rock; an outside tap. **3** a waterfall. **4** a narrow pathway; a gully. **5** a horizontal roof gutter. **6** a razor-fish, a razor-clam. **7** a squirt, a toy (water-)gun, usually made from a plant stem.

8 a small quantity of liquid.

v **1** spout. **2** dart, spring.

spoot fish = **spoot** *n* 6.

spoot gun a popgun.

sporran *n* a purse or pouch, especially the (ornamented) leather pouch worn in front of a man's kilt.

sporrow *see* **sparra.**

sprachle *see* **sprauchle.**

spralloch *v* sprawl, flounder NE.

sprat *n* a coarse or reedy rush or grass.

sprauchle, sprachle *v* move with difficulty or in a hasty, clumsy way (especially upwards), struggle (especially to get out of something), flounder about.

n a scramble, struggle.

spread *see* **spreid.**

spreath [rhymes with 'faith'] *n* (*in past times*) cattle stolen and driven off in a raid, especially by Highlanders; booty, plunder.

spreckle *n* a speckle, spot, freckle.

spreckelt speckled, flecked.

spreid, spread *v, past tense, past participle* **spreidit 1** spread. **2** spread butter etc on (a slice of bread etc). **3** turn the top covers of (a bed) down or up.

spring *n* a lively dance (tune).

sprit-new *adj* brand-new.

sproosh, sprush *adj* **1** spruce. **2** brisk, smart in your movements.

n **1** a spruce (fir). **2** a smartening up, a tidying or setting in order. **3 sproosh** lemonade NE.

sproosh up tidy up.

sprot *n* a rush; name for various reeds.

sprug, spurdle, spurgle NE *n* **1** a sparrow. **2** a small (lively) person, a child.

sprush *see* **sproosh.**

spue, spew *v* **1** spew. **2** (*of liquid, smoke etc*) flow, pour.

spug *see* **speug.**

spuin [rhymes with 'muin'], **spin, speen** NE, **spoon** *n* a spoon.

pit in yer spuin interfere in someone else's affairs.

spulyie [**spool**(y)ie] *v* rob, plunder. *n* booty, plunder.

spunk *n* **1** a spark. **2** a match. *v* spark.

spunkie a lively young person.

spurdle, spurgie *see* **sprug.**

spurtle, spurkle *n* a short round stick for stirring porridge, soup etc.

spurtle shank a thin leg.

sput *see* **spit.**

squaik *v, n* (*of birds or trapped animals*) squeal, squeak, squawk.

squalloch [-a- as in 'cat'] *v* scream, make a noise and disturbance NE. *n* the noise of children playing.

square *n*: **the square** farm buildings, a farm, especially when forming four sides of a square.

square sausage sliced sausage.

squatter [-a- as in 'cat'] *v* flutter in water like a duck, flap about in mud or water, splash along.

n a large number of small creatures or objects.

squeak *n* (*humorous*) a local newspaper.

squeeb *n* **1** a squib. **2** contemptuous term for a person NE.

squeegee *adj* twisted, at the wrong angle, out of shape: '*That picter's hung squeegee*'.

squeenge *see* **scunge.**

squeerie *see* **scurry.**

squeeter *v* spatter, (cause to) fly in all directions NE.

squile *v, n* squeal.

squint *adj, adv* off the straight, set at a slant.

sta, stall, staw *n* **1** a stall. **2 staw** a feeling of sickness or disgust caused *eg* by eating too much, often **get a staw.**

v **1** stall. **2** become sickened by food etc; become bored or fed up. **3** sicken or disgust with too much food.

sta *see* **steal.**

stab *v* a prickle, thorn, a piece of wood in the skin.

stab *see* **stob**.

stacher, staucher *v, n* stagger, stumble.

stack *n* a tall column of rock rising out of the sea SHETLAND, ORKNEY.

stack *see* **stick**[1].

staff *n* a walking-stick.

stalg *n* **1** a young horse of either sex. **2** a stallion. **3** a young castrated horse.

stainch *see* **stench**[1], **stench**[2].

stainchel [**stain**shell] *n* an iron bar (a grating).

stair *n* a staircase, stairs: '*up the stair*'. **stairheid** the landing at the top of a flight of stairs, *eg* in a **tenement**: '*stairheid rammie*'.

stairt *see* **stert**.

stairve *see* **sterve**.

stake *n* a young ling NE.

stake net a salmon-fishing net fixed on stakes in tidal waters.

stakey *n* (*marbles*) a game in which stakes are laid.

stale *n* a foundation of a corn- or haystack.

stalk *n* a chimney-stack.

stall *see* **sta**.

stamach *see* **stamack**.

stamack, stamach *n* the stomach. **hae a guid stamack** have a hearty appetite.

stamagast, stammygaster *n* an unpleasant shock, surprise NE. *v* **1** surprise, bewilder, disappoint. **2** sicken, disgust.

stame *see* **steam**.

stammer *v, n* stumble, stagger.

stammygaster *see* **stamagast**.

stan *see* **staun**.

stance *n* **1** a foundation; a site, *eg* for a market, fair etc. **2** a place where public vehicles stand waiting for passengers: '*taxi stance*'.

stand *see* **staun**.

standard *see* **standart**.

standart, standard *n* **1** a standard. **2** an upright pole or post.

Standard Grade applied to a certificate, examination or course awarded to all pupils in secondary schools at the end of the fourth year.

stane, steen ORKNEY, N, **stone** *n* **1** stone. **2** a testicle.

stondie, stoner a large brown earthenware marble.

stonie a small coloured marble.

stane blin completely blind.

stane chack(art) a stonechat; a wheatear.

stane chipper a wheatear.

stang[1] *v* **1** sting. **2** shoot with pain, throb, ache. *n* **1** a sting (of an insect etc). **2** something which hurts. **3** a sharp pain.

stang[2] *past tense of* **sting** stung.

stang[3] *n* **1** a pole, wooden bar or rod. **2** a spike, prong etc of metal.

stank *n* **1** a street drain and the grating over it. **2** a ditch. **3** a pond, pool; a swampy place. **doon the stank** lost; (*of money*) squandered.

stap[1], **staup** SOUTH *n, v* step.

stap[2], **stop, stoap** *v* **1** stop, block up, halt. **2** push, cram (in(to)). **3** stuff, pack with. **4** stuff yourself with food. **5** tuck bedclothes around (someone) NE.

stappit fou *adj* overfull of food.

stap- *prefix* (*of relatives*) step-.

stap-faither, stapple *n* a step-father.

star *n* name for various kinds of grass growing on moor or boggy ground.

stark *adj* strong, sturdy; strongly made.

starn[1], **stern** *n* **1** a star. **2** a grain, a small amount. **the starn o the ee** the pupil of the eye.

starn[2] *n* the stern (of a boat).

start *see* **stert**.

stashle *see* **stushle**.

stathel *n* a foundation of a stack *eg* of grain.

staucher *see* **stacher.**

staun, staund, stan, stand *v* stand.
n **1** a stand. **2** a stall or booth at a
market etc. **3** a complete set *eg* of
ropes, knitting needles.
standin constant, permanent.

staup *see* **stap**[1].

stave *n, v* sprain, wrench.

staves *npl* (broken) pieces: *'fa intae
staves'.*

staw *see* **sta, steal.**

stay *see* **stey**[2].

stead *see* **steid.**

steal *v, past tense also* **staw, sta,
stealt;** *past participle also* **stow(e)n**
SHETLAND, NE, **stealt** steal.

steam, stame NE *n, v* steam.
steamie a public wash-house.
steamin very drunk.

stech [-ch as in 'dreich'] *v* **1** stuff with
food. **2** fill with bad air or fumes,
stink. **3** gasp, pant, puff.

steek[1] *v* **1 steek someone** *etc* **oot** close
a door on someone etc. **2** close, shut,
fasten.
steekit nieve the clenched fist.
steek an hide the game of hide-and-
seek.

steek[2], **stick** *v, n* stitch.

steel *see* **stull.**

steen *see* **stane.**

steepend *see* **stipend.**

steepid *see* **stupid.**

steer *v* **1** stir. **2** disturb, pester. **3** start
off on a journey.
n a stir, movement, bustle.
steerie lively, bustling, busy.
steerin active, restless, lively.

steet *see* **stult.**

steeth *see* **steid.**

steg *v* walk with long heavy steps,
stride.

steid, stead, steeth SHETLAND, OR-
KNEY, CAITHNESS *n* **1** a site, foundation, base. **2** a **steading.**
steadin(g) the buildings on a farm,
sometimes but not always including
the farmhouse.

stell[1] *v* **1** place in position, set up. **2**
steady (yourself or your feet) by plant-
ing your feet against something firm.
n **1** an open enclosure for sheep on a
hillside. **2** (*mining*) a prop for under-
pinning a roof.

stell[2] *n* a still (for whisky).

sten *see* **stend.**

stench[1], **stainch** *v* **1** stanch, check the
flow of. **2** satisfy with food.

stench[2], **stainch** *adj* **1** loyal, staunch. **2**
serious, severe-looking, rigid NE. **3**
strong, firm; in good health.

stend, sten *v, n* leap, spring, bound.

stent[1] *v* stretch out (a sail, net etc);
pitch (a tent); make taut.
stenter a clothes prop.

stent[2] *n* an amount of work to be
covered in a given time.

step *n* a stepping-stone in a river.

stern *see* **starn**[1].

stert, stairt, start *v* **1** start. **2** startle,
disturb.

sterve, stairve *v* **1** starve. **2 sterve wi
cauld** feel chilled.

steuch *see* **stew.**

stew, steuch [-ch as in 'dreich'] *n* **1** (a
cloud of) dust. **2** an uproar; trouble. **3**
a stench; a suffocating cloud.
v stink.

stey[1] [rhymes with 'gey'] *adj* (*of a hill,
road etc*) (very) steep; difficult to
climb.

stey[2] [rhymes with 'gey'], **stay** *v* **1** stay,
stop. **2** live (in a place), dwell: *'They
stey in Paisley'.*

stibble *n* stubble.

stick[1] *v, past tense also* **stack** NE,
stickit; *past participle also* **stucken,
stickit 1** stick. **2** stab, thrust a knife
into, finish off. **3** (*of a horned animal*)
gore, stab. **4** stop in the middle of (a
job etc).
stickers goose-grass.
stickin stiff in manner, obstinate.
stickit 1 (*of a task etc*) left spoilt or
unfinished. **2** (*of people*) failed: *'stickit
minister'.*

sticky-fingered apt to steal.

sticky-Willie goose-grass.

stick in work hard, go energetically (at): '*Stick in at the scuil*'.

stick[2] *adj* wooden, made of timber.

nae great sticks at not very good at.

stick *see* **steek**[2].

stiddie, studdie *n* an anvil.

stieve *adj* **1** firm, strong, sturdy. **2** steady, loyal, dependable.

still, stull *adj* still.

still an on 1 yet, nevertheless. **2** always, continuously.

stilp NE *v* walk with long stiff steps, stump about.

stilpert *n* **1** a stilt. **2** a tall lanky person or animal.

v walk with long stiff strides.

stilt *n* **1** one of the handles of a plough. **2** a crutch.

v go on stilts or crutches.

stime *n* **1** a tiny amount. **2** a glimmer or glimpse of light.

sting *n* a pole, *eg* used to push off a boat.

stink *v* fill (a place) or affect (a person) with a bad smell.

stinkin haughty, snobbish, supercilious.

stinkin Billy sweet william.

stinkin Willie ragwort.

stint *v* stop, halt NE.

stipend, steepend *n* the salary of a clergyman.

stippit *see* **stupid**.

stirk *n* **1** a young bullock or (sometimes) heifer kept for slaughter. **2** a sturdy young man. **3** a stupid idiot.

stirlin *n* a starling.

stishie *see* **stushie**.

stoap *see* **stap**[2].

stoater *see* **stot**[2].

stob *n* **1** *also* **stab** a stake, a (fence)post. **2** a prickle, a thorn; a splinter in the skin.

stobbie rough and spiky, prickly, bristly.

stock *n* **1** the hard stalk of a plant,

especially of a cabbage etc. **2** a block of wood.

stockin the livestock and gear needed to run a farm.

stockit obstinate, stubborn NE.

stodge *v* walk with a long slow step, stump.

stoit, styte *v* **1** bounce. **2** stagger from drink etc. **3** walk in a casual way, saunter NE.

n **1** blow. **2** a stagger, tottering step. **3** foolish talk, nonsense ORKNEY, CAITHNESS, NE.

stoiter, styter walk unsteadily, totter.

stondie, stone *see* **stane**.

stook *n* **1** a number of cut sheaves, set up to dry in a field. **2** a bundle (of straw).

stookie *n* **1** stucco, plaster of Paris; a plaster-cast for a broken limb. **2** a stucco figure. **3** a slow-witted, dull or shy person. **4 stookies** a children's game in which the players try to remain motionless as long as possible.

stookie eemage *etc* a plaster statue.

stand lik a stookie stand as if unable to move.

stoon *see* **stoond**[1], **stoond**[2].

stoond[1], **stoon** *n* a sharp throb of pain; an ache.

v throb, ache, smart: '*Ma heid's stoondin*'.

stoond[2], **stoon** *v* **1** stun, stupefy. **2** a stunned state.

stoop *n* a wooden post, prop, *eg* a table-leg, gatepost.

stooshie *see* **stushie**.

stoot *adj* **1** fat, stout. **2** in good health.

stoot *see* **stuit**.

stop *see* **stap**[2].

store *n*: **the store** the Co-op, popular name for a Co-operative Society shop.

storm *n*: **storm cock** the missel thrush.

storm windae a dormer window.

story *see* **torie**.

stot[1] *n* **1** a bullock. **2** a stupid, clumsy person.

stot[2] *v* **1** bounce; jump up; walk with a springy step; bound, go by leaps. **2** stagger, walk unsteadily. **3** stutter, stammer.

n **1** a bounce, a spring, a hop in a dance. **2** the beat of a tune, rhythm (of speech or dance). **3** a stammer, stutter.

stotter, stoater 1 a stagger, stumble. **2** (*term of admiration for a woman*) a smasher, looker.

aff the stot out of rhythm; off your stride.

stour [-oo-] *n* **1** dust in motion, flying, swirling dust; (a layer of) dust; any fine powdery substance.

2 commotion, fuss, disturbance.

3 strife, conflict.

4 a storm; a blizzard.

v **1** run, rush (on), bustle (about). **2** (*of dust, spray etc*) swirl, rise in a cloud. **stourie** *adj* **1** dusty. **2** (*especially of a young child*) active, restless.

lik(e) stour like a whirl of dust, with a rush.

stove *n* (*cooking*) a stew.

v **1** (*cooking*) stew. **2** steam.

stovies, stovit tatties dish of stewed potatoes, onions etc, sometimes with small pieces of meat.

stowe [rhymes with 'cow'] *v* fill with food.

stowed oot packed full (with people): '*The pub wis stowed oot wi tourists last night*'.

stowen, stown *see* **steal.**

stowp *n* **1** a wooden pail. **2** a tankard, mug etc. **3** a (milk or cream) jug NE.

strachle *see* **strauchle.**

stracht *see* **straucht.**

strae, straw *n* straw.

v supply with straw.

strae moose a shrew.

strag *n* a stray pigeon.

straik *n* **1** a stroke, a blow etc. **2** a stroking movement of the hand. **3** a stripe of colour etc.

v **1** stroke. **2** smear, sprinkle, spread, streak.

strait, stret NE *adj* **1** strait, narrow. **2** tight, close-fitting. **3** rigid. **4** (*of mountains etc*) steep.

strak *see* **strik.**

stramash [stra**mash**] *n* **1** an uproar, commotion, row. **2** a smash, crash, accident, disaster.

stramp *v* stamp, tread, trample (on); stump about.

strang *adj, adv* strong(ly).

strange *see* **strynge.**

strap, strop *n* **1** a strap, a strip of leather etc, especially a punishment strap. **2 strap** a strip of wood to which something else may be nailed. **3 strap** black treacle, molasses.

strapper a groom.

strath *n* a river valley, especially when broad and flat.

strathspey a kind of dance, slower than a **reel**; a tune for such.

strauchle, strachle *v* **1** move with difficulty sw. **2** straggle.

straucht, stracht, strecht [-ch- as in 'loch'] *adj* straight.

adv **1** straight. **2** immediately, without delay.

v **1** stretch. **2** straighten; smooth, set to rights. **3** lay out (a corpse) NE.

straun *n* **1** a little stream. **2** a (street-) gutter.

stravaig [stra**vaig**] *v* **1** roam, wander aimlessly. **2** go up and down (a place). *n* a roaming about, a stroll.

strave *see* **strive.**

straw *v* strew, scatter, sprinkle.

straw *see* **strae.**

streamer *n* **1 streamers** the aurora borealis, northern lights. **2** a male minnow near spawning time.

strecht *see* **straucht.**

streek *v* **1** stretch. **2** lay out (a corpse). **3** put (a plough etc) into action; start work, get going NE. **4** reach out, be stretched out.

n **1** a stretch. **2** a continuous stretch of time or space.

streen *see* **yestreen.**

street *n*: **on the street(s) 1** in the street, out-of-doors. **2** roaming the streets; homeless, down-and-out.

streetch, stretch *v* **1** stretch. **2** stretch your legs, take exercise by walking or dancing.

streetcher, stretcher a clothes-prop.

streeve *see* **strive.**

strenth *n* strength.

stress *v* overwork, fatigue.

stret *see* **strait.**

stretch *see* **streetch.**

stricken *see* **strik.**

striddle *v* straddle.

stridelegs *adv* astride.

stridlins *adv* astride, with the legs apart.

strik *v, past tense also* **strak** NE; *past participle also* **stricken, strucken** strike.

strucken hour, stricken hour a whole hour by the clock, a long boring time.

strin, strind [rhymes with 'pin(ned)'] *n* **1** a very small stream; a trickle. **2** the jet of milk from a cow's teat NE.

strip *n* **1** a stripe. **2** a long narrow belt of trees. **3** a young fellow, a youth.

strippit baw a round peppermint **sweetie** with black and white stripes.

stripe *n* **1** a small stream. **2** a street gutter. .

strive *v, past tense also* **strave, streeve** NE quarrel, take a dislike (to).

strone *v* (*often of dogs*) urinate.

stroonge *adj* **1** harsh to the taste, bitter. **2** (*of people*) gruff, sullen.

stroop *n* **1** the spout or mouth of a kettle, jug, pump etc. **2** the spout or outlet of a spring or well, a water tap.

stroopach, stroopan a drink of tea HIGHLAND.

stroopie a teapot.

strop *see* **strap.**

strowe [rhymes with 'cow'] *v* strew. *n* a struggle, quarrel; a commotion.

strucken *see* **strik.**

strum *n* a bad mood; the huff, *often* **tak the strum(s).**

strunt[1] *n* a huff, the sulks, *often* **tak the strunt(s).**

v sulk.

strunt[2] *v* strut, walk about in an affected way.

strynge, strange *adj* **1** strange. **2** (*especially of children*) shy, self-conscious.

stranger anything thought to foretell the arrival of an unexpected visitor, *eg* a tea-leaf on the surface of tea.

stucken *see* **stick**[1].

stuckie, stushie *n* a starling.

studdie *see* **stiddie.**

stuff *n* **1** provisions, a store of food. **2** corn, grain, a crop.

stuffie 1 in good health, sturdy, full of vigour. **2** spirited, plucky, game.

stuil, steel NE *n* **1** a stool. **2** a bench, counter.

stult, stoot, steet N *v, n* prop, support.

stull *see* **still.**

stump *n* **1** the core of an apple, what is left after the flesh has been eaten. **2** a short stocky person or animal.

stumpart *v* walk heavily, clumsily NE.

stumparts legs NE.

stumpie 1 the stump of something. **2** a short, stocky or dumpy person.

stumpit short, stunted; stocky, dumpy.

stump an rump completely, absolutely.

stunk *v* sulk, go into a huff NE.

stunks *npl* the stake in a game of marbles; the game itself.

stunt *v* bounce, walk with a springy step.

stupit [-u- as -ew- as in 'stew'], **stippit, steepid** NE *adj* stupid.

sturt *v* trouble, disturb, annoy.

stushie, stooshie, stishie, stashie *n* an uproar, commotion, quarrel; a fuss, bother.

stushie *see* **stuckie.**

stut *v* stutter, stammer.

styte, styter *see* **stoit.**

succar *see* **shuggar.**

sud *see* **sall**.

suddent *adj* sudden.

  on a suddentie all of a sudden N.

suddle *v* dirty, soil.

sudna *see* **sall**.

sugar *see* **shuggar**.

sugg *n* a fat, easy-going person NE.

suin, seen NE *adv* soon.

suit, seet NE, **sit** NE *n* soot.

  Auld Suittie nickname for the Devil.

suit *see* **shoot**.

summer *see* **simmer**.

summons *n* (*law*) the document whereby some court actions are raised.

sumph *n* **1** a stupid, slow-witted person: '*Ye muckle sumph, ye*'. **2** a surly, sullen, sulky person.

  v act like a **sumph;** sulk, be sullen.

sun, sin *n* the sun.

  sundoon sunset.

  sun side sunny side.

  sunweys following the sun, from east to west.

Sunday *n*: **Sunday('s) claes, Sunday braws** your church-going clothes, your best clothes.

  Sunday Monday name of a ball game NE.

  Sunday name your formal first name, as opposed to a familiar form of it: '*When Ah'm bad ma mammie aye cries me by ma Sunday name*'.

sung *see* **sing**[2].

sup *n* **1** a mouthful, a drink: '*a sup tea*'. **2** a quantity, amount (of other liquids, especially rain).

supper *n* **1** in Scotland, usually means a light snack before bedtime. **2** a meal from a chip-shop: '*fish-supper*'; '*puddin-supper*'; '*chicken-supper*'.

sut *see* **sit, sot**.

swab [rhymes with 'stab'] *n* a pea- or bean-pod SW, SOUTH.

swabble [rhymes with 'rabble'] SOUTH *v* beat, thrash.

  n a long supple stick; a tall thin person.

swack[1] *n* **1** (the sound made by) a heavy blow or fall; a sudden or powerful movement. **2** a big mouthful.

swack[2] *adj* **1** soft, moist and easily moulded; (*of cheese*) not crumbly N. **2** easily bent or stretched N. **3** active, supple.

Swad *see* **Swade**.

Swade, Swad *n* **1** a Swede NE. **2** **swade, swad** a swede, the variety of turnip.

swag *n* (the act of) swinging or swaying.

swage [swadge] *v* **1** subside, settle down, shrink. **2** relax after a good meal.

swall [rhymes with 'pal'] *n, v* swell.

swalla [-a- as in 'cat'], **swallow** *n* **1** a swallow, the bird. **2** a martin.

swallae *see* **swallie**.

swallie, swallae [rhymes with 'pally'] *v* swallow.

  n **1** a swallow. **2** a drink, especially an alcoholic one: '*D'ye fancy gaun fur a wee swallie?*'.

swallow *see* **swalla**.

swalt *past tense* swollen.

swang *see* **swing**.

swank *adj* agile, strong; (*especially of a young man*) smart, well set-up.

swankie *adj* = **swank**.

  n a smart, active, strapping young man.

swap [rhymes with 'cap'] *v* **1** strike, hit. **2** fold or wind (a rope, strip of cloth etc) over on itself, criss-cross.

sware *see* **sweer**.

swaree *n* a social gathering, especially one organized by a church, Sunday school etc.

swarf *v* faint.

swarrach [-ch as in 'loch'] *n* a crowd, swarm (especially of young children in a family) NE.

swat *see* **sweit**.

swatch [rhymes with 'match'] *n* **1** a typical piece, example, selection etc. **2** a glimpse.

tak (a) swatch o take a critical look at: '*Tak a swatch o his new computer*'.

tak the swatch o take the measure of, be a match for NE.

swats [rhymes with 'cats'] *npl* (*in past times*) newly-brewed weak beer.

swatten *see* **swelt.**

swatter [rhymes with 'batter'] *n* a large collection or crowd, especially of small creatures NE.

swaver *v* totter, sway SHETLAND, ORKNEY, NE.

sweamish *adj* squeamish.

swee *see* **swey.**

sweel[1] *v* **1** swill; wash (the throat) down with liquor. **2** wash away; wash (food) down with a drink. **3** dash or throw (water) about. **4** (*of water, waves*) roll, flow with a swirling motion. **5** swirl, spin (quickly), whirl.
n **1** swill. **2** a large amount of drink NE: '*a gweed sweel*'. **3** a rinsing, washing or swilling. **4** a swirl, spin, twist.

sweel[2], **sweevil** *n* a swivel.

sweem *see* **soom.**

sweeng *see* **swing.**

sweep *see* **soop**[2].

sweer *v, past tense also* **swure, sware** swear.
n **1** a bout of swearing. **2** a swear-word.

sweerie word a swear-word.

sweet *adj* (*of milk*) fresh, not skimmed or sour; (*of butter*) fresh, unsalted.

sweeten *v* bribe.

sweet-breid fancy cakes, pastries SHETLAND, ORKNEY.

sweetie *n* **1** a sweet, a small piece of sweet food. **2** a large sum of money NE.

work for sweeties work for very little money.

sweetie-wife 1 a female sweet-seller. **2** a gossipy (effeminate) man.

sweevil *see* **sweel**[2].

sweir *see* **sweirt.**

swelt, swite NE *v, past tense* **swat**; *past participle* **swatten** sweat.

n **1** sweat. **2** stress, exertion; a state of anxiety or excitement.

sweirt, sweir *adj* lazy, unwilling (to work), reluctant.

sweirtie laziness SHETLAND, NE.

sweir-arse, sweir-draw, sweir-tree a game in which two people sitting on the ground, holding a stick between them, try to pull each other up.

swelchie [-ch- as in 'dreich'], **swelkie** *n* a whirlpool in the sea ORKNEY, CAITHNESS.

sweltrie *adj* oppressively hot, sultry.

swey, swee, swy(e) SHETLAND, NE *v* sway.
n **1** a sway; a swerve. **2** a swing for children. **3** a movable iron bar over a fire, on which pots, kettles etc can be hung.

swey boat a swingboat at a fair.

swick *n* **1** (a piece of) deceit, trick, swindle. **2** a cheating rogue.
v cheat, swindle, deceive.

swidder *see* **swither.**

swiff *n* the hissing or whizzing sound of an object flying through the air, a rush of air, a whirr SHETLAND, NE.

swine *n* a pig, pigs.

swine crue, swine cruive a pigsty.

swing, sweeng *v, past tense also* **swang** SHETLAND, NE swing.
n **1** a swing. **2** *also* **swing rope** a rope for tying up a boat.

swinge *n* a heavy blow.

swipper, swippert *adj* quick, nimble, active NE.

swire *n* a hollow or slope in or between hills.

swirl, swurl *n* a twist, twirl, coil; a twisted or tangled state.
v (cause to) move round and round, whirl, eddy; wave, brandish.

swirlie 1 curly, frizzy. **2** tangled, twisted.

switchbell *see* **coachbell.**

swite *see* **swelt.**

swith *adv* quickly, at once.

swither, swidder NE *v* **1** be uncertain, hesitate, dither. **2** (*of things*) be uncertain, have a doubtful appearance. *n* **1** a state of indecision or doubt, hesitation, uncertainty. **2** a state of nervousness, a panic, fluster. **3** a state of confusion. **4** a dithering, undecided person.

sword *see* **swurd**.

swurd, sword *n* a sword.

sword dance a Highland dance, usually solo, consisting of a series of steps between swords laid crosswise on the ground.

swure *see* **sweer**.

swurl *see* **swirl**.

swy, swye *see* **swey**.

swype *see* **soop**².

sybies *see* **syboes**.

syboes, sybies *npl* spring onions.

sye *v* pass (liquid) through a sieve, drain, filter.
n a strainer or sieve.

syes *npl* chives.

syke *n* **1** a small stream etc, especially one on flat, boggy ground. **2** a marshy hollow, especially one with a stream.

synd, syne [rhymes with 'mind' or 'mine'] *v* **1** rinse (a container etc), wash out. **2** wash (the face, clothes etc), give a quick swill to (something). **3** wash (food) down with drink, swill (something) away or out with water etc.

n a washing or rinsing out, a swill, a hasty wash.

syne, sin, seen NE *adv* **1** directly after, next, afterwards: '*an syne they cam hame*'. **2** in that case, so, then: '*an syne, ye're no gaun*'. **3** ago, since, before now. **4** from then, since, thereafter.
n that time, then: '*fae syne*'.
conjunction **1** since, from the time that. **2** *only* **sin** since, because, seeing that.
preposition since (the time of): '*Ah've no seen him syne the Christmas pairtie*'.

sinsyne since then, after that time.

syne *see* **synd**.

synod *n* (*Presbyterian Churches*) a court between the **presbytery** and the **General Assembly**.

sype, seep *v* **1** soak, ooze. **2** (*of a container*) drip, leak. **3** cause to drip, ooze; draw liquid from, drain; drip-dry (clothes).
n **1** an oozing, leakage. **2** a small trickle of water; a drip.

sypin, sypit soaked SHETLAND, NE.

sypins oozings, leakage; the last drops from a container.

syre *see* **syver**.

syver, syre *n* **1** a ditch, drain, water-channel, a (covered-in) stone-lined field-drain. **2** a street-gutter. **3** a street-drain and the grating over it.

T

tablet *see* **taiblet.**

tacht *adj* taut N.

tack *n* **1** a lease, tenancy. **2** a period of time, a spell of weather.

tacken *see* **tak.**

tacket *n* a small nail often on the sole of a shoe.

tacketie studded with **tackets,** hobnailed: '*tacketie buits*'.

tadger *n* the penis.

tae¹**, toe** *n* **1** a toe. **2** a prong of a fork etc.

tae² *adj* one (of two): '*It gaes in at the tae lug an oot at the tither*'.

tae³**, tee** NE, **to** *preposition* **1** to.

2 (*of food*) with, for: '*an egg tae his tea*'.

3 (*with verbs of looking*) at: '*look tae that picture*'.

4 by: '*He's a jiner tae trade*'.

5 with (a specified person) as the father, by: '*She had a bairn tae her cousin*'.

6 compared with: '*Ah'm jist a puir man tae you*'.

7 for, on behalf of, for the use of: '*He worked tae Mr G*'.

8 (*expressing family relationships*) of: '*son tae the Sheriff*'.

adv **1** to.

2 (*of a door*) so as to shut or close, closed: '*close the door tae*'.

3 close, on, together, in contact NE.

4 too, also, as well.

conjunction till, until.

tobackie one of the actions in a children's ball game.

tae-fa 1 a lean-to porch or outhouse. **2** an addition; an extra charge, burden.

tee-name an additional name, a nickname SHETLAND, ORKNEY, NE.

be tee be up to schedule NE.

weel tee up to time, well in hand NE.

tae *see* **dey, tea.**

taen *see* **tak.**

taft *see* **thaft.**

tag *n* the strap formerly used for punishment in schools.

taiblet, tablet *n* **1** a tablet. **2** a kind of hard fudge.

taickle *n, v* tackle.

taid *n* **1** a toad. **2** a sheep-tick. **3** an unpleasant, trouble-making person. **4** term of endearment NE.

taigle *v* **1** tangle, confuse, muddle. **2** get in the way of, keep back. **3** get the better of (in an argument), bamboozle. **4** delay, dawdle, hang about.

n a tangle, muddle.

taigelt tired, harassed.

taiglesome 1 time-consuming, causing delay. **2** tiring, boring.

taik *v, n* stroll SHETLAND, N.

taiken *n* a token.

tail *n* **1** a long narrow piece of land jutting out from a larger piece. **2 tails** onion leaves. **3** the end (of a period of time or of an activity). **4** a prostitute.

tailie (day) 2 April, when children fix paper tails with various messages to the backs of unsuspecting victims.

tailor *see* **teylor.**

taings *see* **tangs.**

tairge *see* **targe.**

tairt, tert *n* a tart.

taisle *v* entangle, mix up.

tait, tit NE *n* **1** a small tuft or bundle of hair, wool etc. **2** *also* **a (wee) tait** a small amount (of something); somewhat: '*a wee tait bacon*'; '*a wee tait tipsy*'.

taiver *v* wander about aimlessly; waste time.

197

talvert muddled, bewildered.

talvers *npl* rags, tatters, shreds, (*often of meat*) **biled tae talvers.**

tak, take *v, past tense also* **taen, teen** SHETLAND, N; *past participle also* **taen, teen** SHETLAND, N, **tacken, tooken 1** take.
2 catch (your foot) on; be tripped by.
3 (*of water*) come up as far on a person as: '*That pool will tak ye*'.
4 tak yersel stop yourself from doing or saying something which you might later regret.
5 marry.
6 catch fire.
n **1** an act of seizing, a capture, catch; a catch of fish. **2** a state of growth, the sprouting of a crop.

taen(-like) surprised, embarrassed.

takkie the game of tig; the pursuer in the game NE.

tak aboot take care of; handle, manage.

tak aff resemble.

tak awa eat or drink up.

taen-awa a fairy changeling.

tak the door wi ye leave a room, closing the door behind you.

tak doon weaken, cause to lose weight.

tak yer hand aff (someone's face *etc***)** slap, smack someone.

tak yer heid go to your head, make you giddy.

tak ill become ill.

tak in bring in, welcome (a new day, year etc).

tak on 1 buy on credit or account. **2** affect physically. **3** have (a person) on, tease. **4** get excited or emotional, be worked up; mope.

tak on wi take a liking to, be attracted by.

tak tae yersel admit the truth of (an accusation), feel guilt or remorse, be sensitive about.

tak up 1 take (a collection) at a meeting. **2** (*of a school or college*) reopen

after a holiday. **3** understand, get the meaning of. **4** run into debt, live on credit.

be taen up wi be charmed by, be pleased with.

tak wi 1 admit; admit that you are the father of NE. **2** find agreeable, take kindly to.

tale *n*: **tale-pyot** a tell-tale.

Taillie *n* (*humorous or contemptuous, especially of a seller of ice cream, fish and chips etc*) an Italian.

Tam *n* Tom.

Tam o Shanter a round, flat woollen cap often with a **toorie 1** (*see* **toor**[1]).

Tammie *n* **1** Tommy. **2** a kind of beret.

Tammie cheekie NE, **Tammie norie** a puffin.

tammie reekie a kind of smoke gun made from a cabbage stem.

Tamson's mear *see* **mear.**

tane, teen NE *pronoun* one (of two): '*The tane wad tell a tale, the tither sing a song*'.

tang[1] *n* large, coarse seaweed growing above low-water mark SHETLAND, ORKNEY.

tangle 1 *also* **sea tangle** = **tang.** **2** a tall, lanky person. **3** an icicle.

tang[2] *n* the prong of a digging- or pitchfork.

tangs, taings, tyangs [teeangs] NE, **teengs** SHETLAND, ORKNEY *npl* tongs.

tansy *n* ragwort.

tantersome *adj* exasperating, annoying NE.

tap[1], **top** *n* **1** the top. **2** a tuft of hair, feathers etc; a forelock; a bird's crest. **3** the head. **4** a tip, an end. **5** the surface of water.
v **1** top. **2 top** (*golf*) hit (the ball) on its upper part, making it spin rather than fly forward.

tappin 1 a tuft or crest on a bird's head. **2** the peaked top of a hill; a cairn on a hilltop.

tappit crested, tufted.

tappit hen 1 a tufted hen. **2** a kind of

(pewter) container, containing a standard measure, its lid knob shaped like a chicken's tuft.

taptaes tiptoes.

never aff someone's tap always criticizing, continually quarrelling with someone.

on someone's tap attacking, severely scolding someone.

tap² *n* a top, the toy, especially a whipping top.

tape *v* measure exactly (with a tape-measure); deal out or use sparingly.

tappletoorie *n* something which rises to a peak; an ornament on top of something *eg* a tassel, pompom.

tapsalteerie *adj, adv* upside down, topsy-turvy; chaotic, muddled.

tar, taur, ter *n* tar.

tarry, taurie *adj* **1** tarry. **2** *also* **tarry-fingered** light-fingered, likely to steal.

tarry breeks nickname for a sailor.

tarbert *see* **tarbet**.

tarbet, tarbert *n* (*in place-names*) an isthmus or neck of land between two stretches of water.

targe, tairge *v* treat strictly or severely; question closely, cross-examine; scold severely.

n a violent, scolding woman.

targer a violent, quarrelsome, domineering person, especially a woman.

target *n* a long narrow shred of cloth, a tatter; an oddly- or untidily-dressed person.

tarragat *v* question closely, pester.

tarrock, tirrick *n* **1** a tern. **2** a (young) kittiwake.

tartan *n*: **fireside tartan, grannie's tartan, tinker's tartan** coloured skin on the legs caused by sitting too close to an open fire.

tash *n* damage; a stain, smudge; a blot on your character.

v **1** spoil; stain (clothes etc) by rough or careless handling. **2** weary (with hard work).

tashie tattered, slovenly in appearance, untidy.

tassie *n* a cup, goblet etc.

taste *v* drink alcohol in small amounts. *n* **1** a small quantity of alcoholic drink, a **dram**. **2** a small quantity.

taste yer gab cause a pleasant taste in your mouth, whet the appetite.

tatterwallop *n* **1** a rag, tatter. **2** a ragged person, ragamuffin ORKNEY, NE.

tattle, tawtle *n* **1** a potato. **2** (*contemptuous*) the head; a stupid person.

tattle-beetle a (wooden) potato-masher.

tattle-bogle, tattle-bogie, tattle-boodie NE **1** a scarecrow. **2** a ragged, untidy or strangely-dressed person. **3** a large raw potato with matchsticks stuck in it as a toy.

tattle-broth potato soup.

tattle-champer, tattle-chapper a potato-masher.

tattle-doolie a scarecrow; a ragamuffin.

tattle hoalidays an autumn school holiday (to allow children to help with the potato harvest).

tattle howker a person who works at the potato harvest, especially a temporary worker from Ireland.

tattle howkin, tattle liftin the potato-harvest.

tattle-peelin *n* a potato peeling. *adj* (*of speech*) affected, prim.

tattle-scone a (flat) **scone** made of flour, milk and mashed potato.

tattle-trap (*contemptuous*) the mouth.

the (clean) tattle the right person, one who can be trusted or relied on.

tatties an dab potatoes boiled in their skins and dipped in melted fat, gravy etc.

taucht, teacht *past tense, past participle* taught.

tauple *n* a scatterbrained, untidy, awkward or careless person, especially a young woman.

taur *see* **tar.**

taut *n* a tangled, matted tuft or lock of wool, hair etc.

tautit, tautie matted; shaggy.

taw *v* **1** knead, draw out, twist (*eg* dough, toffee); pull and tug at. **2** work with great effort, struggle. **3** *also* **tawse** beat, whip with a **tawse**. *n* **tawse** a leather punishment strap with thongs, which was used in schools.

tawtie *see* **tattle.**

tchop *see* **shop.**

tea, tae SHETLAND, N, ULSTER *n* **1** tea. **2** *also* **high tea** a meal eaten in the early evening, usually consisting of one cooked course followed by bread, cakes and tea.

tea-bread buns, **scones** etc eaten with tea.

tea-hand, tea-jennie a person (male or female) who drinks a lot of tea.

tea an till't tea served with a cooked meal, **high tea.**

teacht *see* **taucht.**

tear *see* **teir.**

tedder *see* **tether.**

tedisome *adj* tedious, tiresome, boring.

tee *n* **1** (*golf*) the peg or (formerly) the small heap of sand from which the ball is driven; the patch of ground from which this is done. **2** (*curling*) the target, a mark on the ice. **3** (*quoits, carpet bowls*) the target or goal.

tee *see* **tae**³.

teel *see* **tuil.**

teem *v* **1** empty (a container); empty out (the contents) from a container. **2** drain water from (potatoes). **3** (*of rain*) pour, come down in torrents. **4** (*of water*) flow or gush. *n* a very heavy, long-lasting downpour of rain.

teem *see* **tuim.**

teen *see* **tak, tane, tune.**

teengs *see* **tangs.**

teenie *n* **1** (*contemptuous*) a junior domestic servant; an effeminate man. **2** a little girl: '*C'mon, teenie, I'll gie ye a sweetie*'.

teenie-bash familiar, often insulting term for a woman or girl E CENTRAL.

Teenie f(r)ae Troon, Teenie f(r)ae the neeps an odd-looking, oddly-dressed or over-dressed woman.

teentie *numeral* (*children's rhymes*) two.

teep *n, v* (a) type.

teep *see* **tuip.**

teepical *adj* typical.

teer *n* tare, wild vetch.

teerie-orrie *n* throwing a ball against a wall, catching and bouncing it in various ways E CENTRAL.

teet¹ *v* peep, peer, glance slyly. *n* a shy peep, a sly, secretive glance.

teet(ie) bo (the game of) peep-bo.

teet² *n* the smallest sound, a squeak.

teeter hesitate.

teeth *see* **tuith.**

teetle *n* a title.

teewheet, teewhip *see* **teuchit.**

teir, tear [rhymes with 'beer' or 'bare'], **terr** *v* **1** tear, rip. **2** (*of wind*) blow hard, gust, rage. **3 tear awa, tear on** work energetically and with speed (at). **4** rage (at). *n* **1** a tear, a rip. **2** a piece of fun, a spree, joke: '*a rerr terr*'. **3** a lively entertaining person, a comic. **4** a (great) quantity.

tore *past tense, past participle* torn.

get tore intae attack vigorously.

torn face (a person with) a bad-tempered, sulky glum face.

teistie *n* a black guillemot SHETLAND, ORKNEY, CAITHNESS.

tell *v, past tense, past participle also* **telt** tell.

tellin a warning, lesson: '*Let that be a tellin tae ye*'; '*tak a tellin*'.

it would be tellin (someone) it would be better for (someone).

tell on tell tales about, inform against.

tenaby *numeral* (*children's rhymes*) ten SHETLAND, ORKNEY, CAITHNESS.

tend *v* attend (to), look after, see (to).

tender *adj* sickly; in poor health.

tenement *n* a large building, usually of three or more storeys divided into flats; the section of such a building served by one staircase.

tenon *n* a tendon.

tent *n* attention, heed, care.
v **1** pay attention to, listen to. **2** watch over, take good care of.
tentie 1 watchful; attentive. **2** cautious, careful.
tentless inattentive, careless.
tak tent 1 be careful, beware. **2** notice, take note.
tak tent o 1 take (good) care of, heed. **2** pay attention to, keep watch on. **3** beware of, be on your guard against.
tak tent tae listen to.

ter *see* **tar.**

term *see* **thairm.**

terr *see* **teir.**

terrible, terrel *adj* terrible.
adv very much, awfully: '*It's terrible wet*'.

tersie versie *adj, adv* topsy-turvy.

tert *see* **tairt.**

tether, tedder SHETLAND, ORKNEY, N *n* **1** a tether. **2** scope, the limits: '*His mither gied him ower lang a tether*'.
tethery *numeral* (*children's rhymes*) three.

teuch, cheuch [teeooch, teeuch, chooch, chuch] *n* **1** tough. **2** (*of people*) rough, coarse. **3** (*of weather*) rough, wet and windy.
teuch Jean a kind of sticky, chewy **sweetie.**

teuchit [teeoochit], **teewheet, teewhip** ORKNEY *n* a lapwing, peewit.
teuchit('s) storm a period of bleak wintry weather in March (when the **teuchits** arrive and begin to nest).

teuchter [teeoochter] *n* contemptuous term for a Highlander, especially a Gaelic-speaker, or of anyone from the North; a countrified person.

teug *see* **chug.**

teven *numeral* (*children's rhymes*) seven.

teylor, tailor *n* a tailor.
tailor's gartens ribbon-grass.

thack *n, v* thatch.

thae *pronoun, adj* those, these.

thaft, taft SHETLAND *n* a rower's bench, thwart.

thaim *see* **them.**

thairm, term SHETLAND *n* a human or animal bowel, gut, intestine.

than, an *adv* then.
conjunction than.
noos an thans now and then.
than-a-days in those days, at that time.
weel than in that case; yes indeed, very much so.

thank *n, v:* **thankrife** very grateful.

thanksgiving (service) *n* (*Presbyterian Churches*) the service after Communion.

give thanks say grace before or after a meal.

that, at N, **dat** SHETLAND *pronoun* **1** that. **2** this: '*That's a braw day*'. **3** used to emphasize a previous phrase: '*It's very cold. It is that*'.
adj **1** that. **2** those: '*that men*'. **3** *also* **thattan, that a** ... such, so much: '*She had that a cauld*'.
conjunction that.
adv so, to such a degree; to that extent; very: '*He was that feart*'.
relative pronoun **1** that, who(m), which; often left out in Scots. **2** *as possessive* (1) **that** *with possessive adj* NE, ULSTER: '*The crew that their boat wis lost*'; (2) **that's**: '*The woman that's sister mairried the postie*'.
an that and so on, et cetera: '*He'll bring the milk an that*'.
or that or the like, or something similiar: '*a visitor and maybe a painter or that*'.

thaw *see* **thowe.**

the, de SHETLAND, E COAST, **da** SHETLAND, **e, ee** N *definite article* **1** the.

2 used with names of relatives: '*Have ye met the sister*'.

3 used with the names of parts of the body: '*keep the heid*'.

4 used where English leaves out, *eg* referring to public institutions: '*He's at the school now*'; in the home: '*up the stair*'; '*sit at the table*'; '*fish for the tea*'; things you buy: '*the price o the milk*'; a fit of temper: '*tak the huff*'; with names of diseases etc: '*He's got the measles*'; '*He was a terrible man for the drink*'; '*the dry rot*'; with names of activities: '*You've been at the smokin*'; trades or crafts: '*They're at the fishin*'; of language etc: '*the Gaelic*'; of sports, games etc: '*They were playing at the chess*'; before a surname to indicate the leading member of a family: '*Robert the Bruce*'; '*the Chisholm*', and to indicate the chief of a Highland clan: '*the Mackintosh*'; with certain placenames: '*the Langholm*'; before the names of schools or colleges: '*at the Waid Academy*'; **the baith:** '*the baith o them*'; **the maist:** '*the maist fowks*'.

5 used where English leaves out or uses **a**: '*He wears the kilt*'; '*They tell me you're to be the great surgeon*'.

6 the noo now: '*He's here the noo*'.

7 there: '*the ben*'.

8 the day today, **the morn** tomorrow, **the nicht** tonight, **the year** this year.

the *see* **there.**

thee *n* the thigh.

thee *see* **thou, thy.**

theek *v* **1** roof, cover (a building, hay- or peat-stack) with (thatch). **2** cover, protect with a thick covering of hair, clothes etc.

n **1** thatch. **2** any thick covering of hair etc.

theer *see* **there.**

theevil *n* a short stick used to stir food, especially porridge.

thegither, thegidder, thegether *adv* together.

their, thir, der SHETLAND *adj* their.

theirsel, theirsels themselves.

them, thaim, dem SHETLAND *pronoun* **1** them. **2** those: '*Them at sent it kens*'.

there, theer SOUTH, **der(e)** SHETLAND, **therr** WEST, **err** WEST *adv* **1** *also* **the, they, de(y)** there: '*They'll be nae peace*'; '*Dey wir no a flooer tae be seen*'. **2** *also* **dir** SHETLAND, ORKNEY there is, there are: '*There naebodie in*'.

there awa away to or in that place; in that general direction.

there in indoors, at home.

there oot 1 out of doors, in the open. **2** out of that; out of that place.

therecklie *adv* directly sw, SOUTH.

therr *see* **there.**

therteen *see* **thirteen.**

thertie, threttie, trettie SHETLAND *numeral* thirty.

thesaurer *n* a treasurer.

these *see* **this.**

the streen *see* **yestreen.**

they *see* **there.**

thick *adj* thickset, muscular, burly.

thickness a dense fog or sea-mist.

thief *n:* **the auld thief, the black thief** the Devil, Satan.

thig *v* beg, cadge.

thimmie *see* **thummle.**

thin, tin SHETLAND *adj* **1** thin. **2** (*of wind, weather*) cold, bitter, piercing.

the thin(s) diarrhoea NE.

thing, ting SHETLAND, ORKNEY *n* **1** a thing. **2** amount, number: '*an awfu thing o tatties*'. **3** kind: '*Ah'll tak the big thing*'.

a wee thing(ie) rather, a little: '*a wee thing earlier*'.

thingmy, thingwy, hingmy thingummy.

think, tink SHETLAND *v, past tense, past participle* **thocht, tocht** SHETLAND think.

I'm thinkin I presume, it's my opinion.

think lang (for) long (for).

think on think of or about.

thir *possessive adj* their.

thir *see* **their, this.**

thirl[1], **tirl** SHETLAND *v* pierce, bore through, make holes in.

thirl[2] *v* bind with ties of affection, sense of duty or loyalty etc.

　thirled, thirlt bound by ties of affection, duty etc; hidebound by an idea, belief etc.

thirteen, therteen, tretten SHETLAND *numeral* **1** thirteen. **2** thirteenth.

　therteent thirteenth.

this, dis SHETLAND, **is(s)** N *pronoun, pl also* **thir 1** this. **2** this time, this place, now, here: '*He gaed fae this tae Ayr*'. **3** these SHETLAND, N: '*This flooers is past.*'

　adj **1** this. **2** these: '*this bonnie boys*'. **3** **these** those NE: '*These seeds in my hand are better than these on the table*'. **4** **this day** today; **this nicht** tonight.

　adv so, to such a degree or extent: '*this auld*'.

　this o't this state of affairs.

tho, to SHETLAND *conjunction* though.

thocht, thoucht, tought SHETLAND [-ch-, -gh- as -ch in 'loch'] *n* **1** thought. **2** care, trouble; (a cause for) anxiety, worry. **3 a** (**wee** *etc*) **thocht** a very small amount (of), a little; rather. *past tense, past participle of* **think** thought.

　thochtie *adj* heedful, attentive; serious-minded; anxious.

　ill-thochtit having nasty or suspicious thoughts, nasty-minded.

thole *v* **1** suffer, have to bear (pain, grief etc). **2** suffer with patience or bravery, put up with. **3** be able to endure; manage.

　tholeable bearable.

　thole wi put up with: '*Ah cannae thole wi screamin bairns*'.

thon *pronoun, adj* (*usually indicating a thing or person further away from the speaker than another or others*) that; those.

thonder, thonner *adv* over there, at some distance, yonder.

thoo *see* **thou.**

thoomie *see* **thoum.**

thoosan, thoosand *numeral* thousand.

thorow, thorough *preposition* through.

　adj **1** thorough. **2** mentally alert, sane SW, SOUTH.

thorter *preposition* on or to the other side of, across, over.

　v **1** cross the path of; thwart, oppose. **2** do something in a direction at right angles to what you have done before.

thou, du SHETLAND, **thoo** ORKNEY *pronoun* thou.

　thee ORKNEY, **dee** SHETLAND thee: used *eg* between close friends, or by adults to children etc.

thoucht *see* **thocht.**

thoum [-oo-], **thumb, toom** SHETLAND, ORKNEY *n* **1** the thumb. **2** in reference to the practice of confirming a bargain etc by licking and joining thumbs: '*There's ma thoum*'; '*weet thoumbs*'.

　thoomie a wren NE.

　thoum-hand the right hand NE.

　put yer thoum on keep secret, keep silent about.

　crack yer thoums snap your fingers in pleasure or derision SHETLAND, NE.

　no fash yer thoum pay no heed, never worry or concern yourself.

　no be able to see yer thoum be unable to see ahead of you (in the dark).

thoumart *see* **foumart.**

thowe, tow SHETLAND [rhymes with 'cow'], **thaw** *v, n* thaw.

　dirty thowe a thaw brought on by rain.

　dry thowe a thaw after a high wind.

　weet thowe a thaw without wind or rain.

thowless *adj* lacking energy or spirit.

thraa *see* **thraw.**

thrae *see* **fae**[2].

thran *see* **thrawn.**

thrang, trang SHETLAND, ORKNEY *n* **1** a throng. **2** pressure (of work) *adj* **1** crowded (closely together); full. **2** in crowds, numerous. **3** (*of places*) thronged, crowded with people. **4** busy, fully occupied. **5** on very friendly terms.

thrapple, trapple SHETLAND, ORKNEY *n* the windpipe, the throat, the gullet. *v* throttle, strangle.

weet yer thrapple have something to drink, quench your thirst.

thrash, thresh, tresh SHETLAND *v* English distinguishes between *thresh* beat (corn) and *thrash* beat, punish; in Scots the distinction is not made and the form is now usually **thrash.**

thrash *see* **rash**[1].

thrave *see* **threave.**

thraw, thraa ORKNEY N, **traa** SHET-LAND, **throw** *v, past tense also* **thrawed, thraad** ORKNEY, N **traad** SHETLAND *past participle also* **thrawn, traan** SHETLAND, ORKNEY

1 *not* **throw** (1) twist, turn; wring. (2) turn (a key) in a lock, (a knob) on a door. (3) twist (a part of the body) wrench, sprain.

2 *not* **throw** turn, twist; curl.

3 *not* **throw** (1) oppose, cross. (2) be contrary, quarrel, grumble. (3) quarrel with.

4 throw.

5 throw throw up, vomit.

n, not **throw** *in all meanings except* 1: **1** a throw.

2 a turn, twist.

3 a wrench of a muscle etc, a sprain.

4 a twisting of the face, a wry expression.

5 a twisting of the body in pain, a spasm.

6 a fit of obstinacy or bad temper, the sulks.

7 a dispute, quarrel.

thrawcruik 1 an implement for twisting straw etc into rope. **2** a twisted straw rope.

thraa moose a shrew NE.

helds an thraws lying in opposite directions; higgledy-piggledy.

thraw yer face screw up, twist the face as a sign of pain etc.

thrawn, thran, traan SHETLAND, UL-STER; *see also* **thraw** *adj* **1** obstinate, contrary; cross, sullen. **2** twisted, crooked, distorted. **3** (*of the mouth, face*) twisted with pain, rage etc, surly. **4** (*of the weather*) disagreeable, bad NE.

threap, traep SHETLAND, ORKNEY *v* **1** keep saying (something) very firmly. **2** argue, quarrel. **3 threap at** nag at, be insistent with.

n **1** a strongly held opinion. **2** an argument; a quarrel.

threap doon someone's throat force your opinions on someone.

threave, thrave, trave SHETLAND, ORKNEY *n* **1** a measure of cut grain, straw etc. **2** a large number or quantity SHETLAND, ORKNEY.

three, threy SOUTH, **tree** SHETLAND *numeral* three.

threesie 1 a move in the game of **chucks. 2** *also* **threele** the third square or box in the game of **peever**[1].

threesome (of) a group or company of three.

three-fower three or four, a few.

threeple *adj* triple, three times over NE.

v treble NE.

threeplet a triplet.

threld, treed SHETLAND *n* thread.

threld dry completely dry.

threlt *n* a threat.

thresh *see* **rash**[1], **thrash.**

threttle *see* **thertie.**

threy *see* **three.**

thrissel, th(r)ustle, tistle SHETLAND, ORKNEY *n* a thistle; the emblem of Scotland.

thrist SHETLAND, ORKNEY, NE, **trist** SHETLAND *n, v* thirst.

throttle *n* the throat, gullet, windpipe.

throu, trou SHETLAND, **throuch, through** *preposition* **1** through.
2 further into, inside, in another part or end of: '*throu the hoose*'.
3 across: '*throu the bridge*'.
4 on the other side of (a wall), in the next room, next door.
5 during, in (the course of): '*through the day*'.
adv **1** through. **2** (*referring to the length or direction of a journey*) across country: '*They came throu from Ayr*'. **3** at or near your end, done for.

througate a passage(way), lane.

througaun connecting one street, house to another.

throu-hochle (*marbles*) a throw in which the marble is thrown through the legs from behind NE.

throu hoose a house whose rooms lead off one another, with no hall.

throu-pit 1 production, output. **2** energy, activity, capacity for or progress at work.

throu the boil up to boiling point and allowed to boil for a short time.

throu the cauld (*of speaking*) thickly, in a choked way.

throu time in time, eventually.

throu the week during the week: on a weekday; on weekdays.

throuither, throwder NE *adv* jumbled or mixed up (together), higgledy-piggledy.
adj untidy, disorganized, confused.

throw *see* **thraw**.

throwder *see* **throuither**.

thrustle *see* **thrissel**.

thumb *see* **thoum**.

thummle, thimmle *n* **1** a thimble. **2 thummles** name for various plants, *eg* the foxglove, raspberries.

thunner, thunder, tunner SHETLAND *n, v* thunder.

thunner-plump a sudden heavy thunder-shower.

thunner-an-lichtenin lungwort or other plant with white spotted leaves.

thustle *see* **thrissel**.

thwang *see* **whang**.

thy, dy SHETLAND, **dee** SHETLAND, **thee** ORKNEY *pronoun* thy (used between *eg* close friends or by adults to children).

Tibble Thiefie *n* a sandpiper NE.

tice, tize SHETLAND, ORKNEY *v* coax, wheedle.

ticht, tight [rhymes with 'licht'] *adj* **1** tight. **2** (*of things*) in short supply. **3** mean, close-fisted. **4** short of money. **5** strict.
adv tightly, closely, neatly.
v tighten, make close, secure or watertight.
n a tightening.

tichten *v* tighten.
n a tightening.

ticht-hauden hard-pressed, harassed SW, SOUTH.

tick[1] *n* **1** *also* **tickie** a small quantity, a grain, drop. **2** the game of tig SHETLAND.
v tap lightly, especially in the game of tig.

tickie-tak the game of tig.

tick[2] *n*: **play the tick** play truant FIFE.

ticket *n* a person dressed in a slovenly, untidy or odd way, a sight.

tickle *v* puzzle.

tickler a problem, puzzle.

tickly 1 tickly, ticklish. **2** puzzling, difficult.

tid *n* **1** a favourable time or season, an opportunity. **2** a mood, humour.

tidder *see* **tither**.

tide *n* the foreshore, the land between high and low water marks.

tift *n* **1** a tiff, a quarrel. **2** a fit of bad temper, the sulks.

tig *v* **1** touch lightly with the hand, especially in the game of tig. **2** take a sudden whim, go off in a huff. **3** flirt with.

n **1** a light playful touch, slap; the tap given in the game of tig, usually accompanied by the call tig. **2** a sudden mood or humour; a fit of sullenness. **3** used as a call in the game of tig when the pursuer touches someone.

chain(ie) tig, high tig, lame tig variations of the game of tig.

tak the tig take a sudden whim or notion; get a fit of the sulks.

tight *see* **ticht.**

tike¹ *n* **1** a contemptuous term for a dog. **2** a rough person, a clumsy, ill-mannered person. **3** a mischievous child.

tike² *n* a tick, a mattress cover, ticking; the mattress itself: '*Turn the tike*'.

till, tull *preposition* **1** till. **2** to: '*He'll be a credit till us aw*'. **3** with (a specified person) as the father, by SHETLAND, N: '*She had a lassie till him*'. **4** for, for the benefit of: '*a cradle till her*'. **5** with, for, as an accompaniment of (food): '*tak some saut till't*'.

conjunction **1** till, until. **2** before, when: '*It was not till I was cosy in bed*'. **3** in order that: '*Gie me a match till I light the gas*'.

tim *see* **tuim.**

Tim *n* (*contemptuous*) a Catholic CENTRAL.

time *n*: **timeous** [rhymes with 'primus'] at the proper time.

at aa time at any time, at all times.

at a time at times, now and again.

time o day 1 a clock. **2** the right time.

the time that while, during the time that.

timmer *n* **1** timber. **2** wood as a material.

adj **1** wooden, made of wood. **2** *also* **timmer-tuned** unmusical, tone-deaf.

v **1** beat, thrash. **2 timmer up** go at (something) vigorously NE.

timorsome *adj* nervous, timid.

tin *see* **thin.**

ting *see* **thing.**

tingle *v* (cause to) tinkle, ring or chime.

tink *see* **think, tinker.**

tinker, tink, tinkler *n* **1** *also* **tinkie** a travelling pedlar or trader, living in a tent, caravan etc, and dealing in small metal wares, brushes, baskets etc. **2** *now usually* **tink** contemptuous term for a person, especially a foul-mouthed, quarrelsome, vulgar person.

tinker's tartan *see* **tartan.**

tinker's tea tea brewed in a pan rather than in a teapot.

tinnie *n* a small tin mug, especially one used by children.

tint *see* **tyne.**

tip¹ *v*: **tippertaes** tiptoes.

tippertin *n* a piece of cardboard pierced by a pointed stick on which it is spun NE.

tippin (*fishing*) the cord attaching the hook to the line.

tipple fashionable, stylish.

tip up dress up, smarten yourself.

tip² *v* (*football*) kick lightly with the point of the toe SHETLAND, NE.

tip *see* **tuip.**

tippence *n* twopence.

tippenie-nippenie *n* a kind of leap-frog.

tippertaes, tippertin, tippie *see* **tip**¹.

tire *v* tiredness, weariness.

tirl¹ *v* **1** pull or strip off (a covering *eg* clothes, bedclothes). **2** strip the covering off (a person or thing).

tirl² *v* **1** cause to spin, turn, twirl. **2** knock, rattle on (a door etc). **3** turn over, spin, roll, whirl.

n **1** a turn, twirl. **2** a breeze; a flurry of snow etc NE. **3** a knock, rattle (on a door etc).

tirlie-whirlie an ornament, knick-knack.

tirl *see* **thirl**¹.

tirr *v* **1** take the top layer off. **2** strip or tear off (a covering). **3** strip, undress NE. **4** strip (a room, bed etc).

tirraneese *v* harass with overwork.

tirrick *see* **tarrock.**

tirrivee *n* **1** a fit of rage or bad temper; a wild mood. **2** a state of excitement; a disturbance, fight.

tirr-wirr *n* a disturbance; a noisy quarrel, scolding match.

tishie *n* tissue: '*tishie paper*'.

tistle *see* **thrissel.**

tit[1] *v* pull, tug, jerk, twitch SHETLAND, NE.

tit[2] *n* a teat; a nipple.

tit *see* **tait.**

titch *v, n* touch.

tither, tidder SHETLAND, NE *pronoun*: **the tither 1** (the) other, second of two (or more), another. **2** additional, yet another, next.

titlin *n* **1** a meadow pipit CAITHNESS. **2** the smallest and weakest in a brood, especially a litter of pigs.

tittie *n* familiar name for a sister.

tittle *v* gossip, tell someone something, especially by whispering in their ear; whisper, chatter.

tize *see* **tice.**

to *see* **tae**[3], **tho.**

toalie *n* **1** a lump of excrement. **2** contemptuous term for a person.

toatie *see* **tot.**

tobacco fleuk *n* a lemon sole.

tobackie *see* **tae**[3].

toby *n* **1** a stopcock or valve in a water- or gas-main. **2** the penis NE.

tocher *n* a dowry.

tod *n* a fox.

toddie's grund (*children's games*) a place of sanctuary, a 'den'.

tod-lowrie a fox.

hunt the tod the game of hide-and-seek NE.

(the) tod and (the) lambs a draughts-like board game, fox and geese.

tod-i-the-faul(d) name of various games.

toe *see* **tae**[1].

toit *v* walk unsteadily, totter NE.

tolbooth *n* a building used as a town hall, often including the town prison.

tongue *n* impudence, abuse, violent language.

v scold.

tonguie talkative, fluent.

tongue-tackit tongue-tied, having a speech impediment, dumb.

tooch *n* a bang, the sound of a shot SE.

tooder *see* **toother.**

tooel *n, v* towel.

tooken *see* **tak.**

toom *see* **thoum, tuim.**

toon, toun, town *n* **1** a town. **2** an area occupied by a number of farmers, a cluster of houses belonging to this; a village. **3** a farm with its buildings and the area round about.

toondle the person left in charge of a farm when the rest of the household are away NE.

toonie, toonser a town-dweller as opposed to a country person.

toon heid the higher or upper end of a town.

toon hoose a town hall.

township especially in Highlands, a group of crofts.

toon's speak the talk of the town, the local scandal.

toople, tooplcan *n* any high pointed object, a knob on the top of something.

toor[1], **tower** *n* a tower.

toorie *n* **1** a pompom on a hat. **2** a top-knot or bun of hair. **3** a little tower; something rising to a point.

toor[2], **tower** *n* a tour, a circular route.

toosh *n* nonsense word used in children's games.

toosht *n* **1** a loose untidy bundle (of straw etc). **2** a slut; a nasty unpleasant person.

toot[1]**!, toots!** *interjection* nonsense!

toot[2] *v* drink too much.

n a drink (of alcohol).

tooter *v* **1** work unskilfully, potter or mess about. **2** toddle, walk with short prim steps.

n NE **1** an unskilful piece of work. **2** a tottery walk.

toother, tooder *v* handle roughly.

n a rough handling; disorder, a mess.

top *see* **tap**[1].

torie NE, **story** SHETLAND, CAITHNESS *n* the grub of the cranefly or daddy-longlegs.

torsk *see* **tusk**.

tore *see* **teir**.

torter *n, v* torture.

tortie *n* a tortoise.

tosh *adj* neat, tidy, smart.

v make neat or tidy, smarten up.

tossel *n* **1** a tassel. **2** the penis. **3** a tuft or fringe of hair.

tot *n* **1** a small child, toddler. **2** (*child's word*) the penis N.

tot(t)ie, toatie *n* = **tot** 1.

adj small, tiny: '*a toatie wee boy*'.

totum *n* **1** a small child. **2** any very small, neat person, animal or thing.

tought *see* **thocht**.

toun *see* **toon**.

touse [rhymes with 'lose'] *v* **1** pull or knock about, handle (especially a woman) roughly. **2** disorder.

tousle (*usually the hair*) untidy, tangled.

tousle tea high tea.

tousle *v* tousle, pull about (roughly); rumple.

n **1** a struggle, tussle, contest. **2** a rough romp with a person of the opposite sex.

touslie (*of the hair*) dishevelled, ruffled.

tove *v* rise into the air, stream out.

tow *see* **thowe**.

towe [rhymes with 'cow'] *n* **1** a rope, cord, string. **2** a skipping-rope. **3** a whip, whiplash.

tower *see* **toor**[1], **toor**[2].

town *see* **toon**.

towrow [-ow- as in 'cow'] *n* a noisy uproar, disturbance.

towt *n* **1** a slight illness. **2** a sudden (usually bad) mood, huff.

towtie 1 subject to frequent attacks of slight illness. **2** touchy, irritable.

traa *see* **thraw, thrawn**.

traan *see* **thraw**.

trachle *see* **trauchle**.

track *n* a poorly- or untidily-dressed person NE.

trade, tred, tread *n* **1** trade. **2 the Trades = trades holidays**.

trades holidays the annual summer holiday, originally of the craftsmen of a town, especially Edinburgh, later extended more generally.

tradesman a person who practises a trade, craftsman.

to trade by profession or occupation: '*a painter to trade*'.

traep *see* **threap**.

traffeck [trafeck], **trafike** [trafike] NE *n* **1** traffic. **2** dealings, familiar communication SHETLAND, ORKNEY, N.

v deal, have to do or have relations (with) SHETLAND, NE.

traicle, trekkle *n* treacle; in Scotland always means molasses.

traicle gundie candy or toffee, made from treacle.

traicle scone a scone made with treacle.

black traicle molasses.

traik *v* **1** roam, wander about idly or aimlessly, prowl. **2** tramp, trudge, walk wearily or with difficulty. **3 traik efter** follow, run after.

n **1** the act of **traiking**. **2** a person or animal who is always roving about. **3** a long tiring walk, a trudge.

trail *v* tramp, trudge; wander about idly.

n **1** a large collection of articles, a haul. **2** a long tiring walk, a tramp, trudge.

trailep *see* **trollop**.

traipse *v* tramp, trudge wearily; shuffle through mud and dirt; go about, gad about.

n a long weary trudge, a tiring walk.

traison *n* treason.

trait *n, v* treat.

trallop *see* **trollop.**

traivel, travel *v* **1** travel. **2** walk; go on about or make a journey on foot; walk back and forth, pace up and down.

n **1** travel. **2** a walk, journey on foot.

tra(i)veller 1 a hawker, tinker, gipsy. **2** a head-louse. **3** a travelling salesman.

tram *n* **1** a shaft of a barrow, cart etc. **2 trams** the legs. **3** a very tall, thin, clumsy person (with long legs).

tramp *v* stamp or tread heavily on, trample on.

trampers the feet.

trample a tramp, vagrant.

trance *n* a narrow passage, *eg* between buildings, an alley, lane.

trang *see* **thrang.**

transack, transact *n* a transaction, matter of business.

v transact.

trap, trap stair(s) *n* a ladder, a (movable) flight of steps (leading up to a loft etc).

trapple *see* **thrapple.**

trath *see* **trith.**

trauchle, trachle *v* **1** exhaust, harass; hamper, trouble, worry: *'I'm fair trauchelt'*. **2** labour on, toil. **3** bedraggle, injure, spoil (by dragging, knocking about etc).

n **1** a state of complete muddle caused by having too much to do. **2** tiring labour, drudgery. **3** a long, tiring trudge or walk.

trave *see* **threave.**

travel *see* **traivel.**

trawn *see* **thrawn.**

tread, tred *see* **trade.**

tree *see* **three.**

treed *see* **threid.**

treeple NE *v* treble, triple.

treesh NE *v* **1** *often* **treesh wi** beg, wheedle. **2** run after, court.

treetle, trytle *v* **1** trickle SHETLAND, NE. **2** walk with short steps, trot NE.

trekkle *see* **traicle.**

tremendous, tremendious *adj* tremendous.

adv very much, extremely.

tremmle, trimmle *v* tremble.

trimmlin tam *n* **1** another name for **pottit heid. 2** a fruit jelly.

tremmlin tree an aspen.

tresh *see* **thrash.**

tress *n* a trestle.

tretten *see* **thirteen.**

trettle *see* **thertle.**

trews [trooze] *npl* **1** trousers. **2** short tartan trunks worn under a kilt. **3** (*in past times*) close-fitting trousers with the legs extended to cover the feet, worn by Highlanders; *later* tartan trousers worn by certain Scottish regiments.

tribble *see* **trouble.**

tricker *n* the catch or trigger (of a gun).

trid *numeral* third SHETLAND.

triffle *n* a trifle, a small amount.

trift SHETLAND *n* thrift.

trig *adj* **1** trim, neat; tidy. **2** active, nimble, lively, alert.

v, often **trig up, trig out** smarten up.

trimmle, trimmlin *see* **tremmle.**

trink *n* **1** a trench, channel, ditch, gutter. **2** a narrow coastal inlet. **3** a rut in a road.

trinkle *v* **1** trickle. **2** sprinkle, scatter over.

trinnle *n* a wheel or similar circular object.

v, also **trintle 1** (*of an object, vehicle etc*) roll, trundle, bowl along. **2** (*of people etc*) move along; waddle; straggle. **3** (cause to) roll, flow, trickle.

trist *see* **thrist.**

trith, trath SHETLAND, ORKNEY *n* truth.

troch, trough [rhymes with 'loch' or 'cow'] *n* **1** a trough. **2 trochs, trows** a wooden channel for water. **3** the channel or bed of a river.

troddle *see* **trottle.**

troke *v* **1** bargain, barter. **2** trade, deal

in a small way with. **3** associate with, have evil or unlawful dealings with, be on friendly terms with.

n **1** barter, exchange; a bargain or business deal. **2** *usually* **trokes** haberdashery, odds and ends, trinkets. **3** any worthless or rubbishy goods; trash. **4** improper dealings, association. **5** a small piece of work or business, a task, errand.

troll *n* an untidy, slovenly person.

trollie-bags *npl* **1** the guts of people or animals. **2** a fat, unshapely person.

trollop, trallop, trallep NE *n* **1** a trollop. **2** a long, clumsy person or animal. **3** a long, trailing piece of cloth etc.

v hang or trail loosely or untidily.

trollopie (*of clothes*) hanging loosely and untidily: '*a trollopie dress*'.

tron *n* **1** (*in past times*) a public weighing machine, near a market-place for weighing goods. **2** the place or building where the **tron** stood: '*Tron Kirk*'.

trone, troo *see* **troon.**

troon, trone, troo *n* a truant: '*play the troon*'.

v play truant (from): '*troon the scuil*'.

troot *n* **1** a trout. **2** *often* **trootie** term of endearment to a child.

trot[1] *n*: **back-door trot** diarrhoea.

short in the trot *see* **short.**

trot[2] *n* the throat SHETLAND, ORKNEY.

trottle, troddle *n* a small ball of dung, especially of sheep.

trou *see* **throu.**

trouble, tribble *n* **1** trouble. **2** sickness, disease; an ailment.

through *see* **troch.**

trowe *n* (*in Shetland, Orkney folklore*) a mischievous fairy, hobgoblin SHETLAND, ORKNEY, CAITHNESS.

trows *see* **troch.**

trumph *n* a trump, the chief suit in a card game; a splendid person.

trusdar [**troo**ster] *n* an untrustworthy person N, HIGHLAND.

tryst [rhymes with 'priced'] *n* **1** an

appointment to meet at a specified time and place.

2 an appointed meeting or assembly, a rendezvous.

3 an appointed meeting-place; a conspicuous object chosen as a rendezvous.

4 a market, especially for the sale of livestock, a fair.

v **1** make an appointment, arrange a time and place of meeting.

2 meet with by pre-arrangement.

3 engage to be married.

4 order or arrange (something) in advance.

5 fix, arrange (a time or occasion).

trystin the place or time for a **tryst**: '*trystin place*'; '*trystin tree*'.

trytle *see* **treetle.**

tuckle *adj* awkward, clumsy; (*of a limb etc*) disabled, deformed NE.

tull, teel NE *n* **1** a tool; (*humorously*) any piece of equipment etc. **2** term of contempt for a person.

tulm, tim, toom, teem N *adj* **1** empty. **2** fasting, hungry. **3** echoing.

v **1** empty (a container); empty (a glass etc) by drinking. **2** empty (the contents) from a container. **3** (*of rain*) pour, come down heavily.

n a place where rubbish is emptied, a dump.

tulp, tip, teep NE *n* a ram.

v (*usually of a ram*) mate; sire.

tulp-lamb a male lamb, a young ram.

tulth, teeth *n* **1** a tooth. **2** a part of a rainbow seen near the horizon, regarded as a sign of bad weather NE.

tulthfu(l) a mouthful.

tull *see* **till.**

tulloch *n* a mound, hillock; often a fairy mound.

tulyie *n* **1** a quarrel, uproar; a struggle. **2** trouble; toil, exertion.

v quarrel, fight; argue, squabble.

tumfle *n* a dull, stupid, fat person.

tummle *v, n* tumble.

tummle the cat do a somersault, go head over heels SHETLAND, NE.

tummock *n* a small hillock, a tussock; a molehill.

tumshie *n* **1** a turnip. **2** a dull, stupid person.

tumshie heid a stupid person.

tune, teen NE *n* **1** a tune. **2** mood, humour, temper: '*in guid tune*'.

tunner *see* **thunner.**

turbot *n* a halibut.

turk *adj* fierce, truculent, sullen NE.

turmit *see* **turneep.**

turn *v* become, grow: '*It was a dark night turned*'; '*Ye're turnin a big boy*'.

turnpike a spiral staircase.

the day *or* **year is on the turn** the days are changing in length of daylight, temperature etc.

dae the turn serve a (useful) purpose, meet a need.

turn someone's heid make someone feel giddy or drunk.

turn up the wee finger have a habit of drinking too much.

the turn o the year the time of year when the days begin to lengthen.

turneep, turnip, turmit *n* a turnip, in Scotland usually a swede.

turr *n* **1** turf. **2** a surface peat or turf cut as fuel.

v remove surface turf from.

tushilago [-laygo] *n* **1** coltsfoot. **2** a butterbur.

tusk, torsk SHETLAND *n* a ling-like fish of the cod family, found mainly in northern Scottish waters.

tusker *n* a peat spade SHETLAND, OR-KNEY, CAITHNESS.

twa, twae, two *numeral* two.

twosie the second move etc in various games.

twosome, twasome, twaesome 1 (of or for) a pair, a group or company of two. **2** (a Scottish country dance, especially a **strathspey** (*see* **strath**)) performed by two people.

twa-bedded twin-bedded.

twa-eyed (beef)steak (*humorous*) a herring or kipper.

twa-faul(d) 1 twofold. **2** bent double. **3** deceitful, two-faced.

twa-hand(it) crack a conversation between two people.

two or three, twa-three two or three, a few, several.

nane o the twa neither.

onie o the twa either.

twal, twel *numeral* **1** twelve. **2** a set or group of twelve persons or things. **3** **the twal** twelve o'clock, especially midnight.

twelt, twalt twelfth.

twelvesie the last move in the game of **chucks,** in which uncaught stones must be laid in a row.

twal hours, twaloors 1 twelve noon (or occasionally midnight). **2** a midday snack or drink; a midday meal.

twang *n* a sudden sharp pain, an acute pang.

tween *preposition* between.

tween hands between times, meantime.

tweetle *v* whistle, warble, sing.

twel, twelvesie *see* **twal.**

twicet, twict *adv* twice.

twiser (*in the game of* **buttons**) a button valued at two shots.

the twice(t) for a second time.

twig[1] *v, n* jerk, tug, twitch.

twig[2] *n* a quick or sidelong glance; a glimpse NE.

twin, twine *v* **1** divide, separate, part: '*Twin thae knives an forks*'. **2** take (something) from.

twine *n* string.

twine *see* **twin.**

twintie, twuntie *numeral* twenty.

twit *see* **white**[2].

two, twosie *see* **twa.**

twuntie *see* **twintie.**

tyangs *see* **tangs.**

tyauve [teeawve], **chaave** *v* **1** knead, work (dough). **2** struggle physically, tumble or toss about. **3** strive, struggle (frequently with little result), live or work hard, exert yourself NE.

n labouring, exertion, a hard struggle;

a laborious walk NE: '*Ye know the chaave it is to work a ferm*'.

tyne *v, past tense, past participle also*
tint 1 lose, suffer the loss, destruction or disappearance of, mislay; cause the loss of. **2** lose or miss (your way), lose (your footing). **3** lose by letting fall; (*knitting*) drop a stitch NE.
tint lost; bewildered.
type NE *v*: **typin** toilsome.
typit worn out by hard work.
Tysday *n* Tuesday.

U

ug *v* **1** be sickened. **2** disgust, sicken; annoy, upset, exasperate.
n **1** a dislike; a feeling of sickness, *often* **tak an ug at** take a dislike to. **2** an object of disgust; a person with disgusting manners NE.
uggin disgusting, horrible, annoying.
uggit upset, annoyed; disgusted; fed up.
ug(g)some disgusting, horrible.
ugly, ooglie *adj* ugly.
n (*in past times*) a kind of high, framed sunhat, worn by female field-workers.
uilie *see* **ile.**
uil *see* **ill.**
umberella, umberellae *n* an umbrella.
umman *see* **wumman.**
unable *adj*: **unable for** unfit for, incapable of; having no appetite for (food).
unbekent *see* **unkent.**
unbonnie *adj* ugly: '*That's no unbonnie*' = That's pretty.
unbraw *adj* plain, unattractive.
uncannie *adj* **1** (*of people*) mischievous, malicious; not safe to meddle with, because thought to have connections with witchcraft, the devil etc. **2** (*especially of things*) mysterious, ominous, eerie. **3** dangerous, unreliable, threatening; (*of things*) unlucky, tempting fate. **4** (*of things*) awkward, not easy to manage. **5** (*especially of a blow or fall*) hard, violent, severe.
unchancie *adj* unlucky; dangerous, threatening, not to be meddled with.
unco *adj* **1** unknown, unfamiliar, strange. **2** unusual; odd, strange, pe-

culiar. **3** remarkable, extraordinary, great, awful.
adv very, extremely.
npl **uncos** strange or unusual things, rarities, novelties; news, gossip.
unco fowk strangers.
the unco guid the self-righteously moral or religious.
unction *n, v* auction.
undecent *adj* indecent.
une, ovven *n* an oven.
unfarrant *adj* unattractive, unpleasant; not refined.
unfreend *n* someone who is not a friend, an enemy.
unhonest *adj* dishonest.
unkent, unbekent *adj* unknown, strange, unfamiliar (to).
unless, onless *conjunction* unless.
preposition except, but (for).
unner *preposition, adv* under.
unnerstan, unnerstaun(d) *v* understand.
untowtherlie [-ow- as in 'cow'] *adj* NE **1** big and clumsy, badly-shaped. **2** slovenly, untidy in dress or appearance.
unweel, unwell *adj* not in good health, ill (suggesting a more serious illness than in English).
unwicelike *adj* unwise, foolish, indiscreet.
up *adv* **1** (*of a river*) in flood. **2** (*of people*) in a state of excitement or irritation. **3** *also* **up in life, up in years** (*of a child*) growing up; (*of an adult*) advanced in years, elderly. **4** (*of a chimney*) on fire.
oople stiffie, oopsie doopsie (*encouraging a child to get to its feet etc*) upsadaisy.

neither up nor doon 1 nowhere. **2** (*especially of feelings etc*) unaffected by events, the same as before.

up-the-gates *see* **upple.**

up the hoose into the inner part of a house, from the door inwards.

up wi 1 as good as, equal to, fit for, capable of: '*I'm no up wi dealin wi computers*'. **2** even with, quits with.

upbring *v* bring up, rear.

n training, education, maintenance during childhood.

upby *adj* up there, up the way, up at or to a place, especially somewhere thought of as being higher or better than where the speaker is, *eg* Heaven; upstairs.

upcast *v, n* taunt, reproach.

upfeshin, upfessin *n* upbringing, the rearing and training of young people NE.

uphaud *v, past tense, past participle also* **upheeld** NE **1** uphold. **2** look after, maintain. **3** raise, lift up.

Up-Helly-Aa *n* a festival held in Lerwick on the last Tuesday in January.

uplift [upl**ift**] *v* **1** pick up, *eg* take on (passengers), collect (tickets, parcels). **2** collect, draw, take possession of (money, rents etc). **3** dig up, harvest (potatoes and other root crops).

special uplift refuse collection of bulky articles.

upon, upo *preposition* **1** upon, on. **2** about, concerning: '*think upon it*'. **3** (*of time*) during, on the occasion of SHETLAND, ORKNEY, NE: '*sleep upon the day*'. **4** (*of place or manner*) in: '*meet someone upon the street*'.

upper *adj* applied to the higher section of a divided estate, often in farm-names: '*Upperton*'.

upple, up-the-gates *n* (*in the game of hand-ball*) a member of the team playing towards the upward goal, the **upples** usually coming from the upper part of the town ORKNEY, SOUTH; *compare* **doonie** (*see* **doon'**).

upple *v* (*mainly of rain or snow*) stop falling, clear N.

upredd *n* a cleaning, tidying.

upreddin a scolding.

upset [upset] *n* = **upset price** (*see adj* 2).

adj **1** set up, raised. **2** (*of a price at an auction*) which will be acceptable to the seller; (*of a price of property*) below which bids will not be accepted: '*The upset price was £60,000 but the best bid was £75,000*'.

upsides *adv*: **be upsides wi, be upsides doon wi** be even with, have your revenge on.

upstandin *see* **upstanding.**

upstanding, upstandin *adj* (*of wages*) regular.

n (*usually of foodstuffs*) substance, solidity NE.

be upstanding stand up, rise to your feet, *eg* ceremonially to drink a toast, for a prayer etc: '*Will you please be upstanding for the benediction*'.

uptail *adj*: **be uptail and awa** leave in haste, flee at once.

uptak *n* **1** the capacity for understanding, intelligence, *often* **gleg in the uptak, slow in the uptak. 2** the gathering of a crop, especially a root-crop SHETLAND, NE.

ur *see* **be.**

ure [rhymes with 'poor'] *n* **1** a damp mist; fine rain, drizzle. **2** a haze, especially when lit by sunbeams.

urnae *see* **be.**

us, uz, wis, wiz, wir, iz, s, z, oo SOUTH, *stressed* **hiz** *pronoun* **1** us. **2** we: '*us Edinburgh girls . . .*'. **3** me, *eg* '*I telt him a lee . . . he jist felled iz like a herrin*'.

us anes, us yins we, us, those of our group etc.

us *see* **use.**

use, yeese N, **eese** N, **us, yuise** *n, also* **yis(s) 1** use. **2** need, occasion, reason for or to.

v, also **yaise 1** use. **2** *mainly* **yaised**

wi, eest wi N made familiar with, accustomed to. **3** be or become accustomed (to).

eesage usage NE.

useless, yissless, eeseless, yalseless *adj* **1** useless. **2** ill; unable, owing to illness or exhaustion N.

adv exceedingly, far too: '*He's pit on useless monie coals*'.

usual, yaisual, eeswal NE *adj* usual.

yer (auld) usual your state of health, frame of mind; your old self: '*He's in his usual*'.

uz *see* **us.**

V

valg *v* wander about idly, roam aimlessly; gad about.

valge SHETLAND, **veage** E CENTRAL *n* **1** a voyage. **2** a journey; a trip, outing, expedition.

vainish *v* vanish.

varlorum *n* a decoration (in furniture, handwriting etc), an ornament, trinket.

vauntie *adj* proud, boastful.

vawse *n* a vase.

veage *see* **valge**.

veecious, vicious *adj* **1** vicious. **2** (*of weather*) very bad, severe.

veesion *see* **vision**.

veesit *v, n* visit.

veet *n* a vet.

veeve *adj* **1** (*of pictures, images*) lifelike, closely resembling the original. **2** bright, clear, vivid, distinct.

vennel *n* a narrow alley or lane between buildings.

vent *n* **1** the flue of a chimney; the duct used to let smoke out of a room. **2** the opening of a fireplace. **3** a chimney head or stack.

v (*of chimney, room etc*) give out smoke, let smoke pass through or from it.

vermin *n* a large quantity, swarm, crowd N.

verra *adj, adv* very.

veshel, vessel *n* **1** a vessel. **2** the udder (of a cow etc).

vex *n* a source of regret, sorrow or annoyance: '*It wis a sair vex*'.

be vext for be sorry for (a person).

vicious *see* **veecious**.

virr *n* vigour, energy, force, impetuosity.

vision, veesion, weeshan NE *n* **1** a vision. **2** a puny, painfully thin person or animal, an unimportant characterless person.

vizzle *v* look at carefully, inspect, examine.

n **1** a look, glimpse. **2** a view. **3** an aim (with a gun etc).

voar *n* (*the season*) spring; work done then SHETLAND, ORKNEY.

voe *n* an inlet of the sea, a fjord, a sea loch SHETLAND, ORKNEY.

voo *v* **1** vow. **2** curse, swear ORKNEY, NE.

n a vow.

vrack *see* **wrack**.

vraith *see* **wreath**.

vrat *see* **write**.

vratch *see* **wratch**.

vreet *see* **write**.

vricht *see* **wricht**.

vrutten *see* **write**.

vyow [veeow] *n* a view NE.

W

wa[1], **waw** *n* a wall.

wa[2], **waw**, **way** *adv* away.

(gae) wa (wi ye)! (*expressing disbelief, impatience etc*) go away!

wa-gang departure, leave-taking NE.

wa-gaun *n* a departure, going away.

waar *see* **ware**[2].

wab, wob, wub *n* a web.

wabbit *adj* exhausted, weak, feeble: '*She wis wabbit efter the operation*'.

wabble *v* wobble; walk unsteadily, totter, waddle.

wabblie wishy-washy, thin: '*wabblie beer*'.

wabster, wobster *n* **1** a weaver. **2** a spider.

wachle *see* **wauchle**.

wacht *see* **wecht**.

wad[1] [rhymes with 'sad'] *v* **1** wed, marry. **2** bet, wager.

n **1** a stake, bet. **2 wads** name for various games in which forfeits are demanded.

waddin a wedding.

be in (a) wad be liable to a forfeit in a game.

wad[2], **waddin** *n* cotton wool.

wad *see* **wade**, **will**[1].

wade, wad, wide, wed SHETLAND, ORKNEY *v* **1** wade, cross by wading. **2** (*of the moon or sun*) move through cloud or mist.

n wading.

wadna *see* **will**[1].

wae *n* woe.

waesome sorrowful; causing sorrow.

wa'er *see* **water**.

waff[1] *v* wave, move to and fro, flap.

n **1** a flapping, waving movement. **2** a puff, blast (of air etc). **3** a slight smell, illness etc.

waff[2] *n* **1** a waif. **2** a worthless person.

waffle [rhymes with 'baffle'] *v* **1** wave about, flap. **2** waver, hesitate.

wag *v* **1** (*of a leaf, plant etc*) wave to and fro. **2** shake; brandish (a weapon). **3** beckon, signal to.

n a signal made with the hand.

waggle, waggltie a pied wagtail.

wag-at-the-wa, waggltie-wa a wall clock with an uncovered pendulum.

walk, wyke NE *adj* weak.

wait, wyte NE *v* **1** wait. **2** await, wait for: '*She's waitin ye in the hall*'. **3** lodge, live temporarily.

wait on wait for, await: '*Wait on me!*'.

waiter, waitter *see* **water**.

wake *see* **wauk**.

walcome *n*, *v* welcome.

wale, wile *n* choice; the thing chosen as the best.

v **1** choose, pick out. **2** arrange, separate into lots, sort.

walk *n* a ceremonial procession: '*the Orange Walk*'.

wall, well *n* **1** a cold-water tap at a sink. **2** a natural spring of water. **3** a well. **4** a drinking fountain.

v weld.

wall grass, wall girse kail watercress N.

wallie *adj* **1** made of porcelain, china, glazed. **2** fine, pleasant, beautiful. **3** big and strong, thriving, sturdy, plump.

n **1** porcelain, glazed earthenware or tiling; a dish or ornament made of such. **2 wallies** a set of false teeth. **3 wallies** broken pieces of china used as toys.

wallie close a tiled **close**[2].

wallie money broken pieces of china used as toy money.

walloch[1] [-a- as in 'bad'] *v* make violent heavy movements, especially in water or mud, move clumsily.

walloch[2] [-a- as in 'bad'] *v, n* shriek, howl NE.

wallop [rhymes with 'gallop'] *v* **1** gallop. **2** move clumsily and very quickly NE. **3** struggle violently, thrash about. **4** (*of the heart*) throb, beat violently. *n* a violent jerky movement SHETLAND, NE.

wallopie [-a- as in 'bad'] *n* a lapwing.

wallydrag, wallydraigle [-a- as in 'bad'] *n* **1** a good-for-nothing NE. **2** an undersized person or animal.

walyl [rhymes with 'Sally'] *interjection* (*cry of sorrow*) oh dear!, alas!

wame, wime *n* **1** the belly, the tummy. **2** the womb.

wammle *v* **1** (*of the stomach or its contents*) stir uneasily, rumble queasily. **2** roll, wriggle; toss, twist and turn; turn over and over. **3** stagger. *n* **1** a churning of the stomach, a feeling of sickness. **2** a rolling or unsteady motion, a wriggle.

wammlle tottery, weak, feeble.

wan [rhymes with 'can'] *numeral* one WEST, SW, ULSTER.

wan *see* **win**[1], **win**[2], **wand, wund.**

wan- [rhymes with 'can'] *prefix* un-, not without.

wance *see* **aince.**

wand, wan [rhymes with ban(d)] *n* a wand, stick, rod.

wander, waun(n)er *v* **1** wander. **2** get lost. **3** confuse, bewilder.

wandert lost, confused, bewildered; senile.

wanluck *n* bad luck SHETLAND.

want [rhymes with 'pant'], **wint** NE *v* **1** want.
2 lack the basic necessities of life: '*I've plenty o siller and I dinna want*'.
3 lack, be without, be free from: '*The cup wants a handle*'.
4 able to do or go without: '*We cannae want the car the day*'.

5 wish to go or come (in, out, home etc): '*The dug wants oot*'.
n **1** want. **2** a defect, a missing or faulty part of something.

wantin 1 not having, without. **2** mentally defective.

dae wantin do without.

hae a want be mentally defective.

wap[1] *v* **1** throw violently, thrust, fling. **2** flap, wave, move to and fro.

wap[2] *v* **1** wrap, fold. **2** bind, tie, join, especially by splicing; whip with cord.

wap *see* **wasp.**

wapinschaw *n* a rifle-shooting competition.

wappen *n* a weapon.

waps *see* **wasp.**

war *see* **be, waur.**

ware[1] *n* a kind of seaweed, often used as manure.

ware[2], **waar** SHETLAND, ORKNEY *adj* aware, conscious, cautious.

ware[3] *v* **1** spend (money etc). **2** spend, waste (time, efforts etc).

wark [rhymes with 'bark'], **wirk, wurk, work** *n* **1** work. **2** a building, especially a public or large impressive one. **3** a fuss; goings-on; trouble.
v, past tense, past participle also **wrocht 1** work. **2** affect physically or mentally, especially for the worse; trouble, annoy.

warld, world *n* the world.

warldlik(e) normal in appearance, like everyone else.

like the warld (*often of a child*) like everyone else, normal.

warlock [-a- as in 'car'] *n* the male equivalent of a witch; a wizard, magician.

warm [rhymes with 'farm'] *v* beat, thrash, hit.

warmer (*of a person, used in admiration or disapproval*) an exceptionally good or bad person.

warrior *n* **1** humorous or affectionate term for a lively, spirited person, often a child. **2 the Warriors** nickname for various football teams, especially Stenhousemuir and occasionally Third Lanark and Dumbarton.

warse [-a- as in 'car'], **worse** *adj* worse.

the worse o drink the worse for drink, having drunk too much alcohol.

warst *adj, adv, v* worst.

warsle *v* **1** wrestle.
2 manage to do something by great effort.
3 labour, try hard, exert yourself physically and mentally.
4 struggle, wriggle, sprawl about.
5 make your way through life with much effort and difficulty, scrape along.
n **1** a wrestling match, a physical tussle; a struggle, effort. **2** a mental or moral struggle, a fight against circumstances or hardship.

warslin struggling; energetic, hardworking.

warsle throu scrape through, get by.

warst *see* **warse.**

wase *n* a bundle or band of straw.

wash [rhymes with 'bash'] *v, past tense* **washt, weesh** NE; *past participle* **washt, washen** NE wash.

washer-wife a washer-woman, laundress.

wash its face (*of a business*) pay its way, break even.

wasna, wasnae *see* **be.**

wasp [rhymes with 'clasp'], **waps, wap** [rhymes with 'top(s)'] *n* **1** a wasp. **2** **the Wasps** nickname for Alloa Athletic football team.

wasp bike wasps' nest.

wast [rhymes with 'fast'], **west** *adv* west; away from the speaker or the person to whom you are speaking.
preposition above, along, across, over, to the west side of.

waster, wester lying towards the west, western.

wastert westward.

waste *v* **1** spoil by ill-usage or misuse. **2** spoil, pamper (a child, pet etc).

yer heid's wastit you're stupid.

waster *n* a fishing spear with several prongs.

wat *see* **weet.**

watch [rhymes with 'catch'] *v:* **watch yersel** look after yourself, be on your guard, watch out: '*Watch yersel or the parkie'll catch you*'.

water, watter, wait(t)er, wa'er *n* **1** water. **2** a stream, a river, *latterly usually* a small one: '*Afton Water*'; '*Water of Leith*'. **3** a river valley, the area and its inhabitants bordering a river SOUTH.

watery *n* **1** a pied wagtail NE. **2** a lavatory.

watery wagtail a pied wagtail; a yellow wagtail.

water bobble, water craw a dipper.

water brash heartburn.

water clearer one of the small insects that skim over the surface of the water and are said to clean it.

water dog a water-rat; a water-vole.

water fit the mouth of a river.

water gate a fence or grating over a stream to keep animals or floating rubbish out of a mill-race.

watergaw a rainbow which is not complete.

water heid the source of a river, the upper end of a valley.

water horse, water kelpie (*Celtic folklore*) a mythical spirit in the form of a horse found in lakes and rivers.

water mouth the mouth of a river.

water water river water SOUTH.

Waterloo *n* (*marbles*) a soft, brittle, clay marble.

wather *see* **weather.**

watter *see* **water.**

wauch [-ch as in 'loch'] *adj* (*of a taste or smell*) unpleasant, stale NE.

wauchle, wachle *v* **1** walk clumsily; stumble with fatigue etc. **2** plod on amid difficulties, struggle with a situation or task; last out (a period of time) in a weary way.

n **1** a struggle, effort. **2** a staggering awkward movement, a wobble.

wauchelt perplexed, bewildered, muddle-headed.

waucht [-ch- as in 'loch'] *n* **1** a swallow or gulp of a drink. **2** a deep breath of air.

wauk, wake *v* **1** wake. **2** be or stay awake, be sleepless or have wakened from sleep. **3** guard, watch over (places, animals); watch over (a sick person or corpse).

n a wake, watching over a corpse.

waukrif(e) not ready or unable to sleep; able to do with little sleep; watchful.

wauken *v* waken, wake.

waukened awake.

waukenin 1 wakening. **2** a severe scolding, a talking to.

waulk *v* make (cloth) thick and felted by soaking, beating and shrinking, full (cloth).

waulking song any suitable rhythmic Gaelic song formerly sung by a team of women engaged in **waulking** cloth in the Hebrides.

wauner, waunner *see* **wander**.

waur, war *adj, adv* worse.

v get the better of, overcome, outdo.

n the worse.

waur-faured uglier NE.

(the) waur o (the) worse for: '*Ye'll be nane the waur o that*'.

waw *v* (*of cats and children*) mew pathetically, wail.

waw *see* **wa**[1], **wa**[2].

wax cloth *n* oilcloth.

way *see* **wa**[2], **wey**[1].

Waysiders *npl* nickname for Airdrieonians football team.

we *see* **wi**.

wean [WEST, ULSTER rhymes with 'rain', NE rhymes with 'Ian'] *n* a child, especially a young one.

wear *see* **weir**[2].

weary *adj* **1** depressing. **2** annoying.

wearifu troublesome, annoying; sad.

weary for long for.

weather, wather, wither NE *n* weather.

this weather just now, at the moment.

weave, wyve NE *v* **1** weave. **2** knit (usually stockings or socks) NE.

weaver, wyver NE **1** a weaver. **2** a spider.

weaver-kneed knock-kneed.

wecht, wacht NE *n* **1** weight. **2 wechts** a pair of scales. **3** a large amount, a great number (of things).

v weigh.

wed *see* **wade**.

wee *adj* small, tiny, little; **wee wee, little wee, wee tottie** very small, tiny.

n **a wee** a small quantity of something or of time, distance etc: '*Wait a wee*'.

wee hauf a nip of spirits, a small whisky.

wee heavy a type of strong beer, usually sold in small bottles of 1/3 pint (approx. 0.2 litre).

wee hoose an outside lavatory.

wee man 1 the Devil: '*in the name of the wee man!*'. **2** term of address to a small man or boy: '*C'moan then, wee man*'.

the Wee Rangers nickname for Berwick Rangers football team.

wee scull the infant department in a school.

wee team (*football*) the reserve team: '*wee Celtic*'.

wee thing a small child.

wee yins younger children.

wee *see* **wey**[2].

weeack *v, n* chirp, squeak NE.

weed *n* a (sudden) high fever.

weedow *see* **widow**.

week *see* **wick**.

weel[1], **well** *adv* **1** well. **2** very, quite, much. **3** then: '*We're awa, well*'.

adj **1** well. **2** healthy.

weel-daein well-to-do, prosperous.
weel-faured 1 good-looking. **2** decent, respectable.
weel-galthert *see* **galther.**
mak weel succeed.
no weel, nae weel unwell, in poor health.
weel a weel very well, all right.
weel tae be seen having a good appearance, very presentable.
weel² *n* a deep pool; an eddy, a whirlpool.
weemen *see* **wumman.**
ween *see* **wind.**
weer *n*: **on (the) weers o** in danger of, on the brink of, just about to NE: '*I wis jist on the weers o callin for help*'.
weer *see* **oor², wire.**
weesh *see* **wash.**
weeshan *see* **vision.**
weet, wat [rhymes with 'cat'], **wet** *adj* wet.
n **1** wet. **2** rain, drizzle, dew.
v, past tense, past participle also **wat, weetlt 1** wet. **2** celebrate with a drink, drink to the success of (a bargain etc).
weetle wet, damp, rainy.
watshod wet-shod.
weet the bairn's held toast the health of a newborn baby.
weezer *v* ooze.
weigh *see* **wey².**
weir¹ *v* **1** guard, defend. **2** watch over. **3 weir aff** keep off, hold at bay.
weir², wear *v, past participle also* **wurn** wear.
wearin (*of clothes*) for everday use, especially outside working hours.
wear awa 1 leave quietly, slip away. **2** die, pass away.
weird *n* fate, fortune, destiny.
weird wife a prophetess, fortune-teller.
weirdie *n* the smallest of a brood of animals, especially pigs or birds E CENTRAL.
well *see* **wall, weel¹.**
wench *see* **winch.**

werna, wernae *see* **be.**
wersh *adj* **1** (*of food or drink*) tasteless, insipid; cooked without salt; (*of beer*) flat. **2** bitter, harsh in taste, sour. **3** (*of life, activity etc*) dull.
wes *see* **be.**
weskit *n* a waistcoat.
west *see* **wast.**
wet *see* **weet.**
wey¹, wye [rhymes with 'gey'], **way** *n* **1** a way. **2** your way of life, business.
weys -wise, in the manner specified: '*says he, affhand weys*'.
aw wey, a'wey everywhere.
ae wey one way.
a(w) weys in every way or respect.
by his wey o't according to him, by his account.
be in the wey o have a habit of.
be oot the wey o be out of the habit of.
naewey nowhere.
say ae wye agree.
some lther wey somewhere else.
that wey in that manner, so.
the wey (that) because of the way in which, from the way (that).
the wey at the reason why.
the wey o in the direction of.
wey², wee, weigh *v* weigh.
n **weys** a weighing-machine.
wey bauks a pair of scales.
wey butter, wey cheese a game in which two people stand back to back with arms linked and lift one another alternately until one gives in.
wha, whae, fa NE *pronoun* who.
whase, whaus whose.
wha (i)s aucht? who is the owner, parent etc of?
whaal, faal NE *n* a whale.
whack, whauk *v* whack.
n **1** a whack. **2** a cut. **3** a great number, a large quantity.
get yer whacks be punished.
whae *see* **wha.**
whalp, folp N *n* **1** a whelp. **2** contemptuous term for a person.

whammle *see* **whummle.**

whan, whun, fan N *conjunction, adv* when.

whanever 1 whenever. **2** as soon as, at the very moment when.

whang, fang N, **thwang** *n* **1** a thong. **2** a leather bootlace; any kind of shoe-tie. **3** the penis. **4** a long stretch of rather narrow road. **5** a large thick slice of food, especially of cheese; a chunk. **6** a stroke, blow; a cut with a whip.

v **1** cut, slice; slash, chop, snip. **2** beat, lash, whip; defeat.

whar, whaur, far N *conjunction, adv* where.

whase *see* **wha.**

what[1] [rhymes with 'cat'], **whit, fat** N, **fit** N *pronoun, adj* **1** what. **2** (*exclamation*) how!, how very!: '*Whit pretty it is!*'. **3** as much, as far or as hard as: '*She cried what she could cry*'.

whatever, whitivver in any case, however, under any circumstances.

but what that: '*I dinnae think but what it'll be rain*'.

what a! how many!, what a lot of!: '*what a hooses!*'.

whit . . . at? why?: '*Whit's she roarin and greetin at?*'.

whit for? why?, for what reason?

whit for no? why not?

fit ither what else?, of course.

whit like 1 what sort of?, like what in appearance, nature etc? **2 fit like** how are you? NE.

what o'clock is it? a popular name for a dandelion as used by children as a clock.

fit time when, whenever, as soon as NE.

whit wey? 1 how?, in what manner? **2** why?, for what reason?

what[2] *v* whet.

whatna *see* **whitna.**

whauk *see* **whack.**

whaup[1], **faap** N *n* a curlew.

whaup[2] *n* the seed-pod of peas, beans etc.

whaur *see* **whar.**

whaus *see* **wha.**

whauze *see* **wheeze.**

wheeber *v, n* whistle.

wheech [rhymes with 'dreich'], **wheek** *v* **1** move through the air, dash with a whizzing sound, rush. **2** sweep, snatch or whisk away. **3** beat, hit.

n **1** a soft whizzing sound. **2** a blow which makes a whizzing sound; *usually* **wheechs** strokes with the **tawse. 3** a sudden sweeping movement, a whisk.

wheef *see* **whiff.**

wheek *see* **wheech.**

wheen *n*: **a wheen (o)** a few, a small number, several.

a gey wheen, a bonnie wheen a considerable amount or number.

wheep *v* whistle; make a shrill noise, squeak, buzz.

n a sharp cry or whistle.

wheeple *v, n* whistle.

wheep *see* **whip.**

wheeriorum *n* a toy; a thingumajig.

wheesh *see* **wheesht, whush.**

wheesht, wheesh, whisht *interjection* be quiet!, shut up!

v **1** call for silence. **2** silence, quieten. **3** be quiet, remain silent.

haud yer wheesht! be quiet!, keep silent!, hold your tongue!

wheetle *adj* mean, stingy, underhand, shifty NE.

wheeze, whauze NE, **foze** NE *v, n* wheeze.

the wheezles asthma; bronchitis.

whid[1] *n* a squall, (sudden) gust of wind SHETLAND, ORKNEY.

whid[2] *n* a lie, exaggeration.

v lie.

whidder, fudder NE, **futher** NE *v* move violently; rush about; hum or whizz through the air.

whiff, whuff, wheef *n* **1** a whiff. **2** (*of illness, mood etc*) a slight attack, a touch.

whigmaleerie, figmaleerie *n* **1** a

fanciful decoration, ornament or contraption. **2** a whim, fanciful idea, fad.

while, file N *n* a while.

conjunction **1** while. **2** until, up to the time that.

whllie, fllie N a little while.

a while back some time ago, in the past.

a while syne a certain time ago, for some time past.

whiles, files, fylles NE *adv* sometimes, at times, occasionally.

whilk, filk N *pronoun* which.

whin[1], **whun, fun** NE *n* one of several hard rocks, *eg* basalt, flint.

whin[2], **whun, fun** NE *n* gorse; **whins** a clump or area of gorse.

whip, wheep NE, **whup, fup** NE *n* **1** a whip. **2** a sudden quick movement, a start, jerk.

v whip.

whipper-in *n* a school attendance-officer.

whirl, whurl, furl NE *v* **1** whirl. **2** wheel, trundle, cart; drive on.

whirligig *n* a complicated ornament, design or diagram.

whisht *see* **wheesht.**

whisky, whusky, fuskie NE *n* an alcoholic drink distilled from malted barley **(malt whisky)**, or with the addition of unmalted grain spirit (usually maize) **(blended whisky).**

whistle, whustle, fussle NE *v, n* **1** whistle. **2** cuff, hit, wallop NE.

whit *see* **what**[1].

white[1], **fite** NE *adj* **1** white. **2** (*of coins*) silver.

white breid white wheat bread etc as opposed to oat or barley cakes.

white gowan *see* **gowan.**

white hoolet a barn owl.

white iron tin-plate, tinned iron.

white lily *see* **lily.**

white puddin a kind of sausage stuffed with oatmeal, suet, salt, pepper and onions.

white siller silver money, cash in silver.

white[2], **fite** NE, **twit** SHETLAND, ORKNEY *v* cut with a knife, pare, whittle.

whither, fither NE *conjunction* whether.

whitna, whatna [-a- as in 'cat'], **fatna** NE *adj* what kind of, what sort of.

whitrat, futrat NE *n* **1** a weasel, a stoat; a ferret. **2** a thin, small, sharp-featured, inquisitive person.

Whitsunday *n* 15 May, a Scottish quarter day.

whitterick *n* a curlew.

whittle-whattle *n* excuses, stories which hide the truth; indecision.

whittle[1], **futtle** N *n* **1** a knife. **2** a sickle, scythe.

whittle[2], **futley** NE, **whittle beal(in)** *n* a whitlow.

whole *see* **hail**[1].

whuff *see* **whiff.**

whummle, whammle, fummle NE *v* **1** capsize, overturn. **2** empty (a container) or its contents. **3** turn round and round or inside out. **4** go head over heels, fall suddenly.

n **1** a capsizing, upset. **2** a tumble, fall.

whun *see* **whan, whin**[1], **whin**[2].

whup *see* **whip.**

whuppitie-stourie *n* **1** name for a kind of household fairy. **2** a light-footed nimble person.

whurl *see* **whirl.**

whush, wheesh *n* a whish, a rushing noise; a stir, commotion.

wheesher something large of its kind, a whopper.

whusky *see* **whisky.**

whustle *see* **whistle.**

why *adv*: **why for (no)?** why (not)?: '*Why for no couldn't ye come yesterday?*'.

wi, with, we *preposition* **1** with.

2 by means of, by the action of: '*eaten wi the mice*'.

3 by reason of, through: '*Wi being ill he couldna come*'.

4 (*referring to parents*) by: '*a woman with whom he had fower children*'.

5 by (bus, train etc).
6 (*with 'not'*) because of; on account of: '*They coudna fecht wi cauld*'.
dee wi die of.
mairrie wi marry, be married to.
be used wi be used to.
wice *see* **wise**.
wicht [-ch- as in 'dreich] *n* **1** (*often with contempt or pity*) a human being, person. **2** a supernatural being; a person with supernatural powers.
wick, week *n* **1** a corner of the mouth or the eye. **2** a cleft in the face of a hill.
wick *see* **ook**.
wicked, wickit *adj* **1** wicked. **2** bad-tempered, viciously angry.
wid *see* **will**[1].
widd *see* **wuld**[1].
widdershins *see* **withershins**.
widdle *n* **1** withy, willow. **2** a twig or wand of willow or other tough but flexible wood; several such twigs intertwined to form a rope. **3** the gallows. **4** the gallows rope.
widdie *see* **widow**.
widdle *v* move slowly and unsteadily.
wide *adj*: **wide tae the wa** (*of a door*) wide open.
wide *see* **wade**.
widna, widnae *see* **will**[1].
widow, weedow, widdie *n* **1** a widow: '*weedow wumman*'. **2** *also* **widow man** widower.
wife *n, pl also* **wifes** a woman, now usually a middle-aged or older woman.
wifie, wifock, wifockie N a woman (as above); a little girl.
wiggietie-waggietie *adj* very unstable, tottery.
adv unsteadily.
wild, wile ARGYLL, SW, ULSTER, **will, wull** *adj* **1** wild. **2** strong-tasting.
adv extremely, very.
will cat, wullcat a wild cat.
tummle the wullcat, tummle ower yer wullcat(s), tummle ower yer wilkies tumble head over heels, somersault.

wildfire 1 summer lightning, lightning without thunder. **2** (*mining*) firedamp. **3** name of various wild flowers.
wild rhubarb butterbur.
wile *see* **wale, wild**.
wilk *see* **wulk**.
wilkies *see* **wild**.
will[1], **wull** *v* will.
wiltu?, wilter? will you?
winna, winnae, wunnae, wunna, willint will not.
wad, wud, wid would.
wadna, wudnae, wudna, widnae, widna would not.
wullint willing.
it will be . . . I think or expect it is . . . , it is approximately . . . : '*It will be about forty miles frae here*'.
will[2], **wull** *n* will, wish, intent.
get yer will(s) o get your own way with.
will[3], **wull** *adj* **1** going or gone astray, wandering. **2** bewildered, at a loss.
gae will lose your way.
will *see* **wild**.
Willie, Wullie *n*: **willie goo** NE **1** a herring gull. **2** a lost- or stupid-looking person.
willie wagtail a pied wagtail.
Willie Wassle a children's game (*similar to English* Tom Tiddler's Ground).
Willie Winkie a nursery character supposed to send children to sleep, the sandman.
willie-waught [-gh- as -ch in 'loch'] *n* a hearty swig, usually of beer etc.
willint, wilter, wiltu *see* **will**[1].
wime *see* **wame**.
wimple *n* (*of a road or stream*) a twist, turn, winding.
v (*of a river etc*) twist, turn, ripple.
win[1] *v, past tense also* **wan 1** win.
2 beat, defeat N.
3 earn, gain by labour.
4 gather in (crops etc), harvest.
5 make your way; reach (with difficulty); be allowed to go.

6 win to do *etc* manage to do etc SHETLAND, ORKNEY, NE.

winnie (*marbles*) a game in which the winner keeps his or her gains.

win aboon, win abeen overcome, recover from (an illness etc) SHETLAND, NE.

win asleep get to sleep.

win at reach, get at or to.

win awa 1 leave; escape, be allowed or find it possible to go. **2** die, especially after great suffering.

win by get past; overtake.

win in get in.

win in wi find favour with.

win on mount (a horse) N.

win oot get out, escape.

win ower 1 (be allowed to) cross. **2** recover from, overcome.

win tae, win till arrive at.

win[2] *v, past tense also* **wan**; *past participle also* **win 1** (*of hay, peats etc*) dry. **2** dry out, season (wood, cheese etc).

win *see* **wind**.

winch, wench *n* a wench, a little girl. *v* court, go with someone of the opposite sex.

wind, win, wun WEST, **ween** NE *n* **1** wind. **2** breath, the air breathed. *v* exaggerate, boast NE.

wind and watertight (*usually a house, especially in leases*) secure against wind and rain or flood.

winda *see* **windae**.

windae, winda, winnock, windock *n* a window.

windae-sole a windowsill.

wunda-swalla a house-martin.

windle *v* make up (straw or hay) into bundles.

windlestrae 1 a tall, thin, withered stalk of grass. **2** name given to various kinds of natural grass with long thin stalks. **3** (*contemptuous*) a very thin or weak person.

windock *see* **windae**.

winna, winnae *see* **will**[1].

winner *see* **wunner**.

winnie *see* **win**[1].

winnock *see* **windae**.

wint *see* **want**.

winter *n* the last load of grain to be brought to the stackyard in harvest.

winter-dykes a clothes-horse.

Ah never died o winter yet I survived, pulled through all difficulties.

wi'oot *preposition* without.

wir *see* **oor**[2], **us**.

wird *see* **word**.

wire, weer NE *n* **1** wire. **2** a knitting needle.

wirk *see* **wark**.

wirm *n* a worm.

wirr, wurr *v, n* growl, snarl.

wirricow *see* **worricow**.

wirry *see* **worry**.

wis *see* **be, us**.

wise, wice *adj* **1** wise. **2** clever, knowing, well-informed. **3** sane, rational. **4** skilled in magic or witchcraft: '*wise wife*'. *v* guide, direct, show (a person) to (a place etc).

wicelike 1 sensible, reasonable, prudent. **2** respectable, proper, decent. **3** of good appearance, handsome, pretty.

no wice off your head, insane.

wish *see* **wiss**.

wisker *n* a bunch of straw etc, used as a brush or as a holder for knitting needles.

wisna, wisnae *see* **be**.

wiss, wish *v* **1** wish. **2** want, wish for: '*Do you wish any more?*'.

wit, wut *n* **1** wit. **2** sanity, reason, your senses. **3** intelligence, wisdom, common sense.

get wit learn, find out.

lat wit let (a person) know something, inform of.

witch, wutch *n* **1** a witch. **2** *used of various animals, insects and objects associated with witches, eg* a moth NE, a tortoiseshell butterfly SOUTH, a pole flounder, a dab; a red clay marble.

witches' paps, witch(es')-thimmles a foxglove.

with *see* **wi.**

wither *see* **weather.**

withershins, widdershins *adv* in a direction opposite to the usual, the wrong way round; anti-clockwise, in a direction usually suggesting bad luck or disaster.

within *preposition*: **within itsel** (*of a house*) complete in itself, **self-contained.**

witter *n* a restless, impatient person. *v* grumble.

wittin *n* **1** knowledge. **2 wittins** information, news.

wiz *see* **us.**

wizzen *n* **1** the gullet. **2** the windpipe; breath, life itself.

wob *see* **wab.**

wobster *see* **wabster.**

woman *see* **wumman.**

woo *see* **oo**[1].

wood *see* **wuld**[1].

word, wird *n* **1** a word. **2** something said, a remark. **3 words** prayers.

put up a word say a prayer.

work *see* **wark.**

world *see* **warld.**

worricow, wirricow *n* a hobgoblin, a frightening or repulsive-looking person.

worry, wirry *v* **1** worry. **2** choke, suffocate.

worse *see* **warse.**

woun [rhymes with 'moon'] *v, n* wound.

wowe [rhymes with 'cow'] *v, n* howl, bark.

wowff *n* a low-pitched bark.

wrack, vrack NE *n* **1** a wreck. **2** fresh- or salt-water weed, algae. **3** seaweed and flotsam washed up by the sea. *v* wreck, ruin.

wrait *see* **write.**

wran *n* **1** *also* **wrannie** a wren. **2** term of endearment.

wranch, runch *n, v* wrench.

wrang, wrong *adj* **1** wrong. **2** crooked, deformed, out of joint. **3** *also* **wrang**

in the heid (slightly) mad. *v* **1** wrong. **2** damage, hurt; spoil.

no come wrang (tae) not be unwelcome (for).

gae wrang (*of food*) go off.

rise aff yer wrang side get up in a bad temper.

no say a wrang word not use harsh or bad language.

wrannie *see* **wran.**

wrapper *n* **1** a loose dressing-gown or bed-jacket. **2** a woman's household overall, a smock.

wratch, vratch NE *n* a wretch.

wreath, vraith NE *n* **1** a wreath. **2** a bank or drift of snow.

wricht, vricht NE [-ch- as in 'dreich'] *n* **1** a wright, a craftsman. **2** a carpenter or joiner.

v work as a carpenter or joiner NE.

writ *n* a formal or legal document (used more generally than in English where it is now usually restricted to written orders of a court).

write, vreet NE *v, past tense also* **wrait, wrut, vrat** NE; *past participle also* **wrutten, vrutten** NE write.

n **1** writing, as opposed to speech. **2** handwriting.

writer a lawyer.

writer to the Signet (W.S.) a member of a society of solicitors in Edinburgh (which originally had the exclusive privilege of preparing certain legal documents, *eg* signet writs).

wrocht *see* **wark.**

wrong *see* **wrang.**

wrunkle *n, v* wrinkle.

wrut, wrutten *see* **write.**

w.s. *see* **write.**

wub *see* **wab.**

wud *see* **will**[1], **wuld**[2].

wudd *see* **wuld**[2].

wudna *see* **will**[1].

wuld[1], **widd, wood** *n* wood.

wood hyacinth an English bluebell, wild hyacinth.

wuld[2], **wud(d)** *adj* **1** mad. **2** fierce,

violent, wild. **3** furiously angry. **4**
wuld for *etc* eager, desperately keen
to.

wulk, wilk *n* **1** a whelk. **2** the periwinkle mollusc and shell. **3** (*humorous*)
the nose: '*Stoap pickin yer wulk*'.

as fou as a wulk very drunk or full of
food.

wull *see* **wild, will**[1], **will**[2], **will**[3].

Wullie *see* **Willie**.

wullint *see* **will**[1].

wumman, umman NE, **woman** *n*, *pl*
weemen 1 a woman. **2** a wife.

wumman-bodie a woman.

wumman-grown, wumman-muckle
grown to womanhood, adult.

wun *see* **wind, wund**.

wund, wun NE *v*, *past tense also* **wan**
NE wind, turn.

wunda-swalla *see* **windae**.

wunna, wunnae *see* **will**[1].

wunner, winner NE *n* **1** wonder. **2**
contemptuous term for a person.

I widnae wunner but what I shouldn't
be surprised if.

wup *v* **1** bind together by wrapping
string, tape etc round and round a
join. **2** wind (a cord etc) round an
object tightly. **3** coil, become en-
tangled or involved.

n a tying or binding with coils of
string etc.

wur *see* **be, oor**[2].

wurk *see* **wark**.

wurn *see* **weir**.

wurnae *see* **be**.

wurr *see* **wirr**.

wus *see* **be**.

wut *see* **wit**.

wutch *see* **witch**.

wye *see* **wey**[1].

wyke *see* **walk**.

wynd, wyne [rhymes with 'line(d)'] *n* a
narrow (winding) street.

wynt [rhymes with 'pint'] *v* (allow) to
go bad or sour.

wyte *v* blame, accuse.

n **1** blame, responsibility for some
error or mischief. **2** **yer wyte** your
fault.

wyte *see* **wait**.

wyve *see* **weave**.

Y

yabber *see* **yabble.**

yabble, yabber E CENTRAL *v* **1** talk excitedly, chatter, gossip. **2** (*of animals, birds*) chatter, bark etc excitedly ORKNEY, NE.

yable *see* **able.**

yae *see* **ae.**

yaff *v* **1** bark, yelp. **2** chatter on, talk cheekily.
n a chatterbox, a cheeky person.

yair *n* a fish-trap across a river or bay SW.

yaird[1], **yard, yird** *n* **1** a yard. **2** a garden. **3** a churchyard.

yaird[2], **yard** SOUTH *n* a yard, the measure.

yairn *n* yarn.

yaise *see* **use.**

yaisual *see* **usual.**

yaldie *see* **yoldrin.**

yall *v, n* yell, howl SHETLAND, N.

yalla, yallochie *see* **yella.**

yammer *v* **1** howl, whine, whimper, complain. **2** make a loud noise, talk on and on (senselessly).
n a great outcry, endless talk.

yank *v* **1** pull sharply, jerk, twitch. **2** drive or force on energetically.
n a sudden jerk or pull.

yap[1] *n* **1** a chatterbox; a windbag. **2** talking without stopping.

yap[2] *n* child's word for an apple EDINBURGH.

yard *see* **yaird**[1], **yaird**[2].

yark *see* **yerk.**

yatt *n* a yacht WEST.

yatter *v* **1** chatter, ramble on. **2** (*of a person*) gabble; (*of an animal*) yelp. **3** nag, scold.
n **1** continuous chatter, talking on and on. **2** a person who talks on and on; a gossip.

yaul *see* **yauld.**

yauld, yaul *adj* active, alert, vigorous, healthy.

yaw *see* **awe.**

ye, you, yow SOUTH *pronoun, pl also* **youse, ylz, yeez** you, ye.

Yeel *see* **Yule.**

yeese *see* **use.**

yeez *see* **ye.**

yeld, eild *adj* **1** (*of animals*) barren, not having young because of age or accident. **2** (*of cows etc*) not giving milk because of age or being in calf.

yella, yalla *adj* yellow.

yallochie yellowish.

yella fish, yella haddie smoked (now also dyed) haddock.

yella gowan *see* **gowan.**

yella gum *see* **gum**[1].

yella lily *see* **lily.**

yella lintie the yellowhammer.

yella ylte *see* **yite.**

yella yoldrin *see* **yoldrin.**

yer, eer SOUTH *adj* your.

yerk, yark *v* **1** bind tightly. **2** beat, whip, strike. **3** throb, ache, tingle. **4** snatch, tug, pull. **5** drive hard, put pressure on.
n **1** a blow, a hard knock. **2** a jerk, tug. **3** a throb of pain; an ache NE.

yersel *pronoun* yourself.

yesk, esk N *v, n* hiccup, belch.

yestreen, the streen ORKNEY, N, **estreen** NE *adv* yesterday evening; last night; yesterday.

yet, ylt *adv* **1** yet. **2** up to now, at the present time, still: '*Are ye at the scuil yet?*'.

yett *n* **1** a gate. **2** a natural pass between hills.
(as) daft as a yett on a windy day scatterbrained, crazy.

yeuk, yuck *v* **1** itch, feel ticklish or itchy. **2** be keen or eager. **3** scratch. *n* itching, the itch; an itchiness.

yeukie 1 itching, itchy. **2** excitedly eager; sexually aroused. **3** shabby, rough, filthy.

yibble *see* **able.**

yill *see* **ale.**

yin *see* **ane**[1].

yince *see* **aince.**

yird, yirth *n* earth.

v bury.

yird the cogie (*children's game*) a rhythmic chant and quick stamping (to warm the feet) NE.

yird *see* **yaird**[1].

yirn, earn *v* (cause to) solidify, set or curdle; (*of milk*) form curds with rennet and heat SHETLAND, ORKNEY.

yirnin 1 setting, curdling. **2** rennet.

yirn *see* **earn.**

yirth *see* **yird.**

yis, yiss *see* **use.**

yit *see* **ait, yet.**

yite, yoit *n* **1** *often* **yella yite** a yellow-hammer. **2** a small person; contemptuous term for a person.

yitter *v* chatter.

yiz *see* **ye.**

yo *adv* (*contradicting another's 'no'*) but yes: '*Aw no!*' '*Ah bit yo!*'.

yoam *see* **oam.**

yoit *see* **yite.**

yoke *v* **1** start on some activity, set to, go about something (vigorously). **2 yoke on, yoke tae** set on (a person), attack.

yokin the starting of a spell of work, *often* **yokin time.**

yoldrin, yorlin, yaldie NE, *also* **yella yoldrin** *n* a yellowhammer.

yole *n* a kind of small boat SHETLAND, ORKNEY, N.

yon, on, yun SHETLAND *adj, pronoun* that (one), those over there, usually indicating a person or thing further away than **that** *etc*.

adv **1** over there, yonder SHETLAND, N.

2 to that place over there.

yon kind used to describe people or things in a poor state: '*Oh, dinna speak about that. Ye mak me yon kind*'.

yon time: '*It'll be yon time before they come*' They won't come for a long time.

yonder, yonner *adv* in that place, over there, indicating a person or thing at some distance.

adj that (over there), distant, there or thereabouts.

far frae aa yonder half-witted, not all there NE.

yont *adv* **1** farther away or along, beyond, aside. **2** yonder, over there, on or to the other side.

preposition beyond, on or to the other side of.

yont by over yonder, across.

yorlin *see* **yoldrin.**

you *see* **ye.**

younker *n* **1** a youngster, a young lad or girl, a youth. **2** a young bird, a nestling.

youse *see* **ye.**

youth *n*: **youthheid** youth.

youthie young, youthful, especially looking younger than you are.

yow *see* **ye.**

yowdendrift [-ow- as in 'cow'] *n* snow driven by the wind.

yowe [rhymes with 'cow'] *n* **1** a ewe. **2** *often* **yowie** a fir cone NE.

yowe-lamb a female lamb.

yowf *v, n* bark.

yowff [-ow- as in 'cow'] *n* a sharp blow, a swipe, thump.

yowie *see* **yowe.**

yowt *v, n* shout, roar, yell, cry.

yuck, yucker *n* a stone, pebble: '*He hut me wi a big yucker*'.

yuck *see* **yeuk.**

yuffie *n* a lavatory, especially one on a **tenement** stair.

yuise *see* **use.**

Yule, Yeel N, **Eel** N *n* Christmas; the

day itself; the festive season associated with it.

yun *see* **yon.**

yunk *n* (*marbles*) a stake marble.

Z

z *see* **us.**

English-Scots
Dictionary

A

aback *adv*: **taken aback** mesmerised, dumfoonert, stammygastered.

ability *n* abeelitie, can N.

able *adj* yable SOUTH, yibble SOUTH; (*competent*) lik(e)ly.

be able to get: '*Ye'll get swimmin the morn*'.

abnormal *adj* no richt, orra, by-or(di)nar.

abortion *n* slip.

about *preposition, adv* aboot; (*concerning*) anent: '*anent your job application*', on, o.

above *preposition, adv* abuin, abeen N, ower.

abreast *adv* abreist.

abscess *n* bealin, income.

absence *n*: **note explaining absence from school** line.

absent-minded forgettle, nae in.

absent-mindedness forget.

absolute *adj* fair, evendoon; (*in bad sense*) black: '*black lees*'.

absolutely fair, evendoon.

abstract *v* abstrack.

abundance *n* rowth, fouth, feck.

abundant rowth(ie), ruch.

abuse *v* abuise, abeese N; (*verbally*) misca(w), tongue, ill-tongue N.
n abuise, abeese N; (*abusive language*) snash, ill-tongue, tongue.

abusive ill-tonguit.

accent *n* (*of speech*) tune, tin, teen NE, souch.

accept *v* accep.

access *n* wey in, ingang.

accident *n* stramash, mishanter.

accidental casual NE.

accommodation *n* up-pittin.

accompany *v* convoy, set, get: '*We'll get ye doon the stair*'; (*as a friend*) chum: '*chum ye tae the café*'; (*part*

of the way) see by the hen's mait, see the lenth o . . . : '*We'll see ye the lenth o the bus stop*'.

accompanying of a person convoy; (*part of the way*) Scotch convoy.

accomplished *adj* far seen: '*He's far seen as a pianist*'.

accordion *n* box.

account *n* **1** accoont; (*long description*) scrift. **2** (*in a shop*) line: '*Pit it on the line*'.

accuse *v* wyte, faut.

accused *n* (*law*) panel.

accustom *v*: **accustomed (to)** yaised (wi), eest (wi) N.

ache *n, v* stoon(d).

achieve *v* get roon(d), pit ower.

acorn *n* (*large, ripe, on its stalk*) pipe SE.

acquaint *v* acquant, acquent.

acquainted acquant, acquent.

across *preposition, adv* throu, athort.

act *n, v* ack.

active *adj* acteeve; (*of people*) stourie, swack; (*of children*) steerin, steerie NE.

activity acteevitie, throu-pit.

acute *adj* **1** (*mentally*) gleg, snack. **2** (*of pain etc*) fell.

add *v* (*to something*) eik.

addition addeetion; (*something added*) eik.

in addition (to) forby, an a(w).

adder *n* ether, edder NE.

address *n* (*on a letter*) backin.
v (*a letter*) back.

familiar, friendly term of address (*to a man*) Jimmie; (*to a woman*) hen CENTRAL; (*to a small man or boy*) wee man; (*to a big man*) big man.

administer *v* admeenister.

administration admeenistration.

admire *v* respeck.

admirable braw.

admit *v* awn.

I admit that Ah winna say but (whit).

admission admeeshion.

adult *n* man-bodie, wumman-bodie. *adj* muckle, man-grown, wumman-grown.

advance *v* (*further*) forder.

advertise *v* adverteese.

advertisement adverteesement.

advise *v* speak a word tae.

aeroplane *n* airieplane.

affect *v* affeck; (*physically*) tak on: '*The whisky really took on im*'; **affect with** smit wi.

affected (*in manner*) mim, pitten-on; (*in speech*) tattie-peelin, mim-mou'd.

speak affectedly hae a bool in yer mou(th), talk pan loaf.

be affected pit it oan.

affection *n* hert-likin.

affection for notion o.

afford *v* affuird.

afraid *adj* feart (at, for, o), faird SHET-LAND, ORKNEY, frichtit (for).

aft *adv* eft.

after *preposition, adv* efter, aifter, ahin(t).

afternoon *n* efternuin, efterneen N.

afterwards *adv* efterhin, syne.

a little after, not long after (at) the back o: '*the back o six*'.

again *adv* agane.

against *preposition* agin, conter.

age *v* (*of a person*) get up in years.

old age eild.

under age within eild.

be the same age as be ages wi.

aggressive *adj* randie.

agile *adj* soople, swack, swipper(t) NE.

agilely soople, swipper(t) NE.

agitate *v* 1 (*make nervous*) flocht NE. 2 (*shake*) jummle, shoogle.

agitated skeer(ie).

agitation (*mental*) carfuffle, feem NE.

in a state of agitation up tae high doh.

ago *adv* syne, sinsyne.

a moment ago eenoo, ivnoo NE.

some time ago a while back, a filie back NE, no lang syne.

agree *v* gree, say thegither; (*be in harmony (with*)) say ae wey (wi).

agreeable 1 (*pleasant*) couthie. **2** (*in agreement*) greeable.

agreement (*harmony*) greement.

agree to meet tryst.

ahead *adv* aheid, afore.

aim *v* **1** (*a blow etc*) ettle, mint NE. **2** (*a weapon etc*) ettle, wice. **3** (*curling, bowls: a shot to land near the tee*) draw. **4 aim at** *or* **to** ettle at *or* tae, mint at *or* tae.

n **1** (*act of aiming*) gley. **2** (*intention*) mint.

aimless knotless.

aimless person knotless threid.

take aim mark, gley NE.

aisle *n* pass, trance.

ajar *adj* ajee.

alarm *v, n* alairm.

alcoholic *adj* (*of a person*) droothie, drucken.

alcove *n* bole, neuk.

alder *n* aller, arn.

ale *n* yill.

alert *adj* gleg, smairt, smert.

on the alert on the keevee.

alike *adj, adv* equal-aqual; (*all alike*) eeksie-peeksie.

alive *adj* tae the fore, in life, on fit.

all *adj, n* aw, aa, aal.

All Saints' Day Hallowday.

eve of All Saints' Day Halloween.

all kinds of orra.

all the . . . the hail . . .

alley *n* close, pend, entry, wynd, vennel.

allow *v* alloo, lat.

be allowed get: '*Can we get tae the park the noo?*'.

almost *adv* amaist, near(aboot(s)), (gey) near.

alone *adj, adv* alane, aleen NE, (by) his etc lane, im etc leen NE.

along *adv* alang, yont, awa: '*Come awa tae yer bed*'.

right along endlang.

aloud *adv* alood.

already *adv* a'ready, areddies.

also *adv* anaw, forby.

alternately *adv* time aboot, tour aboot; (*in a game etc*) shots each.

altitude *n* heicht, hicht.

altogether *adv* a(w)thegither.

always *adv* aye, ayeweys, still an on.

am *v* (*emphatic*) ur WEST: '*Ah'm ur*'.

am not amnae, amna, urnae WEST: '*Ah'm urnae gaun tae the dentist!*'.

amaze *v* dumfooner.

ambition *n* ambeetion, ettle, ettlin.

ambitious ambeetious.

amiable *adj* douce.

ammunition *n* ammuneetion.

among *preposition* amang.

amorous *adj* fain.

amount *n* amoont, thing: '*Will ye hae a wee thing soup?*', daud: '*a big daud cheese*'.

large amount lump, feck, wecht.

small amount pickle, drap, drop: '*a wee drop cheese*'; (*very small*) tait; (*of liquid*) spark.

ample *adj* (*in quantity*) luckie, foothie, lairge NE.

amuse *v* haud oot o langour SHET-LAND, ORKNEY, N.

amusement divert, ploy.

amusing shortsome, pawkie.

amusing person *or* **thing** divert.

amuse yourself play yersel.

ancestors *npl* forefolk.

ancient *adj* auncient.

and *conjunction* an.

anger *n* birse: '*His birse is up*'. *v* fash.

angry (*furiously*) bealin.

anglicized *adj* Englified.

animal *n* baist, beas; **animals** cattle, beas.

animated *adj* skeich, on the keevie, heich.

ankle *n* cuit, cweet NE.

announce *v* annoonce, lat ken.

announcement (*from the pulpit*) intimation.

annoy *v* fash; (*especially with talk or noise*) deave; (*tease*) kittle.

annoyance fash(erie), deavance.

annoyed mad.

annoying fashious, weary.

annual *adj* ilka year, ilkie ear N.

another *pronoun, adj* anither, anidder SHETLAND, NE.

answer *v* (*in argument or rudely*) speak back.

ant *n* eemock, emmerteen N, pismire.

anticlockwise *adv* withershins, widdershins.

antique *adj* auld-warl(d).

anvil *n* stiddie.

anxiety *n* anxeeitie, thocht.

anxious thochtie; (*restlessly*) lik(e) a hen on a het girdle.

any *adj, adv* onie.

anybody oniebodie, emdy.

anyone onie ane, onie yin, oniebodie.

anything oniethin(g).

anyway, anyhow oniewey(s), onie road.

anywhere oniegate, oniewey(s), onie road.

in any way onie: '*He canna fish onie*', oniewey(s).

apart *adv* apairt, sindrie.

apart from leave aside.

apologise *v* apologeese.

appear *v* kythe.

appearance (*look*) cast.

appetite *n* appeteet.

having an appetite for able for: '*Are ye able fur yer tea?*'.

having a good appetite hertie, maithail.

apple *n* aipple, yap *child's word*, EDIN-BURGH.

apple core stump, runt, casket.

appoint *v* appint.

appointment appintment; (*to meet at a certain time and place*) tryst.

make an appointment (with) tryst (wi).

April *n* Aprile.

April fool huntiegowk, gowk.

April Fool's Day huntiegowk, gowk's day, magowk's day.

April fool's errand gowk's errand, huntiegowk, gowk.

make an April fool of magowk, gowk.

apron *n* peenie.

arch *n* airch, pen(d), bow.

Arctic skua *see* **skua.**

are *v* ur.

are not arnae, arna, urnae.

argue *v* argie, argie-bargie, threap.

argument airgument NE, threap.

arithmetic *n* coonts: '*Dae yer coonts*'.

do arithmetic coont.

arm *n* airm, erm.

armful oxterfu.

armhole (*of a garment*) oxter.

armpit, underpart of the upper arm oxter.

walk arm-in-arm, link arms cleek, link.

hold *or* **carry under the arm** oxter.

army *n* airmie.

join the army go for a sodger, jine.

around *adv* aroon(d).

arouse *v* **1** (*from sleep*) raise. **2** (*sexually*) kittle.

sexually aroused radg(i)e, yeukie.

arrange *v* (*put in order*) redd (up), sort.

arrest *v* (*of police etc*) lift, tak in.

arrive *v*: **arrive at** win at, win till.

arrival (*act of arriving*) income.

arrogant *adj* pridefu, heich-heidit.

arrow *n* arrae, arra WEST, airra NE.

arse *n* erse.

arson *n* (*law*) fire-raising.

article *n* airticle.

artificial *adj* artifeecial.

as *adv, conjunction* is, in: '*in a gift*'.

as if as.

as well an a(w).

ash[1] *n* (*tree, wood*) esh.

ash[2] *n* (*from burning*) ass, ess SHETLAND, NE.

ashamed *adj*: **be ashamed** hae a rid face.

aside *adv*: **set aside** (*for future use*) pit past, pit by, lay past.

ask *v* speir, ax; (*a person*) speir at *or* o.

ask after ask for.

ask for seek.

asleep *adj, adv* awa(y): '*Is he awa yet?*'.

fall asleep fa(w) ower, dwam ower.

aspen *n* esp, tremmlin tree.

aspirin *n* asp(i)reen.

assemble *v* forgaither.

assembled in: '*The scuil's in*'.

assembly forgaitherin.

assistance *n* (*helping hand*) cast, heeze NE.

associate *v*: **associate with 1** troke wi, neibour wi. **2** (*connect with*) liken wi *or* tae.

assure *v* asseer NE.

asthma *n* the wheezles.

asthmatic *adj* pechie.

astonish *v* dumfooner, ca(w) the feet fae, stammygaster.

astonished bumbazed, dumfoonert, stammygastered.

astute *adj* cannie, pawkie.

at *preposition* it.

at all at a(w), ava.

ate *see* **eat.**

athletic *adj* swankin, swack.

atmosphere *n* (*warm, stuffy*) (y)oam SHETLAND, NE, moch; (*thick, stuffy*) smuchter NE, N; (*thick, suffocating*) smore, scomfish.

attach *v* (*fasten*) steek.

attack *v* (*physically*) set tae; (*vigorously*) get tore in(tae).

n **1** onding. **2** (*of illness*) drowe; (*slight*) towt.

attempt *v, n* ettle, mint, offer.

attend *v*: **attend to** see efter, tend, tent.

attention tent.

pay attention to tent, tak tent o.

attentive tentie, gleg.

attractive *adj* bonnie, no bad; (*mainly of people*) sonsie, wicelik(e).

attractive woman stoater, brammer.

auction *n, v* roup, unction.
 sell by auction roup.
audience *n* owdience SHETLAND, NE.
aunt *n* auntie.
aurora borealis *n* merry dancers SHET-
 LAND, ORKNEY, N, streamers.
author *n* owthor.
authority *n* (*power*) heid room.
 those in authority (high) heid yins,
 heid bummers.
autumn *n* hairst; (*late*) back-en(d).
 autumn holidays (*from school*) tattie
 holidays.
avalanche *n* whummle.
 v shuit.
avarice *n* grippiness.
 avaricious grippie, hungry, nippit.
avenue *n* (*leading to a house*) inlat,
 entry.

average *n*: **on the average** owerheid.
avoid *v* miss.
await *v* wait on, wait, bide (for).
awake *adj* waukened.
 easily awakened waukrif(e).
 awakening waukenin.
 be awake wauk.
 stay awake wauk, keep up.
award *n, v* awaird.
aware *adj* awaur; **aware of** ware o.
away *adv* awa, wa; (*distant*) hyne;
 (*further away*) yont.
 away from aff o.
awful *adj* awfu, awfie, aafu NE.
awkward *adj* ackwart; (*of a person*)
 han(d)less, thrawn, fushionless, tuckie NE.
axe *n* aix, bullax N.
axle *n* aixle.

B

baa *v, n* mae, meh.
babble *v* (*chatter*) blether, yatter.
n blethers, yatter.
babbler blether, clatterer NE.
baby *n* bairn, wean WEST, ULSTER, get, geet NE.
bachelor *n* lad.
back *n* 1 (*rear*) hin(t), hin(t)-side; (*back part*) hinen(d), hinneren(d), hinderen(d). 2 (*of a person or animal*) rig, riggin.
adj hin(t).
backbone rig, riggin.
back garden back green, backie, kail yaird.
backward 1 backart; (*of crops*) blate. **2** (*of a person*) glaikit.
be backward hae a want: '*Her wee laddie has a want*'.
backwards backarts, backarties, hint-side foremaist, backlins.
backwards and forwards back an fore.
backyard back coort, back green.
back to front backside foremaist, hint-side foremaist.
bacon *n* ham.
bad *adj* baud; (*evil*) ill, ill-deedie, coorse, shan *originally gipsy*.
badly bad, baud, ill, sair.
badly-behaved coorse, ill-trickit, ill-contrivit SHETLAND, N.
badly off ill-aff, sair aff.
badness ill.
bad-tempered crabbit, wickit, girnie.
in a bad mood in (a) bad cut.
badger *n* brock.
bag *n* poke, pyoke NE; (*small*) pokie; (*polythene*) poly poke.
bagpipes pipes.
bagpipe band pipe band.
bass pipe of the bagpipe drone.

melody pipe of the bagpipe, separate pipe for practice chanter.
classical music of the bagpipe pibroch.
play on the bagpipe pipe; (*shrilly*) skirl.
bail[1] *n* (*law*) caution.
bail[2] *v* (*bail a boat*) lave.
bake *v* byaak NE, fire: '*weel-fired rolls*'.
baked *past tense* beuk NE.
past participle baken.
baking board bake-board, bake-brod.
baking plate (*used over fire or other heat*) girdle.
balance *n*: **in the balance** on the hing.
lose your balance fa(w) aff yer feet.
bald *adj* bauldie(-heidit), beld NE.
ball *n* ba(w).
keeping a ball in the air keepie-up.
ballad *n* ballant.
balmy *adj* (*of weather*) leesome NE, saft.
bamboozle *v* bumbaze, taigle.
banana *n* banannie.
band[1] *n* (*which binds*) baun(d), ban.
band[2] *n* (*group*) baun(d), ban.
bandmaster (*of a pipe band*) pipe major, pipie *informal*.
bandage *n* cloot.
v rowe.
bandy-legged *adj* bowlie(-leggit), bowdie(-leggit).
bang *n, v* dunner, rattle; (*a door*) dad.
bank[1] *n* baunk; (*of river etc: steep sloping*) brae.
bank[2] *n* (*financial*) baunk; (*in a game*) puggie; (*child's*) lucky box.
banknote (*for £1*) note.
bankrupt *adj* broken.
v runk.
banns *npl* cries: '*Pit in the cries*'.

have the banns proclaimed be cried.
baptize *v* bapteese, kirs(t)en.
 baptism bapteesim, kirs(t)enin.
 offer (*a child*) **for baptism** present.
bar *n* baur; (*long, wooden*) stang.
barbed wire *n* pikit weer NE.
barber *n* baurber.
bare *adj* (*of land*) scabbit.
 barefoot barfit.
 bare feet baries.
 bare skin (*bare*) scud(die).
bargain *n, v* (*agreement*) troke.
 bargainer troker.
 strike a bargain with chap.
barge *n* bairge, scowe.
 v breenge.
bark *v, n* (*of a dog etc*) wowe, yowf;
 (*especially of a large dog*) bowf.
barnacle *n* claik SHETLAND, ORKNEY,
 NE.
barrel *n* bowie.
barren *adj* **1** (*of animals*) yeld, eil(d). **2**
 (*of land*) dour, scabbit; (*of soil*) deef,
 hi(r)stie.
barrister *n* advocate.
barrow *n* (*wheelbarrow*) barra(e), borra; (*handcart*) hurlie, hurl-barra.
base *n* **1** (*foundation*) foon(s),
 foond(s). **2** (*in games*) den, dale.
 basement laich, dunnie.
basin *n* bowl(ie).
basket *n* (*especially for meal, potatoes*)
 skep; (*shallow, scoop-shaped, eg for
 fish*) scull; (*deep, carried on back*) creel.
bastard *n* bastart.
bat *n* (*animal*) backie, bawkie.
bath *n*: **take a bath** dook.
bathe *v, n* dook.
batter *v* massacker, cloor, mell.
battle *n* stour.
bawdy *adj* ruch, coorse.
bawl *v, n* goller, gowl, buller NE.
beak *n* neb, gob, gab.
beaker *n* bicker.
beam *n* **1** (*of wood*) bauk. **2** (*of light*)
 leam.
bear *v* (*endure*) thole, bide.
 bearable tholeable.

beard *n* baird.
 bearded bairdie.
beast *n* baist, beas.
beat *v* **1** (*strike, thrash*) bate, dunt,
 bash; (*a person*) skelp. **2** (*of rain etc*)
 blatter. **3** (*overcome*) cowe, ding.
 past tense bate.
 beaten *past participle* bate.
 beating skelpin, lick(in)s.
beauty *n* brawness.
 beautiful bonnie, braw.
because *conjunction* cause, kis.
 because of ower the heid(s) o, for.
become *v* turn, get: '*She's awfie cheeky gettin*'.
bed *n* (*built into wall*) box-bed;
 (*truckle-bed*) hurlie-bed.
 bedcover (*especially thick woollen*)
 (bed-)mat.
 bedridden bedfast.
 bedroom chaumer.
 out of bed oot ower.
 get(ting) up out of bed rise.
 get out of bed in a bad temper rise aff
 yer wrang side.
bee *n* (*honey-bee*) skep-bee; (*wild bee:
 see also* **bumblebee**) bumbee, bummer.
 beehive skep, byke.
 bee in your bonnet maggot, pliskie
 NE.
beetle *n* clock; (*large*) clo(c)ker.
before *preposition, conjunction* afore,
 or, gin.
beggar *n* thigger, sorner, gaberlunyie
 (man).
begin *v* stert, stairt; (*vigorously*) yoke
 (tae).
 beginning *n* stert, stairt.
behave *v* guide yersel.
behind *preposition* ahin(t).
 adv ahin(t), aback.
 behind you *etc* at yer *etc* back.
belch *n, v* rift, boak, byock NE.
bellow *v, n* buller.
belly *n* wame, wime N, painch, kyte.
 bellyflop gutser.
 bellyful wamefu.

belong v belang.
  belongings (*personal*) guids an gear, graith.
  belong to (*a place*) belang, belong: '*He belangs Glesca*'.
below *preposition* (in) ablow.
  adv ablow.
bench n bink.
bend v boo; ((*part of*) *the body*) loot.
  n (*curve*) boo NE.
benefit n: **get the benefit of** get *or* ken the guid o.
bent *adj* (*crooked*) bowlie, bowlt; (*with age*) cruppen doon; (*over a task etc*) oot ower.
  bent double *see* **double.**
beret n tammie, Tam o Shanter.
berry-picking n the berries.
beside *preposition* aside, forby.
  besides forby, ana(w).
best *adj*: **best clothes** braws, Sunday('s) claes.
  best room room, ben.
betting slip n line.
better *adj*: **better-class** bettermais(t).
  I had better I'm better tae, I better.
  get better (*from illness*) mend (o), haud forrit.
between *preposition, adv* atween, tween, atweesh.
beware v bewaur.
  beware of tak tent o.
bewilder v stoon(d), stammygaster.
  bewildered bumbazed, dumfoonert, raivelt.
beyond *preposition, adv* ayont, yont, beyont.
  beyond the limits of outwith.
bib n **1** daidle, brat. **2** (*fish*) jackie downie.
Bible n the (Guid) Buik.
bid v (*invite*) seek.
  n (*especially at auction*) bod(e).
big *adj* muckle, mickle, meikle.
bilberry n blaeberry.
bill n (*of a bird*) neb, gob, gab.
bind v bin; (*tightly*) yerk, yark SHETLAND, N.

bound *past tense* band.
  past participle bun(d); (*with ties of affection etc*) thirlt.
birch n birk.
bird n burd.
birth n hamecomin, howdiein.
  birthplace cauf kintra, cauf-grun(d).
  give birth to bring hame.
biscuit n (*usually thick or soft*) bake; (*oatmeal, ginger*) parkin, perkin.
bisect v half, hauf.
bit n (*small*) bittie, bittock; *see also* **piece.**
bite v gnap NE, chack; (*especially of a dog*) snack.
  n **1** gnap NE, rive; (*especially of a dog*) snack. **2** (*on a fishing line*) rug.
  biting (*of wind*) snell, haarie.
bitter *adj* **1** (*to taste*) wersh, shilpit, soor as roddens. **2** (*of beer*) heavy. **3** (*of weather*) snell, thin. **4** (*of people*) snell, soor as roddens; (*of speech*) nebbie.
  n (*beer*) heavy: '*a pint o heavy*'.
bittern n bog-bleater.
black *adj* bleck, mirk.
  v (*boots etc*) bleck NE.
  blacken blecken; (*dirty*) coom, barken; (*especially the face with soot etc*) bleck(en).
  blackberry brammle, bramble.
  blackbird blackie.
  blackcurrant blackberry.
  black eye (blue) keeker.
bladder n blether.
blame n wyte, dirdum.
  v wyte, faut.
  blame someone for something wyte someone for *or* o *or* wi something.
bland *adj* wersh.
blanket n hap; (*tartan*) (bed) plaid.
blast n (*explosion*) pluff; (*of wind*) skelp, howder NE.
blaze n, v bleeze, lowe.
  blazing (*of a fire*) reevin NE, rovin NE.
bleak *adj* dreich, dour, (*especially of weather*) oorlich N.
bleat v, n mae, meh.

bleed *v* bluid, blood.

blend *v* bland, mell.

bless *v* bliss, sain.

blessing blissin; (*act*) sain.

blind *adj* blin; (*completely*) stane blin(d).
v blin.

blind man's buff jockie blindie, belly-blin(d).

blink *v* blent; (*of the eyes*) glimmer NE, pink.

blinkers blinners, goggles NE.

bliss *n* seil.

blissful seilfie.

blizzard *n* stour.

bloated *adj* fozie; (*with too much food*) brosie, hoven.

blob *n* (*of moisture*) blab NE, glob, drib.

block *n* (*of wood*) stock.

block up stap, clag.

blockhead *n* stookie, sumph, neep(heid).

blood *n* bluid, blid CENTRAL, bleed N.

bloody bluidie, bleedie NE.

bloody nose jeelie nose, jeelie neb.

bloodshot bluid-shed.

it makes my blood run cold it gars me grue.

bloom *n, v* bluim, bleem N.

blossom *n* flourish.

blot *n* **1** spleyter NE. **2** (*on character*) tash.

blow[1] *v* **1** (*of wind etc*) bla(w), byauve NE; (*very hard*) tear, rive, bla(u)d; (*in gusts*) dad, flaff. **2** (*the nose*) snite.

blow[2] *n* **1** (*hit*) bla(w), chap, belt.
2 (*heavy*) dunt; (*especially with a whip*) whang.
3 (*sharp*) jag, knap, snap SHETLAND, N, knack; (*glancing*) skite.
4 (*resounding*) dirl, rummle; (*whizzing*) sing, wheech.

blubber *v* (*weep*) bubble, bibble NE, snotter.

blubbering *adj* bubbly, bibbly NE, snotterie.

blue *adj, n* bew, blyew; (*dark, greyish*) blae.

bluish blae.

bluebell (*Scottish*) harebell, gowk's thimmles NE; (*English*) wood hyacinth.

bluebottle bummer, muck flee, mauk flee.

blunt *adj* (*of a knife etc*) bauch.

bluntly richt oot, stra(u)cht oot.

blush *n* (*blushing face*) rid face, beamer, ridder, riddie.
v get a rid face, get a beamer.

blustery *adj* gurlie, scoorie, grummlie NE, gowsterie.

boar *n* gaut.

board *n, v* brod, buird, boord.

boast *v* bla(w), bum, craw croose.
n bla(w), roose, reese NE.

boastful great, massie.

boastful person, boaster bum, bla(w).

boat *n* bait N.

bob *n, v* boab.

bob up and down hobble, hotch.

bobbin *n* pirn.

body *n* (*of a person*) buddie, boadie, bouk.

bog *n* moss.

boggy mossy.

boggy ground moss, flow.

bogey, bogy *n* bogle, bockie, boodie NE.

bog(e)yman black man.

boil[1] *v* bile; (*slowly*) sotter; (*steadily*) hotter.

boiled sweet boilin, bilin.

up to the boil throu the boil.

boil[2] *n* (*on the skin*) bile, bealin, income.

boisterous *adj* bowsterous, randie.

bold *adj* baul(d); (*and impudent*) gallus, forrit(some), facie; (*rash*) frush, raucle.

bollard *n* (*mooring post*) pall.

bolt *n, v* bowt, slot; (*small*) snib.

bone *n* bane, been N.

bonnet *n* bannet, bunnet; (*traditional Scottish, flat woollen*) Tam o Shanter; (*with tassel*) toorie bunnet.

book *n* buik, b(y)euk.

boor *n* tike, cowt.

  boorish coarse, orra.

boot *n* buit, bit CENTRAL, beet N.

  bootlace whang, pint.

  bootnail tacket, seg.

border *n* (*of land*) mairch, march.

bore[1] *v* (*hole*) thirl; (*with drill*) kirn.

bore[2] *v* (*weary*) sta(w); (*especially with talk*) deave.

  n sta(w).

  bored scunnert.

  boredom langour.

born *adj*: **be born** come hame.

borough *n* burgh.

borrow *v* borrae, get a len (o).

boss *n* maister; (*often sarcastic*) heid bummer; (*male*) himsel(f); (*female*) hersel(f); **bosses** high heid yins.

botch *v* (*spoil*) bootch.

both *pronoun, adj, adv* baith.

  both of them, us, you baith the twa o them, us, ye.

bother *v* (*annoy*) fash, bather, budder SHETLAND, N.

  n fash, bather, budder SHETLAND, N.

  don't bother dinna fash yersel.

  not bother (your head) no jee yer ginger.

bottom *n, see also* **buttocks**; boddam; (*lowest part*) grun(d).

bought *see* **buy.**

bounce *v* stot, stoit.

  n stot.

  bouncing stottin.

bound *n* **1** (*limit*) boon. **2** (*leap*) lowp, spang.

  v spang, lowp; (*of an animal*) stot.

bound *see* **bind.**

boundary *n* (*border*) march, mairch.

bouquet *n* flooer, flooerie NE.

bout *n* (*of something*) match: '*greetin match*'.

bow[1] *n* (*of ribbon etc*) doss NE.

  bow-tie made tie.

bow[2] *v, n* (*respectfully*) boo, beck.

bowel *n* thairm; **bowels** booels, painches.

bowl *n* bowlie.

  bowls (*game*) bools.

bowl over (*physically*) whummle, ca(w) the feet fae.

box[1] *n* boax; (*tin, with a lid*) mull(ie) NE.

box[2] *n, v* (*on the ear*) scoor NE, sclaff.

boy *n* lad(die), boay, loon(ie) N; (*small*) laddie, loonie N, boyackie N.

  boyfriend lad(die), click, cleek.

  get a boyfriend click, cleek.

braces *npl* (*for trousers*) galluses.

bracken *n* fern.

brain(s) *n*(*pl*) harns.

  brainless boss, harnless.

  brainy heidie.

bramble *n* brammle.

branch *n* (*of a tree*) brainch.

brand-new *adj* split-new, spleet-new.

brass *n* bress.

  brass neck hard neck.

brat *n* (*rascal*) get.

brawl *n, v* rammie, tulyie.

bread *n* breid; (*of wheat as opposed to oats etc*) laif(-breid), (*baked in batch loaves*) plain breid; (*baked in separate tins*) pan breid.

  piece of bread (*spread with butter, jam etc*) piece: '*jeelie piece*'; '*piece an jeelie*'.

breadth *n* breid(th).

break *v* brak, brek; (*snap*) knack.

  n (*from work*) speel; (*in school day*) leave, meenit NE.

  broke *past tense* brak.

  broken in (*of a horse*) drachtit NE.

  breaker (*large wave*) jaup, jaw NE.

  breakfast brak(e)fast, pottitch NE.

  breakdown (*in health*) foon(d)er.

  break even (*of an enterprise*) wash its face.

  break up (*of a meeting etc*) skail.

  break wind lat aff, rift, pump, rowt.

breast *n* breist.

breath *n* braith, win(d).

  breathless, out of breath pechin, fobbin NE.

  under your breath intae yersel.

breathe v (*hard*) pech, fob NE.
  breathing n (*heavy*) souch.
breeches npl breeks.
breeze n tirl NE.
brew v (*ale etc or tea*) mask.
bribe v sweeten, creesh (someone's) luif.
bridesmaid n best maid.
bridge n brig.
  bridge a gap *see* **gap.**
bridle n branks.
brier n breer.
bright adj 1 bricht; (*of colours*) veeve, (*showily*) roarie, skirie ORKNEY, NE; (*of weather*) leesome. 2 (*of personality*) gleg, mirkie NE, lifie.
brim n: **brimful** adj lip-fou.
  brimming over lipperin, lip-fou.
bring v: **brought** past tense brocht, brang.
  past participle brocht, brung.
  bring up (*rear*) fess up NE.
bristle n birse, birsle; **bristles** birse.
  v birsle.
  bristly jaggie, jobbie NE, stobbie NE.
brittle adj bruckle; (*of wood etc*) frush, freuch NE.
broad adj braid.
broke, broken *see* **break.**
bronchitis n broonkaities, the wheezles.
brood n brod, breed NE; (*of animals, contemptuously of people*) cleckin; (*of chickens etc*) lachter.
  v (*of birds*) clock.
  broody (*of a fowl*) clockin, sittin.
  broody hen clocker, clockin hen.
brook n burn, rin, stripe SHETLAND, N, straun SW.
broom n 1 (*plant*) breem NE. 2 (*brush*) besom.
broth n NB 'broth' in Scotland means a thick vegetable soup, usually made with mutton or other meat.
brother n brither.
  brother-in-law guid-brither.
brought *see* **bring.**

brow n broo; (*of a hill*) broo, brae.
brown adj, n broon.
bruise v brizz, knuse, pran NE.
  n brizz, birse; (*by nipping etc*) chack, check.
brush n (*broom*) besom.
  brush against skiff.
  brush off scuff.
brute n breet NE.
bubble n bibble NE, blob, bell.
  v bibble NE; (*especially in cooking*) hotter, plapper NE, sotter.
bucket n, see also **pail** (*which, in Scotland, is commoner than 'bucket'*); bowie, cog.
budge v jee, mudge.
  refuse to budge (for) no jee: '*He winna jee*'.
build v big; (*roughly and hurriedly*) rickle.
  n (*of a person*) set.
  building n biggin.
  built past tense biggit, bug.
  past participle biggit.
  badly built ricklie.
bulge n bumfle.
  bulging bumflie.
bulk n, v bouk.
  bulky boukit.
bull n bul, bill.
  bullock nowt; (*young*) stot, stirk.
  bull's eye (*sweet*) black man.
  bullfinch bullie FIFE.
bully n, v ool, hatter.
bum *see* **buttocks.**
bumblebee n bumbee, bummer.
bump v dunt, dird NE.
  n 1 dunt, dunch, dird NE. 2 (*swelling*) knap, knoit.
bun n NB in Scotland usually less sweet than in England; (*plain, round, glazed, of yeast dough*) cookie: '*cream cookie*'.
bunch n toosht NE; (*of flowers*) flooer: '*Here a wee flooer tae ye*'.
bundle v, n bunnle, pauchle.
bungle v, n blooter.
  bungler footer, scutter.

bungling *adj* footerie, footerin.
burden *n* lift, cairrie, fraucht.
 v (*with work etc*) tra(u)chle.
burial *n* beerial NE.
burly *adj* muckle-boukit, thick.
burn *v, n* birn, scowder.
 burnt *adj, past tense, past participle* brunt.
burrow *v* howk, burrae.
burst *v* brust, birst, rive; (*out of a container*) lowp.
 past tense burstit.
 past participle burs(t)en.
 n brust, birst.
 burst open leap.
bury *v* beerie, yird.
bus *n*: **bus station** *or* **terminus** (bus-)stance.
bush *n* buss.
business *n* (*piece of business*) ploy, handlin.
bustle *n, v* steer, bizz.
 bustling (*of a person*) breengin, steerie; (*of a place*) thrang.
busy *adj* thrang; (*occupied*) fest NE; (*working hard*) eydent.

busybody (*talkative*) clishmaclaver NE.
but *conjunction* bit.
butcher *n* flesher.
 butcher's meat butcher meat, beef, flesh.
butt *v, n* (*of an animal*) dunch.
butter *v* (*a slice of bread etc*) spread (a piece).
 butter biscuit butterie.
 butterbur tushilago, wild rhubarb.
 buttercup yella gowan.
 butterfly butterie NE.
 buttermilk soor dook.
buttocks *npl* dowp, hurdies, dock, hint-en(d); (*often to a child*) behoochie, bahookie.
buy *v* coff.
 bought *past tense, past participle* bocht, coft *literary*.
 buyer (*customer*) merchant NE.
 buy on credit *see* **credit**.
buzz *v, n* bum, bizz NE.
buzzard *n* gled N.
by *preposition, adv* be; (*of paternity*) tae; (*before*) gin: '*gin this time*'; come: '*come Sunday*'.

C

cabbage *n* cabbitch, kail.
  cabbage stalk castock, runt.
cabin *n* caibin.
cackle *v, n* keckle; (*with laughter*) keckle, guff.
cahoots *npl*: **be in cahoots with** collogue wi, colleague wi NE.
cake *n* kyaak NE; (*sponge, with paper band*) sair heid(ie); (*small iced sponge*) French cake; (*very rich fruit, in pastry case*) black bun, bun, Scotch bun. *v* (*of soil etc*) lapper NE.
  cakes snashters *often contemptuous;* (*fancy*) gulshichs NE, funcie pieces NE, sweet-breid SHETLAND.
calculate *v* coont.
  calculation wirkin oot.
calf *n* **1** (*animal*) cauf, caffie NE, ca; *pl* caur. **2** (*of leg*) cauf.
call *v* **1** ca(w), cry; (*of birds*) clatter; (*of birds, animals: loudly*) rair, roup, yammer; (*shrilly*) wheep. **2** (*give a name to*) cry CENTRAL; **be called** get: '*He aye gets Jockie fae her*'. **3** (*pay a short visit*) cry in. *n* **1** ca(w), cry. **2** (*short visit*) cry. **3** (*to a cat*) cheet(ie-pussy).
  call in (*make a short visit*) cry in (by).
  call on (*a person for help*) cry on.
  call (someone) names misca(w), cry (someone) names.
calm *adj* (*of weather*) lown, quate; (*of a place*) lithe; (*of the sea etc*) sma. *n* lown.
  calm down be at peace.
  calm yourself sattle.
  keep calm keep a calm souch.
came *see* **come**.
can¹ *v*: **cannot** cannae, canna.
  could *past tense* cud.
  could not cudnae, cudna.
can² *n* (*for liquids*) tinnie.

canal *n* canaul WEST, nollie WEST.
candid(ly) *adj, adv* (*frank*) furth the gate NE.
candidate *n*: **list of candidates** leet: '*short leet*'; '*long leet*'.
candle *n* cannle, caunle WEST.
candy *n* gundie.
caning *n* hazel oil.
canister *n* mull(ie) NE.
cannot *see* **can¹**.
canvas *n* cannas NE.
cap *n* bunnet, kep; *see also* **cloth cap**.
capable *adj* feckfu, lik(e)ly; (*and energetic*) fell.
  capable of up wi: '*She's no up wi that job*'.
capacity *n* (*for work*) throu-pit.
caper *v* flisk, fling, daff. *n* pant, kick; **capers** jeegs NE.
capsize *v* cowp, whummle.
captain *n* (*of a curling rink*) skip.
capture *v* (*lands, goods*) tak, grip. *n* tak.
car *n* caur.
carcass *n* (*of a slaughtered animal*) bouk; (*of a fowl*) closhach NE.
card *n* caird; (*especially playing card*) cairt.
  pack of cards pair o cairts.
care *n* **1** (*anxiety, worry*) thocht. **2** (*attention*) tent. *v* **1** (*trouble yourself*) fash. **2** (*pay attention*) tent.
  carefree lichtsome.
  careful carefu, carefae, cannie, eydent, tentie NE; (*scrupulously*) perjink; **careful!** mind yersel!, ca cannie!
  carefully cannie (lik(e)).
  go carefully ca cannie, watch yersel.
  careless hashie, tentless, haiveless N, owerlie, hither an yon(t).
  carelessly owerlie.

245

work done carelessly hash.
caretaker (*especially of a school*) janitor, jannie *informal*.
care for keep, see till: '*See till yer bairns!*'; (*especially children, animals*) guide.
not care a fig no care a docken.
take care of tak tent o, leuk ower, keep.
carpenter *n* joiner, wricht.
carpet *n* cairpet.
carriage *n* cairriage.
carrion crow *n* hoodie (craw), corbie.
carry *v* cairrie, cerrie; (*goods*) convoy; (*loads, parcels*) cadge; (*something very heavy*) humph; (*under the arm*) oxter: '*Ah oxtered the paper*'.
carrying cairryin; (*of a child on the shoulders*) shooderie: '*Gie me a shooderie*'.
carry on (*continue*) haud on; (*with difficulty*) chaave NE, haggle SOUTH.
carry-on oncairrie, set.
carry under the arm *see* **arm.**
cart *n* cairt; (*child's home-made*) cairtie, hurlie (cairt), piler, guider E CENTRAL.
v cairt, lead, whurl.
carter cairter.
cart-load cairt-draucht, cairtle NE.
cartilage *n* girsle.
cascade *v* plash.
n spoot, jaw, plowt.
case *n*: **in any case** oniewey.
in that case syne.
cash *n* clink; (*in silver*) white siller.
ready cash lyin money.
cast *v* kest, kiest NE, thraw, skail; (*fishing lines or nets*) shot NE; (*fishing line*) wap.
past tense kiest NE, cuist.
past participle casten, cassin, cuisten.
cast iron yetlin SHETLAND.
cast on (*knitting*) lay up SHETLAND.
casting on (*knitting: of first row of stitches*) oncast.
castanets *npl* crackers.
castrate *v* (*livestock*) sort.

casual *adj* happenin; (*of a job*) orra.
casually owerlie.
cat *n* cheet(ie-pussy); (*affectionate name*) (pussy-)baudrons; (*especially castrated*) gib(bie).
let the cat out of the bag lat the cat oot o the poke.
catapult *n* guttie, cattie; (*forked stick for making*) shangie.
cataract *n* (*on the eye*) pearl.
catarrh *n*: **speak through catarrh** slorach.
catch *v* **1** nick, nip, grip; (*as with a hook*) cleek; (*as by a loop*) hank; (*a falling or thrown object*) kep; (*a person, in order to punish*) get yer hands on. **2** (*fish: by groping under banks of streams*) guddle, gump SE. **3** (*eg fingers in a door*) check, chack.
n **1** (*act of catching*) kep. **2** (*of fish*) drave, tak. **3** (*of a window etc*) snib, sneck. **4** (*drawback*) thraw i the raip.
caught *past tense, past participle* caucht, catchit, cotch, claucht.
become caught in a net (*of fish*) strik(e).
catch up on 1 (*overtake*) mak up on, tak in NE. **2** (*a piece of work*) owertak.
caterpillar *n* kailworm; (*hairy*) hairy oobit, hairy worm, grannie; (*large hairy*) hairy grannie.
Catholic *n* (*contemptuous*) pape CENTRAL, ULSTER, left-fitter CENTRAL, Tim CENTRAL, Dan(nie) boy CENTRAL, green grape *rhyming slang* (*for* '*pape*').
be a Catholic kick wi the left fit.
cattle *n* kye, baists, beasts, beas.
cattleman herd, (cow) bailie.
cattle-raider (*in past times*) reiver.
cattle-raiding (*in past times*) reivin.
cattle-shed byre.
caught *see* **catch.**
cauliflower *n* cauliflooer.
cause *v* caase SHETLAND, ORKNEY, N; (*someone to do something*) gar.
cautious *adj* cannie, cowshus, sicker, tentie NE.

cautiously cannie, cannilie, sickerlie NE.

cave *n* cove, clift.

ceiling *n* ruif; (*sloping in an attic*) coom, camceil WEST.

with a sloping ceiling coomceiled, camsiled CENTRAL.

celebrate *v* (*something new*) han(d)sel; (*with a drink*) slocken.

cellar *n* laich, laich hoose; (*in a shop*) laich shop.

cemetery *n* ceemeterie, kirkyaird.

centipede *n* Meg(gie) wi the monie feet, Jennie-hun(d)er-feet, Jennie-monie-feet.

centre *n* mids.

certain *adj* **1** sicker. **2 a certain** . . . ae . . . , yae . . . WEST, SOUTH.

certainly certie, atweel, fine at N.

certainly not nivver at NE, na-say: '*Are ye gaun tae the picters?*' 'Na-say'.

make certain mak siccar.

certificate *n* (*legal*) brief; (*of church membership*) lines.

marriage certificate mairriage lines.

chafe *v* chaff, freet.

chafed chattit NE.

chaff *n* **1** (*of corn etc*) caff, sheelins. **2** (*banter*) heeze NE.

v tak on.

chaffinch *n* chaffie, shilfa, spink SOUTH.

chain *n, v* cheen, chine.

chair *n* cheer, chyre.

chairperson preses; (*especially of a committee etc*) convener.

draw in your chair (*to a table etc*) sit in.

chalk *n, v* cauk, kalk.

challenge *n* (*to a feat of daring*) hen, henner EDINBURGH, coosie ANGUS.

chamber *n* chaumer.

chamberpot chantie, mickey.

chance *n* **1** cast; (*to improve*) scowth. **2** (*probability*) lik(e)ly.

adj antrin.

change *v* cheenge, chynge; (*clothes, house, job, etc*) shift.

n cheenge, chynge; (*of house or job, or of clothing*) shift.

changeable 1 (*of a person*) aff an on. **2** (*of weather*) tooterie NE.

change your clothes chynge yersel, shift.

change your mind tak the rue.

change places (with) shift (wi).

change your shoes chynge yer feet, shift yer feet.

channel *n* (*water*) trink; (*small*) rin.

chaos *n* reel-rall, heeliegoleerie.

chaotic throuither, throwder NE, tapsalteerie, mixter-maxter.

in a chaotic state in a snorl.

chap[1] *n, v* (*(in) the skin*) hack, gaig.

chap[2] *n* (*fellow*) carle, chiel(d), loon NE.

character *n* (*reputation*) word; (*strength of character*) fushion NE, smeddum.

characteristic *n* (*personal*) particularity, set.

charge *v* **1** chairge. **2** (*recklessly*) breenge, ramp.

charity *n* chairitie, chiritie NE.

charm *n* chairm; (*magic*) cantrip.

v chairm.

charmed (with) taen up (wi), browden (on).

chart *n* ca(i)rd.

charwoman *n*: **work as a charwoman** gang oot amang fowk.

chasing game *n* chasie, leave-o, jinks, jinkie.

chat *v* crack, blether, news.

n crack, blether, gab, news.

chatty bletherin, gabbie, newsie.

chatter *v* **1** shatter, yitter, yabble; (*of teeth*) chitter, chack NE, yatter. **2** (*chat*) blether, gab, gibble-gabble, tittle, clishmaclaver, claik; (*endlessly*) paiter, yatter, crack lik(e) a pen-gun; (*irritatingly*) natter, nyatter NE.

n blethers, clack, clatters, gab, yatter, gibble-gabble; (*aimless*) natter, nyatter NE, jibber.

chatterbox blether(er), yap, yatter, haiver.

cheap *adj* chape.

cheat *v* chate NE, swick, nick, pauchle. *n* chate NE, chet: **1** (*act of cheating*) swick. **2** (*person who cheats*) swick, intak.

cheating cheatrie.

check[1] *v* chack; (*oppose*) conter. *n* chack.

check[2] *n* (*pattern*) chack.

black-and-white check shepherd's tartan.

cheek *n* **1** (*side of the face*) haffet; **cheeks** chowks, ginnles, chafts. **2** (*impudence*) snash, tongue.

cheeky facie, sneistie, forrit.

cheep *v* peek, wheetle, queek NE. *n* peek.

not a cheep nae a chowp NE.

cheer *v* lift.

cheered liftit.

cheerful hertie, cantie, croose, joco, lichtsome, shortcome.

cheering *adj* hertsome, lichtsome.

cheerless dreich, unheartsome, hertless.

cheers! slàinte (mhath)!, here's tae us!

cheese *n* (*whole, especially home-made*) kebbock; (*soft*) crowdie.

cherry *n* (*wild*) gean.

chest *n* **1** (*box*) kist, chist; (*especially one used as a seat*) bunker; (*for meal etc*) ark, girnel. **2** (*of the body*) kist, chist.

get something off your chest hoast something up.

chew *v* chaw, chow, hash.

chewing gum chuddie.

chick *n* chuck(ie) NE, E CENTRAL, chookie CENTRAL.

chicken chucken, chuck(ie) NE, E CENTRAL, chookie CENTRAL; (*as food, often*) hen.

chicken soup hen broth, hen bree; (*with leek*) cock-a-leekie.

chief *adj* heidmaist, (*person*) maist.

n himsel(f), hersel(f), heid bummer; (*of a clan*) chieftain.

chilblain *n* moul, mool.

child *n* bairn, wean WEST, ULSTER, chile NE; (*small*) bairnie, wee thing, littlin N, E CENTRAL, smowt, tottie, peerieting SHETLAND, wee loon NE, wee quine NE; (*mischievous*) tike, smatche(r)t, sorra; (*spoilt*) sookie.

children childer; (*young*) wee yins.

childish bairn(l)ie.

childishness bairnliness.

childlike bairnlie, bairnlik(e).

last child of a large family *see* **family.**

chill *v* daver NE.

n (*coldness, illness*) jeel.

be *or* **feel chilled** sterve (wi caul(d)).

chilly shill, greeshach N; (*of weather*) oorie.

chimney *n* lum, chim(b)ley.

chimney-cowl grannie.

china *n* cheenie, wallie CENTRAL, SOUTH, lame SHETLAND, ORKNEY, N; (*everyday*) delft.

china dogs wallie dugs, cheenie dugs.

broken pieces of china (*as used as toys*) wallies, lames N.

chink *n* jink, bore, gaig.

chip *n* (*of wood*) spail.

v (*a blade*) lip.

chirp *v, n* chirl, chirm, chilp NE.

chitchat *n* clack, claik, clash, claver.

chives *npl* sybes NE.

choice *n* chice, wale, wile.

adj han(d)-waled.

choir *n* (*mainly church*) ban(d).

choke *v* chock, chowk SW, SOUTH: **1** (*a person*) tak (someone's) breath, smuir, smoor SHETLAND, NE. **2** (*of a person*) scomfish, smuir; (*convulsively or with laughter*) kink; (*on food*) worry.

choked 1 (*with weeds etc*) grown-up. **2** (*with the cold*) smorin.

choose *v* chuse, chyse NE, E CENTRAL, wale, (*especially sides in a game*) chaps.

chop *v* chap, champ, hack, hash; (*especially wood*) hag.

chopping block hackin stock.
choppy sea jaup, jap.
chop off sned.
christen *v* kirsten, gie (a bairn) a name.
  christening kirstenin.
Christmas *n* Yule, Yeel N.
  Christmas Day Yule Day, Yeel Day N.
  Christmas Eve Yule Een, Yeel Een N.
  Christmas present Christmas: '*Whit wad ye like for yer Christmas?*'
chubby *adj* pluffie, chibbie; (*of a child*) sonsie.
chunk *n* junk, da(u)d, fang NE, whang.
church *n* kirk.
  church service diet o worship.
  churchyard kirkyaird.
  move to another church lift yer lines, shift yer lines.
churn *v, n* kirn.
cigarette end *n* dowp, dowt, dottle.
cinder *n* cinner, shinner NE.
Cinderella Rashiecoat.
circular *adj* roon(d).
  circular motion birl, sweel.
circumstance *n*: **not under any circumstances** at nae rate.
claim *v* (*lay claim to*) awn, own.
  I claim chaps me.
clamber *v* sclammer, sclim, spra(u)chle.
  clamber up speel.
clammy *adj* clam.
clamour *n* sclammer NE, stramash; (*of voices*) yabble, yammer.
  v yammer, sclammer NE.
clank *n* (*eg of a chain*) rackle N.
clannish *adj* hing-thegither.
clasp *n* clesp; (*hasp*) hesp.
  v clesp, hesp.
  clasp hands (*eg to seal a bargain*) chap han(d)s.
class *n* cless.
clatter *v* brattle, reemis(h) NE; (*of crockery etc*) rees(h)le.
  n brattle, reemis(h) NE, swack; (*clattering noise*) clitter-clatter, rees(h)le.

claw *n, v* clowe, cleuk, claut.
clean *adj* claen SW, SOUTH.
  clean(ing) dicht(in).
  clean out redd (oot), dicht; (*with a shovel*) shuil; (*especially a stable etc, of dung*) muck (oot).
clear *adj* **1** clair; (*of light etc*) skire. **2** (*cleared*) redd (oot).
  v **1** (*eg a space, a passage*) redd; (*a fireplace, pipe of ash*) ripe. **2** (*the throat, nose etc*) redd N.,
  clearance redd(-oot), redd-han(d).
  cleared redd: '*Get that table redd!*'.
  clearing (up) (*act*) redd(in) (up).
  clear away set by; (*to get more space*) redd.
  clear out 1 (*ditch etc*) redd (oot); (*bowels etc*) scoor. **2** (*go away*) skice NE.
  clear up 1 (*tidy*) redd (up). **2** (*of weather*) fair (up), harden (up), cast up.
  as clear as crystal *see* **crystal.**
cleavers *npl* sticky-Willie, guse-grass.
cleft *n* clift.
clenched fist *n* steekit nieve.
clergy *n*: **member of the clergy** (*especially of a Presbyterian church*) meenister, minister.
clever *adj* clivver, heidie, gleg (in the uptak), wice; (*shrewd*) fell, pawkie.
  cleverness glegness, ingine.
click *v* (*make a clicking sound*) knick, knack, chack NE.
  n (*clicking sound*) knick, knack.
cliff *n* clift, clint, craig, sker SOUTH; (*especially above sea or a river*) heuch.
climb *v* **1** clim, sclim, speel, rink NE, rise SW; (*with difficulty*) spra(u)chle. **2** (*of plants*) ramp.
  n speel.
  climbed *past tense* clam(b), climmed, sclimmed.
cling *v, past tense* **clung** clang.
clip *v* (*especially hair*) cowe; (*very short*) rump, dock.
  clipped (*of speech or hair*) dockit.
  clippers (*sheep-shearing*) shears.

cloak *n* clock, hap.

clock *n* cloak, knock.

clod *n* claut.

clog *v* clag, cleg.

clogs *npl* clampers.

close[1] *adj* **1** nar. **2** (*of a friend*) hameower. **3** (*of atmosphere*) smochie; (*and damp*) mochie, muithie.

closely-related near, sib, near freen(d)s.

closer nar.

close-fitting strait, jimp, nippit.

close by nar, nearhan(d), in aboot, at yer lug, aboot hands (wi).

close to inby, nar, nearby, nearhan(d), aside.

close together (*of persons*) cheek for chow(l).

be close friends (with) be great guns (wi), be far ben (wi).

sit close cuddle, coorie in.

sitting close together curcuddoch.

close[2] *v* steek; (*the mouth*) dit NE. *n* (*end*) hin(d)maist.

clot *n* **1** clat; (*of blood, milk*) lapper. **2** (*stupid person*) bawheid, heidbanger, eejit; (*clumsy*) muckle sumph. *v* (*of blood, milk*) lapper.

cloth *n* **1** claith. **2** (*piece of cloth*) cloot; (*coarse, for domestic purposes*) dud NE.

cloth cap skippit bunnet, cadie, hooker-doon CENTRAL, snootit bonnet NE.

clothe *v* cleed, cleethe, hap.

clothed cled, cleed.

clothes claes, clathes; cloots *contemptuous*; (*best*) (Sunday) braws; (*Sunday*) kirk claes; (*everyday, working*) ilkaday('s) claes; (*second-best, especially after work*) weirin claes.

clothing cleedin, claith.

clothes-brush claes brush.

clothes-horse claes-screen, winterdykes.

clothes-line (claes) raip.

clothes-prop claes pole, stenter, heyser NE, greenie pole.

cloud *n* **1** clud. **2** (*dense: of smoke, snow, etc*) smuir.

cloudy drumlie.

cloudburst (thunner-)plump, plowt.

rise in a cloud (*of dust etc*) stour.

clove *n* (*spice*) clowe.

clover *n* claver, sookie, curl-doddie; (*flower*) sookie-soo.

be in clover live at heck an manger.

clown *n* (*idiot*) hallion, eejit, feel NE. *v* noise NE.

club *n* (*stick*) mell.

cluck *n* (*of a broody hen*) clock.

clumsy *adj* tackie NE, ill-setten; (*incompetent*) han(d)less; (*at doing something*) ill (at); (*in walking*) shauchlin; (*and stupid*) gawkit; (*of things*) untowtherlie NE.

work clumsily hash.

clumsy person ba(u)chle, gawk(ie); (*large coarse man*) caber NE.

clung *see* **cling**.

cluster *n* boorach.

clutch *n, v* cleek, cla(u)cht, grup.

in the clutches of i the cleuks o N, i the grips o.

coal *n* coll, quile NE.

coal-box (coal) bunker.

coal-bucket baikie, backet.

coal-dust dross.

coalfish saithe, rock-halibut NE; (*young*) cuddie, podlie NE, E CENTRAL.

coarse *adj* coorse; (*of persons, manners etc*) teuch, ruch, raucle, illfaured; (*of language*) randie; (*of texture*) groff, ramsh, great; (*of flax, fibre*) haskie.

coat *n* cot, cwite NE; (*animal pelt*) sloch.

coating (*surface, of paint*) skaik NE; (*thin, of snow etc*) skliff(er), skirvin SOUTH, skimmin SHETLAND, NE.

coat-hanger shooders.

coax *v* fleetch, cook NE.

cobble *v* souter.

cobbler souter.

cobblestone *n* causey stane, cassie, sett.

cobweb *n* moose wab.

cock *n* (*bird*) cockieleerie.

cocky croose, massie.

cockade *n* hackle, heckle.

cockroach *n* clo(a)ker.

cod, codfish *n* (*large*) keelin.

coffin *n* kist, deid-kist.

  laying a corpse in a coffin kistin.

cohabitee *n* bidie-in *originally* NE.

coil *v* pirl, wammle; (*a rope*) faik.

  n pirl, swirl, fank.

coincide *v* complouter.

cold *adj* caul(d), cald, caal N, cowl(d) SHETLAND, ORKNEY, CAITHNESS, ROSS, ARGYLL, ULSTER; (*causing or likely to feel cold*) cauldrif(e); (*feeling very cold*) stervin (wi caul(d)), perisht wi caul(d); (*looking cold and miserable*) nithert, oorie; (*in manner*) cauldrif(e); (*of the weather: bitterly*) snell, thin; (*and raw*) oorie; (*and showery*) bleeterie NE.

  n **1** (*extreme*) jeel. **2** (*illness*) dose o the caul(d); (*severe*) snifters, sneevils, snochers; (*thick, choking*) smuchter NE; (*slight*) glisk o caul(d).

  cold as ice *see* **ice.**

  run cold (*of blood etc*) grue.

  infected by a cold cauldit: '*Ye're still cauldit*'.

collapse *v* come in; (*of a person: from exhaustion etc*) foon(d)er.

collar *n* (*of a coat or shirt*) neck.

  collarbone hausebane.

collect *v* **1** lift; (*goods or persons*) uplift; (*money etc*) ingaither; (*eg subscriptions*) gaither; (*eg at a meeting*) tak up; (*taxes, wages etc*) uplift. **2** (*in crowds*) hatter.

  collection (*of things*) menyie N, smytrie NE; (*confused, of things*) mixtermaxter, hatter.

  collection plate brod.

colour *n*: **colourless** (*pale*) peelie-wallie, fauchie N; (*of personality*) peeliewersh.

  brightly coloured roarie, skirie ORKNEY, NE.

colt *n* cowt, clip NE.

  coltsfoot tushilago, shilagie.

columbine *n* grannie's mutch(es).

comb *n* kaem; (*of bird*) tap.

  v kaem.

combat *v* kemp.

combine *v* gae thegither.

come *v* win.

  came *past tense* cam, come.

  come *past participle* came.

  come back soon! haste ye back!

  come in come in by.

  come on! come awa(y)!, c'wa! NE; (*in encouragement etc*) gaun yersel!

  come together gae thegither, ging thegither NE.

comfort *n* easement; **home comforts** thack an raip.

comfortable 1 (*cosy, snug*) bien, fine, cannie, cantie, croose NE. **2** (*well off*) richt eneuch, nae ill aff.

comic *n* (*amusing person*) tear, divert: '*Yer faither's a richt divert*'.

command *n* biddin.

  Ten Comandments Comman(d)s.

  person in command heid bummer.

comment *n* observe, speak.

commerce *n* traffeck, mercat.

committee *n* comatee.

common *adj* **1** cowmon NE. **2** (*jointly owned*) mean.

  n (*land*) muir.

  commoner carle.

common sense *n* smeddum, mense, wit, rummle-gumption.

commotion *n* stushie, stashie, stour: '*raise a stour*', tirr-wirr, hurry.

communal staircase *n* (*into a block of flats*) common stair; (*along with entrance*) close.

communication *n* traffeck.

Communion *n* (*in the Presbyterian churches*) sacrament.

  service held before communion preparatory service.

compact *adj* (*neat*) snod.

companion *n* marrow, compaingen N, fere *literary*.

company *n* (*of people*) gaitherin; (*especially sociable*) core, quorum NE.

company of two, three *etc* twasome, threesome etc.

compare *v* even (wi).

in comparison with by, by's, tae, forby.

compass *n*: **point of the compass** airt.

compensation *n* mends.

compete *v* (*especially in work*) kemp.

competition competeetion.

competent *adj* lik(e)ly, nae bad (at).

complain *v* compleen, murn, grudge; (*at length*) rant; (*bad-temperedly*) girn; (*whine*) yammer, peenge, pewl.

always complaining girnin.

someone who is always complaining girn(ie), greetin Teenie, greetin face.

complaint *n* mane.

complete *adj* (*whole*) hail; (*absolute*) fair: '*Ye're a fair disgrace*'.

completely fair, hail, haillie.

complex *adj* (*intricate*) quirky, fikie; (*tricky*) pernicketie, kittle.

comply *v* come tae, complouter.

composition *n* composeetion.

compost heap *n* midden.

comprehend *v* tak up.

comprehension ken, uptak: '*slow i the uptak*'.

conceal *v* dern; (*by covering*) hap.

conceit *n* consait.

conceited conceitie, big: '*He's awfie big on it*', croose NE, pitten-on, set-up, cairried, saucy.

concentrate *v*: **concentrate on** (*intently*) gang hail-heidit for N.

concert *n* (*of Scottish, especially Highland music*) ceilidh.

conclusion *n*: **come to the wrong conclusion** hae the wrang soo by the lug, gang up the wrang dreel NE.

condensation *n* (*vapour*) (y)oam SHETLAND, ORKNEY, NE; (*eg on a glass*) gum N.

condescend *v*: **condescending** heich(-heidit).

condition *n* condeetion.

in good condition bien; (*of animals*) gawsie.

out of condition (*of people or animals*) (fat an) fozie.

conduct *v* conduck; (*escort*) convoy. *n* (*behaviour*) gate NE.

conference *n* collogue.

confide *v*: **have confidence in** lippen till.

confident croose.

confidently heid-heich.

confidential parteec(u)lar.

confound *v* confoon NE.

confuse *v* 1 (*muddle*) taigle, taisle. 2 (*a person*) confeese, raivel, ramfeezle.

confused 1 (*in a muddle*) throuither, throwder NE, mixter-maxter, reel-rall. 2 (*of a person*) bumbazit, waun(n)ert, moidert, in a creel, taivert; (*especially because of age*) donnert.

confused story *etc* ham-a-haddie.

confusion 1 (*muddle*) hurry-burry, swither, kirn, picher NE, heeliegoleerie. 2 (*of a person*) throuitherness.

congenial *adj* couthie.

congregate *v* forgaither.

connect *v* conneck.

conscience *n*: **conscientious** eydent.

be conscience-stricken tak guilt tae yersel.

conscious *adj*: **be conscious of** find.

consecrate *v* sain.

consequence *n*: **consequences** efterins.

in consequence of ower the heid(s) o.

take the consequences (of something) dree yer weird, dree the dirdum(s).

consider *v* conseeder, consither N.

considerable gey, bonnie, queer; (*of sums of money etc*) braw.

considerable number gey wheen, hantle.

considerably gey.

console *v* mane.

conspicuous *adj* conspeecuous, kenspeckle.

conspire *v* collogue, colleague NE.

conspiracy pack.

constant *adj* **1** (*of work etc*) close. **2** (*faithful*) leal.

constantly aye '*He's aye at me for sweeties*', even on, everly.

consult *v* inquire at, speir at.

contact *n*: **come into contact with** awn, own.

contagion *n* smit: '*gie someone the smit*'.

contagious smittin, smitsome.

infect by contagion smit.

contain *v* (*hold*) conteen.

contaminate *v* smit.

contemporary *adj* (*of the same age*) ages wi.

contempt *n* sneist.

contemptuous sneistie.

contemptuous term for a person nyaff, skite, waff, toalie, wunner N.

exclamation of contempt yer grannie!: '*hopeful yer grannie*'.

content *v* pleesure.

adj, see **contented.**

contented cantie, fine.

contest *n* tousle; (*eg for first place*) kemp.

continue *v* conteena, haud.

continually ivver an on, aye.

continuous eend on SOUTH; (*especially of rain*) eydent.

continuously even on, still an on.

contort *v* thraw.

contortion (*especially of the face*) thraw.

contract *n* contrack.

v contrack; (*shrink*) gae in.

contradict *v* conterdick, conter, contrair, na-say.

contradiction na-say.

contraption *n* (*fantastic*) whigmaleerie, ferlie NE.

contrary *adj* **1** (*opposite*) contrair, conter. **2** (*perverse, wilful*) contrair, thrawn, contermacious, maggotive NE.

n contrair, conter NE.

go contrary to contrair.

contribute *v* contreebute.

contribution (*of money for some purpose*) inpit.

control *v* guide, maun, haud.

n owerance.

have complete control hae (the) heft an (the) blade in yer han(d).

beyond control neither tae haud nor tae bind.

under control sicker.

have (someone) under control lead (someone) by the neb.

keep under control keep *or* haad in his *etc* ain neuk SHETLAND, NE.

controversy *n* threap, collieshangie NE, argie-bargie.

engage in controversy threap.

convene *v* (*meet*) forgaither, tryst.

convenient *adj* hantie.

conversation *n* crack, gab, news, speak; (*intimate*) corrieneuchin; (*whispered*) collogue, toot-moot; (*between two people*) twa-handit crack.

get into conversation (with) get on the crack (wi), hae a news (wi).

convict *v* convick.

convivial *adj* conveevial, hertie, joco.

convulsion *n* thraw; (*in coughing*) kink.

coo *v* (*of an infant*) goo; ((*as*) *of a pigeon*) rookettie-coo, curdoo.

cook *v* cuik, ready; (*badly*) mismak.

cooked meal made diet SHETLAND, NE.

cooking pot (*large*) kettle, muckle pot.

cool *adj* cuil, cweel NE; (*of air, water etc*) caller.

cooperate *v* complouter; (*with neighbours*) neibour (wi).

cooperative society (shop) coperative, store, co, copie NE, sosh ANGUS, FIFE.

copious *adj* lairge NE, rowthie; (*of a drink*) heavy.

copy *n* neibour, marrow.

cord *n* towe.

cordial *adj* (*friendly*) hertie, sonsie, guidwillie.

cormorant *n* scarf, skart, Mochrum elder sw.

corn *n* (*grain*) stuff.

corncrake craik.

corn-dolly *see* **last sheaf of corn at harvest** *below*.

cornflower blawort, blaver, blue bonnets.

last sheaf of corn at harvest, corn-dolly cailleach, clyack (sheaf) NE, carline NE, kirn (dollie).

corner *n* **1** (*of or in a building*) gushet; (*of the mouth or eye*) wick. **2** (*remote place*) neuk.

cornerstone scuncheon.

having corners neukit.

corpse *n* corp, bouk.

correct *adj* correck.

v correck, sort.

corridor *n* (*in a building*) trance, througaun, pass ULSTER.

cost *n* chairge.

cosy *adj* bien, cosh, snod.

cottage *n* cot(tar) hoose; (*two-roomed*) but an ben.

group of farm cottages cot-toon.

people living in farm cottages cot(tar)-fowk.

row of farm cottages hinds' raw SE.

row of miners' cottages miners' raw.

cotton *n*: **cotton-grass** *n* bog-cotton.

cotton wool wad(din), cotton oo.

cough *v* coaf, hoast; (*loudly*) bowf (an hoast); (*violently*) husk; (*huskily, with a wheeze*) craighle; (*especially to clear the throat*) hauch; (*asthmatically, especially to clear the throat*) pyocher SHETLAND, NE; (*in a subdued asthmatic way*) pech; (*sharply, with a tickle*) kicher.

n coaf, hoast; (*loud*) bowf; (*slight*) crickle: 'a crickle i the thrapple'; (*so bad as to cause anxiety*) kirkyaird hoast.

fit of coughing kink.

cough up hoast up, hask.

could *see* **can**[1].

coulter *n* cooter.

council *n* cooncil.

council house estate (*housing*) scheme.

counsel *n* coonsel.

count *n* coont.

countless coontless.

count out (*money*) tell doon SHETLAND.

counter *n* coonter.

counteract *v* conter.

country *n* countra, kintra, cwintry N. *adj* lan(d)wart.

country person teuchter.

towards the country lan(d)wart.

county *n* coontie.

couple *n, v* kipple.

courage *n* saul; (*spirit*) smeddum.

courageous croose NE; (*ready to fight*) fechtie, nae fleggit NE.

course *n* coorse.

in due course in coorse, syne.

of course in coorse.

court *n* coort; (*supreme civil in Scotland*) Court of Session; (*supreme criminal in Scotland*) High Court of Justiciary, *informally* High Court; (*presided over by a sheriff, criminal and civil*) Sheriff Court; (*lowest criminal*) district court.

v gae thegither, winch; (*someone*) coort (wi), gae (oot) wi, be thrang wi.

courting winchin.

courtyard close EDINBURGH.

courteous *adj* hamelie, mensefu, gentie.

courtesy mense.

cousin *n* kizzen.

second cousin half-cousin.

cover *v* kivver, hap; (*thickly with snow etc*) smore.

n kivver, hap, **covers** (*of a book*) batters.

covered over happit.

covering (*especially for protection against cold etc*) hap; (*especially outer*) huil; (*thin, of soil, snow etc*) skirvin SOUTH, skimmer.

covet *v* hae yer ee in.

cow *n* coo, baist, beast; *pl also* **kye.**
  cow-dung sha(i)rn.
  cow-lick coo's lick.
  cowshed byre.
coward *n* feardie, feartie, cooard, cootcher, fugie.
  cowardly cooard(l)ie, hen-hertit, hennie, fugie.
cower *v* coor(ie), slootch, jouk.
  cower down coorie doon.
cowl *n* cool.
cowrie, cowrie shell *n* John o Gro(a)t's buckie, groatie buckie SHETLAND, ORKNEY, N.
coy *adj* skeich.
crab *n* (*especially large edible*) partan, poo SE.
crab-apple *n* scrab, scrag SE.
crabbed *adj* crabbit.
crack *v* creck, rive; (*make a cracking sound*) knack, knick ORKNEY, N, nicker SHETLAND; (*a whip*) cleesh SOUTH.
  n creck: **1** (*split*) gaig, jink, rive SHETLAND. **2** (*cracking sound*) knick SHETLAND, ORKNEY, NE.
  cracked (*of the skin*) hackit.
crackle *v* crunkle; (*eg of ice when trodden on*) crump NE; (*of food when frying*) skirl, sotter.
  n (*of fat etc in a pan*) skirl, sotter.
  crackly (*eg of snow or ice*) crumpie, crumshie NE.
craft *n*: **crafty** sleekit, slee(k)ie, gleg, pawkie(-wittit), soople.
  craftiness sneck-drawin.
  craftsman tradesman, wricht.
crag *n* heuch, scaur, sker SOUTH.
cram *v* stap, pang; (*especially with food*) stowe, stech.
crane *n* (*hoist or bird*) cran.
  v (*the neck*) rax.
cranny *n* bore, jink.
crash *n* stramash.
  v (*crash about*) breenge.
crave *v*: **crave (for), have a craving for** (*of a pregnant woman for certain foods*) hae a greenin for, green for.

crawl *v* crowl; (*laboriously, clumsily, eg through something*) spra(u)chle.
crazy *adj* daft (aboot), gyte, radge, feel NE.
creak *v, n* craik, chirk, jirg.
cream *n* ream.
  creamy reamie.
  cream jug (*ream*) poorie.
crease *v* runkle, cress, gruggle NE.
  creased runklie, runkelt.
creature *n* craitur, baist, beast.
credit *n* (*honour*) mense.
  buy on credit tak on.
credulous person *n* bluff NE.
creek *n* slock, gote, geo SHETLAND, ORKNEY, CAITHNESS.
creep *v* (*of the flesh*) grue.
  crept *past tense* creepit, crap NE.
  past participle creepit, cruppen.
crest *n* (*of a bird*) tap, tappin; (*of a hill*) rig, kame.
  crested (*of a bird*) tappit.
  crested hen tappit hen.
  be crestfallen hing yer lugs.
criminal *n* creeminal.
cringe *v* creenge, coorie, sneevil, snuil.
  cringing person snuil.
crinkle *v* crunkle.
crippled *adj* cripple.
  crippled person lameter.
crisp *adj* crumpie, crumshie NE; (*of ice, in curling*) keen.
  fried until crisp weel-birselt.
  make crisp (*food by heat*) harn.
critic *n* creetic.
  take a critical look at (*appraisingly*) tak (a) swatch o, (*scrutinize*) scance.
  criticize criticeese, quarrel, be at; (*severely*) hae yer horn in someone's hip.
  never finished criticizing never aff someone's tap.
  criticism (*sharp*) heckle.
croak *v* roup; (*of a bird*) craik; (*of a person coughing*) craighle.
  n craik.
crockery *n* cheenie; (*everyday*) delft.
croft *n* craft NE.

crook *n* **1** (*shepherd's*) nibbie, crummock. **2** *see* **criminal**.

crooked thrawn, gley(e)d, neukit.

crop *n* **1** crap. **2** (*bird's*) gebbie.

v (*very short*) rump.

cross *v* **1** (*eg the legs*) plet. **2** (*stop someone doing something*) thorter. **3** **cross yourself** sain yersel.

adj crabbit, canker(i)t.

cross your mind come up yer back: '*Ye only phone yer mother when it comes up yer back*', come up yer humph.

crouch *v* crootch, coorie (doon), clap (doon), hunker (doon).

crow[1] *n* (*bird*) craw, craa N.

crowbar gavelock, pinch(er).

crow's feet craw-taes.

crowsteps crawsteps, corbie stanes.

gathering of crows craws' waddin.

crow[2] *v* **1** (*of a cock etc*) craw. **2** (*boast*) blaw, bum.

n (*of a cock etc*) craw, cockieleerie (law).

crowd *n* crood, menyie, mardle NE, thrang, clamjamfrie *contemptuous;* (*especially of children*) smarrach NE.

v (*together*) hotter; (*from cold*) hugger NE.

crowded thrang, ho(a)tchin.

crowded out stowed oot.

crown *n* croon; (*of the head*) powe, cantle NE.

v croon.

crude *adj* (*especially of character*) coorse, ruch, roch, raucle.

cruel *adj* ill, ill-set, fell, coorse.

cruelly sair: '*He treated her sair*'.

treat cruelly mischieve SHETLAND, NE.

crumb *n* moolin, meelack(ie) NE.

crumble *v* crummle, murl; (*away*) moot.

crumbly bruckle, frush.

crumpet *n* crimpet NE; NB in Scotland usually refers to a large thin **dropped scone**.

crumple *v* runkle.

crumpled runkelt, runklie.

crunch *v* crinch, crump.

crunchy crinchie.

if it comes to the crunch if hard comes tae hard.

crupper *n* crupple sw, SOUTH, curpin NE.

crush *v* runkle, smush, pran NE; (*flat, with a slap*) scone.

crust *n* (*surface layer*) scruif; (*of a loaf: flat bottom*) sole.

crutch *n* stilt.

go on crutches stilt.

cry *v* **1** (*shout, scream*) roup; (*shrilly*) skirl, scronach. **2** (*weep*) greet, bubble, walloch NE; (*loudly*) roar an greet. **3** (*of a bird or animal*) yowt; (*shrilly*) skraich, claik NE; (*feebly*) peek; (*harshly*) craik.

n **1** (*shout, scream*) yowt; (*shrill*) scronach NE, skirl, claik NE; (*sharp*) wheep; (*wailing*) pewl. **2** (*weep*) greet: '*hae a guid greet*'. **3** (*of a bird, shrill*) skraich, peek; (*especially of curlew*) wheeple.

cry-baby greetin Teenie.

about to cry great-hertit.

apt to cry greetie, bubblie: '*She's awfie bubblie since her man died*'.

bout of crying greetin match.

crystal *n* kirstal.

as clear as crystal as plain as parritch.

cuckoo *n* gowk, gowkoo.

cuckoo-spit gowk-spit(tle).

cud *n* cood, cweed NE.

cuddle *v* knuse, oxter; (*amorously*) smoorich, soss NE.

n smoorich, bosie.

cuddle in coorie in.

cudgel *n* rung.

v loonder, rung, timmer.

cuff[1] *n* (*of a shirt*) han(d)-ban(d).

cuff[2] *n* (*slap*) fung, ringer.

v fung NE, ring, soose, cloor.

culvert *n* cundie.

cunning *adj* sleekit, sleek, soople, quirkie.

n sneck-drawin, slicht.

cup *n* tass(ie) *literary*; (*especially of wood*) bicker, cap; (*shallow, two-handled, often used as a trophy*) quaich.

cupboard *n* aumrie; (*especially in wall*) press, bole.

curb *v* crub, pit the haims on, pit the branks on.

n crub.

curd *n* **curds** cruds, yirned milk.

curdle lapper, yirn; (*of milk*) rin SHETLAND.

curdled cruddie; (*of milk in churn*) broken.

cure *v* **1** (*heal*) cuir, keer NE, mend. **2** (*meat, butter etc*) poother; (*fish, ham etc, by drying or smoking*) reest; (*fish etc, by drying*) rizzer.

n cuir, keer NE.

curio *n* ferlie.

curious *adj* (*inquisitive*) kwerious NE.

curiosity 1 keeriositie NE. **2** (*marvel*) ferlie.

curl *n* (*eg of hair*) pirl SOUTH, link SHETLAND, swirl.

v (*eg of hair*) pirl, runkle, wimple.

curly (*especially of hair*) swirlie, pirlie SOUTH.

curling (*the game*) the roarin gemm.

curling game (*one of a series in a match*) rink; (*part of, from one end of the rink to the other*) en(d).

curling match bonspiel.

play at curling curl.

curlew whaup, whitterick.

cry of the curlew wheeple.

currant *n* curran, curn SOUTH.

current *n* (*strong, in sea*) rug; (*of air*) guff.

currency siller: '*Whit kinna siller dae they yaise in France?*'.

curry favour *v* sook in, sook up, haud in, smool, sleek.

curse *v* jeedge NE, VOO ORKNEY, NE.

cursory glance *n* (quick) swatch.

curt *adj* nippit, cuttit NE.

curtains *npl* hingers.

curtsy *v, n* beck, jouk.

curve *v, n* boo.

cushion *n* cushin, cod.

custody *n*: **take into custody** lift: '*The polis has liftit her man*', tak in.

custom *n* (*habit*) haunt; (*in business*) cheenge NE.

customer merchant NE.

cut *v* (*whittle with a knife*) white, fite NE; (*cut with a knife or hook*) scutch; (*cut short or off*) snib; (*very short*) rump; (*roughly*) hagger NE, risp; (*unevenly*) haggle; (*hair etc*) cowe, coll; (*peats*) cast; (*cloth to a pattern*) shape.

past tense, past participle cuttit.

n **1** sned, whack; (*slight*) sneck; (*deep, jagged*) hagger NE. **2** (*act of cutting*) sneck.

cut down (*trees*) hag.

cut the hair of poll.

cut into sneck.

cut off nick, snib, sneck, sned.

cuttlefish *n* ink-fish, hose-fish.

cylinder *n* ceelinder.

D

dab *v, n* (*light touch*) daub, pap.

dabble *v* **1** (*in liquid*) slaister, slitter, skiddle, plowter, plyter NE; (*in something messy*) slatch. **2** (*potter, waste time*) dauble NE, pingle SE.

dad *n, see also* **father;** dey, paw CENTRAL.

daddy-long-legs *n* jennie-lang-legs, jennie spinner, speeder jennie, spin(nin) maggie.

daffodil *n* (yella) lily; (*pheasant's eye*) white lily, fite lily NE.

daft *adj* glaikit, no wyce NE.

dagger *n* (*short, worn as part of the Highland dress: in belt*) dirk, durk, (*in stocking*) sgian dubh.

dainty *adj* dentie, conceitie; (*of people*) jimp, gentie; (*especially of women*) dink.

daisy *n* gowan.

  ox-eye daisy horse gowan; (*large*) white gowan.

dam *n* (*of stones in a river*) stem. *v* dem NE.

damage *v* skaith, tash, connach. *n* skaith; (*to clothes etc*) tash.

  damaged fruit chippit fruit.

  damages (*compensation*) mends.

dame *n* deem NE.

damn *v* (*in oaths*) dang.

  damned dampt.

  not give a damn no care a docken, no jee yer ginger.

damp *adj* dunk, clam; (*of weather*) saft, drowie, weetie SHETLAND, NE; (*and raw*) oorlich N.
n (*mouldy*) dunk.

  damp down (*a fire*) smoor, reest.

dance *v* birl, shak a fit.
n bob; (*Scottish country dance: lively*) reel, (*slower*) strathspey; (*kind of solo Highland*) Hieland fling.

dancing (*eg at a dance-hall*) jiggin: '*We're gaun tae the jiggin*'.

dandelion *n* dentylion, pee-the-bed.

dandle *v* (*a child*) diddle, daidle, showd NE.

dandruff *n* scruif.

danger *n*: **dangerous** uncannie, unchancie, nae mows NE, sair: '*It's sair climbin up Arthur's Seat*'; (*insecure*) crankie.

  free from danger sicker.

dangle *v* hing.

dapper *adj* (*neat*) trig, feat, perjink.

dare *v* daur; (*mainly negative*) dow: '*I downa dae it*'; (*past used as present*) durst: '*He durstna*'; (*challenge to do something*) hen.

  daring *adj* derf, gallus.

dark *adj* daurk, derk; (*gloomy*) mirksome, douth SOUTH.

  dark(ness) mirk(ness).

  grow dark gloam: '*I dinna like drivin when it's gloamin*', mirken SHETLAND.

  sit in the dark sit lik craws i the mist.

darling *n* dautie, hinnie, doo, jo, cushie(-doo).

darn *v* ranter.

dart *n* dert, dairt; (*in game*) arra(e); (*weapon*) prog SHETLAND, ORKNEY, CAITHNESS.

v dert, dairt, skite, skoosh: '*bairns aye skooshin aboot under yer feet*'; (*especially of people*) spoot, jouk, skilt SOUTH; (*especially from side to side*) jink; (*in and out of sight*) cook.

  darts (*game*) arra(e)s.

dash *v* **1** (*of liquid*) jaw, jaup, spairge. **2** (*with violence*) ding, dad, wap. **3** (*hurtle*) hurl.

n **1** (*of liquid*) sloosh, skoosh: '*a wee skoosh o water in ma whisky*', jaw, jaup, plype NE. **2** (*with violence*) swinge.

date *n* (*meeting*) tryst: '*Ah've a tryst at eight o'cloak*'.

daub *n* sclatch, slair.

daughter *n* dochter, lass(ie), lass(ie) bairn, lass(ie) wean WEST, ULSTER, quine NE.

daughter-in-law guid-dochter.

dawdle *v* daidle, diddle, dachle NE.

dawdler jotter.

dawn *n* (day-)daw.

v daw, gray.

day *n*: **daydream** dwam, sloom.

daydreaming *adj* in a dwam, nae in.

daylight daylicht, sky; **broad daylight** fair daylicht.

day's work (day's) darg.

on alternate days day an day aboot.

during the day throu the day.

in those days than-a-days NE, aan NE: '*Fit did e dee aan?*'

daze *v* donner, stoon(d).

dazed bumbazit, dozent, doilt.

dazed-looking wull-lik(e) NE.

dazzle *v* daizzle; (*with wonder etc*) glamour.

dead *adj* deid, gane awa.

deadly deidlie.

deaf *adj* deef, corn beef *rhyming slang*.

deafen deefen; (*especially with noise*) deave.

deaf person deefie.

deal *n* dale, troke.

v **1** (*trade*) dale, traffeck. **2** (*a blow etc*) len, reak.

dealer dailer, cowper, troker.

dealings traffeck; (*sometimes undesirable*) troke.

have dealings with mird wi NE, mell wi, parry wi; (*often undesirable*) troke wi.

a great deal a gey wheen, a fair few, a fair fyeow NE.

dear *adj* (*expensive*) saut.

n: **my dear** my jo *in poetry*.

death *n* daith, deid, hame-gaun, hinneren(d).

decay *v* murl, moze SHETLAND, ORKNEY, CAITHNESS; (*slowly*) moot.

decayed mozie.

deceit *n* cheatrie, joukerie-pawk(e)rie, swickerie NE.

deceitful sleekit, slidderie, twafaul(d) NE.

deceitful person sneck-drawer.

deceive *v* swick, jouk, mislippen, blear (someone's) ee.

decent *adj* dacent, weel-faured, honest, wicelik(e).

decency honesty.

deception *n* intak, swick, sook NE.

decision *n* deceesion.

decline *v* (*in health*) dwine, fa(w) awa; (*of things*) tyne.

decrease *v*: **stitches decreased** (*knitting*) intaks.

decrepit *adj* decrippit NE.

dedicate *v*: **dedicate yourself to** stick in wi.

deduce *v* jalouse.

deep *adj* howe.

deep (in) up tae the oxters (in), ower the hurdies (in): '*ower the hurdies in debt*'.

deep-set howe.

defeat *v* defait, warsle, win N, baist NE.

defeated defait, defeat, bate.

defecate *v* shite, keech, kich NE, cack(ie).

defect *n* defeck, defection, gaw; (*eg in a fishing line or net*) want.

be mentally defective hae a want.

defence *n* fend.

defend fend, weir.

defend yourself haud aff (o) yersel NE; (*especially in a fight*) keep aff o yersel.

defendant (*law, in a civil case*) defender; (*in a criminal case*) accused, panel.

defiance *n*: **defiant** forritsome, facie.

act in defiance of maugre NE.

definition *n* defineetion.

deformed *adj* palie, wrang NE, camsha(u)chelt; (*especially of a limb*) tuckie NE.

defraud *v* swick, snipe NE.

deft *adj* knackie, gleg, slee.

defy *v* thraw (wi).

dejected *adj* disjaskit, hingin-luggit, hingin-mou'd NE.

delay *v* taigle, latch NE, hing (someone) on NE.

n aff-pit, hing-on.

  cause of delay hinder, affset.

  causing delay taiglesome.

  without delay in a couple of hurries.

deliberate *adj* deleebrit, cannie.

delicate *adj* **1** (*in health*) dowie, peelie-wallie CENTRAL, peelie-wersh SOUTH, shilpit, dortie NE. **2** (*difficult, awkward*) kittle, tickly NE, fykie.

delicious *adj* deleecious.

delight *v, n* delicht.

  delighted suitit, hert-gled.

  delightful loosome, lichtsome.

delirious *adj* deleerit, raivelt, cairried, ree.

  delirium raverie.

delusion *n* phrase NE.

demeanor *n* cast.

demon *n* wirricow; (*living in water*) kelpie, water horse.

demure *adj* perjink, mim (as a Mey puddock).

denounce *v* misca(w), wyte; (*publicly and violently*) sherrack WEST.

dense *adj* **1** (*closely-packed*) thrang; (*of growth*) ruch; (*of mist etc*) blin(d) NE. **2** (*stupid*) glaikit, steekit.

dent *n* dunt NE, dinge; (*especially in metal*) cloor.

v cloor, dunt NE, dinge.

dentures *npl* wallies, seam o teeth.

deny *v* na-say.

  denial na-say.

depart *v* depairt, tak the gate, leg aff.

  departure ootgang.

depend *v*: **depend on** lippen.

  dependable sicker, stench NE, stieve.

depress *v*: **depressed** disjaskit, doon o mooth.

  depressed dreich.

  depression 1 (*hollow*) howe. **2** (*state of*) howes: '*be i the howes*'.

deprive *v* (*a person of something*) twin(e); (*of everything*) roop.

  be deprived of tyne NE.

deputy *n* depute *often after its noun:* '*principal depute*'.

deranged *adj* gyte, wud, wrang NE.

descend *v* gang doon.

desert *v* gie ower, forleet.

  deserter fugie.

desire *v* wiss, seek (tae); (*very much*) ettle efter.

n ettle, will.

  mad with desire gyte.

desolate *adj* (*of a place*) gowstie.

destiny *n* weird: '*dree yer weird*'.

destroy *v* hash: '*Dinnae hash yer new fitba bits*', malafooster.

destructive *adj* sair: '*She's sair on her claes*'.

detach *v* lowse, twine SHETLAND.

detective *n* snoot.

detention *n*: **pupil in detention after school** keepie-in.

deteriorate *v* gae back; (*in health, fortune*) gae doon the brae: '*She's gaun doon the brae since she had a shock*', fail.

determined *adj* dour, positive.

detest *v* laith, ug.

  detestation scunner, ug NE.

  detestable laithsome, scunnersome, ugsome, pooshionous SHETLAND, N.

development *n* oncome SHETLAND, NE.

devil *n* deil, divil, deevil, the bad man, Auld Nick, Auld Cloots, Auld Hornie.

  devilish deevilish, divilish.

  devilry deviltrie.

  devil-may-care ramstam.

  gone to the devil gane tae potterlowe NE.

devise *v* think on NE.

devoted *adj*: **devoted to** (*a person*) browdent on.

devour *v* devoor, gilravage, worry NE.

devout *adj* gracie; (*very*) far ben.

dew *n* weet.

dialogue *n* twa-handit crack.

diarrhoea *n* skitter, skit, backdoor trot(s), the thin(s) NE; (*especially in birds or animals*) scoot.

  have diarrhoea skitter, skite.

dictate *v*: **dictate to** (*order about*) come the peter ower.

dictionary *n* dictionar.

did not *see* do.

die *v* dee, weir awa; (*peacefully*) slip awa; (*especially after great suffering*) win awa.

  die down (*of wind etc*) lowden, lown, quall NE.

  die in harness dee i the harrows NE.

  die of dee wi: '*He'll dee wi the drink*'.

difficult *adj* defeeckwalt, crank; (*tricky*) fickle, kittle, tickly NE; (*troublesome*) ill; (*of tasks*) nae handy, fykie, dreich NE.

  difficulty diffeecultie.

  in difficulties raivelt, in a haud.

  having difficulty (in) ill: '*ill at gyaun*'.

  involving difficulty sair, ill.

  do something with difficulty warsle throu, wa(u)chle throu.

  difficult to please ill tae dae till *or* wi: '*Her man's awfie ill tae dae wi*'.

diffident *adj* blate.

dig *v* howk, hole, sheuch, dell SHETLAND, ORKNEY, N.

  dug *past tense, past participle* howkit: '*Ah howkit the tatties last week*'.

  digger (*person who digs*) howker: '*tattie howker*'.

  dig up (*eg potatoes*) howk, lift, hole NE.

digest *v*: **let food digest** swage ORKNEY, N.

dignified *adj* (*of a person*) pretty, mensefu.

dignity *n* mense SOUTH.

  with dignity heid-heich.

diligent *adj* eydent.

dilute *v* (*especially spirits*) mak doon, tak doon.

din *n* reemis(h) NE.

dine *v* denner.

dinner *n* denner, dine, kail.

  dinnertime dine, kail time.

dip *v* dook.

  n **1** (*in water*) dook. **2** (*in the ground*) sneck.

  dipper (*bird*) water craw.

direct *adj* direck: **1 most direct** soonest, seenest NE. **2** (*in manner*) plat (an plain).

  v direck, (*guide*) airt, wice; (*eg a blow*) ettle.

  direction (*way*) airt.

  in the direction of the wey o, -wan: '*east-wan*'.

  in that general direction there awa.

  directly direck, therecklie SW, SOUTH.

  directly after *adv* syne.

dirt *n* (*filth*) cla(i)rt, keech, goor SHETLAND, N; (*wet, dirty state*) slaister.

  dirty *adj* cla(i)rtie, mirkie; (*grimy*) brookie NE; (*dirty and wet*) slaisterie, cloiterie; (*greasy*) creeshie.

  v (*make dirty*) cla(i)rt, mairtyr; (*especially clothes*) drabble, slaister, slaiger; (*clothes*) scuddle; (*blacken*) bleck, coom, brook NE.

disabled *adj* (*of a limb*) tuckie NE.

disagree *v* (*quarrel*) cast oot, differ, skew NE.

  disagreeable coorse NE; (*of people*) menseless, ill-thraan SHETLAND, ORKNEY; (*of weather*) thrawn NE, thraan SHETLAND, ORKNEY, N.

  disagreement (*quarrel*) ootcast.

disappear *v* (*suddenly*) cook; (*very quickly*) disappear lik snaw aff the dyke.

disappoint *v* disappint, begeck, gie (someone) the gunk; (*greatly*) stammygaster.

  disappointed disappintit.

  disappointment disappintment, dunt; (*great*) sair hert; (*sudden, great*) stammygaster; (*bitter*) het hert; (*source of disappointment*) hert-scaud.

disarray *n*: **in disarray** throuither, throwder NE.

disaster *n* mishanter, stramash.

disbelieve v misbelieve, misdoot.

discipline n discipleen; (*very strict*) norter NE.

v discipleen, keep in aboot, pit the haims on; (*very strictly*) targe, norter NE.

discourage v daunton.

discouraged hertless.

discouraging hertless.

discreet adj cannie.

discretion n mense.

discuss v (*at length, in great detail*) summer an winter.

discussion (*talk*) collogue.

disdainful adj heich, sanshach NE; (*especially of women*) skeich.

disdainfully heich.

act disdainfully sneist.

disease n 1 tribble. 2 (*of animals, feverish*) weed.

disentangle v redd.

disgraceful adj michtie, awfu.

disguise v guise.

disgust v scunner, scomfish, ug, set NE, granich NE; (*intensely*) gar (someone) grue; (*with too much food*) staw.

n scunner, set NE, hert scaud, forlaithie NE, grue; (*for something edible*) skeichen NE.

disgusted scunnert, uggit NE.

be disgusted at tak a scunner at, tak the grue at, tak an ug at NE.

disgusting scunnersome, ugsome, uggin, foosome, feechie.

disgusting person or **thing** scunner, ug NE.

cause disgust to someone gie someone the (dry) boak.

exclamation of disgust feech!, peuch!; (*especially as a warning to a child*) keech!

object of disgust scunneration.

dish n (*wooden, deep*) cap: '*brose cap*'; (*wooden, especially for milk*) cood; (*wooden, with handles*) luggie; (*oval serving*) ashet.

dishcloth dish-cloot, daily dud NE.

dishearten v disherten.

disheartened hertless.

dishevelled adj (*especially of hair*) hudderie, tous(l)ie.

dishevelled person ticket.

dishonest adj unhonest, lowse.

disintegrate v gae (a(w)) tae staps, murl.

dislike n: **take a dislike to** hae a pick at, tak an ug at NE; (*strong*) tak a scunner at.

dislocate v ca(w) oot, rack.

dislocation (*of a joint etc*) rack.

disloyal adj slidderie.

dismal adj dreich, dowie, hertless, oorie NE.

dismiss v (*a meeting etc*) skail.

dismissal (*from a job*) leave.

dismount v (*from a horse*) lowp aff.

disorder n carfuffle: '*Whit a carfuffle this hoose is in!*', sotter, hatter, guddle. v carfuffle, raivel, guddle.

disordered, in disorder throuither, throwder NE, guddelt, tousie, sotterie.

disorderly throuither, throwder NE, huggerie(-muggerie); (*rough*) ramstougar.

disperse v (*of a crowd*) skail: '*The scuil's skailin*'; (*scatter*) sperfle *literary*; (*of cloud*) rive.

dispersal (*of a crowd etc*) skail(in).

display n shaw.

displease v misfit NE.

displeasure displeesure.

dispose v: **dispose of** get redd o, pit by SW, ULSTER; (*money, goods, etc*) ware.

dispute v argie-bargie, thraw, differ, strive SHETLAND, NE.

n argie-bargie, tift(er), threap; (*violent*) collieshangie.

disreputable adj coorse, orra, ruch.

disrespect n disrespeck.

disrupt v (*a group*) skail.

dissatisfied adj no (awfie) taen (wi).

dissect v disseck.

dissent n, v differ.

distance n (*length of way etc*) lenth: '*this lenth*', gate; (*short*) bittie, bittock, piece.

distant 1 yonder. **2** (*in family relationship*) far oot.

at a distance ootby, oot ower; **at a great distance** hyne awa, hyndies (awa) *child's word*, NE.

distaste *n* scunner; (*specifically for food*) skeichen NE.

distinct *adj* sindrie.

distort *v* showl, bauchle; (*the face*) girn; (*especially a meaning etc*) thraw.

distorted thrawn, camsha(u)chelt, bauchelt.

distortion thraw.

distract *v* distrack.

distracted distrackit.

distraction fry.

distressed *adj* made (wi) NE.

distressing sair.

distribute *v* distreebute.

district *n* destrick, kintra, airt.

distrust *v* misdoot, mislippen.

disturb *v* (*annoy*) fash, steer; (*startle*) start; **disturb yourself** mismak yersel.

disturbed (*of the mind*) ajee.

disturbance rammie, stushie, stramash, collieshangie, ca(w)-throu, carrant NE.

create a disturbance stramash.

ditch *n* dutch NE, sheuch, gote, trink.

dither *v*, *n* swither, footer, daiker.

ditherer swither.

dithering switherin, footerie.

dive *v* dook.

diver (*bird: great northern*) Allanhawk; (*great northern or red-throated*) loom NE.

diverge *v* twin(e), sinder, sinner.

diverse *adj* sindrie.

diversion (*entertainment*) divert.

divide *v* twin(e), sinder, sinner; (*into parts*) pairt; (*into two or more parts*) half; (*divide equally*) halve(r).

division *n* (*part, not necessarily one of two equals*) half.

division sums gizinties.

divulge *v* lat ken, lat licht NE, moot, leet SHETLAND, ORKNEY, N: '*nivver leet*'.

dizzy *adj* deezie, licht, waumish.

dizziness deeziness, mirligoes.

do *v* dae, dee.

does dis; **does not** disnae, disna.

do not dinnae, dinna, divna

did not *past tense* didnae, didna.

done *past participle* duin, deen NE, don SHETLAND.

done for awa wi't, puggelt, deen for NE.

done with past, by (wi('t)).

to do adae, adee NE: '*I'll hae naethin adae wi ye*'.

docile *adj* ill-less SHETLAND, NE, quate.

dock *n* (*plant*) docken.

doctor *n* doacter.

dodder *v* dotter, hochie.

dodge *v* jink, jouk; (*doing something*) scoff.

n (*trick*) prottick NE, gink NE, fuppertie jig NE.

dodge in and out jouk.

does *see* **do.**

dog *n* dug, dowg N, hund, tike *contemptuous*.

dogfight collieshangie NE, gurrie.

dogfish *n* hoe SHETLAND, ORKNEY, blinnd hoe SHETLAND.

dole *n*: **on the dole** on the b(u)roo, on the box.

dole money b(u)roo money.

doll *n* (*toy or girl*) dall(ie) NE.

dollop *n* slap, da(u)d.

dolphin *n* dunter.

dominate *v* maugre NE, maun SHETLAND.

domineering *adj* ringin, maisterfu, magerfu NE.

domineering boss master *or* mistress an mair.

domineering woman drum major.

act in a domineering way towards come the peter ower *or* wi: '*He thinks he can come the peter ower me!*'.

dominoes *npl*: **tap the table in a game of dominoes to indicate you cannot play** chap: '*I'm chappin*'.

done *see* **do.**

donkey *n* cuddie (ass), lang lugs *humorous*.

doom *n* weird.

door *n* door-cheek; (*to a single dwelling, as opposed to a block of flats*) main door.

door-catch sneck, snib.

door-handle hannle.

door-key check.

door knocker chapper.

doormat bass (mat).

door-post door-cheek, standart.

doorstep door-stane.

doorway door-cheek; **front doorway** entry.

dormer (window) *n* storm windae.

dote *v*: **dote on** daut.

doting fond, daft (on, aboot *or* for), saft (on).

in your dotage dottelt.

double *adj, adv, n* dooble.

bent double (*especially with age*) twafaul(d).

doubt *v* doot; (*disbelieve, distrust*) misdoot: '*Ah widnae misdoot ye fur a minute*', misbelieve, mislippen; (*be in doubt*) swither.

n doot, misdoot: **state of doubt** swither.

doubtful dootsome.

without doubt (for) shair.

dough *n* daich.

doughy daichie.

dove *n* doo.

dovecot doocot.

down[1] *n* (*soft plumage*) doon.

down[2] *adv* doon.

downfall whummle.

downpour plump: '*It looks like a plump*', poor, onding, plash.

downright ringin, evendoon.

downstairs doon the stair.

downtrodden sair hauden doon (by the bubbly jock).

down-and-out *adj* on the street(s).

down-at-heel 1 (*of shoes*) ba(u)chelt, sha(u)chlin. **2** (*of a person*) scuffie, ill-faured.

down the road doon-by.

down there doon-by.

doze *v* dover, snotter, dove NE, gloss NE.

n dover: '*Ah'll just have a wee dover in the chair*', gloss, slug WEST, SW.

doze off dover ower.

dozing (nid) nid noddin, neebin SHETLAND.

dozen *n* dizzen.

drab *adj* dreich.

draft *n, see also* **draught;** (*rough draft*) scroll.

drag *v* **1** rug; (*violently or roughly*) harl; (*through mud etc; something heavy*) tra(u)chle; (*yourself laboriously*) harl, haik. **2** (*a river etc, for a corpse*) grapple.

n (*act of dragging*) harl.

dragon *n* draigon.

drain *v* **1** (*a glass etc*) tuim, teem N. **2** (*pour liquid from, especially potatoes*) dreep, poor: '*poor the tatties*', teem.

n (*drainage channel*) sheuch, dreep; (*covered*) cundie, syver.

drainpipe (*from a roof-gutter*) rone pipe.

drank *see* **drink.**

draught *n* draucht.

draughts *npl* the dams, the dambrod NE.

draw *v* rug; (*of a chimney*) vent, pou: '*The chimney needs swept, it'll no pou*'.

drawer (*small, in a chest etc*) shottle.

dread *v, n* dreid.

dreadful awfu, awfie, aafu NE, dreidfae.

dreamy *adj* dwamie, dwamish; (*of the eyes*) far ben.

away in a dream awa in a dwam.

dreary *adj* dreich, drearifu.

dredge *v, n* (*especially for shellfish*) dreg.

dress *v* hap.

dressed set-on; (*finely*) weel-pit(ten)-on.

dressed-up brammed up WEST; (*especially of women*) dink.

oddly-dressed woman Teenie fae Troon, Teenie fae the neeps E CENTRAL.

dresser (*kitchen*) bink.

dressing-gown wrapper NE.

dressy fussy.

dress up tosh up, tip up NE.

dribble *v* **1** dreeble, driddle; (*messily*) slitter, slabber. **2** (*in football*) pirl NE. *n* dreeble.

dribbler slitter.

drift *n* (*of snow*) wreath.

drill *v, n* dreel.

drink *v* (*greedily*) slorp; (*quench thirst*) weet yer thrapple; (*drink alcohol in small amounts*) taste; (*continuously in small amounts*) sirple.

n **1** (*a drink*) slock, sowp; (*wishy-washy*) skink, blash, skiddle; (*thirst-quenching*) slockener. **2** (*alcohol, a drink*) dram (NB *any size*), sup, drappie; (*large quantity of drink*) bucket: '*He can tak a guid bucket*', blash NE.

drank *past tense* drunk: '*She drunk aw the juice*'.

drinker (*heavy*) drouth.

on a drinking bout on the bash.

drip *v* dreep, sype; (*of small drops*) pink ORKNEY, NE.

n **1** dreep, sype. **2** (*person*) Sammy Dreep, sumph.

dripping *adj* sypin, sappie.

n (*fat*) rander, dreepin.

drip-dry *v* sype.

drive *v* **1** (*cause to move*) (1) (*a vehicle, animals, a plough, a load*) ca(w). (2) (*specifically in a wheeled vehicle*) hurl. **2** (*be conveyed, in any vehicle*) sail SW, SOUTH. **3** (*push forward: violently*) ding; (*especially with blows*) skelp; (*hustle*) dreel NE; (*hard*) haik. **4** (*of wind, rain*) dad.

n **1** (*in a wheeled vehicle*) drave, hurl, sail SW, SOUTH. **2** (*energy*) smeddum, virr, throu-ca(w), ca-throu NE.

drove *past tense* drave, dreeve NE.

drive away (*by frightening*) fley (awa), gliff SOUTH; (*in terror*) ramscooter; (*illness etc*) fleg.

drive in (*nails*) ca(w).

drivel *n* haivers, styte, gyter NE.

v haiver, slaver, rhyme, gyter NE.

drizzle *v* smirr, dreezle, dribble; (*persistently*) smuchter NE.

n weet, smirr, dreezle, dribble, drowe, rag SHETLAND, ORKNEY, NE; (*often with mist*) skiff, mug NE.

drizzly muggie, drappie NE.

drone *v* **1** (*make a droning sound*) bum, souch. **2 drone on** rhyme, rame.

drop drap: *v* **1** (*drip*) rap. **2** (*a stitch in knitting*) lat doon; (*something into a liquid*) plunk; (*suddenly*) plype NE. **3** (*eg from a wall*) dreep.

n blob, drib NE, spark; (*small amount poured out: especially of alcohol*) nebfu, skite NE, skirp NE; **drops** (*of wind-driven rain or snow*) spitters; (*of spilt food*) drabbles.

droppings (*of animals: of sheep, rabbits etc*) purls; (*especially of sheep*) trottles.

drove see **drive**.

drown *v* droon.

drowned droondit, droont.

drowsy *adj* droosie.

drudgery *n* tra(u)chle: '*Spring cleanin's an awfie trauchle*', pingle, chaave NE.

drug *n* drog NE.

drunk *adj* fou, steamin, drucken; (*very*) bleezin (fou), fou as a puggie, fou as a wulk, miraculous, mingin; (*hilariously*) fleein; (*at the tearful stage*) greetin fou.

drunkard drouth.

dry *adj* (*of weather*) drouthie; (*of wind*) hard; (*parched, shrivelled*) gizzen; (*dry and brittle*) freuch NE; (*of soil*) hirstie; (*thoroughly, of clothes etc*) hert-dry NE, horn-dry, threid-dry.

v (*by wiping or rubbing*) dicht; (*clothes partially*) in open air) haizer; (*fish, ham etc*) reest; (*peats, hay etc, in open air or sun*) win.

dried (*sun-dried, of fish or clothes*) rizzert.

dried fish hard fish; (*and split*) speldin SHETLAND, N, speldrin.

drystone wall dry (stane) dyke, rickle.

dry weather drouth.

duck[1] *v* (*eg to avoid a blow*) jouk, loot; (*in water*) dook.

duck[2] *n* (*bird*) deuk.

duck pond deuk's dub.

ducks and drakes (*game*) skifflers, skifters.

play at ducks and drakes sk(l)iff (stanes), scud, skiffies NE.

flat stone used in ducks and drakes skiffer, skiffler, skiffie NE.

due *adj* (*of direction*) plat SHETLAND.

dug *see* **dig.**

dull *adj* dreich, dowie; (*of people*) dowf; (*stupid*) fozie, blate; (*of actions, writings etc*) fushionless, wersh; (*of the sky*) loorie; (*of weather, and chilly*) oorie; (*of sound*) dowf.

dulse *n* dilse N.

dumb *adj* (*struck dumb*) tongue-tackit.

dumbfound dumfooner, mesmerise, kittle.

dump *v* (*put down heavily*) plank, plowt, dowp.

n (*for rubbish, or dismal place*) cowp.

dunce *n* dult, dobbie.

dunes *npl* (*area of dunes on E Coast*) links: '*Lundin Links*'.

dung *n* muck: '*hen's muck*', fulyie; (*especially of cattle*) sha(i)rn.

dung-fly muck flee, midden flee.

dunghill midden, muck midden.

(small) balls of dung purls; (*of sheep*) trottles.

large piece of dung doll NE.

clear dung from muck (oot).

smeared with dung sha(i)rnie.

spread with dung *v* muck.

duplicate *n* (*of a document*) dooble.

during *preposition* throu: '*throu the week*'.

dust *n* dist NE; (*especially in the air*) stour, stew SHETLAND, N; (*especially of coal or peat*) coom.

dusting (*quick*) skift, dicht.

dusty stourie, stewie NE.

dustbin (ass) bucket, (ass) backet, midgie(-bin), midden CENTRAL.

dustbin man scaffie, midgie man WEST.

like a whirl of dust lik(e) stour.

dwarf *n* droich.

dwarfish drochlin NE, nirlie.

dwell *v* stey, bide, dwall.

E

each *pronoun* ilka, ilkie N, *(apiece)* the piece: *'five pund the piece'*.
 each one ilk ane, ilkie een N.
 each other ilk ither, ither.
eager *adj* willin, aiger SE; *(foolishly)* fond; *(madly)* gyte.
 eagerly snell.
 eager for on for.
 be eager for ettle efter.
 eager to ettlin tae, keen o, wuid tae.
 be extremely eager m(y)ang NE.
eagle *n* aigle, earn.
 sea eagle earn.
ear *n* lug.
 earwig eariwig, clipshear, forkie (-tail(ie)), forker SE, golach, hornie golach.
 long-eared lang-luggit.
early *adj* airlie.
 adv air: *'late an air'*, ere.
 very early hours of the morning (wee) sma oors.
 early part *(of a period of time)* foreen(d).
earn *v (wages etc)* yearn, win.
 earn your livelihood mak saut tae yer kail.
earth *n* erd, yird; *(mould, soil)* muild, mool(s).
 earthenware pig, lame SHETLAND, ORKNEY, N.
 earthenware container crock, pig.
 earthy yirdie.
 earth up *(plants)* set up, furr up.
easy *adj:* **easy-going** jack easy, eedledoddle N; *(and lazy)* easy-osie.
 do something easily skoosh (it).
 take it easy ca(w) cannie.
east *n, adj, adv* aist.
 eastward eastart, eastlins NE.
 eastwards eastle, east the road.
 east wind easter NE.

Easter *n* Pace.
 Easter egg Pace egg.
 Easter Monday Pace Egg Day.
 Easter Sunday Pace Day SHETLAND, ORKNEY, NE.
eat *v* **1** aet, corn. **2** *(quickly)* snap (up); *(greedily)* lay intae, guts, rive. **3** *(with the mouth nearly closed)* mimp. **4** *(messily)* slaiger, slitter, slaister; *(messily and noisily)* slubber, slabber, slorp, sloch, slorach; *(noisily)* slork.
 ate *past tense* ett.
 eaten *past participle* etten.
 eater *(messy)* slaister, slitter.
 eating *n* intak; *(messy, noisy)* slubber.
 eat a meal mait SHETLAND, NE.
eaves *npl* easin(s), aesin(s).
 eavesdrop eariwig, hearken (tae).
 eavesdropper hearkener.
ebb *v:* **ebbing** *(of the tide)* ootgaun.
 ebb-tide *(at lowest point)* grun(d)-ebb SHETLAND, N.
eccentric *adj* unco, orra.
eddy *n, v* swirl, pirl, weel.
edge *n (of a stream, pool etc)* lip; *(of a piece of land, of a peat-bank)* rind.
Edinburgh *n* Edinburrae, Embro, Auld Reekie.
educate *v* eddicate.
 education eddication, (buik-)lair.
eerie *adj* oorie.
effect *n* effeck, ootcome.
 effective feckfu; *(of a blow)* sicker.
effeminate *adj* sapsie.
 effeminate man (big) Jessie; *(gossipy)* (auld) sweetie-wife: *'Whit an auld sweetie-wife her man is'*.
 effeminate boy lass(ie) boy.
efficient *adj* feckfu, eydent.
effort *n (attempt)* ettle, fend; *(struggle)* wa(u)chle, pingle.

make an effort turn yer thoum; (*great effort*) warsle: '*warsle tae get away on holiday*'.

egg *n* goggie *child's word*, WEST.

elder duck *n* dunter SHETLAND, ORKNEY.

eight *numeral* aucht, echt, aicht.

eighth aucht, echt, aicht.

eighteen auchteen, echteen.

eighteenth auchteen(t), echteen(t).

eighty echtie, auchtie.

either *pronoun* aither, ether, edder SHETLAND, NE, onie (o) the twa.

elastic *n* elaskit, eleskit SOUTH.

elbow *n* elba(e), elbuck.

v oxter.

elder[1] *n*: **elderly** up in years.

elders of a church kirk session.

elder[2] *n* (*tree*) boortree.

elect *v* eleck.

elegant *adj* gentie.

eleven *numeral* eleeven, aleeven.

eleventh eleevent, aleevent.

elope *v* skirt.

elude *v* jouk, jink.

embarrass *v* gie (someone) a rid face, gie (someone) a riddie, gie (someone) a beamer.

embarrassed taen(-lik(e)).

become embarrassed get a rid face, get a riddie, get a beamer; (*greatly*) gae throu the flair.

ember *n* aizle, gleed.

embezzle *v* pauchle.

emphatic *adj* evendoon.

empty *adj* empie, tuim, teem N, tim CENTRAL, boss; (*of speech*) pyot.

v **1** empie, tuim, teem N, tim CENTRAL, SOUTH; (*a container by pouring*) poor; (*by tilting*) cowp, whummle. **2** (*become empty*) tuim, teem.

empty-handed tuim-handit.

enchantment *n* glamour(ie).

encourage *v* gie a lift tae.

encouraging hertsome.

encouragement lift, hertenin; (*opportunity*) inlat.

end *n* en, eyn NE: **1** (*of a period of time*) hint, hin(d)maist, tail; (*of the working day*) lowsin time; (*of a season, tenancy*) ootgang; (*especially of life*) hinneren(d). **2** (*lower part*) fit; (*of a loaf*) heel, sole; (*eg of a used candle*) dowp. *v* en, eyn NE.

bring to an end mak throu wi.

on end oweren(d).

stand on end en, oweren(d).

endure *v* (*tolerate*) thole, bide, dree.

enemy *n* unfreend, fae *literary*.

energy *n* smeddum, virr, ca(w)-throu, fushion.

energetic furthie NE; (*and capable*) fell.

energetically fell.

do something fast and energetically leather, skelp on, gae yer dinger, gie it laldie.

work energetically (at) skelp (at), stick in (tae).

give all your energy to gang hailheidit for *or* intil N.

without energy thowless, fushionless: '*Ah'm sae fushionless efter a migraine*'.

engaged *adj* (*to be married*) trystit.

engine *n* ingine.

engineer ingineer.

English Sassenach, Southron.

English person Sassenach.

enormous *adj* (great) muckle.

enough *adj, adv, n* eneuch.

enrage *v* raise.

ensure *v* mak siccar.

enterprise *n* (*undertaking*) ploy, han(d)lin.

entertain *v* enterteen.

entertaining shortsome; (*person*) knackie.

entertaining person divert.

entertainment divert, han(d)lin.

enthusiasm *n* birr.

entire *adj* hail-heidit N.

almost entirely gey near, maistlins, maist han(d) NE.

entrance *n* (*way in*) ingaun, ingang SHETLAND, NE; (*to a house etc*) entry; (*to a stairway of a block of flats*) close (mou).

entrust *v* lippen.

Episcopal(ian) *adj, n* (*of the Scottish Episcopal Church*) Piskie *informal*.

equal *adj* aqual; (*in age or height*) heidipeer; **equal to** up wi.

n aqual; (*of a person or thing*) marrow, maik.

v (*match*) peel, marrow.

equally aqual, equals-aquals.

equally balanced eeksie-peeksie, equal-aqual; (*on an equal footing*) a(w) ae oo.

without equal marrowless.

equipment *n* graith, orders, haudin SOUTH.

era *n*: **the end of an era** the end o an auld sang.

erratic *adj* ragglish NE.

errand *n* message, eeran(t), troke.

errand-boy message-boy, message laddie, eeran loon NE.

go an errand gae a message.

error *n*: **in error** in a mistak.

escape *v* win oot, win awa; (*something or someone*) miss, jouk; (*eg a disease*) get throu: '*She got throu the measles*'.

escort *v* convoy.

n (*escorting*) convoy; (*halfway home*) Scotch convoy.

especially *adv* maistlie, parteec(u)lar.

establish *v* estaiblish.

become established sit doon.

establishment estaiblishment.

estate *n* (*of council houses*) (housing) scheme.

estuary *n* firth.

et cetera an (th)at, an siclik(e), an a(w).

eternally *adv* till the morn-come-never, for aye.

etiquette *n* honesty, mense.

evade *v* jouk, jink.

even *adj, adv* e'en; (*level*) evenlie; **even with** (*quits*) eens wi, upsides wi.

even if suppose: '*He widna tell ye suppose he kent*'.

evening *n* eenin, een; (*especially winter as a time of relaxation*) forenicht.

in the evening at een.

eventually *adv* at *or* i the hinneren(d).

ever *adv* ivver, aye.

for ever for aye, till the morn-come-never.

every *adj* ivverie, ilka, ilk, ilkie N.

everybody a(w)bodie, ilk ane, ilkie een N.

every kind (of) a(w)kin kind (o).

everything a(w)thing(s).

and everything else an a(w).

(in) every way a(w) weys.

everywhere a'where, a(w) wey, a(w)gate, a(w) roads.

evident *adj* weel seen.

evil *adj, n* (*wicked, malicious*) ill.

evil-looking ill-faured.

ewe *n* yowe.

exact *adj* exack, nate; (*of a person*) pointit.

exactly exack.

exaggerate *v* blaw; (*a story*) pit airms an legs tae.

exaggeration whid.

examine *v* exaemin, exem, leuk, see, sicht.

examination exemination NE, exa(e)min, sicht.

exasperate *v* fash, deave, ug SHETLAND, NE.

exasperating chawin, tantersome NE.

excel *v* bang, bear the gree *literary*.

excellent braw, barrie *used by schoolchildren* LOTHIAN, gallus *used by schoolchildren* WEST, peesie *slang or child's word*.

something excellent (*of its kind*) stoater, beezer.

except *preposition* excep, by('s), forby.

exceptional(ly) by-or(di)nar, by-common.

excerpt *n* swatch.

excessively *adv* owerlie.

exchange *v* change, troke.

exciseman *n* gauger.

excite *v* kittle (up).

excited up NE; (*excessively*) up tae high doh, raised; (*violently or sexually*) radg(i)e; **easily excited** kittle.

become excited roose, flichter.

excitement go: '*in a go*', feerich NE, flocht SHETLAND, NE; (*great*) tirrivee, ree; (*panic*) panshit NE; (*pleasurable*) kittle.

over-excited raised, ree, yivverin NE.

excrement *n* shite, keech, kich; (*specifically human*) cack(ie), geing; (*lump of*) toalie, jobbie.

excuse *v, n* excaise, exkeese NE.

exercise *n, v* exerceese.

exercise book jotter.

exert *v*: **exert yourself** fash (yersel), fyke, warsle, chaave NE, kyauve SHETLAND, NE.

not exert yourself no cruik a finger.

with great exertion sair NE.

exhaust *v* exowst.

exhausted wabbit, puggelt, disjaskit, foonert, (sair) forfochen.

exhausting tra(u)chlesome NE.

exhibition *n* exhibeetion.

make an exhibition of yourself mak a puppie-show o yersel.

exit *n* ootgang.

exotic *adj* fantoosh, ootlan(d).

expand *v* (*swell*) hove; (*stretch*) rax SHETLAND, NE.

expect *v* expeck; (*rather think*) doot: '*I doot he'll be here by 8*'; (*hope for: confidently*) lippen.

expectation lippenin, ettlin.

expedition *n* expedeetion, carrant.

expend *v* ware.

expense (*cost*) chairge, ootgang.

experience *n* expairience.

experiment *n* prattick NE.

expert *adj* cannie, slee.

explode *v* **1** pluff; (*with a sharp hiss*) flist N. **2** (*with rage*) lowse, flist N.

explosion (*mild*) pluff; (*loud explosive noise*) reboon(d).

exploit *n* splore.

explore *v* reenge.

exploration explore.

explosion *see* **explode.**

express *v*: **try to express** ettle at.

expression (*on the face: pathetic, to gain sympathy*) sair face.

extend *v* (*stretch, reach*) stent, rax, rack.

extension eik.

extent (*amount*) thing; (*limit*) stent.

to some extent some: '*She cam tae hersel some*'.

to that extent that: '*He wis that scared*'.

extinguish *v* (*a fire etc*) smoor SW.

extra *adj* extrae, tither, tidder SHETLAND, NE.

extra charge tae-fa(w).

extract *v* (*a tooth*) pou.

extraordinary *adj* extraordinar, by-or(di)nar, nae or(di)nar, unco.

extraordinarily by-or(di)nar, forby: '*He wis forby kind*'.

extravagant *adj* expensive, haveless N.

live extravagantly live at heck an manger.

extremely *adv* terrible, unco, sair.

exuberant *adj* cadgie, on the keevee, croose.

eye *n* ee, blinker, een-peeper *child's word; pl also* **een.**

eyebrow broo, ee-broo.

eyelid eelid.

F

face *n, v:* **facing** *preposition* forenent.
(flat) on your face breidth an lenth.
make a face thraw yer gab.
factory hooter *n* bummer.
fad *n* whigmaleerie, fyke.
faddy fykie: '*He's fykie aboot his claes.*'
be faddy stan(d) on freits.
faddy eater fyke.
fade *v (of colours)* dowe.
faded *(of colours)* casten; *(withered)* dowit.
fail *v* miss: '*They nivver miss tae find oot*'; *(go wrong)* misgae NE; *(cause to fail)* misgie.
failed *(in a profession)* stickit: '*stickit minister*'.
faint *v* fent, gang awa.
n (fainting fit) fent, dwam.
adj (weak) dwamie, wauch, waumish.
fair[1] *adj* **1** *(just)* jonick. **2** *(tolerable)* middlin.
a fair number *or* **amount** a gey wheen.
fair[2] *n* ferr; *(funfair)* the shows.
fairy *n (benevolent, household)* broonie, whuppitie-stourie.
fairies guid fowk(s), little fowk(s).
fairyland Elfin.
faith *n:* **faithful** aefauld, leal-hertit, leal.
have faith in lippen tae *or* on.
fall *v* **1** fa(w). **2** *(of rain, heavily)* plump, ding (on *or* doon); *(of snow etc)* smore.
n fa(w), cowp; *(especially when skating)* lander; *(heavy)* dunt, plunk; *(violent, especially into water or mud)* sclatch NE, plowt; *(with a splash)* clash; *(of rain, snow: heavy)* plump, onfa(w); *(of snow: slight)* skiff(in).
fall out cast oot: '*Her and her new*

boyfriend are aye castin oot!*'.
fall over cowp, whummle.
false *adj* fause; *(underhand)* sleekit.
falseness pit-on.
false teeth wallies CENTRAL.
falter *v, n (stumble)* stammer.
familiar *adj* fameeliar, (weel-)kent, kenspeckle; *(homely)* hameower, couthie.
familiar with used wi, yaised wi, eest wi N.
family *n* faim(i)lie; *(ancestry)* kin; *(your relatives)* yer fowk; *(of small children)* sma faimilie.
last child of a large family poke-shakkins, shakkins o the pok(i)e.
famine *n* faimine.
famish *v* faimish, hunger.
famished howe.
famous *adj* faur kent, weel kent, namelie.
fan *v* waff; *(a flame)* flaff.
fancy *adj* fantoosh, wallie.
v (a person of the opposite sex) lik(e).
far *adj* faur, fer SOUTH.
farther farder, faurer.
farthest farrest, ferrest SOUTH.
far away hyne-awa NE.
as far as the lenth o.
far too yaiseless, eeseless NE, useless: '*yaiseless monie cats*'.
farewell *interjection* fareweel, fare ye weel.
farm *n* ferm, fairm, room, grun(d).
v ferm, fairm.
farmer fermer.
farmer's wife dame NE, FIFE, guid-wife.
farm animal baist, beast.
farm buildings *(with or without farm-house)* (ferm) steidin, steadin, steid.
farm cottage cot hoose.

farmhouse ha.

farm-land grun(d).

farm overseer grieve.

farmworker (*male*) jock(ie), joskin; (*female*) jennie; (*adolescent*) halflin, loon; (*doing odd jobs*) orraman, orra loon NE.

farmworkers' quarters (*for unmarried men*) bothy, chaumer NE.

farmyard yaird, close.

fashionable *adj* tippie.

fast *adj, adv* **1** fest. **2** (*of a watch*) forrit.

fasten *v* steek; (*with a catch*) snib, sneck; (*with a hook*) cleek.

fastidious *adj* perjink; (*about food*) skeichen NE.

fat *n* creesh.

adj **1** (*greasy*) creeshie. **2** (*of persons*) bowsie; (*flabby*) fozie.

fatten mend.

the fat's in the fire the ba(w)'s (up) on the slates.

fat clumsy woman clatch.

big fat woman hoose-en(d).

fat sluggish person sumph, hillock.

fate *n* weird: '*Ye maun dree yer (ain) weird*'.

fated (to die) fey.

father *n* faither, fader SHETLAND, NE, auld yin CENTRAL, aul een NE.

v faither, fader SHETLAND, NE.

father-in-law guid-faither.

fathom *n, v* faddom.

fatigue *n, v* tash.

fault *n* faut: **1** (*in character*) shortcome. **2** blame: '*It's no ma blame*', wyte.

find fault with faut, be at (someone about something).

favour *v* (*someone to the exclusion of others*) no see past (someone).

n (*act of kindness*) obleegement.

favourable cannie.

general favourite a(w)bodie's bodie.

in great favour faur ben.

curry favour sook in: '*Stoap sookin in wi the teacher!*', smool.

fearful *adj* **1** (*afraid*) skeer, timorsome, fleggit. **2** (*dreadful*) awfie, affu N.

feasible *adj* faisible.

feat *n* (*difficult*) kittle; (*acrobatic, gymnastic*) henner LOTHIAN.

feather *n* fedder SHETLAND, ORKNEY.

featherbrain sodie-heid.

February *n* Februar.

feckless *adj* haiveless, knotless.

fed *adj*: **fed up** scunnert, uggit.

become fed up sta(w).

looking well fed lik(e) yer mait.

feeble *adj* (*of people*) fushionless, dwaiblie, doweless.

feed *v* mait; (*a horse with oats or grain*) corn NE; (*cattle with turnips*) neep.

feel *v, n* fin(d).

fellow *n* fella, fellae SE, chiel(d), call-an(t), loon *mainly* N.

female boss, female head *n* (*of something*) hersel(f).

fencepost *n* (fence) stob, pailin stab.

fend *v* fen(d).

fend for yourself fork.

fern *n* rannoch.

ferret *n* whitrat, futrat NE, foumart.

fertile *adj* (*of vegetation*) growthie.

fester *v* beal, etter.

festering sore bealin.

festive *adj* blithe, rantin.

period of festivities at Christmas and the New Year the Daft Days.

fetch *v* fess, fesh.

fetter *n* hapshackle.

fever *n* fivver.

few *pronoun* fyow N.

a few a (wee) pickle, a puckl(i)e, a wheen, twa-three.

fib *n* feeb.

fiddle *n* (*cheating*) pauchle.

v **1** (*play the fiddle*) diddle. **2** **fiddle (about)** footer, plowter. **3** (*cheat*) pauchle.

fiddling, fiddly footerie, pernicketie, skitterie.

fidget *v* fidge, fyke; (*especially restlessly*) rowe; (*especially impatiently*) hotch.

the fidgets the fykes.

fidgety fykie.

field *n* park.

  fieldfare skitterie feltie, feltie, feltie-flier.

fiend *n* fient.

fierce *adj* 1 fell, turk NE, ramsh. 2 (*of a battle, struggle*) sair.

fiery *adj* (*in temperament*) het-skinned.

fifteen *numeral* feifteen.

  fifteenth feifteen(t).

  fifth fift.

  fifty fuftie.

fight *v* fecht; (*quarrel*) tulyie.

  n fecht; (*scuffle*) rammie, tulyie.

  fought *past tense* focht.

  past participle fochten.

  fighter fechter, kemper.

figure *n* feegur; (*stucco*) stookie.

  v feegur, jalouse.

file[1] *n* (*row*) raw.

file[2] *v* (*smooth off*) risp.

  n (*coarse*) risp.

fill *v* prime, fou; (*a container*) eik up; (*to capacity*) stap; (*especially the stomach*) stowe, stech; (*eg a hole*) colf NE.

  n fou.

  filling *adj* (*of food*) foosome.

film *n* (*thin layer*) scruif, screef NE; (*of vapour etc*) (y)oam, gum NE.

filter *n, v* sye, sile.

filth *n* cla(i)rt.

  filthy cla(i)rtie, foosome NE, maukit, maukie; (*of people*) brockit; (*especially with excrement*) keechie, dirten.

final *adj* hin(d)ermaist.

  finally at the hinneren(d), hin(d)maist.

finance *n*: **your finances** yer pootch.

find *v* fin; (*by looking*) get, git.

  found *past tense, past participle* fun(d).

fine *adj* 1 braw, gey (lik(e)), gran(d). 2 (*of weather*) braw, leesome NE. 3 (*in texture*) sma.

  finery (*in dress*) braws: '*Wear yer braws tae the waddin*'.

  become fine (*of weather*) fair (up).

  stay fine (*of weather*) keep up.

finger *n* (*little*) pinkie.

  fingertip finger neb.

finicky *adj* (*fussy, intricate*) fykie, (*fussy*) perjink.

finish *v* feenish; (*food, drink*) perish *humorous*.

  finished 1 gaed duin; (*of a meeting etc*) oot. 2 (*done for*) awa wi't.

  finishing time (*at work*) lowsin time.

fir cone *n* fir yowe NE, yowie NE, (fir) tap, peerie SOUTH.

fire *n* lowe; (*on a hearth*) ingle.

  fireplace chim(b)ley NE, brace.

  fireside ingle(-neuk), ingle-cheek.

  firework (*squib*) squeeb; (*homemade*) peeoy.

  catch fire gae on fire, tak lowe, tak lunt.

  make a fire big a fire.

  on fire on haud: '*Yer lum's on haud*'; (*of a chimney*) up.

  set on fire (*chimney*) set up: '*Set the lum up*'.

firm *adj* (*stable, secure*) sicker, stench NE, solvendie, stieve.

  firmly (*securely*) hard, stieve(lie).

  firmly fixed stieve.

first *adj* (*foremost*) forehand.

  first light (*of the day*) keek o day.

  first-rate tap, nae din-bonnets NE.

fish *n* fush.

  v fush; (*with the hands*) guddle.

  fisherman fisher.

  fishing boat (*kind of small*) skiff, yole SHETLAND, ORKNEY, N; (*line-fishing*) liner; (*flat-bottomed for salmon fishing*) (saumon) coble.

  fishing line (*inshore*) sma line; (*handline*) handlin.

  cord etc attaching fishing line to hook snuid, tippin N.

  place a fishing net in water shuit a net.

  fishing rod (fishin) wan(d).

  fish-hawker (fish-)cadger.

  fish-spear (*with several prongs*) leister, waster.

  fish-and-chips fish-supper.

fist *n* nieve.

clenched fist steekit nieve.

fistful nievefu.

fisticuffs nieves.

fit[1] *v* **1** (*of clothes*) ser. **2** (*a bootlace, cart-wheel, with metal tip, band etc*) shod.

adj **1** (*suitable*) settin; **2** (*physically*) able, kneef N.

badly-fitting (*of shoes*) sha(u)chlin.

fit in with complouter wi.

fit[2] *n*: **fit of rage** tirrivee, radge: '*tak a radge*'.

five *numeral*: **group of five** fivesome.

fix *v* (*in position*) stell.

fixed (*of wages*) upstandin.

fizz *v* (*of liquids*) bizz; (*make a fizzing noise*) fiss NE.

fizzy fuzzie NE.

fjord *n* sea loch, VOE SHETLAND, OR-KNEY.

flabbergast *v* dumbfooner, stammy-gaster.

flabby *adj* fozie.

flabbiness foziness.

flag *v* (*become weary*) fag.

flail *v*: **flail about** (*with the limbs*) spra(u)chle, spralloch NE.

flake *n* (*especially of snow*) flicht, pirl; (*thin slice*) skelf, skelb, skelp.

flamboyant *adj* (*especially in dress*) prinkie; (*of colours*) roarie, skirie OR-KNEY, NE.

flame *n* lowe; (*very small*) peep, peek.

burn with a bright flame lowe.

go up in flames tak lowe.

flannel *n* flannen.

flap *n* **1** (*of a shoe, cap etc*) lug. **2** (*flapping motion*) waff.

v flaff, fluffer NE, waff, waffle, wap; (*especially of birds' wings*) flochter; (*cause to flap*) flaff, wap.

flare up *v* **1** lowe, bleeze. **2** (*in anger*) flist NE, loss the heid.

flash *n* (*of light*) gliff, glisk, skime, glent; (*of lightning*) (fire-)fla(u)cht.

flashy fantoosh; (*of colours*) roarie, skirie NE.

flask *n* flesk SOUTH.

flat *adj* flet: **1** (*level, even*) plain; (*of a dish*) skleff. **2** (*dull*) fushionless. **3** (*of beer*) wersh.

n (*apartment*) hoose, hoosie; (*one-roomed*) single en(d); (*two-roomed*) room an kitchen.

flatten flet; (*crops*) lay.

flat foot sclaffer.

block of flats (*usually three or four storeys*) tenement.

flatter *v* sook in wi, claw someone's back, fleetch, fraik, phrase NE.

flatterer sook, fraik; (*excessive*) plaist-er.

flattery ruise, reese NE, fraik.

flatulence *n* pumpin.

relieve flatulence pump, brak the win(d).

flavour *n* (*unpleasant*) kneggum.

add flavour to kitchen.

flax *n* lint.

flea *n* flech, flae.

fleas cattle.

rid (*a person or animal*) **of fleas** flech.

fleck *n* spreckle.

v spreckle; (*especially with snow*) grime.

fledgling *see* **nestling** (*under* **nest**).

flee *v* (*at once*) be uptail an awa; (*from justice*) tak leg bail.

flexible *adj* dwaible, swack N.

flibbertigibbet *n* sodie-heid.

flick *v* flisk.

n flisk; (*especially of the fingers, to move a marble*) plunk.

flicker *v*, *n* flichter.

flight[1] *n* **1** (*act of flying*) flicht. **2** (*flock of birds*) flocht.

flighty flichtie, flauntie, fliskie, (as) daft as a yett on a windy day.

flight[2] *n* (*act of fleeing*) flicht.

flimsy *adj* silly; (*especially of clothes*) slim SHETLAND, N.

fling *v* wap, hove, fung.

flirt *v* tig, daff(er).

n (*girl*) jillet.

flirtation dafferie.

float *v* fleet SHETLAND.
flock *n* paircel; (*especially of sheep*) hirsel.
flog *v* leather, whang.
flood *n* flude, fleed N.
  v flude, fleed N.
floor *n, v* fluir, flair, fleer NE.
  ground floor first flair.
  on the ground floor laich.
flop *v*: **flop down** clap doon; (*especially to hide*) flap.
flounder[1] *v, also* **flounder about** floonder, spra(u)chle, wallop, spralloch NE, plowster SOUTH.
flounder[2] *n* (*fish*) floonder, flunner N, fleuk, grayback NE, FIFE.
flour *n* flooer.
flourish *v* **1** (*of plants*) bluim, bleem N. **2** (*thrive*) dae guid, mak oot.
  flourishing 1 (*of plants*) raffie NE. **2** (*of a business etc*) guid gaun.
flow *v* pirr, trinnle NE.
  n (*of water*) rin.
flower *n* flooer.
  flowery flooerie.
  flower vase vawse, pig.
fluent *adj* (*in speech*) gabbie, glib, tonguie.
fluff *n* (*from cloth etc*) oos(e).
  fluffy oos(s)ie.
flurry *n* **1** (*of snow etc*) tirl NE, waff; (*especially of sleet*) snifter. **2** flocht, swither.
flush *v* (*with clean water*) synd.
fluster *n* swither.
  v fluister, flochter.
flutter *v* **1** fluther, flichter, flaff, fluffer; (*of a leaf etc*) wag; (*especially of birds in water*) squatter. **2** (*be excited*) flichter.
  n (*flapping*) flichter.
fly[1] *v* flee, flicht; (*lightly*) skiff; (*off at an angle*) skite; (*of birds, awkwardly*) flichter.
  n (*in trousers*) shop door, spaiver, ballop.
  send flying skite, skail.
fly[2] *n* (*insect*) flee.

foam *n, v* faem, fro, freith, ream.
  foaming (*of beer etc*) nappie.
fodder *n, v* fother.
fog *n* rouk; (*thick*) smoch; (*cold, especially on the East Coast*) haar; (*dense, from sea*) thickness.
  foggy haarie, roukie.
fold[1] *v* faul(d); (*cloth*) faik; (*fold back*) flype; (*wrap*) wap, wup; (*work into folds*) ruckle; (*arms*) plet.
  n faul(d); (*of a garment*) faik NE, flype; (*crease*) lirk, gruggle NE.
fold[2] *n* (*for animals*) faul(d), crue, lair.
folk *n* fowk.
follow *v* follae, fallow.
fond *adj*: **fond of** browden on NE, fain o, keen o; (*extremely*) daft aboot.
fondle culyie, daut; (*a child*) daidle.
food *n* fuid, mait, scran; (*small amount*) drabble; (*messy*) plowter, soss; (*sloppy*) slaiger.
fool *n* fuil, feel N, daftie, gawpus; (*simpleton*) coof, gowk(ie), gumph.
  foolish fuil, feel N, daft(-like), glaikit, gawpit, menseless, unwicelik(e) N.
  make a fool of tak the rag (oot) o.
  play the fool act the daft lassie *or* laddie.
foot *n* fit; (*of an animal*) luif.
  footling footerie, scutterie NE, skitterie.
  football fitba(w), kick-ba(w); (*especially as (formerly) played on Shrove Tuesday*) the Ba.
  foothold fit: '*miss yer fit*'.
  footpath fit-road, pad.
  footstep (*heavy*) clumph.
  footstool creepie (stuil).
  change your footwear shift yer feet, chynge yer feet.
  on foot Tamson's mear, shanks'(s) naig(ie).
  journey *etc* **on foot** *n* traivel.
  travel on foot *v* pad, traivel.
for *preposition* fur, till SHETLAND, N, tae: '*He worked tae Mr G*', on: '*Wait on me*'.
  forever 1 (*for all time*) for aye. **2** (*continually*) aye.

force *n* (*energy*) birr, virr, smeddum, fushion NE.

v (*make to do*) gar, dwang.

force your way into breenge in(tae), mak intae.

force your way through rive throu.

ford *n, v* fuird, f(y)oord N, rack.

forecast *v* spae *literary*.

forehead *n* foreheid, broo.

foreign *adj* furrin, fremmit, fremd, ootlin.

forelock *n* tap, swirl SHETLAND.

foremost *adj* forehan(d), foremaist.

forenoon *n* forenuin, for(a)neen NE.

foreshore *n* ebb.

foretell *v* spae *literary*.

forewarning *n* moyen NE: '*get a moyen o*'.

forfeit *n* (*in a game*) wad.

v tyne NE.

game in which forfeits are demanded wads.

forgave *see* **forgive.**

forget *v* foryet SHETLAND, disremember, misremember, lose min(d) o.

forgetful forgettle.

forgetfulness forget.

forgive *v* forgie.

forgave *past tense* forgied.

forgiven *past participle* forgien.

fork *n* **1** (*for digging*) graip. **2** (*of a tree*) glack NE.

forkful fork.

fork up graip.

forlorn *adj* tint, disjaskit.

form *n, v* furm, firm.

forsake *v* forsak, forleet, quat.

forth *adv* furth.

fortify *v* fortifee NE.

fortnight *n* fortnicht.

fortune *n* (*fate*) weird; (*good*) seil, sonse.

fortunate seilie, happy, cannie.

fortune-teller (*female*) spaewife, weird wife.

forward *adv* forrit, furrit.

adj forritsome, gallus.

rush forward impetuously breenge.

fought *see* **fight.**

foul *adj* fool, mingin.

foul-mouthed ruch, coorse.

found *v* foon(d).

foundation foond(s); (*of a stack*) stathel, stale.

foundation stone grun(d)-stane.

found *see* **find.**

founder *v* foon(d)er.

four *numeral* fower.

fourteenth fowerteen(t).

fourth fowert.

group of four people fowersome.

fowl *n* fool.

fox *n* tod.

v quirk NE.

foxglove lady's thummles, witches' thimmles, deid man's bells NE.

foxhunt tod-hunt.

fraction *n* (*small amount*) stime, haet.

fractious *adj* fashious, greetin-faced, girnie, peengie, pe(r)neurious NE.

fragile *adj* bruckle.

fragment *n* nip, murlin, nimsh N, mote.

frail *adj* silly, dwaiblie.

frank *adj* fair-spoken, frugal SHETLAND, CAITHNESS, NE, furthie, furth the gate NE, evendoon; (*of speech*) fair oot.

fraud *n* cheatrie, intak.

fray *v* (*of cloth etc*) faize, frizz.

frayed (*of cloth etc*) chattert, chattit NE; (*of rope*) fozie NE.

freckle *n* ferntickle, fairnytickle, spreckle.

freckled ferntickelt, fairnytickelt.

free *adj* quat (o).

v (*yourself or another*) redd (o).

become free lowse.

freedom (*scope*) scowth.

free-for-all rammie, reerie NE, stramash.

freeze *v, see also* **frozen**; jeel, lapper NE.

fresh *adj* (*of air, water, fish, vegetables etc*) caller; (*of milk: new*) green; (*untreated, not sour*) sweet; (*especially herring: unsalted*) green.

freshen caller; (*of wind*) kittle NE.

fret *v* freet, girn, peenge, canker NE.

fretful girnie, canker(i)t.

be fretful girn.

friable *adj* frush, murlie, knappie; (*of soil*) moolie.

friend *n* freen(d), billie, fere *literary*; (*female*) cummer.

friendless freen(d)less.

friendly (*intimate*) freen(d)lie, great, chief, cosh, pack WEST, SOUTH, ULSTER; (*very*) far ben, thrang; (*towards others*) couthie, hamelie, fairspoken; (*in appearance*) sonsie, smirkie.

be very friendly with be gey chief wi, be great guns wi, be gran billies wi NE.

friendliness freen(d)liness.

fright *n* fricht, fleg, fley, gliff: '*get a gliff*', fear.

frighten fricht(en), fear, fleg, fley, gliff.

frightened feart (for), frichtit (for), fleggit.

frightening frichtsome, fleysome.

frill *n* frull.

fringe *n* freenge.

frisk *v* (*caper*) flisk, fud, daff.

frisky hippertie-skippertie NE; (*especially of a horse*) fliskie, skeich.

fritter away *v* moot awa.

frivolous *adj* freevolous, daft, hippertie-skippertie NE.

frivolous person (*silly*) sodie-heid.

frizzy *adj* swirlie.

frog *n* puddock, paddock, paddie.

frogspawn puddock cruddles, (puddock) redd.

frolic *n* cantrip, tear, jink, set.

v daff, splore.

from *preposition* fae, frae, thrae SE, furth.

away from aff.

out from oot.

front *n* (*of something*) foreside.

front garden front.

front part fore-en(d).

in front afore.

in front of afore, forenent.

frost *n* freest NE.

frosty rimie.

frostiness jeel.

Jack Frost nip-nebs.

froth *n*, *v* fro; (*especially on ale etc*) ream.

frothing reamie.

frown *v*, *n* skook, froon.

frozen *adj* jeelt.

fruit *n*: **fruitcake** (*rich, spiced*) black bun.

fruit-machine puggie.

fruit-slice fly cemetry.

frustrate *v* pall SHETLAND, NE.

fry[1] *v*: **small number of fish for frying** fry: '*Here a fry o haddies tae ye*'.

sound of frying sotter.

fry[2] *n* (*of the minnow etc*) peen-heid; (*newly-hatched, especially of herring*) sile.

fuddled *adj* moidert, ree, reezie.

fudge *n* (*of a crisp, crumbly consistency*) ta(i)blet.

fuel *n* fire.

fugitive *n* fugie, rinagate.

full *adj* fou, ful; (*quite full, full to the brim*) bung-fou, lippin(-fou) SHETLAND, ORKNEY, NE; (*of a place*) stowed (oot); (*of frothy liquid*) ream-in-fou; (*of a person: of food*) stappit (fou), (*to bursting point*) riftin fou, fou as a wulk.

fully fou, fullie.

fullness footh.

fulmar *n* mallimoke SHETLAND, ORKNEY.

fumble *v* fummle, ficher SHETLAND, NE, footer, thrummle NE.

fumbling *n* fummle.

adj han(d)less, picherin NE.

fume *v* feem; (*with anger*) beal, reek.

fumes *npl* smuik, smeek, guff.

fumigate *v* (*with smoke*) smeek, smuik SW, SOUTH.

fun *n* dafferie, daffin, gyper NE.

piece of fun ploy, tear.

funny *adj* (*of conversation etc*) knackie.

funny bone dirlie-bane.
funny story baur CENTRAL.
funfair the shows.
make fun of tak the nap aff, geck.
fund *n* foon(d), fond.
funeral *n* fooneral SOUTH, beerial NE.
funnel *n* **1** (*of a ship etc*) lum. **2** (*for pouring liquids*) filler.
furious *adj* radge, dancin mad, gyte, bealin.
furnish *v* (*a house*) plenish.
furniture *n* plenishin, haudin.
furrow *n* (*made by the plough*) furr, sheuch, scart; (*for drainage*) gaw (furrow), watter furr.
v (*make furrows in*) furr.
furry *adj* oos(s)ie.
further *adv, adj* forder, farder.
v forder.
furthermore forby.
furtive *adj* sleekit, hidlin, huggerie (-muggerie).

fury *n* tirrivee.
furze *see* **gorse**.
fuss *n* carfuffle, stushie, stashie, stooshie, souch, fizz, palaver.
v **1** (*make a fuss*) fizz, mak (a) maitter, gae on; (*doing very little*) peuther; (*about nothing*) (mak a) fyke, stan(d) on freits. **2 fuss over** connach. **3 make a fuss of** (*pet*) daut: '*Dinnae daut that bairn efter he's been bad.*'
fussy fykie, footerie, perjink, phrasie NE; (*about food*) pe(r)neurious NE, skeich NE.
fussy person, fusspot fyke, finick, palaver.
fussy eater fyke, pike-at-yer-mait, pickie.
fussiness fykerie; (*about food*) skeichen.
fusty *adj* foostie, mozie, mochie NE.
fustiness foost.
futile *adj* knotless.

G

gabble *v* blether, yatter, slaver, clishmaclaver NE.

gable *n* ga(i)vel, gale NE, hoose-en(d).

gable-end ga(i)vel-en(d).

gad about *v* stravaig, traik, traipse, haik (aboot).

gadabout haik: '*He's an awfu haik*', shanker NE.

gadfly *n* (*horsefly*) cleg, gled SOUTH.

Gaelic *n, adj* Gylick NE.

Gaelic music heedrum hodrum *contemptuous*.

gaff *n* (*salmon-hook*) cleek, clep.

gain *v* (*earn*) win.

gait *n* gang.

gale *n* gell, gurl.

gallery *n* (*in a church*) laft, bauks.

galley *n* (*ship*) gaillie.

gallop *v* skelp, wallop.

gallows *n* widdie.

gallows rope widdie, towe.

game *n* gemm.

adj (*plucky*) stuffie.

gamekeeper gamie, gemmie, gamewatcher NE.

gander *n* (*male goose*) ganner.

gannet *n* gant; (*young*) guga HEBRIDES.

gap *n* open NE; (*eg in a wall, hedge etc*) slap.

bridge a gap kep a slap.

gape *v* **1** gaup, gowp. **2** (*of clothes*) girn.

garden *n* gairden; (*especially of a cottage*) yaird.

gardener gaird(e)ner.

garish *adj* roarie, skirie NE.

garter *n, v* gairter, ga(i)rten.

garter-tab (*of a kilt stocking*) flash.

gas *n*: **small jet of gas** peep: '*The gas is at a peep*'.

gash *v* gulliegaw N.

n screed.

gasp *v* (*for breath*) pech; (*in coughing*) kink.

n pech, hauch.

gate *n* yett.

gatepost stoop.

gather *v* gaither, gadder SHETLAND, NE; (*of people*) forgaither.

gathering gaitherin; (*noisy*) hurroo, helm NE.

gaudy *adj* skirie NE; (*specifically of colour*) roarie.

gave *see* **give.**

gay *adj* (*merry, cheerful*) croose, lichtsome.

gaze *v* (*especially vacantly*) gove; (*intently*) glower; (*open-mouthed*) gowp. *n* (*especially vacant*) gove, gowp; (*intent*) glower.

gear *n* (*equipment*) graith, orders.

general store *n* (*small*) Jennie a'thing(s), Johnnie a'thing(s), shoppie NE.

generous *adj* hertie, guidwillie, lairge, furthie.

genial *adj* hertie, lithesome, lithe NE.

genitals *npl*: **female genitals** fud.

gentle *adj* lithe(some); (*of a person*) douce, cannie; (*of wind*) lown.

gently huilie, cannie; (*especially of wind*) lown.

genuine *adj* jonick, rael, evendoon.

the genuine article the real Mackay.

germinate *v* breird, braird, come awa.

gesture *n* gester; (*feeble*) paw; (*with the hand*) wag.

get *v* git.

got *past tense* gat.

past participle gotten.

get at (*try to express*) ettle at.

get away win awa.

get by warsle throu, chaave awa NE.

get off with (*a person of the opposite sex*) click, cleek, lumber.

get out (*escape*) win oot.

get the upper hand of get ower.

get up 1 (*stand*) lift. **2** (*in the morning*) rise.

get-up (*odd clothes*) paraffin: '*Whit a paraffin she had on*'.

ghost *n* ghaist, bogle, boodie NE, doolie.

ghostly eldritch *literary*.

giblets *npl* harigals.

giddy *adj* (*especially from drink*) capernoitie, reezie.

gift *n* (*small, eg as a token of goodwill*) mindin: '*It's jist a wee mindin*'; (*for luck for something new or just beginning, eg a coin in a new purse*) han(d)sel; (*especially from a fair*) fairin; (*at New Year, especially of food or drink*) Hogmanay: '*Gie them thir Hogmanay*'; (*at Christmas*) Christmas: '*He wants it for his Christmas*'.

gift in order to celebrate something new han(d)sel: '*a handsel for yer new handbag*'.

give as a gift gift: '*£1 000 was gifted to the society*'.

give a small gift to mind.

giggle *v, n* keckle, kicher, snitter, geegle.

ginger *n* ginge.

ginger beer ale NE.

gingerbread gingebreid, gibberie N.

ginger snap snap.

girl *n* lass(ie), quine NE, bird *contemptuous*; (*small*) lass(ock)ie, quinie NE; (*older*) deem N, dame NE; (*attractive*) stoater, brammer; (*lively, tomboyish*) gilpie; (*giddy*) taupie, hallock, lintie; (*mischievous*) hempie, limmer, clip.

girlfriend lass(ie), quine NE, click, cleek.

give *v* gie; (*hand to*) see.

gave *past tense* gied, gien.

given *past participle* gien, gied.

give me gimme, gie's, see me, see's: '*See's ower the teapot*'; (*by stretching*) rax me (ower).

give us gie's, see's.

give and take *n* giff-gaff.

give up (*abandon*) quat, gie ower SHETLAND, NE, jeck (up).

glad *adj* gled, blithe, prood; (*to do etc*) fond.

gladly blithe.

gladness blitheness.

glance *v* **1** (*look quickly*) keek, glent; (*sideways*) sklent, gley. **2** (*fly off obliquely*) skite.
n keek, glent; (*sidelong*) sklent, gley, skew NE.

glancing blow scuff, scud.

gland *n*: **swollen glands** kirnels.

glare *n* (*of light*) gliff.

Glasgow *n* Glesca, Glesgie EDINBURGH.

glass *n* gless, glaiss NE.

glasses glesses.

wearing glasses speckie: '*the speckie boy in the first year*'.

glass marble glessie (bool), glesser.

gleam *v* leam *literary*, skime, glint, lowe, sheen.
n glim, leam *literary*, glint, glisk, skime.

glean *v* (*with a rake*) rake.

glide *v* (*move easily and quickly*) scrieve, link, skimmer.

glimmer *v* glent.
n glim, gleet SOUTH, stime *literary*.

glimpse *v* get a sicht O, get a swatch O.
n glimp, gliff, swatch, twig NE.

glint *v* glent.
n glent, gliff, skime.

glisten *v* glister, sheen.

glitter *v* glent, glister, prinkle, skire.
n glent.

glittering *adj* glaizie.

gloom *n* mirk(ness).

gloomy dreich, mirk(ie), dowie; (*specifically of people*) hingin-luggit, drumlie; (*of weather*) drumlie, dour.

glossy *adj* glaizie.

glove *n* gluive, gliv SHETLAND, ORKNEY, N; (*with or without fingers*) mitten.

glow *v* glowe, lowe, leam.
　n glowe, lowe, leam; (*bright, of a fire*)
　gloss, gleed SE.
glowing (*of a fire*) glossy.
glue *n* batter.
glum *adj* dowie, drum, doon o mou.
　why are you so glum? wha stole yer
　scone?
glutton *n* guts(er), midden NE, hecker.
　gluttonous guts(ie), guttie.
　gluttony gutsiness.
　eat gluttonously guts, gorble, heck.
gnaw *v* gnyauve N.
go *v* gae, gang, gan, gyang NE, ging NE;
　(*very quickly*) streek, skelp; (*smoothly*)
　jeck NE; play: '*The door played clink*'.
　n (*energy*) smeddum.
　went *past tense* gaed.
　gone *past participle* gane, geen SHET-
　LAND, ORKNEY, N.
　going *present participle* gaun, ga(a)n,
　gya(u)n SHETLAND, NE.
　going to gaunae.
　goings-on ongauns, wark.
　go away haud awa; (*expressing dis-*
　belief) awa wi ye!
　go off (*of food*) chynge N, gae
　wrang.
goal *n* (*in games*) dale, dool WEST.
　shout when a goal is scored hail.
goat *n* gait.
gobble *v* gorble, lay intae.
goblet *n* tass(ie) *literary*.
goblin *n* black man, wirricow, boodie
　NE.
God *n* Goad, (the) Guid, Dyod NE,
　(the) Almichtie, (the) Michtie.
　godly guidlie NE.
　godforsaken dreich (lik(e)).
　godmother cummer.
going *see* **go**.
gold *n* gowd.
　golden gowden.
　goldfinch goldie, gowdspink.
golf *n* gowf.
　golfer's attendant caddie.
　act as a golfer's attendant caddie.
　golfball gowfba(w), guttie (ba(w)).

golf club (*stick*) gowf stick; **parts of**
golf club: (*flat bottom*) sole; (*socket on*
　head, for shaft) hozle.
gone *see* **go**.
good *adj* guid, gweed NE; (*specifically*
　of character) honest; (*fairly good*) nae
　bad.
　goodly guidlie.
　goodness knows! Deil kens!
　for goodness sake! fur onie sake!
　goods graith, gear: '*guids an gear*'.
　good for nothing *adj* little worth,
　nochtie, waff(lik(e)).
　in good condition bien.
　in good health hardy.
　good-looking weel-faured, braw, son-
　sie, lik(e)ly, pretty.
　good-looking woman stoater, bram-
　mer.
　good person the hert o corn.
　good-sized gey.
　good time rerr terr.
　good turn cast.
　not very good at nae great sticks at
　SHETLAND, NE.
goose *n* guse, geese SHETLAND, OR-
　KNEY, N.
　gooseberry groset, groser, grosart.
　gooseflesh cauld creep(s), hen's
　flesh, hen('s) picks NE, hen('s) plooks
　SOUTH.
gorge *n* (*ravine*) cleuch, heuch.
　v stap, pang NE.
gorgeous *adj* braw.
gorse *n* whin(s), fun(s) NE.
gosling *n* gaislin.
gossamer *n* slammachs NE.
gossip *v* blether, clash, news, clishma-
　claver NE.
　n **1** clavers, cleck, clatter(s), clish-
　clash, news, clishmaclaver(s); (*of the*
　district) countra clash; (*of the town*)
　toon's speak. **2** (*piece of gossip*) say,
　raverie NE. **3** (*person*) cracker; (*man or*
　woman) (auld) sweetie-wife.
　gossipy newsie, clashie, glib-gabbit.
got *see* **get**.
Gouda (cheese) *n* goudie.

gouge *v, n* gudge SHETLAND, ORKNEY, NE.

grab *n, v* grabble, cla(u)cht.

grace *n* (*mealtime prayer*) bethankit.

graceful jimp, gentie.

grace note NB in piping = a short note played over a melody note; series of these are essential to a piping melody.

gracious *adj* couthie.

(good) gracious! michtie (me)!, losh!, fegs!

grain *n* **1** tick, starn NE; (*of oats, barley, wheat*) pickle; (*of oats*) corn. **2** (*cereal crop*) stuff.

grammar *n* gremmar NE.

granary *n* grainerie.

grand *adj* gran, graun(d).

grandchild gran(d)-bairn, gran(d)-wean.

grand-daughter grandochter.

grandfather gran(d)faither, grandaddie, aul(d) faither, guidsire, deyd(ie) NE.

grandmother gran(d)mither, aul(d) mither, luckie (minnie) NE, deyd(ie) NE, grannie.

grandson nevoy.

grapple *v* graipple.

grasp *v* gresp, cla(u)cht NE, tak a ha(u)d o.
n gresp, cla(u)cht.

grass *n* gress, girse.

grassy girsie.

grate[1] *n* chim(b)ley NE.

grating (*in or over a stream*) heck, watter gate; (*over a street-drain*) syver, stank WEST, brander, cundie.

grate[2] *v* (*make a grating sound*) risp, chirk, scart; (*also teeth*) jirg.

grating sound risp SHETLAND, NE, screeve, screed; (*eg by scraping on wood*) scrunt.

grateful *adj* thankrif(e).

gratuity *n* (*from an employer*) pauchle; (*for drink*) drink siller.

grave[1] *n* (*the grave*) mool(s).

graveyard graveyaird.

grave[2] *adj* (*of a person*) thochtie.

gravel *n* graivel, channel, chingle(s) NE; (*fine*) grush.

gravelly chinglie ORKNEY, NE; (*of soil*) shairp, sherp.

gravy *n* bree.

graze[1] *v* (*touch lightly*) scuff, skiff, scutch N; (*the skin*) screeve; (*the ground with a golf club*) sclaff.
n (*light touch*) scuff, skiff.

graze[2] *v* (*of animals*) gae NE; (*nibble*) nip.

grazing girsin ORKNEY, N.

grease *n, v* creesh.

greasy creeshie, glittie.

great *adj* **1** gryte NE; (*in size, amount*) muckle, bonnie, gey, queer; (*remarkable*) unco. **2** (*of relationships*) auld-: 'auld-uncle'.

the greater part (of) the (muckle) feck (o), the maist (o).

great-aunt aul(d)-auntie.

great-grandson nevoy.

great northern diver *n* emmer guse SHETLAND, ORKNEY.

great-uncle aul(d)-uncle.

greed *n* (*for food*) gutsiness.

eat greedily guts, heck (in).

greedy gutsie, hungry, grabbie, ill-hertit NE.

greedy person gled, gutser.

green *adj*: **greenish** greenich(t)ie NE.

greenfinch green lintie, greenie.

greet *v* goam: '*She nivver goamed them*'.

pass on greetings min(d): '*Mind me tae yer mither*'.

grey *adj* gray.

greyhound grew, grew hound.

greyhound racing the grews.

griddle *n* girdle.

gridiron *n* brander.

grief *n* sair; (*constant*) hert-sair; (*source of bitter grief*) hert-scaud.

grief-stricken (hert-)sair: '*She's been hert-sair since her man died*', doilt NE.

grieve *v* fyke; **grieve over** mane (for).

grievance grummle.

deeply grieved hert-sorry, sair vext.
be grieved grudge.
grill v brander.
grim adj (of a person) dour, raucle.
grimace n girn, showl; **grimaces** mudgins.
v girn, murgeon, sham; (in disapproval etc) mak a mowe NE; (from pain, disdain etc) thraw yer gab; (from vexation, bitter taste etc) showl.
grimy adj brockit, brookit.
grin n, v girn.
grind v 1 (to smaller fragments) mak doon, chap. 2 (two surfaces together) scrunt, (also teeth) risp NE.
(back to) the daily grind, (back to) the grindstone (back tae) auld claes an parritch.
grip v, n grup.
gripped past participle gruppen.
grist n girst.
gristle n girsle.
grit n grush.
v (teeth) cramsh.
gritty (of soil etc) shairp.
groan v, n grain.
groin n lisk.
groove n (scratch, score) rit; (deep) rat SOUTH.
cut a groove in rat; (stone or wood) raggle.
grope v growp, fin(d), grapple; (indecently) fin(d), ficher wi SHETLAND, NE, graip SOUTH; (in streams for fish) guddle.
gross adj (of a person: coarse) guttie.
ground n (land) grun(d); (poor, infertile) scaup SHETLAND, NE; (sandy, rolling, near seashore) links E COAST.
group n boorach, paircel.
groups wheens.
group of four, six etc persons or things fowersome, saxsome etc.
grouse[1] v (grumble) girn, natter, yammer, molligrant, mane.
n mane, girn.
grouse[2] n (bird) groose; (red) muirfowl, (male) muircock, (female) muir-

hen; (black, male) black cock, (black, female) gray hen; (wood-grouse) capercailzie.
grovel v snuil: 'Ye'd better snuil tae yer faither fur crashin the car'.
grow v growe; (of plants, rapidly) come awa.
growing fast (of vegetation) growthie.
stop growing (of plants or animals) set.
grown-up adj up, muckle; (of a man) man-grown, man-big; (of a woman) wumman-grown, wumman-muckle.
growth growthe.
grow longer (of days in spring) creep oot, rax.
grow old see old.
grow shorter (of days in autumn) creep in.
grow smaller creep in, crine.
growl v, n gurr, gurl, wurr; (of a dog) nurr.
grub n (of the cranefly) torie NE.
grudge n grummle.
grudging ill-willie.
bear (someone) a grudge hae a pick at, tak a pike at.
gruel n blearie, lithocks.
gruesome adj ug(g)some, growesome.
gruff adj stroonge.
grumble v, n grummle, grumph, girn, mump, witter.
grumbler grumph, girn.
grumbling adj girnie.
n girn.
grumpy adj grumphie, greetin-faced, torn-faced, girnie.
grunt v grumph, grunch, gruntle; (like a pig) grumphie.
n grumph, grunch, gruntle.
guarantee v uphaud, caution.
guard v gaird; (especially at night) wauk.
n gaird.
guess v jalouse, ettle.
guffaw v, n gaff(aw), guff, heffer E CENTRAL.
guide v (a person to a place) airt, wise.

guillemot *n* queet NE, marrot.

guillotine *n* (*in past times: for beheading*) maiden.

guilty *adj*: **feel guilty about** tak tae yersel.

gull *n* goo N, sea goo NE, (sea) ma(w).

gullet *n* thrapple, hause, craig, reid brae.

gullible *adj* fond.

gullible person daft Erchie: '*That daft Erchie believes aw ye tell him*'.

gulp *v* gowp, gollop, glog (ower).
n gowp, glog NE, glut.

gum *n* (*in the mouth*) goom, geem NE.

gumboil gumbile.

gurgle *v* gurl, glog, clunk; (*in the throat*) souch, glag(ger) NE.
n gurl, glog NE, clunk; (*in the throat*) glag(ger) NE.

gurgling *adj* gurlie.

gurnard *n* gowdie.

gush *v, n* **1** (*of liquid*) teem, pish; (*in spurts*) skoosh. **2** (*in speech*) phrase NE.

gushing (*of a person*) phrasie NE.

gusset *n* gushet, eik, (*triangular*) gair.

gust *n* (*of wind etc*) gowst, gliff, flan; (*sudden*) brash; (*with rain*) flaw, bluffert; (*slight*) skiff; (*howling*) gowl; (*of hot air*) (y)oam SHETLAND, NE.
v (*of wind*) dad, teir, flaff, hushle; (*with rain*) scudder NE, (*strongly*) snifter.

gusty gowstie, blashie.

gusty wind hushle.

gut *n* thairm SHETLAND; **guts** puddins.

gutter *n* gitter, trink, channel; (*in a cowshed*) gruip, greep NE; (*roof-gutter*) rone (pipe), spoot; (*street-gutter*) syver, stank WEST, brander NE, cundie.

guzzle *v* guts: '*He gutsed aw the crisps*', gilravage.

gym *n*: **gymnastic feat** henner.

gymshoes sannies, san(d)shuin, san(d)sheen, gutties.

H

habit *n* (*custom*) haunt, trade NE: '*mak a trade o*'; (*whim*) kick NE; **habits** (*manners*) gates NE.

have a habit of be in the wey O.

hack *v, n* hawk, hag, haggle.

had *see* **have.**

haddock *n* haddie, hoddock NE; (*unsplit, smoked*) (Arbroath) smokie; (*split, smoked in peat smoke etc*) Finnan haddie; (*split, dried or smoked*) speldin SHETLAND, N.

haggard *adj* shilpit, shirpit SE.

haggle *v* haigle, argie-bargie, prig.

hail *n*: **hailstone** hailstane.

hailstorm blatter.

hair *n* herr WEST.

haircut cowe, dock.

hair-splitting pea-splittin.

hake *n* herrin hake.

half *n, adj* hauf.
adv halflins NE.

halves haufs.

half-grown boy halflin.

work half-heartedly plowter, plyterNE.

half-holiday halfie: '*We've got a halfie fae the scuil the day*'.

half-past four *etc* hauf fower etc.

halfpenny bawbee, maik.

halfway half-road(s), halflins, half gaits.

halfwit halflin, daftie.

halfwitted half-chack(it), no richt, feel N, far frae aa yonder NE.

go halves gae halvers.

halibut *n* turbot.

hall *n* ha.

halt *v* haut: **1** deval, huilie, stint NE; (*temporarily*) ha(u)d (aff). **2** (*bring to a halt*) reest, stell.
n (*stopping*) haut, deval, stick.

halter *n* (*for horse etc*) helter, mink, branks.

v helter, brank.

halve *v, see also* **half;** hauf, halver.

ham *n* **hams** hunkers.

hamstring *v* hoch.

hammer *n* haimmer, hawmer NE, Glesca screwdriver *humorous*, Paisley screwdriver *humorous* WEST; (*heavy*) mell.

hand *n* haun(d), han, handie *especially to a child;* **hands** (*raised to fight*) gardies.

v, see **hand over** *below.*

handful haunfae, nievefu, luiffu; (*the fill of two hands*) gowpen(fu).

handball (*as played at certain holidays in the Borders and Orkney*) the Ba; (*as played in the Borders with a small ball*) handba.

handcart hurlie(-barrow).

handcuffs snitchers, shangies.

hand-picked han(d)-waled.

handwriting han(d)write, han(d) o write, write.

at hand aboot hand(s), forrit.

hand over lat see.

lend a hand pit tae yer haun(d).

handicap *n* (*burden*) doon-haud, haud-doon.

handkerchief *n* naipkin, snochterdichter.

handle *n* haunle, hannle; (*eg of a cup*) lug; (*of an implement*) heft.

v haunle, hannle; (*especially children, animals*) guide.

handlebars guys NE.

handsome *adj* braw, bonnie, weelfaured.

hang *v* hing.

hung *past tense, past participle also* hingit.

hanging untidily (*of clothes etc*) trollopie.

hangman (*in past times*) hangie.
hangnail ragnail.
hang about haingle, hanker.
hanker *v* ettle, green, m(y)ang NE.
haphazard *adj* antrin.
happen *v*: **happen to** happen, come o: '*Whit'll come o them?*'; (*mainly of misfortune*) come ower; (*mainly in curses, blessings*) fa(w): '*Foul fa her*'.
happy *adj* blithe, blide SHETLAND, ORKNEY, seilie.
  happily blithe.
  happiness seil.
harangue *n* screed, la(m)gammachie NE, scrieve.
harass *v* tra(u)chle, hash, deave, taigle.
  harassed tra(u)chelt: '*trauchelt wi bairns*', deaved, focht(en) NE, taigelt, hauden-doon.
harbour *n* herbour, hythe NE, (the) shore.
hard *adj* (*of a struggle etc*) sair, stieve; (*of a blow etc*) uncannie; (*trying*) coorse NE; (*difficult to understand*) crank; (*of a bargain*) strait; (*of people, actions*) dour.
  adv (*laboriously*) sair.
  harden (*your heart*) steek.
  hardly scantlins, jimp.
  hardship hard.
  hard cash dry siller.
  hard-pressed wi yer back tae the wa, sair pit(ten) tae: '*sair pitten tae, tae fin a babysitter*'.
  hard-up ticht, plackless.
  hard-worked sair wrocht.
  hard-working warslin.
  hard-working person hinger-in.
  be hard on (*clothes*) be sair on, be heavy on, be a heavy neibour on.
hardy *adj* derf.
hare *n* bawd, maukin, bawtie SOUTH, puss(ie).
  harebell bluebell, gowk's thimmles, lady's thummles.
  hare-brained cat-wittit, hallirackit, cude.

harm *v* hairm, herm, skaith, bla(u)d, mischieve SHETLAND, NE.
  n hairm, herm, skaith, ill; (*physical*) mischief.
  harmful sair, ill.
  harmless saikless, ill-less SHETLAND, NE, mows NE.
harness *n* harnish, graith.
  v (*a horse*) graith.
  harnessed (*of a horse*) dra(u)chtit.
harp *n* hairp, herp; (*wire-strung Highland*) clarsach.
  harp on threap, be on (aboot): '*She's aye on aboot the price o fish*'.
  play on a harp hairp, herp.
harrow *n* harra; (*large, heavy*) drag, grubber.
  v (*land*) harra, straik.
  harrowing sair.
harry *v* herrie.
harsh *adj* (*severe*) sair, ill, fell; (*of the voice*) groff SHETLAND, N; (*to the taste*) ramsh; (*of weather etc*) snell.
  harshly sair, snell.
  make a harsh noise chirk, jirg.
  not speak harshly to no say a wrang word tae.
harum-scarum *adj* hawkit.
harvest *n* hairst, hervest; (*potato*) tattie-howkin, tattie-liftin.
  v hairst, hervest, lift, win.
  harvester (*person*) hairster.
  harvest-home (festival) kirn, clyack NE, meal an ale, cailleach.
has *see* **have**.
hash *v* hag, haggle.
haste *n* heest, hist NE.
  hasten heest, hist NE, lick.
  hasty heestie; (*and sharp-tongued*) whippert.
hatch *v* (*eggs*) cleck, clock.
hate *v* ill-will.
  hatred *n* ill will.
haughty *adj* heich, hauchtie, heidie, primp.
  haughtily heich.
  act haughtily cairry a heich heid.

haul *v* hail SHETLAND, NE, harl.
n (*of fish*) drave.
haunches *npl* hainches, hurdies; (*of an animal*) rumple.
　on your haunches on yer hunkers.
　squat on your haunches hunker doon.
haunt *v* hant.
n hant, howf.
have *v* hae, ha, hiv *especially emphatic or interrogative*: '*Hiv ye seen im?*'.
　has *3rd person singular present* his, hes.
　has not hisnae, hisna.
　had *past tense* hid, haid.
　past participle haen.
　had not hidnae, hidna, hadnae, hadna.
　have not hinnae, hinna, hivnae, hivna.
havoc *n* dirdum.
hawk[1] *n* (*bird*) gled.
hawk[2] *v* (*clear the throat*) clocher.
hawk[3] *v* (*sell, peddle*) cadge.
hawser *n* swing rope.
hay *n* hey.
　hay harvest hey.
　hay harvesters hey-fowk.
　haystack ruck, cole.
hazardous *adj* unchancie.
haze *n* gum N; (*frosty*) rime.
hazel *n* hissel.
he *pronoun* hei SOUTH.
head *n* heid, powe, tap.
v (*a ball*) heidie, heider.
　header (*a ball*) heider.
　headache sair heid.
　head-butt *v* pit *or* stick the heid on, gie (someone) a Glesca kiss.
　headlong ramstam.
　rush headlong breenge, skelter.
　headmaster heidie, heidmaister; (*at a small country school*) the maister, dominie.
　headstrong heidie, ramstam.
　headteacher heidie; (*of a secondary school*) rector.
　go to your head (*make giddy*) tak yer heid.

head for airt for, draw till.
head off kep.
head over heels heelster heids, heelster gowdie.
heal *v* hail, sort, mend.
　skilled in healing skeelie.
health *n* (*good*) (guid) heal, weelness; (*normal state of*) usual: '*He's in his usual*'.
　healthy *see also* **in good health** *below*, hail, caller, weel, at yersel, fere.
　in bad health nae weel, badly, hingin (-lik(e)).
　in good health braw (an weel), hardy, stuffie; (*especially after illness*) stoot.
　good health! (*as toast*) slàinte (mhath)! [**slantye** (**va**)].
　in poor health hard up, hingin(-lik(e)).
　improve in health haud forrit.
　ask about the health of ask for: '*Tell him I'm askin fur him*', inquire for, speir for.
heap *n* haip; (*round*) roon(d)el; (*small*) hot, humplock WEST; (*confused*) rickle, boorach; (*of stones, especially as a marker or memorial*) cairn; (*of waste from a mine*) bing.
v haip, hot, hudge NE, boorach; (*untidily*) hudder.
hear *v*: **hard of hearing** deef.
　hear yourself speak hear yer ears.
heart *n* hert, hairt.
　hearty hertie, hertsome, sonsie, guidwillie; (*of a meal*) hertsome SW.
　heartily hertilie.
　heartache hert-scaud.
　heartburn water brash, hert-scaud.
　heart-sore hert-sair.
　suffering from a weak heart hertie.
hearth *n* hairth, herth, chim(b)ley NE.
heat *n* hait; (*sudden state of*) feem NE.
v het, hait; (*partially*) leep; (*a house*) fire: '*Keep the place fired*'.
　heated *past tense, past paticiple* het.
　heating (*act of*) heat: '*Come awa in an get a heat*'.
　heat haze (y)oam SHETLAND, NE, simmer cowt.

be on heat (*especially of a sow*) breem.

heather *n* hedder SHETLAND, NE.

flower of heather heather bell.

heave *v* have ORKNEY, NE; **heave (up)** heeze, hoise, hodge SHETLAND, NE; (*with the shoulder*) hunch.

n heeze, heezie, hizie NE: '*Gie's a hizie up*', hoise; (*with the shoulder*) hunch.

heaven *n* heiven; **the heavens** the lift.

heavenly heivenlie.

heavy *adj* hivvie; (*of a person*) gurthie; (*of dough*) sad, saddit.

hedge *n* dyke sw.

hedgehog hurcheon.

hedge-sparrow hedgie, (hedge-)spurdie.

heed *n* tent.

v tent, tak tent o, leet; **not heed** nivver heed, no fash yersel.

heedful tentie.

heedless ramstam: '*He jist went ramstam ower the road*', regairdless.

give heed to tak tent tae.

heifer *n* heefer.

height *n* heicht, hicht; (*of a person*) lenth.

heighten heicht, heichen, hicht(en).

held *see* **hold**[1].

hell *n* the bad place.

go to hell! gae tae Freuchie (an fry mice)!, gae tae Buckie (an bottle skate)! NE.

help *v* (*lend a hand*) pit tae yer han(d).

helpful helplie.

helping (*of food*) raik.

give a helping hand to gie a lift tae.

helpless mauch(t)less, doweless; (*unable to cope*) silly.

made helpless owertaen.

help yourself (*to food or drink*) mak a lang airm, pit oot yer han(d).

hen *n* chookie (hen); (*broody hen*) clockin hen.

hen-coop (hen-)cavie, hen-crae.

hen-harrier gled.

henpeck drum-major, hoolet, craw in someone's crap.

hen-roost hen-laft.

hen-run (hen-)ree.

hence *adv* (*of places*) hyne.

her *possessive adj* hir, hur; *see also.* **herself.**

herald *n*: **chief herald in Scotland** Lord Lyon (King of Arms).

herd *n* paircel.

v wirk.

herdsman herd, hird.

hereabouts *adv* hereawa.

heron *n* hern, heronshew, (h)erle, cran.

herring *n* herrin.

herring fishing drave.

herself *pronoun* hersel.

by herself (by) her lane, er leen NE.

hesitate *v* swither, hover, swander SHETLAND, N.

hesitant sweirt: '*I'm sweirt tae leave ma job*', sweir-drawn, ergh.

hesitation swither.

hiccup *n*, *v* hick, yesk.

hid *see* **hide**[1].

hide[1] *v* hod NE, dern, scug; (*especially something for later use*) plank, plunk, pose; (*duck out of sight*) jouk.

hid *past tense* hed, hod NE, hoddit SHETLAND, NE, hidit N.

hidden *past participle* hid, hod NE, hoddit SHETLAND, NE, hidit N.

adj (*also good for hiding in*) hidie, dern.

hiding place hidie-hole, hideance.

hide-and-seek hidie, Hi-Spy, keehoy, hidie-go.

hide[2] *n* (*skin*) leather.

higgledy-piggledy *adj, adv* hickertie-pickertie, throuither, throwder NE, heids an thraws.

high *adj* heich; (*of wind*) teirin; (*especially of prices*) lang NE; (*of taste*) humphie.

highest heichmaist.

highest part heid.

highest up heidmaist.

Highland Hielan(d).

Highlander Hielander, teuchter *con-*

temptuous; (*male*) Hielan(d)man; (*especially Gaelic-speaking*) Gael.

Highlands Hielan(d)s.

high-pitched sound skirl; (*especially of a bird*) wheeple.

high-rise flat multi.

hill *n* hull, heich; (*especially higher*) ben.

hillock knowe.

hilly hill-run.

hillside brae, sidelin(s).

himself *pronoun* himsel, hissel.

by himself (by) his lane, him lane, im leen NE.

hind *adj*: **hind leg** (*of an animal*) hoch.

hindmost hint-han(d).

hindquarters (*buttocks*) hinten(d).

hinder *v* hinner, hender, taigle; (*delay*) hing (someone) on NE, (*with something unimportant*) scutter.

hindrance hinner, hing-on, taigle.

hint *v* mint (at) NE, moot SHETLAND, NE.

n moot SHETLAND, NE, mump NE.

not a hint nae a cheep.

he never gave a hint he nivver loot myowt NE.

hip¹ *n* **hips** hurdies.

hip-bone hurkle-bane.

hip² (*fruit*) hap, buckie, dog(gie)'s hip; **hips** hippans NE.

hire *v* (*something in advance*) tryst.

hiss *v* (*of liquid*) bizz; (*of a cat etc*) fuff; (*to drive away an animal etc*) hish.

n (*eg of a cat*) fuff; (*to drive away animals etc*) hish; (*of an object flying through the air*) swiff SHETLAND, NE.

hissing *adj* fuzzie NE.

hit *v* gowf, skite, ding, swap, lift yer han(d) (tae); (*hard*) melt, stookie.

past tense hut, het, hat.

past participle hutten, hitten, hut.

hit out loonder.

hit out at lat at.

hitch *v*: **hitch up** hotch up, hodge up, hilch up.

n (*movement*) hotch.

hive *n* byke.

hoard *n* huird, hoord NE, rake; (*especially for later use*) pit-by, plank, pose.

v huird, hain; (*especially for later use*) plank, pose.

hoarder gear-gatherer.

hoar-frost *n* haar(-frost), cranreuch, rind.

hoarse *adj* hairse, roupie.

speak hoarsely croup NE, FIFE.

hobble *v* **1** habble, hirple, lamp, hilch. **2** (*an animal*) langle, hapshackle.

n (*for an animal*) langle, hapshackle, hoch ban(d).

hobby-horse *n* habbie-horse.

hobgoblin *n* worricow, boodie NE, trowe SHETLAND, ORKNEY, CAITHNESS.

hobnail *n* tacket.

hobnailed boots tacketie buits.

hoe *n* howe, hyowe N, paidle, claut.

v howe, hyowe N, paidle; (*slightly*) scutch N.

hog *n*: **hogweed** humlock, kex SHETLAND, ORKNEY, coo-cakes.

go the whole hog gae yer dinger, gie it laldie.

hoist *v* hyste, heeze, hize NE; (*a sail*) hoise; (*a load*) humph, hulster; (*a person by the buttocks*) dook(ie) (up) SE, punt-up WEST.

n (*lifting-up*) hyste, heeze, hoise, hulster.

hold¹ *v* haud, had, howl(d) SHETLAND, ORKNEY, CAITHNESS, ROSS, ARGYLL, ULSTER.

n (*grasp*) haud, had, howl(d) SHETLAND, ORKNEY, N, ARGYLL, ULSTER, catch, claut.

held *past participle* hauden, hadden.

hold on to haud till, grip till SHETLAND, NE.

hold your tongue haud yer wheesht, steek yer gab.

hold under the arm *see* **arm.**

hold up uphaud; (*hair, with a comb etc*) kep.

catch hold of grip, cla(u)cht.

hold² (*of a ship*) howld.

hole *n* (*especially as a hiding place*)

bore; (*in ground, for marbles game*) kype, mug.

full of holes holiepied NE.

holiday *n* hoaliday; (*annual summer*) the Trades *especially* EDINBURGH, the Fair: '*the Glesca Fair*'; (*from school for potato harvest*) tattie hoalidays.

hollow *n* (*especially in land: on side of a hill*) corrie.

v **hollow (out)** howk, gowp, hallow.

adj howe, boss, hallow; (*of sound*) tuim, teem N, dowf, howe.

holly *n* hollin NE.

holy *adj* halie.

home *n* hame, yer hoose at hame.

homely hamelie, hamit, hameower; (*especially of a person*) hame-made.

home comforts *see* **comfort**.

home farm mains.

home-loving hamit.

home-made hameart, hamit.

homesick hame-drachtit NE.

homeward hamewith.

homeward bound hame-gaun.

homewards hamewith NE, hameower.

at home hame.

away from home ootby.

make your home sit doon.

see (someone) home set (someone) hame.

seeing someone halfway home Scotch convoy.

honest *adj* jonick, furth-the-gate NE, rael; (*sincere*) aefauld, evendoon, leal.

honey *n* hinnie.

honour *n* (*decency*) honesty; (*credit*) mense; (*eg in a contest*) gree: '*win the gree*'.

honourable honest, guid.

hood *n* huid.

hooded huidit.

hooded crow huidie (craw), hoodie craw, grayback, corbie.

hoof *n* huif, hiv N, luif, cloot.

hook *n* heuk, cleek, click; (*especially for a pot*) cruik, clep; (*for hanging things on*) knag.

v cleek, click.

hoop *n* gird.

hoot *v* (*of or like an owl*) hoo.

hop *v* hap, hip SOUTH, hitch.

n (*act of hopping*) hap, hip SOUTH; (*eg in hopscotch*) hitch; (*in a dance*) stot.

hopscotch peever(ie) beds, peever(s), beds, pallal(s) E CENTRAL, skeetchers N, FIFE, hap-the-beds SW, hoppin beddies NE.

stone *etc* **used in hopscotch** peever, pallal E CENTRAL, skeetcher N, FIFE.

hop about lowp.

hop, step and jump hap, step an lowp.

hope *v, n* howp, hoop SHETLAND, ORKNEY.

in a hopeless situation up a clos(i)e.

in the hope of doing in howp(s) tae dae.

hopscotch *see* **hop**.

horrible *adj* ug(g)some, scunnersome.

horribly laithfu NE.

horror *n* (*feeling of*) grue.

feel horror grue: '*It gars me grue*'.

horse *n* **1** cuddie, naig, gry *gipsy;* (*small, sturdy, used in hills*) garron; (*kept for odd jobs*) orra horse. **2** (*gymnasium horse*) cuddie.

horse-collar brecham.

horsefly cleg, gled SOUTH.

hospitable *adj* cadgie, guid-willie.

hospital *n* hoaspital, ospital.

hospitality *n* mense.

hostile *adj* ill-willie, ill.

hostility hosteelitie.

hot *adj* het; (*uncomfortably*) roastit, sweltrie.

hot-tempered birsie.

hot-water bottle (*earthenware*) pig.

hotel *n* hottle.

hound *n, v* houn, hoon(d).

hour *n* oor; (*whole (long) hour*) strucken oor.

keep irregular hours mistime NE.

house *n* hoose, hoosie; (*large, belonging to a landowner*) big hoose, ha(ll); (*one apartment*) single-en(d); (*having *separate entrance etc*) self-contained hoose, hoose within itsel; (*on ground floor*) maindoor (hoose), maindoor flat.

v hoose.

housing estate (*local-authority*) (housing) scheme.

housebound hoose-fast, hoose-tied.

head of the household (*male*) himsel; (*female*) hersel.

houseman (*in a hospital*) resident.

house-martin wunda-swalla.

house-warming (party) hoose-heatin.

housewife guidwife, dame.

change of house shift: '*We want a shift tae a main door*'.

in(to) a house inby.

move house flit.

set up house, become a householder tak up hoose.

how *adv* hoo, foo SHETLAND, N, whit wey, fit wye NE.

conjunction hoo, foo SHETLAND, ORKNEY, N, hoo that, foo that NE.

however hooivver, howanever, foosomever SHETLAND, ORKNEY, N.

how are you? hoo's a(w) wi ye?, foo's a wi ye? N, fit like? NE.

howl *v* gowl, yowt, yammer; (*of the wind*) gurl, hoo.

n gowl, wow, yowt.

huddle *v* hiddle, hunker, coorie in; (*with cold*) nither, hugger NE.

n hiddle; (*eg of buildings*) rickle.

huff *v* fung, strunt.

go into a huff strunt, tak the strunts, tak the tig, tak the gee.

huffy snotty.

hug *v* smoorich.

n bosie, smoorich, lovie *child's word*.

huge *adj* great muckle, muckle big, wappin.

hull *v, n* (*shell*) huil.

hum *v* (*a tune*) souch, sowff NE, sooth NE; (*to accompany dancers*) diddle.

n (*humming sound*) bum; (*low singing*) sooth, sowff NE.

human *adj*: **human being** bodie, buddie; **human beings** fowk.

human race, humanity Jock Tamson's bairns: '*We're aw Jock Tamson's bairns*'.

humble *adj* hummle; (*of people*) lown.

v hummle, tak doon a hack.

humid *adj* mochie, growthie.

humorous *adj* pleasant.

hump *n* humph, hulk.

humpback(ed) *see* **hunch.**

hunch *v*: **hunched** humphed.

hunchback hump(h)ie(-back), hunchie.

hunchbacked hump(h)ie(-backit), humph-backit.

hundred, hundredth *numeral* hunder, hunner.

hung *see* **hang.**

hunger *n* (*ravenous*) hert-hunger NE; (*growing*) curnawin NE.

hungry hungert, tuim, teem N; (*very*) gleg as a gled.

hunk *n* (*lump*) daud.

hunt *v* (*prowl*) snoke.

n fork.

hunt for reenge for: '*Whit are ye reengin fur?*', fork for.

hunt through ripe.

hurry *v* lick, streek; (*cause to hurry*) heeze, gie heels tae.

n lick.

hurt *v* **1** (*injure*) skaith, wrang, mischieve SHETLAND, NE; (*especially on the head*) brain; (*badly*) kill, mairtyr. **2** (*offend*) heelie.

past tense, past participle hurtit.

n **1** (*injury*) skaith, mishanter. **2** (*to feelings*) scaud.

hurtful sair.

hurtle *v* hurl.

husband *n* man, guidman, neibour.

my husband oor ane, oor yin.

hush *v* (*a child to sleep*) ba(w), hushieba.

interjection hish!, wheesht!

hushed wheesht, lown.

husk *n* huil, sloch.

v huil, pilk.
husky roupie.
huskiness the roup.

hut *n* (*fishermen's, climbers'*) bothy.
hysterics *n*: **go into hysterics** gae hyte.

I

I *pronoun* A(h).
Ice *n* frost; (*icy surface*) s(c)lidder NE.
Icicle (ice-)tangle, ice-shogel.
ice-cream cone pokey hat.
ice-cream shop Tallie shop *humorous*.
ice-cream wafer slider; (*two with marshmallow filling and chocolate edge*) black man.
cold as ice jeel caul(d) NE, fair jeelit NE.
idiot *n* eejit, daftie, heidbanger, bawheid, neep-heid, numptie; (*clumsy*) muckle sumph: '*Ye muckle sumph, ye!*'.
idiocy eediocie.
idiotic eediotical, feel NE.
idle *adj* (*completely*) horn idle.
v sloonge.
idleness idleset.
If *conjunction* gin.
ignore *v* (*a person*) (sling someone a) deefie: '*He deefied me*'.
ill *adj* ull, nae weel, unweel, badly; (*slightly*) hingie, hingin; (*seriously*) far awa wi't; (*dangerously*) far throu.
be ill traik.
become ill tak ill, tak nae weel.
illness ill SHETLAND, N, unweelness NE; (*slight*) tribble; (*especially of unknown origin*) income; (*in children, with no particular cause*) hives; (*sudden*) owercome, brash; (*slight*) towt, skiff.
ill-looking hingin-lik(e), hingie, peelie-wallie, nae weel lik(e).
ill-mannered ignorant.
ill-treat ool.
image *n* eemage.
the (very) image of the spitten eemage o, the marrow o: '*She's the marrow o her mither*'.
imagine *v* jalouse: '*Ah cannae jalouse her mairriet on him!*'.

imbecile *n* daftie, haiverel, feel NE; *see also* **mentally handicapped person** (*under* **mentally handicapped**).
imitate *v* eemitate.
immature *adj* bairnlik(e).
immediately *adv* richt noo, in a crack, stra(u)cht, immedantlie NE.
immoral *adj* lowse.
live immorally gae an ill gate.
imp *n* deevilock NE, limb o the deil.
impatient *adj* (*short-tempered*) on nettles, fuffie; (*restless*) lik a hen on a het girdle.
be impatient with fash at.
exclamation of impatience ach!, och!, in the name (o a(w))!, michtie (me)!
impetuous *adj* heidie, ramstam, breengin.
impetuously fiercelins, ramstam, breengin.
import *v* (*into a place*) inbring.
think yourself important hae a guid consait o yersel.
impose *v*: **imposing** (*of things*) vogie, gawsie.
imposition imposeetion, humbug NE.
impossible *adj* (*out of the question*) oot the windae.
impress *v* pit on.
imprison *v* (*put in prison*) nick, prison SHETLAND; (*shut away*) steek.
improve *v* impruive; (*character etc*) mend; (*in health*) mak better SHETLAND, kittle NE; (*continue to get better*) haud forrit.
improvement (*in health*) betterness: '*There's nae betterness for him*'.
not improve no mak a better o't; (*in health*) nae mak muckle o't SHETLAND, NE.
impudent *adj* impident, gallus, forrit(some).

Impudence impidence, snash, back-jaw.

speak impudently gange; (*in reply*) speak back.

Impulsive *adj* furthie, raucle, ramstam.

In *preposition* i; (*inside, forming a part of*) in o, intil: '*There's tatties intil't*'; (*in respect of*) o(f): '*It's a queer thing o me*'.

ins and outs oots an ins.

Inability *n* inabeelitie.

Inactive *adj* thowless, daichie; (*and fat*) brosie-heidit NE.

remain inactive lie by.

Inadequate *adj* (*not enough*) scrimpie, scrimpit, jimp; (*of a person*) fushionless.

Inattentive *adj* tentless.

Incapable *adj* haiveless N; **incapable of** unable for.

Inclination *n* inklin, list.

follow your own inclination gang yer ain gate.

Income *n*: **constant source of income** dreepin roast.

Incomer ootrel; (*to Shetland*) soothmoother; (*to Orkney*) ferry-lowper.

Incompetent *adj* han(d)less.

Incompetence han(d)lessness.

Inconvenience *n, v* fash, footer.

Increase *v* (*in length*) rack; (*make bigger*) eik (tae).
n eik.

Indecent *adj* undecent, footie.

Indecency (*especially in language*) sculdudderie.

Indecision *n* swither, whittie-whattie; (*fussy*) haiver(s), aff-pit.

Indeed *adv* atweel.

interjection fegs!, hech ay!, na! SHETLAND, NE, yea!

Indifferent *adj* (*not caring*) jack easy; (*cold in manner*) cauldrif(e); (*of health etc*) siclik(e).

be indifferent no jee yer ginger.

Indirectly *adv* (*of speech or look*) sidelins.

Indiscreet *adj* unwicelik(e) N.

Indiscreetly braid (oot).

Indoors *adv* inby, therein.

Industrious *adj* eydent.

Inefficient *adj* han(d)less, kirnin NE; (*disorganized*) throuither, throwder NE.

Inefficiency throuitherness.

he's very inefficient he couldnae run a menodge.

Infant *n* bairn(ie), wean CENTRAL, ULSTER, geet NE.

Infant school wee scuil, little skweel(ie) NE.

Infect *v* smit, infeck.

Infected (*of a wound etc*) atterie, bealin: '*That plook's bealin*'.

Infectious smittle, smittin.

Infested *adj* hoatchin, hotchin, lowpin.

Influence *n*: **use influence** mak moyen(s) NE.

Inform *v* **1 inform of** lat wit. **2** *see* **tell (tales).**

Information wittin; (*got by enquiry*) speirins; (*in advance*) moyen NE: '*get moyens o*'.

ask for information from inquire at, speir (at).

not inform no lat dab.

Infuriate *v* raise.

Infuse *v* (*tea*) mask, mak, scaud SW.

become infused (*of tea*) draw.

Inhuman *adj* ill-set.

Inject *v* jag.

Injection jag.

Injure *v* skaith, mischieve SHETLAND, NE, blaud, mittle, malagrooze NE.

Injury ill, mischief, skaith, mishanter SHETLAND, ORKNEY, N; (*severe*) massacker SHETLAND, ORKNEY, NE.

-in-law *suffix* guid-: '*guid-faither*'.

Inlet *n* inlat; (*of the sea: narrow, rocky*) gote; (*steep-sided*) geo SHETLAND, ORKNEY, CAITHNESS; (*long, deep between rocks*) slock.

Inner *adj*: **in the inner part** ben, inby.

Innocent *adj* ill-less SHETLAND, NE.

play the innocent act the daft laddie *or* lassie.

Inoculation *n* jag.
Inquire *v* speir.
　Inquire after ask for, see aboot.
Inquisitive *adj* inqueesitive, queesitive, speirin, nebbie; (*rudely*) lang-nebbit.
Insane *adj* daft, awa wi't, gyte, no wice, wrang NE, awa in the heid.
Insect *n* beast(ie).
Inside *preposition* inower, intil, in o.
　adv ben, inby, inower.
　inside out backside foremaist.
　turn inside out flype.
Insincere *adj* pitten-on, sleekit.
　insincerity pit-on.
Insipid *adj* (*especially of food*) wersh, fushionless, saurless; (*of liquor*) shilpit; (*especially of people*) fushionless, palie, peelie-wersh SOUTH; (*of things*) smeerless N.
Insist *v* (*strongly*) threap.
　be insistent with threap at *or* wi.
Insolent *adj* ill-mou'd.
　insolence, insolent language clack.
Insomniac *adj* waukrif(e).
Inspect *v* leuk, see, sicht, vizzie.
Instant *n* crack, rap.
Instead *adv* insteid.
Insufficient *adj* scrimp, jimp.
Insult *v* lichtlie, misca(w).
　n dunt; (*insulting remark*) snash.
Intact *adj* intack.
Intellect *n* intelleck.
Intelligent *adj* heidie, mensefu.
　intelligence mense, wit, harns.
Intend *v* ettle, mint.
Intent *adj* eydent; **intent on** browden on NE.
　intentionally willintlie.
Intercourse *n*: **have (sexual) intercourse with** mell wi.
Interest *n*: **take an interest** leuk the gate o.
　take no interest in someone no leuk the road someone is on.
Interfere *v* pit in yer spuin, mak or meddle; **interfere with** middle, parry wi.
Interrogate *v* speir, tarragat.

Interrogation speirin(s).
Interrupt *v* interrup.
Interview *n* (*private*) collogue.
Intestines *npl* painches, puddins, intimmers *humorous*.
Intimate *adj* (*friendly*) far ben, chief, pack.
　n (*female*) cummer.
Intimidate *v* coonger, daunton.
Into *preposition* intae, intil, in.
Intolerable *adj* past a(w).
Intonation *n* (*nasal*) sneevil.
Intricate *adj* kittle, fykie, pernicketie, quirky.
Introduction *n* innin.
Invent *v* (*think up*) cleck.
Investigate *v* pit throu han(d)s, howk, speir oot.
　investigation speirin.
Invite *v* inveet, seek, speir; (*to a wedding etc*) bid.
　invitation inveet; (*to do something*) biddin; (*last-minute*) fiddler's biddin, piper's biddin.
Iris *n* (*flower, especially wild yellow*) seg, seggan WEST.
Iron *n* airn.
　v airn; (*cloth*) dress: '*Dress yer suit fur the waddin*'.
　ironing airnin.
Irregular *adj* (*at irregular intervals*) orra.
　irregularity gley NE.
Irresponsible *adj* glaikit, rhymeless NE, rudas NE.
Irritate *v* fash.
　irritable *adj* crabbit, carnaptious, capernoitie.
Is *v*: **is not** isnae, isna.
It *pronoun* **1** hit, hut, 't. **2** (*children's games*) het, hit, mannie NE.
Italian *adj, n* Tallie *humorous or contemptuous*.
Itch *v* yeuk.
　n yeuk, fykes.
　itchy yeukie.
Itself *pronoun* itsel.
　by itself its lane.

J

Jab *v* job, prog.
  n **1** job, prog. **2** (*injection*) jag.
Jack *n* **1** Jock. **2** jack (*bowls*) kittie. **3** jack (*cards*) munsie NE.
  jackdaw kae.
  Jack Frost nip-nebs.
Jacket *n* jaicket.
Jagged *adj* pikie.
Jail *n, v* jile.
  Jailer jiler.
  be sent to jail get the jile.
Jam *n* jeelie.
  Jamjar jeelie-jaur, jeelie-can.
  jam pan jeelie pan.
  bread and jam jeelie piece, piece on jeelie, piece an jeelie.
January *n* Januar.
Jar *n* jaur; (*especially earthenware*) pig, crock.
Jaundice *n* jandies, gulsoch.
Jaw *n* **jaws** chowks, chafts.
  Jawbone chaft-blade.
Jealous *adj* jeelous.
  make jealous chaw.
Jell *v* jeel.
  Jelly jeelie, jeel; (*specifically table-jelly*) trimmlin tam(mie).
  Jellyfish scalder, scowder.
Jerk *v* fidge, yerk; (*up and down*) hotch.
  n yerk, jink, hotch; (*sharp, forward, especially of a marble with finger and thumb*) plunk.
  jerky movement hirtch.
  move jerkily hainch, hodge.
Jersey *n* (*fisherman's etc*) gansey.
Jet *n* (*of liquid*) skoosh, scoot.
Jewel *n* jowel NE.
Jib *v* (*of a horse*) reest.
Jiffy *n* glisk.
  In a jiffy in a crack.
Jig *v, n* jeeg.
Jilt *v* gie (someone) the fling, fling, gie (someone) the gunk.
  be jilted get the fling.
Jingle *v, n* tingle.
Job *n* **1** (*situation*) joab. **2** (*task: fiddly*) footer.
  job centre b(u)roo.
Jocular *adv* jokie, pleasant, joco.
Jog *v* **1** shog. **2 jog along** shoggle.
  n (*push*) dunch, shog.
Join *v, n* jine.
  Joiner jiner, wricht NE.
  Joint jint; (*of the body*) lirk; (*of the finger or toe*) lith; (*especially in backbone*) link.
  Join in hing tae; (*to the company*) come intae the body o the kirk.
Joke *n* baur: '*jist a baur*', mows; (*practical joke*) ploy, heeze NE.
  no joke nae mows NE.
  enjoy a joke at the expense of hae a rag oot o.
Jolly *adj* (*of people*) sonsie, gawsie, joco.
Jolt *v, n* shoggle, hotter.
Jostle *v* oxter; (*football*) rummle up.
Jot *n* dottle, stime.
Journey *n* traivel, gang.
  set out on a journey steer, road NE.
Joyful *adj* blithe, blide SHETLAND, ORKNEY.
Judge *n* (*of the Court of Session*) law lord.
Jug *n* joug; (*especially milk- or cream-*) stowp NE; (*especially cream-*) poorie.
Juggle *v* joogle.
Juice *n* bree, broo, joice SHETLAND, N.
  Juicy (*of meat*) sappie.
Jumble *v* jummle, taigle, taisle.
  n jummle, mixter-maxter, taigle.
Jump *v, n* lowp, jimp.
Junction *n* (*where a side road meets a main one*) road-en(d).

junk food *n* snashters, gulshichs NE.
just *adj* jonick.
　adv jist, juist, jeest NE, e'en, nae bit NE;
　(*newly*) new.

just now the noo, ivnoo NE.
just so ay ay.
justify *v* justifee.

K

keel over *v* cowp, tirl, whummle.

keen *adj* **1** (*excessively*) hyte; **keen on** on for, ill aboot NE; **keen to** wuid for, wuid tae. **2** (*in seeing, thinking etc*) gleg. **3** (*of wind etc*) snell, thin, fell, haarie.

keenness (*sharpness*) glegness.

keep *v* **1** (*guard*) kep. **2** (*continue*) haud.

kept *past tense, past participle* keepit, keppit.

keepsake mindin.

keep away haud aff; (*keep someone away*) herd fae; **keep away from** haud by NE.

keep going shog, keep the puddin het.

keep in order coonger, haud in aboot.

keep in with haud in wi, sook in wi.

keep out haud oot.

keep up haud on.

kerb *n* crib.

kernel *n* kirnel.

key *n* (*for a door*) check.

kick *v* dump; (*especially of a horse*) fling, fung; (*a football etc, hard*) blooter.

n fung; (*from an animal*) fling.

kick about (*restlessly*) wallop; (*especially in bed*) fowe NE.

kill *v* en(d), fell, nail.

kiln *n* kill.

kilt *n*: **man wearing a kilt** kiltie.

kind[1] *n* (*sort*) kin, thing: '*Wull ye hae white breid or the broon thing?*'.

all kinds akin-kin(d) NE.

kind[2] *adj* couthie, cannie, furthie.

kindly *adj* hamelie, guidwillie, lithe.

take kindly to tak wi.

act of kindness obleegement.

kindle *v* kennle, kinnle.

kindling kennlin, kinnlin, kinnlers NE.

king *n* keeng.

kink *n* (*twist, coil*) kinch, snorl, jink NE; (*in character*) lirk NE.

kipper *n* twa-eyed (beef) steak *humorous*.

kiss *v* pree the lips o; (*loudly*) smack; (*sloppily*) slaik; (*exchange kisses*) smoorich.

n smoorich, smirk NE; (*light*) (wee) cheep(er).

kissing game bee-baw-babbitie.

kitchen *n* kitchie N; (*of a but-an-ben*) but, but the hoose N.

kitchen-maid scodgie; (*on a farm*) (kitchie) deem NE.

kite *n* **1** (*toy*) (fleein) draigon. **2** (*bird*) gled.

kitten *n* kittlin.

kittiwake *n* kittie, tarrock.

kitty *n* (*in a game*) puggie; (*for a social gathering etc*) jine.

knack *n* slicht.

having lost the knack aff the fang.

knead *v* kned, kyauve NE, chaave N, taw.

knew *see* **know**.

knife *n* whittle, futtle N; (*large*) gullie (knife); (*weapon*) chib *slang;* (*worn in kilt stocking*) sgian dubh; (*pen-knife*) jockteleg.

v chib *slang.*

knife-throwing game knifie.

knight *n* knicht.

knit *v* tak a loop; (*especially stockings*) wyve NE; (*stockings*) shank.

knitting wyvin NE.

knitting needle wire, weer NE; **set of knitting needles** wires, weers NE.

knob *n* (*bump, lump*) knoit.

knock *v* chap, dunt, ding, ca(w);

(*sharply*) knap, rap; (*at a door*) chap. *n* chap, dunt, ding, ca(w); (*sharp*) knap.

knock off (*work*) lowse.

knocking-off time lowsin time.

knock-kneed in-kneed, sha(u)chlin.

knock down ca(w) doon, whummle; (*specifically a person*) cowp.

knoll *n* (*hillock*) knowe.

knot *n* **1** (*running*) kinch. **2** (*in wood*) knag, swirl.

knotty (*of wood*) swirlie.

know *v* ken, knaw.

knew *past tense* kent.

knowledge ken, wittin(s), lair.

known kent.

knuckle *n* (k)nickle, knockle; (*of beef*) skink.

L

labour *n* lawbor.
  v lawbor, warsle.
  laborious typin NE, pinglin.
  laboriously sair NE.
lack *v* want, wint NE.
  n inlaik, scant, ingang, haud-in;
  (*especially of food*) faut.
lad *n* lawd, laddie, chiel(d), callan(t),
  loon N.
ladder *n* ledder; (*eg to a loft*) trap.
lady *n* leddy.
  ladybird leddy launners, sodger.
  lady's smock spink.
lain *see* **lie**².
lake *n* loch; (*small*) lochan, peel NE.
  lake-dwelling (*on artificial island*)
  crannog.
lamb *n* lammie(-meh) *especially as pet
  name;* (*female*) yowe lamb; (*male*)
  tuip-lamb; (*reared by hand*) pet
  (lamb).
lame *adj* cripple, palie, hippitie; (*especially of a horse*) cruikit.
  walk lamely hirple, cripple.
  lameness hainch.
lament *n* croon.
  v greet, yammer, croon N.
  lamentation greetin, scronach NE,
  yammer.
lamp *n* (*oil*) (eelie) dolly NE; (*in past
  times: boat-shaped with rush wick*)
  cruisie.
  lamplighter leerie.
lancet *n* lance.
land *n* lan, laun(d).
  landing (*on a staircase*) plat, plettie
  DUNDEE; (*at top of common staircase*)
  stairheid.
  landing place the shore N, FIFE.
  landlady (*of an inn*) luckie, guidwife.
  landlord (*of property*) laird.

landmark (*especially used by sailors*)
  meith; (*heap of stones, especially on
  hill top*) cairn.
landowner laird.
language *n* leid, langage.
lap *v* **1** (*drink*) laip, laib. **2** (*of water*)
  lapper.
  lapping sound lapper.
lapwing *n* peesweep, peewee(t), peesie,
  teuchit, teewheet, wallopie.
larch *n* larick.
lard *n* (*swine's*) same.
larder *n* aumrie, spence.
large *adj* muckle, meikle, lairge.
  something large of its kind beezer,
  wheesher.
lark¹ *n* (*bird*) laverock, larick NE.
lark² *v* daff.
lash *n* (*with a whip etc*) screenge,
  cracker, whang, leerup N.
  v **1** leash, leerup N, whang. **2** **lash
  down** (*of rain*) plash, leash, ding
  doon.
last¹ *v* (*endure*) lest.
last² *adj, adv* hin(d)maist, hinnermaist,
  lest.
  v **1** lest. **2** **last out** get ower NE, dree.
  last night yestreen, the streen OR-
  KNEY, N.
  last part hinderen(d), hinneren(d).
  last year fernyear.
  at last at (the) lang lenth, at lenth an
  lang.
latch *n* sneck, cleek.
  v sneck, snib.
late *adj* (*after the event*) ahin(t): 'She
  arrived ahint for the waddin'; (*after the
  expected time*) yon time: 'He didnae
  get hame till yon time'.
  adv hyne NE, ower SHETLAND, NE.
  later (*at a later time*) again: 'Keep it
  an Ah'll get it again'.

late hours (*of the night*) (wee) sma oors.

lather *n* (*soap suds*) (saipie) sapples, (saipie) graith.
v freith.

Latin *n* Laitin.

latter *adj* hinner.

latterly at *or* i the hinneren(d).

laugh *v* la(u)ch; (*heartily*) heffer; (*noisily, excitedly*) keckle; (*when trying not to*) smudge, smue.
n la(u)ch; (*hearty*) heffer; (*loud*) keckle.

laughed *past tense* la(u)cht, leuch N. *past participle* la(u)cht, la(u)chen NE.

get a laugh out of hae a rag oot o.

no laughing matter nae mows NE.

laughter *n* la(u)chter; (*irrepressible*) kink: '*gae intae kinks*'; '*He went intae a kink*'.

choke with laughter kink.

shake with laughter hotch, hotter NE, hodge NE.

launch *v* lench.

law *n* laa NE.

lawyer lawer, lawvyer, writer, man o business.

lawful lawfu, lawfae.

lawless lowse.

law-abiding leal.

lay *v* (*a table*) set in.

layer (*thin*) skliffer; (*thin surface layer*) scruif, screef NE.

lay aside pit by, set by.

layout ootset.

well laid out snod.

lazy *adj* sweir(t), doxie NE, haingle NE, daeless; (*very*) hert-lazy, stane-tired SOUTH; (*apt to be lazy*) easy-osie.

laziness idleset, sweirtie SHETLAND, NE; (*fit of laziness*) lazy.

lazy person snuil, sloonge.

be lazy snuil, sloonge.

lead[1] *n* (*metal*) leid.

lead pencil keelivine.

lead[2] *v* (*guide, direct*) wice.

leader (*manager*) (high) heid yin, heid bummer.

leaf *n* (*of a cabbage, turnip etc*) blade;
leaves and stalks (*of potatoes, turnips etc*) shaws.

leak *v* leck, laik, seep, rin oot, (*especially slowly*) sype; (*of a boat*) tak in.

leakage seep(age), sype.

leak out skail; (*of news*) spunk oot NE.

lean[1] *n, v* (*out of a window to watch*) hing.

lean-to tae-fa(w), fa(w)-tae.

lean[2] *adj* (*thin*) tuim, teem NE, nakit, slink.

leap *v* lowp, sten(d), spang.
n lowp, sten(d), wallop.

leapfrog lowp-the-cuddie, cuddie-lowp(-the-dyke).

learn *v* lairn, leern NE; (*find out*) lear.

learning lair; (*education*) buik-lair.

leather *n* ledder SHETLAND, NE.

leave *v* lea, lave; (*abandon*) quat; (*go away*) win awa; (*in a hurry*) be uptail an awa.

lecture *n* lecter; (*scolding*) hearin, chaw N.

left *adj* (*opposite of right*) car.

left-handed car(rie), corrie(-fistit), car(rie-)handit SOUTH.

leftovers *npl* orts, orra(l)s, pan-jotrals.

leg *n* (*long, thin*) spurtle shank; (*of meat*) shank; (*of lamb or pork*) gigot; (*of a sock or stocking etc, especially while being knitted*) shank; (*of a table etc*) stoop.

leg-up hainch, dook(ie)-up, punt-up WEST.

lemon *n* leemon, limon.

lemonade skoosh, leemonade, ginger WEST, sproosh NE, ale NE.

lemon sole *see* **sole.**

lend *v* len.

length *n* lenth.

lengthen rax; (*especially of days*) creep oot; (*eg clothing*) eik.

lengthwise, at full length en(d)lang.

full length streek.

your full length breadth an lenth.

let *v* (*allow*) lat.
past tense lat, loot, leet NE.
past participle latten, letten, lat.

let fly lat skelp.

let-down snipe NE.

let go lowse.

letter *n* (*postal*) scrieve; (*short, hasty*) scrape o the pen.

lettuce *n* laituce.

level *adj* (*smooth, even*) snod, evenlie NE, skleff SOUTH.

level-headedness rum(mle-)gumption.

lever *n* gavelock.

v pinch.

liar *n* leear.

libel *n* (*law*) defamation (NB also covers English 'slander').

liberal *adj* leeberal, hertie, guid-willie.

liberate *v* leeberate.

liberty *n* leebertie.

library *n* leebrarie.

lice *npl, see also* **louse**; cattle; (*head lice*) beasts in the heid.

person with head lice scabbie heid, beastie heid.

licence *n* leeshence.

license *v* leeshence.

lichen *n* fog; (*used for dyeing*) crottle.

lick *v* slaik; **lick up** laib, lerb NE.

n slaik, lerb NE.

lick of paint *see* **paint**.

lie[1] *v, see also* **liar**; lee, whid.

n lee, whid; (*mild*) slide NE; (*deliberate*) made lee.

tell a mild lie slide NE.

lie[2] *v* (*be horizontal*) lig *now literary*; (*lie down*) lean.

lain *past participle* lien NE.

lie-in long lie.

life *n*: **full of life** lifie, green.

lift *v*: **lift (up)** heeze, heyze NE, hoise; (*something heavy*) humph.

n **1** (*heave up*) heeze, hoise. **2** (*in a vehicle*) cairrie, hurl.

light[1] *n* (*brightness*) licht, leam *literary;* (*faint*) gloam, (*quick flicker*) spunk(ie); (*for a cigarette etc*) lunt.

v licht(en); (*a fire, match*) spark, sperk SOUTH, SW.

adj licht.

lightning fire-fla(u)cht; (*without thunder*) wild fire.

flash of lightning fla(u)cht.

light[2] *adj* (*not heavy*) licht.

lighten lichten.

lightly licht(lie).

light-fingered tarry-fingered, sticky-fingered.

light-footed lichtsome.

light-headed (*especially from drink*) reezie.

lightning *see* **light**[1].

like[1] *adj, preposition* lik.

n maik: '*They nivver saw the maik o't*'.

likely lik(e).

likelihood lik(e)ly.

more like (mair) liker.

likeness (*exact*) spitten eemage.

likewise siclike, an a(w).

like[2] *v* lik.

likeable fine.

liking goo (of *or* for); (*affection*) notion (o *or* tae), dint (o) NE.

have a liking for be keen o; (*special liking*) hae a saft side tae.

like very much lik(e) fine: '*We lik it fine*', fair lik(e).

lilac *n* laylock.

limit *n, v* leemit.

limp *v, n* hirple: '*hirplin alang*', lamp, hilch, hainch.

limpet *n* lempit.

line *n, see also* **fishing line** (*under* **fish**); (*boundary line*) ma(i)rch.

out of line aff the straucht.

linger *v* hinder, taigle, dachle NE.

lingering (*slow*) lag.

link *v*: **link arms (with)** cleek (wi).

linnet *n* lintie.

lip *n* (*especially of a cow*) mull.

liquid *n* bree, broo; (*quantity of*) sup; (*in which something is dipped*) dook; (*stirred up with sediment*) jabble; (*small quantity*) jibble.

be covered in liquid sail: '*The flair's sailin*'.

liquorice *n* lickerie, sugarallie, black sugar.

liquorice drink sugarallie watter.

liquorice root (*chewed by children*) lickerie stick.

list *n* (*of candidates for a post*) leet: '*long leet*'; '*short leet*'.

put on a list of candidates leet.

listen *v*: **listen to** hark (tae), hearken, tent; (*carefully*) tak tent tae.

just listen to him *etc*! hear till him etc!

refuse to listen steek yer lugs.

listless *adj* hingin, fushionless, thowless.

litter *n* (*of animals*) brod, cleckin.

smallest of a litter rig, shargar, the shakkins o the pokie.

little *adj* wee, peedie ORKNEY, CAITHNESS, FIFE, peerie SHETLAND.

a little (*a (very) small amount*) a wee (bit), a bittie, a (wee) tait, a (wee) thocht, a (wee) pickle; (*somewhat*) a piecie, a (wee) bit, a (wee) tait: '*a wee tait bigger*', a (wee) thocht, a (wee) thing(ie).

little finger pinkie, crannie(-doodlie) N.

little girl lassock(ie), wee quine NE.

little lamb lammie.

little man, little boy mannie.

every little helps monie a mickle maks a muckle.

live[1] *v* leeve; (*in a place*) stey, bide, haud oot.

make a living mak saut tae yer kail, mak oot.

live from hand to mouth pewl.

live on leeve aff.

live[2] *adj*: **lively** (*active*) gleg, leevin-lik(e); (*of an animal*) keen; (*spirited*) cantie, skeich, lifie; (*in conversation*) knackie; (*bustling*) steerie; (*restless*) steerin.

liveliness smeddum, lifiness.

livestock gear, cattle-baists, (ferm) stockin.

load *n* laid, draucht, lift; (*amount carried at one time*) raik, gang, fraucht; (*small load*) pauchle; (*full load*) fou.

v laid, prime.

loaf *n* laif, half-laif; (*old enough to cut*) cuttin laif; (*white, baked in tin*) pan laif; (*white, baked in batch*) plain laif.

loan *n* len; (*brief use*) shot: '*Gie's a shot o yer bike*'; (*of a book*) read(in).

loath *adj* laith, sweir(t).

loathe *v* laith.

loathing laith, scunner, ug NE.

a person or thing you loathe scunner: '*Ma man's a richt scunner*'.

lobby *n* entry, trance.

lobster *n* lapster, labster.

lobster trap (lapster) creel.

local *n* (*pub*) howf.

lock[1] *v, n*: **fastened by a lock, secure under lock and key** lockfast.

lockjaw jaw-lock.

lock[2] *n* (*of hair*) tossel, swirl.

lodge *n, v* ludge.

lodger ludger.

lodging(s) ludgin(s).

loft *n* laft.

log *n* (*of wood*) clog, stock NE.

loiter *v* (*dawdle*) lyter, haingle, haik.

lonely *adj* lanelie, lanerlie, lanesome, hertalane.

long *adj* lang.

v **long (for)** green (for), think lang (for), mang (for), myang (for) NE.

long ago lang syne, lang back.

a long time a guid bit.

long-eared *see* ear.

long-winded (*of a person*) en(d)less; (*of speeches etc*) dreich.

look *v* leuk, luck, deek.

n leuk, luck, deek; (*close*) sicht; (*quick*) scance, swatch.

-looking *in compounds* -lik(e): '*daftlike*'; '*queerlik*'.

look after leuk ower, guide, tend, tent; (*a person*) see efter, see aboot.

look at leuk till.

look for (*search for*) seek, fork for.

look here! leuk see!

look like (*of weather*) mak for: '*It's makkin for snaw*'.

look out! watch yersel!, mind whaur ye're gaun!, mind yersel!

be on the lookout be on the haik (for), keep shot(tie) (for): '*keep shot for the polis*'.

It's a poor lookout for it's a(w) up a clos(i)e wi.

look out of the window leuk ower the windae.

loom *n* luim, leem N.

loop *n* kinch, mink N; (*especially for fastening*) latchet; (*to attach a fishing hook*) snuid.

v hank.

loose *adj* lowse.

loosen lowse, lowsen.

loose-fitting (*of clothes*) lowse.

become loose lowse.

lop (off) *v* sned, sneck.

lop-sided *adj* lab-sidit, skellie, a(w) tae the one side lik Gourock.

lord! *exclamation* losh (me)!, laird!, lorie! SHETLAND, N.

lorry *n* larrie; (*refuse collector's*) scaffie('s) cairt, midgie motor.

lose *v* loss, loass, tyne.

lose ground gae back.

loss *n* loass, miss: '*She's a big miss*'; (*by being cheated*) snipe NE.

cause the loss of tyne.

lost *adj* tint, loast.

get lost! gae tae Freuchie (an fry mice)!, gae tae Buckie (an bottle skate)!

horse *or* **dog which has lost a race** binger.

lot[1] *n*: **a lot** a lump, an awfie, an awfu: '*There an awfu wasps here the day*'.

the lot he hail jing-bang, the hail clamjamfrie.

lot[2] *n*: **lottery** lucky pot.

cast lots draw straes.

loud *adj* lood, fell.

loudly, in a loud voice lood oot, heich.

speak loudly bairge NE.

lounge *v* loonge, sloonge, floan NE.

louse *n, see also* **lice** *pl;* loose, Jerusalem traiveller, poolie; (*head louse*) tra(i)veller *humorous*.

lout *n* keelie, cowt, NE, coof.

love *v* luve, loo *literary;* (*especially a person of the opposite sex*) lik(e).

n luve, hert-likin SHETLAND, NE.

lovable loosome, douce, leesome.

lover lovie, chap, jo *literary*.

ex-lover auld shuin.

loving *adj* fain.

lovely bonnie.

lovesick gyte.

fall in love get the smit.

make love curdoo FIFE.

low[1] *adj* laich, law; (*in spirits*) doon o mou.

lower *adj* (*especially of a place*) nether; (*of a river*) sma.

v laich; (*the head*) loot; (*the price of*) lat doon.

low-class waff, schemie.

low-class-person keelie, schem(i)e, scaff.

lowland lawlan(d), lallan.

low-lying inby.

low[2] *v* (*of cattle*) rowt, belloch.

loyal *adj* leal, sicker, stench NE, stieve.

loyally leal.

loyalty lealtie.

lozenge *n* (*sweet*) lozenger.

luck *n*: **good luck** sonse; **piece of luck** luck SHETLAND, nibble SOUTH.

bad luck misluck, wanluck SHETLAND.

have bad luck be ill-luckit (wi).

lucky cannie, sonsie, seilie.

lucky dip lucky poke.

be lucky luck.

lug *v* humph, haigle SOUTH.

lukewarm *adj* lew (warm).

lull *v* (*to sleep*) ba(w), hushie-ba(w).

n (*in weather*) daak N; (*at sea*) sma.

lullaby hushie-ba(w), baloo.

lumber *n* troke, rottacks NE.

lump *n* (*large piece*) da(u)d, claut, knoit, kneevle, toldie NE, doldie; (*of mud etc*) clag; (*of something soft*) gob; (*especially of food*) dunt, junt NE; (*eg of cheese, butter*) skelp; (*especially of cheese*) kneevlick NE; (*in porridge etc*)

knot; (*bump*) knurl, knap ORKNEY,
NE; (*caused by a blow*) cloor.
v 1 (*form lumps, of porridge etc*) knot.
2 lump together slump.
lumpy knottie: '*This custard's aw
knottie*', knappie NE; (*of a person's
shape*) bumfie.
lungs *npl* lichts, buffs.
lurch *v* rowe, stoiter, hyter NE.

n stoit NE, hyter NE; (*especially of a
ship*) howd.
lurk *v* lirk.
luscious *adj* maumie.
lush *adj* (*of vegetation*) grushie,
growthie.
lustful *adj* radg(i)e.
luxuriant *adj* (*of vegetation*) ruch,
grushie, growthie, go(r)skie NE.

M

machinery *n* graith.

mad *adj* daft, gyte, wuid, feel NE; (*especially with excitement, rage*) hyte, radge; (*completely*) reid wuid, horn daft.

madden raise.

mad person bampot, bammer, radge; *see also* **idiot**.

go mad gang gyte.

like mad lik(e) a hatter.

mad with desire *see* **desire**.

made *see* **make**.

maggot *n* mauk, maithe SHETLAND, ORKNEY, N.

maggoty maukie; (*especially of sheep*) maukit.

magic *n* glamour(ie).

magician warlock.

magnificent *adj* magneeficent.

magpie *n* maggie, pyot, deil's bird.

maid *n* (*servant*) lass(ie), quine NE, kitchie deem NE.

main *adj*: **mainly** maist.

mainlander sooth-moother SHETLAND, ferry-lowper ORKNEY.

majority *n* feck.

make *v* mak; pit: '*He pits me mad*'; (*compel*) gar: '*It gars me greet*'; (*a bed*) mak up.

made *past tense, past participle* makkit.

make-believe mak-on.

make do pit by, shuit by.

make for haud for, airt for.

make much of daut.

male *n* he.

malice *n* ill(-will).

malicious *adj* maleecious, ill-hertit.

mallard *n* mire-duck, muir-duck.

malt *n* maut.

man *n* carle, he, chiel(d), gadgie SE *originally gipsy*; (*as opposed to a wo-*man) man-bodie; (*as a form of address*) min, mon; (*informal*) Mac, Jimmy; (*to an older man*) callan(t) NE.

mankind fowk, Jock Tamson's bairns.

manly pretty.

manslaughter (*law*) culpable homicide.

manage *v* manish; (*arrange, direct*) guide, cast aboot; (*look after*) tak aboot; (*cope*) shuit by, mak a fen(d); (*succeed*) win: '*win tae dae it*', maun, get: '*He couldna get sleepin*'; '*He couldna get sleepit*'.

manager guider, heid bummer *often sarcastic;* (*of an estate*) factor.

mangle *v* (*damage*) massacker; (*cut roughly*) hash, haggle.

mangy *adj* scawt.

manner *n* mainner, gate, shape.

mannerly mainnerlie, mensefu.

manners mainners, mense.

manoeuvre *v* wice, airt.

mansion, mansion-house *n* big hoose, ha (hoose).

mantelpiece *n* brace, chim(b)ley-heid, lintel.

manure *n* muck, manner, shairn.

many *adj* monie, plenty.

(a good) many a hantle.

many a monie's the.

many a person monie ane, a hullock N: '*a hullock o loons*'.

map *n* caird.

marble *n* (*toy*) bool, ruckie SOUTH; (*thrown rather than rolled*) pick NE, pitcher NE; (*large*) dabber SOUTH; (*small*) peasie, peever; (*glass*) glessie (bool), glesser; (*steel*) steelie; (*clay*) clayey; (*red clay*) reidie WEST; (*earthenware*) jaurie, pottie (bool) NE; (*large brown earthenware*) stondie, stoner;

(*small earthenware*) peerie NE; (*small coloured earthenware*) stonie.

game of marbles bools; (*played along a road*) chasie NE; (*with circle on ground as target*) ringie; (*in which winner takes all*) rookie; (*played by flicking with the thumb and forefinger*) plunkie.

march *v* mairch, merch.
n mairch, merch; (*eg in protest*) parawd.

March *n* Mairch, Merch.

mare *n* mear(ie).

marguerite *n* white gowan.

marigold *n* yella gowan.

mark *n* merk; (*of a burn*) scam; (*distinguishing mark*) kenspeckle; (*of ownership on an animal*) kenmark; (*in a game*) gog; (*starting line*) score.
v merk.

market *n* mercat; (*especially for sale of livestock*) mart, tryst.

market cross (mercat) cross.

marriage *n* mairriage, merriage.

marriage certificate *see* **certificate.**

marrow *n* (*in bones*) mergh SHETLAND, mergie SHETLAND.

marry *v* mairry, merry, marrow (wi).
married to merrit on *or* wi.
get married get wad.

marsh *n* slump; (*marshy ground*) moss; (*especially with a stream*) syke.
marshy mossy, slumpie.
marshland moss; (*very wet*) flow.
marsh marigold wildfire.

martin *n* (*housemartin*) (hoose-)mairtin, swalla, wunda-swalla.

martyr *n, v* mairtyr.

marvel *n, v* ferlie.

mash *v* (*vegetables*) chap, champ, rummle; (*malt*) mask.
mashed potatoes champit tatties, chappit tatties.
masher (*for vegetables*) bittle; *see also* **potato-masher** (*under* **potato**).

mask *n* (*face-shaped*) fause face.

mass *n* (*of tiny crushed fragments*) smush; (*untidy*) hushle; (*of something soft*) sklone NE.

mast *n* (*of a boat*) most NE.

master *n* maister.
v get roon(d): '*Ah just cannae get roond maths*', maugre NE.
master of the house guidman.

matted *adj* tautit, tautie; (*of wool*) waulkit.

match[1] *n* (*for lighting*) spunk, lunt.

match[2] *n* **1** (*curling*) bonspiel. **2** (*equal*) marrow, neibour, maik: '*There wisna his maik at waddins*'.
v marrow, neibour, peel.
not matching (*eg of gloves*) mar(row)less, neibourless.
be a match for tak the swatch o.

mate *n* (*marriage partner*) neibour.

matron *n* (*older woman*) wife, wifie, guidwife, mistress.

matter *v, n* maitter.
it doesn't matter there's nae (muckle) maitter, it disna mak N.
what does it matter? whit maitter?, whit's adae?, fat's adee? NE, fit dis't mak? N.

mattress *n* mattrass, tike.
mattress cover tike.

mature *adj* (*adult*) muckle; (*of fruit*) maumie.

maul *v* massacker, mell.

may *v* mith NE.
might *past tense* micht, mith: '*I mith a geen*'.
maybe mibbie, mebbe.

May *n* Mey.

maybe *see* **may.**

mayor *n* provost.

me *pronoun* us, iz: '*Come wi us tae the pictures*'.

meadow *n* meedow, meeddie E CENTRAL, haugh.
meadow pipit moss cheeper.
meadowsweet queen o (the) meedow.

meagre *adj* scrimp(it), seldom.

meal[1] *n* male, diet; (*main meal*) kail; (*cooked*) made diet SHETLAND, NE; (*heavy*) rive.

meal[2] *n* (*especially oatmeal*) male.

mean[1] *adj* **1** (*miserly*) grippie, ticht, scrimpit, moolie, ill-willie. **2** (*contemptible*) footie.

meanness grippiness.

mean person nipscart, scrunt.

act meanly snuil, pinch.

be mean hae a guid grip o (the) gear.

mean[2] *v* (*to do something*) ettle.

meaningless haiveless NE, rhymeless NE; (*of speech*) pyot.

what do you mean? whit are ye at?

means *npl*: **by means of** wi: '*eatin wi the mice.*'.

by no means nane.

meantime, meanwhile *adv* (a)tween han(d)s.

measles *npl* maisles, mirls.

measure *n* mizzer SHETLAND, NE.
v mizzer SHETLAND, NE; (*exactly, with a tape measure*) tape.

meat *n* mait, flesh, beef.

mechanism *n* intimmers.

meddle *v* pit in yer spuin, mak or meddle, mell, middle.

medical certificate *n* (*that you are unfit to work*) (doctor's) line.

medium *adj* (*of medium size, quality etc*) middlin.

meet *v* (*encounter*) meet in wi; (*a group*) convene; (*meet together*) forgaither; (*by arrangement*) tryst.

meeting forgaitherin, tryst; (*informal gathering*) sederunt.

meeting place tryst, trystin place, (*especially a pub*) howf.

arran   meeting tryst.

time f   meeting trystin time.

last meeting (*of a council before an election*) greetin meetin.

melancholy *adj* dowie, oorie, dowf.

melodeon *n* box.

melody *n* souch.

memory *n* (*recollection*) mind(in): '*Ah've nae mindin o where ma car key is*'.

have memory of remember o, min(d) on.

menace *v* mint.

mend *v* sort; (*by sewing*) ranter, (*patch*) cloot.

mentally handicapped *adj* wantin, no richt, feel NE.

mentally-handicapped person daftie, saftie, gowk(ie), eediot, feel NE.

be mentally handicapped hae a want, be feel NE.

mention *v* mint, mou, mooth; (*a person*) lift someone's name.

not mention no say cheese, nae say eechie nor ochie.

merge *v* gae thegither.

merit *n* mense SOUTH.

merry *adj* joco, croose, hertie, rantin, mirkie NE.

merrily mirkie NE.

merry-making daffin, dafferie; (*noisy*) rant, gilravage.

mesh *n* (*of a net*) mask SHETLAND, N.

mess *n* midden, guddle, Paddy's market, Annicker's midden, boorach(ie) N, HIGHLAND; (*wet*) slitter, skiddle; (*wet and dirty*) slaister, soss; (*of food*) plowter; (*disgusting*) slaiger, slorach.

work, eat, drink etc messily slaister, slitter.

messy (*and wet*) slitterie; (*and dirty*) slaisterie; (*and muddy*) gutterie.

messy person slitter, slaister; (*slobberer*) slabber; (*worker*) gutter.

messy work kirn NE, sotter.

it's messy it's a(w) mince.

make a mess of slaister: '*Ye've slaistered yer shirt*', soss SHETLAND, NE, scutter SHETLAND, N.

mess about guddle, plaister; (*with housework*) scuddle.

mess about with skiddle, poatch: '*The baby's potachin his porridge*'.

method *n* road, gate.

methodical purpose(lik(e)).

lack of method throuitherness.

mew *v, n* (*of a cat*) miauve NE.

midday *n* twaloors.

middle *n* mid(s): '*in the mids*'.

midge *n* midgie, mudge HIGHLAND.

midst *n* mids.

midwife *n* howdie.

midwifery howdiein.

midwinter *n* the howe o (the) winter.

might *n* (*power*) maucht.

mighty michtie.

might *see* **may.**

mild *adj* (*of weather*) saft, maumie; (*and bright*) leesome NE.

mildew *n* foost, foosht NE.

milk *n, v* mulk.

milk jug (*small*) poorie.

milk pail milk bowie.

add milk to milk, mulk: '*Mulk the coffee*'.

give milk (*of a cow etc*) milk, mulk.

mill *n* mull.

miller millart, mullert NE.

millrace (*into wheel*) (mill) lade, (mill) lead.

millstone stane, steen NE.

mimic *n* (*person*) afftak.

mince *v, n* minch.

minced meat mince, minch.

mind *n*: **bear in mind** keep mind o.

call to mind mind.

change your mind tak the rue.

never mind nivver heed, nivver leet.

out of your mind by yersel, oot o yer rizzon.

mine[1] *pronoun* mines.

mine[2] *n* heuch AYRSHIRE.

v howk.

miner pickman, Jock brit *contemptuous*.

mineral *n* meeneral.

minimum *n* meenimum.

minister *n* meenister.

minister's house manse.

son or daughter of a minister son *or* daughter o the manse.

minnow *n* minnon, mennen(t) SOUTH; (*large*) baggie (minnon); (*redbreasted*) sodger.

mint imperial *n* pan drop, grannie's sooker, auld wifie's sooker.

minute[1] *n* meenit, minent.

minute[2] *adj* (*very small*) totie-wee, peerie-weerie.

miracle *n* meeracle.

mirror *n* keekin glass, seein glass.

misbehave *v* gae ower the score.

miscall *v* misca(w).

miscarriage *n* (*abortion*) slip.

miscarry miscairrie: **1** (*suffer a miscarriage*) pairt wi bairn. **2** (*of a plan etc*) gley, misgae.

miscellaneous *adj* orra.

mischief *n* **1** ill. **2 piece of mischief** cantrip, prattick NE.

mischievous mischievious, ill-deedie, ill-contrivit SHETLAND, N; (*especially of a child*) royet, roit NE, ill-trickit SHETLAND, ORKNEY, N.

mischievous person *or* **animal** limb o the deil; (*especially a child*) tike N; (*especially a girl*) clip.

miser *n* nipscart, grab, scrunt, misert.

miserly grippie, near the bane, near the bit, meeserable, misert.

miserable *adj* **1** meeserable, ill-aff; (*from cold etc*) oorit. **2 miserable looking** oorie, oorlich.

miserable-looking person greetin face, torn face, soor face.

misery *n* meeserie, pine SHETLAND, NE.

in (a state of) misery in the sheuch.

misfortune *n* **1** mischief, misluck, mishanter SHETLAND, ORKNEY, N. **2** (*a misfortune*) begunk.

mismanage *v* misguide.

mispronounce *v* misca(w).

miss *v* (*fail to get*) tyne; (*fail*) misgae NE.

missed (*because of absence*) misslie.

missing amissin.

miss something good (*by not being there*) miss yersel: '*Ye fair missed yersel at the pairtie*'.

missel-thrush *n* storm-cock.

mist *n* rouk; (*haze*) gum N; (*cold, from sea, especially on East Coast*) haar; (*cold, wet*) drowe SE; (*cold, with breeze*) gull NE; (*thin, light*) smuchter NE.

misty reekie, roukie, haarie, daggie NE.

mistake *v, n* mistak.

mistaken mistaen, aff (o) yer eggs, up the sheuch WEST, SW.

I'm very much mistaken I'm cheatit, it cheats me: '*It cheats me gin he disna fin oot*'.

make a mistake mistak yersel.

by mistake in a mistak(e).

say by mistake lee, skellie.

mistress *n* (*of a house*) guidwife, hersel.

misty *see* **mist.**

misunderstood *adj* (*of a remark etc*) mistaen.

mitten *n* pawkie, hummel-mitten NE, hummel-doddie NE.

mix *v* mell; (*especially liquids, messily*) soss; (*flour etc with water*) draigle NE.

mixture mixter-maxter; (*messy, of food*) soss, slaister, slitter.

mix up taigle, taisle; (*messily*) keeger NE.

mix-up complouter, snorl N, keeger.

moan *v, n* mane.

moaning *adj* greetin-faced.

mock *v* tak the nap aff, lant NE, geck at, lichtlie.

mockery afftakkin.

moderate *adj* middlin.

moderately middlins.

moderation mense.

modern *adj* modren.

modest *adj* blate.

moist *adj* sappie; (*of warm atmosphere*) moch(ie).

moisten slock(en).

mole[1] *n* (*animal*) mowdie, mowdiewort, mowdiewarp.

molehill mowdie(wort)hill.

mole[2] *n* (*on skin*) rasp.

mollycoddle *v* fraik.

moment *n* blink, rap, crack: '*in a crack*', mament.

at the moment the noo, eenoo, ivnoo NE, this weather.

in a moment, a moment ago the noo, eenoo, ivnoo NE.

Monday *n* Monanday.

money *n* siller, bawbees, penny: '*a bonnie penny*'.

moneybox (*earthenware*) pig.

moneygrubber grab, lick-penny.

make money mak rich, mak siller.

without money boss, sillerless.

mongrel *n* tike *contemptuous*, messan *contemptuous*.

monkey *n* pug(gie).

monotonous *adj* dreich.

talk monotonously boo.

monument *n* moniment.

mood *n* **1** muid, meed NE, tune, teen NE, key, tid: '*ill tid*', bin(ner) NE, tift. **2 bad mood** bad cut, gee.

moody tiftie.

moon *n* muin, meen NE.

moor *n* muir, mair CENTRAL, meer NE.

moorland muirland

mooring post *n* pall.

mop *v*: **mop up** dicht up, swaible SOUTH.

mope *v* mump, hing the lugs, peenge.

more *adj, adv* mair, mae.

and more so an some, by's (th)at.

morning *n* mornin; (*very early hours of*) (wee) sma oors.

moss *n* fog.

mossy foggie.

become moss-covered fog.

most *adj, adv* maist.

mostly, for the most part maistlie, maist.

most of the feck o.

most of all maistlie.

moth *n* moch; (*clothes moth*) mowd.

moth-eaten mochie, moch-etten.

mother *n* mither, midder SHETLAND, NE, auld wife, auld yin, minnie *affectionate name*.

mother-in-law guid-mither.

motion *n* (*sudden*) stot; (*of an object flying through the air*) swiff.

mottled *adj* marlie, spreckelt.

mottled skin on the legs *see* **skin.**

mould[1] *n* (*fungus*) foost, foosht NE; (*on cheese, jam etc*) hair(y)-mool(d).

mouldy foostie, fooshtie NE, moolie,

310

mochie NE; (*covered with mould*) (hairy-)mooldit.

become *or* **smell mouldy** foost, foosht NE, mool.

mould[2] *n* (*earth*) mool, moold, meel(d) NE.

　moulder muilder, mooler, moost NE.

　moult *v* moot.

　n the moot, pook: '*in the pook*'.

mound *n* moond, humple, humplock, knowe; (*especially fairy mound*) tulloch.

mount[1] *v* munt, rise; (*a horse*) lowp on, win on N.

mount[2] *n* (*mountain*) munt.

mountain *n* muntain; (*one of the higher Scottish mountains*) ben, (*over 3 000 feet, 914m*) Munro, (*2 500-3 000 feet, 762-914m*) Corbett.

　mountain ash rowan(-tree), rodden (-tree).

　mountain pass bealach.

mourn *v* murn, croon, mane (for).

　mournful dowie, dool.

　mournful sound mane.

　mournfully dowielie.

　mourning murnin.

mouse *n* moose.

　mousetrap (moose-)fa(w).

moustache *n* mouser, fusker NE.

mouth *n* mou, mooth, gab, gob, geggie; (*of an animal*) mull; (*of a river*) watter-mou.

　mouthful moufae, moothfae; (*especially of liquid*) laib, lerb NE, sup(pie): '*a sup tea*'.

　mouth-organ moothie.

move *v* muive, meeve NE, mudge; (*budge*) jee; (*recklessly, carelessly*) breenge.

　movement mudge; (*quick, noisy*) bicker NE; (*sudden, erratic*) stot.

　move about (*awkwardly*) walloch, hodge; (*awkwardly, quickly*) wallop; (*fidget*) rowe; (*quickly, lightly*) skiff, link; (*nimbly*) jink; (*quickly, energetically*) skelp, spank, leash SHETLAND, N; (*quickly, noisily*) bicker.

　move house flit.

　moving house flittin.

　on the move on the leg.

mow *v* maw.

　mower mawer.

Mrs *n* Mistress.

much *adj, adv* muckle, meikle, mickle; (*with comparative*) hantle (sicht): '*a hantle sicht caulder*'.

　much alike eeksie-peesie, neibours, gey sib.

　very much fine, a heap: '*a heap better*', richt NE.

mud *n* cla(i)rt, glaur, gutters, dubs; (*soft, sticky*) glaur.

　muddy *adj* cla(i)rtie, gutterie, glaurie, clattie, clatchie NE; (*full of sediment*) g(r)umlie, jummlie; (*splashy*) jaupie, platchie SOUTH; (*of a road*) slabberie.

　muddy puddles *see* **puddle**.

　sink in mud lair.

　walk in mud plowter, platch.

muddle *n* fankle, midden, carfuffle, guddle, soss, boorach(ie) N, HIGHLAND.

　v raivel, taigle, ramfeezle.

　muddled 1 raivelt, throuither, throwder NE, guddelt, hither-an-yon(t). **2** (*in mind*) bumbazed, taivert, wauchelt.

muddy *see* **mud**.

mug *n* (*drinking*) moog N, joug; (*small, tin*) tinnie.

muggy *adj* mochie, muithie, roukie.

mum, mummy *n* mam(mie), maw CENTRAL, minnie *affectionate name*.

mumble *v* mump, mummle.

mummy *see* **mum**.

mumps *npl* branks.

munch *v* hash, gumsh NE.

murder *v, n* murther.

　murderer murtherer.

murk *n* mirk.

　murky mirkie, drumlie.

murmur *v* croon, murmell.

　n (*of talk*) curmurrin; (*murmuring sound*) murr.

　not a murmur nae a myowt NE.

mushroom *n* puddock stuil, puddock steel NE.

music *n* muisic, meesick NE.

 musician musicianer, musicker.

mussel *n* (*large*) clabbydhu WEST; (*large freshwater*) horse-mussel SHETLAND, N.

must *v* maun.

 must not maunna.

musty *adj* foostie, fooshtie NE, foostit, fooshtit NE.

mutter *v* mump.

mutton *n*: **leg of mutton** gigot.

muzzle *n*, *v* mizzle.

my *possessive adj* ma, mi.

 myself masel, mysel.

N

nag *v* natter, nyatter NE: '*aye nyatterin on*', yatter, nip someone's heid; **nag at** haud at, threap at.

nagging *n* natter, nyatter NE, yatter.

naked *adj* nakit, nyakit NE, scuddie, in the scud.

state of nakedness (bare) scud(die).

name *n, v* nem, neem SHETLAND, ORKNEY, CAITHNESS.

nap *n* dover, dot, slug.
v dwam (ower), dover (ower).

nape *n*: **nape of the neck** cuff o the neck, howe o the neck NE.

napkin *n* servit, naipkin, neepyin; *see also* **table napkin** (*under* **table**).

nappy *n* hippin, cloot.

narcissus *n* lily.

narrow *adj* nairra(e); (*of things*) sma.

narrowly near.

narrow-minded nippit.

nasty *adj* nestie, naistie, scunnersome.

national *adj* naitional.

native *adj* (*belonging to, grown or made at home*) hameart.

native district cauf kintra.

natural *adj* naitral; (*plain, simple*) hameower.

nature *n* naitur.

naughty *adj* coorse NE, ill-trickit, ill-contrivit SHETLAND, N.

near *preposition* nar, nearaboot, aside, inby.
adv nar, nearaboot(s), aside.
adj nar, nearhan(d).

nearer narrer; (*closer to the speaker*) nar.

nearest narrest.

nearby nar(by) NE, narhan(d), near aboot(s).

nearly near, nar, nearhan(d), narhan(d), near aboot(s), gey near, verra near.

very nearly gey near, verra near.

be near neibour wi.

near enough as near.

neat *adj* **1** nate; (*and small*) cantie; (*tidy*) ticht, perjink, conceitie, snod; (*of a person*) gentie, jimp; (*especially of women*) dink; (*especially in dress*) trig, feat. **2** (*of spirits*) nakit.

neatly ticht, triglie.

necessary *adj* necessar.

necessity needcessitie; (*unavoidable*) maun-be.

neck *n* craig, hause.

need *v, n* (*lack*) want.

needy needfu, scrimp, skybald NE.

still in need of no oot o (the) need o.

supply the needs of see till.

needle *n* (*knitting*) wire, weer NE.

needlework shewin, seam.

neglect *v* negleck; (*overlook*) mislippen; (*treat badly*) misguide.
n negleck.

neglected disjaskit.

neigh *v, n* nicher.

neighbour *n* neibour, neiper NE.

neighbourhood neibourheid, pairt SHETLAND, NE.

neighbouring nearhan(d).

neighbourly neibourlik(e).

have as neighbour be neibours wi.

neither *adv, pronoun* naither, naider SHETLAND, NE, nane o the twa.
conjunction naither, naider SHETLAND, NE, nor.

neither one nor the other neither eechie nor ochie.

nephew *n* nevoy.

nervous *adj* nervish, aff (o) yer eggs, timorsome, skeichen NE.

be very nervous be sittin on preens, be lik(e) a hen on a het girdle.

nest *n* (*wasps' etc*) byke.

nestling younker, gorb, gorblin NE, scud(die) WEST, get SW, SOUTH, goggie *child's word.*

nestle *v* coorie (in), hiddle NE.

nettle *n* jaggie nettle, jobbie nettle, jennie nettle.

never *adv* nivver.

nevertheless still an on, hoo an a(w) be, for a' at NE, whitivver.

never a . . . deil a . . . , fient a . . .

never mind never heed, nivver leet.

new *adj (completely)* split-new CENTRAL, spleet-new SHETLAND, ORKNEY, N.

newly new, newlins.

newfangled new-farran(t) NE.

New Year's Day Ne'erday.

New Year's Eve Hogmanay.

New Year gift *(especially of food or drink)* Ne'erday: *'We'll gie ye yer Ne'erday'.*

(be) the first visitor in the New Year first fit: *'We're gaun first-fittin'*; *'He wis oor first fit'.*

do something to celebrate something new handsel: *'I handselled ma new dress at the pairtie'.*

news *n* uncos, speirins; *(news in advance)* moyen NE: *'get a moyen o'*; *(piece of surprising news)* ferlie.

tell your news gie yer crack: *'Gie's yer crack'.*

newt *n* ask, mankeeper.

next *adj* nixt, neist; *(of days of week)* first: *'Monday first'.*

next but one *(of days of week)* next: *'Monday next'.*

nib *n (of a pen)* neb.

nibble *v* moup; *(of an animal: graze)* pike, nip; *(like a rabbit or sheep)* map; *(like a rabbit)* mump.

nice *adj* clivver.

nickname *n* tee-name NE.

niggard *n* niggar.

niggardly nippit, scrimp.

night *n* nicht, mirk.

nightgown goon(ie).

nightingale nichtingale.

last night yestreen, the streen ORKNEY, N.

the night before last erethestreen.

nimble *adj* nimmle, knackie, gleg, licht-set.

nine *numeral*: **ninth** nint.

nineteenth nineteen(t).

ninepins kyles.

group of nine ninesome.

nip *v (eg a finger in a door)* sneck, chack, check.

n chack, check, nib.

nippy 1 *(of weather)* snell. **2** *(of people)* gleg.

nit *n (louse-egg)* neet.

no *adj, adv* nae.

negative reply na(w).

no one, nobody naebodie.

no fear (of) nae frichts (o).

not take no for an answer tak nae na(e)-say.

say no (to) na(e)-say: *'He'll no can nasay ye'.*

nod *v*: **nodding** *(repeatedly, as when dozing)* (nid) nid noddin.

nod off dover (ower).

noise *n (din)* dirdum, yammer, reemis(h) NE; *(loud, rattling)* blatter.

noisy roarie.

move (about) noisily breenge.

talk noisily blatter.

annoy with noise deave.

make a loud noise yammer, mineer NE.

none *pronoun* nane, neen SHETLAND, N.

nonsense *n* blethers, haiver(s), mince.

nonsense! blethers!, haivers!, hoot(s)!, toot(s)!, fine day!

nonsensical haiverin, gyte.

talk nonsense haiver, blether, gyper NE.

nook *n* neuk.

noon *n* nuin, neen N, twaloors.

noose *n* kinch, mink N, fank.

normal *adj* warldlik(e); *(especially of a child)* lik(e) the warl(d).

north *n, adj* nor-.

northern lights merry dancers SHET-LAND, ORKNEY, N, streamers.

northwards northart NE.

nose *n* neb, snotterbox, snoot *contemptuous*, wulk *humorous*: '*pick yer wulk*'.

v **nose about** snoke.

nosy nebbie, lang-nebbit.

speak *or* **breathe through your nose** sneevil.

not *adv* no, nae.

not any nae, nane, nae neen NE, deil a . . . , fient a . . .

not at all nane: '*She can sing nane*'.

notable *adj* namely, markit.

notch *n* natch, nitch SHETLAND, OR-KNEY, N, gneck NE, sneck.

v natch, sneck; (*a blade*) lip.

note *n* 1 (*short letter*) scrape o the pen; (*explaining a child's absence from school or from a doctor, confirming illness*) line.

notebook (*school*) jotter.

notepad scroll NE.

take note tak tent.

nothing *n* naethin, nocht, nowt SOUTH.

nothing at all deil a haet, neither hint nor hair NE.

notice *v* tak tent; **not notice** no goam.

n (*attention*) tent.

take notice of leuk efter NE; (*take an interest in*) leuk the gate o, see till.

nourish *v* mait.

nourishment fushion.

novel *adj* new-farran(t) NE.

n novelle.

novelty newfangle, unco.

now *adv* noo; (*just now*) the noo, eenoo, ivnoo NE, presently, this weather: '*Hoo are ye this weather?*', this: '*atween this an Sunday*'.

nowadays nooadays, thir days.

now and then noo(s) an than(s), noo an aan NE, whiles, files N, filies N.

nowhere *adv* nae place, naewey.

nudge *n, v* nidge, nodge, dunt, dunch, putt.

nuisance *n* scunner, fash, vex, plaister; (*a person*) sorra.

number *n, v* nummer.

considerable number hantle, (gey) wheen.

large number heap, feck, whack, hullock N.

numerous *adj* lairge NE, thrang.

nurse *v* (*tend*) cuiter, sort NE; (*too carefully*) soss NE.

nut *n* nit; (*without a kernel*) deef nit.

nuzzle *v* snoozle.

O

oak *n* aik.

oar *n* air.

oats *npl* aits, yits, corn, haver.

oatcake aitcake, bannock, kyaak (o breid) NE.

oatcakes breid N, cakes NE, kyaaks NE.

oatmeal 1 meal, male; (*coarsely-ground*) pinheid (oat)meal. **2** (*oatmeal dish: with boiling water*) brose: '*kail brose*' = brose made with liquid from boiled kail.

object *n, v* objeck.

what objection do you have (to) . . . ? whit ails ye (at) . . . ?

oblige *v* obleege.

obligation obleegement.

be under an obligation (to) hae a day in hairst (wi).

obliging helplie.

obnoxious *adj* ill-faured.

obscene *adj* (*especially of language*) coorse, randie, ruch, roch.

obscenity sculdudderie.

obscure *adj* mirk, dern; (*puzzling*) kittlie.

obser uk till SHETLAND, NE, see at.

obse tentie.

obse on observe.

obstina *adj* thrawn, dour, positive, contermacious.

obstruct *v* mar, stap.

obstruction hinder, mar.

obtain *v* obteen.

obvious *adj* as plain as parritch.

occasion *n* **1** tid. **2** (*need*) use: '*There was nae use for it*'.

occasional orra, happenin, antrin.

occasionally at a time, whiles, files NE.

occupy *v* occupee.

occupied (*busy*) fest NE.

occupied with in han(s) wi, in the heid o.

ocean *n* dub *humorous*.

odd *adj* **1** (*unmatched*) orra. **2** (*strange*) unco.

oddity (*thing or person*) queerie, magink, ferlie.

odd jobs jots NE.

odd-job man orraman, jotter.

odd-looking person ticket, track NE, munsie NE; (*especially overdressed woman*) Teenie fae Troon, Teenie fae the neeps E CENTRAL.

odd person queerie.

odds and ends orras, trokes.

of *preposition* o; often omitted in Scots in expressions of quantity: '*a drap milk*'; '*a bit breid*'.

off *adv* aff, oaf.

preposition aff (o).

off your head aff at the heid.

offend *v* pet, misfit NE.

take offence tak the gee.

offer *n* bode.

offer (*a child*) **for baptism** *see* **baptize.**

offhand *adj* affloof, jack-easy.

often *adv* aften.

oil *n* ile, uilie, eelie NE.

v ile, uilie, eelie NE, creesh.

oily 1 (*greasy*) ilie, glittie, creeshie. **2** (*of a person*) sleekit, slid.

ointment *n* eyntment.

old *adj* aul(d), ald, aal N, owl(d) SHETLAND, ORKNEY, CAITHNESS, ROSS, ARGYLL, ULSTER.

oldest (*in a family*) aul(d): '*auld brither*'.

old age eild.

old-fashioned aul(d)-farran(t), auld-warld.

old-fashioned little girl grannie mutch(ie).

old-fashioned-looking woman Auntie Beenie.

old-maidish primsie.

old man bodach.

old woman cailleach HIGHLAND, N, WEST, ULSTER, grannie mutch(ie), luckie: '*Luckie Broon*', deem NE, carline *contemptuous*.

grow old gang doon the hill.

on *preposition, adv* in; (*along*) awa: '*Come awa tae yer bed*'.

once *adv* aince, yince E CENTRAL, wance WEST, ULSTER, eence SHETLAND, ORKNEY, NE.

at once in a crack.

once or twice a time or twa.

one *numeral, pronoun* ane, yin CENTRAL, SOUTH, wan WEST, SW, ULSTER; (*mainly emphatic*) ae: '*the ae wey*', yae CENTRAL, SOUTH; (*in children's rhymes*) eentie, eendie.

one another ither, ilk ither.

oneself yersel.

onion *n* ingan.

only *adj* (*child*) ae SHETLAND, N, E CENTRAL, yae CENTRAL, SOUTH: '*oor ae bairn*'.

ooze *v* weeze, sype.

n seep, sype; (*from a wound etc*) glit.

open *adj* apen; (*of a door: partly*) ajee, (*wide*) wide tae the wa.

v apen; (*a bag etc, to search*) gae intae.

opening (*gap*) open NE; (*eg in a wall*) slap.

openly fair.

in(to) the open air furth.

stare open-mouthed gype.

wide open (*of a door*) wide tae the wa.

opinion *n* opeenion.

have a good opinion of yourself hae a guid consait o yersel.

my *etc* **own opinion** ma etc ain think NE.

opportunity *n* (*chance*) inlat, cast NE; (*scope*) scowthe; (*favourable time*) tid.

oppose *v* (*contradict*) conter, contrair; (*stop someone doing something*) thorter, thraw (wi).

opposite *adj* opposeet, conter N.

preposition forenent.

n **the opposite** the opposeet, the contrair.

opposition opposeetion, haud-again.

optician *n* opteecian.

orange *n* oranger.

order *v* (*goods etc*) speak; (*in advance*) tryst; (*drinks*) ca(w).

in order that till.

keep in order haud in aboot, keep in aboot, pit the hems on.

put in order redd (up), sort, snod.

ordinary *adj* oardinary, ordinar.

organ *n* (*musical*) kist o whustles.

organize *v* guide.

origin *n* (*descent*) oreeginal NE.

original *adj* oreeginal.

ornament *n* (*decoration*) affset, ootset, whigmaleerie; (*especially spiral or fancy*) whirligig.

v (*with a chequered pattern*) dice; (*with a knitted border*) pearl.

ornamental wallie CENTRAL, SOUTH: '*wallie dugs*'.

orphan *n* orphant.

other *adj, pronoun* ither, idder SHETLAND, NE.

the other the tither, the tidder SHETLAND, NE.

otherwise itherwise, idderwise SHETLAND, NE, ithergates, ither-roads.

ought *v* ocht.

our *possessive adj* oor, (*unstressed*) wir, wur, (*stressed*) weer NE.

ourselves oorsels, wirsel(s).

ourselves (alone) oor lane, wir lane.

out *adv* oot.

out of oot (o), ooten; (*a door etc*) oot at.

out of doors ootby, oot aboot, ootwith NE, oot ower the door; (*in a town*) on the street(s).

outburst *n* (*especially of noise*) onding; (*of rage*) rampage, fuff, flist NE; (*of emotion etc*) spate; (*of weeping*) blirt.

outdoor *adj* ootby, oot aboot NE.

outer *adj* ooter.

outlet *n* ootlat.

outlive *v* ootleeve.

outlying *adj* ootby, oot SHETLAND, ORKNEY: '*oot isles*', ootwith NE.

output *n* throu-pit.

outrageous *adj* maroonjous NE.

outright *adj* ootricht, richt oot.

outset *n* affset.

outside *adv* ootside, ootwith NE; (*out-of-doors*) ootby, furth SHETLAND, NE. *preposition* furth; (*beyond*) outwith, furth o(f).

　outsiders the fremmit.

outskirts *npl*: **on the outskirts of** ootby: '*ootby the toon*'.

outstanding *adj* by-or(di)nar, sad NE.

outwards *adv* ootby, ootwith NE.

outwit *v* raivel SHETLAND, N, begowk.

oven *n* ovven, une.

over *preposition* ower, oot ower. *adv* ower; (*past*) by: '*when the holidays are by*'; (*of a meeting etc*) oot.

　over and done with by wi.

　over the top of, over to the other side of oot ower.

　over the way owerby.

overall *n* carsackie; (*especially household*) wrapper.

overbalance *v* cowp.

　cause to overbalance cowp, ca(w) ower, ca(w) the feet fae.

overbearing *adj* ringin.

overcast *adj* overcast, loorie, hingin.

overcharge *v* saut.

overcome *v* (*defeat*) overcome, bang, warsle, waur.

overcooked *adj* (*of meat*) sair duin.

overdressed *adj* fantoosh.

overeating *n* gutsin; (*bout of*) guzzle.

over-excited *see* **excited.**

overflow *v* skail, ream ower.

overhang *v*, *n* owerhing.

overlook *v* owerleuk; (*neglect*) mislippen.

overrun *v* ower-rin. *adj* hoatchin, hotchin: '*The hoose is hoatchin wi mice*'.

oversleep *v* sleep in.

overtake *v* owertak; (*catch up with*) mak up on, tak in NE; (*be better than*) mak by.

overthrow *v* owerthraw, whummle, ding doon.

overturn *v* cowp, owercowp, whummle.

　easily overturned cogglie.

　overturning *n* cowp, whummle.

overwork *v* (*cause to work too much*) hash, tirraneese NE, hatter SOUTH.

　overworked tra(u)chelt, sair hauden doon (by the bubbly jock).

owe *v* awe, yaw NE, be due: '*He's due me wages*'.

　owing owe: '*He's owe me £5*'.

　owing to wi: '*Wi the rain we hid tae cancel the barbecue*'.

owl *n* hoolet, ool SHETLAND, NE, oolet; (*barn owl*) white hoolet; (*long-eared owl*) hornie hoolet.

own *v* awn, awe, yaw NE. *adj* ain: '*It's ma ain hoose*'.

　owner awner.

　ownership aucht: '*in yer aucht*'.

　of my *etc* **own** o ma etc ain(s).

　own up to haud wi.

ox *n* owse, nowt NE.

　oxen owsen.

　ox-eye daisy *see* **daisy.**

oyster-catcher *n* sea-pyot, skirlie-wheeter NE, shalder SHETLAND, ORKNEY.

P

pace *n* **1** (*step*) pass, spang. **2** (*speed*) raik; (*steady*) jundie.
 v pass; (*back and forth*) reenge.
 keep pace with haud up wi.
pack *v* (*stuff*) stap; (*full, tightly*) pang.
 packed (*of a room etc*) stowed (oot), ho(a)tchin.
 packed lunch piece(-denner), denner-piece.
 packed-lunch box piece box.
 pack of cards pair o cairds.
paddle *v* paidle.
paddock *n* parroch SE.
paid *see* **pay**.
pail *n* (*bucket*) cog, bowie.
pain *n* **1** (*sharp*) steek, catch; (*sudden, sharp*) twang; (*as of a sting*) stang; (*sharp throb*) stoon(d); **sharp pains** (*especially in the bowels*) grups. **2** (*trouble*) fash; (*grief*) hert-sair.
 painful sair.
 painful injury sair yin.
 painfully sair.
 causing pain sair (on): '*It's sair on the back*'.
 exclamation expressing pain oh-ya!, it-ye! NE.
 take pains fash.
paint *n, v* pent.
 painted pentit.
 paintwork pent.
 lick of paint slairie.
pair *n* perr, twasome, twaesome.
 one of a pair neibour, marrow: '*Thae gloves are nae marrows*'.
palace *n* pailace.
pale *adj* whitely; (*of a person*) peelie-wallie, paewae.
palm *n* (*of the hand*) luif, loof.
pamper *v* (*spoil*) cuiter (up), daut, dossach wi NE, pettle SOUTH; (*especially a child*) waste.

pancake *n* English pancake; NB *in Scotland refers to a small round cake of thickish batter baked on a girdle etc, also known as a* dropped scone, bannock NE.
pane *n* (*of glass*) peen.
panic *n* swither, pirr.
pant *v* pech, hechle, fob NE: '*fobbin lik a fat kittlin*'.
 n pech.
paper *n* (*brown, for wrapping*) gray paper SHETLAND.
 paper bag poke: '*piece poke*', pyoke NE.
parade *n* parawd.
paralyse *v* paraleese.
 paralysis paraleesis.
 paralysed palie.
parcel *n, v* paircel.
pare *v* white, fite NE, skive.
parent *n* pawrent.
parish *n* pairish.
 parishioner pareeshioner.
park *n* pairk, perk.
 park-keeper, (public) park attendant parkie.
parlour *n* room, chaumer, spence.
part *n* pairt; (*share*) dale; (*one of two unequal parts*) half.
 v pairt, twin(e), sinder (wi); (*hair etc*) shed, split.
 parting (*in hair etc*) shed, seam, score.
 partly pairtlie, halfways, halflins, kinna.
particular *adj* parteec(u)lar.
 particularly particular, parteec(u)lar.
partner *n* pairtner, neibour.
partridge *n* pai(r)trick.
party *n* (*social gathering*) pairtie, awthegither, shine: '*tea shine*' = tea party; (*with music etc*) ceilidh; (*especially one organized by a church etc*) swaree.

pass *v* 1 (*spend time*) pit by. 2 (*overtake*) win by. 3 (*hand to someone*) see: '*See's ower the jeelie*'.

n (*mountain*) bealach, slack, slap.

in passing in the bygaun.

pass by haud by NE.

passageway *n* throate, trance.

passion *n* feem NE.

passionate birsie, heidie.

past *preposition* by: '*by their best*'; (*beyond*) yont; (*of hours*) efter: '*hauf an oor efter ten*'.

adj (*of time*) bygane.

things past *or* **in the past** (*eg offences, injuries*) byganes.

get past get by, win by.

paste *n*, *v* (*eg as adhesive*) batter.

pastries *npl* snashters, gulshichs NE, fine pieces NE, sweet-breid SHETLAND.

pasture *n* paster; (*in past times: remote summer*) shielin.

v girse, gress.

pasty *n* (*meat*) (Forfar) bridie.

pat *v*, *n* (*stroke affectionately*) clap: '*Gie the dug a clap*'.

patch *v* cloot, eik, lap, spatch SOUTH. *n* 1 (*mended*) cloot, eik, spatch SOUTH. 2 (*part of a surface*) platch: '*an ugly platch on his cheek*'.

patch up (*a quarrel*) sooder, sowther.

path *n* pad, road, gate.

patience *n*: **patient** (*very*) patientfu, tholin

be p   thole.

have   nce with forbear.

patte   iitter; (*of feet*) fitter; (*of rain etc*) ra

pattern *n* paittern, pattren; (*checked, in tartan*) sett; (*dressmaking*) shape; (*sample of cloth*) swatch.

paunch *n* painch, wame.

pause *v* (*hesitate*) hover, huilie.

pave *v* causey.

pavement causey, plainstanes.

pavilion *n* paveelion.

paw *n* luif, spag N.

v (*the ground, of a horse*) pawt.

pawn *v*, *n* pawnd.

pawnshop pawn(d).

pay *v*, *n* pey.

paid *past tense, past participle* peyed.

payment peyment.

pay for pey: '*It'll pey the gas*'.

paid in advance forehandit.

pea *n* pey SOUTH, pizzer NE.

peas pizz, pizzers NE.

pea-pod (pea-)cod, (pea-)shaup, (pea-)huil.

peashooter scoot(er), pluffer, pluff (-gun), skiter SHETLAND, NE.

pea soup pea bree.

peace *n* lown.

peaceful(ly) lown.

peaceful place lown.

peak *n* (*something which rises to a peak*) tappietoorie; (*of a hill*) kip SE; (*of a cap*) skip, snoot.

peaked (*of a cap: see also* **cloth cap**) skippit, snootit.

peal *n* (*of a bell*) jowe; (*of thunder*) brattle.

v (*of a bell*) jowe; (*of thunder*) dinnle.

pear *n* peer, perr WEST.

pearl *n* purl.

peat bog *n* (*where peat is cut*) (peat) moss, (peat) hill SHETLAND, ORKNEY, N; (*very wet*) flow.

pebble *n* chuckie (stane).

pebbly rocklie.

peck *v*, *n* dab, dorb NE.

peculiar *adj* unco.

pedestrians *npl* fit-fowk.

pedlar *n* cadger, packman.

peel *v* pilk.

peep *v* (*glance*) keek, teet, deek.

peeping Tom keeker.

peep-bo keek(ie) bo, teet(ie) bo.

peephole keekhole.

peer *v* (*look closely*) pie.

peg *n* (*for hanging things on*) (k)nag, nab; (*wooden, on a plaster wall, for holding a nail*) dook.

insert pegs into (*a wall*) dook.

take someone down a peg pit someone's gas at a peep, tak someone doon a hack.

pelt *v* **1** (*with missiles*) clod, da(u)d. **2** (*of rain*) blatter, bicker, plowt.

pen *n* (*enclosure*) cruive, crue, ree(ve).

pencil *n* pincil, keelivine.

  pencil-point neb.

penetrate *v* thirl, prog.

penis *n* pintle, tossel, tadger.

people *npl* fowk, cattle *contemptuous*.

pepper *n* spice.

  peppery spicy, nippy.

  peppermint sweet (*mint imperial*) pan drop; (*bull's eye*) black-strippit ba(w).

perch *n* (*bird's*) spaik.

perfect(ly) *adj, adv* perfit.

perforate *v* thirl.

perhaps *adv* maybe, mibbie, aiblins *literary*.

periwinkle *n* (*winkle*) wulk, buckie.

perk[1] *v*: **perk up** spunk up.

  perky birkie.

perk[2] *n* **perk(s)** chance(s).

permit *v* lat, leave.

  permission permeeshion, freedom.

perplex *v* (*confuse, bewilder*) kittle, tickle, waun(n)er, bumbaze.

  perplexed bumbazed, will NE.

  be perplexed swither.

  perplexity swither.

persecute *v* murther, pursue, pook at.

persevere *v* hing in, stick in; **persevere in** haud at.

persist *v*: **persist in** haud at.

  persistent (*dreary*) dreich; (*of a cold*) sitten-doon.

  persistently even on.

person *n* bodie: '*Could ye no leave a bodie in peace?*'.

persuade *v* perswad.

pert *adj* forritsome.

perverse *adj* thrawn, dour, camstairie, contermacious.

pest *n* (*nuisance*) scunner, sorra.

pester *v* pest, deave, steer, soss.

pet *v* daut.

  petted deltit NE.

  petted child sookie.

petition *n* peteetion.

petticoat *n* coat(s), cwite(s) NE.

pew *n* dask.

pheasant *n* phaesan(t), feesant.

phlegm *n* fleem, glit.

photograph *n* photie.

pick *v* pike; (*fruit, flowers*) pou. *n* pike.

  pick at food smurl.

  pick and choose lift an lay.

  pick out chaps NE, wale.

  pick up (*stitches in knitting*) lift.

pickle *n* (*muddle, confusion*) picher, steer.

picture *n* picter.

pie *n* NB *in Scotland often refers to a round individual* mutton pie, *also known as a* Scotch pie.

  pie dish ashet WEST.

piece *n* (*small*) bittie; (*very small*) nip, (n)imsh; (*especially of food*) snap; (*large*) da(u)d, doll NE; (*long piece of string etc*) leash.

  all to pieces tae pigs an whustles, a(w) tae crockaneetion.

pierce *v* jag, prog; (*slightly*) dab; (*with emotion*) dirl, thirl.

  piercing (*of wind*) snell.

pig *n* swine, grumph(ie), gruntie *humorous;* (*especially young*) gussie; (*especially young suckling*) grice; (*smallest of a litter*) poke-shakkins.

  piggyback backie, coalie-back; (*on the shoulders*) shooderie, high shooder.

  pig-headed (*stubborn*) thrawn, positive.

  pigsty cruive, crue, pig-hoose, ree(ve).

  pigtail pleat.

  pig in a poke blin bargain.

pigeon *n* doo; (*tame*) rookettie doo; (*wood pigeon*) cushat, cushie (doo), croodlin doo NE.

  pigeonhole *n* doocot.

  pigeon-toed hen-taed, in-taed.

pile *n* (*heap*) bing; (*especially loose*) rickle.

  v **pile up** bing; (*loosely*) rickle.

pilfer *v* pauchle, sneck, pike.

pill *n* peel.

pillar *n* stoop.

from pillar to post hither an yont: '*Ah went hither an yont tae pick up the bairns*'.

pillow *n* pillae, cod.

pimple *n* plook.

pimply plookie, plookit.

pin *n, v* preen, peen.

pincushion preen-cod.

pinhead preen-heid.

pinpoint *n* neb.

game played with pins heidicks an pinticks NE.

have pins and needles prinkle.

pincers *npl* pinchers.

pinch *v* 1 (*squeeze*) nevel. 2 (*with cold*) nither. 3 (*steal*) skech, wheech, wheek. *n* (*of meal, salt etc*) nip; (*of snuff*) sneesh(in).

pinched (*with cold, ill-health etc*) shilpit, shirpit.

pine *v* (*waste away*) dwine, peenge; (*of an animal*) pewl.

pip *n* (*of a fruit*) paip.

pipe *n* 1 (*tobacco*) gun; (*short, stumpy, clay*) cutty (pipe), cutty clay. 2 (*of the bagpipes: on which melody is played, or separate pipe for practising*) chanter; (*bass pipe*) drone. 3 (*pipe from a roof gutter*) rone-pipe.

piss *v, n* pish.

pit *n* 1 (*coal mine*) heuch, winnin. 2 (*hole*) delf.

pitted (*roughened*) pickit.

pitch *v* 1 (*throw*) pick, lab. 2 (*of a boat*) howd.

pity *n* peety.

v peety, mane, be vext for.

pitiable peetifu.

to be pitied tae mane: '*They're muckle tae mane*'.

it's a pity it's a sin.

pivot *n, v* peevot.

place *n* 1 (*spot*) bit, spat. 2 (*area*) pairt, airt.

v (*put in position*) stell, plank.

all over the place a(w) roads, a(w) wye(s).

in that place yonner(-aboots).

put someone in his *or* **her place** pit someone's gas at a peep, sort someone.

plaice *n* splash(ack) N.

plain *adj* (*ordinary*) hameart; (*also of food*) hameower.

n (*along a river*) carse.

plait *n, v* plet, pleat.

plan *n* (*especially light-hearted*) ploy. *v* ettle: '*Whit are ye ettlin?*', mak it up (that).

plantain *n* (*greater or ribwort*) curl-doddie, carl-doddie; (*stems and flowerheads, used in a game*) sodgers; (*hoary*) lamb's lugs.

plaster *n* plaister; (*eg for a broken limb*) stookie.

v 1 plaister; (*smear*) skaik NE. 2 (*a broken limb*) stookie.

plate *n* (*large oval, for serving*) ashet; (*soup-plate, or other hollow plate*) deep plate.

play *v* 1 (*roughly, boisterously*) rampage. 2 (*a bowl, curling stone*) rowe.

playing cards cairts, cairds.

play fair play fair hornie.

plead *v* (*with someone for something*) fleetch, prig.

pleaded *past tense, past participle* pled.

please *v* pleesure, kittle (up).

pleasant cantie, cannie, couthie, lichtsome; (*especially of a person*) douce, fine; (*especially in appearance*) sonsie; (*especially of weather*) braw, nae (that) ull.

pleased prood, suitit, set NE, cantie; (*very*) fair awa (wi): '*She's fair awa wi her new computer*'; **pleased with yourself** croose, joco.

not be pleased no please: '*He wadna please*'.

pleasure pleesure.

do what you please gang yer ain gate *or* road.

pleat *v, n* plet.
pledge *v, n* wad.
plenty *n* footh, rowth, feck.
  plentiful rife, rowth, lairge NE.
  having plenty of rife wi.
pliable *adj* dwaible, swack.
pliers *npl* pinchers.
plod *v* stodge, plowd(er).
plop *v* plowp, plowt, plunk; (*of small drops*) pink.
  n plowp, plowt.
  make a plopping noise plump.
plot *n* (*of land*) dale NE.
  v collogue, colleague.
plough *n* pleuch, ploo.
  v pleuch, ploo, furr.
  ploughman pleuchie, hind, Jock hack NE.
plover *n* plivver.
  green plover *see* **lapwing**.
  ringed plover sandy laverock.
pluck *v* pook; (*especially fruit or a bird*) pou.
plum *n* ploom.
plume *n* pen.
plump *adj* pluffie; (*and healthy(-looking)*) sonsie, gawsie; (*well-nourished*) lik(e) yer mait.
plunder *v* spulyie, reive; (*also a nest*) herrie.
  n spulyie.
  plunderer (*in past times, especially in Border raids*) reiver.
plunge *v* dook, plype NE, plowt.
  n plype NE; (*noisy*) plowt, dook.
pocket *n* pootch, poacket.
  v pootch.
  pocket money Saturday('s) penny.
pod *n* huil, cod, shaup.
poet *n* makar *literary;* (*especially in Gaelic contexts*) bard.
point *n* pint; (*eg of a pen, pin, knife*) neb.
  v pint.
poison *n, v* pooshion, pushion, puzzen SOUTH.
  poisonous pooshionous.
poke *v* powk, prog; (*with a stick*)

poatch; (*with the elbow etc*) punce; (*with the nose*) snoozle.
  n powk, prog; (*with the elbow etc*) punce.
  poke about ruit, kirn, reemage NE.
pole *n* powl, pall, stang; (*eg to push off a boat*) sting; (*long, heavy, as thrown in Highland games*) caber.
police *n* polis.
  policeman polis(man), hornie *slang*.
  police station nick.
polite *adj* mensefu, discreet.
pollack *n* lythe.
pollute *v* smit, fyle.
pompom *n* (tappie)toorie.
pompous *adj* fou, poochle NE, massie.
pond *n* dub, stank.
pony *n* pownie; (*especially Shetland pony*) sheltie.
pooh! *interjection* (*nonsense!*) hoot(s)!
pool *n* puil, peel NE, pound, stank; (*below a waterfall*) linn; (*from a natural spring*) wall; (*of stagnant water*) stank; (*especially of muddy water*) dub.
poor *adj* puir, peer NE; (*hard-up*) ill-aff, sober NE.
  poor fellow puir sowl, peer breet NE.
pop *v:* **pop out** lowp.
  popping sound (*of a cork*) plunk.
  popgun spoot-gun.
pope *n* pape.
poppy *n* puppie.
porcelain *n, adj* (*dish, ornament etc*) wallie.
porch *n* entry.
pork *n* purk SHETLAND, NE.
porpoise *n* pellock, dunter.
porridge *n* parritch, gruel SHETLAND, ORKNEY, poshie *child's word*.
  porridge bowl (parritch) cap.
  stick for stirring porridge spurtle, spurkle, theevil.
positively *adv* positeevely, fairly: '*He'll fairly dae it*'.
possess *v* aucht, aicht NE, belang.
possibly *adv* maybe, mibbie.
post *n* stoop, pall, stob: '*fence-stob*', stab; (*upright*) standart.

postman *n* post(ie).
pot *n* pat; (*large cooking*) kettle.
pot-bellied guttie.
go to pot gae gyte, gae worth NE.
keep the pot boiling keep the puddin het.
potato *n* tattie, tawtie; **potato dishes** (*cooked in skins*) skinny tatties; (*dipped in gravy etc*) tatties an dab; (*mashed*) champit tatties, chappit tatties; (*mashed with mashed turnip*) clapshot; (*stewed with onions and sometimes meat etc*) stovies, stovit tatties.
potato-digger (*person*) tattie howker.
potato harvest tattie howkin, tattie liftin.
school holiday when children helped with potato harvest tattie hoalidays.
potato leaves and stalks (tattie) shaws.
potato-masher tattie-champer, (tattie-) chapper.
potato skin tattie peel(in).
potato soup tattie soup.
potter about *v* footer, plowter, gutter.
pouch *n* pootch, poke.
pound[1] *n* (*weight or money*) pun(d).
pound note note, single (note).
pound[2] *v* (*mash*) champ, chap.
pour *v* 1 (1) (*from a container*) poor, tuim, teem, tim. (2) (*gush*) poor, spue. 2 (*of rain*) poor, tuim, tim.
pour the liquid from poor: '*poor the tatties' bree*.
pour out (*tea*) poor: '*poor the tea*'.
poverty *n* puirtith, scant.
poverty-stricken ill-aff, in the grubber SE.
powder *n* poother, pooder; (*fine*) smeddum.
v poother, pooder.
powdery pootherie.
power *n* pooer.
powerful pooerfae; (*strong*) maisterfu; (*forceful*) feckfu.
powerless mauch(t)less.

practice *n* (*habit*) haunt.
practise *v* practeese.
praise *v, n* (*especially flatteringly*) roose, reese NE.
prance *v* link.
prank *n* pliskie: '*play a pliskie on*', cantrip, pant, prattick NE.
prawn *n* praan N.
prayer *n* prayers (*especially children's*) guid words.
say a prayer mak a prayer, pit up a word.
precious *adj* praicious.
precipice *n* heuch, scaur, clint.
precise *adj* preceese; (*of a person*) perjink.
precocious *adj* (*of a child*) auld-farran(t), ancient.
pregnant *adj* on the road, (muckle-) boukit.
become pregnant fa(w) (wi bairn).
make pregnant bairn.
premature *adj*: **give birth to a premature baby** pairt wi bairn.
premonition *n* forego, warnin.
preoccupied *adj* taen up (wi), jammed.
prepare *v* redd (up), graith; (*a meal*) ready.
prepare for mak for.
prescription *n* (doctor's) line, receipt.
present *n* praisent; (*small, eg as a memento*) mindin; (*especially of food, eg from a fair*) fairin.
v gift.
adj (*at hand*) forrit.
presentable weel tae be seen, gate farrin NE, faisible.
at present presently, the noo, ivnoo NE, meantime.
president *n* preses, convener.
press *v* (*squeeze*) chirt; (*especially with the feet*) paidle.
pressure *n* 1 (*especially with the knee*) knidge SHETLAND, N. 2 (*of work*) thrang(itie); (*excessive*) hash.
presume *v*: **I presume** I'm thinkin.
presumptuous ignorant.

pretend *v* mak on, lat on, pit on.

pretence pit-on, mak-on, phrase NE.

pretentious fantoosh.

pretty *adj* bonnie.

adv (*very*) gey (an), lucky SHETLAND, NE.

pretty well geylies, no bad.

prevent *v* kep.

price *n* (*very high*) ransom.

high price bonnie penny.

prick *v, n* jag, prog, job, dob.

prickle *n* jag, job, prog, stab.

v prinkle.

prickly jaggie, jobbie, stobbie.

prickly feeling prickle.

pride *n*: **full of pride** pridefu.

prim *adj* perjink, mim (as a Mey puddock), primsie; (*in speech*) mim-mou'd, tattie-peelin.

primly perjink, mim.

primrose *n* spink.

principal *adj* heid, maist.

n (*of a secondary school*) rector.

print *n, v* prent.

prison *n* jile.

prisoner (*at the bar*) panel.

be sent to prison get the jile, be nickit.

privet, privet hedge *n* privy hedge.

probable *adj* lik(e): '*It's like Ah'll go tae the jiggin the nicht*'.

problem *n* (*puzzle*) tickler; (*difficult problem*) kinch.

procession *n* (*ceremonial*) walk, parawd.

proclaim *v* lat wit NE.

prod *v* prog, poach.

n prog, nib.

produce *n* ootcome.

production ootcome; (*output*) throupit.

produce young (*of animals*) ferry; (*of small animals*) kittle.

profit *n* ootcome; (*unreasonably high*) rug.

profound *adj* (*of a person*) lang-heidit.

progress *n* oncome SHETLAND, NE.

make progress (*eg in business*) forder.

we're not making any progress we canna(e) get oot (o) the bit.

project *n, v* projeck.

prominent *adj* (*conspicuous*) kenspeckle.

promote *v* (*encourage*) forder.

prompt *adj* (*quick, ready*) gleg, yare.

prong *n* (*of a fork etc*) tae, grain, stang NE; (*especially of a digging- or pitchfork*) tang.

pronounce *v* pronoonce.

pronouncement speak NE.

proof *n* pruif, prief.

prop *n* prap, haud; (*eg for a beached boat*) steet N; *see also* **clothes prop** (*under* **clothe**).

v prap, stuit, steet N, stell; (*eg a building*) rance.

propel *v* (*eg a swing with the body*) pile, beam SE.

proper *adj* (*respectable*) wicelik(e).

properly richt; (*very*) fine an . . .

property *n* (*possessions*) gear: '*guids an gear*'; (*property held*) haud, haudin.

proportion *n*: **a large proportion of** plenty o: '*Plenty o them play fitba*'.

propose *v*: **propose to** (*a woman*) seek, speir (for).

proposition *n* proposeetion.

prosecutor *n*: **public prosecutor** procurator fiscal.

prosper *v* come (guid) luck.

prosperity seil, sonse.

prosperous bien, weel-daein.

prostitute *n* hairy, tail, cookie.

protect *v* (*shelter*) scug.

protest *n* (*loud outburst*) reird SOUTH.

Protestant *n* (*contemptuous*) Prod(die).

proud *adj* prood; (*conceited*) ful, conceitie; (*haughty*) proodfu; (*self-confident*) poochle NE.

proudly heich, heid-heich.

prove *v* pruive, prieve.

proved *past participle* proven.

proverb *n* say SHETLAND, N, speak NE.

prowl *v*: **prowl about** scunge, screenge NE; (*like a dog*) skive, snoke, ratch SOUTH.

on the prowl on the skech.

prudish *adj* mim.

prune *v* sned, sneck, snod.

pub *n* howf.

pucker *n*, *v* bumfle.

pudding *n* (*rich fruit, steamed*) dumplin, (*boiled in a cloth*) clootie dumplin; (*steamed in a cloth bag*) poke puddin; (*of oatmeal, suet etc*) white puddin, fite puddin NE.

puddle *n* dub, hole; **muddy puddles** gutters.

puff *v* (*blow gently*) pluff, fuff; (*breathe heavily*) pech, stech.
n (*of air, wind etc*) pluff, fuff, gliff; (*of smoke, steam*) lunt.
puffy pluffie; (*of the face*) chuffie.
puffball blin man's buff.
puff candy pluffie.
puff out pluff.
puffed out 1 bumfelt. **2** (*breathless*) pecht, puggelt.
with a puff pluff.

puffin *n* Tammie norie, norie SHETLAND, Tammie cheekie NE.

pugnacious *adj* randie.

pull *v* pou, pul; (*haul*) harl; (*vigorously*) rug, (rug an) rive; (*suddenly, sharply*) pook, yank, yerk; (*stretch*) rax, rack.
n pou, pul; (*vigorous*) rug, rive; (*sudden, sharp*) pook, yank, yerk.
pull someone's leg draw a bodie's leg, tak a bodie on.
pull to pieces rive, knip.
pull through (*an illness*) ca(w) throu.
pull yourself together gaither, tak yersel up.

pulp *n*: **reduce to pulp** pran NE.

pulpit *n* poopit.

punch *v*, *n* nevel.

Punch-and-Judy show *n* puppie show.

punish *v* pey, sort, pran NE, norter NE.
be severely punished get yer heid in yer han(d)s.
punishment peys, fairins, laldie: '*Gie him laldie*'.

puny *adj* shilpit, shilpie, shirpit, peeng(e)in.

pupil *n* **1** scholar; (*top of a class or school*) dux; (*bottom of a class*) fits, fittie, dult; (*kept in as a punishment*) keepie-in. **2** (*of the eye*) sicht, starn o the ee.

puppet show *n* puppie show.

purchases *npl* (*shopping*) messages: '*Pit the messages doon here*', eeran(t)s.

purl *n* (*knitting*) pearl.

purple *adj*, *n* purpie.

purpose *n* mint, ettle.
without purpose, purposeless lik(e) a knotless threid, fushionless.

purr *v* curmur.

purse *n* pootch; (*especially ornamental, worn with kilt*) sporran.
v (*the lips*) thraw.

pus *n* humour, etter.

push *v* pooss; (*a person*) gie (someone) the heave; (*gently*) putt; (*shove*) dab, ram; (*forcibly*) ding, dush, dird NE.
n pooss; (*gentle*) putt; (*heavy*) doose SHETLAND, ORKNEY, NE; (*sharp*) ding, dush NE.

put *v* pit.
past tense pit, put, pat.
past participle pit, pitten, putten.
put aside (*for future use*) pit by, set by.
put down (*with a thump*) plank, plunk, plype NE.
put in order redd (up).
put out (*a fire, light*) smore.
put yourself out (*trouble yourself*) mismak.
put together (*prepare hastily*) rattle (up).
put up with thole (wi), bide: '*He cannae bide his mither-in-law*'.

puzzle *v* fickle, tickle, kittle.
n (*problem*) tickler.
puzzling (*difficult*) kittle, kittlie, ticklie.

Q

quack *v* quaik NE.

quake *v* quak, grue.

qualify *v* qualifee.

quandary *n* swither.

in a quandary switherin.

put in a quandary jam.

quantity *n* (*considerable*) hantle, kit SOUTH; (*vague*) da(u)d; (*large*) feck, lump, muckle; (*small*) pickle, (wee) tait, lick.

quarrel *n* thraw, threap, ootcast, argie-bargie; (*noisy*) catterbatter FIFE, SOUTH, collieshangie.

v argie-bargie, thraw, threap, cast oot; (*violently*) flyte; (*noisily*) catterbatter SOUTH.

quarrelsome carnaptious, camsteerie, argle-barglous, tiftie.

quarrelsome woman randie.

quarry *n* (*stone-quarry*) quarrel, heuch.

quarter *n* (*of a round of oatcakes*) farl, fardel.

quay *n* shore N, FIFE.

queer *adj* unco, orra.

quench *v* (*thirst or a fire*) slock(en).

quench your thirst weet yer thrapple, slocken yer drouth.

query *n, v* speir.

question *n* speir.

v speir (at); (*closely*) tarragat.

questioning speirin(s), speir.

quick *adj* gleg, clivver, swith; (*active*) swipper(t) NE.

quickly swith, swipper(t) NE.

quick-witted gleg (i the uptak), snack(ie), sparkie.

quiet *adj* quate, quietlik(e), lown.

n quate, lown.

quietly quate, quietlik(e); (*especially of wind*) lown; (*in speaking*) sma: '*speak sma*'.

be quiet haud yer gab, steek yer gab.

be quiet! (haud yer) wheesht!, quate wi ye!

quit *past tense* quat, quate.

quits equal-aqual.

quite *adv* (*rather*) gey an . . . : '*It's gey an hot*'.

quiver *v* queever, dirl.

R

rabbit *n* bawtie SOUTH; (*pet name*) mappie, map-map.
  rabbit's tail bun, fud.
rabble *n* clamjamfrie.
race *n*: **the human race** Jock Tamson's bairns.
rack *n* heck.
racket *n* (*noise*) ricket.
raffle *n* lucky-poke.
rafter *n* bauk, raft.
rag *n* **1** cloot; (*long, trailing*) trollop, trailep NE. **2 rags** cloots, duds, tatterwallops.
  ragged raggit, raggetie, raggie, duddie.
  ragwort ragweed, tansy, stinkin Willie.
  ragamuffin *n* tattie-bogle, tatterwallop NE.
rage *n* tirrivee, feem NE; (*sudden*) pirr, flist NE.
  v fizz; (*of a storm*) tear.
  fly into a rage gang gyte, fuff, flist NE.
  in a (towering) rage bealin, dancin mad, wuid, reid mad.
rail *n* (*in a fence etc*) spar NE.
rain *n* weet, saft, pani SOUTH, *originally gipsy*.
  v (*heavily*) teem, plump, pish doon, plas g on *or* doon; (*violently*) bla (*gently*) smirr; (*slightly*) skiff, irp NE, spark.
  rainy saft, blashie, weetie; (*very wet*) trashie.
  raindrop spark.
raise *v* heeze, heyze NE, uphaud.
rake *n* (*for scraping*) harl.
  rake together harl.
ram *n* tuip, teep NE.
  young ram tuip lamb.
ramble *v* **1** (*wander*) dander, stravaig, rammle. **2** (*in speech*) raivel, rander, rove. **3** (*of plants*) ramp.

ramshackle *adj* ricklie, sha(u)chlie.
ran *see* **run.**
randy *adj* radg(i)e.
range *v* (*wander over*) reenge.
  n (*distance, limit*) reenge.
ransack *v* ranshackle, ripe NE.
rap *v* (*knock*) knap; (*at a door*) chap, rees(h)le SOUTH; (*your knuckles*) clyte.
  n knap.
rapid *adj* fest.
rare *adj* rerr, seendil, antrin.
rascal *n* laidron, rinagate; (*mischievous child*) limmer, sorra, tike.
rash¹ *n* hatter.
rash² *adj* (*reckless*) ramstam, raucle, ootheidie.
  rashly ramstam.
rasp *v* (*make a grating sound*) risp.
raspberry *n* rasp.
  raspberry-picking berry-pickin, the berries.
rat *n* ratton.
rate *n*: **at any rate** oniewey(s).
rather *adv* **1** (*sooner*) raither. **2** (*somewhat*) raither, gey an . . .
  rather than or.
ration *n* raition.
rattle *v* dirl, brattle; (*of rain, hail*) blatter; (*of doors, crockery etc*) rees(h)le, rickle.
  n **1** (*sound*) dirl, blatter, clitter-clatter, rees(h)le, rickle. **2** (*wooden, as used eg by football supporters*) ricketie.
rave *v* rame, raivel, rove.
raven *n* corbie.
ravenous *adj* geenyoch.
ravine *n* cleuch, heuch.
raw *adj* **1** (*of weather*) oorie, oorlich N. **2** (*of liquor*) hard.
ray *n* (*of light*) leam; (*small*) peek.
razor *n* (*as a weapon*) chib, malky *rhyming slang*.

razorbill scoot, marrot.
razor-fish spootfish, spoot.
slash with a razor chib, malky *rhyming slang.*
reach *v* reak, win at, win tae.
n **1** reak. **2** (*of a river*) rack.
reached *past tense, past participle* raucht.
reach out (*the hand or arm*) **to grasp** rax (oot).
reach over (*stretch out*) rax ower.
ready *adj* (*to do something*) free.
ready cash *see* **cash.**
get ready rank NE.
make ready for mak for.
real *adj* rael.
really! (*expressing surprise*) fegs!
reap *v* raep, share.
rear[1] *n* **1** hin(t), hin(t)side, hin(t)-en(d), hinneren(d). **2** (*buttocks*) hin(t)-en(d), hinneren(d), behoochie, bahookie.
adj hin(t), hinder, hin(d)maist.
rear[2] *v* (*children*) fess up NE.
reason *n* rizzon NE, raison; (*sanity*) judgement, wit; (*for something*) use.
reasonable (*of a person*) wicelik(e).
for what reason? whit wey?, fit wye? NE.
the reason why the wey at, foo NE: '*Foo e's deein't, 's . . .*'.
receive *v* (*stolen goods*) reset.
receiver (*of stolen goods*) resetter.
receiving of stolen goods reset (of theft).
recent *adj* raicent.
recently (in the) new, newlins NE, shortlins, short (sin)syne.
recess *n* (*in a wall*) neuk; (*especially used as a cupboard*) bole.
recipe *n* receipt.
recite *v* rame.
reckless *adj* ramstam, rhymeless NE, gallus, rackless.
recklessly ramstam, racklessly.
move recklessly breenge: '*He breenged in*'.
reckon *v* rackon.

recognize *v* ken; (*as a relation etc*) own.
not recognize misken, nae ken.
recognition kennin SHETLAND, ORKNEY, N.
recollect *v* mind, mine, recolleck.
recollection mindin, mind NE, mine NE.
recommend *v* (*a person*) moyen NE.
recover *v* (*from illness*) win ower; (*your health or spirits*) cantle up.
recover from (*illness*) get throu, come throu, mend o.
recovered (*from illness*) till yer fit; (*completely*) better; (*and going about*) aboot: '*Tam's aboot again*'.
recovery betterness: '*There's nae betterness fur him*'.
red *adj* reid, rid.
redcurrant rizzar.
redshank pleep.
reduction *n* inlaik.
reed *n* sprot.
reef *n* skellie NE, skerrie SHETLAND, ORKNEY.
reel *n* (*of thread, for fishing-rod*) pirn.
v (*stagger*) stotter, swaver SHETLAND, ORKNEY, NE.
reel off screed aff.
refined *adj* (*prim*) perjink.
reflect *v* refleck.
reform *v* (*a person*) mend; (*yourself*) mend.
refreshing *adj* caller.
refund *v* repeat.
refuse[1] *v* refuise, refeese NE, na-say; (*to do work*) renaig.
refusal refuise, refeese NE, na-say.
refuse to move reest.
refuse[2] *n* (*rubbish*) hinneren(d), hinderen(d), redd, bruck SHETLAND, ORKNEY.
refuse collection (*of bulky articles*) special uplift.
refuse-collector scaffie.
refuse-collector's cart *or* **lorry** scaffie('s) cairt, midgie motor.
regard *v, n* regaird.

region *n* kintra, countra, cwintry N.

regret *v* rue; (*a promise*) rue.

regular *adj* reglar, raiglar; (*of wages*) upstandin.

reign *v* ring.

reject *v* rejeck, ort.

relapse *n* back-gang(in).

relate *v*: **related** (*by blood*) sib, kin.
  relation, relative (*blood*) freen(d).

relax *v* (*after a good meal*) swage ORKNEY, N.

release *v* lowse.

reliable *adj* sicker; (*of a person*) cannie.

relief *n* (*from physical discomfort*) easement.
  relieve (*a person at work*) speel.

religion *n* releegion.
  religious releegious, guidlie; (*churchgoing*) kirkie.

reluctant *adj* thrawn, sweir(t), dour.

rely (on) *v* lippen (till).

remain *v* bide, stey.
  remainder lave.
  remains (*of a meal*) orrals.

remark *n* observe, say, word.
  remarkable unco.

remember *v* mind (o *or* on), keep mind o.
  I remember (*doing something*) I've seen masel: '*I've seen masel gaun on a Sunday*'.
  remember (someone) to (someone) mind tae: '*Mind me tae yer mither*'.
  remind *v* mind, remember: '*Remember me tae pey the milkman*'.

remnant *n* (*of cloth*) remainder.
  remnants orrals.

remote *adj* farawa, faur oot aboot, hyne awa.

remove *v* remuve, remeeve NE; (*clear away*) redd; (*from one place to another, to another house*) flit.
  removal (*to another house*) flit(tin), shift.

rendezvous *n*, *v* tryst.

rennet *n* yirnin.

renounce *v* renunce.

renovate *v* replenish: '*Ah've replenished that auld hoose*'.

reopen *v* (*of a school etc, after a holiday*) tak up.

repair *v* (*mend*) sort, replenish.
  keep in good repair uphaud.

repay *v* repey, repeat.

repeat *v* **1** (*monotonously*) rhyme; (*again and again*) rame. **2** (*of food*) come back on a person: '*Ingans come back on me*'.

repent *v* remorse NE.

repetition *n* repeteetion; (*monotonous*) rame.

reply *v* (*in argument*) speak back.

report *n* (*account*) din.
  v (*tell*) clype.

repulsive *adj* ugsome, ill-faured, scunnersome.

request *v* seek, speir.

resemble *v* (*a person*) tak aff, kin(d) tae SOUTH.

reserve *v* hain, pit by, set by.
  reserved (*in manner*) stench NE.
  reserve team wee team.

reside *v* stey, bide, haud oot.
  resident *n* residenter, indwaller.

resin *n* roset.

resistance *n* fend.

resolve *v* (*a problem*) redd up.

resource *n*: **resourceful** quirkie.
  at the end of your resources puggelt.

respect *v*, *n* respeck.
  respectable douce, honest(-lik(e)), weel-faured, wicelik(e).
  respectability honesty.
  in every respect a(w) weys.
  in that respect that wey.

responsibility *n* responsibeelitie.

rest[1] *n* (*remainder*) lave.

rest[2] *n* (*time of rest from work*) speel.
  rested sleepit oot.
  restless fykie, fliskie; (*especially of a child*) steerin, stourie.
  restlessness fyke.
  fit of restlessness the fykes.
  in a state of restlessness lik(e) a hen on a het girdle.

restrain *v* pit the haims on, pit the branks on, haud in aboot.

restrict *v* restrick.

restricted scrimpit.

result *n* affcome, ootcome.

end results efterins.

retch *v* boak, byock NE, reach.
n boak, byock NE.

retch(ing) with nothing to bring up dry boak.

retirement *n* retiral.

return *n* (*home*) hamecomin.

revenge *n*: **be revenged on** be upsides wi, be upsides doon wi N.

take revenge on saut.

review *v, n* scance.

revolve *v* birl, wammle, whummle.

rheumatism *n* rheumatise.

rhododendron *n* roddie, rosidandrum.

rhythm *n* lilt, stot.

out of rhythm aff the stot.

ribwort plantain *see* **plantain**.

rich *adj* (*well-off*) bien, (weel-)gaithert; (*of food*) foosome.

rickety *adj* ricklie, cogglie, shooglie.

rid *v* redd.

get rid of redd o, tyne; (*a person*) gie the heavy dunt tae.

be rid of be shot o.

riddle *n* (*puzzle*) guess, quirk.

ask riddles speir guesses.

ride *v* (*in a wheeled vehicle*) hurl.
n (*in a wheeled vehicle*) hurl; (*in a wheeled vehicle or on horseback*) sail.
rode *past tense* rade.

riding equipment ridin graith.

ridge *n* **1** (*of land*) soo('s) back, shin; (*high*) rig(gin); (*long, narrow*) kame. **2** (*in a cultivated field*) rig. **3** (*of a roof*) riggin.

ridiculous *adj* rideeculas.

riff-raff *n* scuff, scaff (an raff), clamjamfrie.

right *adj* richt.

rightly richtlie, richtlins SHETLAND, NE.

right hand thoum-han(d) NE.

all right (then) weel a weel.

rigid *adj* **1** stieve; (*taut*) strait. **2** (*in manner*) stench NE.

rigmarole *n* raible, say-awa.

rind *n* huil; (*of a cheese*) heel.

ring *v* **1** (*of a bell*) tingle, jowe; (*ring when struck*) dirl. **2** (*a bell*) tingle, jowe.
n (*ringing of a bell*) ringle, jowe.

rinse *v, n* syne, synd, reenge, sweel.

riot *n* hurry, gilravage.
v gilravage.

riotous randie, camstairie.

rip *v* rive, screed, raip NE.
n rive, raip NE.

ripe *adj* (*of fruit etc*) maumie.

ripple *v, n* lipper, lapper, pirl.

rise *v* (*above the surface*) heave, hove.
n (*of water in a river: sudden*) spate.

take a rise out of tak the nap aff.

risky *adj* mischancie, unchancie.

river *n* wat(t)er: '*Water of Leith*': '*Black Water*'.

riverbank (*steep*) brae.

rivermouth wat(t)er mou(th).

riverside (land) (*low meadow*) haugh, carse, merse SW.

road *n* gate.

road-fork sindrins.

on the road roadit NE.

middle of the road croon o the causey.

roam *v* stravaig, traik, reenge; (*aimlessly*) vaig, scurrievaig.

roaming *n* stravaig.

roar *v* rair, goller, gollie, buller NE; (*of cattle*) rowt; (*of other animals*) rowt, roup; (*of wind etc*) rowt, gurl.
n rair, reird, goller, gollie, buller NE; (*of cattle*) rowt.

roaring *adj* roarie.

roast *v* plot; (*on embers*) harn.

rob *v* reive, rook, spulyie, roop; (*bird's nest*) herrie.

rock[1] *n* **1** (*crag*) craig, clint SW, SOUTH; (*very steep*) scaur. **2** (*tall column rising out of the sea*) stack ORKNEY, N.

rock[2] *v* **1** shoogle, shog, coggle, howd

NE, showd; (*of a boat*) jowe. **2** (*cause to rock*) coggle NE, shoogle, shog, showd N.

rocking (motion) shog, showd; (*especially of a ship*) howd.

with a rocking motion rocketie-rowe.

rod *n* stang, wand.

rode *see* **ride.**

rogue *n* skellum, loon.

roguery joukerie-pawk(e)rie.

roguish pawkie, ill-trickit SHETLAND, ORKNEY, N.

roll *v* rowe, pirl, trinnle; (*at play*) rowe-chow; (*of waves etc*) sweel.

n **1** rowe. **2** (*of bread*) rowe, bap, skinny; (*flaky, made with a lot of butter*) butterie, rowie NE, butterie rowie NE.

rolling pin (*especially grooved for oatcakes*) rower.

roll along trinnle.

roll towards the jack (*of a bowl*) rowe.

roll up untidily bumfle.

Roman Catholic *see* **Catholic.**

romp *v, n* rant, heeze NE; (*boisterous(ly)*) ramp.

roof *n* ruif, reef NE, riggin, hoose-heid.

roof-gutter rone(-pipe), spoot.

rook *n* craw, corbie.

room *n* **1** (*of a house*) en(d); (*best room*) chaumer, ben, the room; (*of a but-and-ben*) room-en(d); (*living, sitting or dining room*) public room. **2** (*scope*) scowthe.

roomy sonsie, scowthie NE, gawsie.

in *or* **the inner room, in** *or* **to the best room** ben: 'They're aw ben the noo'.

in *or* **to another room** ben (the hoose).

roost *n* reest NE; (*hen-roost*) bauk, hen-laft.

root *n* **1** ruit, reet N.

rope *n* **1** raip; (*for lowering coffin into grave*) cord. **2** (*farming: of twisted straw*) strae raip, thrawcruik.

v raip.

rope-twister thrawcruik.

rose *n*: **rosebush** (*wild*) breer, buckie (-breer) SW, ULSTER.

rosehip *n* dog-hip, buckie; **rosehips** hippans NE.

rotate *v* birl.

rotten *adj* (*mouldy*) mozie; (*of wood, cloth etc*) frush.

become rotten (*of meat, meal etc*) moch(t) NE.

rough *adj* ruch, roch; (*of people*) raucle, teuch, groff, randie; (*in manner*) coorse, ramstouger; (*of speech*) raucle; (*of the voice or throat*) roostie; (*of weather*) ill, teuch, gurlie.

roughen (*of the skin*) hack.

handle roughly rummle, toother.

treat roughly toother.

roughcast *n, v* harl.

rough and ready hielan.

round *adj, adv, n, v* roon(d).

rounders hoose-ba.

round-faced (*and usually stupid*) ba(w)-faced.

round-shouldered howe-backit.

rouse *v* roose; (*to action etc*) rowst.

route *n* road, gate.

routine *n* or(di)nar.

old *or* **usual routine** auld claes an parritch.

out of your routine aff the stot.

rove *v* raik, haik.

rover traik, rinthereoot NE.

roving rinaboot.

row[1] *n* **1** raw. **2** (*in knitting etc*) gang.

row of houses raw; (*mining*) (miners') raw.

row[2] *n* (*quarrel*) stramash, stooshie, stushie, stashie.

row[3] *v* (*a boat*) rowe, oar.

rowing boat oarie-boat.

rowan *n* (*tree*) rodden(-tree).

rowan berry rodden N.

rowdy *adj* bowsterous.

rowdy behaviour ongauns.

rub *v* (*in order to dry*) dicht; (*vigorously*) screenge; (*wear*) chaff.

n dicht.

rubber *n* cahootchie, guttie.

made of rubber guttie, guttie-perkie: '*guttie-perkie ba*'.

rubbish *n* rubbage, muck; (*(to be) cleared away*) redd; (*domestic*) midgie.

rubbish! blethers!, hoot(s)!

rubbish dump cowp: '*Tak aw thae auld claes tae the cowp*', tuim.

rudder *n* rither.

rude *adj* (*impudent*) misbehadden SHETLAND, NE.

ruffian *n* rochian, randie; (*from Glasgow*) (Glesca) keelie.

ruffle *v* runkle, snorl, touse.

ruffled (*of the hair etc*) touslie.

rug *n* (*for wrapping*) hap; (*floor rug: made of rags*) clootie rug.

ruin *n* **1** (*building etc*) rummle SHETLAND, NE. **2** (*state of ruin*) crockaneetion NE, potterneetion NE, stramash. *v* cowp, malafooster, wrack.

ruined awa wi't, by wi't, in the sheuch, awa for ile, gane tae potterlowe NE; (*bankrupt*) broken.

go to ruin gae tae pigs an whustles.

in ruins hyter NE.

rumble *v* rummle, dunner; (*of thunder etc*) hurl; (*of the stomach*) wammle. *n* rummle, dunner NE.

rummage *v* reenge, rummle: '*Whit are ye rummlin in that cupboard fur?*', howk, ripe NE.

rummage through rees(h)le throu.

rumour *n* clatter, souch.

rump *n* curpin.

rump-steak heukbone, Pope's eye, round steak.

run *v* rin, leg; (*quickly*) stour, chase. *n* rin, race; (*for a particular purpose*) raik.

ran *past tense* run, rin.

runny (*of a nose*) snotterie, snochlie.

in the long run at the hinneren(d).

run away tak leg, tak leg bail, tak yer heels.

rung *n* spar, spaik.

runt *n* (*of a litter*) poke-shakkins, shakkins o e pokie NE.

rush[1] *n* (*plant*) rash, sprot; (*coarse*) sprat.

rush[2] *v* stour, whidder; (*recklessly*) breenge; (*violently, headlong*) skelter; (*through the air*) wheech; (*of liquid*) jaw, pish. *n* scoor N; (*violent*) breenge, rummle; (*of work*) hurry, hash; (*of water*) jaw **with** *or* **in a rush** lik(e) stour.

rust *n, v* roost.

rusty roostie.

rustle *v, n* rees(h)le, souch.

rut *n* trink NE, rat SOUTH.

ruthless *adj* fell.

S

sack *n* **1** seck; (*small*) poke, pyoek NE.
2 (*dismissal*) **the sack** the heave: '*They gied him the heave*', yer jotters, the road: '*She got the road*'.
v (*dismiss*) seck, pit awa.
sad *adj* dowie, dowf, sod N.
saddle *n, v* saidle, seddle.
safe *adj* sauf, sicker.
  place of safety (*in games*) den.
said *see* **say**.
sailor *n* tarry-breeks.
saint *n* saunt.
sake *n*: **for goodness sake** for onie sake.
saliva *n* slavers, slivver(s) NE.
  salivate slerp.
salmon *n* saumon, fish; (*young, at early stage, with dark stripes*) parr; (*at next stage*) smowt; (*on first return to fresh water*) grilse.
  salmon fishing boat (saumon) coble.
  salmon leap saumon lowp.
salt *n* saut.
v saut; (*to preserve*) poother.
  salty sautie.
same *adj, pronoun*: **all of the same kind** a(w) ae oo.
  all the same still an on.
  much the same muckle aboot it, siclik(e).
  in the same way siclik(e).
sand *n* san, saun.
  sandy sannie.
  sand-eel san(d)le.
  sand-flea sand(y) lowper.
  sandman Willie Winkie.
  sandpiper sandy laverock NE.
  sandpit (*on a golf course*) bunker.
sandwich *n* piece: '*egg-piece*'; '*piece on cheese*'.
sane *adj* wice(lik(e)).
  sanity wit, judgement: '*lose yer judgement*'.

  not quite sane no wice.
sat *see* **sit**.
satin *n* saitin.
satisfy *v* saitisfee, pleesure; (*especially with food or drink*) ser, stench; (*thirst*) slock(en): '*slocken yer drouth*'.
  satisfaction saitisfaction.
  satisfied suitit; (*with food*) fine; (*of thirst*) slockit.
  satisfying (*of a meal*) hertsome.
  satisfactory no bad.
  satisfactorily bonnilie, richt.
Saturday *n* Saturday.
saucer *n* flat, flet, flattie NE, shell NE.
sausage *n* sassenger; (*sliced*) Lorne sausage, square sausage; **sausages** links, slingers, hingin mince *humorous*.
save *v* sauf; (*money*) gaither.
  savings hainins.
  savings club menodge, menadge.
  save money fog: '*We'll hae tae fog a wee*'.
  save up hain (in), pose (up) N.
saw *see* **see**.
say *v*: **said** *past tense, past participle* sayed.
  saying say SHETLAND, N, word; (*popular*) speak.
  say no more about it lat that flee stick tae the wa.
scab *n* scur(l), scruif.
  v (**form a**) **scab** scur NE.
  scabbed scabbit.
  scabby scawt.
scabious *n* curl-doddie.
scald *v* sca(u)d; (*in hot water to clean etc*) plot, leep.
  scalding (hot) plot(tin) het.
scales *npl* wechts, wey-bauks.
scallop *n* (*shellfish*) clam(shell).
scalp *n* scaup, powe.

scalpel *n* lance.

scamp *v* (*work*) slim (ower), skiff (by). *n* (*rascal*) nickum, loon, skellum.

scamper *v* skelter.

scan *v* scance.

scandal *n* clatter(s), souch.

spread scandal clash, clatter.

scant *adj* scrimp.

scanty scrimpit: '*That's a scrimpit dress*', jimp.

scanty measure scrimpie (measure).

scantiness scrimpness.

scar *n, v* scaur.

scarce *adj* scrimp, jimp.

scarcely scantlins, jimp.

scarcity scant.

scare *v, n* scar, skeer, fleg, fear.

easily scared skeichen NE, easy fleggit.

scarecrow (tattie-)bogle, (tattie-)boodie NE.

scarf *n* (*especially woollen*) gravat.

scatter *v* skail, splatter; (*coins to children at a wedding*) logan NE. *n* (*of coins to children at a wedding*) poor-oot, scoor-oot E CENTRAL, scramble WEST, logan NE.

scatterbrain sodie-heid.

scatterbrained sodie-heidit.

scatter about straw, strowe.

scheme *n* (*idea, plan*) ploy.

school *n* scuil, skweel NE, skeel N, *north of Moray Firth,* SW; (*infant school*) wee scuil.

school lunch hall dinner scuil.

schoolmaster dominie, maister.

school pupil scuil bairn, scuil wean, scholar.

be a pupil at school learn the scuil.

scissors *npl* shears.

pair of scissors shears, scissor: '*Gie me the scissor*'.

scold *v* scaul(d), tongue, sort, be intae; (*severely*) gie someone his heid in his han(d)s, gie someone it het an reekin.

scolding *n* scaul(d), redd(in) up.

scolding match flytin(g).

get a (severe) scolding get yer heid

in yer han(d)s, get it het an reekin, get hey-ma-nannie NE.

scone *n* (*triangular*) farl.

round of six scones cat's face.

scoop *v*: **scoop out** howk. *n* scuip.

scope *n* scowthe.

scorch *v* birsle, scowder.

score *n, v* (*groove*) rit.

have equal scores (*in a game etc*) stan(d) peels, peel.

what's the score? whit's the Hampden (roar)? *rhyming slang*.

Scots (language) *n, adj* Scoats, Scoatch, Doric (*now usually referring to* NE *Scots*), Lallans *literary* (*used by writers*).

scoundrel *n* scoon(d)rel, skellum.

scour *v* scoor, reenge; (*energetically*) screenge.

scowl *v, n* skool, gowl.

scramble *v* **1** (*climb clumsily*) spra(u)chle, scra(u)chle, scrammle. **2** (*eggs*) scrammle, rummle. *n* scrammle; (*struggle*) spra(u)chle.

scrap *n* perlicket N, nick; (*of food*) pick, snap; **scraps** orrals, smush; (*of food*) brock, scran NE.

scrape *v* scart; (*eg to clean*) claut; (*scrape skin off*) peel.

scraper claut.

scraping noise screeve, screed.

scrape through warsle throu.

scrape together (*gather*) scart; (*in little bits*) scran.

scratch *v* scart, scrat, screeve; (*gently, eg to relieve itch*) claw. *n* scart, scrat, rive; (*large*) screeve; (*deep*) rit.

scrawl *n* (*hasty letter*) scrape o the pen; **scrawls** hen's taes.

scream *v, n* skirl, skraich, skelloch, squalloch NE.

screech *v, n* skreek, skraich; (*especially of a bird or animal*) squaik.

screen *v* (*hide*) scug.

screw *v* **1** (*twist*) feeze. **2** screw (up) (*the face*) thraw, shevel, showl N.

scribble *v* scart.

  n scart; *(hasty note)* scrape o the pen.

scrimp *v* jimp, pinch, haud in aboot.

script *n* *(piece of writing)* scrieve.

scrounge *v* scroonge, scunge, skech, scran.

  scrounger skech, scranner; *(in dustbins etc)* bucket-scranner, midgie-raker.

  scrounging skech: '*on the skech*', scran.

scrub *v* screenge; *(eg a pot)* reenge.

scruff[1] *n* *(of the neck)* cuff (o the neck).

scruff[2] *n*, *see* **scruffy person** *below*.

  scruffy waff(lik(e)), schemie.

  scruffy person tattie bogle, ticket; *(very)* scaff, scheme, schemie.

scuffle *n* *(disturbance)* rammie, tulyie.

  v *(fight)* tulyie.

scurry *v* skelter, whidder, fudder NE.

scythe *n* hey-sned, whittle.

  v maw.

sea *n* sey MORAY COAST, SOUTH, tide.

  sea anemone (sea-)pap.

  sea-eagle earn.

  sea fog (sea-)haar E COAST.

  seagull (sea-)maw, maa SHETLAND.

  seaport (town) sea toon.

  seaside *(as holiday area, on the Clyde coast)* doon-the-watter.

  seaweed *(coarse)* tang(le); *(types of edible)* badderlocks, daberlacks NE.

  arm of the sea sea loch.

seal *n* *(animal)* selch, selkie SHETLAND, ORKNEY, silkie SHETLAND, ORKNEY.

  seal people *(imaginary race of seal-like sea creatures)* selkie folk, silkies SHETLAND, ORKNEY.

search *v* fork (for), kirn SHETLAND, N; *(a place, thoroughly)* reenge, range, ripe, seek; *(noisily)* reemage; *(a person)* rake.

  n reenge, fork.

  search for seek.

season *n* saison, sizzon NE.

  v saison; *(food)* kitchen.

  seasoning kitchen.

seat *n* **1** sate; *(long, wooden)* bink;

(formed by two people crossing hands) queen's chair. **2** *(spell of being seated)* sit-doon. **3** *(of trousers)* dowp.

  v set.

  be seated set.

  take a seat lean.

second *adj, n* saicant.

  second cousin half-cousin.

secret *adj* saicret, hidlin(s), dern.

  n saicret.

  secrecy hudge-mudge.

  secretly, in secret (in) hidlins.

secretary *n* secretar.

secure *adj* sicker.

  securely sicker.

sedate *adj* douce.

sediment *n* grummel, grun(d)s.

  full of sediment g(r)umlie.

see *v* sei SOUTH.

  saw *past tense* seen, seed.

  be unable to see *(in the dark)* no be able tae see yer thoum.

  you see? seestu?

  see to notice SHETLAND, ORKNEY, NE, own.

seed *n*: **seedy** *(ill, weak)* bauch.

  seed potato set.

seek *v*: **sought** *past tense, past participle* socht.

seep *v* sype.

seesaw *n* shoggie-shoo.

  play seesaw cowp the ladle.

seething *adj* *(swarming)* ho(a)tchin.

segment *n* *(eg of an orange)* leaf, lith, pap NE.

seize *v* cleek, cla(u)cht, grip, nick.

  seized *past tense, past participle* cla(u)cht.

seldom *adv* seendil.

select *v* wale.

self *pronoun* sel; *(emphatic)* ainsel, nainsell NE: '*her nainsell*'.

  by yourself yer lane: '*He wis aw his lane*', im leen NE, er leen NE, on yer ain.

  selfish hame-dra(u)chit NE.

  self-confident croose (i the craw).

self-conscious (*especially of children*) strange.

self-righteous people the unco guid.

self-satisfied croose, kirr sw.

sell *v* (*by auction*) roup.

sold *past tense, past participle* selt, sald SHETLAND.

semi-detached house *n* hauf-hoose NE.

send *v* sen, set, hae: '*He wis had tae bed*', pit: '*It pits me tae sleep*'.

send flying skite.

send off set (aff); (*eg on an errand*) road; (*on foot*) shank.

senile *adj* donnert, doitert.

sensation *n* (*pleasurable*) kittle.

cause a sensation set the heather on fire.

sense *n* sinse NE; (*good sense*) mense, wit; **senses** judgement: '*oot o yer judgement*'.

senseless (*mad*) glaikit, smerghless N; (*meaningless*) haiveless.

sensible mensefu, wice(lik(e)).

sensibly wice(lik(e)).

sensitive kittlie.

separate *v* sinder, twin(e) SHETLAND. *adj* sindrie.

separately sindrie.

septic *adj* atterie, etterie, bealin.

sergeant *n* sairgint.

serious *adj* sairious; (*no laughing matter*) nae mows NE.

servant *n* (*girl*) (servan(t)) lass, quine NE; (*servant who does rough work*) scodge, scodgie.

serve *v* ser, sair; (*food at table*) lift.

serve someone right be the price o someone.

serve a (useful) purpose dae the turn, dae a turn.

service *n* (*church*) diet o worship.

serviette *n* servit.

set *v* (*of jam etc*) mak, jeel. *past participle* setten. *n* pair (*not necessarily two*): '*pair o bagpipes*'; (*eg of knitting needles*) stan(d).

set aside set by, pit past, pit by.

set off set awa, tak the road, tak the gate.

settle *v* sattle; (*affairs*) redd (up); (*make your home*) sit doon.

become settled (*in a place*) heft; (*of weather, after rain*) harden up.

seven *numeral* seeven, siven N; (*in children's rhymes*) seater, teven.

seventeenth seeventeen(t).

seventh seevent.

seventy seeventie.

group of seven seevensome.

several *pronoun* (*several people*) severals.

severe *adj* (*harsh*) snell, dour, ill; (*strict*) snar; (*of laws, weather*) sicker; (*of weather*) snell, soor, thrawn NE; (*of a blow*) uncannie.

sew *v* shew, steek; (*hastily*) ranter.

sewing shewin; (*act of*) shew.

sewer *n* jaw-hole.

sex *n* (*sexual intercourse*) houghmagandie (*see also* **intercourse**).

sexually excited radg(i)e, yeukie.

shabby *adj* (*scruffy*) scuffie, schemie, orra, shan.

shabby person ticket: '*He looks an awfu ticket*'.

shade *n* (*shelter*) scug.

shadow *n, v* sha(i)ddae SE.

shaft *n* **1** (*of a cart etc*) tram, stang; (*of a scythe*) sned; (*of a brush etc*) shank. **2** (*in a mine*) shank.

shag *n* (*cormorant*) scarf, skart, scrath NE.

shaggy tautit, tautie, hudderie; (*dishevelled*) tousie.

shake *v* shak, shog, shoogle; (*totter*) coggle, jossle; (*with laughter*) hodge NE, hobble NE, (*also with cold, fear*) hotter NE. *n* shak, shog, shoogle.

shook *past tense* shakkit, shuk.

shaken *past participle* shakken, shooken, shucken.

shaking *n* hotter.

shaky shooglie, cogglie, jeeglie; (*especially of a person*) sha(u)chlie.

shake hands chap han(d)s.

shall v will, sall; (*after personal pronouns*) s(e): '*Ye'se hae yer supper*'; *see also* **should**.

shall not winnae, winna.

shallow *adj, n* shalla, shaul(d).

shambles *n* (*confusion*) Paddy's market, Annicker's midden.

shame *n*: **feel shame** get a rid face.

it's a shame it's a sin: '*It's a sin, so it is*'.

share v pairt.

n dale; (*half*) halvers, halfies.

in equal shares eeksie-peeksie.

share equally gae halvers, ging halvers NE.

shark *n* sherk.

sharp *adj* shairp, sherp; (*sharp-edged*) gleg; (*mentally*) gleg, snack(ie), sparkie; (*in manner*) nebbie, nippit, snell; (*of or to the senses*) snell.

sharpen shairp(en), sherp(en).

sharpening *n* shairp, sherp.

sharp-eyed gleg-eed.

sharp-pointed (*of a tool*) gleg.

sharp tongue tongue that wad clip cloots.

sharp-tongued snippit, nebbie, birkie.

shatter v chatter NE, smatter.

shavings *npl* (*wood*) spail(in)s.

shawl *n* hap, faik NE; (*small*) shawlie; (*worn on the shoulders*) shooderie; (*especially long rectangular tartan*) plaid.

she *pronoun* shae, sheu SHETLAND, ORKNEY.

sheaf *n* shaif.

group of sheaves stood to dry stook.

shear v share.

shearing (*of sheep*) clippin.

shed *n* (*for cattle*) byre; (*for fishermen, climbers etc*) bothy.

sheep *n* sheepie(-meh) *child's word;* (*young, until first shearing*) hog(g): '*yowe hog*'; '*tuip hog*'.

sheepdog collie.

sheep dung (sheep) purls, (sheep) troddles.

sheep enclosure (*for dipping, shearing etc*) (sheep) fank, (sheep) stell.

sheepfold sheep (bucht), faul(d), ree.

sheep-shearing (sheep) clippin.

sheep-shears shears.

sheep-tick (sheep) taid, keb, ked.

sheldrake *n* burrow duck, stock annet.

shelf *n* skelf, dale; (*eg on a wall, for plates etc*) bink.

shell *n* shall SHETLAND, ORKNEY.

v shall SHETLAND, ORKNEY, N, sheel; (*peas, etc*) huil, shaup.

shelter v 1 (*from weather*) lown, lithe N; (*a criminal*) reset. 2 (*take shelter*) hiddle, scug, howf.

n (*sheltered place*) lown, lithe N; (*rough: see also* **hut**) howf.

sheltered lown, lithe N.

shepherd *n* herd, hird.

shepherd's crook nibbie, crummock.

shift v mudge; (*awkwardly*) hirsel; (*cause to move*) mudge, jee, fotch; (*along, to make room for others*) hotch yersel.

n (*at work*) yokin: '*Ma yokin wis ten till three last week*'.

shiftless knotless.

shifty loopie.

shine v sheen, glent; (*brightly*) skire; (*of the sun: brightly*) beek.

n glent.

shiny skirie NE.

shingle *n* (*gravel*) chingle NE, channel.

shirk v renaig, jouk.

shirker slootch.

shirt *n* sark, serk.

shiver v, *n* chitter, grue, hotter NE, shither SOUTH.

shivery oorit, oorie, greeshach N.

shoal *n* (*of fish*) drave.

shock *n* gliff: '*get a gliff*', stammygaster; (*disappointment*) dunt.

v stammygaster.

shocking awfu.

shoe *n* shae, shee NE, *pl also* shuin, sheen NE; (*old, worn*) ba(u)chle, sha(u)chle.

v (*a horse*) shae, shee NE, shod.

shoelace (shae) pint.

shoemaker souter, cordiner.

change your shoes chynge yer feet.

shook *see* **shake.**

shoot *v* shuit, sheet N; (*a missile*) pap. **shot** *past tense* sheetit NE.

past participle shotten NE, sheetit NE.

shop *n* chop NE; (*small, general*) Jennie a'thing(s), Johnnie a'thing(s).

shopping *n* messages, eeran(t)s.

shopping list line.

do the shopping gang the messages, dae the eeran(t)s.

shop assistant (*female*) shop lassie.

shopkeeper (general) merchant; (*of a small, general store*) Jennie a'thing(s), Johnnie a'thing(s).

short *adj* jimpit; (*stunted*) stumpit; (*of clothes*) scrimp.

shortage shortcome, inlaik.

shorten (*clothes*) dock; (*of daylight hours*) creep in.

shortly shortlins, eenoo, ivnoo NE.

shortbread shortie.

short cut near cut.

short-tempered short i the trot, short i the pile.

a short time a short NE, a wee, a whilie, a fylie NE.

a short time ago short (sin)syne, short ago, nae lang syne.

in a short time shortlins, in a wee.

shot *n* (*sound of a shot*) tooch SE, knell NE.

shot *see* **shoot.**

should *v* shid, sid NE: '*Ye sid dee't*'.

shoulder *n* shooder, shoother, spaul(d); (*of beef, mutton etc*) spaul(d) NE.

shoulder-bone spaul(d).

shoulder joint shooder heid.

shout *v, n* goller, gollie, rowst.

shove *v* oxter.

n (*rough*) hodge SHETLAND, NE.

shovel *n, v* shuil, sheel NE, shuffle, shiffle SHETLAND, N.

show *v* shaw, kythe, lat see.

n shaw.

showy fantoosh; (*of colours*) roarie, skirie NE.

show off *v* splore, kick N.

show-off *n* primp SOUTH.

shower *n* shooer; (*of rain: especially gusty*) scoor; (*slight*) skiffle, spitter; (*short, sharp*) skite; (*heavy*) blash, oncome; (*sudden, heavy*) plype NE; (*often with thunder*) (thunner-) plump; (*very heavy*) plash, poor.

showery plowterie, scoorie.

shred *n* shreed, screed, target.

shreds taivers: '*bil't tae taivers*'.

shrew *n* (*animal*) shear-moose, thraa-moose NE.

shrewd *adj* cannie, pawkie, lang-heid-it, fell.

shriek *v, n* skirl, skreich, skraich, skelloch NE.

shrill *adj* skraichie.

shrill cry skelloch, squalloch NE.

shrink *v* **1** creep in, crine (in). **2** (*in disgust, fear etc*) grue.

shrivel *v* crine.

shrivelled shrunkelt; (*with cold etc*) scruntit.

Shrove Tuesday *n* fastern's een.

shrug *v, n* hotch.

shrunken *adj* (*of a person or animal*) shilpit, scruntit; (*of a person, with age*) cruppen doon.

shudder *v, n* (*with fear, disgust*) grue, shither, hotter NE.

shuffle *v* **1** shiffle, sha(u)chle, scush(le) NE. **2** (*cards*) pauchle.

n scush NE.

shuffling *n* scush NE, skliff.

shuffling walk sha(u)chle.

shut *v* **1** steek; (*a door*) pit tae, pul tae, (*properly*) shut tae; (*the eyes*) steek, faul(d); (*a book*) steek. **2** (*of a door*) sneck, gae tae.

shut up (*not speak*) (haud yer) w(h)eesh(t), save yer breath tae cool yer parritch.

shut the door as you leave tak the door wi ye.

shy *adj* blate; (*especially of animals*)

scar; (*of children*) strange.

v (*of a horse*) funk.

sick *adj* seeck, bad(ly); (*slightly*) nae weel.

sicken *v* scunner, scomfish SHET-LAND, NE, seecken.

be sickened (by) scunner (at), ug (at).

sickly unweel, peelie-wallie, peelie-wersh SOUTH, hingie, hingin.

side *n* (*especially of a door, fireplace etc*) cheek; (*of the face*) haffet.

sideways sidieweys, sidelins.

at your side at yer lug.

choose sides chap.

side by side han(d) for nieve.

to one side ajee, skellie.

sieve *n, v* sye, seeve, search NE.

sigh *v, n* souch.

sight *n* **1** sicht. **2** (*odd-looking person*) ticket, tattie-bogle.

a welcome sight a sicht for sair een.

signal *n* seegnal; (*made by waving*) waff; (*with the hand*) wag: '*gie a wag*'.

silence *n* seelence, lown; (*absolute*) neither hishie (n)or w(h)ishie.

v w(h)eesh(t).

interjection w(h)eesht!: '*Wheesht wi ye!*'.

silent seelent SHETLAND, NE.

be *or* **keep silent** (haud yer) w(h)eesh(t), sing dumb.

silly *adj* daft, feel NE, sullie.

silly person bawheid, gomerel, sumph: '*Ye muckle sumph, ye!*', gype NE.

silver siller.

adj si   ; (*of coins*) white.

silvery (*of the hair*) lyart.

silver coins white siller.

similar *adj* siclik(e).

similarly siclik(e).

simmer *v* sotter, hotter; (*of a pot*) prinkle.

simple *adj* semple.

since *conjunction, preposition* **1** (*from that time*) sin, syne, fae: '*She's been awa fae this mornin*'. **2** (*because*) sin.

adv sin, syne.

sincere *adj* aefauld, evendoon.

Yours sincerely (*in letters*) Yours aye, Aefauldlie.

sing *v* (*in a low clear voice*) lilt; (*badly*) bummle NE; (*a tune, without words, especially for dancing*) diddle.

singe *v, n* sing, scowder, scam.

singed *past tense, past participle* sung, singit.

single *adj* (*unmarried*) free, his *or* her lane, im *or* er leen NE.

sink *n* (*kitchen sink*) jawbox.

sip *v* (*especially continuously*) sirple.

siren *n* (*factory*) bummer.

sissy *n* (big) Jessie, sweetie wife.

sister *n* tittie.

sister-in-law guid-sister.

sit *v* **1** *see also* **sit down** *below;* (*in a crouching position*) hunker, hurkle; (*lazily*) clock N. **2** (*make to sit*) set.

sat *past tense* sut.

past participle sutten.

sitting room (public) room.

sit in the dark sit lik(e) craws i the mist.

sit down (*to a meal, at a table*) sit in.

sit still! (*eg to a child*) sit at peace!

site *n* (*of a building*) stance, steid(in), lan(d).

situation *n* (*job*) bit, joab.

six *numeral* sax; (*in children's rhymes*) heeturi.

sixteen saxteen.

sixteenth saxteen(t).

sixth saxt, sixt.

sixty saxtie.

group of six saxsome.

six and half a dozen eeksie-peeksie, sixes an saxes.

size *n* bouk.

sizzle *v* seezle; (*especially in cooking*) papple, skirl.

skate *v* skeet, sketch, skeetch N, scly. *n* **1** (*blade*) sketch, ske(e)tcher. **2** (*act of skating*) sketch.

skater skeetcher.

skeleton *n* (*very thin person*) rickle o banes.

skid *n, v* skite, scurr NE.

skill *n* skeel, slicht, can NE.

skilful skeelie, knackie, gleg.

skim *v* **1** (*remove scum from*) scum. **2**
(*move lightly*) skiff(le).

skin *n* **1** (*of a person or animal*) huil,
leather, ledder SHETLAND, NE. **2** (*of a
plant*) huil.

v (*remove skin from*) scruif, screef N;
(*in strips*) flype; (*especially accidentally, eg from a leg*) peel.

skinny skrankie, shilpit, shirpit.

skinny person skinnymalink(ie), skelf.

mottled skin on the legs (*from sitting
too near the fire*) grannie's tartan,
tinker's tartan, fireside tartan.

skip *v* **1** (*move lightly*) skiff; (*hop*) hip. **2**
(*pass over*) hip.

skipping game (*jumping over waving
rope*) pavey-waveys; (*with fast turns of
the rope*) bumps EDINBURGH, firies
ANGUS; (*with two ropes turned in opposite directions*) londies SHETLAND,
NE.

skipping rope jumpin raip, skip(pin)
raip.

skipper *n* (*of a curling team etc*) skip;
(*of a fishing boat*) mannie.

skirt *n* coat, cwite NE.

skittish *adj* fliskie, skeer(ie).

skittles *npl* kyles.

skua *n* (*great*) bonxie SHETLAND,
ORKNEY; (*Arctic*) Allan SHETLAND,
ORKNEY, scootie allan SHETLAND, OR-
KNEY.

skulk *v* skook, jouk.

skull *n* (harn)pan, powe.

sky *n* lift.

skylark laverock.

slab *n* (*large slice*) skelp.

slack *adj* **1** (*of shoes*) sha(u)chlin. **2**
(*lazy*) haingle.

slacker *n* footer.

slag-heap *n* bing.

slam *v* (*a door*) clash, dad.

slander *n* ill-tongue; (*law*) defamation
(NB also covers English 'libel').

v misca(w).

slant *v* (*slope*) sklent; (*move slantwise*)
s(k)lent, skew.

at a slant, slanting squint, skellie,
sklent.

slap *v* skelp, sclaff, scud.

n skelp, sclaff, scud; (*hard*) sclype NE.

slapdash *adj* (*of a person*) hashie; (*of
work*) yeukie, hairy.

adv (*rashly*) ramstam.

slash *v* (*cut*) hash, screed, gulliegaw N.

n screed, sned.

slash with a razor *see* **razor**.

slat *n* (*of wood*) rin(d), reen N.

slatted *adj* sparred.

slate *n* sclate, scailie, skylie NE.

slaughter *v* sla(u)chter, fell; (*an animal
for meat*) butch.

n sla(u)chter.

slaughterhouse butch-hoose, skemmels NE.

slaver *v* slabber, slivver NE.

n slavers, slabbers, slivver(s) NE.

slay *v* en(d), nail.

sledge *n* sled.

sleek *adj* sleekit.

sleep *v* (*lightly*) dover, gloss NE,
snoozle; (*fall asleep: see also* **get to
sleep** *below*) fa(w) ower.

n slug WEST, SW; (*child's words*) baw-
baw(s), beddie-ba(s), Willie Winkie;
(*light*) dover, gloss NE.

sleepless, unable to sleep waukrif(e).

get to sleep win asleep, get sleepit NE.

having slept your fill sleepit oot,
sleepit.

wink of sleep blink.

slender *adj* sma, sclinner NE, jimp(ie),
spirlie.

slice *n* sclice, sleesh; (*large*) skelp,
whang, fang N; (*of bread, cheese etc*)
shave; (*of bread with butter, jam etc*)
piece; (*end of loaf*) heel; (*of meat*)
collop.

v sclice; (*thinly*) skive; (*thickly*)
whang.

slick *adj* gleg, snack, soople.

slid *see* **slide**.

slide v (*(as) on ice*) scly; (*suddenly on a smooth surface*) skite; (*on ice, in a crouched position*) hunker-slide.
n (*(as) on ice*) scly; (*skid*) skite.
slid *past tense* slade, sled.
past participle slidden.

slight *adj* slicht; (*of a person, slightly-built*) sma, smallie, sober NE.

slightly some, a piec(i)e, a wee.

slim *adj* sma.

slime n glaur, goor; (*eg on fish*) glut.

slimy glittie, goorie N; (*especially from a runny nose*) snotterie.
  make slimy glaur.

slink v sleek, smook aboot, smool NE.

slip v (*slide*) sklyte; (*cause to slip*) s(c)lidder; (*on a slippery surface*) skite.
n (*sliding*) s(c)lidder, (*sudden*) skite.

slippery 1 slippy, skitie, slidy, s(c)lidderie. **2** (*of a person*) sleek(it).

slip-knot (*pulled tight*) rin-knot.

slipper n baff(ie); (*loose, worn*) ba(u)chle, sclaff, sha(u)chle.

slit n (*in a skirt etc*) spare, fent.

slither v, n s(c)lidder, sclither, hirsel.

sliver n (*of wood*) spail, splice SE.

slobber v (*in eating or drinking*) slabber, slitter, slaister, slorach.

sloe n slae.

slope n **1** sklent. **2** brae; (*on hill(side)*) sidelins.
v sklent.

sloping sidelins.

sloppy *adj* **1** (*of food etc*) slidderie, slitterie. **2** (*sentimental*) sapsie.

sloppy mess kirn, slaister; (*of food*) plowter.

slouch v sloonge, lootch, s(c)lutter.

slovenly *adj* throuither, throwder NE.

slovenly person guddle, trollop, trailep NE; (*very messy*) midden, slitter, slaister.

do something *or* **work in a slovenly way** guddle, clart, slitter, slaister.

slow *adj* slaw; (*of a person*) lag, latchin NE.

slowly huilie, heelie NE.

slow-worm slae.

slow down (*go more slowly*) ca(w) cannie.

slug n snail.

sluggish *adj* thowless.

slush n (*especially in running water*) snaw-bree.

slut n clatch.

sluttish slaigerin, slutterie.

sly *adj* sleekit, sleek, slee, s(c)lidderie.

smack v skelp, skeeg NE, scuff.

smacking skelpin, skelpit leatherin.

smack someone's bottom skelp someone's dock, scone someone's dock, pey someone's dowp.

small *adj* wee, sma, peedie ORKNEY, CAITHNESS, FIFE, peerie SHETLAND; (*very*) wee wee, little wee, wee sma, tot(t)ie (wee).

small amount (wee) tait, (wee) pickle.

small person *or* **thing** smowt, dottle.

small change smas.

smallholder crofter, crafter NE.

smallholding croft, craft NE.

smart *adj* smairt, smert: **1** (*in appearance*) snod, perjink, knackie. **2** (*lively*) gleg.
v nip.

smash v smush, smatter; (*to pieces*) ding tae scowes.
n (*accident*) stramash.

smear v sclatch, straik, skaik NE; (*very messily*) slaister, slaiger.
n sclatch, skaik NE.

smell n **1** (*slight*) waff; (*bad*) guff; (*very bad*) goo, stew, steuch; (*of decay*) humph. **2** (*act of sniffing*) snoke.
v **1** (*have a certain smell*) saur. **2** (*sniff*) snoke.

smelly mingin, bowfin, smeekie.

smile v (*pleasantly*) smirk.

smithereens *npl* shivereens, crockaneetion, potterlowe NE.

smithy n smiddy.

smoke n **1** reek, rick NE, smeek, smuik; (*thick, choking*) smoch; (*stifling*) smoor. **2** (*at a pipe*) draw, reek, rick NE.
v **1** smeek, smuik, reek, rick NE; (*give*

out smoke) smeek; (*of a chimney*) reek.
2 (*a pipe*) reek, blaw. **3** (*dry food in smoke*) smeek, smuik, reest.
smoky reekie, rickie NE, smeekie.
smolt *n* smowt.
smooth *adj* sleekit, smuith, smeeth N; (*smooth and glossy*) sleekit; (*even*) evenlie.
smother *v* smoor, smore.
smoulder *v* smooder, smuchter NE.
smudge *n* tash, slair; (*large*) sclatch.
smug *adj* croose, kirr SW.
smut *n* bleck.
smutty brookie NE, mottie SHETLAND, NE; (*of language*) groff.
snack *n* piece, chack, chat NE; (*eaten during school break*) play-piece, school-piece, leave-piece E CENTRAL; (*eaten after a swim*) chitterin bit(e), shivery bite; (*break for a snack*) piece-time.
snag *n* thraw *or* whaup i the raip.
snap *n* knack; (*especially of a dog*) snack.
v knack, knip; (*with the teeth*) snack, hanch.
snapdragon grannie('s) mutch(es), mappie('s)-mou(s).
snap your fingers crack yer thoums.
snare *n, v* girn.
snarl *n, v* girn, habber N, wurr NE.
snatch *n* glamp, glaum.
v sneck, hanch, snap NE, glaum.
snatch away wheech awa, wheek awa NE.
sneak *n* hinkum sneev(l)ie, pick-thank NE.
v sleek, smook, smool NE.
sneeze *v, n* sneesh, neeze SHETLAND, ORKNEY, NE.
sniff *n, v* snift(er), snoke.
snigger *n, v* snicher, sneeger, nicher, sneeter.
snip *v* nick, sneck.
snipe *n* heather-bleat(er), moss-bluiter SW.
snivel *n, v* bubble, sneevil, snifter.
snivelling *adj* sneevlin, bubblie.

snobbish *adj* pridefu, stinkin, wallie-close-gless-door WEST, fur coat an nae knickers EDINBURGH.
snooze *n, v* dover, gloss NE.
snore *n* snocher.
v snifter, snoit(er), snork; (*especially loudly*) snagger NE.
snort *n, v* snirt, snifter, snocher.
snot *n* snotter, bubbles, snochter, snochles NE.
snotty snotterie, bubblie(-nosed), snochlie NE.
snout *n* snoot.
snow *n, v* snaw, snyauve NE.
snowy snawie, snyauvie NE.
snow-bunting snawflake.
snowdrift (snaw-)wreath, blin smoor.
snowfall (*heavy*) oncome, onfa(w).
snowflake pile, flichan, fla(u)cht; (*large*) flag N.
snowstorm stour.
snub *n* chaw, sneck, snotter.
v saut, snot.
snuffle *n, v* sneevil, snifter, snocher, snochle NE.
snug *adj* snog, snod, couthie, ticht.
snuggle (down) coorie (doon).
snuggle up coorie in.
so *adv* sae, sic NE; (*to such a degree*) that: '*that big*', this; (*in that case*) syne: '*an syne ye're no gaun*'.
so-and-so sic-an-sic.
it is so! it is sot!, it is sut!
soak *v* drook, dook, sap; (*especially clothes in soapy water*) sapple.
soaked drookit, seepit, sypit SHETLAND, NE.
soaking *adj* (*very wet*) plashin, seepin, in a soom SHETLAND, NE.
n dookin, drook.
soak through seek throu.
soap *n, v* saip.
soapy saipie.
soapsuds (saipie) sapples, saip(ie) graith.
sob *n, v* bubble, bibble NE, greet, sab.
sober *adj* **1** (*not drunk*) richt. **2** (*serious*) douce, richt.

sociable *adj* couthie; (*and cheerful*) hertie, joco.

sock *n*: **pull up your socks** pull up yer breeks.

socket *n* (*for a tool-handle*) hose, ho(o)zle.

sod *n* (*of peat or turf*) clod, fail N; (*thinner*) divot.

soda *n* sodie.

sodden *adj* sappie NE.

soft *adj* saft.

soften saften.

softly saftlie.

soggy *adj* sotterie SE; (*of food*) sappie, sapsie.

soil[1] *n* muild, mool, sile.

soil[2] *v* fyle, suddle, sile; (*clothes*) scuddle; (*with excrement*) fyle, dirt.

sold *see* **sell**.

solder *v* sooder, sowther.

soldier *n* sodger.

sole *n*: **lemon sole** tobacco fleuk NE.

solicitor *n* soleecitor, (law-)agent, writer, advocate ABERDEEN.

solid *adj* (*of things*) sonsie; (*of bread*) sad; (*of a meal*) hertsome sw.

solve *v* (*a problem*) redd (up).

some *pronoun* (*a few*) a wheen.

somehow somewey, somegate.

some time ago a while back, a file back NE, a while syne, a file seen NE.

sometimes whiles, files NE, filies NE.

somewhat some, a bittie, kin(d) o, kinna.

som〔　〕e someplace: '*someplace else*', 〔　〕gate, somewey.

some〔　〕lt *n* henner EDINBURGH, flippie.

turn a somersault tummle the cat SHETLAND, NE, tummle (ower) yer wullcats *or* wilkies, cowp the creels.

sometimes, somewhat, somewhere *see* **some**.

son *n* sin, lad(die), loon N.

son-in-law guidson.

song *n* sang.

song thrush mavis.

soon *adv* suin, sin, seen NE, in a wee.

sooner than or.

soot *n* suit, seet NE.

soppy *adj* sappie.

sore *n* (*festering*) bealin.
adj sair.

sorely sair(lie).

sorrel *n* soorock(s), soor dock(en).

sorrel seeds rabbit's sugar NE.

wood sorrel gowk's mait, sookie soorocks.

sorrow *n* sorra, sair, dool.

sorrowful sorrafu, sair(ie), dool(some).

sorry *adj* sairie.

sorry for yourself wi yer heid under yer oxter.

be sorry for (*a person*) be vext for.

sort *v*: **sort (out)** redd (up), wale.

nothing of the sort no the like.

so-so *adj* siclik(e).

sought *see* **seek**.

soul *n* sowl, saul.

sound[1] *adj* soon(d).

sound[2] *n* soon(d); (*faint*) peep.

soup *n* bree, kail; (*thick, vegetable broth*) broth.

soup plate deep plate.

sour *adj* soor, shilpit SHETLAND, ORKNEY, CAITHNESS, wersh; (*very*) soor as roddens.

become sour (*of food*) wynt, cheenge N.

south *n, adj, adv* sooth.

south side sunny side.

souvenir *n* mindin: '*a mindin o Arbroath*'.

sow[1] *n* (*female pig*) soo.

sow[2] *v* saw, shaave NE.

spade *n* **1** spaad NE. **2** (*in cards*) pick NE.

span *n, v* spang.

spank *v* (*smack*) skelp, scud, leather, scone, pey (someone's) dock.

spanking *n* skelpin, (skelpit) leatherin, licks, scondies.

spare *adj* orrra.

sparing jimp.

sparingly jimp.

spare time by-time.

spark *n* spunk, sperk SOUTH.

sparkle *v* glent, prinkle, skinkle. *n* glent, glisk.

sparrow *n* sparra(e), sp(e)ug, sprug, spurdie.

spat *see* **spit**[2].

spatter *v* splatter, splairge, spleyter NE; (*with liquid or dirt*) spark.

spawn *n*, *v* redd.

speak *v* spike NE, spick NE; (*a great deal*) blether.

spoke *past tense* spak.

speak affectedly *see* **affect**.

so to speak like: '*jist fur the day like*'.

spear *n*, *v* (*pronged, for salmon-poaching*) leister.

spearmint *n* spearimint.

special *adj* speeshal, by-or(di)nar.

speckle *n*, *v* spreckle.

speckled spreckelt.

spectacles *npl* (*glasses*) spentacles.

speech *n* (*speaking*) say, gab; (*a talk*) speak NE; (*long, boring*) screed: '*He gied me a screed aboot why he wis late*'.

speechless dumfoonert.

speed *n* raik; (*burst of speed*) lick.

speedily at a fair lick, swith.

speedwell cat's een.

heath speedwell Jennie's blue een.

at full speed full pin, full slap, hail-tear.

spell[1] *n* (*stretch of time*) speel; (*of weather*) tack.

spell[2] *n* (*magic*) cantrip.

spellbound taen(-lik(e)).

spelling, spelling lesson *n* spell.

sperm *n* (*of a fish*) melt.

spice *v*, *n* (*food*) kitchen.

spider *n* speeder, wabster, weaver, attercap.

spider's web moose wab, moose web.

spike *n* (*of a railing etc*) pike.

spiked pikie.

spiky stobbie NE.

spill *v* skail, jaw, jibble, skiddle; (*with a splash*) jaup; (*dribble*) driddle.

spin *v* 1 (*turn round*) birl, pirl, sweel. 2 (*cause to spin*) birl, pirl; (*a top, so fast that it appears motionless*) doze.

spinning wheel (*large, horizontal*) muckle wheel.

spine *n* 1 rig. 2 (*prickle*) prog, pike.

spirit *n* speerit; (*courage*) saul; (*energy*) smeddum.

spirited stuffie, birkie WEST, croose.

drink of spirits dram.

in high spirits heich, on the keevee.

in low spirits doon o mou, hingin-luggit.

raise your spirits heeze (up) yer hert.

recover your spirits cantle (up) NE.

spit[1] *n* (*for roasting etc*) speet.

spit[2] *v* 1 slerp. 2 (*of a cat*) fuff.

spat *past tense* sput.

spite *v* maugre NE.

spiteful cat-wittit, ill-willie.

spittle *n* spittin(s), slaver(s).

splash *v* jilp, splairge, plash; (*messily*) plowt, skiddle, slitter; (*especially with mud*) platch; (*noisily*) splatter; (*spill*) jaw, jilp; **splash about** (*messily*) plowt(er), plyte(r) NE, platch.
n plash, jaw, jilp, jibble; (*especially of mud*) jaup, splairge, platch; (*noisy*) plowt(er).

splendid *adj* braw.

splendour brawness.

splint *n*, *v* ((*for*) *a broken bone etc*) spelk, scob NE.

splinter *n* spelk, skirp NE, splice SE; (*especially in the skin*) skelf, spail, skelp, skelb.
v spelk, sklinter.

split *v* spleet; (*burst*) rive; (*fish*) speld.
n spleet; (*crack*) rive.

splodge, splotch *n* splatch.

splutter *v*, *n* splitter.

spoil *v* spile, hash, mank, tash, connach, malagrooze NE; (*with kindness*) waste, delt NE: '*a deltit bairn*'.

spoilt child mither's bairn, sookie, mammie-keekie.

spoke *n* spaik.

spoke *see* **speak**.

sponge v 1 (*scrounge*) scunge, spoach SE; (*especially food*) scaff. 2 (*wipe*) dicht.

sponger skech, spoacher SE.

spongy fozie.

spool n (*in shuttle or for sewing thread*) pirn.

spoon n spuin, speen NE.

spoonful spuinfae, speenfae NE.

sport n play.

v daff, mird (wi) NE.

sportsman's attendant gillie.

spot n 1 spat, spreckle. 2 (*on the skin*) plook, bealin.

spotted spreckelt, mottie SHETLAND, NE.

spotty plookie.

spout n spoot; (*of a kettle, jug etc*) stroop.

v spoot, scoot.

sprain v, n rax, rack, stave.

sprawl v spra(u)chle, spralloch NE.

spray v spairge; (*with dust etc*) stour.

n (*cloud of*) stour.

device for spraying skoosher.

spread v spreid; (*with something soft*) skaik NE.

n spreid; (*of food*) doon-set(tin).

spread about skail.

spree n splore, skite, bash.

spring n 1 (*of water*) wall(ie), spoot. 2 (*leap*) lowp, sten(d). 3 (*season*) voar SHETLAND, ORKNEY.

v (*leap*) lowp, sten(d), spoot.

spring onions sybies, syboes.

sprinkle v splatter, sp(l)airge, roose NE.

sprinkler skoosher, rooser NE.

sprinkling n splatter, sp(l)airge.

sprint v sprunt.

sprout v, n sproot, breir(d).

spruce adj, v sproosh, sprush.

n (*tree*) sprush.

spry adj sproosh, sprush.

spur n (*for riding*) brod.

spurt v, n scoot, skoosh, jaw.

sputter v sotter; (*of fat in cooking*) papple, skirl.

squabble v tulyie.

n stushie, stashie, tulyie.

squall n skelp, gurl; (*from high land over the sea*) flan.

squally scoorie.

squander v misguide; (*money*) gae throu, perish.

squandered doon the stank.

square adj squerr WEST.

squat v hunker (doon), cuddle.

adj gudgie.

squat on your haunches see haunches.

in a squatting position on yer hunkers.

squawk n, v squaik.

squeak v squaik, wheep NE, weeack NE; (*of things*) cheep, queek NE.

n squaik, weeack NE.

squeal n, v squaik, squile NE.

squeeze v knuse, nevel, pran NE, knidge SHETLAND, N.

n (*forceful*) knidge SHETLAND, N.

squelch v plype NE; (*eg of water on shoes*) slorp SOUTH.

squib n squeeb; (*schoolboy's home-made*) peeoy.

squid n ink-fish.

squint n 1 (*cast in the eye*) skellie, gley. 2 (*glance*) skellie, gley, skew NE.

v 1 (*have a squint*) skellie, skew. 2 (*glance*) sklent, gley, skew NE.

squint-eyed skellie(-eyed), gley(-eed).

squirt v, n (*spurt*) scoot, skoosh.

stab v stick, durk, prog.

n prog.

stable adj sicker, stieve.

stack n (*of hay, corn*) ruck; (*of hay*) cole; (*small, loosely stacked*) rickle.

stagger n, v stoit(er), styte(r) NE, stot(ter), stammer.

staid adj douce, as mim as a Mey puddock.

stain v, n tash, smad SHETLAND, NE.

stairs npl stair.

staircase stair.

spiral staircase turnpike.

foot of the stairs stairfit.

top of the stairs stairheid.
stake *n* stob.
stale *adj* (*mouldy*) foostie; (*of bread*) aul(d).
stale news piper's news.
stale story *etc* caul(d) kail het again.
stalk[1] *n* (*of a plant*) shank; (*hard*) runt, castock, stock.
stalk[2] *v* (*walk stiffly*) steg, stilp NE.
stall *n* **1** sta(w). **2** (*for selling*) stan(d).
stallion *n* staig.
stammer *v, n* stut, stot, habber SHETLAND, N, mant.
stamp *v, n* (*with the feet*) tramp, stramp.
stand *v* **1** stan, staun(d). **2** (*endure*) bide, thole: '*Ah cannae thole porridge*'. *n* stan, staun(d).
stand on end (*of hair*) be in a birr; *see also* **end.**
standard *n* standart, stannert.
standard-bearer (*in some 'Riding of the Marches' ceremonies*) cornet.
star *n* starn, stern SOUTH.
starry starnie.
starfish cross-fit NE.
stare *v* glower; (*open-mouthed*) gowp; (*foolishly*) gype; (*rudely*) geck. *n* gowp; (*wide-eyed*) glower.
starling *n* stirlin, stuckie, stushie.
starry *see* **star.**
start *v* stert, yoke, get yokit; (*work*) jine. *n* **1** stert, affgo, affset. **2** (*fright*) gliff.
startle *v* stert, flichter.
starve *v* sterve, hunger.
starved hungert, nippit.
statement *n* speak NE.
statue *n* (*of plaster*) stookie (eemage).
stay *v* (*remain*) stey, bide. *n* (*time in a place*) stey, bide: '*a lang bide*'.
steady *adj* sicker, stieve; (*in character*) cannie.
steak *n* collop.
steal *v* pauchle, chore *slang*, sneck.
stole *past tense* stealt, staw.
stolen *past participle* stealt, stow(e)n.

steam *n* stame NE, (y)oam SHETLAND, ORKNEY, NE. *v* stove.
steep[1] *adj* stey, stieve, strait.
steep[2] *v* stap, drook, sap; (*clothes in soapy water*) sapple.
steer *v* airt, guy NE.
stem *n* **1** (*of a plant*) shank; (*hollow, used as pea-shooter*) pluffer. **2** (*of an instrument*) shank.
stench *n* guff, humph, stew.
step *n* **1** (*in walking, or on a staircase*) stap, staup SOUTH. **2 steps** (*moveable, to a loft etc*) trap (stair(s)).
stepping-stones steps.
step- *prefix* stap-.
stepchild stap-bairn.
stepfather stap-faither, stappie.
stepmother stap-mither.
stern[1] *adj* dour, raucle, sair.
stern[2] *n* starn.
stew *v, n* stove.
stewed (*of tea*) sitten NE.
stick[1] *n* (*for stirring*) spurtle, spurkle, theevil; (*shinty*) caman.
stick[2] *v* (*in mud*) lair.
stuck *past tense* stickit, stack.
past participle stickit, stucken.
sticky claggie, cla(i)rtie; (*of ice in curling*) bauch.
stickleback *n* banstickle; (*three-spined*) bairdie.
stiff *adj* stieve, stent(it).
stiffly stieve.
stifling *adj* smochie.
still[1] *adj* quate, lown. *adv* yet, aye.
stand still stan(d) lik a stookie.
still[2] *n* (*for distilling*) stell.
stilt *n* stilpert NE, powl.
sting *n, v* stang; (*of acid taste etc*) nip.
stung *past tense* stang.
stinging (*of a wound*) nippy; (*eg of nettles*) jaggie.
stingy *adj* ticht, meeserable, nippit, moolie.
stink *v, n* stew.
stir *v* **1** steer, pirl SHETLAND, ORKNEY,

NE; (*eg with a stick*) poach; (*vigorously*) rummle. **2** (*move*) mudge, jee.
n (*stirring movement*) steer; (*vigorous*) rummle: '*Gie the dishes a rummle in the sink*'.

stitch *n* **1** (*sewing, knitting*) steek, stick; (*knitting*) loop. **2** (*pain in the side*) steek, catch.
v steek, stick; (*roughly and hastily*) ranter.

stitches decreased (*knitting*) *see* **decrease.**

stoat *n* whitrat, futrat N.

stock *n* **1** (*of a farm*) stockin, haudin. **2** (*from boiling*) bree.

stocking *n* (*in the process of being knitted*) shank.

stocky *adj* short-set, laich-set.

stole, stolen *see* **steal.**

stomach *n* stamack; (*belly*) kyte, wame, wime N, painch, peenie *child's word*.

stomach-ache sair wame.

stone *n* **1** stane, steen N; (*small*) chuckie(-stane). **2** (*used in games*) chuckie(-stane); (*for skimming across water*) skiffer. **3** (*of fruit*) paip.
v stane, steen N.

stony stanie, steenie N.

stonechat stane chack(art).

stool *n* stuil, steel NE; (*low, three-legged*) creepie.

stoop *v* coorie, lootch, loot.
n lootch, loot.

stop *v* stap, stoap, deval; (*bring to a stop*) stell, reest NE.
n stap, stoap.

without stopping even on, nivver devallin.

stop for a moment haud a wee.

store *v* kist; (*for future use*) hain.
n pose N.

storey *n* (*of a house*) flat: '*She lives on the third flat*'.

storm *n* snifter; (*of wind and rain*) blatter.

stormy coorse, sair, gurlie.

story *n* crack, clash; (*funny*) farce.

storyteller (*of traditional Celtic/Gaelic tales*) shenachie.

stout *adj* stoot; (*big and stout*) lik(e) a hoose-en(d); (*fat and soft*) brosie.

stow *v* stowe.

straddle *v* striddle.

straggle *v* traik, vaig.

straight *adj, n, adv* stra(u)cht.

straighten stra(u)cht.

straightforward stra(u)cht-forrit.

straight ahead en(d)weys.

straight away stra(u)cht, richt noo.

straight on en(d)lang, even on.

strain *n* (*sprain*) rax.
v **1** rax. **2** (*sieve*) sye, sile, search NE.

strainer *see* **sieve.**

strait *n* kyle WEST.

strait-laced perjink, mim-mou'd, primsie SHETLAND, ORKNEY.

strand *n* (*of rope etc*) faul(d), faik N.

strange *adj* strynge, unco(-lik(e)), fremmit, ferlie; (*uncommon*) orra; (*rather strange*) queerie.

stranger ootrel, ootlin.

strangers unco fowk, the fremd.

strangeness fremmitness, unconess.

strange-looking unco-leukin.

strange person queerie: '*Her man's a bit o a queerie*'.

strange sight ferlie.

strangle *v* thrapple, guzzle.

strap *n* **1** (*formerly school punishment strap*) tawse, the belt, tag NE, Lochgelly. **2 straps worn below the knees by farmworkers** nickie-tams.

straw *n* strae.

streak *n* (*of colour etc*) straik.
v straik, skaik NE; (*with dirt*) slaik.

streaked (*with dirt*) brookit.

stream *n* **1** (*of liquid*) strin(d), strule. **2** (*small river*) burn.
v teem.

stream out (*eg of smoke*) tove SE.

street *n* causey.

street drain, street gutter *see* **gutter.**

street-sweeper scaffie.

strength *n* strenth, poost.

strenuous *adj* sair: '*That's sair climbin thae stairs*'.

stress *n* (*exertion*) sweit.

stretch *v, n* rax, streetch, streek.

 stretch out (*a thing*) streek; (*the hand etc*) rax oot, rax ower.

strict *adj* strick, ticht.

 strictly stricklie.

stride *v* striddle, steg, strod(ge) SOUTH; (*with long steps*) lamp; (*vigorously*) spang.

 n (*long, vigorous*) spang.

 off your stride aff yer stot(ter).

strike *v* **1** strik, chap, paik; (*heavily*) ding, dunt; (*sharply*) knap, knack, crack; (*a person*) skite, lift yer han(d) tae; (*slap*) skelp, sclaff. **2** (*of a clock*) chap. **3** (*a match*) scart.

 struck *past tense* straik, strak.

 past participle strucken, stricken.

 strike a bargain with *see* **bargain**.

strip *v* (*undress*) tirr; (*a room etc*) tirr.

stripe *n* strip NE, straik.

 v straik.

 striped strippit.

stroke *n* **1** (*blow*) straik, skelp, chap; (*sweeping*) swipe; (*on the palm, with a strap*) palmie, luiffie. **2** (*of work*) chap NE. **3** (*of a clock*) ring. **4** (*paralytic*) shock, blast NE.

 v straik; (*an animal etc, affectionately*) clap.

stroll *v, n* dander, stravaig, taik SHET-LAND, N.

strong *adj* **1** strang, stench NE; (*of people*) able, stieve, wallie. **2** (*of liquor*) hard, nappie; (*of tea*) sitten.

struck *see* **strike**.

struggle *v* warsle, fecht, chaave NE, kyauve SHETLAND, NE.

 n warsle, fecht: '*It's a sair fecht*', chaave NE.

 struggling warslin.

 struggle on warsle on.

stubble *n* stibble.

 stubbly stibblie, stobbie NE.

stubborn *adj* thrawn, dour, contermacious.

stucco *n* stookie.

stuck *see* **stick**[2].

stuff *v* stap (*also in cookery*), prime, colf NE.

 stuffed (*also in cookery*) stappit: '*stappit heidies*'; (*full of food*) stappit (fou).

 stuffy (*close*) smochie.

stumble *v, n* stammer, stotter.

stump *n* (*of a tree*) stock.

 v stodge, stilp NE.

stun *v* doze, daver; (*with a blow*) stoun(d).

 stunned state stoon(d).

stung *see* **sting**.

stunted *adj* scruntit, scruntie.

stupefy *v* daver, doze.

stupid *adj* stupit, stippit, daft, glaikit, feel NE, guffie SOUTH; (*very*) thick as mince.

 pretend to be stupid act the daft laddie *or* lassie.

 do you think I'm stupid? I didnae come up the Clyde in a banana boat *or* on a bike, d'ye think I'm feel? NE.

 you're stupid yer heid's fou o mince, yer heid's wastit.

sturdy *adj* stieve, stuffie.

stutter *see* **stammer**.

subject *n* (*of conversation, especially gossip*) speak.

succeed *v* (*be successful*) luck, spin NE, mak weel, come speed.

such *adj, pronoun* sic, sich, siccan, siclik(e).

 such a sic a.

 such a person sic a bodie.

 suchlike siclik(e).

 in such a way siclik(e).

suck *v* sook.

 sucker sooker.

 suck up to sook in wi, smool in wi.

suckle *v* sook.

 suckling sookie.

sudden *adj* suddent.

 all of a sudden on a suddentie N.

suds *npl* sapples, graith, freith.

suffer *v* dree, thole.

sufficient *adj* suffeecient.

suffocate *v* (*with smoke etc*) smeek, smoor.

sugar *n* shuggar, succar.

sugar-candy candibrod.

slice of bread and butter sprinkled with sugar sugar piece.

suit *n, v* shoot, shuit.

blue suits you ye suit blue.

suitable sitable, settin, confeerin NE.

more suitable mair liker: '*It's mair liker it tae wear a kilt tae yer waddin*'.

sulk *v* fung, hing the pettit lip, strunt.

sulks *npl* dods, dorts, strunts: '*tak the strunts*'.

sulky glumsh, hingin-mou'd NE, dortie.

sulky expression torn face, pettit lip: '*hing the pettit lip*'.

sulky person torn-face.

sullen *adj* dour, doon-leukin, stroonge N.

sullenly dourlie.

sultry *adj* smochie; (*and humid*) mochie, muithie.

sum *n* soum; **sums** (*in arithmetic*) coonts.

sum total (the hail) tot.

summer *n* simmer.

summit *n* heicht, heid, tap.

summon *v* cry, warn; (*before a court*) summons, sist.

sun *n* sin.

sunny side sun side.

sunrise keek o day.

sunset sundoon.

gleam of sunshine (sun)blink.

Sunday *n* Sawbath, Sabbath.

Sunday clothes Sunday claes, Sunday braws, kirk claes.

supermarket trolley *see* **trolley.**

supernatural *adj* no cannie, eldritch *literary*.

superstition *n* (*superstitious idea, observance etc*) freit, threap.

superstitious freitie.

supper *n* sipper.

have supper sowp.

supple *adj* soople, swack.

support *n* haud; (*person*) uphaud; (*prop*) prap, stoop.
v (*prop*) stuit, steet N; (*a person, by the arm*) oxter; (*look after*) tend.

sure *adj* shuir, shair, sheer NE, sicker, solvendie NE.

surely shuir(lie).

make sure mak siccar.

surly *adj* dour, maroonjous NE, stroonge N, snotterie.

surprise *v* surpreese, pall; (*unpleasantly*) stammygaster; (*dumbfound*) mesmerise.
n surpreese; (*unwelcome*) conflummix NE, stammygaster NE.

exclamation of surprise michtie!, dod!, govie dick!

survey *v, n* leuk, scance, sicht, vizzy.

suspect *v* suspeck, doot, jalouse.

suspense *n*: **in suspense** on nettles, on heckle-pins.

suspicion *n* suspeecion.

suspicious suspeecious.

be suspicious jalouse.

swagger *v, n* strunt.

swallow[1] *n* (*bird*) swalla.

swallow[2] *v* swalla(e), pit ower yer craig.

swamp *n* latch, slump.

swampy mossie, slumpie, lairie.

swampy place stank.

swarm *n* (*of bees*) swairm, cast; (*of children*) smarrach NE; (*of small creatures*) swatter NE; (*crowd*) swairm, hotterel.
v (*of bees*) swairm, cast, byke; (*of people*) swairm, hotter, howder.

swarming with ho(a)tchin wi, quick wi, heezin wi.

sway *v, n* swey, shog, showd N, shue SOUTH; (*unsteadily*) shoogle, wammle.

swear *v* **1** (*an oath*) sweer. **2** (*use bad language*) sweer, jeedge NE, voo NE.

swear-word sweer, sweerie word, ill word NE.

swear-words ill-tongue, ill win(d) NE.

sweat *v, n* sweit, feem NE; (*profuse(ly)*) broth.

sweated *past tense* swat.
past participle swatten.
sweaty sweitin, feemin NE.
Swede *n* **1** Swade NE. **2 swede** (*turnip*)
swad(e), neep, turneep, turmit.
sweep *v, n* soop, swype NE.
swept *past tense* soopit, swypit NE.
sweet *adj* hinnie; (*pleasant, lovable*)
douce.
n sweetie, sweetenin NE; **sweets**
snashters.
sweet-bag sweetie poke.
sweetshop sweetie-shop.
swell *v, see also* **swollen**; swall, hove;
(*of arthritic joints*) knot.
swelter *v* (*of people or animals*) plot.
sweltering sweltrie.
swept *see* **sweep**.
swerve *v* jee, sklent; (*nimbly*) jink,
jouk.
n swey, jee, sklent, jouk.
swift *adj* clivver, swith, swipper(t) NE.
swig *v* tak awa.
n wa(u)cht.
swim *v* soom, sweem.
snack eaten after a swim chitterin
bit(e), shivery bite.
swindle *v, n* swick, pauchle.

swindler swick.
swing *v* shog, shoogle, showd N,
sweeng NE, shue.
n (*act of swinging, or a child's swing*)
shog, shoggie-shoo, shue, sweeng NE.
swingboat (*at a fair*) sho(o)gie boat,
shoggin boat, swey boat.
swipe *n* wheech, skliff, slype NE.
v wheech, flisk.
swirl *v, n* swurl, sweel, pirl, swither.
swish *v, n* sweesh.
switch *v*: **switch off** (*an electrical appliance*) sneck aff.
swivel *n* sweel, sweevil.
swollen *adj, past participle; see also*
swell; swallen, swallt, hoven, hovie;
(*of a river*) heavy, great, prood NE.
sword *n* swurd.
sycamore *n* plane (tree).
syllable *n* syllab.
sympathy *n*: **sympathetic** couthie, in-
nerlie SOUTH.
show sympathy for mane, mak mane
for.
syringe *n* scooter, scoot, skite N, skiter
SHETLAND, NE, syreenge.
syrup *n* seerup, traicle.
system *n* seestem.

T

table *n* (*especially spread for a meal*) buird, brod.

table napkin servit, daidlie WEST.

tablet *see* **fudge.**

tackle *n, v* taickle.

tadpole *n* poweheid.

tag *n* (*game*) tig, takkie NE, chasie: '*Let's play chasie*'.

tail *n* (*of a hare or rabbit*) fud, bun.

take *v* tak, hae, pit: '*He wis jist pittin aff his claes*'.

took *past tense* taen, teen SHETLAND, ORKNEY, N.

taken *past participle* taen, teen SHETLAND, ORKNEY, N, tacken, tooken.

taken aback *see* **aback.**

take after kin(d) tae: '*That laddie kinds tae his mither*'.

takeaway cairry-oot.

tale *n* sonnet NE.

tell tales *see* **tell.**

talented *adj*: **talented young man** *or* **woman** lad *or* lass o pairts.

talk *n* **1** (*chat*) blether, clash, crack, news SHETLAND, N; (*light, entertaining*) gab; (*non-stop*) yap(-yappin); (*loud, continuous*) yammer. **2** (*of a place*) speak: '*speak o the toon*'.

v crack, blether; (*fluently and at length*) aff: '*He's aye layin aff aboot new job*'; (*in a lively way*) crack, croose.

talkative bletherin, crackie, newsie.

tall *adj* heich, lang.

tall thin person lang drink (o watter).

tangle *n* fankle, raivel, snorl.

v fankle; (*get into a tangle*) fankle, raivel.

tangled fankelt, raivelt; (*of hair*) tousie.

tantrum *n* tirrivee.

tap[1] *v, n* (*strike lightly*) tig, pap.

tap[2] *n* (*water tap*) well: '*The hot well has a drip*', cran.

tar *n* taur, ter.

tarry taurie.

target *n* (*object set up as a target*) prap NE; (*in curling*) tee,

tart[1] *n* tairt, tert.

tart[2] *adj* **1** (*bitter*) wersh. **2** (*in manner*) nippit, nebbie, snippit, cuttit NE.

task *n* handlin; (*hard*) chaave NE.

tassel *n* toorie, tossel, tappietoorie.

taste *n* **1** gust, saur; (*bad*) guff, humph. **2** (*tasting*) preein.

v lip, gust; (*have a certain taste*) saur; (*try by tasting*) pree.

tasteless (*of food*) wersh, fushionless.

tasty gustie.

tatters *npl* taivers, tatterwallops.

taught *see* **teach.**

taunt *v* cry (someone) names, snite someone's niz.

n upcast, sneist.

taut *adj* tacht SHETLAND, N.

tea *n* tae SHETLAND, N; (*high tea*) tea an till't, tousie tea, mait tea.

tea-break piece-time, minute NE.

tea-drinker (*who drinks a lot of tea*) tea-jennie, tea-han(d).

tea-leaf (tea) blade; (*in a cup, indicating the arrival of a stranger*) stranger.

tea party cookie shine, tea shine.

cup of tea, drink of tea stroopach N, HIGHLAND.

teach *v* learn.

taught *past tense, past participle* taucht.

team *n* (*in curling, carpet-bowling, quoits*) rink.

tear[1] *v* teir, terr WEST, ULSTER, rent; (*rip*) rive, screed.

n teir, terr WEST, ULSTER.

tore *past tense* rave, rived.

torn *past participle* tore, riven.
tear apart rive.
tear at rive, rug an rive (at).
tear off (*a covering*) screeve, tirr, tirl.
tear[2] *n*: **tearful** bubblie, bibblie NE, greetin(-faced), greetie, snotterie.
  burst into tears blirt.
tease *v* kittle (up), be at.
teat *n* tit.
tedious *adj* dreich, tedisome.
teeming *adj*: **teeming with** ho(a)tchin wi, heezin wi NE.
teeth *npl*: **set of false teeth** wallies.
television *n* televeesion.
tell *v*: **told** *past tense, past participle* telt, tauld.
  telltale clype.
  tell tales (about) clype (on), tell (on).
  let me tell you seestu.
  not tell no lat dab, no lat on.
temper *n* (*bad temper*) cut: '*She's in bad cut the day*', birse: '*His birse is up*'.
  fly into a temper fuff.
  lose your temper loss the heid, loss yer puggie.
  in a bad temper crabbit, short i the trot, in a bung NE.
tempestuous *adj* (*of weather*) gowst(er)ie.
temple *n* (*side of face*) haffet.
ten *numeral* (*children's rhymes*) tenaby SHETLAND, ORKNEY, N.
  tenth tent.
  Ten Commandments *see* **command.**
tender *adj* (*easily hurt*) frush; (*of a kiss*) sappie.
tendon *n* tenon NE.
tenterhooks *npl*: **be on tenterhooks** be sittin on preens, be on heckle-pins, be on nettles.
tepid *adj* teepid, lew (warm).
term *n*: **come to terms** gree.
tern *n* pirr, pictarnie SHETLAND, ORKNEY, FIFE.
terrible *adj* terrel.
terrify *v* fricht, terrifee.
  terrifying frichtsome.
  terrified fair fleggit.

terror *n* the shakers; (*feeling of*) grue.
test *v* (*by tasting*) pree, pruive.
testicle *n* stane, steen NE.
tether *n* tedder SHETLAND, N, langle.
  v tedder SHETLAND, N, bin(d).
text *n* (*of a sermon*) grun(d).
than *preposition, conjunction* nor.
thank *v* thenk.
  thankful thankfu, thankfae.
that *pronoun, adj, see also* **those;** at, (*unstressed*) it NE; (*usually of something further away than 'that'*) yon, thon, on NE.
thatch *v, n* thack, theek.
thaw *n* thowe, fresh, saft.
  v thowe, fresh NE.
the *definite article* e(e) N, de SHETLAND, E COAST, da SHETLAND.
theft *n* lift, skin, stootherie.
their *possessive adj* thir.
them *pronoun* thaim, dem SHETLAND.
  themselves thirsels, theirsels, thaimsels.
  by themselves (alone) thir lane, their lane, them lane SHETLAND, NE.
then *adv* than, (a)an NE, well: '*We're awa, well*', syne.
there *adv* therr.
  therefore syne.
  there is there: '*There yer tea*', at's N.
  over there yonder, thonder.
these *pronoun, adj* thae, thir, this, is eens NE, this ones HIGHLAND.
thick *adj* (*of people, things*) guttie.
  thicken (*soup etc*) mak, lithe; (*of jam, porridge etc*) mak.
  thickset thick, stumpie.
thigh *n* thee, hoch.
  back of the thigh hoch.
  thigh-bone hunker-bane.
thimble *n* thummle.
thin *adj* **1** (*of persons*) slink, nairraboukit, skleff SOUTH; (*thin and miserable or ill-looking*) pookit; (*of animals*) sma. **2** (*of liquid food*) spleuterie, wabblie.
  v **thin (out)** (*seedlings*) single, sinder NE.

thin person skelf, skinnymalink(ie).

thing *n* ting SHETLAND, ORKNEY.

thingummy hingmy, thingmy, thing-wy.

not a thing nae a docken, deil a haet.

think *v*: **thought** *past tense, past participle* thocht, tocht SHETLAND.

think of *or* **about** think on.

thirst *n* drouth, thrist SHETLAND, NE.

v thrist SHETLAND, NE.

thirsty drouthie.

thirst-quencher slockener.

quench the thirst of slocken.

thirteen *numeral* therteen, deil's dizzen.

thirteenth therteen, therteent.

thirty threttie, thertie, trettie SHETLAND.

this *pronoun, adj; see also* **these;** is.

this time this: *'There's plenty tae dae atween this an Sunday'.*

thistle *n* thrissel.

thong *n* whang, thwang, fang N.

thorn *n* jag, job.

thorny jaggie, jobbie.

thorough *adj* thorow.

thoroughly richt.

those *pronoun, adj* thae, that, at NE, at eens NE, that ones HIGHLAND; (*of something more remote*) yon, thon, on NE.

though *adv* (*at end of phrase*) but: *'It isna me but'.*

thought *n* thocht.

v, past tense, past participle thocht.

thoughtful pensefu; (*considerate*) considerin.

thoughtless daft, glaikit.

thousand *numeral* thoosan(d).

thrash *v* skelp.

thread *n* threid.

threat *n* threit.

threaten threit, threiten, shore, offer (tae); (*a person*) mint NE.

threatening (*dangerous*) unchancie; (*of weather*) canker(i)t; (*of the sky*) loorie.

three *numeral* chree, threy SOUTH, tree SHETLAND, hree WEST; (*children's rhymes*) tethery.

three or four three-fower.

thresh *v* thrash.

threshold *n* lintel, door-stane.

thrift *n* trift SHETLAND.

be thrifty hain (in).

thrill *n* dirl, stoun(d).

v (*with emotion*) dirl.

thrive *v* trive SHETLAND, ORKNEY, thram N.

thriving growthie; (*of animals*) fresh, raffie NE.

throat *n* thrapple, craig, hause.

clear your throat ha(u)ch; (*noisily*) clorach, hask, slorach.

throb *n* stoon(d), dirl; (*of the head etc*) lowp, dunt.

v stoon(d), dirl; (*of the heart etc*) lowp, dunt, wallop.

throttle *v* thrapple, guzzle.

through *preposition* throu; (*to an inner room*) ben.

throw *n* thraw; (*violent*) fung.

v thraw, wap, heave *without notion of effort as in English;* (*suddenly and forcefully*) skite; (*violently*) bung, fung, wap.

throw away ca(w) awa; (*reject*) ort.

thrush *see* **missel thrush, song thrush** (*under* **song**).

thud *n, v* dunt, dad.

thug *n* keelie, schemie.

thumb *n* thoum.

thump *n* da(u)d, dunt, ding; **thumps** (*on the back, to mark a child's birthday*) dumps, bumps EDINBURGH.

v dunt, da(u)d, ding; (*of the heart*) dunt, flichter, gowp.

put something down with a thump plunk, plank.

thunder *n* thunner, brattle.

thunder shower thunner(-plump).

thwart *n* (*of a boat*) thaft, taft SHETLAND.

v conter, pit the haims on, thorter.

tick[1] *v*: **make a ticking sound** knick.

tick[2] *n* (*sheep-tick*) (sheep) taid, keb, ked.

tickle *n* kittle; (*anything causing a tickling sensation*) itchy-coo.

ticklish kittle; (*easily tickled*) ticklie: '*Ah'm ticklie on ma feet*', kittle, kittlie.

tide *n* (*of the sea*) rug.

ebb tide (*low water*) grun(d) ebb SHETLAND, N.

tidy *adj* trig, tosh, weel-redd-up, nacketie NE.

v, also **tidy up** redd (up), sort, tosh, sproosh (up), trig up NE.

tidied redd-up.

tidily ticht.

tidying-up redd(in)-up, sort, trig-up NE.

tidy yourself sort yersel.

tie *v* wap, wup.

tiger *n* teeger.

tight *adj* ticht, tacht N, strait; (*of clothes*) jimp.

tighten tichten, strait(en) SHETLAND, NE.

tightly ticht, hard.

tight-fitting nippit, jimp, strait, scrimp.

tile *n* (*porcelain*) wallie tile.

tiled (*eg of a wall*) wallie: '*wallie close*'.

tilt *v* cowp.

timber *n* timmer.

time *n* (*season*) tid.

time-wasting footerie, scutterie NE.

time-wasting occupation footer, scutter.

old times lang syne, lang seen NE.

this time this.

a long time (*from the present*) yon time.

a long time ago lang syne.

a short time a bittie, a wee (bit), a (wee) whilie, a (wee) filie NE.

a short time ago nae lang syne.

in a short time the noo, eenoo, ivnoo NE.

at the present time eenoo, the noo, ivnoo NE.

at an unspecified time yon time: '*He'll no be hame till yon time*'; '*She's been here since yon time*'.

by the time that gin.

from time to time noo(s) an than(s) NE.

in (the course of) time throu time.

at that time thae days.

since that time (sin)syne.

some time ago while-syne.

timid *adj* blate, timorsome, hen-hertit, shan; (*of animals*) scar.

tin *n*: **small tin mug** *etc* tinnie.

tin box mull(ie) NE.

tingle *v* dingle, dirl; (*especially of the fingers*) dinnle.

tingling sensation (*eg from a blow*) dirl.

cause to tingle nip, dingle.

tinker *n* tink(ie), caird, cyard NE.

tinkle *v*: **cause to tinkle** tingle.

tiny *adj* (little) wee, tot(t)ie (wee), peedie ORKNEY, CAITHNESS, FIFE, peerie SHETLAND.

tip[1] *n* (*end part*) tap; (*iron*) shod; (*pointed end*) neb.

tip[2] *v* (*upset*) cowp (up), owercowp.

tipsy *adj* capernoitie, cornt NE.

tiptoes *npl* taptaes, tippertaes: '*on tippertaes*'.

tire *v* staw SE.

tired forfochen, lowsed, taigelt.

very tired fair forfochen, (fair) wabbit.

tiredness tire.

tiring taiglesome.

tissue *n* tishie.

titbit *n* snag NE.

titbits gulshichs NE.

title *n* teetle.

titter *n, v* snicher, kicher.

to *preposition* tae, till, tee NE; (*after verbs of calling, shouting, knocking etc*) on: '*He's shoutin on ye*'; (*before infinitive: in order to*) for tae; (*in telling time*) o(f): '*a quarter o fower*'.

toad *n* puddock, taid.

toadstool puddock-stuil, puddock steel NE.

toast *n* tost.
  v (*bread etc*) birsle, harn.
  toasted (*of cheese*) roastit.
tobacco *n* tabaccae, tabacca.
today *adv, n* the day, e day NE.
toddle *v* hotter SOUTH, paidle.
  toddler tot(t)ie, totum, bairnie, wean WEST, ULSTER.
toe *n* tae.
toffee *n* taffie, gundie, black man.
together *adv* thegither, (th)egidder NE.
toil *n, v* tra(u)chle, chaave NE.
toilet *n* cludgie, shunkie, yuffie.
told *see* **tell.**
tolerate *v* thole (wi), bide.
  tolerable (*bearable*) tholeable; (*fair*) middlin, geylies.
tomboy *n* gilpie, hallockit.
  tomboyish hallockit, hallirackit.
tombstone *n* lairstane NE.
tom-cat *n* gib(bie)(-cat).
tomorrow *adv* the morn, the morra.
  tomorrow morning the morn's morn, the morra's morn.
  tomorrow night the morn's nicht.
tongs *npl* tangs, tyangs NE.
tongue *n* **1** (*speech*) gab. **2** (*language of a country*) leid.
  tongue-tied tongue-tackit.
  hold your tongue! haud yer w(h)eesh(t)!, save yer breath tae cool yer parritch!
tonight *adv* the nicht.
too *adv* tae, tee NE; (*also*) an a(w); (*excessively*) ower: '*no ower clean*', over.
  too many ower monie.
  too much ower muckle, overly.
took *see* **take.**
tool *n* tuil, luim, leem N.
tooth *n* tuith, teeth.
  toothache teethache, sair teeth.
top[1] *n* (*highest point*) tap; (*higher part, upper end*) heid: '*braeheid*'; (*of a class, school*) dux, heids SOUTH.
  top hat lum (hat).
  top-knot toorie.
  on top of oot ower.

top[2] *n* (*spinning top*) peerie; (*humming*) bummer.
topic *n* speak.
  favourite topic leid N.
topple *v* cowp, whummle.
topsy-turvy *adv* tapsalteerie, heels ower gowdie, heeliegoleerie.
torch *n* (*pocket*) blinkie.
tore *see* **tear**[1].
torment *v* (*with questions*) deave, tarragat.
torn *see* **tear**[1].
tortoise *n* tortie.
torture *v, n* torter.
toss *n* fung.
  v fung; (*the head*) cast; (*of a ship*) howd, jowe.
tot *n* **1** (*small child*) tot(t)ie, totum. **2** (*small drink*) (wee) dram.
total *n*: **the total** the hail, the hail jing-bang.
totter *n, v* stotter, stoiter, styter.
  tottery shooglie, stammerie, stotterie.
touch *v* tig; (*lightly*) scuff, skiff, scutch N.
  n **1** (*slight, in passing*) scuff, skiff; (*light, playful*) tig. **2** (*of illness etc*) whiff, gliff, skiff.
  touchy pernicketie, kittle.
tough *adj* teuch; (*of persons*) raucle.
n keelie.
tow *v, n* towe.
towel *n* too(e)l, han(d)-cloot.
tower *n* toor.
town *n* toon.
  town hall toon hoose.
  townspeople toonsers.
  to the centre of a town up the toon.
  top of a town toon heid.
toy *n* wheeriorum N, playock.
trace[1] *n* (*rope or chain for drawing*) tress.
trace[2] *n* (*small amount*) pick, perlicket N.
trachea *see* **windpipe** (*under* **wind**[1]).
track *n* (*narrow path*) pad; (*especially sheep-track*) roadie; (*for cattle*) loanin.

track down speir oot.

trade *n* tre(a)d, traffeck, mercat.

v traffeck, troke, cowp NE.

tradition *n* tradeetion.

trail *v* tra(y)chle, traipse; (*untidily*) trollop, trailep NE.

tramcar *n* ca(u)r, skoosh-car WEST.

tramp *n* **1** caird, gangrel, gaun(-aboot) bodie. **2** (*long tiring walk*) trail, traik, traipse.

v traik, trail, traipse.

trample *v* paidle, pran NE.

trample on tramp on, stramp.

trance *n* dwam.

translate *v* owerset.

transport *v* convoy, flit; (*in a wheeled vehicle*) hurl.

trap *n* (*snare*) girn, mink NE; (*for mice or rats*) fa(w).

v (*ensnare*) fankle, girn.

trash *n* troke.

trashy food snashters.

travel *n, v* traivel.

traveller (*usually referring to tinkers etc*) traiveller, treveller.

travel on foot *see* **foot.**

treachery *n* traison.

treacherous traicherous.

treacle *n*, NB *in Scotland always refers to molasses;* traicle, trekkle, strap.

tread *n, v* stramp.

tread on stramp; (*heavily*) tramp.

treason *n* traison.

treasure *n* traisure.

treasurer thesaurer.

treat *n* trait.

v trait; (*handle*) guide.

treble *adj* threeple.

v threeple, treeple NE.

tree *n* wood, timber NE: '*That's a fine bit o tree*'.

tree-stump scrunt; (*old or decayed*) runt.

tree-trunk (*long, slender*) caber, shank.

tremble *v* tremmle, trummle.

fit of trembling (fit o) the shakers.

cause to tremble dinnle.

tremendous *adj* unco, by-or(di)nar, tremendious.

trench *n, v* sheuch.

trendy *adj* fantoosh.

trestle *n* tress; (*for scaffolding*) horse.

trick *n* (*piece of mischief*) cantrip, pliskie, swick; **tricks** (*playful*) jinks.

v jink, jouk, swick, quirk NE.

trickery joukerie-pawk(e)rie, swickerie.

tricky (*of a task*) fykie, fickle, kittle.

trickle *n* dribble, trinkle.

v trinkle, seep, sype.

tricky *see* **trick.**

trifle *n* (*thing of little value*) triffle.

v footer.

trigger *n* tricker.

trim *adj* tosh, trig; (*of people*) nate, snod.

v sned, snod; (*hair*) coll.

trip *n* **1** (*journey*) vaige SHETLAND, veage E CENTRAL. **2** (*stumble*) stammer.

v stammer, snapper SHETLAND, NE, hyter NE.

tripe *n* painches.

triple *adj, v* threeple.

triplet threeplet.

trivial *adj* footerie, treevial, skitterie.

trolley *n*: **supermarket trolley** barra(e).

trot *n* jundie.

v treetle NE.

trouble *n, v* fash, tra(u)chle, tribble.

troubled tra(u)chelt.

troublesome fashious, ill, fykie, tribblesome.

have plenty of trouble no hae yer sorras tae seek.

trough *n* troch.

trousers *npl* troosers, breeks.

trouser braces galluses.

trousseau *n* waddin-braws, providin.

trout *n* troot; (*small*) trootie.

truant *n* fugie, plunker, troon, trone.

play truant jouk (the scuil), plunk (the scuil), kip (the scuil), troon, trone.

truce *n* (*in games, also* **cry for a truce**) barley, baurlie, keys, parlie.

trudge *v, n* tra(u)chle, trail, traik.

trump-card *n* trumph.

trundle *v* trinnle, trunnle, hurl.

trunk *n* **1** (*chest*) kist. **2** (*of a tree: long, slender*) caber, shank.

trust *v* lippen.

not to be trusted sleekit.

truth *n* trith, trath SHETLAND, ORKNEY.

try *v* **1** (*attempt*) ettle, mak a shape. **2** (*try out, especially by tasting*) pruive, pree.

tub *n* (*for washing clothes*) boyne, (washin) bine, cweed NE.

tuck *n* (*pleat or fold*) touk.

v, also **tuck up** touk, kilt.

Tuesday *n* Tyseday.

tuft *n* toosht NE; (*of hair, wool etc*) tap, tait; (*of hair*) tossel, swirl, taut; (*of grass*) tait; (*of feathers on a bird's head*) tappin.

tug *v, n* chug, teug, rug, yerk.

tumble *n* tummle, whummle.

v tummle, whummle, cowp.

tummy *n* peenie, wame.

tune *n* tin CENTRAL, teen NE, lilt, souch.

out of tune aff the stot.

tune without words diddle.

tune up (*an instrument*) kittle.

turd *n* toalie, jobbie CENTRAL.

turf *n* turr; (*sod*) fail; (*thinner*) divot; (*surface*) turr.

turkey *n*: **turkey cock** bubbly jock.

turn *n* **1** (*turning*) birl, skew, thraw SHETLAND, N. **2** (*spell*) shot(tie); (*in a game*) crack.

v birl, thraw; (*quickly*) jink; (*a key, doorknob*) thraw.

cause to turn (round) birl, feeze on.

in turn shots each, shottie aboot NE.

turnover 1 (*in trade*) owerturn. **2** (*with savoury meat filling*) (Forfar) bridie.

turn up on end oweren(d).

turnip *n* neep, turneep, tumshie *humorous or informal;* (*swede*) neep, swade, baggie SE.

turnip-lantern neep lantern.

turret *n* tappietoorie; (*round*) roon(d)el.

tweak *v*: **tweak someone's nose** snite someone's niz.

tweezers *npl* pinchers.

twelve *numeral* twal.

twelfth twalt.

twelve hours a roon(d) o the clock.

twelve o'clock twaloors.

twenty *numeral* twintie.

twice *adv* twicet.

twig *n* cowe; (*of willow or hazel, especially for thatching*) scob.

twilight *n* gloamin.

twin-bedded *adj* twa-beddit.

twinge *n* rug, stoon(d); (*sharp pain*) twang.

twinkle *v* glent, prinkle, skinkle.

n glent.

twirl *n* tirl, birl, swirl.

twist *n* skew, cast, thraw.

v **1** thraw, fank, rowe. **2** (*a joint etc*) rax, rack, thraw.

twist the face shevel, sham.

twisted thrawn, squeegee, fankelt.

twitch *n* fidge, pook, tit; (*of the lips or eyelids*) wicker.

v fidge, pook, tit; (*of the lips*) moup, mump.

twitter *v* chitter.

two *numeral* twa, twae; (*in counting rhymes*) teentie.

two-faced sleekit, twa-faul(d) NE.

twopence tippence.

just the two of them baith the twa o them.

two or three twa-three.

type *n* (*kind, printed letters*) teep.

typical *adj* teepical.

U

udder *n* ether, edder NE.
ugly *adj* ill-faured.
ulcer *n* (*on the skin*) bealin.
umbrella *n* umberella, umberellae.
un- *prefix* wan-.
unable *adj* (*because of exhaustion etc*)
useless, yissless, ees(e)less NE.
  unable to awa fae: '*He wis awa fae
  speakin*'.
unaccustomed *adj*: **unaccustomed to**
oot o the road o, no yaised wi, nae
eest wi NE.
unappetizing *adj* wersh, wauch NE.
unattractive *adj* unbraw, unbonnie,
hackit.
uncanny *adj* no cannie, eeriesome NE,
oorie.
uncertain *adj* (*having doubts*) dootsome.
uncommon *adj* orra.
uncouth *adj* coorse, raucle, raploch.
undecided *adj* dootsome, aff an on.
  be undecided swither.
under *preposition, adv* (in) alow, (in)
ablow.
undergrowth *n* scrogs.
underhand *adj* sleekit, hidlins, wheetie
NE.
underneath *adv, preposition* (in) ablow, (in) alow, (in) aneath.
undersized *adj* scrimpit, palie, sharg-
art, shilpit.
understand *v* unnerstaun(d); (*a person, what a person says*) pick up, tak
up.
  understanding *n* uptak: '*gleg i the
  uptak*', rum(mle-)gumption, kennin.
undertaking *n* ploy, han(d)lin, prottick NE.
undiluted *adj* (*of alcoholic drinks*)
hard, nakit.
undo *v* lowse(n).

undress *v* (*yourself, a person*) tirr NE;
(*a person*) tirl.
unearth *v* howk.
uneasy *adj* on nettles.
unemployed *adj* orra.
  unemployment idleset.
  unemployment benefit b(u)roo
  money.
unexpectedly *adv* in a hurry.
unfair *adj* no fair.
unfamiliar *adj* un(be)kent, fremmit,
unco NE.
unfasten *v*: **become unfastened**
lowse(n).
unfit *adj*: **unfit for** unable for, no able
for.
unfortunate *adj* misfortunat, no
chancie, misluckit NE.
unfriendly *adj* ill(-willie).
ungrateful *adj* pick-thank NE.
unharmed *adj* hailscart, hail-heidit N.
unhealthy *adj*: **unhealthy-looking**
pookie; (*ill-looking*) peelie-wallie.
uninteresting *adj* dreich, smeerless N.
university *n*: **a or the university** the
college: '*She's at the college noo*'.
unkind *adj* ill.
unknown *adj* un(be)kent, nae kent,
unco NE.
unless *conjunction* athoot.
unlucky *adj* unchancie, ill, uncannie.
unmannerly *adj* menseless.
unmarried *see* **single.**
unmethodical *adj* throuither, throwder NE.
unnatural *adj* no cannie.
unpredictable *adj* kittle.
unpunctual *adj* mistimeous N.
unravel *v* (*thread etc*) redd.
unreasonable *adj* oot o aa rizzon
SHETLAND, N.
unrelated *adj* (*by blood*) fremmit.

unreliable *adj* (*of a person*) slidderie, kittle.

unruly *adj* ramstam, neither tae haud nor tae bind, maroonjous NE.

unsatisfactory *adj* ill.

unscrew *v* feeze aff.

unsettled *adj* (*of the weather*) grumlie NE.

unskilful *adj* handless.

unskilled hielan(d), ill; (*of a job*) orra.

unsteady *adj* (*of things*) shooglie, cogglie.

untidy *adj* throuither, throwder NE, hither an yon(t); (*especially of work*) hairy; (*of clothes: hanging loose*) trollopie; (*of hair*) touslie, like straw hingin fae a midden.

untidy person ticket.

untidy place Paddy's market, Annicker's midden, guddle: '*Why's this hoose aye sic a guddle?*'

until *preposition* or.

conjunction gin, or, tae.

untrustworthy *adj* sleekit, slidderie.

unusual *adj* by-or(di)nar, unco.

unusual(ly) nae or(di)nar.

unwell *adj* no weel, nae weel, bad.

unwilling *adj* sweir(t).

unyielding *adj* dour, stieve.

up *adv, preposition* (*out of bed*) oot ower.

upsadaisy (*eg encouraging a child to its feet*) oopsie doopsie.

up there upby.

upbringing *n* upfeshin NE.

upkeep keep-up.

upright *adj* (*of a person*) upricht.

standing upright oweren(d).

uproar *n* stushie, stishie, stramash, collieshangie.

uproot *v* (*by digging*) howk.

upset *v* 1 (*overturn*) cowp, whummle. 2 (*a person*) pit aboot.

n (*overturning*) cowp, whummle.

adj uggit, up.

upset the stomach fyle the stamack.

upside down *adv* tapsalteerie, heels ower gowdie, heelster heid(s).

turn upside down whummle.

upstairs *adv* upby.

urge *v* threap at.

urge on ca(w), haud at.

urgently *adv* sair: '*Ye're sair needin a pair o shuin*'.

urine *n* pish.

urinate pish, strone.

us *pronoun* uz, wiz, iz, wir, oo SOUTH; (*stressed*) hiz; (*those of our group etc*) us *y*ins, hiz eens NE.

use *n* yiss, eese N.

v yaise, yuise, eese N.

used to (*accustomed to*) yaised wi, eest wi N, used wi.

he used to be able to he used tae could.

be used up gae duin, gang deen NE.

useful yuisfae, eesefae NE.

useless uisless, yissless, ees(e)less N.

usual *adj* eeswal NE.

usually, as usual for ord(i)nar.

utter[1] *adj, adv* fair: '*Ye're a fair disgrace*'.

utter[2] *v* mint, moot SHETLAND, NE.

V

vagrant *n* gaun-aboot bodie, gangrel.
vain *adj* pridefu, saucy, vauntie.
valley *n* howe; (*especially steep-sided with a river*) glen; (*broad, flat, at lower end of a river*) strath.
vanish *v* vainish.
varied *adj* sindrie.
various *adj* sindrie.
vase *n* vawse, pig.
vault *n* pen(d).
vertebra *n* link.
vertigo *n* mirligoes.
very *adv* verra, gey (an), terrible: '*Whit a terrible bad cauld ye've got*', braw (an), fine an, awfie, aafa NE, richt.
  the very thing the like.
  not very . . . no that . . . , no awfie, nae aafa NE.
vest *n* (*of wool etc, usually men's*) simmit, seemit NE.
vet *n* veet, ferrier.
vibrate *v* dirl, dinnle.
  vibration dirl, dinnle.
vicious *adj* veecious, ill.
view *n* vizzy; (*partial*) swatch.
  v leuk.
vigour *n* smeddum, fushion NE.

vigorous caller, hail.
  do something vigorously gae yer dinger, gie something laldie, skelp, gie something big licks.
village *n* toon.
violent *adj* (*of people*) bang, wuid; (*of wind, storm*) snell.
virtuous *adj* gracie.
vision *n* sicht, veesion.
visit *v* veesit, ca(w) for, leuk the gate o, ceilidh HIGHLAND, ULSTER; (*in passing*) cry in (by), roar (in).
  n veesit; (*in passing*) race, cry (in); (*sociable, evening*) ceilidh HIGHLAND, ULSTER.
  visitor veesitor.
vivid *adj* (*of personality*) gleg.
voice *n*, *v* vice.
vole *n* lan(d) moose.
volume *n* 1 (*size*) bouk. 2 (*book*) buik.
vomit *v*, *n* boak, byock NE.
vow *v*, *n* voo.
voyage *n* veage E CENTRAL, vaige SHETLAND.
vulgar *adj* coorse; (*of language etc*) groff.
vulva *n* fud.

W

waddle *v, n* hoddle, wauchle, showd N.
wade *v* wad, wide, paidle.
  waders widers.
wafer *n* (*ice-cream*) slider; (*with chocolate and marshmallow*) black man.
wager *v, n* wad.
wagtail *n* (*pied*) willie-wagtail, waggie, watery NE; (*yellow*) watery wagtail.
wail *v, n* yammer, walloch NE.
waistcoat *n* weskit.
wait *v* bide, wyte NE, hing on.
  n wyte NE.
  wait a little bide a wee, haud a wee.
  wait for wait on, wyte on NE.
wake *v* wauk.
  wakeful waukrif(e).
  waken wauken, raise.
walk *v* **1** traivel, shank (it); (*go for a walk*) dander, daun(d)er: '*He daundered doon the toon*', streetch.
  2 (*clumsily*) sha(u)chle, skleush N; (*in a flat-footed way*) sclaff; (*through mud*) plowter, plyter NE; (*wearily*) tra(u)chle.
  3 (*slowly*) dander, daun(d)er; (*aimlessly*) traik.
  4 (*with a springy step*) lowp; (*energetically*) spad on NE.
  n traivel SHETLAND, N, range; (*leisurely*) dander, daun(d)er, raik; (*long, weary*) traik, trail, raik.
  walking *n* shanks'(s) naig(ie), Tamson's mear.
  adj (*of a child*) gaun.
  walking stick nibbie staff SW, SOUTH; (*with hooked handle*) crummock, nibbie.
  walk arm in arm *see* **arm.**
wall *n* wa, dyke.
wallop *v, n* loonder.
wallow *v, n* walloch N, plowter, plyter NE.

wand *n* wan.
wander *v* waun(n)er, stravaig, scaff NE, traipse; (*aimlessly*) traik, haik.
  wandering (*in mind*) waun(n)ert, raivelt, cairried.
  wander over reenge.
wangle *v, n* (*dishonest(ly)*) pauchle.
want *v* wint NE, seek, wish: '*Dae ye wish mair tea?*'; (*very much*) ettle (for); (*eg something to eat*) be for: '*Are ye for puddin?*'.
  n wint NE; (*lack*) faut.
warble *v, n* chirm, tweetle.
warm *adj* het; (*cosy*) cosh; (*of weather: warm and damp*) mochie, muithie.
  v (*yourself*) beek; (*warm thoroughly*) birsle; (*become warm*) (get a) heat; (*make warm*) (gie a) heat.
warn *v* wairn.
  warning *n* tellin: '*Lat that be a tellin tae ye*'.
warrant *v* uphaud.
wart *n* mowdiewort *humorous*.
wary *adj* ware, sicker.
was *v, past tense* wis, wus, wes, wur.
wash *v, n* (*quick(ly)*) syne, synd; (*swill*) sweel.
  washed *past tense* washt, weesh NE.
  past participle washt, washen NE.
  washing-tub washin bine.
  wash-house washin hoose; (*public*) steamie.
  wash out syne (oot), synd (oot).
  wash up wash the dishes.
wasp *n* waasp, waps.
  wasp's nest byke.
waste *v* connach, misguide SHETLAND, NE; (*especially food*) ort; (*time*) pit aff, hinder SHETLAND, NE.
  n **1** (*especially from a mine or quarry*) redd. **2** (*of time*) aff-pit.
  wasteful haiveless N.

wastepaper basket bucket.

waste time pit aff (time), play yersel: '*Stoap playin yersel an feenish yer work*'; (*in footling jobs*) skitter.

don't waste your breath save yer breath tae cool yer parritch.

watch *v*: **watch over** tak tent o; (*keep guard over*) wauk, weir; (*protect*) leuk ower.

n (*timepiece: large, pocket*) neep.

watchful waukrif(e), tentie.

watch out! watch yersel!

water *n* watter, waitter SE, pani *gipsy*, SOUTH.

v watter, waitter SE.

watering can rooser.

watery (*of food etc*) wabblie, spleuterie NE.

watery-eyed blearie.

water-beetle water clearer.

waterfall linn, spoot.

water pistol scoot, skiter SHETLAND, NE.

water rat water dog NE.

water sprite water horse, (water) kelpie.

put in boiling *or* **hot water** plot: '*Plot yer pooshiont finger*'.

wave *n* **1** (*of the sea etc*) jaw NE. **2** (*of the hand: as signal*) waff, wag.

v waff, wag; (*wave about*) waffle.

waver *v* swither, waffle, wavel.

way *n* wey, wye SHETLAND, N, gate, road, airt; (*direction*) airt.

all the way a(w) the road.

give someone his *or* **her (own) way** gie someone his *or* her (ain) gate.

in every way a(w)weys, ilkie wye NE.

in your way in yer road.

in no (possible) way nae road, nae gate.

on the way in the gate NE.

a long way (from) hyne fae.

the way in(to) the road in.

W.C. *n* cludgie, shunkie, watery; (*especially on a staircase in a tenement*) yuffie.

we *pronoun* OO SOUTH.

weak *adj* waik, wyke NE; (*physically*) wabbit, fushionless; (*mentally*) saft, silly, feel NE; (*in character*) fushionless, facile; (*of food or drink*) wersh, spleuterie NE.

weaken (*in health*) tak doon.

weakling wallydrag NE, sha(u)chle, shargar NE.

weal *n* (*scar*) score, blain.

wealth *n* walth, gear.

wealthy walthie.

wean *v* spean N.

be weaned spean.

weapon *n* wappen.

wear *v* **1** weir. **2** (*damage: clothes with hard usage*) scuff; (*clothes, shoes out of shape*) sha(u)chle; (*into holes*) hole.

worn *adj, past participle* wurn; (*into holes*) holed.

worn out (*of a person*) (sair) forfochen; (*of a person or thing*) sair awa wi't.

weary *adj* wabbit, forjeskit, forfochen.

v deave, jabb NE; (*with hard work etc*) tra(u)chle, tash.

weariness tire.

grow weary of fash o.

very weary of sick-tired o.

weasel *n* whitrat, futrat NE, foumart, thoumart.

weather *n* wedder, wither NE.

weave *v* wyve NE.

weaver wabster.

web *n* wab, wob; (*spider's*) moose wab.

wed *v* wad.

wedding waddin, mairriage.

wedding cake bride(s)cake.

scattering of coins to children by a wedding party poor-oot, scatter, scoor-oot, logan NE, scramble WEST.

wedge *n, v* wadge; (*as support*) cog.

Wednesday *n* Wadensday.

weeds *npl* growthe.

week *n* ook SHETLAND, NE, wick NE, aucht days.

weekly ilkie wick NE.

weekday everyday, ilkaday NE.

a week on Monday a week come Monday, Monday next.

weep *v* greet; (*childishly*) bubble, bibble NE.

wept *past tense* grat, gret.

past participle grat, gret, grutten.

fit of weeping greet: '*Hae a guid greet tae yersel*', bubble, bibble NE.

weepy greetie.

weepy person greetin Teenie.

weigh *v* wecht, wacht NE, wey, wye SHETLAND, ORKNEY, N, wee SE.

weight wecht, wacht NE; (*heavy*) cairrie.

weird *adj* unco NE, eldritch *literary*.

welcome *n, v, adj* walcome.

weld *v* wall, well.

well *adv, adj* weel; **very well** fine, brawlie; **fairly well** no bad, nae bad. *interjection* weel!; **well then!** noona!

well-baked weel-fired.

well-behaved mensefu, gracie.

well-dressed braw, gash.

well in (*with someone*) fa(u)r ben.

well-informed wice.

well-known (weel-)kent, kenspeckle.

well-mannered mensefu, gentie.

well-off weel-daein, (weel-)gaithert, bien.

as well an a(w).

as well (as) forby.

went *see* **go.**

wept *see* **weep.**

were *past tense* wur, war NE.

were not werna(e), wurnae.

as it were lik(e): '*jist for the day lik*'.

west *n, adj, adv* wast.

west *n, adj, adv* waster, wester.

to the west of wast: '*wast the toon*'.

wet *adj* weet, wat, weetie, sappie; (*soaking wet*) drookit, sypit; (*rainy*) saft, blashie, plowterie; **wet and windy** blashie.

v weet, wat, plash.

past tense weetit, wat.

past participle weetit, wat, wutten NE.

n weet, wat.

whack *v, n* whauk.

whale *n* whaul, whaal SHETLAND, NE, FIFE, faal NE.

what *pronoun, adj* whit CENTRAL, fat N, fit N.

whatever fitivver NE.

what a . . . whit a . . . , fit a . . . NE.

what else? whit ither?, fit idder? NE.

what kind of whit lik(e), whatten, whitna, fitna NE.

wheat *n* white NE.

wheatear stane chack(art) SHETLAND, NE, stane chipper.

wheedle *v* wheetle, fleetch, smool.

wheel *n* (*in machinery*) whurl; (*on wheelbarrow*) trinnle.

v hurl, rowe, whurl.

wheelbarrow hurl(ie)-barra.

wheeze *v, n* pech, wheezle, whauze NE, foze NE.

wheezy pechie.

whelk *n* wulk, wilk, buckie; (*large*) horse-buckie.

when *adv, conjunction* whan, whun, fan N.

where *adv, conjunction* whar, whaur, far N.

wherever whaurivver, farivver NE.

whet *v* what, shairp.

whetstone set(-stane), shairpin stane.

whether *conjunction* whuther, whither, fither NE, gin.

whey *n* fey N, fy NE.

which *relative pronoun, adj* that, whilk, filk N, fit NE.

whiff *n* whuff, wheef; (*unpleasant*) guff.

while *conjunction* file N, the time at.

little while (wee) whilie, (wee) filie NE.

a while ago a while syne, a while back, a file seen NE.

whimper *v, n* girn.

whin[1] *n* (*bush*) whun (bush), fun (buss) NE.

whin[2] *n* (*rock*) whun, fun NE.

whine *v, n* girn, yammer.

whining *adj* girnie, greetin-faced.

whinny *v, n* nicher.

whip *v* **1** (*beat*) whup, fup NE. **2** (*rope etc*) wup, wap.

n whup, fup NE.

whipping *see* **beating** (*under* **beat**).

whirl *v, n* birl, whurl, furl NE.

whirlpool swirl, swelkie ORKNEY.

whirr *v, n* birr, souch.

whish *v, n* whush, souch.

whisk *v, n* wheech.

whisker fusker NE.

whisky *n* **1** whusky, fuskie NE. **2** (*measure, drink of*) dram, hauf; (*small*) wee hauf.

whisper *v, n* whusper, fusper NE, cheep.

whistle *v, n* whustle, fussle NE, wheeber, tweetle; (*of a bird or the wind*) wheeple.

white *adj, n* fite NE.

whitebeam mulberry.

white-faced (*of animals*) hawkit NE.

white fish (great) fish, fush.

whittle *v* futtle N, white, fite NE.

whizz *v, n* wheech, souch.

who *interrogative, also relative in anglicized usage* wha, whae, fa NE.

relative also that, at NE.

whom that, at N.

whose that's, whase, at + *possessive adj*: '*the crew at thir boat wis vrackit*'.

whole *adj, n* hail.

wholly hail, haillie.

wholesome hail(some).

the whole lot the hail jing-bang, the hail rickmatick.

whoop *v* (*with mirth*) hooch.

whooping couch kink hoast, kink cough.

whore *n* hure, limmer.

why *adv, conjunction* hoo?, foo?, whit wey?, fit wye? NE, whit for?, fit for? NE: '*Fit did ye dee at for?*'.

why not? whit for no?, why for no?, foo nae? NE.

wicked *adj* wickit, ill, ill-deedie, coorse NE.

wickedly ill.

wide *adj*: **wide open** (*of a door*) wide tae the wa.

widow *n* weeda(e), weedow.

widower weeda(e), weedow.

wife *n* wifie, wifockie N, wumman.

wild *adj* (*especially of people*) wull, will,

wile ARGYLL, SW, ULSTER, gallus, randie, maroonjous NE; (*of children*) royet; (*of weather*) gurlie.

wild cat wullcat.

will[1] *v, see also* **won't, would**; wull.

will not willnae, wullnae, winna, wunna.

will you? wiltu?

will[2] *n* wull.

wilful heidie, ramstam, breengin, contermacious.

willing wullint, guidwillie.

will-o'-the-wisp lichtie NE.

willow *n* sauch, widdie.

wily *adj* pawkie(-wittit), quirkie, sanshach NE.

win *v* wun.

won *past tense* wan.

past participle wun.

wind[1] *n* **1** win, wun(d), ween NE. **2** (*sound of wind*) souch.

windy wundie.

windmill win-mull.

windpipe thrapple, throttle, hausepipe, wizzen.

blast of wind skelp.

break wind lat aff, pump, rowt.

wind[2] *v* **1** rowe; (*a cord etc tightly round something*) wup; (*yarn onto a reel*) reel. **2** (*of a river*) wimple.

window *n* winda(e), winnock.

window-sill windae-sole.

wing *n* (*on a wing-chair*) lug.

wink *v* glimmer.

winnow *v* dicht.

wipe *v* dicht; (*mucus from nose*) snite. *n* dicht; (*hasty*) scuff, slaik.

wire *n* weer NE.

wisdom *n* wit.

wise *adj* wice, lang-heidit.

wish *v* wiss, want, wint NE. *n* wiss, wush.

wish someone was out of the way see someone far enough.

wishy-washy *adj* fushionless, wersh.

wit *n* wut; **wits** judgement: '*oot o yer judgement*'.

witty (*cynically or critically*) pawkie.

witch *n* **1** wutch, carline; (*fortune-teller*) spaewife. **2** (*ugly old woman*) rudas NE.

witchcraft glamour.

with *preposition* wi, in: '*providit in*'; (*of food*) tae, till, to: '*an egg tae his tea*'.

wither *v* dwine.

without *preposition* wi'oot, athoot, ithoot, wantin.

do without want, wint NE, dae wantin.

wizard *n* warlock.

wobble *v, n* shoogle, wa(u)chle.

wobbly shooglie, shoggie.

wolf *n* oof.

woman *n* wumman(-bodie), umman (-bodie) NE, wife, wifie; (*affectionate or familiar term of address*) hen CENTRAL; (*formal form of address to a (married) woman*) mistress.

women weemen, weemen-fowk.

womb *n* wame, wime NE.

won *see* **win.**

wonder *v* wunner, winner NE.

n wunner, winner NE; (*something to be marvelled at*) ferlie.

won't *v* winnae, winna, wunnae, wunna.

wood *n* wuid, widd; (*material*) timmer; (*piece of woodland*) buss.

wooden wudden, widden, timmer.

woody widdie, wuddie.

wood grouse capercailzie.

woodlouse slater.

wood-pigeon cushat, cushie(-doo), croodlin doo NE.

wood sorrel *see* **sorrel.**

wool *n* oo, woo.

woollen oo(en): '*oo baw*'.

woolly ooie, oo.

word *n* wird.

not a word no a cheep.

work *v* wirk, darg.

n **1** wark. **2 piece of work** seam. **3 works** (*of a mechanism*) intimmers.

worked *past tense, past participle* wrocht, vrocht NE.

worked up vrocht up NE, on the keevee.

worker (*speedy but careless*) hasher; (*dirty, untidy*) scutter, slaister, slitter.

begin work yoke (tae), streek NE.

time to begin work yokin time.

time to finish work lowsin time.

set to work pit tae yer han(d).

stop work lowse.

work clumsily *see* **clumsy.**

work done carelessly *see* **care.**

work hard stick in, chaave NE; (*until you are exhausted*) knock yer pan in.

work for little or nothing work for sweeties.

world *n* warld.

worldly wardlie.

worm *n* wirm.

worn *see* **wear.**

worry *v, n* fash, wirry.

worse *adj, adv* waur, warse.

(the) worse for (the) waur o: '*Ye'll be nane the waur o that*'.

worst *adj, adv* warst.

v warst, waur.

worth *n*: **worthless person** scum, schemie; (*small*) (wee) nyaff.

worthy honest, braw.

not worth anything no worth a docken, no worth a bodle.

would *past tense* wid, wud.

would not widnae, widna, wudnae, wudna.

wound *v* brain, gulliegaw N; (*severely*) mairtyr.

n (*slight*) scrat; (*from a heavy blow*) dunt; (*from a sting or sharp object*) stang.

wrap *v* wap, hap.

wrap up rowe up; (*untidily*) bumfle; (*a person*) hap.

wreck *v* wrack, vrack NE; (*especially a ship*) perish.

n wrack, vrack NE.

wreckage stramash.

wren *n* wran(nie), cutty wran SW, thoomie NE.

wrestle *v* warsle, chaave NE.

wrestling match warsle.

wretch *n* wratch, vratch NE.
wriggle *v, n* wammle.
wring *v* thraw.
wrinkle *v, n* runkle.
　wrinkled runklie.
writ *n* (*to appear in (a civil) court*) summons.
write *v* vreet NE.
　wrote *past tense* wrut.
　written *past participle* wrutten.
　writer (*especially contemptuous*) scriever.

writing *n* write; (*piece of writing*) scrieve.
writing pad (*for rough notes*) jotter.
wrong *adj* wrang.
　n ill.
be wrong be aff the gley.
go down the wrong way (*of food*) gae doon the wrang hause.
go wrong misgae, gang agley.
what's wrong with her? whit ails her?, whit's adae wi her?, fit's adee wi her? NE.
wrote *see* **write**.

Y

yacht *n* yatt WEST.
yard[1] *n* (*measure*) yaird.
yard[2] *n* (*enclosed ground*) yaird.
yarn *n* **1** yairn. **2** (*tall story*) sonnet NE.
yawn *v, n* gant.
yell *n, v* yall SHETLAND, N.
yellow *adj, n* yella, yellae, yalla, yallae.
 yellowish yalloch(t)ie NE, fauchie.
 yellowhammer yella yite, yella lintie,
 yorlin, yaldie (yite) NE.
yelp *v, n* (*bark*) nyaff, yaff.
yes *adv* ay.
 yes indeed och ay.
yesterday *adv* yestreen, estreen NE.
yet *adv* **1** (*still*) yit. **2** (*nevertheless*) still
 an on.
yoghurt *n* soor dook.
yonder *adv* thonder, yonner NE.
you *pronoun* ye; (*singular, familiar*) du

SHETLAND, thoo ORKNEY, (*objective*)
dee SHETLAND, ORKNEY; (*singular and
plural, informal*) youse; (*plural*) yeez,
yiz.
young *adj*: **young children** wee yins,
weans WEST, ULSTER, geets NE.
your *possessive adj* eer SOUTH; (*unstressed*) yer; *singular only* dy SHET-
LAND, thy ORKNEY.
yours *singular only* dine SHETLAND,
thine ORKNEY.
yourself yersel.
 by yourself yer lane.
 to yourself (*in a whisper*) intae yersel.
youth *n* (*young man*) lad, laddie, loon.
 youthful green, youthie.
 promising youth lad *or* lass o pairts.
 the time of your youth the daft days.
Yule *n* Yeel N, Eel N.

Z

zigzag *v* jink.

Verb List

The following is a list of Scots verbs, selected from the dictionary, which might cause you problems in forming the right past tenses and past participles. Where there is no special Scots form, sometimes the English form has been included, *eg* **be.....***past participle* **been**. For many of the verbs, you can also use the English form, if it fits your sentence better, *eg* **sit.....***past tense, past participle* **sat**.

Most Scots verbs however form the past tense and the past participle by adding -(**i**)**t**, *eg* **clartit**, or -(**e**)**d** as in English, *eg* **breenged**.

Infinitive	*Eng Infinitive*	*Past Tense*	*Past Participle*
bake	(bake)	beuk NE	baken
be	(be)	wes, wis, wus, wur, war	been
beat, bate	(beat)	bate	bate
bide	(bide)	bidit, bad	bidit, bidden
big	(build)	biggit, bug	biggit
birst	(burst)	burstit	burstit, burs(t)en
brak, brek	(break)	brak	brukken
bring	(bring)	brung, brang, brocht	brung, brocht
burn	(burn)	brunt	brunt
can	(can)	cud	
cleek	(seize)	cleekit, claucht	cleekit, claucht
come	(come)	cam, came, come	cam, came, come
creep	(creep)	creepit, crap	creepit, cruppen
dae, dee	(do)	done	done, duin, deen NE
ding	(knock)	dang, dung	dung
drive	(drive)	drave, dreeve NE	drave, dreeve NE
drink	(drink)	drunk	drunk
eat	(eat)	ett	ett, etten, aten SW
fecht	(fight)	focht	focht, fochten
fin(d)	(find)	fun(d)	fun(d)
gae, gang	(go)	gaed, gied	gane, geen SHETLAND ORKNEY, N
gie	(give)	gied	gied, gien
greet	(cry)	grat, gret	grat, gret, grutten
grup	(grip)	gruppit	gruppit, gruppen
hae	(have)	hid, haid	hid, haid, haen
hing	(hang)	hingit	hingit
hit	(hit)	hut, het, hat	hut, hutten, hitten
keep	(tend, take care of)	keepit	keepit
ken	(know)	kent	kent
leap	(leap)	lap, lape, leapit	luppen, leapit
lowp	(jump)	lowpit	lowpit, lowpen

Infinitive	Eng Infinitive	Past Tense	Past Participle
may	(may)	micht	
pit	(put)	pit, pat	pit, pitten, putten
pruive	(prove)	pruivit	proven
quit	(quit)	quat, quate	quat
rin	(run)	run	run
sall	(shall)	sud SHETLAND, sid NE, shid NE	
see	(see)	seen, seed	seen
seek	(seek)	socht	socht
sell	(sell)	selt, sald SHETLAND	selt, sald SHETLAND
set	(set)	set	setten
shae	(shoe)	shod, shoad	shoddit
shuit, shoot, sheet N	(shoot)	shuitit, sheetit NE	shotten, sheetit NE
sit	(sit)	sut	sitten, sutten
slide	(slide)	slade, sled	slidden
speak, spike NE spick NE	(speak)	spak	spoken
steal	(steal)	staw, sta, stealt	stowen, stealt
stick	(stick, stab)	stack, stickit	stucken, stickit
strik	(strike)	strak	stricken, strucken
sweer	(swear)	swure, sware	sworn
sweit, swite NE	(sweat)	swat	swatten
tak	(take)	taen, teen SHETLAND, N	taen, teen SHETLAND, N, tacken, tooken
teach	(teach)	taucht, teacht	taucht, teacht
tell	(tell)	telt	telt
think, tink, SHETLAND	(think)	thocht, tocht SHETLAND	thocht, tocht SHETLAND
thraw, thraa ORKNEY, N, traa SHETLAND	(throw, twist)	thrawed, thraad ORKNEY, N, traad SHETLAND	thrawn, thraan ORKNEY, traan SHETLAND
tyne	(lose)	tint	tint
wash	(wash)	washt, weesh	washt, washen
weet, wat	(wet)	wat, weetit	wat, weetit
win	(get)	wan	won
write, vreet NE	(write)	wrait, wrut, vrat NE	wrutten, vrutten NE
wark, wirk, wurk	(work)	wrocht	wrocht